MW00668652

MARQUE AND REPRISAL

MARQUE AND REPRISAL

The Spheres of Public and Private Warfare

Kenneth B. Moss

 University Press of Kansas

Published by the University

Press of Kansas (Lawrence,

Kansas 66045), which was

organized by the Kansas

Board of Regents and is

operated and funded by

Emporia State University,

Fort Hays State University,

Kansas State University,

Pittsburg State University,

the University of Kansas,

and Wichita State University

Library of Congress Cataloging-in-Publication Data

Names: Moss, Kenneth B., author.
Title: Marque and Reprisal : the spheres of public and private
warfare / Kenneth B. Moss.
Description: Lawrence, Kansas : University Press of Kansas,
2019. | Includes bibliographical references and index.
Identifiers: LCCN 2018058628
  ISBN 9780700627752 (hardback)
  ISBN 9780700627769 (ebook)
Subjects: LCSH: Private military companies (International
law) | Mercenary troops (International law) | War
(International law) | Private military companies—Legal
status, laws, etc.—United States. | Mercenary troops—Legal
status, laws, etc.—United States. | Constitutional law—
United States. | BISAC: LAW / Constitutional. | HISTORY /
Military / Other.
Classification: LCC KZ6418.5 .M67 2019 | DDC 343/.015354—
dc23
LC record available at https://lccn.loc.gov/2018058628.

British Library Cataloguing-in-Publication Data is available.

Printed in the United States of America

10 9 8 7 6 5 4 3 2 1

The paper used in this publication is recycled and contains
30 percent postconsumer waste. It is acid free and meets the
minimum requirements of the American National Standard
for Permanence of Paper for Printed Library Materials
Z39.48–1992.

To Debbie, with love

and

In memory of Kinley J. Brauer
mentor and, most of all, friend

CONTENTS

ACKNOWLEDGMENTS

Researching and writing a book can become a long endeavor. This one started in about 2010, and the work proceeded in fits and starts—*fits* seems the best word—that included the normal obligations of teaching as well as additional tasks in department administration, university responsibilities, retirement and a move to a new home in 2015, and the readjustment that inevitably follows. Throughout this time my wife, Debbie, was the anchor of our house. She engineered the successful accomplishment of the past years in particular while showing great interest in the progress and substance of my work—all of this on top of a health issue that momentarily sidelined her in 2017. It is a small gesture, I know, but I have dedicated this book to her.

Most of the research for this book as well as its conceptualization occurred while I was on the faculty of the Dwight D. Eisenhower School for National Security and Resource Strategy. Formerly known as the Industrial College of the Armed Forces, the school is one of the colleges in the National Defense University (NDU) at Fort Leslie J. McNair in Washington, DC. It is a remarkable setting for teaching and thinking about various aspects of national security, thanks to a faculty that is a mix of academic, military, civil service, and diplomatic professions. The student body contains the same mix of people, although, the US military component is larger in the student body than faculty. For nearly ten months one works with students in seminars that are rarely above sixteen in number. The students average in their early forties and have fifteen to twenty-five years of service or work behind them. I had officers, diplomats, and other career servants who only a few weeks before had been abroad—some in combat zones, others in senior diplomatic posts. I stress this because students like these become one's educators as well. The combination of academic classroom assignments with years of experience can provide immense insight. The substance of this book draws upon these years in seminars. In a nonattribution setting with no emphasis on rank or seniority, students shaped my understanding probably more than I theirs. I cannot cite them by name, but I want to stress my debt to them. You will see some of their names in the press.

Former colleagues, however, do not have to dwell as much in anonymity, and many listened to pieces of my work and thinking as it proceeded.

The university provost, John Yaeger, has known and assisted me for twenty years, going back to his assignment as a student while a captain in the US Navy and advancing subsequently as a faculty member himself and later administrator. Several colleagues in the Eisenhower School followed and commented on my ideas as they started, grew, and sometimes disappeared back into an abyss where they needed to remain. I think in particular of individuals like Greg Foster, Frank Cooling, Alan Gropman, Stephen Kramer, Steve Meyer, Shannon Brown, Steve Randolph, Linda Brandt, Richard Shipe, George Topic, Brian Collins, Bill Fuller, Irene Kyriakopolous, and Don Losman. Some have retired or moved on to other positions, but others remain. Another group of faculty members was uniquely important for this work. These are the judge advocate generals (JAGs, the military lawyers) who came to the faculty for one or two years. For a number of years I taught an elective that examined issues surrounding war powers. This and the work I did on a previous book on the role of undeclared war brought me to realize I needed to understand the law of armed conflict far better than I did. The JAG assigned to the faculty taught this course, and I asked if I could join as a supporting instructor. The several years spent doing this were critical for my thinking. I wish the public at large understood how important the JAGs are not only to the military but for all of us who place trust in a civilian-controlled military. One of them, Harry Dorsey, was dean of faculty in the Eisenhower School and a strong supporter of my work as I started it back in 2010–2012. Those JAGs who enabled me to join them in the classroom included Richard Prevost (who joined me in the war powers course), Denise Lind, Randall Keyes, Tim Cook, Michael Black, Sam Smith, Andrew Norris, and Michael Boock. Most were US Army, but the last two were, respectively, US Coast Guard and US Navy. We also had JAGs in class, US and foreign, who have to remain nameless as sources. During my last three years at Eisenhower I benefited greatly from the presence of Nick Rostow, who was a visiting senior scholar with the Institute for National Security Studies at NDU and also a teaching colleague.

Over the years I have retained some contact with my undergraduate alma mater, Indiana University, and in 2015 after retiring from NDU we moved to Bloomington. Going back, for nearly fifteen years one person has been particularly important in helping arrangements for me: Nick Cullather, a professor in the Department of History who is also the current associate dean in the School for Global and International Studies at Indiana University.

The current chair of the Department of History, Wendy Gamber, and her predecessor, Eric Sandweiss, have gone the extra mile to welcome, support, and encourage me. They and others in the department have invited me to participate in discussions and have commented on my work. In November 2016, after I had begun writing, the department hosted a program for me to present a couple of chapters for comment by both faculty and graduate students. I want to thank in particular Steve Buono, Jake Hagstrom, Cara Caddoo, and Ellen Wu for the suggestions they offered.

One additional benefit of being in Bloomington and affiliated with Indiana University has been the chance to talk frequently with former US Representative Lee H. Hamilton (D-IN), who now resides in the community. Having founded the Center on Congress at IU and joined both the Schools for Public and Environmental Affairs and Global and International Studies as a professor of practice, he actively contributes to the growth of the university, its focus on international matters, and the student body. Over thirty-six years ago, Mr. Hamilton hired me as a staff member of the House Foreign Affairs Committee, and we have remained in touch ever since. He has followed my work with keen interest, and the emphasis I place on congressional responsibility in the decision to use armed force unquestionably reflects what I learned working with him and other members of Congress, and what we sometimes discuss over lunch or in other venues.

Librarians and other staff in the major libraries at the National Defense University and Indiana University have been obvious benefactors to me. The remarkable efforts they take to arrange collections, be they in traditional book or electronic forms, are heroic, especially in light of decreasing budgets and rising prices. Their endeavors helped keep my questions to a few, but on occasion I had to rely on their expertise. I want to thank as well the Lilly Library at Indiana University, in which I spent some time in 2012 looking at manuscripts and rare books related to the War of 1812 and privateering.

To have the University Press of Kansas as a publisher is an invaluable honor. For decades its commitment to the publication of studies in military history, political thought, the US Constitution, the presidency, Congress, legal studies, and other subjects has enabled it to bring forth numerous distinguished titles. A longtime personal friend, Sandra Van Burkleo, and her colleague at Wayne State University, Melvin Small, encouraged me to approach the University Press of Kansas because of their positive experiences with it. David Congdon, Larisa Martin, and their colleagues at the press have worked with me through the different steps of preparing, reviewing, and revising the manuscript. Their comments and encouragement have meant so much, especially to an author who spent some years outside of academic life before returning. I thank them all.

This book rests greatly on the work of many scholars. I have sought to represent their findings and arguments fairly, for without them I would not have come anywhere close to bringing this work to conclusion. If there are misrepresentations of research and interpretation and errors of fact, I take full responsibility for them. Finally, even though I left US government service over three years ago, I want to stress that the content and opinions in this book represent in no way a stated position of the US government or one of its offices.

When I told Debbie I wanted to dedicate this book to her, she was very touched. However, we both thought one other person needed recognition in a different way—namely Kinley J. Brauer, who was my advisor—my *Doktorvater*, so to speak—at the University of Minnesota. Kinley retired in 2000, and he and his wife, Sue, went to the gentler climate of North Carolina for what was planned to be a long, happy retirement. That was not to be. Cancer took Kinley's life in early 2003. I hope he would have been happy with this work if he had lived to see it.

INTRODUCTION

By summer 2015 the United States had been in conflict in Afghanistan for fourteen years; the length of its war in Iraq was only about eighteen months less. Even though the United States had ended military operations in Iraq at the end of 2011, the rise of the extremist group called Daesh, the Islamic State, or the Islamic State of Iraq and the Levant (or Iraq and Syria) by 2014 caused the United States to recommit forces. The end in 2011 had not been much of an end. Not only were these the longest continual campaigns the United States had waged overseas; they were being fought and supported by a very different force than any used by the nation in most of the twentieth century. Gone were the large conscript-based militaries of the two world wars, Korea, and Vietnam. Afghanistan and Iraq witnessed US operations conducted by an all-volunteer military and an assortment of private military contractors. The number of US military personnel in Afghanistan peeked in June 2011 at 98,900; alongside them were 93,118 contractors (both US and foreign nationals) signed up by the Department of Defense (DOD). The number of US military personnel in Iraq reached its peak in 2006 at 187,900; contractors numbered about 100,000. A year later, after the beginning of the reduction of US force levels to 165,700, the number of DOD contractors had risen to 163,591. By June 2015 the total numbers for US forces and contractors were radically different in Afghanistan and Iraq. Afghanistan had 9,060 US troops and 28,931 contractors (again both US and foreign for DOD). Iraq, thanks to the reintroduction of US forces, had 3,550 US personnel and 1,349 DOD contractors.[1] Aside from US operations in the Balkans during the 1990s, the US military had never worked alongside such a proportionate number of contractors.

The obvious question arising from these figures was, what were these people doing? More specifically, were they engaged in the traditional mission of the military—namely to fight? Most, as will be seen in greater detail in

Chapter 6, certainly were not. They were providing maintenance, preparing and serving food, cleaning toilets, doing work on information technology systems or operating them. Some of these were tasks that soldiers for generations would have happily yielded to others. Many civilian and military leaders believed such work could be done more cheaply and efficiently by the private sector, thereby enabling the armed services to concentrate on their core missions: the conduct of military operations. However, the roles were far from being that clear. Readers likely noticed that the aforementioned figures were for contractors supporting only the Department of Defense. There were hundreds of contractors in both countries, as well as nearby, where the United States and its allies and partners had facilities supporting these operations, who were responsible to other departments and agencies of the US government—the Department of State, the Agency for International Development, the Central Intelligence Agency, the Department of Justice, and so on. The Department of Defense had no control over these individuals. Among other duties, the Department of State had selected contractors to provide security for its personnel. The State Department's own security capabilities could not fulfill this need; nor could the US Marines, whose presence at embassies is a long tradition. To whom were these people (DOD and other agencies) accountable, and what were the range and effectiveness of the lines and procedures for accountability?

Such questions especially figured prominently with contractors who carried weaponry. The possession of weapons implicitly recognizes a right of self-defense, but "defense" often has a fluid meaning in times of conflict and war, and both Iraq and Afghanistan offered numerous examples. What seem to be measures of defense in one set of eyes may seem to be aggression in another's. Do both US law and international law allow private contractors or employees to conduct military operations, especially those defined as offensive? Did the authorization to use military force against Al Qaeda and affiliates in 2001 or in the 2002 intervention in Iraq embrace roles for contractors? If so, a host of problems immediately arises. For example, international law does not recognize the right of contractors to be treated as legal combatants.

Numerous incidents in recent conflicts have raised these types of questions—perhaps none more so than the events in Nisour Square in Baghdad on September 16, 2007. Four armored vehicles driven and defended by employees of Blackwater, one of the most widely known of the private contractors, were escorting Kerry Pelzman, an official with the US Agency for International Development (USAID), back to the Green Zone, where the US Embassy and most official offices supporting US operations in Iraq were located.[2] Blackwater's reputation would ultimately become so controversial that its owners first renamed it as XE and then sold it in 2010 to avoid more controversy. A new company, Academi, subsequently emerged.[3] Blackwater's founder and chief executive officer, Erik Prince, has vigorously defended his employees against charges of being trigger-happy by arguing that the company's more frequent reliance on gunfire represented the fact that Blackwater employees were responsible for a noticeably higher number of security escorts than any other US competitor. Furthermore, he argues the employees were not uninhibited "Rambos" running amok in Baghdad streets or elsewhere. While they did not have to adhere to the "rules of engagement"—the rules that govern the nature and potential escalation of an armed response for the Department of Defense—they did have to follow an "escalation of force policy" set out by the assistant secretary of state for diplomatic security as well as the firearms policy stated by the US mission in Baghdad.[4]

Exactly what happened as the vehicles entered a traffic circle in Nisour Square remains debatable. Moving rapidly, as these convoys do, to decrease the possibility of attack by gunfire or an improvised explosive device, the vehicles sometimes draw attention and scorn for their speed and the appearance of the drivers and guards, with their wrap-around sunglasses and/or physically toned bodies. A driver of a Kia sedan came toward the convoy. The Blackwater employees claimed its driver ignored repeated calls and hand signals to halt, and, Paul Slough, a turret gunner in the third vehicle, allegedly fired a shot and killed him. Confusion, ensuing exchanges of gunfire, the calling in of a Blackwater helicopter for observation, and departure of the convoy followed. Seventeen Iraqis were dead.[5]

From the first hour, very conflicting accounts and judgments about the necessity or recklessness of the incident appeared. Some US military regarded Blackwater's response as overreaction and problematic for the ability of US and allied military units to conduct operations among the populace.[6] Many Iraqi witnesses saw the incident in even worse terms—as unprovoked, unnecessary, and tantamount to murder. One point that emerged very early, though, was that Blackwater's employees were operating in a legal fog. The contractors enjoyed exemption from Iraqi law. Furthermore, as they were not working for the Department of Defense, it was doubtful they could be placed under the Military Extraterritorial Jurisdiction Act (MEJA), which did apply to those working for the DOD. Even trying to stretch the coverage of this law by claiming the Blackwater employees were supporting the DOD mission in Iraq did not offer sufficient grounds. The only apparent alternative was for the Department of Justice to try to hold them accountable under US criminal law, which required sentences of thirty years for using a machine gun in a violent crime. This was not an easy path to prosecute. In 2008 a federal judge dismissed the charges because the prosecution appeared to rely on statements made by the defendants under the threat of loss of their jobs. Only in October 2014 did a jury finally find four of the defendants guilty under a combination of weapons charges, manslaughter, and murder. A fifth defendant had pleaded guilty to manslaughter and cooperated with the prosecution. The account that emerged from the trial differed from others. It was Nicholas Slatten who fired the first shots, not Slough, and Slatten was found guilty of murder. The other three faced lesser charges. For the United States the trial's outcome was proclaimed a public relations victory, if nothing else, as it had rested much of its credibility on the argument that Iraqi citizens could trust the US justice system. Yet, the fog reappeared in early August 2017 when the US Court of Appeals for the District of Columbia ruled that Slatten should have been tried separately from the other three and that the latter had suffered cruel and unusual punishment because of the length of their sentences and the dependence of the convictions on federal firearms charges commonly used for gangs and bank robbers rather than security personnel. Slatten's retrial ended in a hung jury in September 2018, but federal prosecutors decided to pursue another trial beginning in November that found Slatten guilty.[7]

The circuit court's review of the verdict did not override a desire to send a strong signal that any person under contract to the US government was not beyond the reach of US law. However, it had not been the jury's responsibility to answer the broader questions about the appropriate place and role of private contractors in conflict and military operations. In the present day, these questions grow daily in size and implication. Advocates of reliance on contractors range from the cautious to the enthusiastic and boundlessly optimistic. Some believe contractors should be prohibited from combat operations and the actual battlefield; others suggest they could be used in such circumstances but only in settings where strict boundaries of authorization and accountability exist. A third perspective favors use of contractors instead of government forces because of the diminished appeal and interest in service in the professional military among the population of modern developed societies; a growing reluctance of the latter's governments to ask their societies for such sacrifices; the comparatively low cost, in the opinions of some, of private militaries in place of government-generated ones for less-developed countries, and even a libertarian conviction that defense is better and less expensive when left to choices in a free, nongovernment market. Erik Prince described with pride a scenario in Najaf, Iraq, in April 2004 where he asserted US (and Salvadorian) military personnel were "commanded" by private contractors. The fact that many of the contractors on hand were former Navy SEALs seems to diminish the value of any question about broader questions of effectiveness, legality, and accountability.[8]

Prince has proved irrepressible in his quest to find business and develop ways to use private forces to replace or supplement both foreign or US military personnel in a variety of settings. In 2010 he relocated to Abu Dhabi. Besides Academi he created Frontier Service Group in 2014, which is sold on the Hong Kong stock exchange and specializes in helping companies operating in "frontier markets." The locations are numerous, including Somalia (an antipiracy force), United Arab Emirates (an alleged "secret army"), and China (security training for Chinese companies). Donald Trump's victory in the presidential election in 2016 certainly pleased Prince, who had donated to Trump's campaign, and some have alleged that the fact his sister, Betsy DeVos, is the secretary of education in the administration has played to his advantage. In late July–early August 2017 Prince and Stephen Feinberg with DynCorp, another major private military firm, met with President Trump's chief strategist, Stephen Bannon, and the president's son-in-law, Jared Kushner, to push for the substitution of 5,500 contractors for US military personnel in Afghanistan. Reports of Trump's desire to reduce, and even end, US involvement in Afghanistan possibly posed an opportunity to reduce controversy by this replacement of most US troops with contractors and Afghan personnel. About 2,000 US Special Operations forces might remain, but Prince claimed the cost would be about a quarter of what the United States was currently paying in Afghanistan and that the reduced visibility of the United States could be enhanced if the administration put these operations under the guise of intelligence rather than military operations. The whole operation would be under the control of a "viceroy" reporting to the president. Bannon reportedly expressed interest in it, but Lieutenant General H. R. McMaster—Trump's national security advisor—and Secretary of Defense James Mattis opposed the idea. Reception on Capitol Hill was mixed. Some members of Congress thought the United States should not rule out the use of contractors, but more appeared to share the opinion of Senator Lindsey Graham (R-SC), who deemed it a vision from a bad novel. Bannon's departure from the White House shortly thereafter may have laid such ideas temporarily to rest, but they will resurface. Speculation surrounds the position of the new national security advisor, John Bolton, on this matter, and indeed Prince tried again in August 2018 to push his proposal, but to no avail. Yet, setting Prince, Bolton, or others aside, the factors behind interest and use in private means in conflict transcend certain personalities. As this book shows, this is an old question that has resurfaced in modern times. It is valuable to look into the past to recognize even more so the duplication and novelty in the present.[9]

This book tries to do something that has not been done extensively before: to look at the questions of why and how private actors using armed force in the past came to fall under the control of state and other forms of public accountability. Particular attention will be given to privateering because of the similarity of its business arrangements to modern contracting, but appreciation of the experiences surrounding mercenaries must occur to provide context and reinforcement for the discussion. More specifically, because the United States is the leading provider and customer of private military firms, this book gives particular attention to how the colonial and revolutionary experiences of the early United States led the writers of the Constitution to tackle the matter of private force directly in the "marque and reprisal clause" in Article I, Section 8 of the Constitution. Today, that clause can seem to be among the most arcane in the document, but viewed in a larger understanding of its origin and purpose, it assuredly is not. We will see that some have claimed the clause should be reasserted literally—in effect, making Prince and his many corporate counterparts the equivalent of eighteenth- or early nineteenth-century privateers. The United States, after all, has never outlawed privateering, which isolates it from almost the entire international community since the Declaration of Paris in 1856 that ended the Crimean War and for all purposes the practice of privateering.

The benefit of examining the marque and reprisal clause is to appreciate the fact that the framers recognized there could be a place for private actors in a declared or congressionally authorized war and that the state, specifically its legislative arm, had the power to authorize these measures and the means to control them. This could be privateering, as understood in 1787, or, arguably, for later forms of private force. To hold the marque and reprisal clause to a strict construction of its purpose is to miss its broader point: there is a right to have a public form of accountability for private action, whether to the state or some other form of publicly organized and recognized body.

Marque and reprisal, keep in mind, was a legal authority and framework provided by princes, monarchs, or governments to privateers. Their land-bound counterparts, mercenaries, did not operate under such strict arrangements. They had contracts and conditions of employment, but a privateer was also supposed to be acting under official authority of a government or legal entity. Both privateers with their licenses of marque and reprisal and contracted mercenaries exercised their private rights and actions in times and settings before modern states even existed. Understanding this can enable one to appreciate more deeply how notions of the cause and conduct of conflict and war have changed. We will see that marque and reprisal rested on the rights of private parties to seek redress or compensation for damages when governing figures, in whatever form, were unable and even unwilling to address these problems. By the late seventeenth century, marque and reprisal had become more of a means of supplementing the resources and capabilities of the state, whether through money for the treasury or additional measures for war at sea. Private means of war fell more and more under state control, and this only began to reverse itself in the late twentieth century. Mercenaries and, more so, private military firms came to be regarded as attractive options to use alongside or in place of the instruments of state, including uniformed military personnel. These considerations were not unlike those pondered in Philadelphia some 230 years ago. How does a government or state take advantage of resources provided by private parties who want to engage in these activities for profit, particularly when the means offered come from incorporated entities with shareholders and governing boards? However, the questions would not end there. What if private actors have the actual capability to wage war without the consent, or maybe even the full knowledge, of the state or international bodies? It is a dawning reality today in the domain of cyber.

While no one has looked at the subject in the way I have done in this book, many scholars have examined and written on aspects of it. This is a literature that encompasses a wide array of disciplines—history, political science, international relations and security studies, law, philosophy, anthropology, technology, business and corporate studies, and pure military science. I have tried to tie these many threads together, and for the recent period I have drawn more on primary sources, especially government and military documents, as well as my own personal experience in senior-level military education. In 1994, when I took a position in the Industrial College of the Armed Forces, part of the National Defense University in Washington, DC, I entered an educational environment that was trying to examine and assess the implications of increased reliance on private means on the development of defense capabilities as well as the actual conduct of military operations. Some of this I observed firsthand, and much of it I was able to discuss with, or witness discussions conducted by, military officers from all branches of the US military as well as many foreign militaries. I cannot attribute their words in seminar or conversation by name, but content from their observations figures prominently in the last third of this book. Thirteen years of experience prior to the National Defense University, particularly with the professional staff of the House Foreign Affairs Committee and as a Washington, DC, representative for the US subsidiary of a large German multinational, Siemens, enabled me to witness and engage in aspects of the policy debates and emergence of policies surrounding business-government relations, the transfer of technology, and the sale and export of both commercial and military goods.

As already intimated, examination of this subject has to begin with discussion of broad questions that invite digression down tempting and diverse paths. For example, one has to consider the meaning of *war*. What is it? Who fights it if force is used? For what end is it waged? To illustrate, international law, if strictly applied, limits the term to conflicts between states, but we use the label of "war" for other types of armed conflicts. Furthermore, "war" itself has become a term to rally support behind a lot of campaigns against drugs, poverty, crime, pornography, and terrorism, among other things. How one defines *war* and *wartime* is going to carry implications on decisions about who wages or fights it.[10] The objective in these pages will not be to settle on a single definition of war; the very diversity and range in definitions and descriptions point to the problems surrounding private actors or any nonstate actors in war and conflict. Assessing the place of the private contractor in war also requires brief consideration of periods of history preceding the existence of states, because they were a time when the right of private war enjoyed recognition. This is important, as legacies of that practice continued into the mid-nineteenth century and reemerged in the late twentieth.

Whether one agrees or disagrees with German political sociologist Max Weber, the analytical starting point for a study of private force has to consider what he wrote in his famous essay "Politics as a Vocation." "Today, however," Weber observed, "we have to say that a state is a human community that (successfully) claims the *monopoly of the legitimate use of physical force* [emphasis is Weber's] within a given territory. Note that 'territory' is one of the characteristics of the state. Specifically, at the present time, the right to use physical force is ascribed to other institutions or to individuals only to the extent which the state permits it."[11] Published in 1919 and based on a lecture of Weber's from the previous year, the essay's argument is not surprising. Development of the German state had been a dominant issue throughout Weber's lifetime, and history was about to enter a period in the twentieth century where "state" would be elevated to its highest levels of profile and command for better and worse. The point here is Weber's emphasis on war as state-sponsored violence. In short, war had become what contemporaries in the United States and elsewhere call "an inherently government function." Weber implies that violence and warlike actions may occur outside the authority or control of states, but, if so, it is not a legitimate form of war: *legitimate war is a state function.* A century later, determination of what exactly is an inherent government function is not so clear. The question has become a contentious arena populated by advocates of free markets and privatization against protectors of the traditional, and in their eyes, necessary powers of government. Yet, in 2018 the United States no longer regards war as strictly confined within Weber's boundaries. In the future, war, too, could be an activity better handled by "outsourcing." Where the standards rest on what should or should not be outsourced is debatable.

A discussion of the types of private actors in war is also in order. The emergence, use, purpose, and replacement of mercenaries by professional or conscript armies must be considered, with particular attention given to that most interesting side of war's private sector: the high seas. One reason for doing so is that the customs, laws, and procedures on the maritime side developed much more than on the land side. A sizable portion of international law emerged as a result of the political and legal questions that arose from the development of European empires and the places and rights of those who were operating and conducting armed operations in their areas of interest and control. These laws created the means by which privateers and vessels operating under letters of marque and reprisal could operate legally on the high seas in a state's name. In similar and diverse ways these types of legal frameworks more closely parallel the types of arrangements and contractors that private military contractors or security firms enter with governments. The law of the sea has become a framework for much of the law and policies surrounding airspace and now, many argue, should serve as the same for the cyber domain. After all, sea, air, and cyber are regions and domains where traditional landmarks of terrain and their uses for boundaries and sovereignty do not easily apply. As war's meaning and conduct become blurred more by new technologies, such as cyber, forms of response by private actors may become more necessary and practical. Certainly, their existence is already reality due to the actions of hackers, companies, and others on the internet that may or may not have state sponsorship.

A second reason to give such attention to letters of marque and reprisal is that the internal business and legal arrangements that existed in these licenses for privateers, more than those for mercenaries, resembled the structure and practice of modern private contractors. Money and personal gain were admittedly a significant part of the story on land and sea. However, those who sought letters of marque and reprisal to commence privateering developed arrangements of finance with investors, shareowners, and distribution of gains or profits. Admittedly, no "Privateering, Inc." ever really emerged. Privateering ventures were usually one-time arrangements, but it was not uncommon to see the same parties reconvene for the same purpose with another vessel and crew or, sometimes, with the same vessel and crew. In short, more than mercenaries, privateering demonstrated the characteristics of a business venture, a corporation, and a legally recognized group of investors. It follows from this that the legal means governments provided to enable privateers to go on their missions resemble some of the policies and practices of the modern day with private military and security firms.

Privateers with letters of marque and reprisal (real and sometimes fake) became important instruments of sea-going powers from the sixteenth century through most of the eighteenth century—surviving longer in many settings than their land-based counterpart, mercenaries. The reasons were not radically different from the arguments made today for privatization: economic and operational efficiency; valuable supplemental components to the existing or standing parts of the navies, which were more expensive to build and maintain; the provision of an armed instrument that sometimes served to obscure state responsibility; and finally, a form of armed force that might prevent escalation of a conflict to an actual state-on-state engagement. The European governments that initially relied on such measures were enthusiastic about them, but by the early eighteenth century a growing unease, even dislike, emerged about their presence and use. Private actors did not always act in the best interests of their sponsoring government or agent. In fact, there were instances where they attacked ships of the same country or vessels owned by merchants or companies from that country. Furthermore, as European colonial empires expanded, so, too, did the conviction that government ministries had to maintain better control over those persons who claimed to be acting on their realms' behalf on the high seas. A form of centralization in imperial authority and a desire to protect and better assert the interests of the parent government and state became paramount.

While several of the European powers relied on privateers and ships operating with letters of marque and reprisal, the experience of the British is especially important for this study. First, given the focus of the last half of this book on the United States, the development of British practice and law heavily influenced the American experience from the colonial period onward. Also, the far-ranging global stretch of British interests as time progressed lent a strategic and political tone to the discussions about use of these types of instruments. That aspect certainly was not absent in the discussions of the Spanish, Dutch, and French, among others, but the British conviction about the strategic dominance of sea power, which was ongoing during these years, elevated strategic implications to more frequent and insightful examination. Such calculations also figured prominently in the creation and operation of the European trading companies, such as the Dutch East India and British East India companies. Their purpose went beyond commercial gain, to the exercise of political power both within Europe and in the foreign zones covered by these companies. However, as the eighteenth century progressed, London became more convinced that its empire and members must ultimately serve the Crown's interests more and those of colony and company less. The thirteen American colonies were key players in this—especially in the licensing of privateers with letters of marque and reprisal, which colonial governors did under the authority of the Crown. When those colonies moved toward independence and the creation of a new government, they logically walked in the steps of their British counterparts in the arguments both for and against use of private means of armed force.

The experience of the United States powerfully illustrates, as well as any country's, the difficulties and controversies surrounding the existence and use of privately owned means of armed force. Initially a very decentralized system operated in the colonies; each colony (later a state) could issue its own letters of marque and reprisal to privateers throughout the American Revolution and under the Articles of Confederation. What were the reasons, then, for the decision of the writers of the Constitution to take that authority away and place it in the hands of Congress? Was this because letters of marque and reprisal were a measure in war-making that, like a declaration of war itself, required congressional action, or, to use terminology unknown to the Founding Fathers, was it to assure that decisions made about "national security" occurred only at the national level?[12] Like other states, the new United States had to create safeguards for its behavior to assure it would be recognized and treated with respect in the international community.

However, in a political system and culture that entertained strong suspicions of central authority and capability, particularly in regard to standing militaries, reliance on the entrepreneur or private sector could be appealing. It seemed cheaper and, as will be shown later, probably was so when the United States only needed particular military capabilities on an episodic, sporadic basis. Furthermore, even though navies did not have the same notoriety as standing armies, the absence of a large fleet and numerous sailors provided a little more security against the prospect of military rule. Like today, some also thought that large militaries inevitably attracted the attention of other powers and encouraged the likelihood of war. During the American Revolution and War of 1812 this "outsourcing," if one can call it that, served the United States rather well. In no way could the nation have been able to raise the revenue to build a fleet. Its puny navy conducted itself very well against the far superior British in both wars, but without the parallel efforts of privateers and vessels operating under letters of marque and reprisal the outcome in both wars might have been less favorable.

It should be no surprise, then, to learn that the United States held onto these practices longer than many of its more powerful competitors or rivals. When the major powers gathered in Paris in 1856 to negotiate a settlement to the Crimean War, they also had to address other issues that had played their parts in the overall actions of the participants and the war's outcome. The United States had not been party to the debacles that occurred on all sides in that war, but as a neutral state it had interests in negotiations that affected trade and the rights of neutral states during time of war. One of the outcomes of the treaty was a ban on the practice of private war at sea— privateering and letters of marque and reprisal. That ban figured prominently in the decision of the United States not to sign the treaty, and to this day it has never signed it, even though Washington would claim, as it has in relation to some other treaties it never signed, it has adhered to the words and practices of the agreement.

Nevertheless, the terms *privateering* and *letters of marque and reprisal* sank into obscurity through the remainder of the nineteenth century and into most of the twentieth. Legal scholars and historians kept them in use for specific purposes, and creators of fictional naval swashbucklers found these seemingly archaic antics could hold the attention of a sizable readership seeking respite from routine office jobs, possibly demented colleagues, and encroaching families. The reference found in Article I, Section 8 of the US Constitution that assigns the power to declare war and issue letters of marque and reprisal followed an almost schizophrenic path. The first half became the foundation for an endless argument over the distribution of war powers in the US system, particularly when placed alongside the commander-in-chief provision that favored the president.[13] The last half dropped almost into complete obscurity. It seemed to be one of the most anachronistic set of words in the Constitution. If a special convention had been called to cleanse the document of the pointless and unnecessary, it assuredly would have been a target for removal.[14] Even today, most legislators would likely designate it this way, as the language seems so bound to circumstances and practices of a bygone time and environment that it is meaningless.

Some of the history, circumstance, and settings may seem to have little to no direct application to the present or future, but the arguments made for development and reliance of such private capabilities and the counterarguments to place these same assets and activities back into the hands of the state do hold a real significance for us. In broadest terms, arguments and discussions, whether from the eighteenth, the twentieth, or the twenty-first century, revolve around an endless debate over the proper role of government. Regardless of assumptions and their starting points, nearly all philosophies of organized government believe its purpose deals partly with the welfare of those living under it as well as their protection from danger from the outside. How this is done, as well as the range and nature of responsibility held by the government, varies widely, so a common answer is elusive. The United States, as well as its global neighbors, has watched the pendulum or meter move from one side to the other at different stages of history.

Arguments over the role and size of government domestically have automatic implications for the standing and capability of a state or government internationally. If one worries about the size of the state and the growing intrusion of government into the private and personal—which has been a visible topic in recent decades, even while its origins go back much farther—the aspiration will be to reduce or eliminate parts of that structure and capability and return it to a more local or individual level. Some individuals believe national defense and security must be exempt from this. Others argue to the contrary and stress that the "national security state" is part of the problem. It, too, must be pared back, and privatization, perhaps, is a part of the answer.

By the 1980s a convergence of domestic and international changes seemed to make this possible and necessary. Arguably in the 1980s, at least for the United States, this reduction occurred mainly in the domestic arena, whereas defense spending increased, especially during the early and middle years of the presidency of Ronald Reagan (1981–1989). The end of the Cold War and the slow dismantlement of parts of the military monoliths the two superpowers possessed created a setting where it became easier to entertain the retreat of the "national security state" and transfer some of it to the private sector, where it was not the "state" per se. Many of the arguments that had been made two or three centuries earlier resurfaced—sometimes in very recognizable forms, while others required closer scrutiny.

Those arguments included concerns driven by the large numbers of former military personnel, now back in the civilian marketplace, who were looking for jobs. Supporters of privatization also drew attention to, and simultaneously benefited from, the growth of nonstate actors who figured more prominently in settings where superpowers had sometimes had control of proxies or nominal control of other actors. Insurgents, freedom fighters, counterinsurgents, terrorists, organized crime, warlords, drug lords, pirates, and, yes, private military companies grew alongside each other in the international system. In reality, nonstate actors such as these had existed throughout history—revolutionaries, guerrillas, partisans, tribal groupings, and fighters for national liberation. Professional military literature was filled with cycles of attention about the conflicts related to these *petite guerre, kleine Kriege*, rebellions and revolutions, wars of national liberation, and insurgencies. Sometimes such conflicts have caused leaders to vow, like the US Army after Vietnam, that they would not fight these types of wars again because of the difficult character of the war, the unclear end-state and conditions allowing an exit, and the social and political cost to the army at home. As Iraq and Afghanistan appeared to wind down after 2011, segments of the US Army revived the vow again. Armies, like most of us, prefer to do the type of things they want rather than the tasks they get. Privatization posed itself as a possible way of creating and sustaining the types of forces that would be necessary. These notions of privatization went beyond the sourcing out of responsibilities and functions that could easily be easily given to the private sector, such as matters related to sanitation, food, and maintenance, and entertained the transfer of actual combat and combat support to the private sector. Most members of the professional military have vigorously opposed the privatization of actual conflict, war, and combat. It is more in parts of the commercial sector and even in corners of the community of policy and defense intellectuals where the case has found its strongest adherents.

Thus, as the United States began to transfer more functions from the military to the private sector, political and military leaders, lawyers, and academic specialists started to examine much more closely the political, economic, and military gains and losses of these changes. You will encounter a number of these political and military leaders, writers, and commentators in the coming pages, as I have chosen to address them when or where their work seems most salient or to have the most impact. Thanks to the role of contractors at Abu Ghraib, Guantanamo Bay, and in various other incidents in Afghanistan and Iraq, such as Nisour Square, law attracted the most immediate attention. The continued ambiguity in current laws needs obvious action, as part of the answer to the challenges and problems of privatization must rest there. However, answers to broader questions about whether to do this must go beyond the "how" or "how not" that is the focus of most law. The historical record is a better source to understand and evaluate the "why," "how," and "whether" (or not) that surround the decisions to rely on privately owned means of armed force. One could do so by tracing the subject from its beginning: such private means were known in the ancient world, and they are also a part of non-Western traditions and cultures. Worthwhile questions obviously appear in these areas of inquiry. This is especially so if this study were to aim its focus at the reasons developing economies and states as well as non-Western cultures might resort to privatization in warfare, as some indeed have. Some discussion of these will occur, but the center of attention here is the United States.

The United States is not the sole actor in the developed world that has turned to private means in warfare, nor was it the first. Other modern states have done so. For those states with constitutional systems that are democratic, republican, or a combination thereof, the questions and controversies are similar to those in the United States. Arguably, though, the United States is very much the trendsetter in this entire area. If it concludes that it can turn to privatization reliably in ways that do not compromise constitutional, legal, political, military, and ethical requirements and principles, other states and government will follow in its wake. To turn heavily to privatization, the United States would arguably have to make remarkable concessions in laws, values, and practice that I truly hope remain insurmountable. However, others disagree and believe that if armed force, conflict, and war are means and instruments that must be retained and kept effective, it is essential to change and adapt in different ways in the spheres where war is conducted. However, to be done, the private sphere must be expanded and adjusted to enable these new capabilities. In reality, the solution appears to rest somewhere in the middle, for private war in certain forms is returning. The historical record urges caution. States and governments benefited from reliance on private means of force, but they almost inevitably confronted problems with control and assurance that state or government objectives were being served. The answer that emerges does not say "never do this," but, if done, it will require a level of attention and commitment not often found in the past. The following chapters will probe much more deeply into this conclusion.

1 DEFINING THE SPHERES OF WAR

The determination of who best fights in war is implied in the very definition of war. Depending on the characteristics one assigns to war and the causes and purposes of it, its actual conduct may rely on a variety of actors. The record of war and the literature examining it is vast. War has undergone, and continues to experience, major transformation. Regardless of all the study and inquiry, no single definition of war exists on which all agree. Whether in the ancient, classical, medieval, early modern, modern, or contemporary periods, as well as in projections about the future of war, we have not been able to agree completely on the terms of its scope, scale, duration, participants, range of damage and death, or now, with subjects like space and cyber, its location. Most of us could easily settle on its major characteristics, but there are aspects of war that puzzle us and invite argument about its existence and place. We may not completely agree on what it is, but we have little doubt about its label when we see it. No final definition of war is attempted here. That is not the purpose of this study. Instead, different definitions of war appear because they have different purposes and application, which, depending on circumstance and focus of the discussion, are important to examining who should bear the burden of fighting it. Even concepts and definitions of war related to early periods in history may appear applicable again. For example, if one believes the authority of states is diminishing in the present day, it could be worthwhile to examine war in the centuries before states existed. The contemporary scholar Philip Bobbitt offers this description of war:

> From the time when the first modern states began to emerge, only states have made war. . . . Since the Renaissance, brigands, pirates, feudal and religious orders, even Corporations (like the Dutch East India Company) might fight but only states could sanction violence as war. War is a matter between states—constitutional entities created by

and wielding law—and war carries with it the constitutional evolution of five centuries of interstate conflict.[1]

Bobbitt's description of war relies on both Max Weber's state-centered framework that places the sanction of violence in the hands of the state and an evolving body of international law that governs the decision for war as well as the measures for its proper conduct. It is a helpful definition for placing boundaries around war's existence and purpose. It is not helpful, though, for defining the status of affairs outside these boundaries—whether they are from today or three hundred years ago. A lot of consequent questions come from this definition, and two will figure with special prominence. What does "sanction" by a state really mean, and, second, is it completely accurate and possible to suggest that war cannot occur between nonstate or private actors? Certainly there have been instances where the participants thought they were genuinely at war as well as cases where private actors believed they had a right to wage war. Furthermore, what does one do with conflicts within one state? Bobbitt would correctly refer to the body of international law, known as the law of war, the law of armed conflict, or international humanitarian law, for answers. Yet, even with those answers, Bobbitt's definition leaves some confusion when addressing scenarios where states do not exist—both in the past, before modern states existed, and in the present, where the authority and framework of the state are in question.

Other students of war have proposed definitions based on characteristics that are not as tied to states. In a classical work from the mid-twentieth century, Quincy Wright recognized attributes that might not automatically be state-driven, even while presenting conditions that suggested states or actors similar to them. "War is seen to be a state of law and a form of conflict involving a high degree of legal equality, of hostility, and of violence in the relations of organized human groups, or, more simply, the legal conditions which equally permits two or more hostile groups to carry on a conflict by armed force."[2] Wright avoids the label *state*, but his references to "organized human groups" and "legal conditions" clearly require some type of authority that has set these standards. Wright's work appeared in 1942, the third year of a world war whose scale and destructiveness was unprecedented. One hopes the world never witnesses its magnitude again, whether between states or other groups. However, words like *groups*, *organized*, and even *equality* are not exclusive to states. These can be found in examples of ancient warfare and tribal warfare, and they reflect as well the premise of proportionality that is a central tenet in the entire concept of modern "just war" theory.[3]

As the various conflicts of the Cold War and afterward illustrated, any definition of war that depended on state control and management of violence was problematic. A contemporary legal scholar, Gary Solis, has observed that the nature of these episodes remind us that "not all armed conflicts are wars, but all wars are armed conflicts."[4] Solis's reference to "armed conflicts" notes the major efforts of the twentieth century to outlaw war, except for purposes of self-defense—the Kellogg-Briand Pact and the United Nations Charter. As these treaties placed the legality of most wars into question, the term *armed conflict* has become the preferred label of the modern day. Such conflicts, however, could embrace both state and nonstate actors.

Scholars during the past few decades have tried to find concepts and terms to push thinking beyond state-on-state conflict and to acknowledge the role of nonstate actors of various types, including contractors and corporations. Mary Kaldor's *New and Old Wars* has been one of the most influential of these works because of its readability and clarity of argument. Kaldor writes, "The new wars involve a blurring of the distinctions between war (usually defined as violence between states or organized political groups for political motives), organized crime (violence undertaken by privately organized groups for private purposes, usually financial gain) and large-scale violence of human rights (violence undertaken by states or politically organized groups against individuals)."[5] "Organized" is a word that runs throughout her description, but it importantly is not a level of organization fully equivalent to states.

Broader concepts of war push the boundaries beyond where Kaldor stands. Jack Levy's and William Thompson's definition initially sounds traditional—"'war' [is] sustained, coordinated violence between political organizations." However, it is their view of "political organizations" that is critical; these wars "include violent conflicts between states, empires, city-states, ethnic groups, chiefdoms, tribes, and hunter-gather groups, as well as many types of violent conflicts within those groups." They add, "For violence to constitute warfare it must be organized and it must have some threshold of magnitude or severity." The reference to violence is not surprising, but Levy and Thompson discount the commonly argued conviction that violence in war must have a "political purpose."[6] Their discussion of war makes no specific reference to private firms or contractors, but as it is a "behavioral definition" its use does not depend on the identity of the parties doing the fighting. "If two or more political units engage in the sustained and coordinated use of violence, it is a war regardless of the motivations for the violence."[7]

Whether a corporation would be a "political unit" in the above discussion is unclear. The right, if there is one, of purely private warfare is not implied by Levy and Thompson. Yet, that right did exist at one time, and it may become difficult today and in the future to rule out its revival in relation to corporations and individuals. Modern corporations do have to be legally chartered and adhere to the laws of where they are incorporated and/or where they act for purposes of business. Those requirements do not automatically make them a "political unit" as such. Indeed, in US law, corporations enjoy the rights and treatment of private citizens.[8] Modern states have laws that obstruct and prevent corporations and individual citizens from acting against law, including of course laws shaped by national security considerations. The interesting distinction Levy and Thompson make, though, is that only the organization has to be "political"—but not the ends or purpose of the violence being done. The ambiguity that rests in this argument resurfaces at different points throughout these pages and ultimately around the matter when corporate attacks and counter-attacks in the cyber realm could or should fall under a definitional umbrella for war or violence. These "private wars" might not have political purposes, but they certainly could have political consequences! In most cases throughout these pages, privateers, holders of letters of marque and reprisal, and contractors acted under the official auspices of a state (a "political organization"), so the prospect of such actors operating as the equivalents of legally free-floating atoms would be unlikely. If they did so on the high seas they became known as pirates, who lacked legal protection anywhere. Yet, at the same time, any privateer or modern contractor has consistently acted out of the hope of making money. Thus the aspiration for lucre is supposed to be subordinate to the "political organization," but what if it is not?

Violence has been a constant quality throughout the commentaries in the literature on war. Its likelihood is there even with the legal technicality that allows a state of war to exist without the actual presence or conduct of violence. The latter point can be set aside for now, but the place of violence cannot, because it, too, is tied to the identity of the actor committing it. For professional students and practitioners of war in Western culture, the starting point for much thought is Carl von Clausewitz's *On War*. Taken literally,

Clausewitz's straightforward definition of war does not seem to confine its practice to a specific group of people. "War," Clausewitz wrote, "is . . . an act of force to compel our enemy to do our will."[9] "Force" may not be equivalent to violence, but Clausewitz's characterization of it leaves no doubt the prospect of violence is on hand. "Physical force . . . is thus the means of war."[10] Thus, when Levy and Thompson argue that the actual exercise of violence may not need a political purpose, they challenge the traditional view on how political groups must use violence. As "war is an instrument of policy," in Clausewitz's words, "it must necessarily bear the character of policy by its standards. The conduct of war . . . is therefore policy itself, which takes up the sword in place of the pen."[11] Here, at least, war and the violence and force that are part of it must have a political end, although it may not necessarily be an end sought by a state. Private war for private, nonpolitical purposes will not stand scrutiny in Clausewitz's model.

The conflicts between World War II and the present have given more reason to question whether violence must have political ends as Clausewitz understood them. Lawrence Freedman stresses that "without the element of violence the study of war loses all focus," but war does "not . . . need states." The violence used must be "purposive," by which Freedman means it "must be to a degree strategic." This is a significant qualifier that may allow broader considerations than the traditional ones of states and political groups. Freedman stipulates that the violence "must be geared to an end other than whatever satisfaction is derived directly from the experience of violence. Street fights, random displays of hostility, or 'letting off steam' do not count."[12] Although unelaborated, a lot of other purposes of violence could count; "purposive" and "strategic" are not attributes of states only. The same range of actors in conflicts made an international legal scholar remind readers twenty years earlier that "parties which engage in war do not have to be recognised as States by their Enemy. A country, nation, or group can be a belligerent in spite of non-recognition." Just how far the meaning of "group" can be expanded is unclear. It excludes mercenaries for sure, but modern-day contractors go to great length to argue they are not mercenaries—a claim that still awaits authoritative resolution. Whoever they may be, nonstate actors cannot issue a declaration of war, which is a power solely retained by states.[13] This position rests on existing international law. Thus, neither Osama bin Laden's declaration of war in 1998 nor a hypothetical declaration made by a private sector actor would have unquestioned legal standing. In a lot of other arenas, though, the use of violence would hold standing—particularly for those at the receiving end of it. War, thus, needs a purpose, but whether that is only for a state to decide is debatable. *Purpose* implies someone or some group has made a decision, and it is how that purpose is maintained and respected that is so critical here.

THE SPHERE OF PRIVATE WAR

What is it about private force that the modern world finds so repugnant? Does the objection originate "from the idea that taking human life in warfare is only morally justified by some attachment to a cause bigger than oneself"?[14] This would be the accusation against traditional mercenaries, but private military firms argue they are serving the interest of their employing state and not just goals of private gain. In fact, many would point out that their employees, especially those more closely tied or integrated with the operations of a national military, are not that different from volunteer soldiers, who have enlisted for a period during which they are paid for their services.[15] Nevertheless, a casual perusal of newspaper headlines and stories in the United States will testify to a major gap in public perception of professional soldiers and private military contractors. We identify those killed in action, and they are listed as part of the fatalities in Afghanistan, Iraq, and elsewhere in the current operations against terrorism. The nation mourns them in an abstract sense, and their home states, communities, and families certainly mourn for them with mounting intensity as the circle of those affected narrows. The death of contractors is scarcely noted or reported; cumulative tallies over the years are not shown, and the mourning is definitely at the level of family and friends. One reaction reflects the conviction that the man or woman died for their country and its defense—a higher purpose; the other mirrors a belief that he or she died because they needed the money.

We are so acculturated to the presence of the state and the role of its constitutions and governmental processes in sanctioning actions taken in the state's name on behalf of its citizenry that it is easy to forget or overlook that states with such capabilities are rather recent in history. A survey of the entire historical record would assuredly be of definite value, but the linkage of history with most law and current practice points to a review of the West beginning in the feudal period and Middle Ages. This has become an important reference point in recent discussion because one of the most important and insightful books on private armies and war, Sean McFate's *The Modern Mercenary*, has especially drawn a parallel with this time in history. McFate observes and warns that "the emergence of private armies heralds the slow return to the status quo ante of the Middle Ages, when states did not enjoy primacy in international politics and instead shared a crowded world stage with other actors." He describes this emerging environment as "neomedievalism" and notes that "a key challenge of neomedievalism will be controlling private military force."[16]

One can embrace the value of McFate's analogy and the warnings he provides and also dispute some aspects of the approach he takes. Whether one accepts his analysis and the consequent label completely, McFate has used it to highlight the arguable erosion of the state system in the international order and the effects of globalization. Scholars, practitioners, the business and economic sectors, and journalists have argued over the specific characteristics of globalization, the magnitude and meaning of its changes, and the comparative power of states in this order. Few would disagree, though, with the assertion that the modern world has more actors operating alongside or opposite and alongside the authority of states. McFate sees reliance on private armies as the consequence of both choice and circumstance. Perhaps the latter is more so with developing states that lack the resources (monetary, technological, and human) among others and thereby turn to private contractors, even armies, to do what would be more difficult for them. For a modern, postindustrial state like the United States the resort to such means is more a matter of choice.

McFate's treatment of the historical period concentrates more on the experience of mercenaries—an alternative that had definitely become more common in the later Middle Ages as the structure of states evolved and new means and measures for developing military capabilities appeared. After all, McFate is concerned with how states control private armies and their experience with mercenaries and the militaries of the major trading companies. He pays less attention to what preceded these developments. Yet the earlier part of the feudal period is important because it is in this setting where concepts of private war developed, took hold, and lasted in select ways into the following centuries. Any understanding of the ramifications of this period requires an examination of both private warfare and the private armies that evolving states and their successors used.

"The medieval state," as David William Bates describes it, "was not a proper state because it was not autonomous and did not have a monopoly over coercive violence within its boundaries or even over the conduct of war." There were other sources of authority—the Church and, depending on one's location and orientation, the Holy Roman Empire. Also, in the absence of strong monarchs and rulers there was the practice of private or seigneurial wars (especially in France), where lords, principalities, and even towns fought one another over rights or title to land, among other things.[17] In fact, the disputes over the location of authority were one of the reasons so many disputes and, arguably, so many variations of warfare appeared. Rulers, practitioners, and commentators believed there were private and public forms of war. A good example of a public form would be the Crusades, in which the Pope had the authority to call for war against infidels, the *bellum Romanum*. While papal authority was not equivalent to what we understand as political sovereignty, the Vatican nonetheless held and claimed authorities that enabled it to announce war and declare it for the common good, in this case the well-being of Christendom.[18] Locating this authority in the more temporal world was problematic. Writing in the fourteenth century, Honore Bouvet came up with a complicated list of types of wars that ranged from those in the heavens to individual duels conducted by wager.[19] The latter was a private conflict between two individuals, and it was a right of both parties.

The authority vested in the papacy to wage war drew greatly from the writing of Augustine, whose life spanned the turbulence of the late Roman Empire in the fourth and fifth centuries CE. Christianity had become the official religion of the Roman Empire during Augustine's life, and his work, particularly *The City of God*, tried to explain what had befallen the empire through repeated foreign invasions and destruction. However, Augustine was also arguing for a form of just war that could allow Christians to fight—something that was not automatically that easy in early Christian belief. If the Greco-Roman world had regarded the state as the highest level of human organization, Augustine subordinated this earthly realm to God's authority. Wars ordained by God would be just. Christians could wage war with the support of God and the assurance of the authority that His support provided.[20]

Arguably, the only temporal source of authority to conduct war with proper authority was the emperor of the Holy Roman Empire. At least that was so until around 1300, when his authority in western Christendom came more into question. Prior to that, against whom would he have declared war, since the other princes in this part of Christendom recognized his authority?[21] The growing powers of princes and monarchs and the ongoing evolution of what became modern states would splinter the Holy Roman Empire and, more important, elevate the state to the level of the actor or entity for which war was being fought. It would also begin to narrow, but not fully eliminate, the practice of private warfare that had actually been a major feature of the feudal and medieval world until this time.

The ongoing frequency of challenges to the authority of the Pope and the Holy Roman Empire from monarchs that occurred in Europe even before the beginning of the fourteenth century was a factor influencing a scholar in the thirteenth century, Thomas Aquinas, to introduce a concept of just war that recognized the emergence of early states and the authority of their rulers. Just war theory is a rich field of inquiry and thought that drew upon Greek and Roman arguments as well as those in the Judeo-Christian tradition. It has counterparts in other religious and non-Western traditions as well. In its simplest form, just war theory tries to identify a set of criteria and standards to be met that enables one to justify the decision to go to war (*jus ad bellum*) and to conduct the war in a just fashion (*jus in bello*). For our immediate purpose, the most important feature of Aquinas's argument was that war had to occur under just authority (divine or secular, such as the state). He did not grant the right for a private actor to initiate and conduct war based on his or her own sanction. Private individuals had to recognize those with greater authority over them. They could not summon an army or wage war. Two other key requisites in Aquinas's argument were a "just cause" and a "right intention."[22] Of course, one can find interpretative holes and flexibility in all of the above, and just war theory did not enjoy universal acceptance at any time in all parts of the world—even in the Judeo-Christian world. I encountered skepticism among German audiences about the weight most contemporary US decision makers place on it, a fact that clearly represents painful memories of earlier historical examples where governments invoked justice in their cause. However, in this book two of the theory's standards are going to reappear at times—legitimate sanction from *jus ad bellum* and proportionality drawn from *jus in bello*.

In his study of the impact of the development of the law of war on war itself, James Q. Whitman observes that "the tale of the law of war . . . was the tale of how sovereigns, and especially monarchs, had acquired the exclusive privilege of pursuing their rights through victory in war. In particular, it was the tale of how monarchs had crushed the cherished historic right of nobles to mount private wars of their own."[23] Such conflicts had been all too common during that time. When they occurred, they did not commence with a declaration but often through what was known as "the defiance." According to Frederic Baumgartner, who has examined war-making in this and the early modern period in Europe, the first written description of "defiance" is in The Song of Roland, which involves an action (vowing three times) by Roland's stepfather to kill him. The practice had originated from the more common circumstance of a feud between a lord and vassal. In most cases it involved the vassal accusing the lord of violating his rights and the breaking of a stick and throwing it at the lord's feet. Often the dispute was resolved by a duel on the spot. Eventually the selection of proxies and the appointment of heralds to carry the accusation developed. In 1356 the Holy Roman Empire announced a requirement of a three-day cooling-off period before physical action and violence could occur.[24] Clearly there was a danger that such feuds could evolve into something worse.

Besides lords and vassals, another group of people also wanted a way to find redress—especially when it came to stolen and destroyed property. The right of self-defense was not in question, but this concern was a step beyond. How could one obtain compensation or redress for damages? By the thirteenth century, laws began to emerge that set forth the measures, including use of force, to get satisfaction for the aggrieved party. In England local legislation tended to clarify the process; in France it was more through law of custom, and Italian city-states tried to handle it by treaty. The name for such measures was reprisal. Reprisals were private actions; principalities, kingdoms, and the states that succeeded them did not get involved directly in these steps. Many of these actors did not yet have that strong a sense of obligation to act in the welfare and interest of the overall populace, and often they lacked the means as well to do this. In fact, in some parts of Europe, such as the Germanic states, private wars were regarded as the right of a lord. Reprisals would remain a common practice for three more centuries, by which time growing states arguably had more "national consciousness" and began to reexamine the wisdom of leaving such measures in private hands.[25]

The resources required to take on these types of private conflicts were not that extensive in many cases. In struggles involving a feudal lord, vassals owed the lord forty days of service a year, which was fine for limited, short conflicts. An important factor to remember, though, is that these forces were in the control of private parties—nobles, knightly orders, and even ecclesiastical groups. In the hierarchical structure of the medieval world, only people of certain standing could resort to duels; they were not a recourse for peasants. Aristocrats regarded themselves primarily as a warrior class. War was their mission and duty, and war was a way of expanding the control of territory—a source of power and wealth in the temporal world. This presents a troubling facet of feudal war that just war theory highlights. A just war has a legitimate foundation under it that rests on both the legal authority of the initiator and a measure of consent from those involved in the fighting. Knights, for example, customarily enjoyed some form of a title. Their code of war rested heavily on the principles of chivalry, which governed how they fought each other and treated civilian noncombatants. Common soldiers who fought on the ground rather than horseback enjoyed less protection. It could be a cruel, merciless outcome for them. War was an expected, even desirable, attribute for knights and aristocrats. Consent might not be a major consideration for them, as they expected war. However, for the commoner consent was essentially nonexistent. They rarely received such a question. Coercion to serve and fight could come by force or by economic necessity. The range of consent offered to the average citizen remains debatable to the present day, even in modern democracies, but the common person of the feudal world would not have known the choice.[26]

The needs of larger-scale conflicts, though, could not be met as easily by the time-restricted frameworks for vassals and lords. As monarchs with growing responsibilities of sovereignty, including defense, had to fill their ranks, they began to turn to inducements to attract men to service—land (including fiefs offered in the Holy Land during the Crusades) and money. War in the feudal period or in the early Middle Ages had not been that resource-demanding, but larger-scale conflicts serving the ambitions of rulers or needs of emerging states could be. Promises of knighthood might work, too, as an incentive, but that only went so far. By the fourteenth century it was apparent that the traditional lines of feudal obligation no longer could serve the requirements of monarchs, kingdoms, and states.[27]

Thus, in a growlingly complex world one observer identified three different types of warfare that arguably seemed both just and legal. John of Legnano in 1360 designated them as wars involving nation against nation, wars of reprisal—which Legnano noted could also involve a government act on behalf of its subjects—and private war (self-defense).[28] As the practice of war developed, it relied greatly on concepts from dueling. Looking at this nearly six hundred years later, Quincy Wright argued that three forms of the duel coexisted: "State duel[s]" in which a "champion fights in behalf of the state"; "Judicial combat or trial by battle . . . to prove guilt or innocence"; and the "duel of honor," whose focus on self-honor was evident. As war ascended more to the monarch-on-monarch or state-on-state levels, it retained aspects of all three of these. States had their champions—armies; wars sought to support and prove the justice of a cause, and states often thought their national honor was at stake.[29] Wright was concerned mainly with the first form of wars in Legnano's categorization, but concerns of justice and honor were also interwoven into wars of reprisal and private self-defense.

A case can be made that this evolution of war to the state-on-state level, where its origins and conduct would become the focus of international law, actually made war more destructive. War by wager could be limited and decisive. The nature of a wager invites fast rather than belabored and extended settlement. People are not going to slaughter one another for something that can be resolved rather clearly and early. War in the Middle Ages also frequently revolved around questions of property. If James Whitman's characterization of both these wars and the available writing about them is accurate, their conduct and settlement sought an end-state closer to terms over injuries than determination of "criminal guilt." War's advance more and more into the public arena—that is, onto the stage of state-on-state and international conflict—would move it away from injuries to matters of guilt, self-defense, and honor.[30]

It is hard to accept the implications of such an argument about international law and the scale of war for the present and future world. Nor is an argument being made to reverse the clock, restore some of these forms of conflict, and dismantle the institutions, procedures, and laws that govern the conduct of war in the present and future. The primary purpose here is a reminder that the aforementioned were issues and attributes of the world from which the use of mercenaries, privateers, letters of marque, and trading companies emerged and functioned. Today we exercise a "tendency to associate the private sphere with the individual and freedom of markets and economic exchange, while the public sphere is associated with state authority and legitimate compulsion." Yet, today, many other types of "legitimate authority" claim to exist, and many of them are nonstate actors.[31] In terms of the relationship between war and the public sphere, we believe, as Claire Cutler writes, that "only public authorities are entitled or empowered to prescribe behavior for others because only public authorities are accountable through political institutions. Private entities, such as corporations or business associations, are not entitled to act authoritatively for the public, because they are not authorized by society and are thus not subject to mechanisms of political accountability."[32] It was not always so simple.

These assumptions and views govern most of the literature written about private means of armed force in academic, political, and legal circles in the United States and nearly the entire postindustrial world. That applies to this work as well, because of my recognition of the role of private actors but strong suspicions about their accountability. An example of clear usage of the term *public* is in Laura A. Dickinson's *Outsourcing War and Peace*, in which she sees private means as dangerous to "public values," which include "fundamental respect for human dignity," "public participation in decision making," and "transparency and anticorruption."[33] The validity of this assessment is weighed later, but grasping the importance of such assumptions that govern much of what we think is important here. "The concept of national security," the Danish scholar Karen Lund Petersen writes, "has historically entailed an understanding of the state as the protector of individual security" and "freedom." Ideas about "national interest and *raison d'état*" are part of our framework about national security.[34] To appreciate the historical world in which private actors in war acted, we have to set aside these assumptions and beliefs and consider why they were used and only later abandoned for the "public" or state options.

In reality, the definitions and boundaries of what is "private" and "public" have changed through history and may well be changing again. Today we think of it as between the government and the private sector (or the market), or between government and the rights of the individual, including notably the right of privacy opposite the government. The ancient Greek world defined these distinctions very differently, between the "household" and what was occurring in the common world. Only slaveholders could participate fully in this public world, while slaves and women addressed the needs of the private. If one lived in the private realm, he or she was not a full person.[35] Today some of that distinction would still arguably apply—the emphasis on what benefited the city-state overall being in the public—but laws to insure equality of citizens have broken down the distinctions between private and public in other ways.

If conflict today between states is being conducted in accordance with international law, it is occurring in the public sphere. The law of armed conflict does not provide full combatant status to private actors, and it does not recognize a legal place for war between private entities. Thus, it should be no surprise that in earlier stages of international law, as it developed alongside the structure of those actors affected by it, there was a parallel status for both private and public war. The most influential of the commentaries recognizing this was made by a young Dutch jurist, Hugo Grotius, in his *The Rights of War and Peace*. Grotius will appear again in this book in relation to the practices of the Dutch East India Company. Born in 1583 in Delft, Grotius had been a precocious young man, to say the least. By age fifteen he had completed his doctorate; he was practicing law a year later. One of the questions confronting Grotius on his return to The Hague was literally the legal status of the Dutch Republic, which Spain, its ruler, regarded as still being in a state of revolt. Grotius thus had to develop arguments that could win the republic international acceptance. In 1604 Grotius, now a seasoned twenty-one, was approached by the directors of the Dutch East India Company to write a justification for the attack and capture of a Portuguese ship by an officer of the company's navy. The Dutch wanted to challenge Portuguese dominance in the East Indies trade, and the Portuguese had attacked Dutch vessels and interests to prevent it—thus the Dutch attack on the ship, the *Santa Catarina*. The Portuguese were not pleased by this act, and neither were the Mennonites who owned shares in the Dutch Company, because they did not believe in war. Grotius had to make an argument showing that the war, and actions taken by the Dutch officer, was legal.[36] The answer did not come as quickly as Grotius's client wanted—certainly not the first or last time in the profession of law and policy. When it did come, with the title of *De Jure Praedae*, known in English as *Commentary on the Law of Prize and Booty*, it was not a concise answer on the technical points of the seizure of the Portuguese ship but a discussion of the "universal law of war." It was a subject that would occupy Grotius for years to come, and his work would be a milestone in the development of the body of law related to war and conflict.[37]

The critical point Grotius made was that a private party, in this case "a trading company," "might legitimately engage in a private war against other merchants, or even against the agents of a sovereign state, in order to enforce the natural law, which mandated freedom of trade and navigation." Grotius recognized this right even for those from the Dutch provinces whose international status was still in question. The argument rested on natural law, where the rights of trade and navigation were inherent to free people everywhere. Equipped with a right to defend oneself, the company's representatives could pursue these natural rights on their own if no "independent" or "effective judge" existed (the words are Martine Julia van Ittersum's, not Grotius's). The waters of the Indian Ocean, the East Indies, and Southeast Asia lacked a ruling authority, whether local or that of a European power. Ship captains for the company had to act in their interests and not wait for any distant government officer.[38]

Grotius developed themes and facets of his analysis and argument in both the *Commentary on the Law of Prize and Booty* and a much larger work twenty years later, *De Iure Belli ac Pacis* (*The Rights of War and Peace*). In Chapter II of the *Commentary* Grotius stated a definition in one paragraph that is worth quoting.

> Armed execution against an armed adversary is designated by the term "war." A war is said to be "just" if it consists in the execution of a right, and "unjust" if it consists in the execution of an injury. It is called "public" when waged by the will of the state, and in this latter concept the will of magistrates (e.g., princes) is included. Moreover, public war may be either "civil" (when waged against a part of the same state) or "foreign" (when waged against other states). What is known as a "war of allies" is a form of foreign war. Those which are waged otherwise (than by the public will), are "private" wars, although some authorities have preferred to describe such conflicts as "quarrels" rather than as "wars." These conflicts, too, may be either civil or foreign. In the present work, the terms "seizure of prize," [and] "seizure of booty" are used to refer to the acquisition of enemy property through war.[39]

Public war is thus dependent on actors and a process that reflect the "will of the state." This is quite different from the view of war drawn across the English Channel by Thomas Hobbes, who described war as "the time men live without a common power to keep them all in awe." When this occurs, "they are in that condition called war, and such a war as is of every man against every man." In such war, Hobbes wrote, "nothing can be unjust.

The notions of right and wrong, justice and injustice, have there no place."[40] Grotius, Philip Bobbitt observes, made very different assumptions forty to fifty years earlier that assume existence of a sovereign or sovereigns, of rules, and an environment that, while chaotic, is not a wild, unregulated world of all against all.[41] Of course, Grotius had experienced comparative tranquility in contrast to Hobbes's world that was so shaken by the English Civil War and the Thirty Years' War.

Grotius's elaboration of private war raised important attributes that played significantly in the years, and even centuries, to follow. Whether privateers or captains of merchant ships carrying letters of marque or reprisal knew Grotius's work directly is not as important as the fact his thinking reflected broader views on practice and law. Although his analysis had been prompted by a trading company, Grotius wrote that *"private wars . . . are justly waged by any person whatsoever, including cases in which they are waged in conjunction with allies or through the agency of subjects"* (italics are by Grotius). This definition allows the conduct of war, therefore, not only by those directly affected but by other actors the latter party might select. This significant allowance could permit privateering as well as letters of marque and reprisal. The example Grotius drew upon was the story of Abraham from the Bible. Not only did Abraham and his allies wage war, so, too, did "the young men," who because they were slaves had little choice.[42] Privateers and others during the sixteenth through early nineteenth centuries were not slaves in most instances. They acted by choice, albeit a choice that may sometimes have resulted from dire circumstance. Again, even though it is not Grotius's focus, questions about the meaning of consent reside in the shadows in this discussion. It always does, whether discussing mercenaries, privateers, or employees of contractors.

Grotius details at different times the types of actions allowed in private war, which include the obvious measures for personal self-defense, the "defence or recovery of one's property," or "even private exaction of a penalty for crime." The latter could fall upon "adulterers [in certain cases], robbers, rebels, or deserters." Furthermore, he adds that "as certain private wars are just by virtue of their cause, so public wars are unjust in the absence of due cause." A private war proceeds without the sanction or "the power of judgment" that the state holds. In Grotius's view, if the war reflects that, it is not a private war but rather a public one. Yet, this does not give a private actor a free hand to act regardless of the state's position. Based on "the authority of sages and of civil law," "no one is given power to set armed forces in motion when the ruler has not been consulted." If this occurs, the act is merely "private robbery." If it is private war, though, its conduct can last for some time—at least "up to the point where we shall have obtained value comparable to that debt."[43]

An ambiguity easily stands out in the aforementioned description and conditions. The private actor cannot just take unilateral action. He or she must consult or inform authorities in some fashion; however, the exact nature of this is unclear. What is the difference between a state being informed about a desired act and consenting to it and the actual outcome of a process that represents the will of the state, which means public war? That was a question, as will be seen, that was already in play by the time Grotius had written his work. The Spanish monarchy, for example, had wondered repeatedly about the exact terms and conditions of the relationship between British privateers and His or Her Majesty's (usually Her) official position in London. Whether it is Queen Elizabeth I in the 1580s or any number of governments in the early twenty-first century, questions of attribution, responsibility, and intent arise. The old questions have indeed come back to us.

This argument makes a case for the prospect of nonstate violence being consciously prompted and rewarded by the state. Janice Thomson in a study of mercenarism argues that such forms of violence were "not an identifiable problem . . . because practical distinctions between societal and state violence were difficult to make." The latter form of violence "was exerted on behalf of the personal interests of the sovereign," while violent societal action was encouraged, sponsored, and exploited by the state. Thus, differences between these forms of violence "were blurred." Thomson astutely observes that "societal violence [what Grotius would more often label as "private"] sometimes made it difficult to determine whether a state was at war or at peace with another state."[44] Yet, that ambiguity may well have been the very point, even in a period when concepts of sovereignty, boundaries, and law were not well-evolved. "Societal" or "private" violence may have been used even more proactively than Thomson states. To be fair, Thomson focused more on the eighteenth century, a good one hundred to two hundred years after the events shaping Grotius's writing. Yet, the characterization she provides for the 1700s would have been stronger at this earlier time. She attributes the problem in discerning sources of violence partly to an historical environment that is witnessing "the transformation of the state and the subject into the citizen." With such changes emerged stronger borders that specified "the physical limits of state authority" and "citizenship" that set forth "the political limits of state authority."[45] Thomson's interpretation carries much value, but its claims that distinctions between sources and types of violence were "not an identifiable problem" must be taken carefully. There were examples where there were problems.

Some can be found in Grotius's later scholarship that widened the scope of private war in important ways. In *The Rights of War and Peace* Grotius elaborated an argument that allowed a private actor, the East India Company being the obvious one, to use private war to punish others. This is a different condition than self-defense or the seizure of items to compensate for damages. Richard Tuck comments in his introduction to the edition of Grotius I use that Grotius in effect had created an argument to allow a private actor to "make war as if it were a state when it encountered any people with whom it did not already have some kind of civil association." Taking his analysis further, Tuck points out that this allowed "European traders" and others "to make judgments about the morality of the various parties and to punish those who seemed to be violating other people's rights, even if there was no immediate threat to the Europeans themselves." The range of these actions could include pirates, tribal groups, and other groupings that had not entered into any relationship with the company or actor. Reflecting the lessons drawn from the Netherlands' own experience as well as that of the then ongoing Thirty Years' War, Grotius ruled out religion as a justification for such actions.[46]

Grotius's argument drew from a body of argument, law, and religious writing that had dealt with the Crusades and the conquest of non-Christian and native peoples in both the Old and New Worlds. The implications of this line of argument would carry immense implications for the fate of native people, for example, throughout the Americas. However, it likewise raises questions about the exact relationship between the state and private actors (or "societal" actors) under its auspice. Thomson's analysis concentrates on the emergence of states, nation-states, and their citizens that operate on a comparable plain. The argument Grotius made regarding the status and treatment of those people and groups outside of that system reflects a distinction in types of violence and war. It may be a distortion to treat such a matter from the vantage point of the present century, where the lines between public and private are different and when centuries of intervening history have so greatly affected the human, legal, ethical, and political landscapes. Yet, from the beginning, both tension and harmony existed between the aspirations of governments, rulers, and emerging states and the desires and goals of the private individual or company. Even while such actors enjoyed great freedom and leeway well into the eighteenth century, as Thomson shows, an ongoing assessment about the relationship between the state and the individual and the degree to which private actions should reflect and represent the beliefs and objectives of the state was occurring. The conviction that war must be a public matter in service of something greater than the private or individual aspiration or grievance was developing alongside the arguments supporting the benefits of private war for both states and citizens.

THE SPHERE OF PUBLIC WAR

One of the political writers and thinkers of the eighteenth century who thought seriously about the development of states, war, and the security of both the state and the people was Adam Smith. Commenting at different places in The Wealth of Nations on the chaos and absence of effective control by sovereigns over their nobility and lords and the ensuing wars, the Scottish economist proclaimed emphatically that "the first duty of the sovereign, therefore, that of defending the society from the violence and injustice of other independent societies, grows gradually more and more expensive, as the society advances in civilization."[47] Smith's theory of history and political economy, which placed much emphasis on the role of evolution and development, paralleled the spirit and content of many writers in the Enlightenment—a fact that might be lost today on some enthusiasts who would see his argument as a rationale for ever-increasing defense spending.[48] In reality Smith was grappling with one of the ongoing questions about the reasons behind the emergence of modern states and the content and form they, individually and collectively, have tried to place on war and conflict. In fact, in the next paragraph Smith wrote of a "revolution" in war brought about the introduction of firearms and the mounting expenses that accompanied them.[49] He also highlighted the importance of a standing army, not a mercenary one, which would serve "the law of the sovereign."[50] This was public war—war in the interest of many and not the few.

The relationship among security, protection, the people, and the state is the subject of rich scholarship and commentary. The object here is not to settle upon one interpretation over others but to illustrate how these arguments have influenced the development and treatment of war and examine why war's conduct became more a matter for the governments of those states to control.[51] In *The Prince*, Niccolo Machiavelli, reflecting in the early sixteenth century on the experiences of the Italian city-states, observed that "the primary foundation of all states—new, old, or mixed—is good laws and a good army. And as there cannot be good laws where there is not a good army, and where there is a good army there have to be good laws, I will omit any discussion of laws and speak only of armies."[52]

Machiavelli's concept of the state related it directly to matters of security and war. In elaborating that relationship and purpose, Machiavelli posed lines of argument that have continued into the present day about the tie between war and the state. In 1990 the political sociologist and historian Charles Tilly essentially presented a similar relationship in his work *Coercion, Capital, and European States* when he wrote that "extractions and struggle over the means of war created the central organizational structure of states." Rulers of states operated with three approaches on creating, managing, and mobilizing the domestic resources they needed to wage war. One was through coercion, literally the squeezing of "the means of war from their own populations and others they conquered, building massive structures of extraction in the process." Tilly offered Russia and Brandenburg as examples of this. The second was a "capital-intensive" route in which the ruler depended on arrangements and the support of capitalists "whose interests they served with care—to rent or purchase military force, and thereby warred without building vast permanent state structures." City-states could be in this category, and Tilly cites the Dutch Republic as a prominent example of this model in that form of government. The third approach, not surprisingly, was a hybrid of the first two—"capitalized coercion," which, once enabled, the ruler hoped would provide the maximum advantages adopted from the other two models. France and Great Britain were examples of this combined method.[53]

Bruce Porter makes similar observations in his *War and the Rise of the State* by describing how an "iron triangle of arms, capital, and bureaucracy was forged at the very birth of the modern state." Porter clearly chose the term *iron triangle* intentionally as a reference to a label Americans have become so accustomed to using in relation to the current environment and structures that shape defense spending. President Dwight D. Eisenhower assigned it an even more popular name—the "military-industrial complex." Porter writes that "in a self-perpetuating cycle, the need to wage war impelled rulers to accumulate capital in order to fund bureaucracies; these in turn extracted more capital, which brought armies, which made possible greater wars."[54]

Tilly and Porter, of course, benefit from the vantage point of nearly another five centuries, and they are not writing with a particular political climate or needs of particular political personalities in mind. Machiavelli certainly did not dismiss the importance of law. He stressed its place, and, in what some scholars regard as evidence of his republican leanings, Machiavelli's comment that a prince "who obtains a state with the help of the people maintains his position with less difficulty than a prince who acquires it with the help of the nobility" implies his preferences for order.[55] Nevertheless, scholars disagree about the extent to which Machiavelli recognized a difference between the interests of the ruler and those of the ruled. Quentin Skinner, David William Bates, and others have argued that Machiavelli drew no such distinction; there was no "separation of the institutions of rule from the interests of those who rule and of those who are ruled."[56] Martin van Creveld in *The Rise and Decline of the State* takes an even harsher view of Machiavelli and charges that he ignored the fact that the Romans he so admired had ruled as magistrates and not as "kings who ran the city as their private property."[57] Philip Bobbitt disagrees with much of this and states, quite to the contrary, that Machiavelli made his "prince" act for reasons of state and not just for himself. If one does not find this in *The Prince*, Bobbitt suggests it can be found in other writings, such as a statute Machiavelli drafted for Florence in 1505 to organize a militia and to insist a republic must embody "justice and arms."[58]

These arguments matter in the consideration of private and public war because as the concept of a state as an entity separate from the ruler evolved, so, too, did the perceived need for public war. Public wars certainly had been fought between rulers and others before modern concepts of the state existed, but the characteristic of what the term *state* meant, particularly in its representation of interests beyond the ruler and tied to the population and the survival of the system and principles of government, required different measures of preparing for, conducting, and sustaining war. These conditions demanded, as well, reassessment of the private means and measures that had been part of conflict. Were they still usable? If so, when, how, and where? Would it become necessary to eliminate them or to place them under tighter control by the state to serve?

Just what the state represented and the character of its relationship to its population is at the heart of a different framework of analysis that places less emphasis on the role of war in state development and more on a bargain or purposely determined relationship between the governed and the governing. In his discussion of the origins of the French state, Hendrik Spruyt sees less influence from factors of war and more from a type of bargain that arranges for "exchange of revenue for the provision of security by the monarch." As "military security became increasingly expensive because of the ever-rising costs of warfare, taxes had to be raised accordingly." Not surprisingly, bureaucracy and centralized administrative abilities had to develop as well to handle all of this. If war and military technology had been such dominant drivers, Spruyt asks the reader to ponder why the German and Italian states did not follow France's path but remained comparatively decentralized until the nineteenth century.[59]

Such arrangements would assuredly expand the "public" dimension of war in particular ways, especially in the need to have the agreement and support of key sectors of the population to help fund the costs. Indeed, one sees dimensions of the factors of consent and legitimate authority from just war theory in such a discussion. Spruyt describes how a "confluence" between the "material interests of monarchy and towns" developed through a process of "regularized taxation" that would strengthen both the climate for commercial prosperity and the treasury for expenses related to protection and war. As towns liked greater independence in their affairs, Spruyt argues it would have been in their interest to submit to the promise of protection from the monarch rather than from the local lord. By the late thirteenth or early fourteenth century, Spruyt claims, "taxation, judiciary, police and military functions had to a considerable extent been centralized and affected the activities of society on a regular basis."[60] If one concurs with Spruyt's analysis, the foundation of a modern state that would practice war more and more in a public arena was the result of the need for order and protection rather than the circumstances of war.

The coexistence of the objectives and desires of both the ruler and ruled suggested a level of consideration that surpassed or even overshadowed the interests of the specific ruler. The term *reason of state* began to appear in the sixteenth century; some trace it to contemporaries of Machiavelli, such as

Francesco Guicciardini and Giovanni Della Casa. Their writings implied a reasoning and logic to choices and actions that stood above the preferences of a single ruler. Importantly in the context of the sixteenth century, this line of thought did not rest solely on divine authority or provision of God.[61] Arguably one of the most influential commentators on the ruler and the state was the French writer Jean Bodin. While Bodin did not coin the term *sovereignty*, he shaped much of our subsequent popular understanding of it. Rulers would come and go, but the attributes of sovereignty and the interests of the state tied to it would prevail beyond them. How the latter would endure depended, in Bodin's view, on order and the existence and acceptance of law. This view was not original to Bodin; he had borrowed it partly from the Roman politician and writer Cicero, who had regarded a republic as a community "governed by law."[62] Perhaps Bodin did not want to take away all of the monarch's relationship with divine authority, but he was arguing that in the realm of earthly matters, royal authority depended on the ability to establish order and to govern it through law.[63] Authority and use of the instruments of war would become increasingly a question of public authority rather than the mere choice of the ruler or monarch.

Writing several decades later in the turmoil of the English Civil War, Thomas Hobbes amplified this dominance of state interest over the self-motivated, single ruler. To do so Hobbes distinguished between the private and public spheres. War, in fact, was the original condition in which all lived if they did not have "a common power to keep them all in awe." Individuals created the former condition by their own initiative; war was a condition "of every man against every man." It was in some ways the consummate collection of private acts, as its situation operated only on that level. The opposite condition was the commonwealth, in which such actions represent a common objective or good. As Hobbes described it, a commonwealth "*is one person, of whose acts a great multitude, by mutual covenants with one another, have made themselves every one the author, to the end he may use the strength and means of them all, as he shall think expedient, for their peace and common defence*" (italics are by Hobbes).[64] "The state," in Martin Van Creveld's analysis of Hobbes, had thus become "the most important public body of all. It authorized the rest (in the sense of determining whether or not they were lawful) but was authorized by none."[65]

Hobbes also recognized the place and supremacy of law, but its dominance only prevailed within the organized political body in the public realm or commonwealth. As we know, Hobbes regarded the world outside of the boundaries of states as a chaotic state of nature, a world where the acts of the private prevail over the needs and interests of common security and order.[66] A Hobbesian world lacked any international public body; it was that aggrandizing, self-seeking state of nature where gain ruled over any sense of common good or even the various attributes that had created the individual state. The needs of war might not decide the virtual existence and configuration of the modern state, as some argue, but external disorder and the role of war would compel contrasting assumptions, approaches, and treatment of the domestic and international arenas.[67] This array of external circumstances does not mean that war could or would not be "public." "The right of judicature," which Hobbes assigned to sovereignty and the state, involved "hearing and deciding all controversies which may arise concerning law."[68] Without law, the state of nature—war—took over, and the right of protection by "private strength" prevailed over the "end for which every commonwealth is instituted."[69] The authorization or decision to resort to force on behalf of the commonwealth would have to be in a form that supported public war, but beyond that Hobbes did little to delineate how the process might actually work. At the time, that consideration would not have mattered as much as the assurance that war, if used, would be "public," in the interest of the state, and not for the gain of one over the many.

Thus, Hobbes supports state monopoly over the use of force. His concept of the state or commonwealth envisioned public militaries that served the survival and enhancement of the contract that existed between the sovereign and the governed, even if the realities of the time were still varied and evolving. The world of the mid-seventeenth century continually witnessed acts of war by private actors or governments willing to use them. Hobbes assuredly knew there was no effective means in place to prohibit the former, and he likely understood the latter was an option much used by nearly all governments. However, as Elke Krahmann observes in her seminal work on states and the privatization of security, Hobbes solved this by insisting that force is an instrument to support "the Social Contract" and not to protect individual citizens. "If the sovereign does so successfully," she writes, "the security of the citizens is a direct consequence of their own behavior."[70] In fact, Krahmann comments that Hobbes seemed uncertain on the matter of mercenaries as he appeared to accept the right of a person to substitute another in his place while at the same time claiming that the defense of the commonwealth requires all to come to its defense.[71] The critical point, though, is that the authority to decide to use force rests at the level of the sovereign and commonwealth. How it is exactly to be done is unclear.

Hobbes entrusted the sovereign to make the decision to use force. To modern ears this rings heavily of supreme executive authority, and that matched very well the circumstances and institutions Hobbes knew. Students of war powers and government decision making know that conflicting arguments followed later in the seventeenth century and, more so, in the next century that challenged this placement of such authority. Without getting too far ahead, the key revision in these discussions was by John Locke in his *Second Treatise of Government*, written in the early 1680s, just a few years before the political reforms and changes in 1688–1689 and the Glorious Revolution. Chronologically Locke's world was not far away from Hobbes's, but events had greatly strengthened the legislative branch of the English government, and, thus, it is no shock to find Locke arguing that it is the legislative branch, as the law maker, that holds the supreme levels of power. Many modern US scholars have found in this judgment a basis for the claim that Congress should retain control over decisions to go to war, but Locke's own words can be frustrating, as he clearly regarded foreign affairs and defense as special areas of government responsibility and action. Locke strongly supports the common good and cause that governments must serve. In this regard his view of war as more of a public act taken for common good is clear. Locke specified five powers of government, though, not three, as areas: executive, legislative, judicial, federative, and prerogative. It is the last two that are frustrating to defenders of the legislative branch. Federative power included the making of war as well as the negotiating of alliance and peace, and these powers resided with the executive. Prerogative was a separate category where the executive could act without sanction of law, even against it, if such acts were for the public or common good.[72] Locke's argument thus leaves unclear the question of where the authority to make decisions about private means of force resides; he stresses the supremacy of law and the legislative branch, but he leaves the executive with stronger authority of deciding, declaring, and executing war. The United States would seek to place these decisions under the legislative branch but by the late twentieth century found them mainly in the executive.

Agreement on the desirable public character of war for a common good could also come from perspectives quite different than Locke and certainly

Hobbes. In 1762 Jean Jacques Rousseau published *The Social Contract*, a work that posed a very different state of nature than that of Hobbes. People living in this state—"their primitive condition of independence"—"have no intercourse regular enough to constitute either a state of peace or war. . . . It is conflicts over things, not quarrels between men which constitute war." "Private wars between one man and another can exist neither in a state of nature, where there is no fixed property, nor in society, where everything is under the authority of law." Rousseau concluded that "war then, is not a relation between men, but between states."[73] Rousseau went further and dismissed "the types of private wars that were permitted by the ordinances of King Louis IX" as "no more than an abuse of feudal government, an irrational system if there ever was one, and contrary both to natural justice and to all sound polity."[74] This indictment sounds quite absolute, although in practice it would allow reliance on private actors if serving broader state purpose. In the eighteenth century the French were indeed still dependent on privateers and letters of marque and reprisal.

State monopoly over the use of armed force was critical for Rousseau. Elke Krahmann argues that it was this same consideration that brought Rousseau to revise the notion of the Social Contract and to assure that "the right and control over armed force is to be invested in the general will of all citizens." This contract was not between the ruler and ruled, as characterized by many previously discussed scholars, "but among all citizens who constitute the 'state.' As citizens formed the state, they would decide on and control the means of violence used in their name." The "general will" would enable them to select the course of action preferred. Yet, Rousseau took his argument to another level by adding a third characteristic that would guarantee that violence in the state's name (and the public's) would be protected. This was to urge reliance on citizen militias as the nation's military. In fact, this was a duty derived from their participation in the governing contract. Rousseau strongly preferred this path over dependence on professional or regular soldiers, who were useful only for invading others or repressing and putting down rebellions and actions by the citizenry. The military represented the willing choice made by the citizens; it and the government were responsible for their security; and, lastly, the citizens controlled the military to prevent abuse and to serve their interests.[75]

By the middle of the eighteenth century and the onset of events that would lead to the American Revolution and its aftermath, two paths were emerging that shaped how most of the North Atlantic world would approach questions of state monopoly of force, its composition, and its use. One rested on assumptions identified more with republicanism and the other on those associated with liberalism. The former sees the state and centralized government as the best form of "democratic representation" for the community. The state controls policies and measures related to national security—policy, revenue, mobilization, structure and composition of forces, deployment, and use in times of peace and war. The citizen observes, critiques, and votes for or against the policies of the government and serves as a "citizen-soldier." The citizen has control over the military through elections and government and assures its linkage to the civilian world through the concept of the citizen-soldier. Militias and citizen armies are the preferred means.[76]

Liberalism, and this is not the meaning associated with US politics, emphasizes individual rights more and seeks to protect citizens from unnecessary intrusion or "interference by the state." The liberal model, as explained by Krahmann, stresses the decentralization of government, including even in national defense and security, and its distribution through different geographic sectors and division among government sections and private and government sectors. Limiting state authority is of central importance. National defense is handled by a professional military, which is "politically neutral," and in instances even by private contractors and organizations. The military's service and loyalty to the citizens is provided less by large citizen involvement and control through government and more by an ethos of service, loyalty, and professionalism. Contractors would be responsive more to market conditions and practices than to government authority and decision.[77]

Most modern states with democratic and/or republican traditions and institutions have operated with one model and, more frequently, with a combination of both models. Both models accept and stress the public model of war, which means its service to a commonly determined benefit, national interest, and some form of public determination, announcement, and execution. The republican model has fewer places for the role of private actors, but it certainly does not exclude them. The United States possesses attributes of both frameworks, although it has arguably moved from more of a republican model to a liberal one. Yet, one could argue that through elections, congressional oversight of the defense budget and force structure process, and public discourse aspects of the republican model continue. The debate would be over how well they operate and to what degree these processes and mechanisms actually fulfill substantive responsibility or just re-create the options. A third model would begin to assert itself in the last third of the twentieth century—neoliberalism, which in the opinion of some (both advocates and critics) would replace the role of government that still retained a pivotal role, even in a decentralized environment, with market forces. Some 230 years ago governments on both sides of the Atlantic were thinking primarily in terms of republicanism and strengthening national controls over the use of force. It is critical to understand those developments before examining and evaluating the questions and issues facing the present day.

Whatever the framework or intellectual tradition used—republicanism or liberalism—the preference of both systems to conduct war mainly as a public endeavor creates an expectation that a formal declaration of war must be part of this process. A declaration is essentially an announcement that informs the citizenry, the adversary, and the international community that a state of war now exists. Rousseau claimed, "Declarations of war are warnings not so much to a government as their subjects," but that claim was even a little cynical for Rousseau's day.[78] In contemporary surroundings a declaration, or an authorization that is tantamount to a declaration, can set into motion a series of laws and regulations domestically. It also requires members of the international community to decide and take action to protect their rights in relation to the policies and acts of those who are parties in the conflict.

Declaring war is not a recent practice, although since the end of World War II and the approval of the UN Charter it has become a largely defunct one. Its antecedents can be traced to the ancient and classical worlds. The writings of Cicero laid out the argument that for a war to be just it has to be declared. People in Rome could determine whether they were at war by looking at the Temple of Janus in the Roman Forum. If its doors were open, war was ongoing; if closed, Rome was at peace. During the feudal period and Middle Ages, conduct of a just war, as noted earlier, depended on its declaration in whatever appropriate form.[79] By the sixteenth and seventeenth centuries, when one begins to see the emergence of modern states, political and legal thought had begun to grapple with this question directly and with a variety of answers. A recurrent question, and one that has never been definitely answered to the current day, is whether a declaration of war must always occur. If not, what are the circumstances or the types of conflict that do not require it, and what would be the consequent means or measures allowed in the absence of a declaration? The answers would have significant bearings for an understanding of public and private war as well as the appropriateness or suitability of the instruments used.

Analyses throughout the time discussed repeatedly divided war into different categories. For example, Richard Zouche, a royalist during the English Civil War and a contemporary of Hobbes, referred to "formal" war, "which a state wages after declaring it, or informal, waged by private persons." Reprisals would serve as an example of "informal war." Zouche allowed for three cases where war, even it were on a scale that might equal formal conflict, did not require a declaration: wars for self-defense, wars "made on those already regarded as enemies," and conflicts against rebels.[80] The German legal scholar Samuel von Pufendorf, writing mainly in the 1670s and 1680s, also identified two forms of war, which he labeled as "declared and undeclared." Reflecting the writing on the sovereign and state discussed earlier, Pufendorf stressed that a declared war had to follow a declaration announced by both sides; the war had to "be waged on the sovereign's authority on both sides" as well. Undeclared war meant what it says, and it could also be waged by and against citizens."[81]

In an Atlantic world where the political-economic theory of mercantilism prevailed, an important related question was whether customs and laws that applied on land would necessarily apply on sea. As we have seen, Hugo Grotius had argued that private actors could wage war to protect their rights of freedom of navigation on the high seas or property. They could also so act against indigenous peoples with which there had been no prior or existing formal association. The English jurist Charles Molloy had almost assuredly read Grotius prior to the publication in 1676 of his *De Jure Maritimo et Navali: Or, A Treatise of Affairs Maritime and Naval*. Molloy's argument closely resembled his predecessors and contemporaries in his assertion that a "just war" must be a "solemn war," which meant that it was waged "under the authority of the highest power in the state." However, on turning to practices on the high seas, such as the issuance of letters of reprisal that allowed attacks for recovery of damages, Molloy stated these were not a "breach of the peace." Practices and rules that applied on land did not necessarily apply on the high seas.[82] In practice, there could be two standards for war—one for land the other for sea—a condition that appears very strange and dangerous to a reader in the twenty-first century but not so much to one in Molloy's time, when differences between public and private were significantly different and states purposely licensed or chartered private parties to act on their behalf. Arguably, too, mercantilism's function and perceived success depended on this ability to draw lines differently when it came to acts of war versus measures to defend rights of property and movement on the world's oceans.

This combination of commerce on the high seas, practices of war, and the ongoing development of the body of international law concerned with all of the preceding led to interesting choices as the eighteenth century matured. In 1715–1718 a set of actions by the king of Spain, Philip V, to secure an Italian kingdom for his younger son led to an invasion of Sardinia; a formation of a Quadruple Alliance by Austria, England, France, and the Dutch Republic to oppose this scheme; and a sea battle against the Spanish in 1718. All of this occurred without any declaration of war. King George I of England believed he had to seek a declaration of war against Spain as all attempts to obtain compensation for damages done to British subjects, including commerce, had proved futile. By then, the power of the House of Commons was much stronger than it had been even in John Locke's time, thirty to forty years earlier. Parliament could not block the king, but its members could offer their advice, and they did not hold back. A number of them questioned the need for a declaration, as such an act seemed to serve the interests of the four-party alliance more than it did the interests of England. The king presumably could obtain a "redress of grievances" (meaning English grievances) against Spain without a declaration of war. King George thought differently, though, thanked the members of Parliament for their opinion (which is more than most modern US presidents do), and notified colonial governors in the empire to allow individuals to take measures to harass Spanish interests, which, as the next chapter explains, meant letters of marque and reprisal.[83]

These types of considerations brought about further elaborations on public and private war and the declaration of war by British legal thinkers, such as George Carmichael (a Scot) and Thomas Rutherford, as well as Dutch jurist Cornelius van Bynkershoek. Rutherford regarded the key attribute of public war to be the consequence of an "act of the two states' executive bodies." The rank of those making the decision was not important in itself. He even spoke of "mixed war," in which a state (a public actor) would be using force against a private one, such as pirates. Rutherford also relied on the distinctions of "solemn" and "unsolemn" war discussed earlier. A solemn war had to be a just war, and it had to be declared. It was a public war as well, and the combination of all of these features enabled it to be deemed a "perfect war." An "imperfect war," which was unsolemn, often occurred without declarations. In fact, they were often not wars but rather "reprisals or acts of hostility." A second key distinction between "perfect" and "imperfect" war was the scale of involvement by the nation or state. The former required commitment of the entire or whole state; the latter required the participation of only part of the state. Thus, a state could use its navy or rely on privateers, both which were partial measures, and be engaged in an "imperfect" war that was neither declared nor perhaps even public.[84] Bynkershoek's arguments followed similar directions when he spoke of "general" and "particular" wars. The first was close to "perfect war," and the latter involved use of specific measures, such as marque and reprisal, to commit injury on an enemy. However, the Dutchman took a position that contrasted significantly with most of his contemporaries when he argued that a declaration of war was not mandatory in a general conflict. He argued this practice had come from classical, particularly Roman, times and had been done more for the sake of honor. Arguably the best reason for doing so in the context of the eighteenth century was to inform other states, especially neutral ones, of the imminence of war so they could take appropriate protective measures.[85]

As the middle of the eighteenth century approached, one could argue that the bulk of political and legal writing on war stayed closer to that of Rutherford and earlier proponents of public and declared war while the practice of states had moved more into Bynkershoek's camp. For example, The Principles of Political Law, published in 1748 by J. J. Burlamaqui, used familiar concepts when he spoke of public, mixed, and private wars. Public wars reflected "the authority of the civil power," mixed wars were self-explanatory in character, and "private wars" were among "private persons . . . without any public authority." Burlamaqui's discussion of war that was "solemn" or not closely resembled Rutherford's, as did his use of "perfect" and "imperfect." Perfect war "entirely interrupt[s] the tranquility of the state, and lays a foundation for all possible acts of hostility." War that was imperfect "does not entirely interrupt the peace, but only in certain particulars, the public tranquility being in other respects undisturbed." The latter type of war involved "reprisals," that is, "acts of hostility which sovereigns exercise against each other, or, with their consent, their subjects by seizing the persons or effects of the subjects of foreign commonwealth . . . with a view to obtain security, and to recover our right, and in case of refusal, to do justice to ourselves, without any interruption of the public tranquility." Thus, Burlamaqui did not rule out the fact such measures might be public, but, if so, they were not done with the purpose of becoming a full-scale or perfect conflict.[86]

The practice of states seemed to struggle increasingly with the need to declare war. In the debate in the House of Commons over the declaration of war against Spain in what is popularly known as the War of Jenkins' Ear in 1739, Robert Walpole observed that such declarations increasingly came from the "mouths of cannon" rather than the mouths of kings and politicians. However, Walpole relented in part by acknowledging such a declaration was probably important to be fair to British allies.[87] Debate over a declaration of war involved not only the needs of the international community but also the choice of instruments a state would use in the war. Scale of the war, cost, and the length of conflict could become variables difficult to control. Even objectives may expand or contract depending on circumstance or poorly conceived strategy. If one wanted to preserve "tranquility," to cite Burlamaqui's term, it could be prudent and smarter to rely on more limited measures for more specific, limited objectives. Letters of marque and reprisal and other measures might be the more realistic choice in select cases. At the same time, those same variables could also bring a government to consider their use even in times of declared, perfect, public war. To understand why states might resort to such means it is important to review the characteristics, circumstances, and forms of use of such means—be they mercenaries, privateers, letters of marque, or the resources and means of private trading companies.

2 PRIVATE WAR: WHO ARE THE PARTICIPANTS?

After the Cold War's end in 1989–1991, commentators searched for paradigms and labels to understand the behavior of people fighting in conflicts who seemed unclassified in this new environment or had become products of its disorder. The absence of a great bipolar confrontation of two powers—the United States and the Soviet Union—had not produced a more peaceful world. In fact, it appeared to deteriorate quickly in some areas into unexpected chaos. The Cold War paradigm had told us to look for our adversary behind every regional upheaval or conflict, but, at least for the United States, the primary rival was no longer there. Terms like *rogue state*, *terrorist*, and *transnational crime* assumed greater prominence in explanations for what was now happening, but the label that seemed most helpful, because it was so inclusive, was that of *nonstate actor*. Even today the label seems simple enough in its description. Yet, its applicability goes far back in history, for as long as there have been states, there have been those acting beyond their control. The term *nonstate actor* can both create and conceal confusion. "Non-state actors," writes one authority, (1) "are willing and able to use violence for pursuing their objectives and" (2) are "not integrated into formalized state institutions such as regular armies, presidential guards, police or special forces."[1] This description seems appealing in how it draws a line between the state and those outside its power. However, a problematic word in the description is "integrated," because the link or absence thereof is not always so visible. For example, when speaking of mercenaries, this contemporary definition might make little sense in relation to how governments and evolving states in the past treated them. Historical distinctions may not offer that much value today, either, from the perspective of onlookers and adversaries. Even Ulrich Schneckener, the scholar quoted above, concedes this by acknowledging such individuals "may . . . be supported by state actors whether in an official or informal matter." "State officials," too, may be "directly or indirectly involved in the activities of armed non-state actors."[2] The world of the nonstate actor in whatever category has many shades of activity.

Just consider how various nonstate actors can act outside or beyond state control but also, depending on circumstance, be parallel and even responsive to it. "Rebels," "partisans," and "guerrilla fighters" fight for "the 'liberation' of a social class or a 'nation.'"[3] At the same time they may be receiving assistance, training, and leadership from an outside state that can attest to goals of independence or separation as well as attachment to the supporting state. Such could be the case with the "little green men," the Russian military personnel found as volunteers in eastern Ukraine in 2014. An even more troubling example of the ambiguity in state-nonstate actor relations can be found with "militias" or "paramilitaries"—described as "irregular combat units" acting "on behalf of, or at least tolerated by, a given regime." They often receive training, money, and even leadership from that state but because of the absence of formal state control are treated as nonstate actors.[4] The recent world has had plenty of these organizations, such as some armed groups in the Balkan wars in the 1990s or the widely held analyses made about Iranian and/or Syrian support for the Hezbollah militia in Lebanon.

Leaders of tribes or clans, designated here as "clan chiefs" or "big men," can claim to represent or lead groups of people, and they may be seeking independence or some form of regional autonomy or separate administrative status for their group and the territory it claims to control.[5] Here, too, the leaders or the group may be receiving support from another state and its military, but the absence of integration with the latter can also testify to the limits of what the supporting state and its representatives can do—an experience repeated various times by both the Soviets and later the Americans and their allies in Afghanistan and Iraq. A more advanced and often stronger version of this type of nonstate actor is a warlord. The warlord does "control a particular territory" during or after a conflict, which more importantly means the warlord also controls local resources as well as the population—important resources for both manpower and money. Such a warlord "can hold territory locally and at the same time act financially and politically in the international system without interference from the state in which he is based."[6] Warlords likewise may be receiving assistance for an outside state or states, as examples in Afghanistan prove, but they can also be very difficult for an outside party to control.

During the past four decades the international community has focused on one particular nonstate actor: terrorists. Terrorists are often organized on a smaller scale than the preceding examples; for instance, they could be a subset of a tribal group or independence movement. "International terrorism," writes one scholar, "implies either isolated assassination and 'hostility' missions or the intermittent use or threat of force against person(s) to obtain certain political objectives of international relevance from a third party." While the objectives may be, and often are, political, they can be private as well, such as the gain of money—a dimension of terrorism that sometimes could bring it close to the forms of nonstate actors and action treated in this book.[7] As with the other types noted previously, state support or sponsorship can be present in a terrorist movement and its actions. History has provided many examples, such as the Serbian government's support for the Black Hand, which figured prominently in the assassination of Archduke Ferdinand and his consort in Sarajevo on June 28, 1914. Yet, such actors also often act outside or contrary to any state control, as there seldom seems to be a total convergence of aims. Perhaps one of the obvious measures of a state actor is the latter's formal submission to state control, compensation from it, and the state's certainty about and trust in that actor. None of these categories guarantee those qualities.

Other types of nonstate actors that definitely do not assure easy identity with the state are organized crime or "marauding" groups. Consistent with all nonstate actors, these categories, too, have definitional issues, although Phil Williams's reminder that "transnational criminal organizations are Clausewitzian in that crime is simply a continuation of business by other means" is a helpful, humorous comment on the fact that crime and conflict are often the product of calculated decisions to pursue an objective by less desirable means. Crime is as old as original sin, but the post–Cold War environment generated a set of conditions that raised its scale to levels that made it of concern not only to governments and states but even to the values and institutions of the international community.[8] Of course, criminals can also have ties to states, but more often it is their efforts to circumvent state authorities that attract attention. States may even practice crime; witness recurrent allegations against North Korean counterfeiting. Other nonstate actors also can resort to it for purposes of additional money; thus one reads of accusations against the Taliban for opium or resort by the Islamic State and earlier terrorist groups to hostage taking for ransom payments. Marauders and raiders may be the least organized of all these groups. They may appear both during and after conflicts, especially where there is a lack of any control. They may have ties to other nonstate actors, and even a state, and thus serve sometimes as agents for massacres, ethnic cleansing, rape, or other violations of individual or group rights and dignity. Money and personal gain can be motives, but they are not necessarily the most prevalent ones.[9]

The aforementioned brings the discussion closer to categories of nonstate actors where considerations of money (either saving it or making it), personal gain, and profit figure much more directly, even dominantly, in the organization or membership of these actors. These categories, however, do not see themselves as criminals or even opponents of the state system per se. They are instead private servants accepted or paid by the state. Their numbers include mercenaries, private military and security contractors and firms, and privateers holding letters of marque and reprisal. More obscure variations within these groups include those called corsair, buccaneer, or filibusterer. Some would throw in soldiers of fortune and other freelancers as well as variations of mercenary life. Historically, freelancers were often an individual or a small band, often just three (a soldier with a horse, a page, and perhaps an archer), who sold their services on a case-by-case arrangement.[10] The emphasis on money among these types does not mean cash did not figure in the behavior of other categories of nonstate actors. A government, for example, could believe that by supporting a rebel or independence group it is actually supporting a proxy at lower costs than it would pay if it were using its own military forces. Furthermore, the casualties suffered are those of the rebels or insurgents rather than one's own forces. The recurrent feature, though, with all of these groups, including arguably modern contractors, is that there is no complete integration with the state. Whether nonstate actors are completely beyond state control or act under the auspice or arrangement with a state, their existence and role demonstrate the fact that monopoly over conflict and the violence therein has never existed fully under state control.

A related consideration, even though it is not the focus of this book, is that nonstate actors fall into a less-defined area of law than those who fight in formal state-to-state conflicts, which are governed by the Geneva Convention of 1949. The seventeen years since the attacks of 9/11 have witnessed more arguments as to whether terrorism should be addressed within the context of the law of armed conflict, also known as international humanitarian law, or criminal law, which is largely in national jurisdictions. None of the nonstate actors discussed in this book would automatically enjoy the rights of state combatants under the Geneva Convention, even if they or their predecessor acted in close coordination with or even direction of a state. Unlike their counterparts on land (mercenaries), privateers when possessing letters of marque and reprisal operated in a legal environment that required them to find ways to prevent themselves from being charged and punished for piracy. If they became the latter, they found themselves marked as an international enemy of humanity. Even mercenaries never confronted such a universal label and indictment if caught.

MERCENARIES

The meaning of the term *mercenary* has evolved, as we will see, throughout history. Prior to the eighteenth century, the term could mean a person who fights for money—in short, a mere soldier. The word *soldier* is derived from the Latin *solidus*, a silver coin, a word whose own origins came from the word for salt and the practice of paying people salt for their services; thus, Roman officials could ponder whether the person had been "worth his salt."[11] Early mercenaries could be from the kingdom, principality, or state itself. The purpose of using them was "to complement or replace those armed forces raised from among a state's citizens by voluntary enlistment or conscription." Here one can begin to sense a difference in the nature of the association between this particular type of soldier and those others from the population at large. Some studies have shown that mercenaries often provided certain services or skills not widely available in the population at large. Throughout the sixteenth and seventeenth centuries it became more common for monarchs, princes, and others to look for mercenaries beyond their borders. The fact that "a mercenary may fight in a cause which is not that of his own nation" became an increasingly common attribute. This feature of a hired outsider to do some or nearly all of one's fighting was so common that Voltaire would write in *Candide* of "a million regimented assassins running from one end of Europe to the other, engaging in murder and banditry in a disciplined fashion to earn his crust, since he has no more honest trade." Voltaire represented a growing conviction about mercenaries in the eighteenth century, and so it was no surprise to find mercenaries held in increasingly low regard as the decades progressed.[12]

As the body of international law concerning war began to emerge from the late nineteenth century on, its focus and purpose rested almost totally on state-to-state conflict and those in uniformed service to states. Non-state actors, like mercenaries, who had fallen into such ill repute, did not receive equivalent status in this. Of course, mercenaries did not go away as the twentieth century progressed. Sean McFate reminds his readers of examples before US entrance into World War II like the Flying Tigers, who were American volunteers flying with the Chinese Air Force. WatchGuard International, a British company founded in 1965, offered training and various forms of support to governments throughout much of the developing world, and mercenaries in Africa during the 1960s worked for mining companies, toppled governments, and inspired a genre of novels and entertainment for the popular market.[13]

The events in Africa provided the greatest impetus for the international community to take a closer look at the need for a modern definition of a mercenary, which was placed into Geneva Protocol I in 1977 as an addition to the original Geneva Convention of 1949. This definition and its current standing, including the fact the United States signed it but has never ratified the protocol, will be examined in more depth in Chapter 6. However, it is valuable here to understand what we believe a mercenary is today before we take a brief look at the historical record related to them. Images from the past may confuse our thinking as much as carrying current perceptions into the historical record. The protocol sets forth six criteria for defining a mercenary:

1. Is specifically recruited locally or abroad in order to fight in an armed conflict;
2. Does, in fact, take a direct part in the hostilities;
3. Is motivated to take part in the hostilities essentially by the desire for private gain and, in fact, is promised, by or on behalf of a party to the conflict, material compensation substantially in excess of that promised or paid to combatants of similar ranks and functions in the armed forces of that party;
4. Is neither a national of a Party to the conflict nor a resident of territory controlled by a Party to the conflict;
5. Is not a member of the armed forces of a party to the conflict; and
6. Has not been sent by a State which is not a party to the conflict on official duty as a member of its armed forces.[14]

As we will see in Chapter 6, additional measures to control or eliminate mercenaries have occurred, such as the Convention for the Elimination of Mercenarism in Africa, supported by the Organization of African Unity in 1977, as well as the UN Convention against the Recruitment, Use, Financing and Training of Mercenaries, approved by the UN General Assembly in 1989. The latter document, though, lacks the signature of several key powers, including the United States.[15]

Not being a national of the parties, working mainly for personal gain, and enjoying compensation higher than government personnel are all characteristics of a mercenary in 2018. Those criteria sometimes provide modern contractors reason to argue their employees are not mercenaries, but that may be a selective treatment of present fact and history. US companies in Afghanistan, Iraq, and elsewhere hire many US nationals, and their frequent past service in the US military, along with the terms of contract, provide, in their employers' view, adequate proof that the major goal is not personal gain but support of national policy objectives.[16] Such trust and confidence about contractors today—assuming it is indeed widely held—has not been common in much of the historical record of mercenaries. Whether the distinctions claimed between the contractors of today and the mercenaries of the past are accurate is a judgment that should be made from examination and not acceptance of assertions at face value.

The mercenaries of the ancient and classical worlds only resembled our modern understanding of the term in partial ways. At the risk of overgeneralization, mercenaries were more of a "complement" of the armies of the day. In actual war, rulers might rely on nearly all of the male population to participate, but keeping this much of the population in arms all of the time was not a good way to assure adequate farming of crops, distribution of food, and payment of taxes or revenue. A paid mercenary or soldier—keep in mind the two were interchangeable—could enable most of the civilian population to focus on domestic needs. The later phases of the Roman Empire found the army depending on the recruitment of barbarians, such as members of the German tribes, to fill many of the ranks. Trying to categorize them as mercenaries or regular soldiers along modern terms can be frustrating, as Rome often enabled peoples from other parts of the empire to become citizens. Nevertheless, this type of recruiting did enable other segments of the population to remain in the fields or toiling at the functions that made the empire work and survive for so long.[17] Another type of mercenary hired for different reasons could be found in the court of the Byzantine Empire from the late ninth to the early tenth century. These were the Varangian Guard—Norse Vikings, Russians, and Britons who were in the employ of the emperor. Kept in their own barracks, they were at the service of the emperor and useable for everything from dealing with mobs after sporting events to dispatching of various opponents and problem makers for the emperor. Their example probably comes closer to the modern stereotype of mercenaries. Untoward turns in political events in Constantinople and the lure of asserting their power in Norway convinced their leader to depart for the North, thereby providing an early example of the risks of dependence on mercenaries, who might leave when the political and military winds change to seek better opportunities.[18]

Resort to mercenaries, privateers, contractors, and so on, always reflects a combination of factors and circumstances—the political-economic system in the realm, territory, or state; the availability and absence of resources running from population to money; the values or principles of conduct that are in place; the changing nature of warfare; and the objectives of the use of force. Without question, the importance of each of these varies immensely; there is no set formula. Yet, whether one is examining the practices of feudal Europe, where much of what we discuss today about this subject was set into motion, or the choices in 2018, the interplay of each of these considerations remains. Reliance on private means of force tells us many things about a society and state besides contemporary preferences in how to wage war.

The environment around medieval warfare figured greatly in changing the use of mercenaries from being a complement to that of a supplement for other instruments of war.[19] Depending on the scale of the conflict, it was doubtful that the customary way of obtaining soldiers, via the relationship between a lord and vassal, could provide enough manpower. Furthermore, for various reasons a lord or monarch might not prefer to be so dependent on vassals, thanks to considerations about their age, health, or even level of loyalty. In parts of Europe a practice known as *scutage* developed, in which the vassal could pay the lord money in place of the service owed. For the same reasons, as well as the desire to increase the holding of the treasury, lords often preferred this. Consequently, a practice emerged where the lord turned to recruiting or hiring soldiers to serve during the duration and term of the agreement, thereby commencing the institution of contract warfare, as Sean McFate describes it, in which those desiring to serve looked for the best bargain they could for their skills.[20] Even then, the distinction between mercenaries and what we would regard as traditional soldiers was not always clear. Many of the men probably were subjects of the lord or king, rather than foreigners for hire. The remuneration was not so high that it would meet the standard in today's view of mercenaries. Research suggests that factors of citizenship (to use this more modern term) and loyalty probably figured more prominently in France and England than they did in the assortment of Italian principalities and kingdoms, where service by foreigners became more common. Yet, even there in the thirteenth century, research finds that mercenaries were more of a supplement to armies of citizens.[21]

The growing reliance on mercenaries in Europe in the twelfth and thirteenth centuries resulted in part from a convergence of major economic, social, environmental, political, and technological changes that were occurring. William McNeill attributes much of this change to the impact of the emergence of a capitalist system of economy and its spread with Christianity beyond the Latin parts of southern Europe. A political, social, and military order that depended on rural relationships among lords, vassals, and the rest of the population conflicted with the needs and practices of a world of emerging capitalism that favored commerce and the growth of cities. The latter wanted to control the required sources of food around them, which contributed to rivalries and conflict. As the thirteenth century advanced, climate change, plague, famine, peasant revolts, and other factors contributed to more reasons for change.[22] In much of Europe the institution of knighthood and its place in war began to diminish. Townspeople, merchants, and apprentices did not labor and operate within the older framework.

As kingdoms began to develop and rulers found the need to establish better control over resources, the character and purpose of war also underwent change. What more modern eyes would recognize as state-on-state conflict was developing, and these types of conflicts required fielding larger militaries. So, too, did the demands of the Crusades that commenced at the end of the eleventh century and continued for nearly two hundred years in parts of Europe and in the eastern Mediterranean. Armies became larger. Louis IX of France (1214–1270) took between 15,000 and 25,000 soldiers on his first Crusade. Edward I of England (1239–1307) was able to get as many as 30,000 men on horseback. Yet, this type of warfare could not depend on mounted knights on horseback. It required infantry, such as pike men, archers, cavalry, and others. These types of men did not come from feudal obligations, and even if they did the numbers were insufficient; they would have to be found by other means. Those who tried to depend still on feudal obligations, such as the French, would pay dearly in losses such as at Crecy against the English in 1346.[23]

Technology and its impact on combat also surpassed the abilities of traditional feudal armies to use such weapons or find adequate numbers who even had the skills. Crossbows were an old weapon, but beginning at roughly this same time the manufacture of them in Mediterranean cities such as Barcelona and Genoa made them more widely available in Europe. Originally regarded as more of a weapon for defense of ships, the crossbow quickly lent itself to use in land combat as well. The velocity of the bolt made it a deadly weapon, capable of penetrating armor, even if its rate of fire was slow by the need to "span" it by placing one's feet on the bow to pull up the string and place another bolt for fire. Remaining knights and few others in the population had the skills to use crossbows, at least in their early days, so mercenaries often became the source of the skill. Ultimately, the crossbow would be surpassed by a simpler but equally powerful weapon: the longbow. The irony of the longbow was that it took a longer time to master accuracy with it—time that many mercenaries did not have or preferred not to exercise.[24]

The growing scale and needs of militaries in war created not only a demand for mercenaries but a source of supply for them as well. Not unlike soldiers in the present day, the need for their particular skills decreased when peace took over. An intermission in the Hundred Years' War, for example, would place on French roads in particular men who had fulfilled the requirements of their service. For money, emotional or psychological need, self-identity, and other motives they could seek service with another leader or ruler in a different conflict. Others might remain on a path of pillage and destruction, as medieval warfare did not draw the same lines between combatants and noncombatants that we try to have in force today.[25] Adding to the numbers of men who were on the roads were all the factors that McNeill and others have stressed—regions of overpopulation due to imbalances of numbers of people with available food, lack of opportunity, as various forms of primogeniture existed, and other hardships. The supply of food could be more consistent in an army or from the hands of someone facing a pointed sword. The sources of mercenaries would vary, shifting from the Low Countries and the Italian states to Switzerland and the German states beginning in the fourteenth century and carrying forward into the fifteenth and sixteenth centuries.[26]

Clearly the underlying considerations between mercenaries and the agent or actor willing to use them did not rest on lines of fealty, duty, or service during this time in history. If a prince or ruler thought reliance on mercenaries would strengthen the justification for war within the realm or beyond, he or she would find little foundation. The degree of legitimate consent or sanction to conduct war obtained by using mercenaries would have been tenuous at best. Economic necessity and survival appeared to motivate mercenaries rather than any sense of loyalty, service, or duty. The arrangement was a form of a public-private relationship, to use modern language, and it would usually end on those terms. Thomas Aquinas had conceded that private persons could fight in a war, but they did not have the authority to commence or sanction one. Thus, fighting for booty or a payment for services rendered was not wrong in itself. Having access to mercenaries offered no legitimacy, though, for going to war. That rested with people at higher levels who had the authority to initiate war in a legitimate and just fashion. While we are not yet at a point in history where one can speak of the consent of the governed to make war legitimate, one could not arguably secure consent or authorization for war by simply paying parties to do it. Such terms would not carry the same implications and commitment obtained from a vassal, lord, or a recruited or levied common soldier serving a ruler or kingdom, who, in turn, had to offer explanation for the need for war to make it legitimate.[27] There was a bond between ruler and ruled with such obligations. True, hardship and loss of life were possible outcomes for all involved in war in the Middle Ages, but a soldier of the ruler or prince would still arguably have more invested and more at stake in war than those under contract, such as the security of home and family. Admittedly, seeking greater depth of consent and support from the ruled to obtain service could be risky for the ruler who wanted to avoid unrest or disruption at home. So the mercenary option was a plausible, attractive choice in the feudal period and Middle Ages, but it held its uncertainties, too, that would show themselves as time progressed.

Since mercenaries were part of a system that shared the features of the institutions of capitalism that were developing alongside, one could argue that the demand for them may have been as important as the available supply. Considering the last half of the twelfth century, the historian Michael Mallett

concludes it "is not clear whether the companies of infantry mercenaries
. . . emerged as a result of expanding population and underemployment or
whether royal initiative and deliberate recruitment was the key factor."[28]
Jurgen Brauer and Hubert Van Tuyll discern the same difficulty in measuring
the exact significance of push-and-pull factors or supply and demand in their
study of how economics explains military history.[29] Certainly demand was
part of the appeal of mercenaries and their closely related counterparts at
the time—fully paid soldiers. In his study of the foundations and development of states in this period, Thomas Ertman argues that the English and
Italians seemed to have come to the same conclusion at about the same
time—circa 1270s and 1280s—by developing a type of contract (initially
called an *indenture* in England) for either nobles or actual entrepreneurs
to recruit soldiers for a fixed salary for particular conditions. Money itself
could be a strong inducement for a broader swath of the population, and
one could get volunteers to agree to serve for longer periods of time in the
agreement.[30] There was also a desire to bring order to recruiting and better control over some types of mercenaries, such as a *lance*, or a freelance,
essentially a mercenary knight or a mercenary with a few armed men to
handle horses and to serve in combat. It was arguably better to have these
mercenaries in a unit or company rather than as autonomous actors with
no effective command.[31] The same concern was at hand in trying to place
free companies, what the French called *routiers*, under better control. These
were literally private armies of their own, who often engaged in ravishing
people and the countryside but disappeared when confronted with a real
adversary. They seemed more interested in gains, however defined, than
persistence and dependable service for their employer. They were a particular
curse in France during the turmoil of the Hundred Years' War. One band,
commanded by the Englishman John Hawkwood, who had at his beckon
veterans of these wars, began to pillage Italy so badly that a nun, Catherine
of Siena, beseeched him to turn his group's talents to fighting the Muslim
Turks. Italy, though, was more lucrative, and there Hawkwood remained.[32]

Thus, reliance on mercenaries grew, even though they were supplements
to larger armies. Simultaneously, though, rulers and the structures of early
states were beginning to develop measures to place mercenaries under better
control to secure their service for larger political ends rather than private
ones. Contracts became much more sophisticated; so, too, did some of the
offices and mechanisms that governments created to manage the contracts.

From approximately 1300 to 1500 Europe witnessed the peak of its reliance on mercenaries, although they would retain a prominent place in some armies well into the eighteenth century.

Renaissance Italy had a combination of characteristics and circumstances that made it an especially prominent venue for mercenaries. Urbanization occurred earlier on the Italian peninsula than in many other parts of Europe, which paralleled the growth of trade and the workforce and population involved in and dependent on it. Feudal institutions and customs weakened in the face of this. Rivalries among cities to control the surrounding population and resources as well as each other offered a large number of actors that wanted the services of professionals in combat to supplement the civic militias they often had.[33] William McNeill adds that the comparative prosperity of the growing economies in Europe created enough capital to convince the leaders of wealthier cities to tax their population and use part of the revenue to pay for professional men-of-arms.[34] Certain cities figured prominently in their use of mercenaries—Milan, Florence, and Venice—but the Papal States in central Italy and Naples to the south also used mercenaries in these struggles.[35]

A formal business relationship emerged between the principal (the city-state) offering the contract and the agent (the mercenaries) signing it. The terminology of contracts and contractors became a part of the historical record—the *condotta* or *condotte* (plural) for the principal and the *condottiere* or *condottieri* (plural) for the agent. Brauer and Van Tuyll observe that there was a problem from the very beginning. It would not be easy for the principals to observe what the agent or agents do and how well they did it, especially if it involved actual battle. An impressive array of good-looking horses, well-armed men, and ample equipment was not proof in itself that the contracted mercenary would do what he promised or subsequently claimed. Falsified claims and inflated charges were a risk from the first day. Of course, not all problems were with the agent. Principals might chose to renege or claim falsely that they could not honor the compensation promised. Also, conditions could arise later that might become real problems, such as a *condottiere* holding off from additional action because the number of enemy had increased or circumstances around the battlefield had worsened.[36] Just as contractors and contracting officials struggle today to anticipate all factors in a contract, their predecessors had to do so in fourteenth- and fifteenth-century Italy and other parts of Europe.

The details in these contracts easily suggest some of the types of issues that could arise. If it was a cavalry unit, which was common because warfare at this time had become more dependent on cavalry, one found the expected stipulations related to numbers of men, horses, the value of the horses, compensation for the loss of a horse, the types and value of the required equipment, payment for travel, the pay rate and frequency of pay (including the rates for different ranks or levels), handling of prisoners, and the treatment and status of booty. Contracts were usually for three or six months, and they often had renewal options. A variety of other provisions could be found, including payments of a bond to assure the good behavior of the mercenaries—a not insignificant concern. Sometimes specialists were brought into the process; for example, to establish accurate estimates on the value of the horses. Notaries witnessed the agreements. Provisions existed for breach of contract. The contractor or agent could sometimes have freedom to negotiate and enter contracts with other parties—a potential problem, to say the least, if not closely watched. A contract could set forth the nature of both defensive and offensive capabilities, and provisions did exist that required payment by the mercenary if he decided not to attack. Sometimes both parties entered a contract that limited the service to a particular campaign or even more specifically to a single action.[37] Whatever the details, the negotiation of them involved its own expertise, so it was not surprising to find that some mercenaries, or *condottieri*, employed lawyers as well.[38]

This contract warfare or use of free-market soldiers carried the inevitable seeds of dispute. Seizure of castles, for example, could result in disagreement over the possession of all movables. Mercenaries wanted to claim them, but the Florentine code of 1337 stipulated that such things, just like the permanently fixed items (such as the castle itself), were to be in the hands of the city-state.[39] One should never forget that being a mercenary was supposed to be a money-making endeavor. Fighting to the last man was not a good money-making strategy, and any ruler or principal had better be prepared for disappointment if he expected it. Rather than getting themselves killed, a better course for surviving and making money alongside was to prolong the campaign and live off the land until the enemy surrendered, lost the mercenaries that supplemented his army because of expired contracts, or retreated. The historian Michael Howard suggests that such factors even shaped the course and conduct of war in Europe during most of the 1500s.[40]

In comparison to their modern descendants, the contractors of the Renaissance period, like their feudal ancestors, were not guaranteed pay that surpassed what one might obtain serving in a city-state or civil militia. A lot of German mercenaries worked on the Italian peninsula, and to obtain the equipment they needed they often had to sell possessions before departing their homes. The pay would not necessarily make up for the initial sacrifice. The numerous campaigns and wars in Italy witness repeated cases where soldiers and mercenaries went without pay for weeks or even months, with the predictable results of switching sides or using force to get money. Kidnapping people and stealing livestock for ransom were recurrent means of obtaining more of it. Sometimes advanced pay was extended, but soldiers, whether professional employees of the state or mercenaries, have never been renowned as great savers. Making a living as a mercenary at this time seems to have been a rather difficult path to follow. Evidence suggests that about two-thirds of the German mercenaries in Italy stayed for only a campaign season or two before returning home, for the pay may not have even matched that of a day laborer in much of Italy. Carrying home riches was not the reason they returned to the German states. The leaders and officers, the real *condottieri*, sometimes could secure much more lucrative payments just for themselves that were not distributed to their subordinates.[41]

By 1500 developments in Europe appeared to favor turning from mercenaries to militaries created and paid by emerging states from their populations. Yet, the Thirty Years' War (1618–1648) witnessed battles and armies that were almost entirely mercenary. The coexistence of contradictory paths resulted from a variety of factors—the character and objective of the war, the size and condition of the population, and others—but perhaps none was more dependent than the system used to develop and coerce the required resources, human and monetary, to sustain the war. The three frameworks posed by Charles Tilly and briefly discussed in the previous chapter—coercion-intensive, capital-intensive, and capitalized coercion—were being implemented simultaneously with a variety of results; the first more dependent on the actual population, the second more on capitalist actors and outsiders, and the last a demonstration of a calculated combination of the other two.[42] Thomas Ertman, in his study of the early modern state, describes the situation differently by stressing that rulers had to reconcile two conflicting aspirations. Rulers needed access to resources that would support the state and conflict. Those asked or pressed to make the contributions wanted to make a profit or obtain some form of gain or expanded influence. "The first," Ertman observes, "is the source of a drive towards 'rationalization' in the Weberian sense, while the second is the source of a tendency towards 'irrationalization,' or the expansion of private at the expense of public interests." Maybe because of his historical focus Ertman states this tension was "always present within the medieval and early modern state."[43] But it would clearly reappear in the late twentieth century too.

Thus, the preceding descriptions of efforts to make mercenaries more effective and trustworthy instruments of the state reflected an attempt to control the free-market nature of their activity and establish a more "mediated market," in Sean McFate's words.[44] The quest to align the aspirations of agent and principal is a story with no end, but it was unquestionably made hard by the conflicting realities as well as evolving characteristics of both the client and mercenary. Niccolo Machiavelli (1469–1527) experienced this tension in his own thinking. He looked back nostalgically on the idea of Roman legionnaires fighting for the empire as citizens, but he attributed Rome's downfall partly to overreliance on mercenaries from the German tribes and contrasted them with the often undependable condottieri he had seen or read about. Yet, at the same time, Machiavelli knew that mercenaries were often better troops because of their skills and experience.[45] Machiavelli's perspective reflected he was living in a time when princely realms like Florence were evolving into princely states—a time when the legal and material attributes of a human being were ascribed to the state itself, meaning that one could use words like legitimacy, personality or character, and sovereignty to describe or characterize the state.[46] As we know, some of the Italian city-states were quite prosperous but lacked the size of population to defend themselves independently. Nonetheless, Machiavelli represented a growing conviction that believed that the preservation of the attributes of a state required an army not reliant on mercenaries.

The solution was to develop steps that would invite greater loyalty and identity with the state from those serving it in arms. The methods for creation and coercion of resources and the scale of capital available were critical for providing greater freedom and ability for states. Some of the measures were not that revolutionary or imaginative. Paying soldiers regularly and directly, rather than relaying the money through condottieri, was one way of reducing costs. As the sixteenth century progressed, more and more soldiers in Italy were outside of the condottieri system, even if they were still serving under terms of a contract. Even longer terms of contract with the *condottieri* were better arrangements. Direct, regular pay for longer periods of time seems to have helped establish better bonds of loyalty between the soldier and the state. Billeting troops in a neighborhood or particular area also built stronger ties for the soldier, and the presence of regularly paid troops in an area added to economic growth as they spent money in the locale.[47]

Technology and its impact on war could create both a demand for mercenaries with specific skills and a reason to train local or state soldiers in its use in place of mercenaries. Swiss mercenaries were in much demand in Italy and elsewhere because of their skill with pikes and halberds, fighting in phalanx formation and in close quarter with their enemies. Adding to the uniqueness of the Swiss was the fact that negotiation of their contracts was handled by authorities from the respective Swiss cantons rather than entrepreneurs. Providing mercenaries became a national business for the Swiss. Major competition for their services came from the *Landsknechte*, mercenaries who were mainly from the southern German principalities and represented by traditional entrepreneurs, if they were not the one and same. These men also knew how to use the pike and halberd, but when early firearms began to appear on the battlefield they also developed proficiency in their use.[48] Not all city-states turned to the Swiss and German mercenaries, though, as some recognized the need for developing skills with such weaponry among their own soldiers. The Venetians, for example, used Swiss and German mercenaries as trainers in the use of these weapons—a practice that has followed to the present day with modern contractors.[49]

Warfare in the sixteenth century was undergoing major change. At the century's beginning one could still find retention of some features of feudal warfare and actors. Knights may not have been as numerous, but they were still present in some settings. Cavalry had been a prominent feature of war as the century opened. However, the development of field artillery and firearms that could be carried and fired by a single soldier spelled significant change because they were weapons of distance. Heavy fortifications—fortresses, redoubts, large land works—all became much more important on the battlefield. The number of soldiers and others needed to support war, much less to fight it, grew significantly. A form of war had developed that placed less emphasis on chivalry or proof of one's honor; taking prisoners for ransom, a favorite tactic of mercenaries and others, held less attraction. War had become much more about killing as a measure in the acts of victory and conquest. Emphasis on killing and death were not as appealing features for entrepreneurs who had regarded war as a way of making a living.[50]

In the one hundred years between 1555 and 1655 armies grew by as much as twice or three times. That of Castile/Spain increased from 150,000 in 1555 to 300,000 by 1635; France's tripled from 50,000 to 150,000 during the same time; Sweden's experienced a twelvefold increase in just forty years, expanding from 15,000 in 1595 to 180,000 in 1635.[51] Of course, these increases reflected the impact of the Thirty Years' War, which had begun in 1618 and ended in 1648 with the Peace of Westphalia. In fact, the sizes of armies had declined by 1655. In his study of war and states, Bruce Porter reminds us of the three salient factors that contributed to this growth of militaries. The first was briefly discussed in the preceding paragraph: the military revolution in technology, tactics, and armed forces. The second was the convergence of religious, social, economic, and political tensions that grew out of the Reformation; and the third was a struggle against or for, depending on one's objectives, hegemonic control over Europe, which had been prompted by moves by the Habsburgs to establish such supremacy. All three, of course, converged in and contributed to the length and destruction of the Thirty Years' War, but one should not forget as well the turmoil and violence that occurred often within states and kingdoms that were separate from that horrible three-decade conflict.[52]

As the main actors in this conflict were "tax-and-power" states, to use the description of Lauro Martines, they faced immense hurdles in paying the costs to wage these conflicts.[53] Taxpayers in Europe probably faced an average fourfold increase from 1520 to 1670. (One can only imagine the political fury that might have existed if the same person paid them for all 150 years. Life is mercifully shorter.) The cost of outfitting soldiers may have increased five times during the same period. It should be no surprise that states also had to establish bureaucracies to handle all the revenue, expenditures, provision of equipment, and so on, that became part of war.[54] The phenomena and debate over war feeding on war, the military-industrial complex of the mid-twentieth century, or the self-licking ice cream cone depicted by today's commentators were coming into place by the seventeenth century.

Indeed, as war became more complex and sophisticated, its demands bore implications for how states supported it as well as the type and structure of forces they needed to fight it. The future of the mercenary rested within these changes. Reviewing the changes that occurred, Charles Tilly observes that more sophisticated forms of war meant that fewer people owned or had access to the instruments to fight it. Something that could serve as a sword was more at hand for the average person than a musket. Furthermore, governments were, in effect, beginning to disarm their populations so they could pay the taxes and other costs of an equipped military. Payment of taxes or compensation for provisions was also an easier way for governments to get resources than seizing them arbitrarily, which sometimes resulted in strife. Finally, states were beginning to build for themselves some of the items needed in war. If all of these measures were going to work to the maximum benefit of the state, though, two needs had to be met—a "relatively monetized economy, and the ready availability of credit." Naturally, wars have a way of creating their own momentum, and unless a state chooses to fight only within its means, there is a likelihood of having to exceed its own revenues and resources. Thus, the capability to borrow was important, and, consequently, so was the belief of the creditor that the borrowing party would be able to pay the debt. States with cities often possessed the economic characteristics that gave them higher prospects in being able to serve and meet all of these demands.[55] Market forces, in short, were instrumental in building state power. Even though monarchs might have struggled to understand it, "European states," William McNeill writes, "were strengthened by their involvement in the fiscal web spun by international bankers and suppliers."[56]

In the short term, though, the development of these state capabilities would benefit the profession of the mercenary, for their implementation and practice would help make the Thirty Years' War the "apogee" of the mercenary experience. States either had these capabilities and hired mercenaries as their armies or they lacked them and turned to mercenaries to do the recruiting. Geoffrey Parker, in his study The Military Revolution, estimates that there were as many as 1,500 people recruiting contract soldiers all over Europe.[57] Some of the armies were composed entirely of mercenaries. The army recruited by the most famous and controversial of these entrepreneurs, Albrecht von Wallenstein, may have come to as many as 50,000 men.[58]

Wallenstein, thanks in part to the German Romantic playwright and poet Friedrich Schiller, who depicted him so graphically for the stage, is arguably the embodiment of the mercenary in early modern Europe. A minor nobleman in Bohemia, Wallenstein was born and raised in a Lutheran family but converted to Catholicism as a young man. He cast his support behind the

Habsburg emperor Ferdinand II in the latter's effort to strengthen both the Habsburg and Catholic positions in Central Europe. Wallenstein's armies, like those of other mercenary captains on both Protestant and Catholic sides, were a scourge on the countryside and population. Straight plunder, as Geoffrey Parker points out, probably cost too much time and energy for these mercenaries. The more common approach was to threaten the community with being burned down or sacked in turn for a ransom of money and/or necessary goods. The mercenary captain or even his employer might offer a letter of guaranteed protection for the future, which carried the expectation that the community would provide later supplies as needed. Some communities even tried to save themselves by watching the lines of march of the armies and offering goods as a preemptive concession.[59] Supplying one's own forces arguably was as important, maybe even more so, than military victory, since the preferred goal resembled "economic exhaustion" rather than defeat.[60]

The siege of the Lutheran community Magdeburg in May 1631 illustrated what could befall cities, towns, and people on all sides of the war. Magdeburg had successfully defended itself against Wallenstein two years earlier, but this time the forces of the Catholic League, led by General Charles Tilly, proved too powerful. Of the approximate 30,000 inhabitants in the city, about 5,000 survived. A Jesuit priest urged the army to respect the honor of women in particular, repeating an order given by Tilly, but to no avail. The priest later wrote, "the streets were . . . strewn with dead bodies and the clothes of those who had been robbed. No consideration had been shown for women's honor. In front of the Peterskirche lay a heap of violated and murdered women. Our victorious landsknechts hurled themselves with dog-like lust upon the women of the vanquished city. This lecherous behavior turned our victorious armies into bands of defeated men." Within a year of Magdeburg, opposing armies, led partly by the king of Sweden, Gustavus Adolphus, would destroy several hundred villages and much of their population in central Germany and Bavaria.[61] The killing and slaughter followed a timeworn path taken by nonstate and state actors alike when they are trying with force to show others a better spiritual path from temporal life to the afterlife.

Wallenstein's own path provided lessons in the danger of unchecked mercenary captains. The fact these wars dragged on for so long reflected the fact that those fighting them increasingly had to come from the outside; the population of the German states could not have sustained such losses on their own. The German population was then around 13 million of which 1 million died, 4 to 5 million others became refugees, and maybe 1.5 million were war cripples.[62] Wallenstein made a lot of money in this environment with his recruited solders, even with setbacks such as the Battle of Luetzen in November 1632, which also witnessed the death of Gustavus Adolphus. As Wallenstein's power grew, he appears to have held his sponsor, Ferdinand II, in increased contempt and ultimately thought he could topple him and become emperor. This interpretation became a central thread in Schiller's depiction of the mercenary captain and in popular imagination. The emperor had become aware of Wallenstein's designs and arranged a counterplot against him. In February 1634 he died at a banquet at the hands of Scottish and Irish mercenaries.[63]

If the Thirty Years' War provided one of history's most indelible images of the risk of mercenaries and soldiers out of control, the peace that ended this conflict signaled changes that would bring most mercenary activity to an end within one hundred and fifty years. Although the exact impact of the Peace of Westphalia in 1648 is a subject of analytical debate, there is valid reason to acknowledge it as a pivotal development in the establishment of the state system that shaped Europe's subsequent history. The conferences at Muenster (largely for the Protestants) and Osnabrueck (for the Catholics) set into place the religious boundaries in Europe. The Habsburg-dominated Holy Roman Empire was greatly diminished in fact and symbolism. German states that had once deferred to it now represented themselves in diplomacy.[64] Regarding the peace from the vantage of the evolution of modern states, Philip Bobbitt argues that it was the bridge between the existence of kingly states and the emergence of territorial ones. "Whereas a kingly state was organized around a person, the territorial state was defined by its contiguity and therefore fretted constantly about its borders. For the territorial state, its borders were everything—its legitimacy, its defense perimeter, its tax base." The ultimate example of the kingly state was arguably France under Louis XIV whereas the model of the territorial state could be found in the emerging powers of Prussia and Great Britain.[65]

War itself was still undergoing changes that reflected experience as well as the requirements of the political and state systems that were developing in Europe. The sheer destructiveness of the Thirty Years' War had left a powerful impression that war could not be allowed to become so unchained. The terrible human costs were unbearable by almost any form of measurement. It is no surprise that this conflict generated the body of political, legal, and strategic thought that was briefly examined in the previous chapter. The numerous outrages against civilians were just another factor arguing for better control over the selection and command of men in the military. Conscription of men from the state's territory was one answer to this problem—a practice developed first in Sweden and later by Prussia (1688) and other European states. Mercenaries did not quickly disappear in this environment, but the terms of their selection and use changed. They became parts of permanent standing armies with long-term arrangements for their services—whether individual or by larger unit. Some principalities became known as major suppliers of units to other states, such as was the case of the principalities of Hesse, Brunswick, Hanover, Baden, and Waldeck for the British. These would be the mercenaries so reviled by American colonists in their revolution. At the same approximate time, though, about one-third of the French army was composed of mercenaries before the French Revolution.[66]

Nearly all trends pointed policy and war away from the mercenary. Technology continued to do the mercenary no favors. Newer muskets did not require the levels of skill to load and fire, and yet, they were more accurate and deadlier. Training conscripted soldiers in their use, perhaps firing in three rotating ranks, was not that difficult. A diplomatic system emerged that worked to negotiate the avoidance of war or the fast termination of it before it became too destructive. These so-called cabinet wars were often conflicts seeking minor adjustment, and their settlement sought to preserve a balance of power that proved so central in European state thinking in the eighteenth century. The premise that armies should generally remain within five days of their bases contradicted the earlier practice of living off the land and population and tolerating the destruction that came with it. Frederick the Great observed that if war was conducted properly, the civilians should not even be aware of its occurrence. Reinforcing this measured approach to war and the preference for better control over armies and commanders were economic realities. Standing armies were expensive. One either had the revenue, the means of collecting and administering them, and of providing military capabilities, or one did not. By the middle of the eighteenth century Great Britain had become a power not because of its immense population or inherent military prowess but because of its willingness to tax, its acceptance of public deficit finance, and the existence of a bureaucracy that could make all of this operate. The British state had become the single largest actor in the national economy. Even though they served in the British army, the mercenaries that went to North America and the policies that enabled them faced a short-term future.[67]

The desire to assure that war serves the objectives of the state was the primary reason for the diminished place of the mercenary in land warfare. Certainly other factors had their role. Doubts about loyalty and dependability repeatedly occurred, and the establishment of more permanent forms of service could prevent that. Costs could be better controlled, too, because of longer terms of service, the limited skills required for most men to fight in the infantry, and the elimination of middlemen who had been both recruiters and commanders. Also, even though the feudal traditions of chivalry had disappeared, land war in the European part of the Atlantic world still carried imagery of glory, honor, sacrifice, and stature for those aristocrats and others perhaps capable of purchasing an officer's commission to lead. The growth of modern states and their stronger control over war to serve national ends created a stronger bond between the soldier and the state in this mindset for war. The rise of nationalism and the growth of mass mobilized armies in the early nineteenth century created a ferment that offered little for the mercenary.

Mercenaries had emerged in settings where modern definitions of war had less meaning. In the feudal world models of private and public war coexisted and were sometimes not easy to distinguish. As shown in the previous chapter, private actors could seek reprisal on land if no other means for settlement existed. No doubt mercenaries benefited from such circumstances and needs. Yet, as we have seen, they often complemented or supplemented existing forms of military force and action. Market forces did assume an important part in the relationship between mercenary and employer. Increasingly, the mercenary became a private entrepreneur or actor who sold his service to the ruler and later the state. Sometimes the ends and objectives of both parties converged nicely; making money could serve the realm's or state's purpose. Other times the two conflicted, as the need to protect assets (soldiers) and to make money collided with the needs of the state. As land warfare and strategic thinking about its role and purpose evolved, war as a "public" end—a collective act that must serve the objectives and welfare of the state—required higher confidence and trust in the willingness of soldiers to stand by and defend those public purposes to whatever degree the state believed essential. This was not an environment where a mercenary could make money, even if laws forbidding their existence were not in place. Conceptions of both the state and the word *citizen* demanded wholly different relationships that could be best served by measures like conscription and more effective means of state preparation for war.

Whether speaking of the relations between official or state actors or between public and private warfare, a very different dynamic existed in the maritime world. Considering the world of the sixteenth and seventeenth centuries, William McNeill writes that "in every instance European ventures on the oceans were sustained by a combination of public, quasi-public, and relentlessly private enterprise." No better example of the interplay of private and public sectors exists than the fact that most of the English vessels sailing to defend the realm against the Spanish Armada were armed merchantmen. The English had not drawn clear distinctions yet between their merchant marine and the navy.[68] The capital marketplace held a much greater place at center stage in maritime conflict than it did on land. True, money making was a pivotal factor for the mercenary and his captain, but on the seas the making of money was something that also stood in prominent place for the ruler or state. In instances, as we will later see, it was the primary objective and determinant. In fact, the people who made the very decisions about force could operate from very different perspective of honor and profit. McNeill observes how those "who made decisions about raising armies and planning campaigns were utterly out of sympathy with pecuniary calculation. War was an affair of honor, prestige, heroic self-assertion." For ventures on the high seas, "investors in each voyage measured their costs against prospective returns as shrewdly as they knew how."[69]

How long this dynamic lasted can be debated. Essentially, it was at its end in the late eighteenth century as well, although the United States arguably held onto it into the mid-nineteenth century. It will be no surprise to find that the demand for better state control over the agents and acts of violence in conflict assumed a similar role in the maritime world as well. What is interesting, though, is the way distinctions were drawn between public and private as well as the recognition by most parties of the need for agreements and international law to address the actions of states and private actors and to prevent blurring or seepage of actions between private and public that could result in actual war and conflict. The maritime world would see an earlier development of laws and practice governing private actors in conflict, especially at the international level, than warfare on land.

Whether it is the framework for mercenaries on land or for letters of marque and privateering on sea that provide the best parallel for the present and future status of private military firms and actors in conflict is a matter at the heart of this book. The answer will draw from both. If the framework is more like that of the traditional mercenary, then the answer seems rather straightforward. Governments must either choose to reestablish government actors in those roles—"renationalize" them, as some might say—or develop stronger, more effective measures to assure that private sector actors will respond to consideration of national interest and good rather than corporate or personal gain. If the framework resembles that of the maritime world of letters of marque and reprisal and privateering, a more complicated set of options emerges. It is not just a matter of reestablishing government roles and creating better laws and mechanisms of control; it is also a question as to whether governments want to purposely make private agents responsible for certain types of measures and accept the risk of private wars over which states lack or even abdicate control. To evaluate that question, though, it is critical to understand what these maritime practices were, why they existed, and why they were largely abandoned.

THE MATTER OF PIRACY

As we have seen, the distinction between nonstate actors who are serving within the boundaries of state authority and those acting beyond can be very hard to discern. Mercenary bands acting within the terms of their agreement often pillaged and looted. If they did so without agreement or contract they were just thieves and bandits. However, actions on the high seas were harder to govern and regulate because the ocean did not lend itself to the same applications of sovereignty and rule that land did, even though such features did not stop states and others from trying to impose similar controls and enforce them. (The same dilemma exists in the cyber domain today.) The practice of being a mercenary did not derive or descend from skills of theft and murder. The mercenary had skills or numbers of men provided to an employer. Letters of marque and reprisal and privateering had a close, uncomfortable, and at times even indiscernible relationship with piracy. One can argue war is a crime, but it is frequently done through the involvement of governments and states. Piracy, as understood in popular imagination, is not a state-sanctioned action.

Piracy holds a unique position in international law and politics that goes all the way back to discussion of its status and meaning in the classical and Roman periods, as piracy was certainly a problem throughout the Mediterranean world and beyond.[70] Yet, *piracy* has been fairly elusive to define because of difficulty in specifying the exact spatial boundaries for the term's application as well as stipulating the types of actions or behavior that fall within it. Consider first a modern definition, such as "acts of violence done upon the ocean or unappropriated lands, or within the territory of a state through descent from the sea, by a body of men acting independently of any politically organized society."[71] A critical addition to this in most definitions would be that the acts must be done for private ends. Charles Molloy, writing in the 1670s, described pirates very succinctly as "sea thieves," which certainly plays into the image we hold of them as hairy or shaved-headed men, along with a few colorful women, clambering over decks and seizing vessels and passengers.[72] Contrast these views with a definition from 2013, actually more of a description of piracy and pirates as actors who

> enter into a conflictive "relationship" with the state, especially when the state claims to be the sole source of sovereignty; they operate in an organized manner on uncharted territory, from a set of support bases located outside this territory, over which the state typically claims sovereign control; they develop, as alternative communities, a series of discordant norms that, according to them, should be used to regulate uncharted territory; and ultimately, they represent a threat to the state because they upset the very ideas of sovereignty and territory by contesting the state's control and the activities of the legal entities that operate under its jurisdiction.[73]

Much of the above is grounded in the description of piracy Cicero wrote in 44 BCE in which he remarks on how pirates operate outside of the bounds of government, or what would be later treated as state authority. "A pirate," Cicero notes, "is not included in the number of lawful enemies, but is the common enemy of all." As pirates are not members of city-states, they are not criminals subject to national criminal law. Nor are they an opponent in wartime, since their rootless, stateless qualities make it impossible to be a "lawful" enemy.[74] If a pirate is "the common enemy of all," it is implied there should be no place that offers them safety or exemption. By the sixteenth century, lines of argument had developed in Europe that advocated a form of "universal jurisdiction" in relation to pirates. In short, they could be captured, tried, and punished by whatever state or government that held them, and this has remained in effect to the current day.[75] However, as Janice Thomson has explained, placing pirates under international law is not easily done, as they are not acting on behalf of states, which is the focus of international law. Yet, if their status may not be completely clear, there is no doubt that international law expects states to take actions against pirates.[76]

The discussion of piracy in this chapter sets it almost completely in a maritime world, which is the setting we know so well, but the practices linked to the word have no reason to be limited to the sea. The sea was, instead, the first of several domains that rulers, governments, and states believed they could organize, govern, and expand or consolidate as needed. The discussion of the Atlantic world in the next chapter depicts the plans, efforts, setbacks, and policies surrounding attempts to do this in that world and the role that private force, particularly sanctioned by the state, played in it. With piracy, though, it was resistance to such authority that figured prominently. Piracy challenged that authority, often demonstrated its limitations, and sometimes perfected alternative measures and behavior to circumvent whatever governments attempted. Looking at a variety of pirate organizations, Rodolphe Durand and Jean-Philippe Vergne found several common characteristics. Pirates act

in the gray areas in which norms are not fully established and where the sovereign is unsure of actions it should encourage or discourage. The pirate organization, generally, intervenes when a sovereign first maps a territory for expansion. . . . The pirate organization worms its way into the sovereign state and navigates between its borders. It challenges the sovereign's control. But the pirate organization does not seek to overthrow and replace the system in place, rather it seeks to challenge widespread norms.[77]

Piracy brought confusion into the seventeenth- and eighteenth-century worlds as it has today. Not only is it because of the reappearance of traditional piracy in parts of the world, such as the Straits of Malacca, the Indian Ocean, or the Straits of Hormuz, but also because the term and concept seems to apply so fittingly to other domains—outer space, hacking and cyber, and abuse of biological and medical patents—to mention a few areas. Whether Julian Assange is an early twenty-first-century pirate is a question this study will not try to answer. What will be of concern is whether these types of nonstate actors pose challenges resembling in certain ways their historical ancestors. To what extent can governments and states today and in the future respond solely through state actors? Will they have to rely more on selected nonstate actors to assume these responsibilities? What, too, if various nonstate actors purposely bypass or dismiss state-controlled means and respond with their own capabilities?

In his study of piracy, Daniel Heller-Roazen, a professor of comparative literature at Princeton, observed how piracy, ancient or modern, poses especially challenging problems of definition. "Piracy," he writes, "brings about the confusion and, in the most extreme cases, the collapse of the distinction between criminal and political categories."[78] It is a recurrent problem with nonstate actors, as we witnessed in arguments over how to respond to terrorism—more vigorous laws and law enforcement, or measures of war. Yet, it is a subsequent stipulation made by Heller-Roazen that is especially troubling in a study of the state, war, and private force:

> Piracy entails a transformation of the concept of war. Since "enemies of all" are neither criminals nor belligerents in any accepted sense, the operations carried out against them cannot be formally identical to those employed against a lawful enemy. They must involve the measures used in prosecuting both belligerents and criminals; procedures of external relations and of internal security, technologies of politics, as well as of police.[79]

This environment not only creates ambiguity in times between spheres of war and peace but, as Heller-Roazen implies, requires a different combination of instruments and means. The dilemma is not unique to piracy, though. It is the same set of choices states believe they face with terrorism, cyber attacks, and transnational crime. States recognize that private means are a critical part of this response because they offer skills and capabilities that government may not have at hand and may not be able to create and afford as easily.

In a very different world, rulers and emerging states struggled with similar choices. Just which ruler, kingdom, nobleman, or whomever first decided to give support to capture and thievery for official purposes is lost in the murk of history. Laws against piracy exist in the code of Hammurabi and the laws of ancient Egypt. To infer that sanctioned piracy might have been tolerated at the same time is difficult. We do know, however, that the ancient Greeks supported piracy to capture merchant ships of their enemies. In 594 BCE Athens enacted a law that recognized the legality of contracts between merchants or pirates. Treaties between city-states forbid the capture or taking of merchant vessels by either side.[80] Such practices and agreements continued into the Roman period and thus would have been known to Europeans from the early feudal times onward. Reinforcing this knowledge would have been the patterns of piracy that emerged between the Muslim and Christian worlds in the seventh century. Even though a strong trade existed between the two worlds, Muslim leaders regarded raids and piracy as divinely justified attacks. The Roman Church sought to prohibit trade with the Muslim world but failed, and it simultaneously sanctioned divinely inspired piracy against Muslim vessels.[81]

Whether the captains and crews of these vessels benefited from terms or labels that comforted them with the knowledge they were not common-day pirates is unclear. The word *privateer*, which is the term for officially approved or supported piracy, was not known until the seventeenth century. The practice was known, though, and so too were legal terms that provided through licenses a form of defense against the charge of piracy. For example, in 1243 King Henry III of England gave licenses to Adam Robernolt and William le Sauvage "to annoy our enemies at sea" and to return half of their gains to the crown. At roughly the same time Catholic Church officials had given similar licenses to conduct piracy against Muslim shipping.[82] The terms used for these licenses were *letters of marque* and *letters of reprisal*. The labels could seem interchangeable at the time and have remained so in popular memory, but, as we will shortly see, they did carry different meanings.

The appeal of this option during the medieval period and into the early modern period is not hard to understand. Kingdoms and realms simply did not have navies as we understand them now. Naval warfare is almost consistently the most capital-intensive form of war. Building vessels and recruiting crews for them was more expensive than forces on land. Venice would be the only medieval state that took steps to create an actual navy. The British naval historian N. A. M. Rodger has provided a portrait of the high costs of maritime warfare for England in the fourteenth century. The money Edward III spent on naval operations amounted to around 23 percent of all the king's war expenses, but, in turn, he mainly obtained merchant vessels and their crews. Obtaining professional crews and the warships they could bring was just too expensive. His adversaries, the French, had a national income perhaps three times that of England's, and they could afford such services only intermittently.[83] These were basically mercenary navies, not unlike their landed counterparts, and they no doubt presented the same challenges when relying on them.

If one could not, or did not want to, pay for this with taxes, the crown's own coffers, or the investment of the ship owners, one option was to cover much of the expense through reliance on prize money. As we have seen, Henry III had taken half of the money and left the rest to the licensed parties. Edward II, seventy years later, would allow it all to go to the licensed holders, but a pattern emerged where the monarch received a quarter of the prize, the ship owner a quarter, and the actual captor or prize holder the remaining half.[84] The lure of this magnitude of money, if successful, began to draw a sizable number of traditional as well as aspiring pirates as well as investors and ship owners. Whether the piracy was under the authority of the government or just regular piracy, which was illegal, did not seem to matter to many gentry, landowners, and merchants, who either willingly invested and sold supplies or turned their faces away while supporting illicit activity. Pirates might have their personal companies, as well.[85] A clear entrepreneurial spirit had entered into this practice, whether it was done with official blessing or just out of personal desire. It may not have matched the structure and process between principal and agent that was characteristic of the *condottieri*, but the level of sophistication was evolving along with need and circumstance.

The nature of maritime war and technology in the medieval period also encouraged piracy in legal and illegal forms. Maritime commercial traffic still hugged the coastline as much as possible due not only to navigation but safety. Trying to encounter commercial traffic by encounter on the open seas was a very uncertain endeavor, but striking their home ports was easy and worthwhile, even if the actual ships were not there, since such raids and attacks could destroy supplies and goods and other ships at the location. Raids from the sea were still a common feature of strategy and tactics, which continued a pattern that went all the way back to the ancient world or the later raids by the Vikings throughout Northern Europe.[86] The distinction between illegal and legal piracy (or privateering) was often hard to make in the Middle Ages. Again private actions could become easily confused with more public ones that signaled actual war. Edward I of England queried and criticized the Cinque Ports (a corporate association of ports in Kent) that had supported pirate attacks in 1293 on French vessels in the English Channel and on French ports. Officials from the Cinque Ports responded that they had done so because of French attacks. The inabilities of Edward and Philip IV of France to find a settlement ultimately lead to formal war a year later. The extent of piracy apparently worsened by the early fourteenth century, as one estimate claims around 7,000 pirates operated in the English Channel alone.[87]

While most European realms were not to the point where they wanted full-time navies, they still relied on various means to use private vessels. Even so, government offices were beginning to take shape to administer this better and to pay the accompanying costs. In England, clerks either in the exchequer or chancery handled the money. In the fourteenth century the position of "clerk of the king's ships" evolved to handle these matters. However, monarchs sometimes wanted to circumvent these officials and their procedures, and one option was to establish a fund within the royal household. The Wardrobe became a recurrent place for this money and authority to rest. The evolving capabilities of Parliament were beginning to peer into the monarch's business more, and this was a way of blocking that curiosity and preserving royal control.[88] Much of this was going to change within a hundred years, including the roles of those giving as well as receiving licenses, because of the impact of the voyages of exploration and the accompanying pursuit for empire that depended so greatly on maritime trade and commercial expansion. Piracy, letters of marque and reprisal, and privateering would undergo major changes in this new environment. The reasons for state selection and reliance on privately owned instruments and measures of force would become more sophisticated and supportive of a range of economic and political objectives. Having tried to explain the pertinent aspects of piracy, it is now time to turn specifically to those options that worked with the blessing of official or state authority.

LETTERS OF MARQUE AND REPRISAL AND PRIVATEERING

The previous chapter examined the right of private parties to take action for losses suffered at the hands of others—particularly when government authorities in the perpetrator's home failed to act to compensate the losses of the aggrieved. Just when and where this first occurred is unknown. French practice refers to letters of marque that were apparently derived from laws devised by guilds to enable merchants to seize goods when the other party had failed to pay for an earlier purchase. Ruling authorities used this practice as a form of precedent to permit aggrieved parties to take similar action on the high seas. The term *marque* does not have a clear origin. One scholar claims it came from the Latin *marcare*, which meant to seize goods as a pledge.[89] The more prevalent explanation traces the term to *letter de mark*, a reference to "marcher law," or what was also called the "law of the marches." These were lawless frontier areas that stood beyond the king's rule. The sea, of course, could be a prominent example of such a lawless zone, although medieval Europe presented examples of rulers who thought otherwise—Venice and the Adriatic and Denmark and the Baltic being two examples of regional seas dominated by self-proclaimed rule.[90]

N. A. M. Rodger stresses a couple of critical distinctions for letters of marque. First, military naval warfare was separate from commercial naval warfare in the Middle Ages. The former was an intermittent affair between princes and rulers; the latter was an almost permanent condition. While commercial sea traffic was a business matter, its practitioners had to be ready to fight competitors sometimes; thus, merchant vessels were often armed. They sometimes attacked one another in times of "profound peace" between rulers. If one wanted to obtain compensation for losses resulting from this action or capture by obtaining a letter of marque, he could only obtain it in a period of peace. Letters of marque existed to deal with private claims; they were not a tool to resolve differences between rules and governments. Of course, as one should wisely suspect, realities were not sometimes as clear as the guidelines that existed for their use. Private acts could naturally be a means of trying to conceal a prince's or state's interest and objectives.[91]

The lexicon for these types of measures became more complicated in the thirteenth century and after by introduction of the word *reprisal*. In reality the meaning of the words *marque* and *reprisal* became interchangeable for a few centuries, until at least the seventeenth and eighteenth centuries in English usage, when some distinction began to appear. *Marque* would become a term associated more with letters or a license to inflict actual injury on another party. It was a commission to a private man-of-war; in short, a privateer who would be active during periods of war. *Reprisal* remained to be a term that permitted use of force to "secure compensation for a loss by the taking of property." It is important to understand it was not *retaliation*, which is the intentional inflicting of injury for an injury done by the other party. Authorization by a ruler or the state was critical for the status of reprisal; to act without it was to commit piracy. Unlike the later understanding of marque, reprisals did not have to have a direct tie with war.[92]

Princes and kings nevertheless understood that the character of commercial warfare and the use of reprisals could create the danger of a free-for-all that could cause worse, undesired consequences. The role of official authority was critical, and so too was a clear understanding of what was expected for a satisfactory and acceptable exercise of the right of reprisal. King Edward I of England presented all of this in detail in a letter authorizing Bernard Dongresilli, a merchant in Bayone (part of English-occupied France) to take goods from the king of Portugal or his subjects until he had enough to equal his losses. The instructions were specific and delineated definite limitations on Dongresilli. To be legal, he had to have a precise claim and proof of what had happened, proof that the loss had occurred because of unlawful actions by the other parties, and evidence that reprisals were taken only after failure of legal and diplomatic means. Reprisals were measures of last resort and not alternatives for other choices. King Edward proceeded with more specifications: Dongresilli could act only with official authorization; he had to limit seizures to the parties or people identified in the letter or license; he could seize an amount "sufficient to satisfy the claim, plus reasonable costs; and he had to stop as soon as he had complete compensation.[93]

Scholars have found repeated examples of how rulers and kings relied on developing concepts of their powers and sovereignty to place bounds on the practice of reprisal while still permitting and maybe using it for their ends. After consideration of French, English, Venetian, and Genoese practices, Fredric Cheyette concludes that by the end of the thirteenth century scholars, lawyers, and rulers had made it clear "that it is not the act that renders itself legitimate, nor the actor, but the authorization. Rightful violence belongs only to him who has no superior and to those he appoints. Only Emperors and kings, and the admirals, judges, and assorted officials bearing their commissions, have the right to victimize their fellow men."[94] Reviewing a very different type of authority, the town council of the port of Marseilles, Christopher Beck found that the council suspended all issuance of letters of marque because it wanted a better understanding of the impact of this policy and practice on the overall public good of the city. Beck believes the suspension was done "as a means to create more favorable conditions and to strengthen the council's reputation of just and wise leadership of its citizens," and he attributes this path to the influence of the writings of Augustine and Aristotle, who stressed the importance of a broader good over individual liberty and gain.[95] Of course, such changes may also have resulted from the social and economic changes occurring in the Mediterranean world in the fourteenth century. Whatever the reason, the practice of letters of marque and reprisal had been separated in both convenient and functional terms from the world of piracy. Legal authority was instrumental in its existence and performance, even if those at the receiving end of the reprisals might have had good reason to ask whether they were enduring a form of sanctioned piracy rather than an exercise of a form of maritime law.

Yet, if one holds to a strict legal view of reprisal it was not like the action of a mercenary, pirate, and privateer. Reprisals were not measures to make a profit but a way to compensate for an earlier wrong and loss. Nor were practitioners of reprisal bringing, especially in the Middle Ages, special skills or weapons that complemented or supplemented those held by a prince or king. Ostensibly, they were seeking settlement of a private claim, not acting on behalf of someone else. They might use a different vessel, but many used the same merchant vessel they had earlier, since, as noted earlier, the vessels were usually armed merchant ships. Pirates and privateers could and often did take steps to build or find a vessel with the features necessary for raiding on the high seas. Privateering was to occur under the auspices of war; sailing with a letter of reprisal was a permissible act during a time of peace between rulers, governments, or states.

The outward expansion of European power and the assertion of authority or sovereignty that often went with it were going to have major consequences for the world's seas in which letters of marque and reprisal, piracy, and privateering were in play. Lauren Benton has described the actions taken by growing European empires as a "rationalization of space." With notions of territory, boundaries, and defended borders more fixed in official minds, the effort to try to do the same for the ocean logically followed—helped in part by the later development of measurements of latitude and longitude and the skills of mapping.[96] In an environment of strengthening rulers and growing states, the papacy saw as among its duties a need to try to prevent unnecessary friction and division in the Christian world. Thus, in the final

decades of relative harmony in Christendom, Pope Alexander VI through a
papal bull, *Inter Caetera*, in 1493 and several more bulls and statements created what history calls the Treaty of Tordesillas in 1494.[97]

The treaty's name commemorates the name of the Spanish town where
representatives of the monarchs and Spain met in June 1494 to sign a treaty
based on these papal directions. The circumstance that prompted these
series of events rested ultimately with the first voyage of Christopher Co-
lumbus, who had returned to Europe in 1493. Talk of claims made in Spain's
name and prospects of commerce raised strong concerns in neighboring
Portugal, whose ruler believed earlier papal declarations had given that
country control over any future trade that might develop with new lands.
The papal solution was to draw a line down the middle of the Atlantic that
designated the area east of the line to be Portuguese and that west of it to be
Spanish. Parties who violated or did not respect this division were threatened with excommunication from the Church. This seemed simple enough,
particularly when one did not fully appreciate the size of the globe or know
much about the location and character of some territories and oceans on it.
However, what Portugal did know was that the proposed line could affect
its trade routes around Africa due to the continent's westward push into the
Atlantic. Thus, Portugal agreed to move the line several hundred miles to
the west and unknowingly won itself the basis to claim Brazil.[98] The treaty
was not as ironclad as some Spanish and Portuguese would later argue.
Spanish and Portuguese claims were only for territories they already had
found or their appointed agents would discover in the future. The treaty did
not rule out or forbid voyages by other European realms. Furthermore, one
had to show proof of the claims and of measures to develop and sustain
one's presence there.[99]

This attempt to rationalize order in Christendom and to organize the
space beyond it was about to collide with major changes within Europe itself.
The papacy's own authority and position in Europe was under strong scrutiny
and criticism by rulers who still regarded themselves as faithful adherents
to the Church but who had more defined interests of state to advance and
better institutions through which to do so. France was an ascendant power
in Europe, and within a few decades of the signature of the treaty it had
begun to question its terms. As King Francis I allegedly remarked, "The
sun shines on me just the same as on the other; and I should like to see the
clause in Adam's will that cuts me out of my share in the New World."[100]

Acting under the license of the French government, French privateers were already attacking ships in the Spanish treasure fleets in the eastern part of the Atlantic. A closer look at the political economic conditions of the Atlantic world comes in the next chapter, but the French monarch quickly understood how important Spain's imported wealth was becoming for its treasury and its power.[101] Of course, after 1517, thanks to Martin Luther, there were even more heretics in Europe who challenged both the spiritual authority of the pope and the foundation of any division he made of the Atlantic world. The rising powers of England (later Great Britain) and the Dutch Republic would see no reason to respect the demarcation made in the Treaty of Tordesillas.

By the sixteenth century parts of the Atlantic world were becoming those ill-defined zones where assertions of sovereignty and control were incomplete and very difficult to establish and enforce. The expansion of European empires into the New World as well as into India and the Indian Ocean and the land and seas of southeastern Asia created areas of contested claim and control. Here were settings that were optimal for the practice of piracy. Given the growing competition in maritime commerce, increased capture of vessels and seizure of goods and crew created more grounds for desired reprisal against the violators. Those governments that were interested in challenging the Treaty of Tordesillas proved especially willing to provide the necessary authority. If actual conflict broke out, which it recurrently did, privateering became an option as well.

Privateering, in contrast to mere reprisal, was becoming more common by this time. The word began to appear by the 1660s, just shortly after England had seized the Caribbean island of Jamaica from the Spanish. English captains and seamen continued to attack Spanish ships in the Caribbean, and the English governor of the island declared these were legal acts and provided commissions to the vessels and crews committing them. What had once been piracy was now something else. Those with commissions were called privateers repeatedly by English authorities in Jamaica. Of course, being a pirate one day and a privateer the next could be a life-saving development that set out a safer path for captain and crew alike, which was the fate of one Henry Morgan, accused of being a pirate in 1661, and who may have been the same Morgan who became one of the most famous privateers (a pirate in the eyes of Spain).[102]

We already know from earlier discussion that the practices associated with privateering had been in place long before, certainly in the thirteenth century. The French created prize courts to deal with the settlement of captured vessels and property as early as 1373.[103] The English were not far behind. By this time kings were appointing an admiral of England, and this officer, among other things, was supposed to deal with the settlement of prizes. Kings repeatedly offered commissions for men "to sail and pass to the seas with as many ships, barges, and balingers of war, men-at-arms and bowmen properly equipped, as he may be able to provide himself with, to do all the hurt he can to our open enemies," as Henry IV extended to one Henry Paye in 1404.[104] It had been customary to allow common law to deal with prizes, but this proved inadequate, and the Admiralty Court (literally the admiral of England's court or courts) began in the early fifteenth century to make decisions based on civil and Roman law. The fact that the court as well as the monarch received a share of the value of the prize made this a lucrative practice both for the realm and the officials involved in it.[105]

The attempted expansion of sovereignty and control over both sea and territory made this whole situation more complex. If anyone crossed westward over the line of demarcation of the Treaty of Tordesillas, he was in effect a pirate, unless he was Spanish. As Michael Kempe has observed on this particular situation, "being a pirate was mainly a question of international politics, not of international law." After issuing a letter of marque in 1529 to a merchant from Dieppe whose ship had been seized by the Portuguese, Francis I began to issue routine letters of marque to French sea captains to go after Portuguese and Spanish vessels in the Atlantic. This authority notably included the western Atlantic and Caribbean.[106]

Here, of course, was a very problematic twist, as one can see an intentional blurring of traditional letters of marque or reprisal by support for privateering. The French and their heretic Protestant competitors, the English and Dutch, were insistent on their right to sail the oceans and conduct trade without intrusion from the papacy or any claim made by Spain or Portugal. The letters of marque that some of these vessels carried were not in the hands of captains or owners who had suffered prior damages. This was the use of violence to commit injury for political ends and not private ones. Students of the early modern period have commented extensively on this use and misuse of letters of marque and reprisal. It was a calculated, intentional mixing of public and private concepts of war. Rulers might also use validly licensed privateers in times of war to conduct private reprisals for damages. The injured party in turn could conceivably seek reprisal against the ruler or state who had committed these damages under the umbrella of public war. Thus, the domains of public and private war became intermingled and difficult to distinguish.[107] As one moved into the seventeenth century this coexistence of piracy, privateering, and of letters of marque and reprisal became more common. The historian Mark Hanna has written that "if we define a pirate as a sea marauder who disavowed any association with a particular state, then there were few pirates in the seventeenth century. They almost always held some form of paperwork from a state." Admittedly this was still at a time when it was difficult to define a state exactly. Questions about the extent and source of authority of the state still existed, and additional questions followed in regard to the place and authority of representatives of colonial governments under that state, such as the status of the governor of Jamaica mentioned above.[108]

The option of using privateers for political and state purposes, as well as the expansion of providing letters of marque and reprisal to them, opened avenues for rulers and states that wanted to use maritime capabilities and commerce as instruments of power and war. The Spanish and Portuguese, for example, were the major maritime powers of the sixteenth century. At a time when naval fleets were still a developing institution, it would be inaccurate to expect fleet actions like those of the seventeenth and later centuries. Nonetheless, the French, English, and Dutch, while weaker, still wanted to challenge Spanish and Portuguese dominance and commerce on the seas. They pursued an early form of what the French came to call *guerre de course*; the British equivalent was commerce warfare or commerce-raiding. This particular approach and means of war served the strategies of states that were either weak or unable to afford the costs of building and supporting a sizable navy or of stronger land powers that, because of proximity to the sea, also needed to possess some form of naval capabilities. This form of war has been a classic form of asymmetrical response by the weak against the strong that one can find to the present day, motivating some of today's pirates, whether on sea or in the realm of cyber.[109]

Commerce-raiding or *guerre de course* concentrates on attacking the commercial traffic and shipping of the enemy while clearly avoiding major warships. A clear advantage was the option of outsourcing the mission to private actors—in short, privateers—who would provide and outfit their own vessels, sail under the authority of letters of marque, and provide prizes that could help state revenue for support of this particular strategy as well as for larger national needs. The underlying objective was to make the costs of lost ships, cargoes, and possibly crews so high that the greater power would begin to succumb to pressure and begin to offer terms for an acceptable settlement. This set of measures arguably played a role in imperial German strategy in World War I to use U-boats against the British, French, and, later, the United States.[110] Its application receives closer examination in the following chapters. Before doing so, though, a helpful foundation for understanding the role of privateering in the early application of *guerre de course* emerges if one looks at the actions of England, and briefly France, in the sixteenth century.

The English case is obviously the better known and more deeply studied, but the French record deserves treatment here and later as well because it represents a different approach. The English record illustrates "how private means of violence were put at the disposal of the state" while the French "highlights how state means were put to use in aid of private operators."[111] In plainer terms one could argue that for France, particularly in this earlier period, its navy essentially was privateers and merchant vessels. It purposely tried to avoid the construction of a navy because of concern about cost. The English also did not have much of a navy at their disposal at this time, but London would begin to consolidate its naval policies earlier and take the measures to develop a navy. Privateering would perhaps evolve from being a major source for naval capability to being a supplement used for a combination of economic and political purposes.

In a world that was aggressively expanding its presence beyond its traditional confinement, but doing so without the existence of state-funded navies to keep sea lanes open and secure, a voyage contained elements of adventure and financial risk. A new voyage was also a new venture that required its own investors. As the capital market dominated the development of these voyages, it also significantly affected any measures to provide force to protect ships on the seas. Large profits could benefit future exercise of both dimensions—the commercial and the military.[112] It was a world where piracy and privateering could easily coexist.

England in the early sixteenth century was a relatively weak power. In the early years of his reign, Henry VIII aspired to make England a continental power, but that was not to be. Difficulty in accomplishing that goal through politics or battle, the realm's geographical position, and advice given to him compelled Henry to develop capabilities on the sea. Their purpose would be primarily defensive, a course Henry may or may not have taken after consideration of the success of the Scots with such measures.[113] The Scots resorted to privateers not to obtain dominance at sea but to destroy enemy vessels and inflict enough damage to get the latter to stop the conflict. They knew they lacked the resources and could not match the size of naval forces at the beckon of states like Portugal or Sweden, but they recognized that inflicting a lot of damage on the other's merchant vessels could compel peace and expand commercial opportunity. It was a strategy of the weaker against the stronger.[114] Scotland's senior admiral had two different private options. If it was more pure defense, the Scots licensed armed vessels to serve as "waughters," which were escorts or vessels on watch. For more aggressive measures to attack enemy shipping, privateers, who provided and equipped their own ship, were the path taken. They did this at their own expense. Evidence shows that there were numerous investors and seamen willing to take that risk for the sake of potential gain, as the admiral received only 10 percent of the prize.[115]

Henry VIII had his own problems with the Scots, but his primary nemesis was France. In 1542 England found itself at war with France. Two years later Henry released a proclamation that authorized unlimited warfare by private parties on the high seas. These privateering endeavors received financial support from many prominent figures at court as well as the king himself. The authorization also permitted attacks on neutral shipping, which at this particular time included, significantly, the merchant traffic between Spain and its colonies in the Spanish Lowlands. The war and the privateering that went with it, whether against the enemy or neutral parties, did England little good. When a treaty ended the conflict in 1550, Henry had little to show for his policies.[116]

This strategy of the weak and reliance on the defense of the sea continued under Henry's final successor, Queen Elizabeth I. By the time of Elizabeth's ascent to the throne (1558), Protestantism was a major driver in Europe's political landscape. As Europe's leading Protestant monarch, Elizabeth believed she had to support its cause, especially in light of the determination of most Catholic monarchs to end her rule. She thus intervened in the civil war in France by supporting the Huguenots, which became the reason for her first major use of letters of reprisal as a political instrument rather than a means to collect compensation by private merchants. When the queen announced in 1563 a proclamation allowing for general privateering, she was taking a step that might ultimately promote England's presence in other parts of the world but also cost it potential friends and invite eventual retaliation in the form of the Spanish Armada in 1588.[117]

While Elizabeth's policy provided future stories for novelists and aficionados of naval warfare, it created significant problems in the command and conduct of naval operations. England's government relied on unpaid gentry and nobility, and it was some of these same individuals who chose to invest in the privateering measures Elizabeth encouraged. Elizabeth did not want to antagonize them, and she depended as well on the support of the merchants in London. Whether these people were conducting their operations in the illegal realm of piracy or the ostensibly legal zone of privateering, they were elusive to monitor or prosecute. The notoriety of people like Sir Walter Raleigh and Sir Edward Horsey, the captain of the Isle of Wight who allowed the island to become a no-questions-asked locale for behavior of all types, created opportunities and problems for the English. Privatizing military operations offered definite problems. Commanders had sizable discretion as to what they could do, and such freedom created what one historian, using more modern lexicon, describes as a "confused and weakened . . . command structure."[118] Again, interesting distinctions existed in some of these operations that are largely lost today. Those actions done in the queen's name and under her orders were essentially "partnership operations," but others were conducted simply through the license from the queen. The contemporary term for these seamen was "voluntaries," which resembled the much more traditional world of the privateer.[119] The former may have resembled the command relationship often found with mercenaries, but the latter had an open-endedness and lack of control between principal and agent that could be very problematic.

Elizabeth wanted to fight wars on the cheap. She did not want to impose additional taxes, and she hoped the revenue from privateering would be a substitute in the national treasury. She privatized the navy more extensively than her father had and even provided vessels to privateers. The construction of ships went to private builders without any type of process that we would recognize as bidding; she outsourced the provisioning of vessels as well. This was not done out of any philosophical conviction about the virtues of privatization but from what David Loades has described as "the queen's increasingly neurotic unwillingness to spend money."[120] Such measures might raise questions about the balance between private gain and public good that

Elizabeth's policies created. Yet, if the queen created some disorganization in her command and invited political tension and even war from countries whose merchant ships had been attacked, she also helped establish and operate a system that enabled England to fight above its apparent measurements of power. In the final two decades of her reign, Loades writes, privateers may have "supplied about 50 per cent of the war effort... making it possible for a country with a totally inadequate financial infrastructure to sustain one of the longest wars in its history, and to confront a power [Spain] whose resources were in every way superior."[121] Elizabeth's policies pose an interesting question, even in the present time with very different conditions, as to whether there are circumstances where privatization may serve the needs of a weak state that does not have command of extensive monetary resources.

Privateers operating under Elizabeth's license were active in European waters, even though Elizabeth's own admiral and his vessels patrolled closer to home while privateers went further abroad in the Atlantic, the Caribbean, and beyond. Their attacks on Spanish shipping, reinforced by the desire to challenge the Treaty of Tordesillas, brought Spain and England into a condition of undeclared war waged by private interests. One of the investors in some of these voyages was Elizabeth herself. The English challenged the Spanish in a number of maritime and commercial activities, including the slave trade, which provided an incident that would fuel conflict in the Atlantic and Caribbean. Elizabeth and others had invested in the voyages of John Hawkins, who was breaking the Spanish monopoly over the slave trade in the New World colonies. Sailing in 1568 in the somewhat ironically named, in light of its cargo, *Jesus of Lubeck*, Hawkins had to take his leaky ship into the Spanish port of San Juan de Ulua, an island near modern-day Veracruz, Mexico. The Spanish viceroy was alarmed and unhappy with the presence of the *Jesus of Lubeck* and other vessels accompanying Hawkins, and he ordered an attack on them. Hawkins escaped in another vessel, as did his cousin Francis Drake. Hawkins and Drake would return to England angry and anxious for reprisal.[122]

Hawkins submitted a tally of losses to the Board of Admiralty as a foundation for his claim to seek reprisal. The amount, which would easily surpass $10 million in modern currency, was probably exaggerated. Also, one historian has noted that 76 percent of the amount claimed dealt with losses directly tied to the slave trade, including the cost of seven tons of manacles. The board refused to issue a letter of reprisal to Hawkins, perhaps out of misgivings about the amount he claimed as well as caution about not allowing him to take actions that could pull England into actual war, a situation Elizabeth and her court did not want due to an ongoing uprising by two Catholic dukes, a strengthening of Spain's position opposite the Dutch, and tensions with France over England's support of the Huguenots.[123] However, Elizabeth was willing to allow private actors to act against Spanish shipping, whether in the area of the English Channel or the North Sea. These latter were not so much English captains and crews as they were Dutch—sea captains and crew who had received letters of marque from William of Orange. When they approached the regent of the king of Spain, she, Margaret of Parma, dismissed them as "beggars," thus giving them part of the name history knows them as, the Dutch Sea Beggars. Raiding Spanish shipping and Catholic institutions, they could not find ports in the Spanish Netherlands to accept their prizes. Elizabeth temporarily allowed them to use English ports, so their voyages against the Spanish became a form of unofficial defense against the Spanish.[124]

As relations with Spain and other Catholic realms deteriorated, Elizabeth was in a position where she wanted to preserve peace on paper but use force to strike at Spanish commerce in particular and challenge Spain's claims in the western Atlantic and Caribbean. Her excommunication by Pope Pius V in February 1570, which he apparently did without consulting with his primary enforcer, Philip II of Spain, was enough to persuade many in her realm that the Catholic realms of Europe, and especially Spain, were at war with her.[125] Investors and sea captains like Francis Drake clearly saw these developments as proof of Spain's intentions and war against the English monarchy. Thus, the next several years were going to see a set of actions taken by English ships that obfuscated piracy and privateering. The English saw their acts as more of the latter; the Spanish definitely treated them as the former.

From the perspective of the English monarch and her government, dependence on private actors posed clear advantages. As we already know, if an actual letter of reprisal (later marque and reprisal) was issued, this was not an act of war. It provided official authority to redress private wrongs. If the merchant or captain holding the license overstepped its terms, the licensing authorities could, if they chose, deny responsibility or protection for the perpetrator. This scenario alone had its ambiguities. Others that became very common contained even greater problems. The English could, and did, issue letters of reprisal on very vague, even false claims, which enabled more unlimited actions against the Spanish or others. Obviously, such documents could be shown when convenient to try to justify a capture or seizure. Some did not even bother with getting a license from the admiralty but simply a note from the lord admiral himself. More difficult were those circumstances where the merchant or captain was acting as a pirate, but perhaps doing so in ways that reflected unofficial endorsement and support for his actions. Elizabeth's England practiced all of these, and so did others as well—both ruling governments like France and Spain and representatives of rebellions such as the Huguenots and the Dutch. Here in Peter Earle's words was "a cheap means of waging war by proxy, a process which enabled the Crown to deny responsibility for the uncontrollable activities of those who happened to be English subjects." If a privateer overstepping his license or a pirate operating with the quiet support, maybe even financial backing, of the queen was caught, London could essentially disown them and claim they were responsible for their own actions. Here, too, was a form of plausible deniability that would make practitioners from the twentieth and early twenty-first centuries envious of the skill in which this was done and comfortable in the knowledge that there is such long-standing precedent for it.[126]

A short review of the actions of only Francis Drake between 1570 and 1588, the year of the Spanish Armada, provides a good understanding of how this worked. After Elizabeth's excommunication, Drake headed to the Caribbean, where in three months he raided ports where precious metals and gemstones were gathered to be shipped to Spain and attacked vessels as well. He returned with booty and treasure that may have been worth over $23 million in modern currency. This had been Drake's own war, so to speak, although the absence of arrest or punishment suggests it was very well-received entrepreneurship.[127] Drake followed up with another Caribbean raid in 1572–1574. For a while Drake's energies were directed to assist the advancement of English interest in Ireland and to keep him from worsening relations with Spain at a time when Elizabeth's court was more anxious about avoiding war. However, in 1577 English interest in establishing a presence in the Pacific created an inviting climate for Drake. Drake himself invested in this voyage of circumnavigation, as did some of Elizabeth's close advisers: the Earl of Essex, the Earl of Leicester, Sir Francis Walsingham, and Lord Admiral Lincoln, among others. The voyage, of course, intended to establish English presence in an ocean that had first been explored by Ferdinand Magellan. In the Pacific Drake's vessels seized Spanish vessels along the western coast of South America as prizes and looted their contents. He returned to England in 1580 not even certain if Elizabeth was still queen or whether England was in a state of war or peace. The value of his treasure and prizes amounted to slightly over $50 million in present currency.[128]

Drake's final great adventure in this time frame occurred in 1585, and this time it was in reaction to steps taken by the Spanish that May when they seized several English vessels in ports. One of them, the *Primrose*, escaped and reported these actions on arrival in England. The lord admiral reviewed the claims for redress and recommended they be issued, which the queen signed on July 1. This time the English were operating under letters of reprisal, although, still, this was not an actual act of war. In fact, Elizabeth worried about her ability to wage offensive war, given the small resources she had and competing expenses, such as the Irish campaigns. The path to be taken was *guerre de course* and privateering by depending on "voluntary forces" to strike at Spain's commerce and at the same time pay their way through the value of their prizes. While Elizabeth did have a navy, she was still highly dependent on private actors to supplement her naval capabilities. In 1585, as the prominent British historian of privateering, Kenneth Andrews, has observed, privateering provided Elizabeth with a variety of helpful covers. It did give official sanction to the merchants and sea captains involved; it was also a more limited type of warfare, which, if properly exercised, created less risk of alienating neutral powers; and it offered those same neutrals paths for recourse if such acts did occur. Finally, because it was private shipping it did not require taking money out of the exchequer.[129] Furthermore, customs duties had to be paid on prize goods, and the lord admiral received 10 percent of the value of the prizes to cover his costs. That said, Elizabeth still invested her own money in two vessels in the flotilla that Drake established through the creation of a joint stock company. Drake sailed again into the Caribbean, where he occupied and sacked Santo Domingo and also attacked the port of Cartagena before later appearing along the Florida coast and attacking St. Augustine. Because of disease and dissent among the crews this voyage was not as successful as Drake's earlier ones. Ultimately the value of prizes and booty proved less than the capital investment before the voyage.

War with Spain did follow, however, thanks in part to another papal bull in 1585 to provide Spain with money to bring the "heretical state" under Elizabeth to its end.[130] It lasted through the defeat of the Spanish Armada until Elizabeth's death in 1603 and the treaty of peace signed by James I after he became king. Although the treaty did not end the practice of piracy, it did temporarily suspend to some degree the English reliance on privateering as a form of private war that could serve state ends. It would return in the new century, which would witness both vigorous use of it and more extensive measures to place it under effective state control. The English experience of the sixteenth century had nonetheless established a noteworthy precedent for private war and a set of arguments that made it appealing, which revolved around costs, limited impact on neutral states, and a course for plausible denial if governments and their leaders found it necessary or attractive. The experience of the English would not be forgotten in London or beyond.

Yet, one should not conclude the English were the only practitioners of privateering in the early modern period prior to 1600. References already exist to Scotland's practice of it, as well as actions by the Huguenots, the Dutch rebels against Spain, and the French themselves. A related form of state-supported privacy also existed in the Barbary states along the northern African coast, where pirates, often known as corsairs, with the support of their rulers took hostages from foreign vessels and held them for ransom— a form of piracy that reappeared in the early twenty-first century with the support of various nonstate groups, particularly in the Indian Ocean off of the coast of Somalia. French privateering is particularly worth noting in the context of this time because it was occurring alongside that of the Scots and English, among others. France's Catholic status did not prevent it from sending privateers into Spanish-claimed waters; in fact, Drake's first voyage in 1570 followed in the path of French privateers. The French, too, had created their own legal mechanisms, prize courts, and so on, as noted earlier in this chapter. The French approach to privateering was going to play a prominent role in the Atlantic world of the seventeenth century and after, much more than it had until then.

3 PRIVATE AND PUBLIC WAR IN THE ATLANTIC WORLD AND BEYOND

The desire of King James I to restrict the role of privateering and piracy in wars, such as the recent one between England and Spain, did not even survive a decade. There was no way the king could have envisioned what followed in the new century, when piracy and privateering entered what some (obviously its practitioners and generations of entertained readers) regarded as a virtual golden age. The seventeenth century witnessed major change in the concepts and frameworks that shaped the use of violence on land and sea as well as the institutions that governed it. In land war the major powers moved toward full-time armies. Mercenaries were still present as supplements to armies, but they were less common as the key components of land power by century's end. On the high seas, professional navies became ascendant as powers to varying degrees moved away from dependence on private armed vessels. What had been the responsibility of many private vessels and crews, such as the capture of pirates or the provision of security and escort, was replaced by the practices of naval patrols and convoy escort. Arguably, though these practices were most unique to the Atlantic world, they spread beyond as the rising powers of England, France, and the Dutch Republic (or the Netherlands) would rely on new forms of private activity—chartered trading companies—to assert and expand their interests. This eventful century and the one that followed presented an aggressive expansion of state power and control over the use of force alongside a willingness to have private actors assume responsibility for force in circumstances where the probability of direct state-on-state conflict was low.

The boundaries between the state and the private sector were undergoing continuous change in the seventeenth century. The Elizabethan system had been "noted for its ability to incorporate private ambition into the service of the state," and, while particulars might be modified, the overall content of that observation was not going to change.[1] While privateering did not always add greatly to the royal treasury and the offices of those administering it, it sometimes did, and when news of such gains traveled others took advantage of the potential to provide services as outfitters, shipbuilders, and related tasks. In his study of the emergence of British power, John Brewer notes that until the middle of the seventeenth century most European powers had depended on entrepreneurs to create and raise much of their military power. As other European powers moved to establish government offices and lines of revenue to support and manage war, London lagged behind until the final decades of the century.[2] The provision of charters for trading companies, such as the East India Company, Hudson Bay, and others, also attested to different boundaries between the public and private worlds. Until the end of the seventeenth century, the monarch controlled much of the chartering in person. It was as much a personal decision, perhaps more so, than it was that of the state. However, this changed after 1720, when in the wake of the South Sea Bubble, Parliament asserted control of the charters subsequently given with royal approval.[3]

What was emerging in Great Britain (James I preferred this name, but its use is more accurate only after 1701) and in different forms in Europe was the fiscal-military state with "high taxes, a growing and well-organized civil administration, a standing army and the determination to act as a major European power." By the end of the seventeenth century more than 75 percent of British public expenditures funded the waging of war. The purpose of the government apparatus behind this, which far surpassed the size of the rest of the government, was to bolster military power. As Brewer observes, the "chief task" of this structure "was not to serve the welfare of the nation."[4] England was the beneficiary of several factors that enabled it to expand and to pursue a course to empire—"favorable natural endowments," "a form of early industrialization," an active "community of merchants," and "the construction of responsive financial institutions."[5]

The English path to increased capability and power throughout the seventeenth century was hardly unique, as a study of measures in Sweden, Russia, and France (among others) shows. However, for study of the roles of private force and war, France's course is particularly important. The French monarchy and its ministers had to contend with opposition from the nobility, religious dissent and conflict, peasant revolts, and the ambition of rival states, among other things, to accomplish the centralization of authority that became another model to emulate. Significant portions of this enhanced power relied on intentional expenditure on weaponry for the army and navy as well as the construction of bastions throughout France itself. An expansion of the number and power of provincial *intendants* to collect taxes and to maintain order also helped. In fact, these officials sometimes relied on the army to help enforce payment of taxes.[6] By the time Louis XIV took power in 1661 much of this apparatus and the accompanying procedures were in place. France appeared well ahead of Britain in its construction of the edifices of power. However, its assertive, state-directed forms of capability building were not as strong as they seemed, for France was not as effective in building the fiscal dimensions that could sustain power. The establishment of the Bank of England in 1694 to provide credit in times of war did not have an equivalent in France. Concessions and compromises had to be made. France was a land power, and its strategic mindset carried that proclivity. The maintenance of a full-time standing navy proved costly and arguably unnecessary in the eyes of some. Thus, in 1694 the French purposely decided to resort to private investors and privateering to serve much of their military needs on the high seas.[7] It was a choice that would indeed destroy or damage much foreign commerce but not provide France with the strategic equality or supremacy it hoped to establish.

The driver behind the resurgence of privateering and piracy that James I had not foreseen in 1603 was the growing pressure for empire that figured in the seventeenth century and afterward. As Robert Ritchie has written, "piracy and privateering accompanied the rise of the European empires. Both activities thrived with state sponsorship as the competition for trade and empire caused a scramble for the spoils of the emerging world economy."[8] These agents of state power entered into uncertain zones of control and into arenas where international law was still developing, whether in the Atlantic or other oceans. In their wake both states and private actors would try to set up processes and structures to handle what they now claimed.[9] The theory and assumptions underlying this approach to empire would be instrumental in the use of privateering or other means of private force to expand and sustain state power.

The word *mercantilism* would have drawn puzzled looks if one had mentioned it in the seventeenth century. Its usage comes from Adam Smith's critique in *The Wealth of Nations* of the political economic theory that shaped so much state and strategic thinking well into the last half of the eighteenth century. Amsterdam, London, and Paris were the three cities where the political side of mercantilism's execution primarily resided, but its effect and legacies would be felt worldwide, as its very assumptions and premises compelled powers to raise their focus far beyond their geographical horizons. Mercantilism appears to have originated in part from questions that both intrigued and troubled the English monarch and others in the home islands in the 1620s. Given the understanding of the material foundations of wealth and power at the time, it seemed Spain should still remain powerful, even in the wake of the Armada's defeat and the later peace in 1603. Yet, Spain's decline was becoming evident. At the same time, the Dutch, who were still not completely free of Spanish control—that came in 1648—were now a major maritime power with trading companies that asserted themselves in both hemispheres. How could a country "not fully so big as two of our best Shires" accomplish this, wondered Sir Thomas Mun, a merchant who wrote *England's Treasury by Foreign Trade* in the 1620s and 1630s, a book some regarded as a core argument for mercantilism when it appeared in print in 1664.[10]

In the early seventeenth century the Dutch were clearly the dominant actor in world trade. They overshadowed Portugal and Spain. Their economic system surpassed their Italian or south German predecessors in the sixteenth century. Thanks to the concentration of their agricultural laborers in activities with high value added, they were able to have more of their workforce involved in manufacturing, whether in textiles or shipbuilding. Many of their vessels offered large cargo space and fast speed with lower labor costs, which undercut a fair amount of their competition. Their navy was good and provided convoy escort for shipping. Not surprisingly, such conditions attracted merchants and customers from other European countries to Dutch shipping. The Dutch also realized the potential of penetrating the spice markets in South and East Asian waters. In 1602 the major federal decision-making body, the States General, chartered the Dutch East India Company (the Vereenigde Oost-Indische Compagnie—often identified as the VOC), which received a twenty-year monopoly from west of the Straits of Magellan to east of the Cape of Good Hope. In short, the company claimed special privilege from the Pacific through the Indian Ocean.[11] This was an advantageous position for the Dutch to hold, which their British counterparts and neighbors regarded with envy and suspicion.

The ongoing growth of English and later British interests depended on the maritime tradition. The word *empire* itself began to appear in publications more in the last half of the seventeenth century. Its definition was subject to debate, but many applied it especially in maritime terms with an emphasis and pride not only in naval prowess but commercial gain and expansion. Drawing perhaps from the Elizabethan outlook that treated maritime conflict as a self-paying endeavor, thanks in part to the role of private actors, wars on the highs seas were viewed more positively than those on land. The latter were often endeavors that benefited the monarchy more, whereas the former offered wider gain and benefit. Armies, history proved, could be the tools of despots; navies rarely were. Territorial empire was a dangerous path to pursue, as the record of the Roman Empire seemed to prove. By the eighteenth century, writes the historian P. J. Marshall, the British vision of empire "did not necessarily mean rule over territory, but could also signify power or dominant interests outside Britain." Instead of a single empire, the British understanding of the word also implied a series of empires through the world in different locations and sectors, be it the East Indies, Africa, fisheries, plantations, or elsewhere.[12]

Resources and goods were the foundations of this view of empire and national strength. This was not a novel view of the basis of power, as the discussion in the previous chapter of the Spanish quest for gold and silver in the New World and the attraction of their bullion fleets to pirates and privateers proved. Mercantilism, through its practice in various forms by the Spanish, Portuguese, Dutch, British, and French, among others, extended commercial activity to various items: spices, tea, silk, and so on. The underlying assumption was that these existed in finite amounts. Thus, practitioners of mercantilism engaged in a "zero-sum game" struggle for wealth. Colonies or areas of dominance were "suppliers of raw materials and markets for manufacturers of the 'mother country' alone, with foreign interlopers to be excluded by force if necessary."[13] Mercantilism largely rejected the argument that one could expand or grow the market; instead one had to corner and control it. The potential for conflict was high in order to protect both resources and markets. Mercantilism, at its best, would provide ample resources and enable favorable balances of exports back to the original provider of resources. Prospects of victory were highest for those states that had the necessary fiscal resources, gained in part from commerce, and sent naval and land forces to defeat the rival. As Ronald Findley and Kevin O'Rourke explain in their book, *Power and Plenty*, "Power would be the means to secure Plenty, which in turn would provide Power with its sinews."[14]

Mercantilism was a theory of political economy that would place thousands of ships on the world's oceans to serve its end—merchant ships, war ships, passenger ships, troop ships, and some that combined all or most of the preceding. It created "what could be called an Atlantic System, linking four continents by an ocean and comprised of a northern Anglo-Dutch-French segment, a central Spanish-Mexican zone, and a southern Luso-Brazilian zone [Portuguese], all connected with each other and with Africa via multiple webs of economic relationships."[15] The range of conflicts would extend globally, and by the late seventeenth century a global rivalry was emerging between Britain and France not unlike the Cold War of the last half of the twentieth century, with periods of cold war, hot war, declared war, undeclared war, and, obviously, public and private wars. This environment was one in which private actors in conflict and war would thrive. Just how well they advanced and supported the interests and desired objectives of their state sponsors or creators would become an increasingly complicated question to consider and answer as time progressed.

As privateers took to the oceans in the early seventeenth century, they entered what most assumed to be the aforementioned Atlantic System, but the reality that emerged posed uncertainty about that. Briefly appreciating the resulting complications is important in assessing what privateers did and how different authorities tried to control their actions. Who or what governed conduct on the high seas was an underlying problem. We have seen the attempt by the papacy to resolve this question in relation to Spain and Portugal in the Treaty of Tordesillas in 1494, and we have watched other rulers and states, both Protestant and Catholic, undermine that attempt at order. The maritime practices that underpinned mercantilism would challenge any authority that claimed jurisdiction over the world's oceans. Control of territory was not the sole end state or purpose of the competing empires that emerged. It was control and governance over the routes there that also mattered. Each ruler and state approached control differently—usually by extending present laws and customs from the parent country, but in instances even creating separate entities, such as trading companies, that exercised their own authority and law, rather than those of the founding state.[16]

Law and authority often traveled with the naval vessel, privateer, trading company, and even pirate who asserted such power through their presence and actions. It was not a pure "system" as such. Instead it is easier to imagine it as a set of channels or paths travelled by different and sometimes competing agents who maintained their own practices, laws, and means of enforcement.[17] Thus, as parties from major European powers sailed beyond the Atlantic and Mediterranean they often tried to apply the customs and laws they had developed in those regions. The Portuguese, for example, sold permits that enabled vessels to enter the Indian Ocean, a practice that other Europeans followed. Yet, provision of letters of marque and reprisal could also give a similar legal foundation to a voyage.[18] One can easily imagine the disputes that could emerge, whether between the European actor and indigenous peoples or between competing European actors. This is not to say that absolute legal chaos existed on the sea. Two legal scholars of the late sixteenth and early seventeenth centuries, Alberico Gentile and Hugo de Grotius, elaborated the rights of natural law on the world's oceans. Both, for example, amplified the already established position that pirates were common enemies of all. As competing maritime empires emerged, both also worked to clarify actions of private and public war, such as the right of redress of grievances for lost property on the high seas. As discussed in Chapter 1, Grotius placed importance on the act of official authorization to create a distinction between what could be legitimate reprisal and illegal piracy. Grotius's legal acumen had been called upon by the Dutch East India Company to provide legal justification to Dutch reprisals against a Portuguese vessel because of the failure of the latter's government to permit compensation.[19] Thus, most European actors had some common understanding of the practices related to public and private war that had emerged in their own history and were now in play on seas throughout the world.[20]

To borrow and use a modern expression in trade policy, none of this suggests, though, that the world was an "even playing field." To a degree, as Lauren Benton has explained in her seminal work on sovereignty, empires, and oceans, the Indian Ocean became a different legal space than the Atlantic world, even if the Europeans did try to transfer existing custom and law to this region.[21] The most prominent example of this is the authority and power the British gave to their own East India Company in this part of the world. This company, as explained in more detail later in this chapter, held its own rights of sovereignty, commanded its own army and navy, and negotiated its own agreements with native rulers. It also had its own policies and law affecting the existence and conduct of privateers within the waters under its jurisdiction. To sail and operate with authority of letters of marque and reprisal in the Atlantic world and then enter that of the Indian Ocean and assume the same role proved of sad consequence for more than one privateer or pirate.

For the English the expansion of jurisdiction in their Atlantic world would be accompanied by an extension of the jurisdiction of admiralty. On the surface this development looked advantageous because of its apparent establishment of consistent law and practices throughout the Atlantic and Caribbean parts of the empire, but, ultimately from London's perspective, the assumption of duties of admiralty by colonial governors became a headache. During most of the seventeenth century no formal means existed for the transfer of such authority from London. Colonial governors merely assumed it as the need for law and jurisdiction on the sea grew. By doing so, they claimed the power to make judgment on captures and prizes and to issue letters of marque and reprisal for settlement of compensation or privateering. This was certainly how the governor of Jamaica interpreted the commission of authority he received from the king in 1667.[22] The seventeenth century would teach the British that having multiple figures of authority interpret and execute what seemed to be a common set of law was no guarantee for a harmonious Atlantic System. Just how much authority should rest in London vis-à-vis the colonial seats of government was a question that carried greater implications as this century progressed into the eighteenth.

The seventeenth century in the Atlantic community began optimistically enough with the peace between England and Spain in 1603, but peace inevitably brings its own problems. Captains and crews who had worked as privateers now found themselves unneeded and possessed of skills that easily transferred to piracy, which is the path many took. Some activities could even continue as actual privateering, thanks to the support of men like the English secretary of state, Sir Robert Cecil, or the lord high admiral, the Earl of Nottingham, who, along with London merchants, helped establish trading companies such as the Levant Company in the Mediterranean and the East India Company. The privateers/pirates headed in multiple directions, but the Mediterranean and the Atlantic became their two major theaters. Some attacked vessels from the Venetian and Tuscan merchant fleets and returned to London to claim them as prize. Others actually worked alongside the Barbary pirates, essentially corsairs sponsored by the Barbary rulers along the northwestern and northern coasts of Africa. Barbary ports were a convenient place to settle claims on a prize that might not have passed muster in English or other European prize courts. Some English, Irish, and Scottish pirates even joined the Barbary ranks and raided the European and Christian shipping en route. Those operating in the Atlantic and Caribbean had to engage, momentarily at least, in actual piracy. Ireland became a base for a lot of pirate activity around the home isles and in the North Atlantic. Pirates from the British Isles acted alongside or against pirates from the Netherlands, France, Spain, and other countries.[23]

Lacking an adequate navy, the English ultimately had to commission private vessels, including (no doubt) former pirate vessels and crews, to seek out these pirates and take their ships for prize and compensation. The lord high admiral ordered the commissioning of such ships in 1610. However, problems quickly emerged. The potential of gain attracted more willing participants, and controlling their actions on the high seas proved difficult. Of equal importance is the challenge to this practice that appeared from other parts of the English government and its institutions. Even if it was still small, the navy's objections against private commissions apparently served as enough of a cause to repeal the commissions in 1618.[24] At the same time, the Parliament was asserting itself in more ways to try to gain control over some forms of revenue in order to restrict the range of the monarch's prerogative. Parliament was working to gain more control of taxation and other forms of revenue, such as the monarchy's historic claim to custom duties. Customs duties from seized cargoes were also paid to the Crown, although the lord admiral also received 10 percent of their value. In the short term Parliament did not seem as interested in limiting this particular type of customs duty for the monarch. Money from prize cargo and vessels was not a form of direct taxation; it came from foreign-owned property that was not entering as traditional commerce. Also, too many merchants who swayed voices in Parliament were also investors in the privateering ventures that were making money. It should be no surprise that the Duke of Buckingham purchased the position of lord admiral in 1618 in order to benefit personally from the gain and to help finance his campaigns against Catholic Spain and, later, France. He promised members of Parliament that he would deny no applications for letters of marque. Buckingham's actions were steps toward state-sponsored private violence.[25] The question was, how long would Parliament continue to allow such practices without finding means for its own review and approval?

In fact, Parliament had helped create the problem, for while it urged war against Spain, it refused to provide the money to wage it. Part of the reason was a widely held suspicion of Buckingham as a closet Catholic who wanted to return England to Rome's fold. Another reason, implied above, was that many in Parliament thought the war could be paid for by means other than taxation—privateering being one of the options. Thus, as Buckingham promised, all who wanted letters of marque and reprisal could pay the fee of three pounds, two shillings, and ten pence for a letter good for a year. Applicants also had to post a modest bond that could be taken if the privateer tried to accept the sum of the prize without paying taxes or was found guilty of having attacked ineligible targets. In spite of taking somewhere between 700 and a thousand prizes between 1626 and 1630, the money owed to the admiralty and as customs did not help the treasury very much. Many of the vessels seized were small, and about 15 percent of them belonged to friendly or neutral states. Buckingham, who was assassinated in 1628, did not appear to worry that much about the rights of neutrals. The Spanish and French responded with their own commissions for privateers against British vessels. Privateers acting out of Dunkirk alone may have seized as much as one-fifth of Britain's merchant fleet. Only the Earl of Warwick in the Caribbean and western Atlantic and Sir Kenelm Digby in the Mediterranean conducted operations that were both effective instruments of Protestantism and noticeably profitable for their investors.[26]

The comparatively small size of the English navy, the poor condition of many of its vessels, and London's dependence on privateering had all combined to diminish the reputation of England as a maritime power. King Charles I (1625–1649) acted to correct this by enlarging the fleet. He did not have adequate revenue from taxation imposed by Parliament; therefore, he chose to use a policy known as Ship Money, in which seaports paid to support naval defense. Charles extended this practice to towns in the interior. The payments were not taxes but regarded as payments to substitute for service. At the same time, some revisions of law and practice regarding privateering appeared. An actual distinction between letters of marque and reprisal again emerged. A letter of marque continued to be a means by which a private party could take a vessel in times of war to attack and seize vessels of the belligerents or those of neutrals carrying contraband. For a letter of reprisal, the criteria to prove loss became stricter. Clearly the almost unquestioning attitude of the late Buckingham and others was over. Access to letters of reprisal became more difficult through the remainder of Charles's reign and would become almost nonexistent under the Commonwealth of Oliver Cromwell. Use of English naval vessels for voyages of personal privateering and gain effectively ended by the mid-seventeenth century.[27]

THE GROWTH OF STATE CONTROL AND POWER

The political and religious crisis that played itself out in the English Civil War and the ultimate execution of the king carried immense implications for the level of state control over both the British navy and the policies governing privateering and the issuance of letters of marque and reprisal. When Charles I left London in January 1642, he put the navy in the hands of Parliament. Even though Parliament initially was somewhat inattentive to the navy, its control of it, as well as the army, had turned part of the table in English politics. Parliament, the king, and Irish rebels all issued commissions for privateers, but the fact that overseas trade provided 70 percent of the revenue from customs for the government gave Parliament a strong advantage. Control of the navy enabled parliamentary forces to conduct campaigns at different locales in the British Isles. Even though political and constitutional questions surrounding parliamentary control of both the navy and army remained, the balance in authority and control over war and its instruments had shifted.[28]

Although its implementation traveled an obstructive path, the British Atlantic world experienced something of a tectonic shift in the midseventeenth century. What had been a system of intermittent involvement by the king and government in London had become by 1660, in the words of historian Carla Gardina Pestana, a complicated world that "was more centralized, more diverse, more divided religiously, and more polarized between those who lacked autonomy and those who had power."[29] Pestana's words describe a system under construction, not one that was working, or ever did work, like a tuned engine. Whether on the level of commissioning privateers or defining the political center of gravity between London and the North American colonies, the British Atlantic System was one that would encounter difficult execution and passage. "The Commonwealth" of the Puritan Oliver Cromwell, writes Pestana, "wanted to remake the loose conglomeration of colonies that it had seized into a centrally governed and commercially integrated empire."[30]

All of the measures, accomplished and failed, to integrate the empire are far beyond the purpose of this book, but the steps to make the finances of the state as well as the decision, execution, and instruments of war more accountable to the state are instrumental. As Charles I had already expanded the navy through the use of Ship Money, Parliament in 1650 legislated increases in customs duties to pay for the fleet. A larger fleet could also assume significant new duties, including the escort of expanded merchant fleets. Thus, convoy duty, whether against royalist privateers serving those wanting to restore the monarch or privateers from foreign countries, became a fixed part of English maritime practice by the 1670s. Other European powers soon adopted the practice.[31] The political-economic theory of mercantilism itself almost made this form of state protection of commerce mandatory, as commerce between the parent country and its colonies was so essential for the prosperity and political power of the former. Protection of commerce from attack was only part of the problem. A larger concern was the competition and interference in colonial commerce that could come from other countries—most noticeably the Dutch, whose East India Company and other trading ventures were making inroads into English colonies. To counter this, Parliament passed the Act of 1650 that prohibited foreign shipping from trading with English colonies. A year later it passed the Navigation Ordinance (later known as the Navigation Act) of 1651 that required goods being shipped to and from the colonies to be carried only by English flagged vessels. Imports from elsewhere could move either in ships from the originating country or English ships. Neither of these two laws were an automatic success. London's merchant fleet was not actually big enough to carry all the commerce, and British merchants, and indirectly their customers, had to pay higher prices because their vessels rates were more expensive than the Dutch.[32]

London's clamp on trade only increased, regardless of whether it was through the Commonwealth of Cromwell or the restored monarchy under Charles II. In 1660 the first Parliament under the king passed a new Navigation Act that combined the acts of 1650 and 1651 and added a list of items that the colonies could send only to England. The only exception of note was fish, which had a large market in southern Europe. The Staple Act of that same year prohibited the shipment of goods from any foreign country to the colonies, even if they were to be carried in an English vessel. The law created an artificiality that allowed foreign goods to be brought into an English port, from which they could be legally shipped to the colonies.

These policies did admittedly help English shipping. They also helped create a working segment of the population, perhaps as much as 20 percent of the population not working in agriculture, who were employed in jobs related to shipping.[33] At the same time, though, they helped create attitudes of defiance and lawlessness because of the higher rates and prices that resulted and the imposition of control from London on colonies that had largely been able to develop their local practices and preferences. Thwarting the Navigation Acts became almost as much a badge of honor for colonists in many settings as circumventing Prohibition was for many Americans in the 1920s.[34]

As mentioned earlier, issuing commissions for letters of marque and reprisal and privateering had become practices that colonial governors were accustomed to controlling—usually in accordance with the policies and wishes from the distant mother country, but not always. By the time Charles II ascended to the throne in 1660 the balance between London's authority and that of the colonies was becoming problematic in a number of locations. No setting was perhaps more difficult to resolve than Jamaica, which was probably the leading source in privateers among British colonies in the Caribbean and North America during the 1650s–1670s.[35]

The Spanish trade in the Caribbean and the West Indies was an appealing target to privateers and pirates, and this assembly of English, Irish, French, and Dutch actors frequently settled in the islands of the Antilles (such as Barbados, Martinique, and St. Kitts) because of their proximity to shipping routes from Spanish colonies in the Americas from Mexico south and major colonies in the Caribbean, such as Hispaniola (modern-day Haiti and the Dominican Republic). French pirates and privateers, also known as *filibustiers* (from the Dutch term for freebooter) or *buccaneers* (derived from the word for *boucan*, the places where they dried meat often stolen from the Spanish), often based themselves as well on the island of Tortuga, just off the northwestern coast of Hispaniola. Aside from the island of Santa Catalina (renamed Providence Island fittingly in honor of its apparent divine mission against Spain) off of the coast of Nicaragua, the English did not have another major base. That began to change in 1654, when driven by aspirations for a Protestant counterpart to the Spanish empire in this region, Cromwell attempted to invade Hispaniola. That did not go well, but the invasion of Jamaica, a colony Spain had not paid nearly as much heed to, proved far more successful. As the English historian Charles Leslie wrote a century later in his *New History of Jamaica*, the island seemed to be a magnet for "people of desperate fortunes" from the British Isles.[36]

Thomas D'Oyley, governor of Jamaica, in 1657 created Jamaica's first court to deal with Spanish prizes. D'Oyley had asked London whether he had the authority to do so, and, receiving no answer, he acted on the claim that he possessed the power of prerogative to establish such a court and to commence issuing letters for privateers against Spanish ships and cargo. In fact, D'Oyley went on some of these voyages himself and certainly enjoyed lucrative gains from them. By 1660, when Charles II retook the throne, the governor was issuing commissions for eight to fifteen privateers per year. As no Royal Navy was present, D'Oyley had to rely solely on privateers, and he willingly looked away when on occasion one of them might attack a British ship rather than Spanish. After learning of the peace signed between Britain and Spain in 1660, the governor issued a proclamation to call all privateers home, but ships and crews who relied on privateering for their livelihood did not greet it favorably. Having been appointed by Cromwell, D'Oyley returned to England in 1662 to be replaced by Lord Thomas Windsor.[37]

The continuation of privateering in the wake of the peace in 1660 has created an impression that Charles II and his ministers really did not care what the governor of Jamaica was doing, but practices in seventeenth-century diplomacy and treaties did not make this so clear.[38] Some treaties of the time contained what was known as a "friendship termination line," an imaginary demarcation, in this case in the Atlantic, beyond which there was no guarantee of the preservation of peace. In short, Spain and England might be at peace in the Old World, but there was no certainty it would carry over into the New World. On his own authority Windsor continued to issue commissions for privateering and to operate prize courts—all of this based on the claim of "imminent threat" of Spanish invasion. Keep in mind that this concern existed alongside a situation where the British navy was only beginning to expand; it was not yet that visible, and the fear of possible Spanish invasion was not just a convenient figment of imagination.[39] In reality, the king was unhappy with news of this practice, as it threatened the peace he had negotiated. A letter sent to Windsor's successor, William Lyttleton, expressed the king's wish to have his policy and law obeyed. Lyttleton replied that the privateers did not act under the monarch's authority and that he did not believe he had to recall them—a very aggressive assertion of prerogative by this soon-to-be removed governor.

Charles sacked Lyttleton and replaced him with a Royalist he believed he could trust, Thomas Modyford.[40]

Modyford took office as England was in its second war against the Dutch, which began just a year after the peace signed with Spain and ended in 1667. The Dutch had a sizable presence in the West Indies, including islands such as Curacao and Tobago, and they were allied in this instance with France. Fending off attacks by Dutch naval vessels as well as Dutch and French privateers, Modyford chose to respond with privateer/pirate operations against their possessions. There were plenty of volunteers, including a skilled privateer named Henry Morgan. They attacked Dutch and French vessels and ports but also conducted raids against the Spanish in Nicaragua in 1665. The Spanish retaliated by seizing the island of Providence and reimposing the name of Santa Catalina. Modyford believed the Spanish were about to invade Jamaica; it is possible Morgan told him this to get him to authorize the next measures. In 1668 the governor sent Morgan to raid Cuba. Whether his men were acting as pirates or privateers depended on perspective and also the letters they could show or claim they possessed. As Charles had sought to halt the issue of commissions for privateers to wait for a response on the status of English possessions in the Caribbean, Modyford continued to do so on his own and concealed this practice from London. Morgan and Modyford had discussed a possible attack on Panama, and after a limited Spanish attack on the north coast of Jamaica in June 1670, Modyford appointed Morgan commander of the fleet responsible for protecting the island. The Panama operation was set into motion, and in January 1671 Morgan attacked Panama City with a force of two thousand French and English privateers and pirates. Morgan's attack may have acquired as much as 750,000 pounds in plunder and prize, and Modyford informed the king of the great value gained in spite of the fact he had tried, he claimed, to curtail the raid. This was an awkward embarrassment for Charles II, as England and Spain had signed in July 1670 the Treaty of Madrid, in which Spain recognized England's colonies. Hostilities against Spain in the Caribbean ended, and London promised it would terminate the policy of no peace beyond the imagined line of demarcation. It appeared, too, that reliance on privateering as an instrument of force against the Spanish would end as well.[41]

Yet it did not, because "Jamaican privateering had evolved from an act of military necessity to one of economic opportunity."[42] Privateers who could not depend on the authorities in Jamaica to provide them with commissions could turn elsewhere, especially to the French, who had resorted to the form of pirate and privateer collaboration in their empire that had been practiced by Britain. Between 1678 and 1684 French privateers from Tortuga and Saint-Dominique attacked Spanish shipping and ports. The Truce of Ratisbon ended this particular French-Spanish conflict in both the Caribbean and Europe.[43] Meanwhile London made more effort to place the actions of colonial authorities, merchants, and privateers under stricter control. If privateers were not sailing from Jamaica as much as they had, they, their vessels, and fellow merchants were actively and openly flaunting the navigation laws that tried to protect the operation and foundation of the empire.

The French had turned to privateering as a means to mount an effective force on the high seas without the expense of maintaining a large fleet. France had done so during much of the seventeenth century, but during the 1690s Louis XIV decided to rely on privateering, the practice of *guerre de course*, war on commerce, against its major adversaries—usually Spain or England.[44] There has been debate as to whether France could have afforded the range of investment that its British rival was placing into its navy. One historian has estimated that in relation to the amount of money, the size of the labor force, and the physical resources involved in production, the British navy was probably the world's largest industrial unit by the second half of the eighteenth century.[45] Economic hardship caused by loss of access to some trading markets, closure of fishing areas, and the resulting hardship for seamen also created an interest in privateering. Furthermore, the French, as discussed earlier, simply concluded privateering was the way to go. During the wars of the late seventeenth and early eighteenth centuries, the French purposely loaned ships, as well as their crews, to serve under privateers. It appeared to be an attractive way to outsource some functions and to share costs between the state and private entrepreneurs. The monarch might even select the targets to be attacked but leave the action to the privateer.[46]

In principle, the laws and procedures governing French privateering at this time were quite elaborate. Their detail reflects the intent of the French state to try to maintain control over this form of violence even if the actual reality fell somewhat short in practice. Since the late sixteenth century, French prize law had required privateers to return their prizes to French ports, preferably the one from which they sailed. The French restated this in 1681 in the *Ordonnance de la marine*, often known as the *Ordonnance Colbert*, in reference to Louis XIV's famous minister of finance, Jean-Baptiste Colbert, who played such a central role in the development of the French state. Resolution of the prizes was in the hands of French consuls in various ports, who, thanks to the *Ordonnance*, now held such authority through the admiralty. Privateers had to operate under a license and also had to register their ship. The *Ordonnance* specified what types of ships and cargo could be considered legitimate prizes. On taking a prize, the privateer captain had to seize all papers and passports that related to its status. Not to have them could jeopardize the status and determination of the prize. Customarily, the vessel had to return promptly to its home port with prize and any prisoners, barring factors of weather or pursuit by foreign vessels that would require sailing to a different port. Taking or opening goods before adjudication of the prize was prohibited. Once in port, authorities sealed the prize, examined papers and conducted interviews related to the location and circumstances of its seizure, and spoke with prisoners and the privateer crew to obtain additional information about the seizure. If all seemed in order and legal, the admiralty judged it a good prize. One-tenth of the prize amount went to the admiralty; the rest was divided among investors and owners as well as the ship captain, officers, and crew. Sometimes captain and crew might hold some of these other functions as well.[47]

Of course, this system did not function as cleanly as it read on paper. One can see the loopholes. Weather, for example, can be a very capricious factor that offers opportunity for innovative excuses. Not surprisingly, it was hard for France to have in place a network of consular officials who could cover these duties as efficiently as desired. Circumstances of war could also influence the administration and enforcement of the system. In such periods, elimination of foreign cargoes and the provision of revenue to both the French state and privateers could override adherence to the letter of the law. In fact, throughout the eighteenth century it appears that French policies actually became more lenient and less subject to attempted central control. The French privateer of 1800 arguably operated in a more freewheeling environment than his ancestor a century earlier.[48]

That certainly would not be the case for his British counterpart, who would operate in an increasingly restricted world beginning in the late seventeenth century onward. However, in the early 1680s, to pick an arbitrary date, privateers, whether operating from English, Scottish, Irish, or colonial ports, probably sailed in a less restrictive world on paper and practice than their French counterparts. London had an uphill struggle to conduct against the diffusion of authority and its independent and arbitrary exercise by some officials throughout the empire. While France was acting to empower the privateers, even if the legal framework was rather specific, the British were beginning to take steps that centralized state power, as had the French, but that slowly eroded dependence on privateers and other private actors. The pattern of such actions would naturally occur at different speeds depending on the location as well as the types of actors in play.

One of the problems confronting London, as illustrated already by the circumstances in Jamaica, was the enforcement of royal and parliamentary wishes regarding the Navigation Acts, privateering, and other imperial matters. The arbitrary, even deceptive, actions taken by some of Jamaica's governors had shown the disparity that existed between London's aspirations for greater consistency and unity of rules in the empire and the insistence of some colonial officials that they held their own authority. Added to that, of course, was the resistance of merchants and traders who disliked government intrusion into patterns of trade and commerce that had existed for decades. Complicating this picture was the parallel existence of three different types of colonies just in British North America—royal, proprietary, and charter.

Royal colonies, of which Virginia and New York were leading examples, had governors directly appointed by the king or queen. Their legal structures generally resembled those of London's, and, not surprisingly, they generally had firmer legal ties between themselves and London. Proprietary colonies, of which Pennsylvania was a prominent example, originated from grants of land to investors in order to attract settlers and develop crops and natural resources. The lord proprietors sometimes chose to remain in Britain, which presumably would assure a good relationship between the Crown and the colony, as the proprietors had such strong roles in the governance of the colony. Reality was not always that harmonious, whether with royal or proprietary colonies. Colonial populations became used to a fair amount of leeway in their affairs, and there were instances when they even opposed appointees of the British government and selected a person from their own circle. The third form of colonial structure in North America was that of a charter colony—Massachusetts, Connecticut, and Rhode Island. A charter was a legal agreement, in effect a contract, that bound the colony to English law but allowed it to compose its own government. These colonies enjoyed a special legal status that created both envy and dislike among their colonial neighbors. One factor adding to their disfavor was the impression that charter colonies had become inviting locales for crime, vice, and piracy. London's alarm about the spread of piracy in the Atlantic and Caribbean—even Jamaica now complained about the lawlessness emanating from charter colonies—moved the Privy Council 1684 to depict the charter colonies as a cause of the growth of piracy and advise them to follow the role model of a royal colony like Virginia. That charge proved too much for Rhode Island, in particular, to accept.[49]

Rhode Island believed it had its own right of admiralty jurisdiction, which covered a number of maritime issues besides privateering. History seemed on its side. In 1653, a whole ten years before the colony received its charter, the Privy Council in London told Governor William Dyer to defend Rhode Island from the Dutch (with whom England was at war), which included the right to take Dutch vessels on the sea. The Rhode Island assembly concluded this authority included the establishment of prize courts. The Privy Council had limited privateering to act against the Dutch, but authorities in Rhode Island ports like Newport did not confine it to the Dutch when issuing commissions. Local merchants from the middle and upper classes were the applicants. Rhode Island authorities claimed they had the problems with piracy and privateering under control, but complaints led the Lords of Trade in London to send the surveyor general for customs in the colonies, Edward Randolph, to investigate. Arriving first in Massachusetts, Randolph accused that colony of violating the Navigation Acts and permitting privateering, which resulted in Massachusetts having its charter revoked in 1684. Rhode Island was now in Randolph's sights, and it thus received a letter of warning that same year from Sir William Blathwayt, who was about to become the Privy Council's secretary on trade and foreign plantations. The letter urged a halt to all piracy and privateering from Rhode Island.[50]

This demand really did challenge Rhode Island's capacities and position in fundamental ways. Such a small colony was heavily dependent on maritime commerce for its survival. Relying on privateers was a matter of necessity and not just a quest for more profit. At the time when Randolph and Blathwayt made their threats, London was in no position to defend this colony, or any North American colony, with a fleet. Rhode Island had to turn to privateers to defend itself, as it did in 1690 when the French attacked the colony. Rhode Island responded in a way that arguably complied with London's wishes but that also preserved its authority and controls over privateering. As many admiralty cases fell under the jurisdiction of common law courts, Rhode Island saw no reason to change this practice, which often included matters related to privateers. Until the mid-1690s London accepted this begrudgingly. The colonial assembly's new law also asserted that such cases tried in Rhode Island would carry the same stature as those done in England. Finally, the assembly defined piracy in a narrow way that enabled it to continue the practice of privateering for its own citizens: piracy was committed by those who would leave Rhode Island and offer their services to a foreign leader. No records could be found documenting such a traitor, which meant no prosecutions would occur. This clever evasion did not escape the scrutiny of royal authorities, who had the colony's charter revoked. For two years Rhode Island essentially had no government, but privateers continued to sail from its ports. On having its charter reestablished in 1689 under a new governor, the practices of old seemed to continue as before. As noted, this included commissions to privateers to defend the colony against the French in 1690.[51]

The measures taken in relation to Massachusetts and Rhode Island, as well as the displeasure directed at other colonies, such as Pennsylvania, for harboring pirates under the guise of privateering, were part of an ongoing series of measures to try to place commerce in stronger boundaries that served the interests of the empire. Beginning in 1689 London took steps to assure that the authority of admiralty decisions in the colonies rested more with the Crown than with the prerogative of governors. Each governor, besides receiving his commission, also received a commission as a vice admiral. This had occurred sporadically before, especially with proprietary colonies, but now it would be standard practice. The vice admiral could conduct court in person, but, as the volume of cases grew, it became common to appoint judges to handle some cases.[52] In instances jurisdictions of colonies were combined; for example, between 1697 and 1701 there were eleven jurisdictions in British colonies in the New World for vice-admiralty courts.[53] London acted to restrict the choices for privateering by citizens and colonists by stipulating in measures in 1692, 1694, and 1700 that service under foreign commission would be judged as piracy.[54] In terms of the linkages among trade, piracy, and privateering, the creation of the Board of Trade (the common name for the Committee on Trade and Plantations) was a significant step toward a more centralized system of review and authority. The committee was a replacement for the Lords of Trade, a grouping of people who were often political amateurs and favorites. Now this new structure would bring more knowledge, rigor, and skill to the increasingly complex questions facing it.[55] It needed such abilities, for the board had to compete with a variety of actors—the monarch, the Houses of Commons and Lords, the admiralty, the treasury, customs officials, the secretary of state, and others; the colonies also had avenues to many of these actors and could play them off one another as well.[56]

As always, assurance for good conduct and behavior by privateers was a concern of London and other governments. The English had handled this since the sixteenth century with required pledges or sureties, but by the end of the seventeenth century contracts with privateers required sizable payments of promise for good behavior. A privateer with a crew of more than 150 had to pay 3,000 pounds; if less than 150 the amount was halved. The amounts of money do not appear to have posed insurmountable hurdles to those investing in and owning privateering ventures.[57]

A separate problem, given the ascending importance of the navy, was to prevent privateers from taking too many sailors. Privateering and, even more so, piracy offered more attractive conditions than service in the navy. Working conditions and discipline were harsh in all settings, but because privateering and piracy were forms of business ventures some other factors weighed in their advantage. Food was sometimes better, work shifts might be shorter, and pay could be higher as well. These considerations even held true in spite of the much larger crews on pirate vessels. (Seeing a ship with a crowded deck was sometimes a good indicator of a pirate because of the need for more crew to seize vessels and sail them.) Furthermore, crews had more voice in the governance of the vessel, sometimes even including the selection of officers. As the navy increased in size into the eighteenth century, impressments became a more common means of finding labor. Joining a privateer was a voluntary act; in fact, seamen could sometimes buy a small share in the overall operation. Prize money was a potential in all these lines of work, but its division was least favorable for the majority of the crew in the navy, where a hierarchical command structure directed most of the prize to the officers and the government. Privateers were privately owned and somewhat more democratic in their operations, but prizes and prize money, as we have seen, had to be divided among payment to the admiralty; custom duties; payments to the major investors, captain, and major officer (who might hold both responsibilities); and then the crew. Piracy was certainly the more attractive alternative when one was not caught and suffered the fate of pirates. Assuming the pirate vessel was not operating under a commission (real or feigned), little to no money would go to government offices, and the distribution of the prize and money was often more equitable than it was on a privateering ship.[58] If given a choice, many young men would choose service with a privateer, which was legal, and possibly a pirate, which certainly was not, over being with the Royal Navy. To prevent this the Board of Admiralty began to make it conditional for issuance of a letter of marque that the privateer, or the proper representative agent, would certify that at least 50 percent of the crew were from the land and other nonmaritime parts of the population. The purpose was to guarantee that privateering would not seriously diminish the pool of available men for service in the navy—either as volunteer or impressed seamen.[59]

The problem with the adherence and respect of colonial governments for the Navigation Acts and other laws affecting the administration, revenues, and maritime practices of the empire remained well into the eighteenth century. The patterns of smuggling, piracy, and liberal provision of commissions to privateers continued as the old century ended and the new opened. English merchants complained about lost revenue. Critics of the colonies believed it was time to place them under direct control. Among these was the aforementioned Edward Randolph, who as early as 1695 proposed that all corporate and proprietary colonies be abolished and that charter colonies see their charters revoked. This seemed to be an unduly strong course of action. However, five years later Randolph pressed his proposal again after another visit to the North American colonies. Aside from the governors of Virginia and New York, Randolph regarded the rest as practitioners and enablers of corruption. The Board of Trade used his report, no doubt with other grievances, to propose in March 1701 what became known as the Resumption Bill to accuse all proprietary and charter colonies of flouting law and fostering pirates and to have them placed under direct royal control.[60] Thanks to the lobbying efforts of colonial representatives as well as the fact some in Parliament did not share the depth of the Board of Trade's alarm, the Resumption Bill did not become law. The problems remained. Essentially the mother country and the colonies had different views of piracy and privateering, and they certainly had different perspectives on smuggling and respect for the Navigation Laws. Adding to the justifications most of the colonies held about their actions was the fact that new horizons of activity for piracy and privateering had arisen beyond the Atlantic. Those were far away, they were lucrative, and the perception was that the rules that governed the practice of privateering in the Atlantic could flourish with less restriction and inhibition in locations like the Pacific, the Red Sea, and the Indian Ocean.[61]

An important development for the course of privateering during the next two decades began in 1696 when the French tried one last time to establish a Catholic monarchy in England by the planned murder of King William III. Another of the wars between these powers that occurred so frequently for over a century started with both countries ill-equipped to conduct major naval operations, thanks partly to lack of money. As a result London and Paris resorted to increased levels of privateering as a substitute. It was commercial warfare brought to almost unprecedented levels. The scale of privateering, in fact, required some revision of the terminology. Privateers, especially full-time ones, were commissioned to look for prizes and to seize them. Letters of marque in this conflict took a modified meaning and referred to papers for merchant vessels on their customary routes that nonetheless were armed and could take advantage of opportunities that might come by their way. As N. A. M. Rodger points out, this form of privateering was "a profit-making activity, in which the object was easy victims, not hard knocks and glory."[62] One of the leading newspapers, the *Observator*, which regarded itself as a voice for British merchants, stated that in maritime war "the chief Care ought to be the Security of our merchant Ships, by providing sufficient Convoys, and next to that, the encouragement of Privateers." Another paper instructed members of Parliament to "contribute your utmost assistance for the Encouragement of Privateers."[63] The French ultimately ended up sending out squadrons as large as twelve vessels—some belonging to the French navy, others privately owned privateers—to attack British ships and those of allies and neutrals carrying contraband. Squadrons of this size could often overcome any convoy escort. The revenue gained from this became critical for the continuation of France's naval war. If one measures their gains from 1689 to 1713, when this particular cycle of conflict ended with the Peace of Utrecht, the French had seized around 12,000 prizes. The benefits France gained from this strategy have been debated ever since. While France did not win the naval war, it certainly stayed in the fight, and the privateering strategy provided revenue that France otherwise would not have had. It is probably correct, as Rodger observes in his assessment, that France would

have experienced a more favorable outcome if its state budget and structures had been in better condition. In London one direct consequence was
increased support for the construction of more ships for the navy.[64]

Such a prolonged conflict also invited expansion of privateering into
regions that had not experienced it frequently. Mercantilism had helped
extend commerce throughout the world, and the creation of trading companies by European states added to the magnitude and value of the commerce
involved. Reports spread that vessels in the Indian Ocean and Asian waters
were often larger and not that well-armed (although that practice may not
have lasted very long). The vessels of the trading companies themselves,
although better armed and defended, were also highly appealing. Those
going outward-bound from Europe usually carried gold and silver and then
returned home filled with jewels, spices, coffee, textiles, and other goods and
products. When major European wars occurred the number of pirates often
decreased, as they could turn their skills and resources to privateering, but
by the early 1690s London was receiving reports of privateers, commissioned
by British governors in North America and the Caribbean, appearing in the
Indian Ocean and the Red Sea. Thus began the notorious adventures of the
"Red Sea Men," as these privateers and pirates were known. The first such
voyage may have been that of the Jacob, which received a commission from
the governor of New York to attack French shipping. Nothing of the like
occurred, as the captain sailed his vessel directly into the Indian Ocean and
began to attack native shipping. The prize money was reportedly staggering
by contemporary terms—as much as 400 to 500 pounds per man. An extra
benefit was that the ship and crew could refurbish in Madagascar courtesy
of a trading post owned by the richest merchant in the port of New York. On
returning to New York, the privateers gave the governor some prize money
as well as the ship, which he was able to sell.[65]

This was an unsavory way of conducting business, whether by the privateer or the officials offering him the commission. These vessels combined
traditional merchant activity, the carrying of products and goods, along
with privateering. A number of them also joined in the slave trade as they
returned to their home ports in the Western Hemisphere. They did sometimes attack the vessels of the country, and its trading company, that the
commission specified, but with willpower and imagination it became easy
to attack those of other countries and companies, including one's mother
country. As the British colonial historian I. K. Steele observes, "flags were

often as changeable as the wind" in the Indian Ocean "and depended on the size of the ship on the horizon."[66] Thus, if one sailed from Rhode Island or wherever, having a nice inventory of flags on hand was valuable if one decided it could be lucrative to attack a vessel affiliated with the British East India Company. Admittedly, even a legitimate privateer was at the mercy of distance and the slow speed of news into these distant waters. Peace might have been reached between the warring states in Europe, but privateers this far away could sometimes face a news lag as long as two years.[67] Obviously, this circumstance could sometimes be used to one's advantage. Whatever the explanation or excuse, the Red Sea and Indian Ocean were the type of environments where piracy could flourish—competing and loosely defined areas of responsibility and jurisdiction, with an absence of effective agreements, law, and means of enforcement to resolve differences, and the presence of those willing to circumvent and even establish precedents for new behavior and codes of conduct.

Into this ambiguous but target-rich setting sailed one of history's best-known pirates (or privateer, as he thought himself), Captain William Kidd. He would bring into question the matter as to what degree the world of the Indian Ocean paralleled that of the Atlantic. Kidd was born in Scotland, and as a young man he went to sea, where by the late 1680s he had experience as a pirate and privateer in the Caribbean. By 1694 he was living in New York, a city that had become a popular base for privateers, and reports tell of his departure in May 1694 on his brigantine to pursue French vessels. Kidd was a respected member of New York society, owned a pew in Trinity Church, and was a friend of several local political leaders. In 1695 he sailed to London with the apparent intent of seeking commission as a privateer. A friend in New York wrote him a letter of introduction to Sir William Blathwayt, the same official who had warned Rhode Island in 1684 and who was now secretary of war.[68] Kidd arrived in London just at the time that Anglo-French conflict was again escalating. Faced with the need to recruit more sailors for the navy, the admiralty had stopped issuing commissions for privateers, who drew many seamen to their vessels. However, the damages British merchants and others, including the East India Company, were suffering at the hands of French privateers moved the admiralty to change its mind. Kidd found himself at the mercy of machinations between Tory and Whig politicians who struggled to control Parliament. Thanks to the presence in London of one of his New York friends, Robert Livingston, Kidd fell in with a group of Whigs, of which Richard Coote, the Earl of Bellomont, proved the most important. What happened at this stage varies based on whose account one accepts. One version has Kidd stressing he would go after privateers from New York who acted more as pirates in the West Indies. The other is that the admiralty, pressed to take action to protect commerce and ships in the Indian Ocean, decided to use Kidd as a privateer. In January 1696 Kidd received a commission from the admiralty to hunt for pirates. In order for the senior partners in this venture to profit by bypassing admiralty procedures—including Bellomont; Lord John Somers, Lord Keeper of the Great Seal; Henry Sidney, the Earl of Romney; and Edward Russell, Earl of Oxford—they had to obtain consent from King William. The king gave it and was to receive 10 percent of the prize.[69]

Kidd's experience and understanding of privateering was from the Atlantic and Caribbean, but he was about to enter the Indian Ocean, where his perspective and knowledge might not serve him so well. Remember that many ships in the Indian Ocean, especially those operating with the trading companies, held passes that protected their transit through its waters. Kidd knew about this, and he probably thought this arrangement, combined with his knowledge of letters of marque, would provide him with both the adequate authority for protection and ambiguity to allow for a more flexible exercise of seizure.[70] His first actions were obviously in the Atlantic world, though. He took his ship, the *Adventure Galley*, to the port of New York to get more crew. The crew of seventy given him by the admiralty was not enough; he needed at least one hundred more men who could fight and sail. The Anglo-French war had depressed the port's economy, so Kidd had no trouble finding men who hoped to get decent prize money to go with him.[71]

Kidd's passage through the Atlantic and along the western coast of Africa presented no significant problems. Although his plans for piracy were probably already in place, he seems to have known he should be on good behavior while in the Atlantic. Once he passed around the Cape of Good Hope and made his way to Madagascar, a notorious haven for pirates, his ambition began to reveal itself. Kidd was fully aware that his backers expected money, and after initial consideration of going after a ship of the East India Company, he sailed for the Red Sea, where he believed greater riches could be won at the cost of native merchants and traders. Threatening but not seizing vessels there, he headed on to India, where he fought his first successful engagement against a Portuguese warship, although he did not seize it. Flying French colors, Kidd's first prize was a Dutch-owned vessel whose officer showed a French pass, which he thought would save him and his crew. It obviously did not. Kidd then began to make a series of fatal mistakes. He seized the Quedah Merchant, a merchant vessel with an English captain, carrying a large load of silk that had been leased to Muklin Khan, a high official in the Mughal emperor's court. He also chased, but did not capture, a ship of the East India Company. News of these events quickly gave Kidd a bad name throughout the region. The Mughal emperor in late 1698 issued an order to all European companies to compensate those local merchants who had suffered losses at the hands of pirates or face the risk of being forced to stop business in the region. The East India Company was undergoing economic and political hardships in London, thanks to the trade losses resulting from wars with France as well as growing opposition from British textile manufacturers against textile imported from India. In 1698 the old company had to confront the chartering of a new company alongside of it. Events were also turning against Kidd and his crew.[72]

Perhaps in the waters of the Indian Ocean Kidd was so far away that he could not really understand the changes that were occurring in distant capitals. Kidd's early life in privateering and piracy had been at a time when London and its colonial governments willingly turned to this instrument of force and violence to serve political ends. In a world with elaborate networks of commerce, merchants and other players wanted a maritime world of stability, order, and some predictability. Peter Earle has described it so well in his study of piracy in this period, writing that "trade, shipping and the empire itself would be promoted, protected and controlled for the benefit of merchants and governments alike. The state would provide protection for trade and, in return, would receive a flow of revenue from increased wealth and customs duties and a pool of trained sailors to fight in its naval wars. There was to be no place for pirates in this world."[73] Nor, in reality, would there be much of a place for the type of privateering that Kidd and many of his historical ancestors had enjoyed—a type of nebulous and transitory world between the legal and illegal, between actual authorized force and illegal force covered with a patina of false authorization. "The state would have a monopoly of violence at sea, through its navy at all times and through privateers properly commissioned and policed in times of war."[74] A privateer might be able to go to sea for reasons tied to compensation and redress, but such measures would also have to support state ends. Private war, if it existed, must also be public.

On a less abstract level, British merchants and politicians wanted their government and its navy to act against the depredations of pirates and privateers. After Kidd's actions, the East India Company sought a larger presence of the British navy in the Indian Ocean. Kidd meanwhile headed back to the West Indies with his largest prize, the *Quedah Merchant*, which he ultimately chose to scuttle before proceeding on to Boston, where he hoped to begin settlement with some of his investors and partners. One of those supporters, the Earl of Bellomont, was now lord governor of New York and Massachusetts, an arrangement that reflected some of the changes made in colonial government in the wake of the controversies about the Navigation Acts and privateering from past decades. Bellomont now held different perspectives on the issue of privateering than he had a few years earlier. He represented the concerns and convictions of those who believed the commerce of the empire needed stability and protection from marauders like Kidd. Having received orders from London to arrest Kidd if he was in his jurisdiction, Bellomont arrested him and returned him to London in autumn 1699. The timing of Kidd's return to London could not have been worse, as Parliament was about to legislate a law "for the More Effectual Suppression of Piracy." For those found guilty, the law mandated execution. The law also warned charter and proprietary colonies not to interfere with the operation of the law and its courts. If they did so, London would revoke their charters.[75]

The details of Kidd's return to London, his experiences in the midst of the currents of British politics, and his trial are recounted in the pages of Robert Ritchie's study of Kidd and piracy. The notorious captain even had to go to Parliament, and after that he faced trial for both murder—he stood accused of crushing a gunner's skull with a bucket—and piracy. The two-day trial found Kidd guilty of both charges. Two weeks later he left Newgate Prison for the gallows awaiting him at Wapping. It was a spectacle where the curious and fascinated waited for the government to demonstrate its resolve to enforce the law in the firmest fashion to a hopefully impressed public. They received their entertainment's worth. The rope broke the first time, and Kidd had to climb the gallows again for a second, more successful, effort.[76]

The fate of Captain Kidd was only one step of many in a campaign against piracy that the British waged vigorously during the very end of the seventeenth century and into the early eighteenth. In 1700 alone, even before the passage of the anti-pirate legislation, the North American colonies sent a number of pirates back to London for trial.[77] Of course, political aspirations of officials and the passage of laws did not result in a prompt removal of pirates from the world's oceans, particularly those parts important to the British. Piracy did continue in the Indian Ocean, even if the Royal Navy maintained a presence, and in other parts of the world. When news of the War of the Spanish Succession arrived in the Western Hemisphere in 1702, the governors of Jamaica and the Bahamas began to issue licenses for privateers.[78] These orders fell in with London's wishes, as Parliament itself had debated a privateering bill in May 1702, and even though it failed to pass, many members of Parliament strongly urged the government to authorize privateering, which it did in June 1702. The proclamation came with both incentives and restrictions. Privateers were offered "gun money," essentially the right to retain items that were seized above the levels of the gun decks on ships. At the same time, though, explicit directions prohibited embezzlement, the torture of prisoners on the seized ships, and attacks on British and allied ships. Along with elaborate guidance about the custody and sale of prizes, the combined message was very clear: privateering was an instrument being used to serve and advance state interests.[79] Within a few years of the beginning of the War of the Spanish Succession, Jamaica had thirty licensed privateers, with about three-quarters of its white male population serving on them.[80]

The importance of privateers for Britain grew as the war against France lengthened and French privateers inflicted significant damage on British commercial traffic. Queen Anne issued an authorization in 1708 that provided incentive to privateers by removing the admiralty's portion of the prize money, thereby enabling the captain and crew to take all of it. The queen's order served as a basis for 127 vessels from Bristol, a port seriously affected by French privateers, to obtain letters of marque and head onto the seas.[81] One of the destinations this time was the Pacific. Spain had two treasure fleets in the Atlantic that arrived in or sailed from Veracruz, Mexico, and Cartagena, located in present-day Colombia, and returned to the Spanish port of Cadiz. Those arriving in Spain carried, gold, silver, and other riches; when they returned to the New World the ships carried soldiers, equipment, wine and food that could survive the voyage, and other goods needed in the colonies. A third treasure fleet, however, sailed from Acapulco on the west coast of

Mexico to Manila, Philippines, where it left gold and silver and returned with silk, porcelain, and other goods offered by Asian merchants. These would be carried overland to Veracruz and shipped to Spain. The Pacific treasure fleet was a potentially fat target in a time of war. Indeed, its ships were richly laden but also dangerous, for the Manila galleons were larger than their Atlantic counterparts, weighing up to 2,000 pounds and carrying hundreds of crew. The Spanish enjoyed a monopoly in the Pacific and had not encountered much problem keeping it until the early eighteenth century.[82]

Queen Anne had actively condoned a privateering voyage into the Pacific in 1703 led by William Dampier. Dampier had the backing of the lord high admiral and a number of prominent figures in London society and the royal court. One source of misgiving, however, had been the East India Company, which feared Dampier might infringe on the monopoly it had in trade with India. Dampier and his partners paid securities to assure the company his ships would not harm company interests.[83] Dampier was part of a second voyage, commanded by Woodes Rogers, and, again, the privateers had to contend with the doubts of the East India Company. Waiting off the coast of Baja California in late December 1709, they finally encountered one of the Spanish ships. This one was smaller than the large galleons, and it ultimately fell in their possession. An attempt to capture a second ship later, a large galleon, proved fruitless because of its size and heavy cannon. Rogers headed west to the Dutch East Indies to resupply, repair his ships—he had to scuttle one—and to take his vessels back to London. Representatives of the British East India Company in the port of Batavia (Jakarta), which was now a friendly locale, watched Rogers with strong suspicion because they suspected he was going to try to trade illicitly in East India Company goods. The company also held a monopoly for British trade in Southeast Asia. On returning to London in October 1711, Rogers found representatives of the East India Company waiting for him. They brought a suit against him, which cost Rogers most of his prize money; the crew apparently received nothing, and many, on returning to the port of London, faced another dimension of British power over maritime affairs—impressment into the Royal Navy.[84] With stronger oversight from London, being a privateer now required captain and crew to confront more competition, review by authorities, and acknowledgment of the reality of a larger navy.

The navy had needed many sailors during the War of the Spanish Succession, but its end in 1713 with the Peace of Utrecht found the Royal Navy seriously short of money. It demobilized nearly three-quarters of its men within two years of the peace—nearly 36,000 sailors—who now had to find work in ports or wherever. Privateers also had to get rid of their crews and find other lines of business for themselves. With so many wandering the docks, wages fell for those who did find work. Not surprisingly, piracy became one avenue for them—whether they were former privateer captains or just regular crew. Possibly adding to the luster of piracy was the wreck of the Spanish treasure fleet in July 1715 near the coast of Florida. Ten ships carrying gold bullion and silver coins went down. The Spanish began a salvage operation to recover the treasure, and it was no surprise that real privateers, self-appointed privateers, and plain pirates joined in this effort. One group returning to Jamaica with treasure they claimed to have taken legitimately as privateers found local authorities fully unconvinced. This group, led by one Henry Jennings, sailed to the Bahamas, which for the next several years was going to be one of the leading havens for pirates.[85]

The fifteen to twenty years that followed the Peace of Utrecht presented the world with the legacy and imagery of pirates that has followed us into the modern day, thanks to Daniel Defoe, Robert Louis Stevenson, Hollywood, and the admittedly fascinating historical record surrounding these events and people. Some of the most famous names in the public imagination originated from their exploits. Edward Teach (or Thach) is remembered as Blackbeard, thanks to his commanding height and long black beard, which he wove into braids with ribbons and completed with lighted candles. It was not a visage to encourage hope for mercy. Teach raided and seized vessels and prisoners throughout the West Indies and along the North American coast. Perhaps he recalled the type of support Queen Anne, the last Stuart monarch, had given earlier to privateering, when he and his sailors renamed one of their prizes *Queen Anne's Revenge*. The new monarch, George I, from the House of Hanover, was a vigorous opponent of piracy, and Blackbeard would die at the hands of the Royal Navy in November 1718.[86] His death testified to the growing capabilities of the British navy in combating piracy and maintaining more order on those ocean sectors important to the British.

However, George I, who had become king in 1714, had also tried more peaceful routes to stem piracy. Given the magnitude of the problem, and its relationship to the political and economic changes of the last few years, George offered a general pardon in September 1717. All pirates who willingly surrendered before September 5, 1718, would receive a full pardon, even for murder if it had been done in the context of piracy. Neither would the pirates have to yield the goods they had seized and stolen. The text of the pardon was available in the colonies by the end of the year. Initial response seemed encouraging, and in some locales, the combination of the pardon along with better means of enforcement by the royal governor showed positive results. The Bahamas, now governed by the same Woodes Rogers who had been charged of piracy by the East India Company only several years before, was one such example. However, other pirates dismissed the pardon and laughed it off. Distrust and the lure of old ways made it too hard to change. Interestingly, Teach did accept the pardon and settled in North Carolina. After obtaining a commission to trade with the island of St. Thomas from the Vice-Admiralty Court, Teach took two French ships and on returning to North Carolina claimed one as a prize and insisted the other had been adrift. Maybe a decade earlier this type of story might have passed scrutiny, but it did not now, and two months later Teach was dead.[87]

Ultimately British maritime policy was simply more effective and aggressive against piracy. The British hanged twenty-six pirate captains during the 1720s; twenty-five of the trials were in courts in Atlantic ports.[88] However, the British now had a genuine "blue water policy," to borrow a modern term about a naval strategy. The navy was clearly a component of their political-economic strategy of mercantilism. From the Peace of Utrecht in 1713 to the Peace of Paris fifty years later, which ended the Seven Years' War, the British would acquire a series of locations on which they could develop ports and naval installations. The role of private actors was now more limited and secured in ways to assure support for state objectives. The British replaced their role in part with a larger navy and integrated the remainders into a coordinated naval policy. Their French adversaries had continued to rely greatly on privateers in their pursuit of *guerre de course*, but they, too, had created a stronger and larger system of prize courts to try to assure that the prize and revenue from these measures would land in the state treasury.[89] War, be it declared or not, was an instrument of state policy, and to support that instrument private parties involved in it must be controlled in ways to enable their use of violence to serve state objectives. Private actors could still use violence, but the state increasingly claimed monopoly over the decision of when and how to use it.

Yet, even if the days of rather open-ended privateering were seemingly over—at least for the British—some practices from this era remained. One was prize money, which had been not only a benefit of privateering but also a reward for sailors on regular warships. David Baugh, a historian of the British navy in the eighteenth century, has observed that in war prize money "was the chief attraction of the naval service."[90] With a global deployment of the navy to protect British commerce and interests, some began to think that the quest for prize money should perhaps be less important than other strategic interests. Operationally, the hope for prize money could even discourage captains from taking on enemy vessels in close quarters to disarm or destroy them. The risk of damage to one's own ship, and the consequent inability to seize and take goods from the enemy, were possible and strategically costly restraints in the eyes of some.[91] Queen Anne's order in 1708 allowing privateers and crew to keep all the prize money had found its way into law. Britain still had problems with Spanish privateers in the Caribbean and West Indies, even though the two countries were at peace after the end of the War of the Spanish Succession. Some of the Spanish privateers had British and French crewmen on board—testimony to the combination of economic hardship and opportunistic aspirations that drove some of these men. Privateering seemed a possible solution to the Spanish problem, and the king even extended the pardon to pirates until July 1719 out of the hope that some would return to serve as privateers.[92]

Nearly twenty years later, though, the option of privateering seemed too risky for London. Frustrated by the continued Spanish depredations against British shipping, King George II indicated a willingness to issue letters of reprisal to English merchants to obtain compensation for losses. By 1738 reprisals looked increasingly to be a form of private war that had little place in the modern world, especially since the institutions and practices of diplomacy had developed more effective procedures to deal with such matters between both private citizens and state governments. In the presence of such measures, recourse to reprisals seemed to create an unnecessary risk of war. Only if the Spanish court did not give satisfaction, or the British court as well for a Spanish merchant, would it be appropriate to set reprisals into motion. Yet, even then, the likelihood of war remained high. Fifty or a hundred years before, the distance between private war and public, or official, war had been greater. The certainty of the former leading to the latter was much lower. Governments had even acknowledged the existence of a line that separated the areas where peace was in place by treaty and where its enforcement was in question. A century earlier privateers did not have to worry about the navies of European powers, even smaller ones. Now they did. Furthermore, the merchants who could receive a letter of reprisal expected the navy to be at hand to support their action. They were not going to fight on their own. Merchants and other segments of Britain's population paid for the navy, and it was expected to be there for them. Unless the government was ready for war, it was not likely anyone would be ready to receive a letter of reprisal.[93]

However, as questionable as reprisals and privateering now were, Parliament's behavior could still reveal schizophrenic views on privateering grounded in tradition. Nearly at the same time the king's proposed reprisals were in discussion, Parliament had to consider whether to keep the 1708 law on prize money in place. Supporters believed the prospect of prize money was a real lure for seamen to become privateers. Prime Minister Robert Walpole wanted stronger control over privateers, and he hoped to preserve peace between Britain and its two intermittent opponents—Spain and France. Walpole's position was to restore the right of the government's share in prize money. Parliament, however, chose to retain the law in its current form because prize money was such an enticement. Members did not want to offend friends and officers in the navy, and besides, as Daniel Baugh notes, "it was generosity with the money of France and Spain."[94] Reform of generosity with prize money was just a step too far. Even if British officials and parliamentarians wanted stronger control over privateering and other practices relying on private parties in war, such as the mercenaries who would serve during the American Revolution, there was still value in retaining a relationship with private interests. There were the naval and ground forces of the East India Company, the contractors who built ships and provided supplies to the army and navy, and even financiers who still retained a key place in sustaining government policy. The state, though, had greater strength in shaping and administering these actors and the procedures involved. The fiscal-military state studied so closely by John Brewer in The Sinews of War was falling into place.[95]

A year later, in October 1739, Walpole had to give in and go to war against Spain. Opponents of Walpole, like William Pitt, charged him with inadequate measures to protect British commerce and to halt Spanish violations on the high seas. Episodes like the appearance of Robert Jenkins, a seaman, on the floor of the House of Commons, who showed outraged members a pickled ear ostensibly cut off by a Spanish seaman seven years earlier, inflamed legislative unrest. Now that war was forthcoming and the navy's role was assured, merchants were ready to accept the letters of reprisal issued to them.[96] Also in the wake of these events, George II set explicit instructions to the governors in British North America authorizing them to issue letters for privateers from their ports and detailing the procedures for claiming the prize. Additional instructions could follow, such as a letter sent by George II on April 13, 1743, to the governors (in this copy to Thomas Bladen, the deputy governor of Maryland) reminding them of the treaty signed with the Netherlands and to order commissioned privateers to respect the terms of the treaty and Dutch vessels.[97] Such examples illustrate the degree of control London had established over practices that just fifty years earlier had been rather free-wheeling.

Privateering as it had been known in British history was disappearing. The renewal of Anglo-French conflict in North America in 1754 resulted in an announcement by George II of reprisals in 1755. However, these reprisals had nothing to do with private acts and wrongs but rather with acts of alleged French aggression in North America. The execution of the reprisals was in the hands of the Royal Navy, which did seize French vessels. The initial French acts occurred before the actual declaration of war in 1756. Pitt, now prime minister, explained to the French that the British waged these reprisals not as part of the war but as responses against the earlier aggressive acts.[98] The British had thus turned the concept of reprisals in a different direction by breaking away from the premise of private measures and violence, sanctioned by the state, to compensate for losses suffered by the former party. In this case, the state had assumed the responsibility for exercising the reprisals. It was a fundamental rebalancing of the relationship between public and private. The state had defined the terms of the losses and assumed the responsibility for redress or compensation for them. This was essentially a state-on-state dynamic that was unlike what had been customary in reprisals and privateering since their beginning.

The government in London had little need for privateers. Without question the rise of the fiscal-military state in Great Britain, and its ability to build and place a large navy on the ocean, was a major factor. The navy could do a better job than privateers, particularly if the objective was not only the taking of prizes and the gaining of prize money but the defeat or destruction of the opponent's capabilities. Privateers had never been as committed to that, nor were most of them even capable of doing it. A warship was a different vessel and far too expensive to build for most privateers and investors. In 1780 it required 50,000 pounds to build a seventy-four-gun warship. Arguably, only the state with its sizable fiscal resources could entertain the idea of building and operating such a vessel.[99] If reprisals and privateering were now linked more to actual war, then it was arguably better to leave war to those vessels built and prepared to fight it—the navy. By the time of the Napoleonic Wars, the prospect of a British privateer capturing a prize ship had decreased significantly. Two economic historians, Henning Hillmann and Christina Gathmann, estimate there was a 50 percent probability during the American Revolution; thirty years later the probability was 10 percent.[100] Taking this all into consideration, Hillmann and Gathmann then point to other reasons they believe privateering declined—the expansion of trade, size of markets, and value simply made it too profitable and attractive to sustain interest in privateering.[101] If the navy patrolled the sea lanes, acted against pirates, and enforced the rules of commerce, and if governments were establishing more defined and routine ways to handle claims and damages through negotiation and treaty, where was the potential profit to be had for the investors, captains, and crews who placed their money and hopes in the institution of privateering? It was a question that was harder to answer in the affirmative.

Privateering, of course, had been an endeavor supported and conducted by a small group of individuals. In the British experience, at least, they ultimately had been replaced by larger government organs, such as the Royal Navy, that assumed their mission more effectively and perhaps less problematically. One of the problems privateers had faced, especially when they sailed outside of the Atlantic world, was the presence of the large trading companies that held their own powers and entertained views of privateers that were sometimes very unlike those in London or in colonial capitals in North America. The trading companies were a very different type of private actor than privateers, but one whose role in various ways was supposed to advance the profile and power of the state that chartered it. Much more powerful than a privateer, even if the latter had a following among merchants, in Parliament, or in the royal court, the major European trading companies also found themselves being controlled by and subordinated more to state interest as the eighteenth century advanced.

THE TRADING COMPANIES

Mercantilism as a political-economic theory rested on the aspiration of developing and protecting long-term relationships with suppliers and customers, be they colonies or foreign buyers and sellers. How to do this without creating onerous costs for the state was an important question. An even more attractive question was how to do it in a way that created greater wealth for the state. The push outward by the European powers that began at the end of the sixteenth century and carried, in instances, all the way into the middle of the nineteenth, depended not only on policies like the Navigation Acts or the establishment of large navies to protect the sea lanes, but also on new forms of business relationships that could help overcome factors of time, money, and the ongoing changes in leadership and investors. The answer was a joint-stock company, a business structure that had roots in Italy but found especially welcoming attitudes in the Netherlands (the Dutch Republic) and the British Isles (especially in England and Scotland).[102]

The advantages of a joint-stock company were multifold. Being a long-term structure, it would not only outlast generations of investors but also "dispose continuously of a large stock of fixed assets." As had regulated companies, these companies could also receive particular rights from the government of the state, which included not just a monopoly on trading rights but, more important for this discussion, powers that were customarily held by the state—the right to make treaties, the right to make war against native peoples; the charters prohibited direct war against other European states unless permitted, and the power to build and maintain armies and navies. Limitations on war-making were sometimes facts more on paper than they were in actual practice. A trading company was an illustration of economy of scale, for its size and financial backing would cover the cost of their militaries and commercial ships in addition to the building of shipyards, warehouses, and other buildings as well as services that were necessary.[103] In fact, depending on the state to pay for all of these requirements would probably have been out of the question. The companies usually paid for the costs of their militaries and fortresses from their own resources "instead of being dependent on subsidies from a cash-starved metropolitan government."[104]

Given the fact many of the trading companies exercised powers commonly associated with states, one can fairly ask, what exactly were they—a state or a business? Edmund Burke's famous description of the British East India Company as "a state in the disguise of a merchant" has captured our imagination ever since.[105] While it is not this book's purpose to answer the question, its salience became especially important as the eighteenth century progressed, and it is important today as multinational corporations and other entities are seen as possessing the attributes of states. The decision, for example, of Denmark in early 2017 to appoint an ambassador to represent it and interact with leading information technology firms is an interesting example of the question again in play. Historians have disagreed on these same points in various ways. Andrew Phillips and J. C. Sharman have written that companies "were neither sovereign states themselves, nor were they extensions of their respective home states. Instead, they were hybrid actors without twenty-first century equivalents." Conceding their exercise of certain powers linked with states, they nonetheless conclude that the British and Dutch examples in particular "were also very definitely private companies, owned by shareholders and run for profit."[106] While he would not probably disagree with the assertion that these entities were companies, a prominent historian of the British East India Company, K. N. Chaudhuri, clearly argues for a closer link between this commercial venture and the political interests and aspirations of the state chartering it. In fact, Chaudhuri believes "the political overtones of the east India trade were indeed the strongest weapons in the armoury of those who argued for the continuation and strengthening of the commercial monopoly." It was politics and national interest, not profit, which drove the existence of these companies. "The organization and the conduct of the east India trade could not be strictly separated from the conduct of national foreign policy, and reasons of state dictated that the merchants should look to the government for a large measure of political support."[107] Both sides of the argument actually are important to understand the growing argument over the purpose of the British company in the mid-eighteenth century and the decisions as to what extent, if any, the company should have in decisions that affected the national interest of Great Britain.

Why and how that question developed requires a brief appreciation of the types of companies that existed and the specific reasons for their formation. The first one to appear, and an obstacle to the aspirations of others, particularly, was that of Portugal. Interestingly, but not surprisingly, as the Portuguese had little experience with such arrangements, it was not a joint-stock company. Like Spain and France, Portugal had an aristocracy of blood that had little use for merchants and traders and sought to keep them in their place.[108] These countries envisioned their companies as instruments of state power. The charter of the Companhia da India Oriental gave it control over the trade between Lisbon and India. It built its own ships, and it could charge for private commerce its ships carried. At the same time, these ships, which obviously were large, had to carry three hundred soldiers on them, thereby assuring their use to the interests of the state. The company responsible for trade with Brazil was supposed to provide military assistance to those Portuguese struggling against the Dutch West India Company in Brazil. By the end of the 1640s following the Peace of Westphalia, which also ended the Spanish campaigns in the Low Countries, the Portuguese felt threatened more than ever, since their Iberian neighbor was free to go after them. With Portugal lacking money in its treasury to fight the Spanish, as well as the Dutch, in the western Atlantic, King Joao IV agreed to the creation of a joint-stock company in relation to Brazil, which, he hoped, would alleviate the revenue problem and secure a dominant position in trade. However, the profits from trade would also support the construction of warships to serve as convoy escorts in the Atlantic against the Dutch. The Portuguese benefited from the Anglo-Dutch wars at this time, which required Dutch vessels to return to home waters, but, once the Portuguese were able to prevail over the Dutch in the western Atlantic, their West Indies company seemed to acquire a reputation for being too expensive and unnecessary. What had been a trading company was actually more of a state instrument used in periods of war or undeclared conflict. As a money maker, it did not share the economic success of its Dutch and English competitors in particular.[109]

A similar state-directed approach characterized the French companies. Louis XIV's brilliant minister, Colbert, oversaw the creation and direction of these—the French East India Company and West India Company in 1664, followed by the Compagnie du Nord (Northern Company), which was to challenge Dutch trade and dominance in the Baltic, and the Levant Company for the Mediterranean. Colbert, as Michael Howard writes, regarded these companies as armies to be used against the Dutch. This is not to say, though, that the companies treated commerce as a distant and irrelevant second; the charter of the East India Company (Compagnie des Indes Orientales) gave that company a monopoly of trade east of the Cape of Good Hope, control of Madagascar, tax exemption for ship building, and the power to designate envoys, declare war, and negotiate a peace. The French played a role, alongside that of the British in the early eighteenth century, in diminishing the Dutch position in the Indian Ocean and along the coast of the subcontinent itself. This collision of ambition of the British and French trading companies in India alongside the recurrent wars that broke out between France and Britain in Europe, North America, the Indian Ocean, and beyond would generate discussion, as will be seen, about the priorities of the two companies in relation to the objectives of their parent countries.[110]

Even if the Dutch East India Company was one of the leading examples of joint-stock ventures established arguably more for commercial gain than political advantage, it is important to remember that the Dutch, too, could follow a path tied more to state advantage than profit. This was arguably the case with their West India Company. Established in 1621, nineteen years after the East India Company, the company's initial focus fell partly on conducting privateering voyages against Spanish and Portuguese ships in the Western Hemisphere. Most of the time, the privateering did not generate the wealth the Dutch had expected, even if it did help erode the Portuguese and Spanish positions some, and in 1646 they decided to reassign privateering by the company to other parties. Otherwise, the Dutch endeavors in the Western Hemisphere did not pay off that well; the Portuguese were able to retake most of what they had lost to the Netherlands in Brazil, and, furthermore, the Dutch lost New Amsterdam in North America to the British. Defense of these colonies was beyond the resources the Dutch had—money or human. The islands they acquired in the Caribbean were not large enough to satisfy much of the European demand for sugar or other goods. As a setting for a mercantilistic strategy, the New World did not provide the Netherlands with the resources and money it wanted.[111]

The experience in the Indian Ocean and southeastern Asia proved very different. As we have seen in the context of privateering and naval power, the English in the early seventeenth century had been puzzled by how such a small country could surpass another that seemed to have most advantages to its side. Joyce Appleby in her history of capitalism quotes Daniel Defoe's observations about how the Dutch had made themselves "the Middle Persons in Trade, the Factors and Brokers of Europe." Societies dominated by aristocracies tended to regard the Dutch as uncouth, unclean, and uninteresting, but, even while Portugal still enjoyed a firm hold on trade in the Indian Ocean and southeastern Asia, the arrival of Dutch merchants in these waters by the end of the sixteenth century shook their confidence.[112] By 1602 there were enough trading companies trying to operate in Asia that the States General of the Dutch Republic founded the East India Company to control it. If a Dutch venture wanted to trade in Asia it had to be a part of the East India Company. What resulted was a "federal company structure" that had six regional chambers, including Amsterdam, Rotterdam, and Delft, that held their own capital and controlled their operations. The enticement was unlimited profit aside from a modest amount paid to the state. The magnitude of impact of this company can be found partly in the fact that in its first ten years approximately 8,500 men left the Netherlands on its ships; by the 1650s that would average 40,000 per decade.[113]

The Portuguese were clearly the targeted competitor of the Dutch company, but the target was mainly in commercial terms. The primary purpose of the company was trade, not colonization. The company could negotiate peace treaties and alliances, "wage defensive war," build fortresses, and raise an army and navy whose personnel took a loyalty oath to the East India Company and the States General. In 1621, after Grotius had written much of his argument supporting the right of the company to use reprisals against other ships and property for compensation, the company's new charter made an interesting alteration to the right to wage defensive war by adding that it could "make war and peace" against "indigenous powers."[114] The stress on defensive war could prevent attacks on Portuguese or other European state actors that might spark a conflict. However, the ability to wage war against indigenous or native people rested on assumptions and arguments Grotius and others had stated in their work; these were societies, or entities as such, that were beyond the realm of traditional government or sovereignty as then understood. Janice Thomson notes that the very stipulation of military power scared away some investors who wanted to concentrate solely on trade, but the overall number was not that many. A military presence and force were necessary to protect lanes of commerce, ports, and other installations—a concern clear to all. The military capabilities the Dutch did need often depended upon mercenaries recruited either from the region or from Europe. Spending for these military needs grew to as high as 70 percent of its capital as the company's business and reach expanded.[115]

The historical reality about Dutch company wars that emerged strayed somewhat from the charter, particularly when the interests of other European actors were in play. Defensive war certainly did not apply to the treatment of locations controlled by a rival company. As to the level of concern about war against indigenous peoples, it was not noticeable at first, but its implications became harder to ignore in the eighteenth century as the

British and French companies found their actions with local populations intruding more and more with national interest as seen in Paris and London. When the Dutch East India Company entered the Malay Peninsula and archipelago in 1619 it did find itself in conflict with its British rival. Faced with an imminent war with Spain, the Dutch reached a settlement with their British rival, which enabled the British to get a hold of a sizable percentage of the spice trade in turn for a commitment to the Dutch company to help pay expenses for a joint defensive fleet. Since the Dutch were at war with both Spain and Portugal from 1618 to 1648 almost anything their companies did against these two easily paralleled their government's policy. The Portuguese paid a particularly high price from Dutch East India Company attacks. Furthermore, company interests conflicted at times with national interests, as was evident in 1641 when the Dutch and Portuguese ratified a truce between themselves. Directors from both the East India and West India companies objected by noting the great gains they had made against their Portuguese competitors and the amount of resulting profit. Three years later the Dutch East India Company reminded the States General that the locations and possessions the company had taken in the East Indies were not conquests of the Dutch nation but the property of merchants. Dutch merchants could sell these to whomever they wanted, including enemies of the Dutch Republic.[116] Such an assertion of private interest over that of the state did not seem so out of place in the seventeenth century, when definitions of state and public were still evolving. Furthermore, the development of Dutch institutions and laws followed somewhat different paths than those of France or Great Britain, just to cite two states whose ascendance greatly affected the capabilities and future of the Dutch. The stance taken by the Dutch East India Company shared some of the same spirit of defiance against English laws expressed by some English colonial governors at about the same time for very different reasons. The conditions of the eighteenth century were going to change the balance between state and private actors significantly in much of the Atlantic world.

It is in the path of the English East India Company that one finds a growing tension between state and company that ultimately saw the subordination of the latter to the former. The tension was there from the beginning in 1601 when James I issued the charter for the East India Company. Janice Thomson notes it in her study of nonstate actors when she points out the Crown issued these charters in part because the company's revenues were not controlled by Parliament. Almost from the beginning there were private parties who wanted to participate in the monopoly enjoyed by the company but were unable to do so because of their lack of connections with the king. They pressed Parliament to secure their involvement, and after the Glorious Revolution in 1688 (the removal of James II and the installation of William and Mary), Parliament did obtain the power to determine a monopoly. The fact that the East India Company, along with other companies, was a political pawn of both the monarch and Parliament was going to figure prominently in the unfolding of events in the coming century.[117]

The company's primary purpose was trade. In fact, the charter issued by James I explicitly prohibited attacks on the Portuguese.[118] The company, as noted earlier, received a monopoly over trade in Asia. It received jurisdiction over English subjects in that part of the world, and, like its Dutch rival chartered a year later, the company could use force to defend outposts and trade and wage war against non-European peoples in its area of jurisdiction. It could establish new colonies in its region without London's approval. Negotiations and treaties with the Mughal emperor and other rulers along the coast of India quickly gained trade access for the company as well as the right to build warehouses in locations as dispersed as Bombay, Madras, and Calcutta. Its sea captains, in the tradition of strong powers held at sea, were in complete command of the ship, including cargo and crew. They sailed with a commission from the king (through the company) to wage war on suspicious ships. The company was "a government over its own employees and corporations."[119]

As a joint-stock venture, the company went to great lengths to protect and expand its position in the Indian Ocean and beyond. "Interlopers" were watched closely and often had their vessel and cargo seized and their claims for trading rights challenged. British North America was a recurrent source of these individuals, as seen in the case of Captain Kidd, and the presence of pirates claiming to be privateers and merchants trying to bypass the company monopoly led to a troubled relationship between the East India Company and the American colonies.[120] More significant for its future, though, was the company's attempt to expand its presence and the willingness to use armed force to do it—a course of action that would begin to raise eyebrows in London, especially after the Glorious Revolution and the increased review and authority over the company by Parliament. Since the company had the power to raise its own forces, which it did through the recruitment of mercenaries and use of local military units if available, it chose in 1686 to send an expedition against Bengal. It already had Bombay on the western coast, which it had acquired in 1667. Obtaining Bengal on the eastern coast required the company to go to war against Siam. Some have regarded the company's decision to go to war to signal "the moment when it turned away from its necessarily peaceful commercial objectives toward a misguided attempt at territorial dominion." This was a company war, even though it had the support of King James II, and its purpose served both company and British interests, as Siam was seen as a potential target for French interference in this region. At the same time, a successful outcome would enable the East India Company to expand its commercial presence, thanks to expanded trade and the establishment of more ports and warehouses for business and supply. The turn of events in the 1680s definitely enlarged the company's vision of itself. In 1689 the company issued a declaration of intent in India. The company's leaders in effect "must make us a nation in India. Without that we are but a great number of interlopers, united by His Majesty's royal charter, fit only to trade where nobody of power thinks it their interest to prevent us." Trade arguably remained the focus of the company, but such aspirations signaled that it was beginning to assume broader definitions of its place, role, and rights as a form of governing authority.[121]

Seventy to eighty years later one of the most famous of the critics of the East India Company, Adam Smith, offered a commentary that illustrated the question looming in front of both the company and the government in London. To what extent its declared aspiration to be a "nation" carried within it an understanding of sovereignty is unclear, but the East India Company, with its expanding control over parts of India and influence in others, was faced with that question. It certainly had many of the characteristics that one associated with the responsibilities of government—treaties, war, and coinage (a power it had acquired a few decades after its initial charter). Smith argued that "a company of merchants are, it seems, incapable of considering themselves as sovereigns, even after they have become such." They would still regard trade as their primary focus, with "the character of the sovereign as but an appendix to that of the merchant." Given Smith's dislike of mercantilism, it is no surprise that he claimed the merchants would strive to keep out all competition from the locations they governed. However, Smith continued with another observation that did comment accurately on what the East India Company had done decades before Smith wrote his critique. While being a merchant was "extremely respectable," it was a profession "which in no country in the world carries along with it that sort of authority which naturally over-awes the people, and without force commands their willing obedience. Such a council can command obedience only by the military force with which they are accompanied." Considering all factors, Smith worried that this pattern of rule by merchants "tends to make government subversive to the interest of monopoly."[122]

The East India Company had found it necessary to increase the size of its military forces significantly by the 1660s, when it created its first army from mercenaries and troops from the area around Bombay. A decade later it had its first regular military force composed mainly of men from the Indian principalities and surrounding region. After the elimination of competition from the Dutch, the company began to turn more to recruits from Europe, especially Swiss and German mercenaries.[123] Perhaps the company was not as dependent (yet) on the military instrument as Smith depicted it in the 1770s, but the requirement of larger military capabilities was something its originators had not envisioned at the beginning of the seventeenth century.

Proponents of stronger parliamentary control over the East India Company used the aforementioned characteristics alongside accusations of despotism, tyranny, and absolutism to criticize its ties with the monarchy—particularly the increasingly unpopular Stuart monarchy. Parliamentary forces wanted more control over the company and its money. After the change of monarchs, the gloves, one could say, came off. Critics accused the company of illegally seizing property, of creating an "arbitrary Admiralty court," of fighting an "unwarrantable war"—the war against Siam. William III began to consider terminating the company's charter. This resulted in a very convoluted set of events during the next few years that resulted, at one point, in three competing East India Companies! In 1695 Parliament chartered a Scottish company, but its life was short, and its one colonial effort, a colony of New Caledonia in Panama, which was part of a plan to develop a better route to India, proved to be a dismal failure. Parliament and King William III acted to create a new East India Company in 1698. For a short time it carried the name of the English East India Company while the old one was called the London East India Company. The competition that followed between the two was economically costly, and in 1709 the two were merged into the newly named United East India Company. The significance of these events was that Parliament now had stronger control over the company and its actions in Asia. The charter of the old company had operated under the authority and protection of God; the new one would function under the authority and protection of the monarchy and Parliament.[124]

The Peace of Utrecht had ended the Anglo-Dutch rivalry on the high seas and in the Indian Ocean. The East India Company nonetheless faced two large problems. One was the continuation of piracy by many indigenous actors in the region as well as the continuous arrival of "interlopers" in its commerce from Europe and the British Isles. The company expanded its naval capabilities and operations, which enabled it as well to enlarge its presence in India itself. As the company now operated under a charter offering government protection, it also began to urge British involvement in the affairs of the Indian Ocean and nearby waters. In 1721 the first East Indian Royal Navy squadron sailed into these waters. By 1715 the company had already requested that all outward-bound vessels leaving British ports receive royal commissions so they could act against pirates. Increased dependence on London was a double-edged sword; it increased both the company's power and presence in the Indian Ocean and made the company more dependent on government resources and direction.[125]

The second problem was the increased activity and presence of the French and the consequential placement of this competition in the Indian Ocean in the growing global rivalry between these two powers. As we know, the French Compagnie des Indes Orientales received its charter in 1664 along with the customary powers that other European trading powers held. However, the French company enjoyed additional advantages over its competitors—an interest-free loan, exemption from payment of taxes on shipbuilding, and special concessions on both imports and exports.[126] Initially, the French did not pose that much of a danger to their British competitors. The main French trading port was Pondicherry, located along the southeastern coast of India, in a region known as the Carnatic. The French lost the port to the Dutch in 1693 but regained it as Dutch fortunes waned. They began to cast their eyes on other key ports, including British-controlled Madras, also in the Carnatic. The arrival of Joseph Francois Dupleix in 1722 provided the French with the type of aggressive visionary they needed. While governor of Chandernagore, the French trading post located near the British one in Bengal, Dupleix administered over a threefold increase in French trade in just a decade and founded two more trading posts for his company in India.[127] In 1742 Dupleix moved to Pondicherry. He did so in the midst of an undeclared war between France and Britain that had broken out in Europe in 1740 but that would be formally declared only in 1744. Known as the War of the Austrian Succession, news of the actual declaration did not reach the Indian Ocean until 1745, where it first arrived on the French-controlled island of Mauritius. The company directors had instructed Dupleix not to enter into hostilities with the British, as the company was approaching bankruptcy and the royal palace feared France could not send troops to India in light of the scale of the European conflict, which was underway in the New World as well. Dupleix did propose to his British counterparts in India that there be no fighting east of the Cape of Good Hope. The British rejected this, and Dupleix agreed to the proposal of the French governor of Mauritius to try to take Madras from the British, which fell in 1746. Dupleix may have been angered by an attack by warships of the Royal Navy on French company vessels in the Indian Ocean. Meanwhile the British company found itself at war alongside its government as well.[128]

Both companies found themselves tied more closely to the aspirations and moves of their national governments, which became fully evident in 1748 when the Treaty of Aix-la-Chapelle ended the war and Madras was returned to the British. However, the end of formal conflict in Europe did not automatically carry over into other parts of the world: witness North America and, even more graphically, the continuation of hostilities between the two companies in India and the Indian Ocean. The informal hostilities that existed before 1744 now continued well beyond 1748. Each company continued its diplomatic and military campaigns (with European and British mercenaries and local military resources) to sway or dominate local princes to their side in spite of the efforts of the Nawab of the Carnatic to prohibit conflict in the areas he ruled. London and Paris were actually unaware of this fighting for some time, and on learning of it, they exchanged copies of the letters they had with India to prove the fact there was no government duplicity behind this. Dupleix in February 1751 wrote Paris that his efforts were "directed towards attaining for you vast revenues from this part of India and consequently placing the nation in a position to maintain itself here even when it may lack support from Europe." One of his British counterparts, Governor Thomas Saunders, who was in charge of one of the British posts, Fort St. David, was a little more regretful about the situation, noting "that if Europeans had not intervened in these affairs and had left Indian princes to resolve their own quarrels, that might have been infinitely more beneficial to trade." That said, French actions had made it "essential to thwart their designs lest their success render our situation worse during peace than in time of war."[129]

Neither government was pleased with the continuation of hostilities in India while a fragile peace held in Europe. A clear question arose as to what ultimate purpose such companies should serve—the gains of their investors or the interests of the nation-state. By 1754 both companies had brought themselves close to insolvency, thanks in part to the costs of military operations in India. A truce ended the conflict at ironically about the same time young George Washington was leading a small force from Virginia into southwestern Pennsylvania to examine French intentions there, which sparked yet another round of Anglo-French violence and served as a forerunner to the outbreak of the Seven Years' War in 1756. Dupleix returned to France in 1754, hoping to get the company to pay him for the sum of personal money he had spent to support some of the operations in India. The company did not do so, and on Dupleix's death creditors seized all his possessions to cover their debts.[130]

The future of the relationship between the East India Company and the British government was about to undergo a major change, and the financial hardship the company experienced in the years leading up to 1754 may have enabled some in its leadership to sense it. Up to this point in the eighteenth century the company had enjoyed the reputation of being a leading creditor for the government. As long as it "managed its affairs with tolerable competence, [it] had little to fear from Government intervention. The most that was demanded of it, as in 1730 and 1744, was a financial quid pro quo in return for the periodical review of its Charter." When the renewal occurred in 1744 the company had lent the British state amounts of money that contributed "significantly to its ability to fight and win a series of wars against rival European powers."[131] The economic hardship facing the company in 1754 was not enough on its own to generate a reassessment of the state's relationship with it, but it helped plant questions that figured prominently within several years. Holden Furber in his history of major trading companies in East Asia writes that "the British governing classes became convinced that the company's activities should be made to benefit the 'public' as well as the company and the servants. By the 'public,' these eighteenth century gentlemen mean the 'nation' in the sense which they understood that term." This benefit to the nation would be particularly important in helping reduce national debt.[132]

Clearly a position on private war, which the company conflicts were a variant of, was not completely in place. The company charters had limited what companies could do against other sovereign states in Europe, but even this had been loosely interpreted and enforced depending on circumstance and convenience. The informal hostilities that existed between 1740 and 1744 and, more so, those from 1748 to 1754 illustrated the difficulty of allowing a private war to continue while governments had negotiated an end to the public one. Of course, representatives of both companies would have disputed that if charges had been made with those terms. They thought they did operate with the consent and support of the state, as illustrated by their charters and arguably a past record that had tolerated hostilities against sovereign states by companies when it occurred beyond the Atlantic and Mediterranean worlds. However, that was going to begin to change within a few decades. As to war against indigenous peoples, the development of Western practice and law had so far drawn very distinct differences between the two by essentially claiming that native peoples did not hold and enjoy the same characteristics and rights of states. An emerging lesson, however, was that it was becoming ever more difficult to confine these wars to these peoples without having them spread into the state-on-state relationships of the major powers that were either behind them or parties in them.

From the 1760s until Parliament passed the East India Company Act of 1813, which ended the company's monopoly in trade, except in tea and its conduct of trade with China, the concern of the British government was less the fact that the company waged wars and more on the objective and convergence with British national interests. An indicator of the concern was the fact that the terms of the Treaty of Paris ending the Seven Years' War in 1763 that affected India were not negotiated by the French and British companies but by their governments. After the peace in 1754 the British had sent forces to the region to assist the East India Company. After the Seven Years' War began, representatives of the company inquired about their specific rights. Could they regain control of fortresses in India they had once had? Would their soldiers (most of them Indian) be able to get their share of the booty they had taken? The answers were only partly satisfying—yes to the return of fortresses, but only after royal consent—and yes to the possession of booty, but if British troops had been involved as well the distribution had to be between company and royal troops.[133]

Doubt was growing in London about the wisdom, indeed the strategic benefit, of allowing a company to manage trade, territory, and war. Arthur Young, a contemporary of Adam Smith and a known commentator on politics, economics, and agriculture, wrote in 1772 that "trade and the sword ought not to be managed by the same people. Barter and exchange is the business of merchants, not fighting of battles and dethroning of princes."¹³⁴ Young's observation raised a legitimate question about comparative company and state capabilities. The East India Company had made significant gains in India in 1763, as had the British in North America. The king's ministers were expecting more money from their major colonies or companies, wherever they were, to compensate for past costs and to help prepare for future expenses, and they wanted a stronger voice in the decisions made by these subsidiary units. Like the North American colonies, the East India Company had well-known interests and allies in London who opposed a number of these measures, but ultimately to no avail. William Pitt, now Lord Chatham, was a particularly strong advocate of legislation to require the company to pay some of its revenues to London in return for the retention of its authority in India. The framework might have remained at that, but reports of corruption and mismanagement in the company fed a call for more government oversight and control of the company. In 1773 Lord Frederick North, the prime minister, managed legislation of a Regulation Act that set forth closer government supervision of the company. The Crown now shared responsibilities for the appointment of several senior officials and paid their salaries. In turn, to avoid conflict of interest, these individuals were to refrain from engaging in commercial business or taking gifts from Indian representatives. North hoped this would be a temporary measure, subject to review in 1780, but war broke out in 1775 with most of the colonies in North America.¹³⁵

Prior to the American Revolution and the loss of thirteen of the North American colonies in 1783, most in London regarded British North America and the West Indies as the focus of key British interests. Yet, as H. V. Bowen, a historian of the East India Company during this period, notes, "there was nevertheless growing recognition of the different ways in which East Indian affairs bore ever more directly upon the nation's economic and military fortunes."¹³⁶ A series of wars between 1775 and 1782, initiated by Governor Warren Hastings, as well as more reports of corruption and irregularities, resulted in one more attempt to bring the company closer to London's wishes and interests. The India Act of 1784, initiated by William Pitt the Younger, who had begun his first ministry a year earlier, required the company to pay the government more money, and, more importantly, established a group of commissioners, soon called the Board of Control, that was to read and review all correspondence between the company and London and assume, for all purposes, responsibility over revenue, military, and civil policy in India while leaving the company as the administrator. Pitt had deemed the recall of the company charter excessive and unnecessary, as he hoped these reforms would prove adequate.[137]

Americans easily forget the fact that their revolution was part of a global struggle between France and Britain that was going to abate only temporarily for about a decade before resuming with first the governments of revolutionary France and then that of Napoleon. These latter wars were seen as wars of national survival by the British. In India, what had once been perceived mainly as private company wars, although with obvious dimensions of national interest, became wars where "national interest" was in play. Whether they were directly against the French or against Indian states did not matter that greatly. A major consequence of this assessment was that Britain needed to commit more of its forces into India and the surrounding ocean and, in so doing, also had to consider the merits of relying on company and Indian forces. Even in the 1780s King George III remarked to Pitt that "while the Army in India remains in such unfit hands as those of a company of merchants, I cannot expect any good can be done."[138] The Indian army in 1783 consisted of 100,000 men, of which 90 percent were native sepoys recruited and paid by the company and often commanded by Britons, who were also company employees. By 1805 the size of the army had increased to 200,000—a result in part of fear about Napoleonic operations as well as a decision to deploy the sepoys to locations beyond India where the company had commercial interests, such as Ceylon, Malacca, the Cape of Good Hope, and Java.[139] An interesting pattern was emerging in which colonial forces, like the company army in India, were kept proportionately larger and less demobilized during interludes of peace than British forces at home. The British suspicion of sizable standing armies did not seem to carry over into this setting.[140] There were other suspicions, however. The East India Company tried to equip its sepoys with better muskets and equipment and to train them in European-style formation and operations. Some wondered whether there was the danger of this being turned against the company and British control, but the British were becoming "mesmerized by [their] own military mythology, a combination of racial arrogance and past experience. At its heart was the belief that resolutely led white soldiers would always sweep all before them, regardless of the odds."[141] A growing fear about control over India and the company, the friction that developed between company and British forces, and disagreements between civilian and military figures in India added to the increased strategic focus London had on India and the conviction that the company and its military had to be under London's control.[142]

The wars against revolutionary France and Napoleon only reinforced this view. Pitt pressured the company to give the government money, which it did in what was known as the "Loyalty Loan." Reflecting on the size of the company's fleet and the problems the British were having with French privateers, one commentator noted that if the East India Company were treated as a naval power it would be the third largest in Europe[143] Belief in having the East India Company under control in foreign policy and war was hardening. Since 1769 a Crown plenipotentiary had been appointed so serve as a voice for the government in diplomatic matters in the Indian Ocean, but this measure had not proved very effective. North's Regulation Act in 1773 had enabled ministerial review of incoming correspondence from India. The continuation of company-initiated wars in the 1780s and 1790s, nevertheless, heightened worry about aggressive acts that did not serve British national interests. Pitt's India Act in 1784 had deemed "schemes of conquest and extension of dominion in India" as "measures repugnant to the wish, the honour, and the policy of this nation," and the law specified that the Board of Control and the directors of the company had to approve all wars except those fought for self-defense. However, practice in India did not necessarily comply with law. Governor General Richard Wellesley (the older brother of Arthur, the future Duke of Wellington who also served in India as a general) commenced another war to expand influence in India at the behest of the president of the Board of Control, Henry Dundas. Whether Dundas's support satisfied legal requirements is debatable. Other members of the board apparently did not think so, and they mounted a campaign that finally required Wellesley's return to Britain. The interesting point, though, was that Dundas had justified his support on strategic terms—increased British control of India—rather than the reasons tied just to the East India Company.[144]

Problems like these in the midst of a conflict with Napoleonic France, and in 1812 a much smaller one with the United States, could only reaffirm the desire to place the East India Company under direct state control. This occurred in 1813 with the Charter Act, which extended the company's charter but, as noted earlier, ended the company's monopoly of trade with Great Britain and the Empire. The Crown now had to approve the appointments of the governor general, the governor, and the military commander-in-chief. The Board of Control received full power of review of finances, and, most significantly, the territories controlled by the East India Company would now be held "in trust for His Majesty, his heirs, and successors." The state in the form of the monarch and Parliament were not in full control. While the company remained, there was no longer a government of merchants masquerading, as Burke saw them, as a government.[145]

The Sepoy Rebellion that began in 1857 ended the East India Company for all purposes, although it held on as a legal entity until 1873. In a bloody mutiny that should have tempered British certainty about the superiority of white troops—it did not, as Japan proved in 1941–1942—Parliament in 1858 approved the passage of government in India from the remnants of the East India Company to Her Majesty's government (Queen Victoria). India would come under the authority of a secretary of state, a government ministry that was equal to that of the Foreign or Home Offices. The Court of Directors of the East India Company held its last meeting in India House in London on September 1, 1858.[146]

The experiences of the European trading companies, in particular that of the British East India Company, had begun in a period when the distinctions between private and public were not well-defined. Their first century had paralleled the development and centralization of state authority in much of Europe. The second century and the first half of the third (the nineteenth century) had witnessed the expansion of state interest and control into the private arena because of a mounting certainty that the affairs within that arena had significant bearing for the welfare of the state, its ability to defend itself, and, most importantly, its effectiveness in asserting its interests and objectives in the international system. The companies had always been, in part, an agent of state interest, either as a source of revenue or a means of expansion that did not tap directly into national budgets. The emergence of states that had the resources, capacity, and institutions to muster wealth and create power believed it in their interest to do so rather than to rely as willingly on private actors—be they privateers or trading companies. If they remained, their futures seemed limited and increasingly narrow.

The trading companies and the subsequent assumption of their roles by states, if they lasted long enough and were successful enough to become potential rivals to state authority, had also helped to disseminate a set of laws and customs that had developed largely in the Atlantic world. How well this was done and to what degree it actually occurred is beyond the scope of this book, but as the nineteenth century began the European side of the Atlantic believed its influence and place was in ascent. The British had assuredly centralized portions of their expanding empire, thanks, in part, to granting independence to the most fractious segment in British North America, which became the United States. An unanswered question, though, was whether the Americans would follow in the path increasingly in motion in parts of Europe. The United States represented one of the most obstreperous parts of an empire that was now on its own. Whether it would feel the need to centralize authority along the pasts taken by its European counterparts was unclear. As to war itself, the Americans hoped to avoid it in the international arena and remained quite wedded, it seemed, to a highly decentralized system of volunteers and private actors like privateers.

4 DEFINING THE BALANCE IN A REVOLUTION AND THE CONSTITUTION

In the late twentieth century several legal scholars began a debate over the meaning of the marque and reprisal clauses in the US Constitution. The term is mentioned twice in Article I, which discusses the powers of the legislative branch in the US system of government. In Section 8, marque and reprisal is part of the "declare war" provision, specifically assigning to Congress the power "to declare war, grant letters of marque and reprisal, and make rules concerning captures on land and water." The topic resurfaces in Section 10 with the statement "no state shall enter into any treaty, alliance, or confederation; grant letters of marque, or reprisal." The purposes seem straightforward enough. Clearly declaring and going to war was a national matter, and the decision to do so and to use measures like marque and reprisal that had become commonly affiliated with war by the eighteenth century was significantly assigned to Congress and not the president. Gone were the independent, even defiant, acts of colonial governors that had been so problematic for London in the late seventeenth century. Made even more certain, it seemed, than the contemporary practice in Britain was the absolute dominance of the legislative system. Whereas Parliament had certainly asserted itself over letters of marque and reprisal, the Crown still arguably had a place in the issuance. The US president, it appeared, was at most an agent of Congress who would enforce US law and Congress's instructions.[1]

As undeclared war had become such a recurrent part of US policy by the last half of the twentieth century, scholars, legislators, and practitioners were focused not only on the matter of executive/legislative powers but even more so on the meaning of war and the exact relationship of marque and reprisal to it in the context of both 1787 and the situations confronting the United States in the Cold War and afterward. The ongoing arguments wanted to prove or disprove the control of Congress not only over declaring war, which seemed obvious, but authorizing it if the conflict were to be for whatever reason and purpose undeclared. As the Constitution contains no reference to undeclared war, proponents of this argument had to search for places where it could be inferred. Marque and reprisal could be the terms that answered that need. As we will see later, some scholars argued the term was in effect a label for undeclared war. A subset of this argument claimed the label embraced the type of measures that had become known as "covert operations" short of war. Other scholars, who were not necessarily advocating expanded presidential authority in war, observed that these judgments were ahistorical and neglected both the context and the meaning that the words *marque* and *reprisal* had in 1787. Preponderant evidence would favor the latter conclusions but not completely exclude the implications that late eighteenth-century language and practice might carry into the modern world.[2]

The plain fact is that the American colonists, just like their British counterparts, were acting in a world where the distinctions between private and public rights and powers, or the place of private right and power and state authority, were changing. At the risk of oversimplification, though, the Americans were behind the curve. They obviously understood they were part of an imperial system, but they could not easily perceive and understand issues from the perspective of those responsible for defining the objectives of the system, setting its rules and policies, and administering and maintaining its institutions and actors. Thus, as we have seen, early colonial governors, merchants, and ship owners had seen marque and reprisal largely in terms of the older meaning of reprisal—compensation of damages and claims as well as a source of revenue that could reward the owner and investor and likewise bring extra money into the treasury of the colony. The fact that colonial officials were sometimes the private actors as well added to the difficulty, as it had done in Britain and other European settings. This older understanding of marque and reprisal and privateering increasingly collided with one that wanted these measures to support the advancement of state interest and objectives. Captain Kidd had been on both sides of the Atlantic, and if the older perceptions and practices had survived he might not have dangled from a gallows in London, but the rules and motives of the actors within were changing and Kidd could not be tolerated.

TURNING TO MERCENARIES AND PRIVATEERS

To appreciate what the Americans faced in their revolution and the subsequent writing of the Constitution, it is helpful to understand the practices and institutions they had for their own defense. Contrary to what we might think, based on popular entertainment and even the words of the Declaration of Independence, British North America had not been able to rely much on defenders sent to its shores by orders from London. These were developments during the eighteenth century—first the enlargement of the Royal Navy and then the later deployment of British soldiers in the French and Indian wars. Defense had been very much a local and colonial matter. The British colonies simply used the militia model they inherited from their mother country—a form of universal compulsory service that required male citizens, usually between the ages of sixteen and sixty, to participate in the defense of the British state or colony.[3] No single system for militia existed among the colonies; in fact, each of the thirteen colonies that became the United States had its own variation. Nevertheless, four models with variations coexisted in the seventeenth and eighteenth centuries. They were:

1. Standing militia: Men who actually served under an obligation and who had to meet and train periodically with weapons they usually possessed. If called to duty, they often served for periods of three months.
2. Volunteer militia: Men often drawn from the above group who served in special units, such as artillery or cavalry, and who provided their own uniforms, horses, and, often, special weapons.
3. War volunteers: Men who volunteered for operations and other duties lasting longer than the customary three months. In some cases, depending on the colony, they might even be sent outside of the colony itself.
4. Involuntary servers: Men who might have been impressed into service. They often represented the poorer, more voiceless segments of the population. In instances colonies also just took men from the militias for additional or longer service.[4]

The duties and the quality of the colonial militias varied extensively. Fighting Indians was only one function; some militia had responsibilities in slave catching and other tasks. The historian John Mahon deemed the militia from the New England colonies as generally the best because mobilization through the "political township provided a compact base upon which military organization could rest." In addition, New England had a denser concentration of population, and, according to Mahon, benefited from a Puritan perspective on the shortcomings of human nature that made it emotionally easier to wage war.[5] If Puritanism was so influential, it may have provided one reason for the reluctance of colonial authorities to have their militias be in the presence of regular British soldiers, who began to appear in larger numbers in the mid-eighteenth century. Professional soldiers were moral reprobates in the eyes of some, and the standards of discipline they had to endure were not desirable.[6] British soldiers and officers in turn would come to regard many colonial militias and their commanders with condescension, amusement, and despair. As mentioned previously, service outside of the colony sometimes occurred, but this had to be accomplished through disputes between colonial governors and legislatures over the control and command of the militia. In arguments that precede modern ones between presidents and Congress, governors sometimes wanted to deploy militias beyond their traditional jurisdiction for local defense. Cooperation among colonies could provide for a better response to attacks by Indian or French forces. Douglas Leach, who studied colonial wars in North America for much of his career, points out that colonial legislatures usually viewed this question from the vantage point of their English predecessors and British counterparts. Militias were mainly for local defense. Not surprisingly, they sought to strengthen control over their respective militias. At the same time, the need for a larger perspective and understanding in order to build some unity among colonial efforts at defense was becoming more evident, even while colonies still protected their respective interests.[7]

Nearly all of the aforementioned militias were composed of private citizens who were serving under a widely understood obligation to a colonial government. These were not mercenary units placing their services out for hire. Although not a mercenary unit as portrayed in this book, one unit that offered an interesting combination of the private and public was known variably as the Military Association of Philadelphia, the Philadelphia Association, or just as the Associators. This was an all-volunteer group responsible for the protection of the colony of Pennsylvania. The colony's Quaker heritage discouraged active military defense and measures, although as seen in the previous chapter such pacifism did not necessarily conflict with privateering, which was good business. The Military Association organized itself in 1747. Because Pennsylvania did not even have a permanent militia act until 1777, "the Association," in the words of its major historian, "found itself as the only legitimate military leadership in the colony." Initially concentrating on artillery defense for Philadelphia—artillery being one weapon that was fairly available in the colonies due to the needs of harbor and port defense—the Military Association had a prominent role in Pennsylvania's early contributions to the revolution after fighting broke out in April 1775. Its leaders helped organize horse cavalry and a variety of infantry units that were in place before the 1777 militia law.[8]

Thanks to the Declaration of Independence, Americans automatically associate the word *mercenary* with the British and their use of mercenary troops that came predominantly from the German principalities. However, the colonies resorted to the recruitment of mercenaries too, in different ways. Probably the most frequent was simply the solicitation of alliances with various Indian tribes or groups with offers of bounty, goods, and favorable settlements after the peace. While both sides had political reasons for these arrangements in which a desire for or to be mercenaries usually ranked in a distant second place, the promises of goods and lucrative gain among these allies shared some features with the terms offered to mercenaries. This tactic found use among colonial officials, British authorities, and their French counterparts as the Anglo-French-Indian wars recurred throughout the eighteenth century. The practice continued on both sides—British and American—through the American Revolution.[9] The effectiveness of such alliances covered the spectrum from invaluable to counterproductive, as Native American allies had their own interests and objectives in relation to their ally as well as the opponent. Thus, what military writers today would describe as "unity of effort" was sometimes absent in these operations and campaigns.

The most troubling form of mercenary arrangement, or "outsourcing," especially to modern sensitivities, was the encouragement of scalp hunting, a practice that was becoming more common and popular by the beginning of the eighteenth century. The case for doing so rested partly on a shortage of manpower and money to wage sizable campaigns from colonial coffers. Underneath it was a distinction drawn between the rules of war for Europeans and their descendants and indigenous peoples in North America. If one could not fulfill needs by mustering militia, then other, more lucrative measures might induce men to take up the musket, hatchet, and knife, and collect scalps. "Scalp hunting," writes John Grenier, "offered American frontiersmen acting as *entrepreneurs de guerre* the potential for an economic windfall."[10] The motives were similar to those that had motivated the *condottiere* in Italy and Wallenstein's men during the Thirty Years' War; the problems were also just as abundant. During Queen Anne's War (part of the ongoing wars the British fought against Louis XIV), Massachusetts in 1702 offered ten pounds for every enemy Indian killed and scalped over the age of ten. That did not provide enough motivation, so the bounty went up to twenty pounds and ultimately one hundred pounds for an Indian male capable of carrying a firearm. The worth of a woman's scalp remained at ten pounds. This was certainly more money than one could expect from any colonial government for service alone in the militia; thus, militiamen could collect scalps as well. The practice customarily continued during periods of peace as well as war, and the use of it by both colonial and royal officials became wider with the occurrence of later wars against the French and their Indian allies.[11] The downside of such of such a practice requires little imagination. Scalps were scalps, and no one could easily distinguish among them by source (tribe, age, or gender). No documentation was required about the scalp or the victim; this was not like privateering with its laws and rules. Taking prisoners alive was not as financially rewarding, so one can imagine the likely action taken. Once this particular tactic was set into motion it was hard to stop, and it could undermine other objectives that colonial or government agents might seek.[12] The difficulties were just like earlier interactions with mercenaries and privateers. Whose interests were ultimately being served? Reliance on scalp bounties would continue well into the nineteenth century in some campaigns in the American West.

Whether on land or sea, officials in London and the colonies operated from considerations that were sometimes contradictory. London was obviously more attentive to imperial policies and interests, whereas colonial governors worried more about defense, competing territorial claims in the hinterland, and fulfillment sometimes of personal and financial ambitions, among other things. Lacking sizable resources, it was no surprise, then, that colonial officials frequently turned to private individuals to help advance these objectives, whether they were entrepreneurs in scalps or in commerce and privateering. By the mid-eighteenth century, governors retained more authority as to what they could do on land in contrast to the sea. Initiating operations against Indians was within their powers, but issuing letters of marque and reprisal now depended on sanction from the monarchy. The former, of course, were native peoples, while the latter involved actions against European vessels and states.[13] Events in the previous chapter demonstrate, nonetheless, how appealing privateering remained, even if it were more constrained by London than it had been in the 1690s or early 1700s. When King George's War began in North America in 1740 against France, Britain and its colonies found themselves in two conflicts in the New World—the other being the colorfully named War of Jenkins' Ear against Spain. Merchants and investors in a number of ports in North America saw attractive opportunities in privateering when they learned of King George II's authorizations. Nearly half of the privateers commissioned between 1739 and 1748 in British North America came just from New York and Newport, Rhode Island. Twenty-four percent originated in the British West Indies. Such port cities had the financial resources, shipping, and available pools of manpower to support privateering on the scale that occurred during these years. Carl Swanson, who has closely studied privateering during this war, estimates that American privateers took 829 vessels as prize from 1739 to 1748. The impact appears to have been especially hard on the French; for example, their commerce with the West Indies dropped by one-half in just two years (1743–1745). Fishing fleets sent to the waters off Newfoundland to help feed Catholic France took terrible losses at the same time. To claim that the British might have lost these conflicts without colonial involvement and privateering would be distorting, but London clearly welcomed and relied on the contributions made by the colonial privateers. Here colonial privateering had definitely helped advance imperial interests.[14]

MERCENARIES AND PRIVATEERS IN THE REVOLUTION

The sequence and impact of events that occurred between London and its North American colonies from the start of the French and Indian War in 1754 to the outbreak of fighting in Massachusetts in April 1775 carry far beyond the focus of this book, but it is critical to consider that their collective impact, whether it was the Albany Congress, the reactions to the Stamp Act and other British provisions, or the two Continental Congresses, nurtured a realization that no single colony had the strength (political or otherwise) to challenge Britain's policies and capabilities. Some form of joint collaborative action had to occur, whatever the means taken, to increase the prospect for success against the British.[15] If circumstances escalated to actual conflict, it would be necessary to consider and clarify the proper role of private parties and actors and their relationship with the colonial governments and any central body of government that might take shape. Thanks to their own history and the increasing intrusion of British control, the colonials had a fairly well-founded understanding of what privateering entailed. The term *mercenary*, however, appears to have been less well understood, in spite of the experiences colonial governments had had with Indian allies, scalp hunters, and other actors recruited through such inducement.

One year into the revolution itself, we find use of the word *mercenary* in one of the strongest accusations made against King George III in the Declaration of Independence. The charge is as follows: "He is at this time transporting large Armies of foreign Mercenaries to complete the works of death, desolation and tyranny, already begun with circumstances of Cruelty and perfidy scarcely paralleled in the most barbarous ages, and totally unworthy the Head of a civilized nation." Considering the record of mercenaries in some conflicts going back to the Renaissance and Reformation, incidents that the educated authors of the Declaration assuredly knew about in instances, this is quite a sweeping statement. Indeed, the emotional impact of such an accusation may have been much of its intent, for *mercenary* had become a very inflammatory word.[16] To have endured the accusations of unjust treatment against American subjects enumerated in the Declaration was hard enough, but to be confronted by foreign troops serving the king was a demonstration of contempt and dismissal for the rights of British subjects. The emphasis placed on mercenaries stands out even more when one considers that neither the Constitution nor the debates formulating it mentioned them. Perhaps this was because, as the legal writer Matthew Underwood observes, many during the time of the revolution and the constitution that followed tended to regard standing armies and mercenaries as almost the same. This does not seem so on reading the Declaration, where a separate reference is made to the king's use of standing armies in the colonies without their legislative consent. Yet, in debates related to both documents there are multiple cases where writers and speakers used the terms interchangeably. As the Constitution in 1787 would reflect such a strong suspicion of standing armies (see later in this chapter), it would not be surprising that commentators treated the two as essentially the same.[17] Also, the world of the late eighteenth century was not that far removed from the time when armies had become professional and soldiers were hired for pay. The earlier discussion in Chapter 2 highlights the fact that the distinction between mercenary and soldier had not been clear well into the seventeenth century and arguably beyond. Thus, the conflation of the two words was not completely on purpose. The authors of the Declaration, however, saved their special animus for mercenaries, as they were a particular type of professional soldier—in effect almost the lowest of the low—who could be found in the ranks of a standing army.

Britain's use of mercenaries was not exceptional in the world of eighteenth century warfare, and the role that troops from the German states played was hardly surprising given the German foundations of the House of Hanover in London. The reasons were straightforward. Britain needed them to supplement the soldiers it had from the British Isles and the Loyalists in North America. The British army, keep in mind, served a state that had its own suspicion of large standing armies, and, consequently, it was not that large. Total strength was about 29,000 troops, of which 10,000 were already in British North America when the revolution started in 1775. The second-largest garrison, of 7,700 men, was at Gibraltar. After the costly victory at Bunker Hill in July 1775, London realized it needed additional troops to fight the colonials. Estimates made by the War Office indicated that perhaps only 5,000 troops could be raised from the British Isles within the coming year.[18] Domestic resources simply could not meet the requirements. Interestingly, the East India Company was unwilling to suspend its own recruiting in the British Isles, and the government, unless Parliament had acted, lacked the power to make it stop. Removing troops from Scotland and Ireland raised concerns about keeping control and collecting revenue. An early hope of obtaining Russian troops from Catherine the Great proved fruitless, so London turned to the German states of Hesse-Cassel and Brunswick for soldiers. The original plan was to send them to Ireland in order to redeploy the British forces there to North America, but authorities in Ireland objected. In January 1776 Britain signed treaties to obtain 18,000 German troops to solve its personnel needs. Ultimately, as many as 32,000 German troops may have fought against the Americans.[19]

The Americans would use mercenaries, too, although not as sizably as Britain did. The recruitment of foreign officers by American agents, such as Benjamin Franklin in Paris, to serve with the American army provided important skills in drill, logistics, and other tasks—skills that the British already had on hand with their officer corps. The Americans continued as well the practices they had inherited from the colonial period, such as the use of Indian allies. Given the recurrent need to remuster their armies, due to the wish or need of men to return home to farm, or just the result of desertion, the Americans tried to encourage German mercenaries to desert through various incentives. Approximately 3,000 of them did, but generally not until the closing part of the war when a favorable outcome for the British looked less certain. Rates of desertion by the German mercenaries were no higher than found in German regiments fighting in Europe during the same time.[20]

The incidents at Lexington and Concord were followed within weeks by a convening of the Continental Congress in May 1775 and the designation of the militia gathered around Boston as a Continental Army commanded by George Washington. There was an immediate need for some type of naval presence to monitor British activity in Boston harbor and in nearby waters. Also some supplies for the Americans arrived by water. Yet, the thought of being able to mount any type of effective naval challenge to the British seemed almost ridiculous. Taking the steps to do so required actual illegal activities. Raising militias for defense was a long-recognized right for the colonies, but creating a navy to fight the Royal Navy was a clear step over the line. The British naval historian Sam Willis has written "that the overt establishment of a navy would have been nothing less than a tacit declaration of independence," which would have ended the remaining hope, at least in summer 1775, of reconciliation.[21] Building commercial ships posed no legal or technical problems. Shipbuilding was actually the largest industry in British North America; in fact, the American colonies had built about one-fifth of the entire British merchant fleet.[22] The admiralty had prohibited the construction of warships in the colonies, and to add a certain blanket of security against the conversion of merchant vessels into warships the British had prevented the casting of cannons or larger anchors.[23]

Faced with these obstacles and considerations, it is no surprise that the initial American naval response was decentralized, small-scale, and partly dependent on the contributions of private actors. True, in October 1775 Congress created a naval committee that authorized the purchase and arming of a few vessels, thereby commencing the beginning of the US Navy. The Continental Navy had forty-one ships in service during the revolution, and more than half of those sank or were destroyed. It witnessed heroic actions by officers like John Paul Jones; yet, alone, its impact on the outcome of the revolution was not decisive. Consider that the British used 170 vessels just to evacuate troops and Loyalists from Boston, and one appreciates the disparity in strength and numbers.[24]

However, months before Congress took these steps for a navy, colonies had begun to create navies of their own. In June 1775 Rhode Island commissioned two armed vessels, the largest of which had ten cannons and a crew of eighty. Massachusetts followed in August with two ships of its own.[25] A month earlier Congress had authorized each colony to arm and operate vessels at its own expense to protect harbors and sea lanes. If they were not doing so, most colonies commenced doing so through maritime committees in their legislatures. By 1776 eleven of the thirteen soon-to-be states had their own navies. [26] Navy was perhaps a grandiose term for some of these efforts. A lot of the vessels were boats, row galleys, and barges that were best for shallow waters. There was really no "blue sea" threat to speak of. Pennsylvania, for example, was the first state to try to build a specially designed vessel—galleys that were armed with one cannon in the bow. They were to defend the estuary of the Delaware River. Virginia, partly through the inspiration of Patrick Henry, followed a similar path in the construction of galleys to protect the James River. Virginia, in fact, would have the largest number of vessels of any state in its navy, with over thirty vessels by 1779. However, its navy proved largely ineffective, which was painfully demonstrated when the British burned its shipyard and sank a number of vessels in 1781. Its neighbor Maryland had one of the larger vessels in the state navies, a merchant ship converted into a frigate armed with eighteen six-pound cannons and two four-pound ones that actually took several prizes before the ship received a commission as part of the Continental Navy. Connecticut's navy tried to protect the deep water harbor of New London, using among its vessels the Oliver Cromwell, whose name must have been a poke in the king's eye.[27]

All together, these efforts paralleled the type of semi-independent and, at times, fully free-willed actions that the various states took during the American Revolution. As commander, George Washington could not respond to each and every threat and incursion the British posed. He had to prioritize based on the level of strategic importance and available resources. There were instances when states did act on their own, as was the case with a disastrous invasion of Maine by Massachusetts that the Congress refused to fund. Rhode Island also had to oppose the British invasion of Newport in 1776 without any assistance.[28] It is hard to imagine that any of these state naval efforts posed serious operational, much less strategic, threats to the British. Cumulatively, though, they added to the diversity of challenges the British faced and no doubt required a dispersal of resources.

Operating without a navy by late July 1775, Washington still had to take steps to try to mount a challenge to British dominance in the waters around Boston and beyond. His decision to lease seven merchant vessels, also done by some of the state navies, became part of a wider effort to use private actors and their ships against the British. Leased to the "United Colonies," these ships were to seize vessels going to and from Boston in support of British operations. Technically, these were not privateers, and if they had been, the "United Colonies" still lacked any admiralty courts to deal with seized property. That may have been fortuitous, although it meant Washington had to deal with much of the paperwork himself involving claims. The *Hannah* was the first of these armed merchants ships to go out, and the first vessel it seized belonged to a member of the Continental Congress. Washington realized the ship and its cargo had to be returned to its owner. The *Hannah*'s luck did not seem to start well, as the next seven ships seized resulted in damages being paid to American owners along with the return of the ship.[29] Seizing ships and privateering had never operated with complete certainty, and this had to have been vexing for the new commanding general.

While Washington was handling these actions, others had begun to initiate the first steps of privateering—the measure that would ultimately cause more damage to the British and their Loyalist allies than the Continental Navy or the state navies. Massachusetts had chosen to begin issuing letters of marque and reprisal in November to merchants and supporting investors who wanted to act against the British. Some had not even bothered to wait for this cover and had sailed on their own—riskily placing themselves into the category of pirates. Drafted by Elbridge Gerry, and praised by John Adams as "one of the most important documents of the Revolution," the law claimed the colonial charter for Massachusetts gave it the authority to issue such letters to private persons "for the defence of America." To strengthen its claim on this practice, Massachusetts established three admiralty courts to adjudicate the claims. Like their colonial and European predecessors, the captains had to post a bond, promise to obey the laws of Massachusetts, and present documentation on the circumstances of the capture and the contents of the cargo.[30]

Faced with merchants throughout the colonies who suffered losses at the hands of the British and who wanted to compensate themselves at the expense of the British, Congress agreed on March 23, 1776, to establish a national policy for issuing letters of marque and reprisal. In itself this was a significant gesture, for here was a body representative of those in rebellion, but still a nonstate, taking an act reserved to states—the issuance of commissions to allow nonstate actors (read private persons) to commit violent acts on the high seas. This step, along with the decision to open ports to foreign trade, was suggestive of how close the colonies were moving toward independence and how far they had stepped out of the imperial mercantile system they had operated within.[31] By means of this first law and a second one legislated in early April, Congress set forth a regulated system for privateering that, it hoped, would be restricted to commercial warfare that would damage British interests enough and bring sizable revenue to the coffers. Blank commissions went from Congress to the states for letters of marque and reprisal, which the states completed and provided to qualified applicants. Getting a commission was not cheap; the owner or owners had to post a bond of $5,000 for any vessel below 100 tons and $10,000 for each vessel above that tonnage. This was not an endeavor for the casual small investor. However, both they and the crews recruited hoped the reward would prove rich, for stories circulated of privateers who had made fortunes after just a single voyage. Already there was recognition of the fact such a potential reward could draw sailors away from the fledgling continental or state navies, so at least one-third of the crew had to be men of the land rather than the sea.[32]

The clear purpose here was not to destroy British shipping—military or commercial. The privateers were not to be sea raiders, like the German raiders who caught so much attention during World War I. The armed privateers were to seize ships owned by "British inhabitants." Neutral vessels were off limits. Privateers could not destroy the ship or its cargo but had to bring it into a port for legal adjudication of the seizure and the cargo. Humane treatment of the captured crew was required; evidence to the contrary could result in forfeiting the bond payment and other forms of legal liability. Continental Navy vessels could take prizes as well and bring them into court, but whereas the privateer and crew received all the value of the prize, minus a deduction for court expenses, the navy had to turn over two-thirds of the prize to the Continental Congress. Congress worked to watch these actions closely, and it modified the 1776 law during the course of the revolution. Interestingly, in 1780 it extended marque and reprisal to captures on land as well, and it did try to harden the treatment of the British, but it never abandoned the premise that this was commercial war and that legal process stood at the center of the practice of privateering.[33]

Destruction of British ships could hardly have been a realistic objective anyway. Privateers were more interested in making a profit than in destroying an enemy ship. A Continental Navy vessel could be expected to stand and fight, but the recourse of the privateer was either to avoid action or to sail away and get out of range. Few privateers had the firepower to take on a British frigate, much less a ship of the line (colloquially, "line-of-battle ships," the top-tier warship of the day) with 74 or more guns, which would have simply blown them out of the water. Matching the gunnery skills of the crews of British warships was something privateers could neither do nor wanted to try. Consequently, the ideal privateer ship was built for speed and did not carry large numbers of cannon, even while it had a sizable crew at times to manage both the captured ship or ships and its own vessel. Enemy warships, aside from the ship itself, did not carry the types of cargo and prizes owners, captains, and crews wanted. Knowing these attributes, officers of Continental and state naval vessels were not enthusiastic about joint operations with privateers. They did not take orders well, they preferred to act independently, and discipline on board was often lax in contrast to the navy. An example of these limitations was in the invasion of Maine by Massachusetts in 1779 against the British installation on the Penobscot River. With forty ships in total, of which twelve to sixteen were privateers, this was the largest amphibious operation by the Americans during the entire war. The commander of the naval side of the operation was hesitant to support an attack by the ground forces, as the privateers, reluctant to endanger their ships, urged him to delay. When the British brought reinforcements, the privateers hastily left the scene.[34]

Obviously, another deterrent to close engagement of the British by American privateers was the treatment the captain and crew would receive if taken prisoner. General William Howe, the commander of British forces at Boston, had lamented in December 1775 that he currently could not distinguish in treatment of prisoners taken on land or water. At that stage of the war Howe was much more worried, somewhat mistakenly perhaps, about what the colonials might do to the British on sea than on land. He wanted a change in British law, which Lord North succeeded in accomplishing in early 1777 with language that designated those taken on the high seas as pirates. In principle, this meant privateers could be hanged, and, although this apparently did not occur, the prospect of it, and the reality of harsh treatment in British prisons or prison ships, served as a powerful caution.[35] The British in turn also resorted to privateering to support their own operations. In March 1777 Parliament allowed the commissioning of privateers. As had their Massachusetts counterparts, some British merchants in the West Indies had commenced such activities on their own in late 1776. Now, they, too, had legal cover from Parliament. In the last five years of the revolution, British privateers appeared in large numbers, having obtained their commissions in the West Indies, Halifax, or in British-occupied New York. Exact numbers are hard to determine; Robert Patton has estimated the figure at 2,600, which, if true, surpasses many numbers used for the total number of American privateers (see below). The number of prizes they took is also unclear, but scholarship suggests they concentrated more on foreign shipping, such as that of the French, in both European and Caribbean seas.[36]

There was no problem finding crewmen for the privateers. The possibility of capturing a rich vessel and its cargo offered a powerful incentive to men who otherwise would have had to depend on whatever the navies paid them. It was hardly surprising that earlier American privateers drew heavily from the ranks of sailors in the port, thus creating a competition with the navies for manpower. After a couple of years men from professions on land became common recruits out of the same hope to make money in amounts they could not imagine on land. Keeping men on navy ships was a constant challenge because it was so easy to move from the status of a navy sailor to that of a privateer's crewman. Continental Navy commodore Esek Hopkins urged the assembly of Rhode Island to suspend the recruitment of crews for privateers until the navy's demands were met. It failed because too many members of the assembly had a direct stake in privateering themselves.[37] Naval officers disliked the fact their crews were paid in paper money, whose value was notoriously questionable, while privateer crews received prize money in the form of specie. Deserters from both the navy and army sometimes joined privateers to take advantage of the promised money. An effort by John Paul Jones and others to get Congress to reduce the amount of prize money owed to Congress by naval warships from two-thirds to one-half helped but did not end the problem. Even naval officers were not immune to such temptations, and many had seen service first with a privateer.[38]

We should never forget that while General Washington, the Continental Congress, and young state governments viewed privateering as a private means to both complement and supplement other military efforts, the people who owned the ships and invested in the project to outfit them, acquired weapons, and recruited a crew regarded this as a business. It was an investment made out of hope for gain. Privateering was, in fact, a dimension of commerce itself. The cargoes seized belonged to the owners, captains, and crew, and they sometimes sold the contents at very good prices. In a time of war, privateering provided a source of supplies for people in the states. Nor should it be any surprise to find that merchants turned to privateering as a substitute when the channels and contents of trade dropped; what one lost in one area of business might be compensated in the other.[39]

Just a brief consideration of the experience of Robert Morris shows the fascinating aspects of involvement in the different dimensions of privateering and the war. Morris had begun as a merchant in Philadelphia who would ultimately be cast in public imagination as the financier of the American Revolution. In 1776 he was a member of the Secret Committee on Trade in the Continental Congress as well as the Secret Committee on Correspondence, an antecedent for what we would regard as a foreign ministry or the State Department, as the United States had no executive officer at this time. In September 1776 in a letter to Silas Deane, the American agent in Paris, Morris commented on how people were making so much money quickly in privateering, a "business which I confess does not square with my principles." Within three months, though, Morris's principles had undergone some adjustment, as Morris explained in a long letter to William Bingham, an agent Morris, through the Secret Committee on Correspondence, sent to the French colony of Martinique in the Caribbean. Morris had obtained a commission for Captain George Ord to command a privateer. Morris had very clear notions about the number of cannon and the size of guns on the ship, but Bingham was to purchase and outfit it. The ownership of the ships was to be divided equally among Morris, Bingham, and Cotiney de Prejent, who accompanied Captain Ord to meet Bingham. Morris stressed, "You must observe I have not hitherto had any Concern in privateering and even at this day my Partner Mr. Willing objects possitively [sic] to any Concern. Therefore this has no Connection with the business of my House but is totally distinct and on my own Account." Morris also explained the circumstances that had brought his change of heart on privateering. Acknowledging his original desire to stay out of it, "but having had several Vessells taken from me and otherways lost a great deal of my property by this War, I conceive myself perfectly justifiable in the Eyes of God and Man to seek what I have lost from those that have plundered me."[40] Clearly Morris regarded privateering in both the context of traditional reprisal and as a private measure permitted by governments during times of war. His unease revealed conflict about its propriety, but this misgiving ultimately had to be secondary to the right of compensation for damages and a realization this action could benefit the cause of the revolution, which is apparent in the comments Morris makes about British successes in New Jersey and eastern Pennsylvania.

Support for privateering went up and down with the course of the war and the level of complaints by those who thought it actually impaired the war effort because of its attraction to potential sailors for the navy and the temptation it posed for others to desert. In 1776 support may have been at its peak; a year later some accused it of creating so much greed that it hampered the war effort. Yet, when British actions against American commerce made items scare and expensive, the calls for privateers and investors to support them climbed again.[41]

Assessing the success of privateering and its impact on the outcome of the American Revolution is not easy. Numbers fluctuate in terms of the amount of American-commissioned privateers as well as the count of British ships seized and the value of their cargoes. American privateers operated obviously in Atlantic waters, but two of their favorite areas of activity were in the Gulf of St. Lawrence, where merchant vessels and fishing craft were vulnerable thanks to the foggy weather that sometimes shrouded the privateers; and in the West Indies, where the American could strike at the ships in the valuable sugar trade. There, however, they had to keep careful watch for the Royal Navy's West Indian squadron.[42] A valuable boost doubtlessly came from France in 1777 when it announced its intention to abrogate the Peace of Utrecht of 1713 in which both Britain and France had agreed not to allow their ports to harbor enemies of the other country. American privateers could now make use of French ports alongside the French privateers already operating there.[43] If one uses the records of the Continental Congress, 1,696 privateering vessels operated with commissions it had provided. In his study of the US Navy and privateering during the revolution, James Volo estimates that American agents, like William Bingham, operating in Europe and the West Indies, may have issued enough commissions to raise the total figure to around 2,000. Massachusetts on its own may have issued as many as 1,000 commissions, and several other states issued them as well. Connecticut may have had as many as 500 privateers at sea in 1781. Thus, the total number is elusive.[44] Using the records of Lloyds of London, historians have the Americans capturing 3,087 British vessels; however, the Royal Navy was able to recapture 39 percent of these, which still left 2,208 ships and their cargo taken by the Americans into ports as prizes. Their value may have amounted to $18 million, although Nathan Miller points out this could be low as one American privateer, the *Rattlesnake*, took over $1 million of prizes just on a single cruise. No other American privateer matched that, but there were well over a thousand more on the high seas.[45] It was this monetary cost, more than the number of British merchant and naval sailors taken prisoner—maybe as high as 16,000—that figured into British reactions. Certainly, this was not enough to have decided the fate of the war, but the cost of these losses was high enough to make the British feel them and take notice. Merchants in the British West Indies complained about their vulnerability to American privateers, and insurance rates rose significantly. Even if the ship were in a convoy, by now a common practice on the high seas, merchants and owners had to pay a rate 30 percent higher than it had been in peacetime. The fact that the American Revolution was part of a global war Britain was fighting against Spain and France should not be forgotten. The American theater, its costs and losses, drained human, military, and monetary resources that would have been used elsewhere. Privateering had not been decisive, but the commercial war as part of an overall American strategy helped to erode British capabilities and willpower.[46]

WHO SHOULD CONTROL THESE PRIVATE INSTRUMENTS OF WAR?

Writing to General Horatio Gates on March 23, 1776, John Adams knew that the revolution now underway had to take on more aggressive acts, both politically and militarily, if it had any chance of success, and he fully believed privateering had to be part of this escalation. "We have hitherto conducted half a war; acted upon the line of defence, &c., &c.; but you will see by to-morrow's paper that, for the future, we are likely to wage three-quarters of a war. The continental ships of war, and provincial ships of war, and letters of marque and privateers, are permitted to cruise on British property, wherever found on the ocean."[47] One could parse Adams's words for pages, since his view of what contemporaries regarded as commercial warfare illustrates he did not regard such measures as full-scale conflict, but Adams was part of a world that could still see the coexistence of peace between governments alongside a continued or newly initiated series of acts of force against commerce that preceded actual war. However, even he knew that "three-quarters of a war" was a debatable stretch of this relationship between acts against commerce and real war. Unlike some modern historians who have treated the support of privateering as tantamount to an act of independence, Adams did not. "This is not independency, you know. Nothing like it." Adams did not seem ready for that, and the word "independency" itself was "a hobgoblin of such frightful mien, that it would throw a delicate person into fits to look it in the face."[48] Twenty days later he told his wife Abigail the same thing. "Independency" was a "Government in every Colony, a Confederation among them all, and Treaties with foreign Nations, to acknowledge Us a Sovereign State, and all that." When it might happen was unclear. "Perhaps the Time is near, and perhaps a great Way off."[49]

However, Adams knew the steps taken to independence were imminent and necessary, even if it still pained him a little to consider the action. To Gates in the same March letter he observed, "The success of this war depends on a skilful steerage of the political vessel." The challenge rested in doing the very things he had mentioned to Abigail. "The difficulty lies in forming particular constitutions for particular colonies, and a continental constitution for the whole. Each colony should establish its own government, and then a league should be formed between them all." Thinking of the international implications of these developments, Adams claimed, "Thirteen colonies . . . together in a faithful confederacy, might bid defiance against all the potentates of Europe, if united against them."[50]

By July 1776 the Americans knew they had to take action to redefine their relationship with Britain and to establish a legitimate presence in the international community. If the revolution were to succeed, the newly independent states had to receive assistance and some form of recognition. The revolution against British authority was unprecedented, but, in doing so, the Americans were not rebelling against the international system of custom and law in which they lived and operated. They wanted to be part of that, and they wanted the rights that it offered. Eliga Gould in his study of the American Revolution and the international system has observed "that independence was a condition that required the consent of other governments, not something that they could achieve unilaterally (or solely on their own terms)."[51] These were conditions Adams had clearly understood in his letters to Gates and Abigail. Without independence and the recognition and support of others, the United States were (and in this case and context the plural is still technically correct) helpless.

One of the required subsidiary actions of independence had direct bearing on use of private instruments of war. The evolving body of international law that existed governed the actions of states and offered some protection as well to official state actors. Distinctions between combatants and noncombatants were coming into place.[52] However, as British treatment of Highland Scots in the 1740s or British and colonial treatment of Native Americans in repeated episodes showed, the limits on conduct of war could still leave categories of people at the mercy of state actors. By the time of the American Revolution, a prevalent view had developed in the Atlantic world that the real outrages of war occurred at the hands of pirates, privateers, mercenaries, and native peoples who operated outside the boundaries of state-to-state war. Some attempts were made to bring some of these under the guidance of law. During the 1750s Britain extended coverage, thus the requirements of the articles of war, to the British and colonial militia and private ships.[53] We have seen examples of the British and other Europeans, along with the Americans, requiring adherence to law in granting commissions to privateers before and during the American Revolution.

The point here is that if the Americans, whether the Continental Congress or the states, were going to be so dependent on privateers, they had to place them under better control and create some line of accountability. The Continental Congress began this in March and April 1776 with the release of commissions to the colonial or state governments. The success or failure of such measures, of course, remained for the future. If such control did not occur, privateers would basically resemble pirates and Indians—actors who in the eighteenth-century mind dwelled beyond the desired boundaries of law and standards of international conduct. Each European state that had relied on privateers in war or letters of reprisal during peace had faced mounting difficulty in controlling these actions in ways that served the interests of the state. The Americans themselves had been at the receiving end of this in the late seventeenth and early eighteenth centuries because most of the colonies had become hives of privateering and/or pirate activity. To establish standing in the world, recognition, and support the United States had to have these practices under control—preferably at a national level rather than in the statehouse of thirteen somewhat different states.[54] Otherwise, who would want to deal with this new country?

In less than two weeks after the Declaration of Independence, the Continental Congress had a draft of Articles of Confederation in front of it. The draft simultaneously illustrated how far thinking had evolved in assigning the uses of force and war at a national level and how far this same process still had to develop to place these matters securely at that level. The document's full name, the Articles of Confederation and Perpetual Union, attested to the desired permanence of the newly independent association. Yet, the description of "a firm League of Friendship with each other" pointed to the powers retained by each colony or state. More than an alliance, but not yet a unified nation-state, the draft spoke of "their common Defense, the Security of their Liberties, and their mutual and general Welfare, binding the said Colonies to assist one another against all force offered to or attacks made upon them or any of them." None of the colonies could enter into a treaty with a foreign state or with one another "without the Consent of the United States assembled."[55]

The resources and capabilities of defense were left at the state (or colony) levels. Colonies could not keep standing armies during periods of peace "except such as Number only as may be requisite to garrison the Forts necessary for the Defence of such Colony or Colonies." Each colony was expected to "keep up a well regulated and disciplined Militia." Clearly no place existed for mercenaries. War itself operated in the same confines as treaties. No colony or combination of colonies could engage in war "without the previous Consent of the United States assembled." An obvious exception was if "the Colony or Colonies be actually invaded by Enemies." An additional circumstance, which is interesting in light of more recent controversies in US policy and international law, permitted war if the colony "received certain Advice of a Resolution being formed by some Nations of Indians to invade such Colony or Colonies, and the Danger is so imminent, as not to admit of a Delay, till the other Colonies can be consulted." Whether this meant "preventive" or "preemptive" attack, to use terms from modern international discussion, was not clarified, although arguably the language of the draft leans in the direction of "preemptive" measures. Written eleven years later, the Constitution contains no explicit reference to "imminent threat," as the writers of that document took extra measures to assure that the initiation of war was a congressional matter and not something that could be taken by any state.[56]

Commissions for privateering and the issuance of letters of marque and reprisal were now solely instruments used during times of war. The long-standing practice and the surviving legacy of reprisals as an act rightly taken by a private party to seek compensation for damages during peacetime was no more. This early draft of the articles firmly closed the door on this option; private wars on the high seas against private parties and foreign vessels during times of peace were now past. The phrasing of the draft language left little doubt: "Nor shall any Colony or Colonies grant Commissions to any Ships or Vessels of War, nor Letters of Marque or Reprisal, except it be after a Declaration of War by the United States assembled" (emphasis added by author). The use of or indicates an appreciation of the historical differences between marque and reprisal—the latter being the aforementioned practice of seeking compensation for losses. Admittedly, an American merchant might still seek reprisal out of a financial motive, but the newly emerging government saw reprisal as a wartime measure. Otherwise, it would be piracy. The target of letters of marque or reprisal, and thereby of privateers too, was restricted "only against the Kingdom or State and the Subjects thereof, against which War has been so declared, and under such regulations as shall be established by the United States assembled." Not only was any such act strictly defined in target and purpose; it was also strictly regulated by behavior. The new United States wanted to show it could hold actors accountable and that they would conduct themselves and treat property in accordance with the practices of international custom and law.[57]

Thus, aside from the circumstances acknowledged where states could make war, any decision to change the status for all colonies from peace to war had to be done at the level of the Articles of Confederation themselves—a vote of at least nine of the "United States assembled." Any remaining questions about the issuance of letters of marque or reprisal, the taking of prizes "by land or naval Forces in the Service of the United States," or matters of crimes or piracy on the high seas and navigable rivers were also in the hands of the "United States assembled."[58]

Sixteen months later the Congress approved the Act of Confederation of the United States of America on November 15, 1777. The final document reflected many of the intervening realities—a number of which were quite sobering—in the course of the revolution since July 1776. Overall, the structure and process in the draft from 1776 remained, but the new document reflected a determination to signal not only to its member states but to the international community a commitment to effective and accountable controls over the use of force and war. States were prohibited from maintaining vessels of war or bodies of troops during times of peace, except for those "deemed necessary by the united states in congress assembled." The stipulation of "deemed necessary by the united states in congress assembled" was an addition that provided assurance of accountability at a national level. State maintenance of a "well-regulated and disciplined militia" remained. The right of states to "engage in any war" on their own was strictly limited to the conditions in the original draft—attack or imminent attack. The draft version had referred to an approval required from the "united states assembled" in all other instances. The Act of Confederation changed the wording to "the united states in congress assembled," a clarification that meant the action of a specific body. A subtle change of language still permitted war in self-defense against attack or imminent attack but accepted such measures only "till the united states in congress can be consulted." In short, the Act of Confederation left open the possibility, albeit rather remote, that it might concur with actions taken by a state or states in self-defense. State issuance of any commissions to "ships or vessels of war," as well as "letters of marque or reprisal," had to await a declaration of war by "the united states in congress assembled." Limiting these actions again to the state and its subjects against which war had been declared, the act aimed to strengthen the hands of the congress. Only when a state found itself "infested by pirates" could it fit out vessels of war to take action until either the state believed the problem solved or congress "shall determine otherwise." Any actions taken during periods of peace, such as the capture of vessels, taking prizes, or using letters of marque and reprisal, were to be decided by "the united states in congress assembled."[59]

The elevation and stronger foundation of a congress was an important intermediate step toward the much more formalized place given to Congress in the Constitution. The continued acknowledgment of the right of states to defend themselves against attack illustrated the philosophy and identity of a confederation in which an attack on a state or states, especially by a foreign actor rather than Indians, could still conceivably not be seen by all as an automatic obligation to respond. The sense of "nation" was not fully in place. At the same time, the admission that the congress might grant letters of marque or reprisal as well as commissions to vessels of war during times of peace invited questions. The qualification about vessels of war reflected the opposition to creating a standing navy for peace or war. Navies, like armies, could be created as needed. The Model Treaty that would serve as an aspiration for US foreign policy saw the new nation as one that needed vessels for free trade and commerce with all, including Great Britain, but not for war.[60] Any use of letters of marque or reprisal during a time of peace would raise questions about intent. Was the new United States still committed to the premise that reprisal might still be permitted in order to satisfy a demand for compensation against a foreign actor who had avoided such acts on his own or through the auspices of his government? By this time such a practice had become far less common. The other question, though, was, to what degree did the United States entertain the notion that war against commerce might be a form of *guerre de course*, a more limited, restrained form of war that fell short of actual conflict? These were questions on which both Americans and the international community awaited clarification. However, at least in terms of process in declaring war or issuing letters of marque and reprisal, the Act of Confederation was explicit in its statement that a minimum of nine states had to give "assent to the same." War, and measures related to it, was too important to be left to undefined, ambiguous procedures.[61]

Yet, ambiguity was a constant companion of those Americans abroad trying to represent and explain the position of the United States to foreign governments, thanks to the midcourse development and state of American law and institutions and dependence on sea travel for the flow of information. Also, the policies and laws of other nations could add their own ambiguity at times. Benjamin Franklin, Arthur Lee, and John Adams, the three envoys in Paris, had to try to explain in September 1778 to the French secretary of the navy, Antoine de Sartine, the circumstances affecting an American privateer, the *General Mifflin*, which had taken a French brigantine that had been held for eight hours by a British privateer. Sartine had wanted to know in part what the rights of French privateers were in American waters and courts; did they have the same rights enjoyed by American privateers in French courts? The three Americans assured Sartine of their shared belief in reciprocity. However, they did not have a copy of any of the US laws on hand; furthermore, the *General Mifflin* had received its commission from Massachusetts. Various technical issues were in play in the case of the *General Mifflin*. French law and Massachusetts law offered different percentages for the amount of prize money to be paid, particularly when the recaptured vessel was taken from a pirate rather than another privateer. The amount of money, the Americans assured Sartine, was not an issue. At stake was a much broader question as to whether the British ship was a privateer or pirate and the rights of all who seize vessels during times of war. It appeared the British captain had carried a commission to attack and seize American vessels. However, seizure of a French vessel appeared in France's eyes to be an act of piracy because, it seemed, France did not regard itself as being at a state of war with Britain. Yet, the Americans argued, that position seemed to be a contradiction in fact. Conceding that no formal declaration of war had been made, they observed "that the two nations have been at actual war at least from the time of the mutual recall of ambassadors." If that were not the case, then war was in place "from the moment of the British King's most warlike speech to his Parliament."[62]

The three Americans had posed important questions about the dependence of a state of war upon an actual declaration. Ironically, their argument was to the advantage of the British captain. They observed, "it would be without a precedent in the history of jurisprudence to adjudge the subject of any nation to be guilty of piracy for an act of hostility committed at sea against the subject of another nation at war. . . . It is not the want of a commission, as we humbly conceive, that makes a man guilty of piracy, but committing hostilities against human kind, at least against a nation not at war." Thinking on the characteristic of war, they added, "comissions [sic] are but a species of evidence that nations are at war, but there are many other ways of proving the same thing." Assuredly Franklin, Lee, and Adams were thinking of the standing of the United States, its tiny navy, and its privateers as they wrote this. Britain did not regard its rebellious colonies as a new state; the latter's privateers were mere pirates in London's eyes. While one can argue that the Declaration of Independence was also a declaration of war, the American diplomats in Paris were claiming that documents are a "species of evidence that nations are at war." Other actions and developments could serve the same purpose. This point was obviously not that important to America's new French ally, but it was pivotal to the Americans in a state of rebellion who relied significantly on actors like privateers. They wanted to make certain France understood this position and would accept it, for "perhaps no nation ever punished their own subjects or citizens for making a prize from an enemy without a commission."[63]

The significance of an announcement by a European government to issue letters of marque against Great Britain could be the equivalent of war. That is how John Adams reported the announcement of the Netherlands on January 12, 1781, to enable the commissioning of privateers against the British. Sending the text of the placard announcement, Adams wrote it "looks like war." That was certainly the language in the Dutch statement, which iterated how "we are obliged to neglect nothing which can serve for our defence."[64] Later in the summer, Adams excitedly wrote that the instructions given to Dutch privateers allowing them to use "the ports or roads of the allies and friends of this republic, especially France, Sweden, North America, or Spain" or to sail with privateers from these countries, was "not only an acknowledgement of the independence of North America, but it [the Netherlands] is avowing . . . to be an ally and friend." Technically, these instructions were available to ship owners, who gave them to privateers, but the fact they were official acts and documents was enough to prove the actual intentions behind them.[65]

Thus, the United States had begun obtaining the recognition and support of key actors in the Atlantic world. Doubtlessly, attempts to bring the new nation into the channels of international custom and law had helped create some legitimacy in others' eyes along with an expectation of possible longer-term viability. However, the need for additional clarity and accountability in US institutions, law, and policy remained, whether looking at the new country from the inside or the outside. While the thirteen states referred to themselves as the United States, "united" was much more aspiration than reality. The Articles of Confederation provided Congress with no coercive authority over the states. State governments could largely do whatever they pleased with no authority at a national level to prevent or reverse an undesirable act or policy. Between early spring and late summer of 1781 Congress considered recommendations to do so, which covered a wide array of concerns that ran from the absence of a system of extradition among the states to a need for a common oath that prevented officials from taking gifts or other emoluments from foreign states, the lack of a post office, the value of a mint for currency, and in more traditional defense matters the advantage of "one universal plan of equipping training and governing the Militia" and common rules "for captures on land and the distribution of the Sales." As the country was a "Confederate Republic," it needed a "general Council" with enumerated powers; otherwise the "War may receive a fatal inclination and peace be exposed to daily convulsions." The enumerated powers included the right "to lay embargoes in time of war without any limitation," "to prescribe rules for impressing property in the service of the U.S. during the present War," and the right "to stipulate in treaties with foreign nations for the establishment of [consular?] power, without references to the States individually." The Congress was urged to assure that congressional votes on key war and related issues obtain agreement from "at least two thirds of the U.S." These included "Waging War," "Granting letters of Marque and Reprisal in time of peace," "concluding or giving instructions for any Alliance," and "Fixing the number and force of Vessels of War, and appointing a Commander in Chief of the Army and Navy." Although the "general Council" was hardly an executive body or authority in any meaning of the word, its proposed creation reflected appreciation of the fact the United States needed an organ created by Congress to be able to speak for the United States in matters where both the appearance and reality of national unity was important for national defense and survival.[66]

Privateering, letters of marque and reprisal, and obtaining final legal settlement of claims following the actions of those carrying such papers and authority were just a few of the many problems that illustrated the insufficiency of the Articles of Confederation in deciding and acting on what served overall national interest. Of course, we know from the modern day that even if such perspectives and means had existed, finding agreement on that "interest" and the measures to pursue it would not have been easy. The critical point here is that the mechanisms were not securely in place to resolve differences and to decide settlements that would answer the concerns of both domestic and international parties. Students and historians of the Constitution have explained in many invaluable ways how these considerations almost compelled delegates to assemble in Philadelphia to construct a system that might address many of these concerns and increase the prospect for national success and survival.

Consider, for example, the absence of any national law of policy concerning the treatment of captures and prizes taken on the high seas. Congress had established control over the issuance of letters of marque and reprisal, but there was no national court of admiralty to deal with claims. This was left to the states, with predictable results of disagreement and feuds. The states were to use existing courts or establish new ones for this purpose. Congress had realized that state courts might act in very parochial fashion in prize cases, so it required that state prize decisions be subject to review by a federal appellate court. However, this was placing the bar too high.

States resisted federal review, and Congress had to work to remove most obstacles. Furthermore, two key states, Pennsylvania and Massachusetts, refused to submit any of their cases to federal review. The resistance of these states alone prevented review of a majority of prize cases during the revolution. Of course, decisions by state admiralty courts could have significant implications in relations between the United States and other nations, including key allies, as well as between states themselves. An example was the American privateer Silas Talbot, who seized the *Betsey*, a British privateer. Watching nearby, three other American privateers approached Talbot's ship and seized the *Betsey* for themselves, taking her into the port of New York for adjudication of the prize. Understandably furious, Talbot and his ship's owners brought claims against the three other Americans in a Pennsylvania court. Some cases like this would literally have to await settlement in federal courts established after the Constitution's ratification.[67]

A closely related problem also existed with how states treated piracy. During the revolution, states legislated laws on their own that met their specific concerns and needs regarding piracy. The Congress followed in the wake of these actions. The text for the Articles of Confederation proposed in 1777 did not obtain ratification of the required number of states until 1781. In March and April of that year Congress did approve the creation of courts to try cases of piracy and crime on the high seas. At the same time, Congress encouraged states to create their own courts, if they had not done so, which almost guaranteed that conflicting bodies of law would emerge at the state and national levels. By the mid-1780s, shortly after the revolution's end, it was apparent the United States needed to find a way to assure, as Charles Pinckney of South Carolina expressed it, that "similar crimes should be punished in a similar way." A resolution followed to have the secretary of the Department of Foreign Affairs, John Jay, establish courts to insure consistency in interpretation of law and punishment. Jay himself became a partial obstacle by concurring that Congress had the power to establish the courts but that it lacked the power to define piracy and felony. Nothing was done, and the states remained in charge of this issue for all purposes until the Constitution took effect and placed these matters in the new Congress's hands.[68]

THE CONSTITUTION AND THE CONTROL OF WAR

For those who were convinced the newly independent United States needed stronger authority at the national level to deal with matters that covered currency, revenue, trade, militias, and defense, examples like the above proved how untenable the Articles system was. A letter by an unidentified British merchant in the *New York Journal* on December 6, 1787, just two-and-a-half months after the completion of the Constitutional Convention in Philadelphia, taunted American readers with threats of war resulting from unpaid debts and damages owed British creditors. He offered the scenario that the British would easily retake Rhode Island, destroy American commerce on the high seas, and "collect a large quantity of American seamen for manning our navy." The writer predicted that the entrepreneurial spirit of Americans would convince many of them to seek their commissions from the British rather than the Congress. "The Americans," he speculated, "may be brought to wish for a return to their ancient government."[69] An entirely different concern surfaced in the debates of the New York Assembly in February of that year when Alexander Hamilton expressed concern about a legislative proposal to disqualify from public office in New York any person who had served as a commander of a privateer vessel that had acted against citizens of New York or other states. Hamilton did not have to remind his listeners that the port of New York had been under British occupation. Some of these individuals, he noted, did so because the British forced them; others so acted because they had suffered damages and wanted compensation. Even at the time of their actions, some had harbored quiet support for the American cause, and in the present environment Hamilton believed many more did so. Hamilton decried this desire to "punish the innocent with the guilty." He conceded some "were guilty of a culpable want of firmness. But if there are any of us who are conscious of greater fortitude, such persons should not on that account be too severe on the weaknesses of others."[70]

These, then, were the types of concerns surrounding privateering that were carried into the Constitutional Convention. It was not a major issue; to call it even a secondary-level one would be an exaggeration. However, the questions it and letters of marque and reprisal posed to the framers were components of broader and difficult issues that had to be addressed. We can assume with some confidence that one work of international law several delegates at Philadelphia had read was that by Emer de Vattel, *The Law of Na-*

tions, published in 1758. De Vattel's commentary on what made a sovereign state would have been a good contemporary guide for shaping thinking:

> Every nation that governs itself, under what form soever, without dependence on foreign power, is a *sovereign state*. Its rights are naturally the same as those of any other state. Such are the moral persons who live together in a natural society, subject to the law of nations. To give a nation a right to make an immediate figure in this grand society, it is sufficient that it be really sovereign and independent, that is, that it govern itself by its own authority and laws.[71] [emphasis in the original]

The legal writers Anthony Bellia and Bradford Clark point out that the authors of the Declaration of Independence asserted this understanding of a sovereign state when they referred to the thirteen colonies as "Free and Independent States" that had the "power to levy War, conclude Peace, contract Alliances, establish Commerce, and to do all other Acts and Things which Independent States may of right do."[72] Americans of a more nationalist persuasion who wanted to assure more concurrence and support from the independent states knew the goals set forth in the Declaration were not yet reality, specifically those related to commerce as well as many of the "other Acts and Things" that states could do. In 1784 Spain had closed the mouth of the Mississippi River; in 1786 the United States had been unable to obtain money from unwilling states to fund an expansion of the army to put down a tax rebellion. The Congress could not impose taxes.[73] These were large issues in contrast to states challenging national authority in adjudicating admiralty prizes or retaining separate definitions of piracy, but the implications for the United States were serious regardless of the scale.

War, letters of marque and reprisal, and privateering were practices that now had some common understanding of meaning and circumstances of legal use. While treaties or bilateral agreements on terminology were not common, custom and major works of international law had pushed interpretation and meaning closer together for much of the Atlantic world. A state or government could expect another to respect the rights of custom and tradition on the high seas and in diplomacy and war. In the 1780s, though, that was not a given with the United States. It lacked the authority to override state court decisions or the acts of other state officials, unless the Articles of Confederation prohibited the specific action. Congress could not punish a state for violating a foreign treaty or international law.[74]

John Jay had learned these lessons firsthand during the Articles period, which is one reason he joined Alexander Hamilton and James Madison in writing essays, now known as the *Federalist Papers*, to support the ratification of the Constitution by the state of New York. In the third essay, Jay reflected on the causes of war and asked "whether so many *just* causes of war are likely to be given by *United America*, as by *disunited* America." Just causes of war, Jay noted, were usually the result of "direct violence" or "violations of treaties." The very word "just" illustrated how just war theory and the evolution of international law influenced Jay's thinking. It was clearly "violations of treaties" that worried Jay, for he knew the United States was in no position to commence a war against any power of note. However, American disarray invited trouble. "It is of high importance to the peace of America, that she observe the laws of nations towards all those Powers," and "this will be more perfectly and punctually done by one national Government, than it could be by thirteen separate States, or by four distinct confederacies."[75]

Jay suffered injury in a street riot, a testimony to the political tone of the time, which prevented him from making as sizable a contribution to the essays as had probably been planned, so Hamilton and Madison authored a large number of them. Hamilton had had a different perspective from which to assess national needs—military service on Washington's staff during the revolution—so some of his strong convictions about the need for stronger national authority took shape early. In September 1789 in a long letter to Congressman John Duane, Hamilton expressed his conviction that Congress needed control over matters of war, diplomacy, trade, revenue, and appropriation of money, among other things[76] His Virginia colleague, James Madison, with whom he would later strongly disagree, had developed similar convictions from his vantage point and experience in Virginia and in the spring of 1787 wrote down his concerns in a pamphlet titled *Vices of the Political System of the United States*. Although Madison did not mention privateering or letters of marque and reprisal, the types of concerns he raised pertaining to international treaties would have applied to them as well as other actions. "Such violations posed grave dangers to the peace and security of the United States," he wrote. "Not a year has passed without instances of them in some one or other of the States. . . . The causes of these irregularities must necessarily produce frequent violations of the law of nations in other respects." Madison added that "as yet foreign powers have not been so rigorous in animadverting on us," but he feared "this moderation . . . cannot be mistaken for a permanent partiality to our faults."[77]

Madison would be a forceful, articulate advocate of government. In an exchange in the Virginia convention to ratify the Constitution with Patrick Henry, who had expressed doubt about assigning Congress the power "to raise and support armies," Madison, who held his own misgivings about standing armies, nonetheless defended the provision and added that the maintenance of effective militias was a valuable means in avoiding dependence on standing armies. He then turned his argument more to the realities of government. "There never was a Government without force," Madison observed, and he clearly believed reliance on militias and other safeguards in the Constitution would prevent the type of military tyranny that frightened Henry. "What is the meaning of Government? An institution to make people do their duty. A Government leaving it to a man to do his duty, or not, as he pleases, would be a new species of Government, or rather no Government at all."[78] In *Federalist No. 41* Madison had clearly described the importance of government in national security. He enumerated six categories of power that the new Constitution assigned to the government. The first one was "security against foreign danger." This, he observed, "is one of the primitive objects of civil society. It is an avowed and essential object of the American Union. The powers requisite for attaining it, must be effectually confided to the federal councils." Among the "powers falling within the first class, are those of declaring war, and granting letters of marque; of providing armies and fleets; of regulating and calling forth the militia; of levying and borrowing money."[79] Madison's explanation is critical for understanding what the Constitutional Convention did in relation to letters of marque and reprisal and the vestiges of war waged by private actors or independent states. Even though these practices were, perhaps not as central as the actual declaration of war, raising armies, or obtaining revenue, they were part of a set central to national survival.

By the time the Constitutional Convention convened, there was little doubt the delegates would place decisions about war at the national level. The question, instead, was what part of the proposed government should receive this power. The Declaration of Independence had condemned the king for his war-making powers, and the Articles of Confederation had assigned the authority to go to war to Congress, leaving the states the power in cases of attack or in circumstances where attack, most likely by Indians, seemed imminent. As will be discussed shortly, even these concessions to state power may have been regarded as too open-ended. Remarks by future delegates like James Madison and Charles Pinckney and a respected military figure like Arthur St. Clair during the 1780s had attested to their worry about any retention of war powers by the states.[80] Leaving the war power in the hands of Congress seemed preferable, although some early proposals by Pinckney in late May and Alexander Hamilton in mid-June favored designating the Senate alone as the appropriate location.[81] The delegates also awaited the draft presented to the convention on August 6, 1787, by the Committee on Detail.

That committee's draft clearly reflected the convictions about responsibility for war and national security at the national level and placement of the powers of action in the "Legislature of the United States," which significantly meant both chambers. Here are the powers related to war and the mobilization and uses of force enumerated in the draft:

1. To make rules concerning captures on land and water;
2. To declare the law and punishment of piracies and felonies committed on the high seas, and the punishment of counterfeiting the coin of the United States, and of offences against the law of nations;
3. To subdue a rebellion in any State, on the application of its Legislature;
4. To make war;
5. To raise armies;
6. To build and equip fleets;
7. To call forth the aid of the militia, in order to execute the laws of the Union, enforce treaties, suppress insurrections, and repel invasions.

Clearly war powers were a national, and noticeably, a legislative power. Gone were the days when state governments and courts could define piracy, set and enforce their own laws, and challenge national authority. The reference to "the law of nations" clearly asserted the priority of national power and responsibility. Absent, though, in this section of the draft dealing with legislative power is any reference to letters of marque and reprisal. No explanation appears to be at hand. Either the draft's authors had taken for granted the congressional control over the issue of such letters and commissions set forth in the Articles of Confederation, or they had not regarded them as war-related measures. The latter is very unlikely, since by 1787 the use of letters of marque and reprisal and privateers had largely become actions dependent on a state or declaration of war.

The omission is interesting because the draft section addressing the powers of states does mention letters of marque and reprisal. Specifically the draft states, "No State shall coin money; nor grant letters of marque and reprisals; nor enter into any treaty, alliance, or confederation; nor grant any title of nobility." Elsewhere, restrictions on state activities related to war and conflict were strict. "No State, without the consent of the Legislature of the United States, shall . . . keep troops or ships of war in time of peace; nor enter into any agreement or compact with another State, or with any foreign power; nor engage in any war, unless it shall be actually invaded by enemies, or the danger of invasion be so imminent, as not to admit of a delay, until the Legislature of the United States can be consulted." These were strict guidelines. The national-level authority over letters of marque and reprisal indicated appreciation that such actions affected relations between the United States and other nations and that their implementation on the state level could invite disagreement with foreign governments and violations of international law, but the restriction does not seem to treat them as war-related actions. Otherwise, it would have been best to place them in the paragraph restricting state actions related to war. In relation to the power of a state to wage war, the language stresses actual invasion or invasion "so imminent" the state could not wait for legislative consent from Congress. This was a higher bar for states to meet, even in the world of 1787 when news might need days to reach its destination or Congress was not in session.[82]

The draft's treatment of letters of marque and reprisal does seem to leave them in a nebulous position—a measure the writers obviously believed rested at the national level because such commissions could affect relations between nations and compliance. However, whether they were related to war seemed unclear—at least in this language. Again, the ambiguity, if it was intentional, may not have seemed that troubling to contemporaries. In his study of American thought about military force in this period, Reginald Stuart reminds us that Americans, like their European counterparts, still believed in forms of limited measures that were not the equivalent of war.[83] As shown elsewhere in this book, there was precedent for treating limited retaliation or acts like letters of marque and reprisal as actions that might precede war, prevent it, occur during it, or even be conducted after the traditional state-to-state peace had entered into effect. If one doubted this, again arguments to the contrary could be found in important legal writings from the time—which some in Philadelphia had either read or knew about through secondhand reading and conversation. In *The Principles of Political Law*, written by J. J. Burlamaqui, published in 1748 and translated into English four years later, an argument for this type of measured approach to war awaited the reader. Burlamaqui wrote of public and private wars— the former occurring under "the authority of the civil power and the latter without it"—and he added mixed wars in which one waged it publicly and the other privately. More directly related to the matter of war and phased measures preceding it was the discussion of "perfect" and "imperfect" war. Burlamaqui's use of these words carried no moral or ethical meaning but rather a reference to the scale of conflict. "Perfect" war "entirely interrupt[s] the tranquility of the state, and lays a foundation for all possible acts of hostility." "Imperfect" war "does not entirely interrupt the peace, but only in certain particulars, the public tranquility being in other respects undisturbed." Thus, scale is measured in two ways—the magnitude of disruption of the life of the state as well as the scope and scale of choices used in waging the war. "Perfect" war resembled what the twentieth century would recognize as "total" war. "Imperfect" war meant that boundaries had been set to limit the war's impact on the society waging it as well as the selection of instruments being used. The critical qualification Burlamaqui added is that "imperfect" war "is generally called reprisals," which are "acts of hostility, which sovereigns exercise against each other, or, with their consent, their subjects by seizing the persons or effects of the subjects of a foreign commonwealth . . . with a view to obtain security, and to recover our right, and in case of refusal, to do justice to ourselves, without any other interruption of the public tranquility."[84]

Burlamaqui's description of reprisals matched how most of the framers in Philadelphia would have understood the term, if applied in international law and practice. The requirement of approval by the "sovereign" or state was essential, which reflected practice now centuries old. The matter of approval was much more important than whether the war was declared or undeclared. Burlamaqui had recognized the existence of both types, although he avoided the terms *declared* and *undeclared*. Instead he chose to use the word *solemn* to make the distinction. "Solemn" war was "made by the authority of the sovereign; it usually had certain formalities or events as part of it, including a declaration. If the war was not "solemn" it was being "made either without a formal declaration, or against mere private persons."[85] Burlamaqui clearly had little problem with the practice of undeclared war; it might reflect decisions about intent and scale that did not need or require a declaration. How extensively such an opinion would have been shared in Philadelphia is hard to say, although a number of those present could remember or reflect on experiences from their own lives. George Washington's own command of the expedition to investigate French activity near Fort Duquesne in 1754 had not been intended to commence a war, but it did, and it was a war that remained undeclared for two years—a declaration that carried more meaning for conflict of states in Europe than it did in the forests of North America. Alexander Hamilton within a few months of the convention would observe in *Federalist No. 25* that "the ceremony of a formal denunciation of war has of late fallen into disuse."[86] Just how far back Hamilton's memory had gone is unclear, but clearly his current day seemed to operate without a requirement of declarations. If Burlamaqui and other writers on international law going back to Grotius were any guide, the critical question was more that of approval of the sovereign. Reprisals were measures in an "imperfect" war, but they could be steps found in wars that were "solemn" or not. The one requirement in all was approval by the sovereign. The delegates in Philadelphia were trying to define the best location for these powers to reside.[87]

The discussion on war powers that followed the submission of the draft from the Committee on Detail was not long or intense. Some unease remained about the ability of all of Congress to act in matters related to war. Charles Pinckney favored placement of such powers just in the Senate, as the House might be cumbersome and certainly less experienced in foreign affairs. Perhaps as an overreaction against congressional management of war and military matters during the revolution, Pierce Butler of South Carolina recommended placing war-making power with the president. Elbridge Gerry of Massachusetts found it extremely troubling "to hear in a republic a motion to empower the Executive alone to declare war." The discussion seems to have combined the issues of both declaring and waging war, and it was Gerry along with James Madison who proposed a change to the draft—namely exchanging the word "declare" for "make" in the text. Both, too, could recall the difficulties that had occurred during the revolution as a result of congressional attention or inattention on war-related issues.

Anything that suggested congressional management of the actual operations of war would not have been appealing.[88]

On considering the Committee on Detail's draft, Gerry was troubled by
the absence of a reference to letters of marque and reprisal. Being from Massachusetts, Gerry probably had his own memories of the role of privateering
in the recent conflict and his part in shaping that state's policy on it, and the
omission struck him as serious enough to correct. In James Madison's notes
Gerry proposes that after "declare war" language be added "concerning letters of marque, which he thought not included in the power of war." Also, if
Gerry had not known the literature of international law that well, he almost
assuredly would have known William Blackstone's *Commentaries on the Laws
of England* in which the influential writer wrote that issuance of letters of
marque and reprisal "is nearly related to . . . making war; this being indeed
only an incomplete state of hostilities."[89] This language is not that different
from the characterization found in Burlamaqui. Gerry obviously believed
that letters of marque and reprisal were war-related measures. (His reason
for omitting reprisal is unclear; it may have been Madison's notes or the
fact that the practices had become increasingly blurred by this time.) As the
Articles of Confederation and the Committee on Detail draft treated them,
Congress retained authority over issuing them whether in times of war or
peace. The use during the latter might not appear as likely as it once had,
but by experience or reading Gerry knew that states still relied on reprisals
in circumstances separate from war as well as with it. He wanted to assure
that control over letters of marque and reprisals existed at the congressional
level, whether in times of declared war or otherwise.[90]

Taking into consideration the proposals made by the delegates, the
Committee on Style revised the draft Constitution and submitted it back to
the convention as a whole on September 10, 1787. This draft included the
changes proposed by Madison and Gerry and read "To declare war; and
grant letters of marque and reprisal." It still listed separately the power "to
make rules concerning captures on land and water." The final version of the
Constitution "as agreed upon" a week later (September 17) saw this provision
moved and added to the section dealing with declaring war and letters of
marque and reprisal. The edit was thoroughly understandable, as captures
could be done by either warships or commissioned privateers. Arguably,
again, experience from the revolution and the Articles of Confederation
reminded the delegates that inconsistency in such rules could become a

source of disagreement with other governments. The language in the first draft pertaining to limitation of state powers in war and issuing letters of marque and reprisal remained.[91]

The document that now went to the states for ratification had significantly strengthened the role of the national government over national security and foreign affairs. The establishment and elevation of practices, institutions, and procedures to fashion policy on these issues at the national level would never remain unchallenged by states, groups, or individuals who thought otherwise or who feared the expansion of these powers. However, opposition to the changes regarding letters of marque and reprisal and privateering never appeared. National security and war were matters of national importance and decision, even though the states were still responsible for the provision of militias to serve in the nation's defense when called upon by Congress. When so done, the president, along with whatever standing military units existed, would serve as the commander in chief. Obviously private individuals could still seek commissions in the form of letters of marque and reprisal or to act as privateers commissioned by the US government. Private warfare in these circumstances nevertheless had to be conducted as part of a public action, as the sanction of Congress was required whether in times of war or peace. While a private party could still pursue such measures to obtain compensation for damages, the actions taken had to occur with congressional authority and obviously in a fashion that served national interest as well as private. In principle, Congress would decide the balance between public and private ends as well as means.

Until recently, when the prominence of private military firms and contractors has raised the issue of private and public means and ends in war and conflict, the scholarly discussion of letters of marque and reprisal centered more on the question of whether the power embraced all forms of limited war or just these specific measures. However, interesting variations in these arguments invite questions to the current day and beyond. Arguably, the most sweeping interpretation of the framers' intention in the marque and reprisal is by John Hart Ely. Ely claims "the framers and ratifiers of the Constitution provided that all acts of actual combat performed on behalf of the United States—*even if they didn't amount to 'war'* [emphasis is Ely's]—had to be authorized by Congress." Several pages later Ely amplifies and repeats his point: "The marque and reprisal provision was designed to insure that authority to license such acts of war or lesser hostilities in behalf of the

United States, like the authority to authorize full-fledged wars, would be unambiguously vested in Congress."[92] Ely wishes to support the case for required congressional authorization of the use of force in limited and undeclared wars, and he finds this power residing in the marque and reprisal clause—a seeming label for the various forms of limited military action the United States could take at the time. Other scholars, especially proponents of the requirement for congressional action, have supported Hart's argument—most notably the constitutional expert on executive-legislative relations with the Library of Congress, Louis Fisher, who observed, "any initiation of war, whether by declaration or by marque and reprisal, was reserved to Congress. Thus, both general and limited wars were left to the decision of the representative branch."[93] Fisher's argument strongly rests on a statement made by Secretary of State Thomas Jefferson in 1793 on the seriousness of reprisals that, when implemented, are "act[s] of war." As such an act, Congress's approval beforehand was a requirement.[94] Reinforcing Fisher's interpretation is the fact that Jefferson also most assuredly was using the word "reprisal" in a broader sense than just measures for loss of property. From this interpretation states could use a variety of measures for actions and violations committed by other states.

Others have concurred with Ely and Fisher on the broader coverage of the marque and reprisal clause but have added more claims. Writing in the mid-1980s, actually before both Ely and Fisher, when the administration of President Ronald Reagan was supporting insurgent and counterinsurgent movements in Nicaragua and El Salvador, Jules Lobel argued the marque and reprisal clause provided the legal foundation for congressional control over covert operations, particularly those relying on paramilitary forces. His claim rested on an observation that "in eighteenth century America, the term 'letters of marque and reprisal' lost much of the technical meaning and came to signify any intermediate or low-intensity hostility short of declared war that utilized public or private forces." Seeing a similarity between paramilitary groups and the types of private actors involved in the pursuit of letters of marque and reprisal, Lobel asserted Congress had the power over authorization for such covert operations. He wrote, "covert operations are the modern analogy to the private armies and military operations of an earlier time. If these two methods of 'imperfect war' are functionally related then the Framers' decision to vest the power to issue letters of marque and reprisal in the legislative branch continues to be relevant and mandates that modern-day covert operations be authorized by Congress pursuant to the marque and reprisal clause."[95]

Here it is important to point out Lobel's obvious concern about the perceived inadequacy of existing measures in law to authorize US support for such operations—especially the Intelligence Oversight Act of 1980, which requires an executive report, a "finding" to verify to Congress the value of US support of a particular covert mission. By 1986, when Lobel's article appeared, Congress was divided on the value of continued support for covert missions in Central America. Lobel's purpose was to find a better mechanism for legislative approval than what existed, and he argued that "covert use of paramilitary force to conduct American foreign policy abroad is the modern day analogy to the private wars for which letters of marque and reprisal were historically required."[96] Here his argument requires some stretching to accept. The paramilitaries might be private actors, but they did not operate in the legal frameworks that holders of letters of marque and reprisal did, particularly by the time of the American Revolution and even earlier. Admittedly, the latter were not always pristine and respectful in their interpretation and adherence to law, but there was recourse for their actions, even if it might not have always been successful for the aggrieved party. The letters of marque and reprisal had been a form of agreement or contract with specific terms for operation. Where Lobel's argument may be more valuable is in relation to US contractors used by the Central Intelligence Agency. Twenty to thirty years later the intelligence and military worlds would be much more reliant on private actors and contractors, and Lobel's point could deserve revisiting. Building on Lobel's article, another legal commentator, Kevin Marshall, argued that the primary purpose of the marque and reprisal clause had been to circumvent the power of the purse held by Congress. The Constitution had, in effect, allowed for the use of private actors with private money in limited uses of force, thanks to this very clause. Yet, assignment of this power to Congress had given Congress power over the action and actor even if no money crossed from the government to the privateer. Marshall regarded the marque and reprisal clause as an obstacle to any president arranging for private money to a private party to use force on behalf of the United States. If that is done, it should be through Congress and the channels of the marque and reprisal clause.[97]

The arguments for an expansive interpretation of the marque and reprisal clause often rely on a flexible, open-ended definition of marque and reprisal.

John Yoo, whose writings are strongly associated with vigorous assertions of executive power, stands against these interpretations. This should not be surprising, as full acceptance of them would provide Congress with a strong framework to oppose presidential action, especially in instances where the use of force is limited and sometimes concealed through use of proxies or other nonstate actors. Yet, even if Yoo's preference for a more unhindered executive causes disagreement, his concern about the ahistorical nature of some of the arguments is well-founded. These views "rip the constitutional text from its historical context," Yoo writes. He notes that "by the time of the framing, letters of marque and reprisal had come to refer to a fairly technical form of international reprisal, in which a government gave its permission to an injured private party to recover, via military operations, compensation from the citizens of a foreign nation."[98] Michael Ramsey, a legal scholar who certainly does not walk in step with Yoo, reminds us that "this eighteenth century version of limited conflict, in which nations seized each other's property as a means of redress without invoking full-scaled hostilities, was called reprisal; and the official approval distinguishing it from piracy was the 'letter of marque and reprisal.'" This "specific form of limited hostilities," which could be an "offensive hostility," "was properly a congressional, rather than a presidential responsibility."[99] Other scholars have agreed in various ways. Frances Wormuth and Edwin Firmage likewise noted the specificity of the circumstances of marque and reprisal, but, somewhat like Louis Fisher, they see the real scope in the word *reprisals*, not in the form of marque and reprisal but rather in the broader meaning raised by Jefferson. The application of the former term is fairly narrow, but the use of the latter assuredly is not.[100] In his survey of the marque and reprisal clause, Jay Wexler gives historical context weight when considering the meaning of marque and reprisal, but he acknowledges as well the preference given to Congress in the application of this power.[101] A very different application of marque and reprisal that tries to see parallels in its historical practice for a modern-day issue is the case for stressing similarities between letters of marque and reprisal on the high seas and the role of states and private actors in the ever-expanding domain of cyber. This is significant enough that I choose to focus attention on it in the Conclusion, where I discuss the open-ended, troubling implications of cyber for public and private war.

Historical evidence just does not lend itself easily to arguments that assert that marque and reprisal can stand for limited conflict at large. When

Gerry raised his concern in August 1787 he knew exactly what he meant. The dependence of the united colonies/United States on privateering during the revolution had been significant; the requirement for congressional control of the issue of letters of marque and reprisal by the states had been critical to any level of national effort against the British, and the inconsistencies in state interpretations of law, and even the resistance of states to national review, had been potentially damaging to the interests and foreign relationships of the United States. Gerry and his colleagues understood that letters of marque and reprisal were often war-related measures intended to supplement limited military capabilities; privateering was assuredly a war-related measure. If used in peacetime the captain and owners absolutely needed the approval of a state authority; otherwise, the captain and crew were acting as pirates. Madison and Gerry wanted to secure this power in the hands of Congress, where it had resided during the revolution and since, and not allow it to move into the hands of the president. Their effect and consequences could cause decisions that lead to formal, declared war. The power to issue them in peace and war had to rest with Congress, and these measures had to be used with forethought and caution.

Some scholars may make too much of the projected use through the Constitution of letters of marque and reprisal during periods of peace. It is true this option remained, but the likelihood was not as high as it had been in earlier periods. Marque and reprisal and privateering had increasingly become a dimension of war by the late eighteenth century, unless one wanted to treat periods of undeclared or limited war as periods of peace, which technically they might be if one depended on or expected an actual declaration. However, that specific requirement had become less important as well in warfare. Practitioners knew that other actions and development could signify war; one did not need a declaration to reach that threshold. If Congress were to retain the power to declare war, it had to hold on to those powers that could precede war, possibly instigate it, and assuredly accompany it. Even the British Parliament secured more of a voice in the use of letters of marque and reprisal and privateering as the century advanced. Neither legislative body would allow it to reside solely in the hands of a president or king.

Sometimes it may be too easy to read circumstances of the present into the past. The argument that the intention of the clause in Article I, Section 8 was to bypass the power of the purse by using private funds may be such an example. The objective in the time of the revolution and Constitution was not to bypass the power of the purse but rather to rely on private means to prevent emptying it and maybe even fattening it. The United States had a small navy during the revolution, and after the Constitution entered into effect there was still no agreement on the desirability, or need, for a standing navy. A standing army, many thought, posed a danger of military intervention and occupation, reminiscent of the practices of the British prior to the revolution. A standing navy was expensive, as the British knew all too well, and some worried that American vessels might drag the new country into unwanted conflicts. Reliance on privateers and letters of marque and reprisal could provide an adequate naval capability—certainly a cheaper one—that would fit more with the American desire to be a major commercial actor that posed no military threat to others.

Thus, if marque and reprisal was not a label for all limited war in general, it was clearly a particular type of limited war that needed control by Congress. To say this does not fully invalidate the arguments of those who want to use the clause as an envelope that contains different forms of limited war. The clause does offer a case for obtaining congressional consent in other forms of such conflict or for legislation requiring authorization in the future. However, there is little evidence to support the claim that the later eighteenth century had come to regard marque and reprisal as a catch-all term for limited war. Governments knew what marque and reprisal meant and that in confrontations between states while peace remained technically in place, or in actual war, governments could resort to this particular instrument—even in circumstances on land but much more frequently on sea. War on the high seas had become a major aspect of the global struggle for power that had characterized the eighteenth century. The Americans hoped to avoid that facet of the international scene, but they knew they had to operate and survive in it. It was best that the power to use letters of marque and reprisal be well-defined and clearly grounded in the branch of government responsible for these decisions. Keep in mind that for the Americans not all forms of war would have required formal action by Congress through the use of a declaration or letters of marque and reprisal. Wars and campaigns against Native Americans did not have such a requirement. This was not state-to-state war, but war against indigenous peoples within areas claimed by or actually within US boundaries. The state system and laws of the Atlantic world treated these people differently and at a lower level of recognized rights. The framers of the Constitution almost inherently understood this as well; there could be forms of limited war that would not fall under Article I, Section 8 of the Constitution with congressional power over declaring war, issuing letters of marque and reprisal, and defining policies regarding to capture.

CONTROLLING WAR AND CONFLICT AFTER THE CONSTITUTION

The problem for the Americans was that surviving and trying to conduct commerce on the international stage was not easy. Much to their fortune the British had concluded after the revolution to treat the United States not as a pariah but as a country that could still operate and serve British interests in trade. In a pamphlet in 1783 titled *Observations on the Commerce of the United States*, one of the leading mercantilists, John Holyrod, Lord Sheffield, had pointed to what almost seemed obvious: the Americans had little choice but to continue trading with the British. Sheffield was right, and a number of prominent Americans, such as Washington and Hamilton, not only hoped for the reestablishment of commerce but believed it critical to the survival of the new country. In early July 1783 the British issued orders in council that allowed American materials to enter Britain at duty rates lower than that enjoyed by any other country. American exports to British colonies in the Western Hemisphere would nonetheless have to be carried in British ships.[102]

British encouragement and engagement with the Americans only went so far, however. As the Americans quickly began to assert themselves in the world's carrying trade, they learned that they would be on their own. An early problem was with the Barbary pirates operating along the northwest coast of Africa and along the northern African coast in the Mediterranean. By 1784 their depredations had become serious enough that some believed the United States needed to take military action. Thomas Jefferson, still in Paris as the American representative, believed the European practice of giving tribute to the pirates was intolerable and urged developing the naval power to act. So did John Jay, whose determination increased on learning that Algiers—one of the Barbary states—had declared war on the United States in 1785. However, the prudent course of tribute prevailed; in fact, it prevailed through the first decade after the Constitution entered into effect. Some worried about the cost. Benjamin Franklin noted that the pirates conducted little commerce, so what could the Americans retaliate against? Jefferson even tried to generate interest from Paris in a combined

European-American response to the pirates, but to no avail.[103] These events had been part of the preparatory ground for the empowerment of Congress in the Constitution to provide for a navy, but as the 1790s opened this was a power on paper and not in fact.

The questions of whether to have a standing navy and of what size were part of the much broader and philosophical questions that affected American political discourse at the time. The first was the debate over the range of centralization and authority at the national level. Jefferson and Madison had both supported earlier the establishment of a navy, but now the question became part of whether the navy would signal a disproportionate military presence in the new country. With the Constitution's assignment of letters of marque and reprisal to Congress, Madison thought that privateers could meet the naval requirements of the United States.[104] Of course, the founders' suspicion of a standing army was even deeper. Both Jefferson and Madison remained wedded to a concept of national defense that depended on a mobilization of capability as needed through militias and privateers. Avoiding conflict with a European power was the eminent concern. The preferred instrument, if possible, would be measures tied with economic coercion—embargoes, boycotts, and, obviously, privateering.[105] The example of *guerre de course*—commerce raiding—was an option that still held merit, and, as discussed in the coming chapter, these measures would figure prominently in the presidencies of both men.

The other development so significantly shaping discourse in the United States, as well as shaking the Atlantic world, was the French Revolution. The first stages of it had been even exhilarating—a confirmation of the political steps the Americans had taken themselves just a decade earlier. However, in 1792 with the arrest of King Louis XVI and the establishment of the National Convention that set France on a more republican course and also on a path urging expansion of the values of the revolution, concern in some Federalist circles in the United States mounted. The beheading of the king and the declarations of war by France on Britain, Holland, and Spain that followed created circumstances for President George Washington that posed a serious test of statesmanship that could literally decide national survival. Was the United States required to honor the terms of the Treaty of Alliance and the Treaty of Amity and Commerce it had signed with France in 1778? The system of government that had signed those for France was now destroyed. The former was an alliance that pledged both nations to assist in the defense of the other's possessions. Two articles in the second treaty directly addressed matters related to navies and privateering. Article XVII allowed French privateers and warships into American ports to be refitted and to have prizes adjudicated. France's enemies obviously lost their access to these same ports. The latter point gained more reinforcement from Article XXII, which prohibited France's enemies from having privateers fitted in US ports or having prizes decided in court.[106] So far, the matter of American privateers had not entered into discussion much.

The arrival in the United States in early April 1793 of Citizen Edmond Charles Genet, the French representative, brought these questions to a head. Genet was filled with the fervor of revolution and its ideals. One of his objectives was to stir prorevolutionary ideas in Canada, Louisiana, and Florida, where British and Spanish control remained, and to excite Americans in the West to play a part in pushing the Spanish out of the lower Mississippi region. Genet's objectives did not end there. He hoped to renegotiate the 1778 treaties and to move the Americans to pay off the remainder of the debt they owed France from the American Revolution.[107] The fact that Genet chose to arrive not in Philadelphia, where the US government then resided, but in Charleston, South Carolina, attested to his assessment of American governing institutions and the diffusion of American power, such as it was. Carrying blank commissions for letters of marque and reprisal, he was able to commission four privateers in South Carolina. The state governor saw no harm to US neutrality in this. Genet, who spoke fluent English, made his way to Philadelphia as something of a celebrity. Meanwhile, the frigate that had brought him to the United States, the *Embuscade*, commenced its own capture of British vessels near the American coastline, bringing two ships into Charleston harbor, and in early May, about two weeks before Genet's arrival in Philadelphia, two more British merchant vessels into that port.[108]

These were the types of developments President Washington and his cabinet knew had to be avoided to preserve neutrality and to prevent further deterioration of relations with Britain, with whom the United States had outstanding issues that remained from the revolution, including the ongoing presence of British troops in garrisons in the West that were now inside the United States. The discussions during April 1793 that followed Washington's thirteen questions to his cabinet about the status of the treaties and relations with France as well as the various options to consider have been well studied. Even though Secretary of State Thomas Jefferson and

Secretary of the Treasury Alexander Hamilton entertained different views of the French Revolution, both recognized the importance of neutrality and of not permitting the French to outfit privateers or bring prizes into American ports. Genet learned of the proclamation of American neutrality while he made his way to Philadelphia. Washington had agreed to receive him, but this was not done as a gesture to offer Genet hope for American reversal of its neutrality.[109] Through late May and early June, Genet continued to complain about American obstruction on the licensing and outfitting of privateers in their ports. On June 5, Jefferson defended the US position by stressing "the *right* [emphasis is Jefferson's] to prohibit acts of sovereignty from being exercised by any other within its limits, and the *duty* of a neutral nation to prohibit such as would injure one of the warring powers." Jefferson amplified the point nearly two weeks later when he wrote Genet to stress that the matter of French privateers "was one of arming not for self defense but for the purpose of committing hostilities on nations at peace with the United States." He warned Genet the United States would prosecute not only US citizens involved in these matters but also foreign actors within US jurisdiction who were promoting such measures. Genet's mission was in effect finished, although he remained in his official capacity until year's end. Wisely, he sought to remain in the United States rather than return to France under the Committee of Public Safety, and did so for the remainder of his life.[110]

The arguments Jefferson, Hamilton, and Washington made in relation to the commissioning of French privateers in American ports was a strong illustration of the desire and need of the United States to be taken seriously as a member of the sovereign community of states. Alexander Hamilton stated it very frankly in a letter to a friend, Richard Harison, in mid-June when he described French measures, whether privateering or organizing military expeditions on US territory, as "an offence against the law of Nations—the law of Nations is a part of the law of the land. Hence such an act must be on principle be punishable." He cited de Vattel in making his case, which Jefferson did likewise in his correspondence with Genet at almost the same time. "Our own citizens are guilty of a breach of the peace stipulated by our Treaties with England, Holland and Prussia. The Citizens of France are guilty of a violation of our Sovereignty and Jurisdiction, tending to endanger and disturb our Peace."[111] The Washington administration had in effect told the states that they could no longer do what South Carolina had allowed when Genet arrived in Charleston. These were now decisions for the national level and for Congress to decide, whether it be an American state's commission of a privateer or allowing a foreign government to license such a ship in US waters. By recruiting crews for privateers or licensing ships in American ports, as well as trying to involve Americans in a land expedition against the Spanish in Louisiana, the French had violated US sovereignty. Hamilton had noted that the law of nations was the law of the land. Such a body of law required order within the nation as well as in its interactions with others on the outside.

Across the Atlantic, as well as across the Channel, the British had watched the Franco-American relationship with great interest. As soon as war broke out between republican France and Britain in February 1793, the Royal Navy began to stop US vessels bound for France and to impress crewmen, often alleged British deserters, to become crew on British warships. By June 1793 the British had declared all food bound to France as contraband, regardless of the flag the ship was flying. In early November the British formalized their policy of seizure by allowing seizure of any American vessel headed to France or even carrying French goods. The United States actually did not learn about the official order until early 1794.[112] These events came along with the other existing problems with the British related to garrisons and relations with Indians in the Old Northwest and settlement of debt claims. Jefferson and James Madison urged a set of commercial retaliations against the British, similar to some of the measures the two would pursue a decade later prior to the War of 1812. However, the final preferred course was to pursue negotiations through the appointment of a special envoy, John Jay, to go to London and try to resolve the differences with the British.[113]

One of the sidebar developments during this same period was a decision in Congress to support the construction of six frigates—the beginning of a navy. The real reason was not to counter the British, which would have been hopeless, but to deal with the continued depredations American ships experienced at the hands of the Barbary pirates—particularly those from Algiers. Even in that environment, majority support for the construction of warships was not a given. James Madison headed the opposition in the House of Representatives with a variety of arguments: bribing the pirates would be cheaper and probably more effective, starting a navy would generate future demand for even more ships, maintaining the ships would be expensive, and having them would attract unwanted British attention.

Even John Adams, who had been a supporter of creating a navy, doubted much could be done against the British. To Abigail he wrote that "we have not the smallest Thing to hope unless it be by Privateering, and such is now the tremendous Naval Superiority against Us that we shall loose [sic] more than gain by that." Nevertheless, the impact of the British orders that had expanded seizure of American ships trading with France or carrying French goods added an argument for approval of the legislation in March 1794. Two years later, thanks in part to British intercession with Algiers, a treaty ended the ongoing hostility with that state. Another naval act in 1796 stopped construction of three of the six vessels.[114]

Americans treated Jay's Treaty, signed in November 1794, as everything from a salvation that prevented possible war and protected American commerce to an absolute, disgraceful sell-out of national interests. France regarded it as a virtual alliance with Great Britain and a rejection, as the French saw it, of US treaty obligations with France. The treaty prohibited British enemies from sending warships or privateers into American ports and from seeking adjudication of prizes. Jay had agreed to accept the policy of consolato de mer, which the British used to assert the right of seizing enemy goods found on neutral ships. American critics regarded this as a sacrifice of the American position that neutral ships have the right to carry non-contraband cargo. The French likewise saw this as a measure that favored Britain over them. Interestingly, Article 25 of the treaty stated that nothing in it "shall however be construed or operate contrary to former and existing Public Treaties with other Sovereigns or States."[115] That provision would have had more meaning if the United States and France had had a common understanding of the treaties from 1778.

Jay's Treaty obtained Senate consent in June 1795, and a full year passed before the Directory in Paris provided a response. Issuing a decree in early July, the French stated they would treat neutral vessels the same way the British did in terms of capture, searches, and confiscation of what they found onboard the vessel. Some confusion existed on the American side as to what exactly this meant and how it would be implemented, but the answer became clear on learning that French warships and privateers had begun an indiscriminate attack on American ships. The French had a record of significant privateering before the French Revolution, and the French government in place now pursued it again aggressively. Their hope, accompanied by actual interventions by their ambassador in the United States, for the election of

Thomas Jefferson as president went unrewarded. Instead, they faced the replacement of George Washington by his vice president, John Adams, who was not seen as a friend of France. Two days before Adams's inauguration on March 4, 1797, the Directory escalated the measures against the United States by renouncing the practice of "free ships make free goods," which meant that French vessels would capture American vessels carrying British goods. They additionally warned the Americans that any US ship not being able to present a role d'equipage—a list of passengers and crew that American vessels rarely had—would be a proper candidate for seizure.[116]

Adams completely understood the comparative weakness of the United States opposite France, and he, too, hoped a path of negotiation might resolve differences as had been done with Britain. The urgency for this sentiment no doubt got reinforcement when Secretary of State Timothy Pickering reported to Adams that between October 1796 and June 1797 the French had seized 316 American vessels, in short more than one per day.[117] Adams believed it was necessary to set in motion preparations for a naval response, although full-scale war would never be in his thinking. In May 1797 he told Congress of his plan to send a three-man delegation to Paris to seek a negotiated settlement and then urged action on measures to commence coastal fortifications, the construction of warships, and the arming of merchant vessels for self-defense. The latter, one should note, would not be privateering. His vice president, Thomas Jefferson, and Jefferson's leading ally in the House, Albert Gallatin, questioned both the cost and some of the wisdom of the naval program, particularly in light of Adams's desire to pursue negotiations, but in July Congress approved a naval program that allowed completion of the three frigates that remained after the 1796 law and use of a few revenue cutters the Department of the Treasury had as warships for defense. Congress did not approve the arming of warships.[118]

The adventures and misadventures of the three American representatives in Paris—John Marshall, Charles Cotesworth Pinckney, and Elbridge Gerry—have become lore in the history of the early United States. The French foreign minister, Charles Maurice de Talleyrand-Perigord, refused to negotiate with them based on objections to remarks Adams had made about France as well as overall displeasure with the United States, and he infamously sent three representatives at various times to suggest that a bribe to the Directory might change the tone of their reception. (Talleyrand did briefly receive them on their arrival, and there were several private meetings with Gerry.) The Americans designated these three gentlemen "XYZ" in their correspondence, thus giving the affair the name it has held since. The first correspondence arrived back in the United States in March 1798.[119]

The treatment of the American representatives infuriated Adams, along with the knowledge that the French had escalated their measures against the United States by declaring that French vessels would seize any neutral vessel that had anything from Britain on board. Of course, it would almost be impossible for American ships not to carry something British, given the volume of trade that existed. Meanwhile, Adams faced a divided cabinet. Secretary of State Pickering and Attorney General Charles Lee urged Adams to request a declaration of war; opposed were Secretary of War James McHenry and Secretary of the Treasury Oliver Wolcott. Both of the latter men were very close to Alexander Hamilton, who was now out of government but very much a key political actor in these and other events. Hamilton was arguably the guiding light for arguments that discouraged a declaration of war and promoted a course of limited war or hostilities.[120]

Hamilton was no stranger to this way of thinking about limited forms of hostilities. A few years earlier, when President Washington had faced challenges from both the Algerian pirates and the British, Hamilton had urged a similar course. The cost of actual war could be damaging for the fledgling United States, and Hamilton had thought the population would only be willing to make the necessary sacrifices if the United States were attacked. He had urged reliance on reprisals as a way of dealing with the British, and a couple of years later he added that privateers could be an effective instrument by disrupting British commerce.[121] Hamilton was thinking of reprisals as they had been discussed in the evolving body of international law—Grotius, Burlamaqui, de Vattel, and others—measures that a sovereign authority could order and take when other steps for redress had failed. As we have seen, the discussion surrounding them in the Constitutional Convention had recognized they were tied with the war power either as a component thereof or actions that could precede or occur without actual war. Hamilton had pressed these types of actions in 1796 and 1797 before the XYZ affair and the heightened dilemmas its outcome posed to Adams, his cabinet, and Congress.[122] Hamilton thought stronger military preparations were justified—completion of the three frigates, outfitting twenty sloops for war, purchasing ten ships of the line , and arming merchant vessels. Hamilton also thought it time to raise a regular army of 30,000 troops. The scale of his ideas distressed some, such as Pickering, who feared that arming merchant vessels would endanger their crews even more than actual war.[123]

Even though the discussions centered on limited forms of force and hostilities, privateers for the Americans had not entered prominently into discussion. In reality, what were really being set in motion were the first steps toward an expanded standing military. The unstated assumption in these debates, ongoing since the Constitution, was that the government and the state must take more direct responsibility for national defense and not leave it primarily in the hands of the states or those who came to it out of private initiative. Not only had the problems that had occurred with the British, Spanish, and French since the end of the revolution added to this conviction, but so had developments such as the Whiskey Rebellion and difficult and, at times, costly campaigns against Native Americans.[124] Through a combination of twenty pieces of legislation, Adams from April to July 1798 began to place the United States military more in place—the power to buy, build, or even rent twelve warships; the leasing or buying of foundries for cannon and manufacturers of arms; ammunition; the building or purchase of galley ships for coastal defense; the establishment of the Department of the Navy; and the creation of the US Marines. In late May, Congress provided the authority to order US armed vessels (which would obviously include privateers as the United States virtually had no navy yet) to seize any armed French vessel operating on American coasts and bring it into an American port. In July, Congress authorized extending that power to anywhere on the high seas. At the end of June, Congress authorized Adams to receive twenty-four armed vessels provided as gifts or on loan from private individuals.[125]

The last was an interesting turn to the private sector to assist. Ultimately, ten warships came into service this way during the Quasi-War, the undeclared war with France. Philadelphia even built a thirty-six-gun frigate. Newburyport, Massachusetts, was the first port city to complete a ship, and it loaned a twenty-gun warship to the United States. Frederick Leiner, the historian of these subscription warships, as they were called, has observed that these ships were the result of actions taken by citizens who realized in part that the new government did not have the capabilities, yet, to build many warships. However, many American ports had shipyards or settings for the construction of ships and boats. The US government issued stock, usually at 6 percent interest, to those private investors who took on the construction of these ships. Whether the investors were patriots for profits or profiteers for patriotism is somewhat beside the point. They did so partly because many of them were merchants who had suffered losses at the hands of the French. This was certainly the case with Newburyport. These were also individuals who operated in a cultural and legal setting that had not drawn distinctions between private and public interest as we understand them today. Sometimes the city providing the vessel built them more to the specifications it knew from its own maritime experience, such as Baltimore, which would provide two sloops that could maneuver quickly in shallow waters—an important feature for approaching French privateers near the shore. It is not surprising that some of the cities thought the vessels would be used primarily for patrolling nearby waters, which occurred in some instances. Whether the subscription ships actually saved the government money is unclear. Their future, however, was short lived, since Thomas Jefferson's ascent to the White House in early 1801 brought into office a president who was suspicious of both merchants and the navy.[126]

While Adams was greatly concerned about the ability of the United States to neutralize the danger of French warships and privateers, an entirely different problem arose relating to actions taken by a private citizen in matters of foreign policy and national security. After the American delegation returned from Paris and the unsavory XYZ affair, George Logan, a respected Quaker physician in Philadelphia and friend of Vice President Jefferson, decided to go to Paris in June 1798 to discuss with the French what had gone wrong and whether they would be willing to accept another mission from the United States. A few of the French initially confused Logan with an Indian chief carrying the same last name that Jefferson had mentioned in his *Notes on Virginia*, but once that confusion ended Logan received attention from both newspapers and prominent French figures, who gave him an understanding they were ready to receive another delegation. Logan even believed he had won a reprieve from the Directory to end the embargo against American ships and to release imprisoned crewmen. On his return later that year, Logan met with President Adams, who listened to his account and claims with respect. Secretary of State Pickering had less patience with the impressionable Quaker and told him that the Directory had hoodwinked him. There was no such decree relating to American ships and seamen. Former President Washington, now in the final months of his life, expressed his strong disapproval of such actions by a private citizen, and Adams decided to go to Congress to seek legislation that would halt such "temerity and impertinence of individuals affecting to interfere in the public affairs between France and the United States."[127]

Representative Matthew Griswold of Connecticut introduced legislation in the House just a week after New Year's Day, 1799. The House and Senate approved the legislation respectively after some debate and changes on January 17 and January 25, 1799. The language of the original legislation is worth quoting at length to appreciate the scope of this effort to end acts of private citizens in foreign relations:

> *Be it enacted, etc.*, that if any person, being a citizen of the United States, or in any foreign country, shall, without the permission or authority of the Government of the United States, directly or indirectly, commence or carry on any verbal or written correspondence or intercourse with any foreign Government, or any officer or agent thereof, relating to any dispute or controversy between any foreign Government and the United States, with an intent to influence the measures or conduct of the Government having disputes or controversies with the United States, as aforesaid; or of any person, being a citizen of or resident within, the United States, and not duly authorized shall counsel, advise, aid or assist, in any such correspondence with intent as aforesaid, he or they shall be deemed guilty of a high misdemeanor; and, on conviction before any court of the United States having jurisdiction thereof, shall be punished by a fine not exceeding ___ thousand dollars, and by imprisonment during a term not less than ___ months, not exceeding ___ years.[128]

One has to see the significance of this law in the ongoing efforts of the early United States to centralize the expression, authority, and implementation of foreign policy under the constitutionally designated offices and institutions. The problem is related to the same one raised during the revolution and the Articles of Confederation period: Who speaks for the United States—its officials, or the state governments? The very same question was in motion here, too. The answer in 1799 and today is not to rule out a place for private actors but rather to guarantee that when they had a part they did so as an authorized actor speaking or acting on behalf of the United States. The purpose here is not to defend or attack the role of what has become known as the Logan Act. The Logan Act seems almost to be a living fossil today. It is waved in the air in different circumstances and even threatened, but US officials have never successfully prosecuted anyone in violation of it in over two hundred years. Whether they should do so in the present or future is a question for the last chapter, not here.

The United States and France were now entering into the phase of their dispute that is well-captured in the term *quasi-war*. Congress had authorized US warships, armed merchantmen, and privateers to seize armed French vessels. Following his earlier reservations, as well as those of Hamilton and others, Adams sought no declaration of war. However, the United States suspended relations with France. Combined with the authorizations provided by Congress, France arguably had legitimate reasons to wonder whether the United States was actually at war with it. The question seemed even to play itself out in the exchange between Captain Stephen Decatur Sr., US Navy, and his counterpart on a French privateer in early July 1798 when Decatur's twenty-gun sloop made the first capture by the Navy. When the French commander asked Decatur if the United States was at war with France, he answered "no" but then added that France was. The French commander's retort was that he had a commission for what he was doing on the high seas, to which Decatur responded that so did he! Declared war or not, both commanders were operating within powers given to them by the designated sections of their respective governments.[129]

American warships and privateers did begin to have effect on the presence of French privateers near the coast and also in the Caribbean, where French privateers enjoyed even greater success. One of the ports where French privateers originated was Saint Dominique in Haiti. The rebellion led by Toussaint L'Ouverture on that island presented a real hope to the Americans—the elimination of a key base for French operations—so it was no surprise that Adams in early June 1799 lifted the US embargo on trade with the island out of hope of supporting the rebellion. The British had already tried the same course as part of a campaign going back to 1793 to reduce France's presence in the West Indies. Toussaint and his followers were no more anxious to have British slave masters than French, and the British worried the rebellion could spread antislavery sentiment throughout the region. By the time Adams had acted in 1799 the British military campaign in Haiti had failed, but they successfully placed themselves alongside the United States in its effort to support Toussaint and weaken French control, which now had ascended in importance to London. Toussaint in turn promised to stop French privateering on the island. The French in turn had agreed to another round of negotiations with the Americans to settle differences and end the ongoing conflict. When the Americans left the United States they were preparing to negotiate with the Directory, but by the time of their arrival they found they would have to negotiate with the government of the new First Consul, Napoleon Bonaparte. What his intentions were was unclear.[130]

Whether the United States had been at war or not was a question that figured not only in the conduct of the war itself but also in the settlement of claims that remained afterward. Adams at one point had referred to it as a "half-war."[131] Attorney General Charles Lee concluded in August 1798 that the United States and France were engaged not only in "an actual maritime war" but, more importantly, a maritime war that both nations had authorized. In August 1800 the US Supreme Court in a unanimous decision ruled that France and the United States had been engaged in a lawful war, even if no declaration had occurred. The circumstances that brought the court to this conclusion were complex. John Bas had been the commander of an American cargo ship that a French privateer seized at the end of March 1799. About three weeks later an American public armed vessel, commanded by a Mr. Tingy, recaptured Bas's vessel. The technical issue in the case was the amount of money due to Tingy from the vessel's original owners, which, in turn, depended on which federal statute the court concluded was actually in force when the recapture occurred. The final version of the law came from 1799, and it referred to recaptures from "the enemy." Tingy's claim sought the largest amount of money, and to obtain it the court had to rule that a state of war existed; otherwise, there was no "enemy." In August 1800 the Supreme Court ruled that the right of prize did exist in this conflict even if no declaration of war had occurred. In short, the hostilities we know as the Quasi-War had, in effect, constituted a war.[132]

The Supreme Court's assertion that a state of war existed without a declaration was not an invitation to write Congress out of the decision. The explanations offered in the ruling made clear that the scale or magnitude of war was a matter Congress could address and even define. Justice Bushrod Washington's explanation drew significantly from the arguments of de Vattel and Burlamaqui. Congress could authorize "imperfect" or "perfect" wars. The former were "more confined" as well as "limited as to places, persons and things" beyond which those receiving the commission can "go no further than the extent of their commission." A "perfect" war involved "one whole nation . . . at war with another whole nation." Justice William Paterson iterated Washington's argument with reference to "modified warfare" that is "authorized by the congressional authority of our country." In this case it was "a maritime war, a war at seas as to certain purposes." Justice Samuel Chase's opinion concurred with his assertion that "Congress is empowered to declare a general war, or [C]ongress may wage a limited war; limited in place, in objects, and in time."[133] Thus, if it was a form of war that Congress believed required authorization—which at this time appeared to be all conflicts aside from those against Native Americans—Congress could calibrate the scale and scope of the war. As Justice Paterson's explanation pointed out, this was "a war at seas as to certain purposes," a very apt description of what letters of marque and reprisal and privateering had become—one form of limited war, not the equivalent of all forms—that Congress controlled and exercised as seen fit in its discussions with the executive branch and through its own deliberations and decision.

Thus, as the United States headed into one of its more tumultuous elections in 1800, it believed it had organized itself and its laws in ways that would win respect and equal treatment among the community of nations. This was not an inflated delusion that placed the United States alongside that of Britain or Napoleonic France in terms of military power—far from it—but rather a belief that it had done what was expected of effective sovereign nations. It had created laws, processes, and instruments that placed the use of violence and war under government and state control. Private actors and practitioners might well remain, but law now required them to act within the boundaries set forth in the Constitution and by subsequent law. Building upon the legacies of other European states and obviously Britain's in particular, the United States had accomplished significant measures in a span of twenty-five years.

The single-largest question that remained for the Americans in defining the relationship between the private and public instruments of force and war was whether the new nation would choose to create a larger-scale standing military capability or rely, instead, on the premise that it could mobilize state militias and privateers to supplement what were still a small army and navy. Perhaps the Convention of Mortefountaine in 1800, which concluded the Quasi-War with France and buried whatever remained of the 1778 treaties with France, added reason for new confidence as Thomas Jefferson assumed the presidency. Confidence, it turned out, was not going to last very long. A debate soon ensued over what means of power the United States had in the international arena and what was the place of private means of force within that power.

5 THE RETURN AND RETREAT OF PRIVATE FORCE FOR PROFIT

Americans at the beginning of the nineteenth century were not uncomfortable relying on private actors in war. In fact, many, particularly Jeffersonian Republicans, regarded this as preferable to a large navy. Thanks to the memories of the American Revolution and a parallel retreat from use of mercenaries in European war, the latter had no place in the constitutional design for territorial self-defense. In spite of the initial actions taken by President John Adams, state militias still remained the predominant force alongside a small standing army. Overall, the Americans had reason to think they had created enough control and accountability over the decision to go to war and the choice of relying on private actors on the high seas to meet the requirements of international law at the time.

To a modern reader, the certainty of these assumptions seems almost astonishing. The comparative confidence of two centuries ago that the power to declare war was securely locked in Congress looks quaintly archaic at best when generations of Americans have become accustomed to presidential decisions to use force with little prior consultation with Congress, much less an authorization or the rare declaration of war. Three-quarters of a century of a large standing military whose size would likely terrify the framers, even those like Hamilton, if they could see it has become accepted fact for most of the nation's population. American comprehension of war is still heavily shaped by the four years the nation was in World War II, thereby making use of private actors in war unique and arguably dangerous. There were private contractors and actors who saw conflict in this last global war—the American contractors on Wake Island when the Japanese invaded it, admittedly involuntary participants in a stubborn, but hopeless, defense; or the American "volunteers" from the Army Air Force who served with the Chinese Air Force before the United States declared war on December 8, 1941. However, the efforts of massive state mobilization and the military during the world war and Cold War that followed tower over these people and their circumstances. The eminence of national security—in itself a postwar term—in national priorities and the level of defense spending make the outlook of the United States from two hundred years ago resemble either a modern nostalgic yearning for a world that might have been or a fool's paradise that reflected the nation's innocence and inexperience in the international arena.[1]

Appreciation of the world that immediately preceded the War of 1812 and the course of the war itself—at least on the high seas—is critical for understanding the significance of what followed the conflict. Arguably, the United States experienced its most successful use of letters of marque and reprisal in its history. The constitutional arrangement of placing the issuance of these letters alongside that of the power to declare war arguably worked, even if some thought, as we will see, that President James Madison should have turned earlier to Congress to authorize reprisals before war was declared. This is not to claim that issuance of these commissions for privateering turned the course of the war in favor of the United States, but their actions definitely generated concern and worry in London at a time when the British had far greater matters of national interest at stake in Europe. The point to remember is that the Americans thought the private instrument, so to speak, had served the nation well on the ocean. They carried this notion into the decade before the Civil War and even the war itself—on both sides, but by the closing decades of the century the attraction of private force essentially disappeared. Everything from changing values and law, technology, and national interest and ambition altered the American outlook. Just as privateering had ascended with the growth of mercantile empires, it also then confronted greater challenges and restriction by expanding states that wanted to place more authority over violence in war in the state's hands and not those of privateers and profiteers.

COERCION, PRIVATEERING, AND THE WAR OF 1812

To understand the emphasis Jefferson and Madison placed on privateering as an instrument, it is helpful to appreciate the central importance they and many of their political colleagues assigned to commerce as both the means and objective they envisioned for the United States in the world at large. Whether Federalist or Jeffersonian Republican, these were individuals who had been born in a mercantilistic world that had purposely limited or restricted colonies and could do the same to the United States if permitted to tread on its newly established rights as a member of the community of nations. We saw this conviction emerge during the revolution in both the minds of future Federalists, like John Adams, or a future Jeffersonian, like their own namesake, Thomas Jefferson. There was a confidence that if able to trade in unhindered fashion with the rest of the world, the United States would prosper. Whether Adams found the time to wade through Adam Smith's *The Wealth of Nations* is unclear, but he did have the time to read works by Smith's contemporaries, like Thomas Pownall, a former governor of Massachusetts Bay Colony who echoed Smith's arguments. Adams aspired to have the United States trade with all nations and to remain neutral in times of war. Benjamin Franklin, his Pennsylvania counterpart in Paris during the American Revolution, had thought the same.[2] Prosperity, though, was not the sole purpose in this vision of a commerce-connected world. Picking up on some of the writers of the French and British Enlightenment who decried not only mercantilism but the dynamics of the balance of power, proponents of a diplomacy resting on commerce saw it as a replacement for this older, violent order with one benefiting from the harmony created by the move of goods, capital, and people. Not all critics of mercantilism and the old political/diplomatic order saw commerce as such a guaranteed palliative. Both Smith and his fellow Scot, David Hume, did not share such unguarded optimism, but others, including some Americans, did. Their resistance to the restrictions of British mercantilism and the subsequent steps to craft a new nation with a stronger central government only reinforced these inclinations.[3]

It was in those reservations about the capacities of commerce to change the international system that one could find an emerging division between Revolutionary-era allies and friends. Federalists like Adams or his president, George Washington, believed in the importance of commerce and certainly did not find it to be in the interests of the United States to develop political and military capabilities to insert itself into the affairs of Europe, but as to how to address the prospect of war differences emerged on the American side. While Federalists disagreed over the extent and cost of measures to take, their response was that to defend the nation it had to be prepared for war. As we have seen, Adams, in particular, began taking steps to do this. The Jeffersonian preference was to rely more on the transformative model of diplomacy the Americans had developed during the revolution. This was a worldview that did not accept as a given the need for more defensive preparation but aspired for a newer framework among nations based upon commerce and rule of law.

Rule of law is the underlying foundation of a government based on a constitution. It stands above the actions of individuals as well as those of member states in the political community. In the conduct of commerce, the US Constitution had clearly subordinated the power of the states to that of the national government. States could not make their own currency or enter into agreements with foreign governments, including commerce. This harmonization of policy and instruments was analogous to what had been done in the arena of war and related actions, such as letters of marque and reprisal. Not only did such control through the Constitution assure standing with other nations; it would also promote stability and, it was hoped, prosperity in the United States. Even Jefferson, who was suspicious of overcentralized authority, recognized the importance of such measures as he contemplated the growth of a "republican empire." Commerce and investment would promote prosperity and linkage among the different states. Territorial expansion would assist in the prevention of urban concentrations that Jefferson thought were part of the troubles that plagued Europe and its predominantly monarchical systems. Optimally, Jefferson preferred a world in which the United States would have to depend as little as possible on Europe and the outside. "It might be better for us to abandon the ocean altogether," he once wrote, ". . . to leave to others to bring what we shall want, and to carry what we can spare." Yet, Jefferson even knew this type of semi-autarky was neither feasible nor desirable. In fact its opposite—the opening of the world's seas and ports to American commerce and the same for American ports to that of the world—was what was best for the United States.[4]

It was that vision and the policies set out to accomplish and protect it that brought the United States into collision with its former political master—Great Britain. Certainly, there were many contributors to the War of 1812—American nationalism and expansionism, shifts in the American political landscape, ongoing involvement of the British with Native American tribes in parts of the American West, perhaps a longing in certain circles in London to "correct" the mistakes of just thirty years prior, the disputes over rights on the high seas (part of the larger question discussed in these pages), and London's frustration with a pesky government that did not seem to appreciate the magnitude of dangers the British faced in Europe—but a fact that covers part of the aforementioned is that the United States and Britain just had fundamental disagreements over what was meant by free trade.

Although the most articulate and long-lasting critiques of British mercantilism came right from the British Isles, many in the government and other important circles had not been converted to the arguments. The types of open trade Adam Smith wrote about, or what people thought he wrote about, were not in place in British policy. Nor were they, to be honest, in American minds, as illustrated by the many heated arguments and votes that occurred in Congress over tariffs. That important fact aside, the Americans held to a two-part understanding of free trade. It did not mean just the unhindered movement of goods and products, thanks to the end of mercantilist-like barriers and practices, but also enabled neutral countries to trade with belligerents during periods of war. The notion that "free ships make free goods" was not a novel idea created by the Americans; it had appeared in commercial practice as early as the thirteenth century in the Mediterranean. The British had accepted this practice, too, by the seventeenth century if not before. Neutral vessels could carry goods to belligerents with the exception of contraband—goods and articles that supported the conduct of war. Defining contraband remained a contentious issue into the last century. At times, its definition might be very narrow, as was the case in the Peace of Utrecht in 1713 that excluded food, clothing, and naval stores used for constructing and repairing ships from "contraband."[5]

The British announced the Rule of 1756 at the beginning of the Seven Years' War, and it was still in effect in the opening decade of the 1800s. It was going to have a major impact on the commerce of the United States. The rule stated that trade prohibited to a neutral state during peacetime could not be conducted during periods of war. In practical terms it meant that after Britain effectively stopped the sailing of French ships from French ports, the Americans could not step in as a carrier to take the goods from France to French colonies or reverse. The American argument was that neutrality enabled its goods to practice the "free ships make free goods" claim. During the 1790s and Jefferson's first term in office the British actually tolerated a circumvention of their rule in which American ships would make a brief stop in an American port and thus break up what would otherwise have been a continuous voyage between two French destinations. British tolerance for this wore thin, and in 1805 London announced that American ships would have to carry documents to show the voyage had been broken and not just for a convenient stopover. The British began to seize American vessels, possibly as many as four hundred, although British courts released most of them later. Contraband was a closely related and even more difficult matter. The Americans interpreted the word narrowly; the British did not. If the goods were not contraband, but still French owned, the British insisted they could seize them during periods of war. This was a clear challenge to the American position that ownership of the ship, not the good, determined what could or not be seized. American merchants circumvented British policy by "Americanizing" the goods—purchasing them and making them American owned. The British saw through this charade easily.[6]

The British and Americans tried to negotiate their differences in what is known as the Monroe-Pinkney Treaty of 1806 (named after the two US negotiators, James Monroe and William Pinkney). The British made significant concessions to the Americans on the rights of commerce and seizure, essentially accepting the American re-exports practice and defining contraband narrowly and offering to pay American merchants for vessels detained in violation of this treaty, but they would not yield on impressments—the power to halt foreign vessels and search for British deserters. The Americans actually had to concede their insistence on "free ships make free goods," guarantee their neutrality, implement no commercial sanctions against Britain, and not allow privateers from British enemies to use American ports. Jefferson chose not to submit the treaty to the Senate for its advice and consent. The absence of any concession on impressments was unacceptable. So, too, was the British insistence on no future commercial sanctions, which Jefferson believed would strip the United States of a diplomatic instrument it could use. Also, Jefferson apparently thought France and Russia would emerge as the dominant powers from these wars and in so doing be able to compel the British to announce a more lenient stance on neutral rights.[7]

One can legitimately wonder how well the Americans understood contemporary changes in warfare and their implications for the understanding of international rights that they entertained. The wars begun by the French Republic and now continued by Napoleon were total war for all purposes, dependent on mass mobilization of society and armies whose size would have seemed unimaginable during the eighteenth century, when conflicts in Europe had been fought to resolve territorial differences, compensate for losses, or other finite political purposes. For some these were wars of national survival; for others they were wars of emerging national identity. Perhaps the United States overestimated its ability to stay afar from these conflicts due to distance, its confidence in the potential values of commercial contact with all, and the expectation placed in international law after the American Revolution and the first decades beyond.[8] Without question, Jefferson and Madison carried overly high expectations as to what their measures and instruments could accomplish.

On becoming president in 1801 Thomas Jefferson and his fellow Republicans worried not only about the antidemocratic threat posed by standing militaries but about their cost as well. Within a year the standing army dropped from 5,400 to 3,300. The possibility of war in 1808 with Britain moved Congress to raise the ceiling for the army to 10,000, but Republican politicians primarily treated the enlarged officer corps as a reward for political supporters. Party loyalty rather than competence seemed to be the preferred measure. The navy fared as badly, even in spite of Jefferson's resort to its use against the Barbary pirates from Tripoli during his first term. The president had little trouble using naval force to protect the rights of American commerce against pirates; otherwise, its cost was high and its expansion posed in the eyes of some Republicans a reckless challenge to the British. This was indeed a low-profile strategy that would seem foreign to Americans two hundred years afterward. The Republicans did provide funding for the construction of coastal defenses and gunboats, which could be useful for coastal defense but would easily be swamped in higher seas. The real preference for naval operations was "the militia of the seas"—privateers.[9]

Jefferson's thoughts on privateering had changed based on circumstance and the danger that he thought existed. In 1804, while concerned with the mounting disagreements with the British as well as the Tripoli pirates, Jefferson condemned privateering. Complaints had come to him about US citizens who had so acted, and Jefferson admonished "that individuals should undertake to wage private war, independently of the authority of their country, can not be permitted in a well-ordered society. Its tendency to produce aggression on the laws and rights of other nations and to endanger the peace of our own is so obvious that I doubt not you [Congress] will adopt measures for restraining it effectually in future."[10] However, Jefferson was objecting less to privateering than to the fact it was occurring without proper authority. That was a clear reference to the Constitution. This was 1804. Jefferson still entertained hope of resolving differences with the British over rights on the high seas and other issues. He certainly wanted to avoid war, and he knew the British could demand compensation for the acts of any self-proclaimed privateer.

Eight years later, in fact on July 4, 1812, a month after the actual declaration of war by the United States and on a day that resonated with Jefferson and many Americans, Jefferson praised the prospective role of privateers:

> In the United States, every possible encouragement should be given to privateering in time of war with a commercial nation. We have tens of thousands of seamen that without it [privateering] would be destitute of the means of support, and useless to their country. Our national ships are too few in number to give employment to a twentieth part of them, or retaliate the acts of the enemy. But by licensing private armed vessels, the whole naval force of the nation is truly brought to bear on the foe.[11]

Jefferson makes an interesting choice of words in this article. The description of Britain as a "commercial nation" is not only apt—it ironically parallels Napoleon's about a "nation of shopkeepers," but it is not as dismissive; the characterization attests to Jefferson's lasting confidence even in 1812 that attacking British commerce could produce the desired result. This especially seemed within reach if done by "the whole naval force of the nation." Jefferson certainly was not deluding himself about the capabilities of the US Navy. This confidence reflected, instead, a belief that the cheaper alternative of relying on merchants and their seamen rather than just a navy, owners and investors outfitting merchant vessels to make them warships, and congressional authorization of their use on the ocean could make the British accept American wishes. Without question, the size of the American fleet, if this scale of privateering actually occurred, would be significant, and, as converting or refitting merchant vessels to be more like warships would be cheaper and faster than building the latter, the option of privateering was simply more desirable and obtainable.[12]

Before such calls for force and war could be made with legal as well as political assurance, Jefferson and Madison had to traverse a difficult course that saw their hopes in other commercial measures fall seriously short. Jefferson tried a nonimportation act in 1806 aimed at select British manufactured goods. A year later, in June 1807, the British warship HMS *Leopard* fired upon the USS *Chesapeake* after the latter's captain had refused to allow a British boarding party to come on the vessel to search for deserters (which indeed there were on the American ship). Even though the British would subsequently disavow the attack and offer reparations, the Americans remembered the affair as a flagrant violation of sovereignty, among other insults. In December 1807 Jefferson and Congress responded with an embargo on trade with Britain. This attempt at economic coercion of Britain through self-inflicted denial failed as well, even after Jefferson got Congress to approve sweeping authorities to enforce it, which mainly increased political dissent in the United States. By the time Madison won the election of 1808 and prepared to enter the White House, there was not much left in the inventory of choices in economic coercion except to go with the Non-Intercourse Act, which suspended American trade with all belligerents and their colonies and closed American ports to them. The one thing neither president could do was actually stop American merchants and captains from taking their vessels wherever they wanted once they were beyond national waters. Some trade with Britain continued.[13]

On entering the White House, James Madison faced calls from nationalists who wanted the United States to resort to force, but Madison hoped to avoid such measures through continuation of commercial pressure. In Madison's view, as well as his secretary of state, Robert Smith's, international law set standards that had to be met to justify war against Great Britain.[14] Madison's aversion to war may have been illustrated by his selections for the cabinet positions of secretaries of war and navy—William Eustis and Paul Hamilton—who were about as undistinguished and unprepared a pair the new president could have found.[15] Nevertheless, during his first weeks in office Madison flirted with measures of marque and reprisal that could justify limited war, if the right conditions developed. Several nationalistic Republicans in Congress wanted to authorize the arming of merchant vessels, partly from the hope and conviction that a British attack on them could be a legal cause for war. These discussions occurred alongside those that repealed the embargo of 1807 and replaced it with the Non-Intercourse Act. Opinion on Madison's willingness to support such a form of limited war is divided. Possibly, the president regarded letters of marque and reprisal as measures that accompanied war rather than a form of escalation that some hoped would provoke a British act that could justify war. Congress removed the clause authorizing such measures and proceeded with the Non-Intercourse Act.[16] The expiration of this law within a year required

Madison and Congress to consider another strategy, which was a reversal of the suspension of trade with a restoration of it with all belligerents. If one of the belligerents, Britain or France, recognized the rights of trade by neutrals, the United States would suspend trade with the other—a tactical error that Napoleon quickly exploited when he announced the suspension of the Continental Decrees, in which he had sought to halt British trade with French-occupied sections of Europe as well as those allied with France. Madison was now in an unenviable position. If he thought Napoleon's action would increase pressure on the British to change their position, it proved erroneous. The options left for commercial pressure on the British were disappearing.[17]

By summer 1811 Madison assuredly realized that the likelihood of war was high. Congress avoided the swamp-like heat and humidity of Washington during this time of year, and Madison called it back into session for November 1811. The message he sent it on November 5, 1811, described the failure of the latest negotiations with Britain, and the president told Congress it was now time to prepare the nation for the possibility of war by expanding the army and navy, seeking volunteers, addressing the readiness of state militias, and increasing munitions supplies. Madison explicitly mentioned the likely need to authorize letters of marque and reprisal. Interestingly, both Albert Gallatin, his secretary of the Treasury, and James Monroe, his new secretary of state, cautioned Madison against taking premature warlike stances. Madison by now also thought use of armed merchantmen might serve as a provocation of British action to justify war, but he agreed to drop the reference to their authorization in his request to Congress.[18] In March 1812, as no evidence of British moderation was on hand, Madison told Congress to continue work on legislation to prepare for war. Movement on this was not always as smooth as Madison had hoped. There was resistance to the high cost of building new warships, preparatory measures regarding state militias were not in place, and Congress did not create or expand any taxation. Evidence of the imminence of war could be seen in legislation of an embargo for ninety days to get American merchantmen off of the high seas. Not surprisingly, there was a flurry at American ports as merchants worked to get ships on the way before the embargo entered into effect. Meanwhile, the British began to make incremental changes in policy that suggested accommodation with the American positions. They did not do so dramatically—the most notable announcement coming just two days before the American declaration of war, suspending the Orders of Council affecting American trade. Dramatic public announcements would not have helped in 1812, as the speed of news still depended on wind, sail, and the sea.[19]

It is worth stepping aside briefly to contrast this rather elaborate, cautious route toward war that sought to rest itself on legal claims and causes for war with steps taken in 1811 by the governor of Indiana Territory, General William Henry Harrison, to commence a campaign against the Shawnee under the leadership of Tecumseh and his brother Tenskwatawa, known to most on the frontier as the Prophet. Harrison was an ambitious expansionist. The interaction of the Shawnee and their allies with the British was no secret, but it was arguably expansionism that fed Harrison's proposal to launch a campaign against the Shawnee encampment, Prophetstown, on the Wabash River. There was no consultation with Congress here. Harrison did apprise the secretary of war of the need for such a campaign, which, to be fair, the Madison administration, given other problems, was not anxious to commence but willing to support if the opportunity seemed ripe. Harrison did receive additional troops alongside the state militias and volunteers he commanded. The battle of Tippecanoe, which Harrison depicted in glorious terms, would further inflame expansionist sentiments against both the Indians and the British.[20]

International law, which so concerned Madison and others in relation to war against Great Britain, did not favor the status of the Shawnee or any other Native Americans. In a recent study by Deborah Rosen on the first Seminole War, which occurred only a few years after the War of 1812, the importance of the distinction between the rights of sovereign versus nonsovereign nations and areas is made clear. As discussed earlier in this book, a long tradition already stood in international law that justified different treatment and standards for commencing war against native peoples. The United States did not see those tribes as independent sovereign states comparable to its counterparts in Europe. Dealing with Indians was often depicted as part of protection and maintaining internal order; a declaration of war was unnecessary. Law was a consideration in these arguments, but, unlike treatment of a sovereign state, the prevailing view was that Indians were outside the law—for example, a recurrent argument that Indians were to be treated as outlaws. Some even argued that the United States was in a state of "perpetual war" with the Indians, which also negated any need for a declaration. Treating Indian actions as criminal also placed them outside the jurisdiction of international law as understood at the time. As the United States had shown itself to be a member of the community of sovereign states, it could exercise what was then recognized as a right of sovereign states—the expansion of its territory into areas where rights of comparable sovereignty existed.[21] The dichotomy between concern about law and justification in war with Britain is ironic because Americans actions, like Harrison's, could have repercussions with Great Britain as well, particularly if their effects spread into British Canada proper. The British, though, could not have been overly concerned about this dichotomy, as they, too benefited from the same approach to native populations in regions that were deemed sovereign-free.

On June 1, 1812, Madison sent Congress a message asking Congress to decide whether conditions warranted a declaration of war. The key paragraph is worth quoting in its entirety because it reflects Madison's ongoing caution as well as his respect for the structure and process in the Constitution:

> Whether the United States shall continue passive under these progressive usurpations and these accumulating wrongs, or, opposing force to force in defense of their national rights, shall commit a just cause in the hands of the Almighty Disposer of Events, avoiding all connections which might entangle it in the contest or views of other powers, and preserving a constant readiness to concur in an honorable reestablishment of peace and friendship, is a solemn question which the Constitution wisely confides to the Legislative department of the Government. I am happy in the assurance that the decision will be worthy of the enlightened and patriotic councils of a virtuous, a free, and a powerful nation.[22]

Madison should have had little doubt that Congress would provide a declaration. Even a president in the early nineteenth century, particularly a president who had served in the Constitutional Convention, would know one does not request power from Congress if he does not really want it. In the earlier part of his message Madison emphasized Britain's violations of American sovereignty and right to conduct commerce—rights that he believed nation-states retained. He briefly referred to "warfare just renewed by the savages on one of our extensive frontiers," which covered Harrison's actions as well as events that had followed, but the focus was British abuse of American rights as a nation-state. Before making the request quoted above, Madison summed up the situation with the observation, "We behold, in fine, on the side of Great Britain a state of war against the United States, and on the side of the United States a state of peace toward Great Britain."[23] Whether the United States was going to change that "state" because of the "progressive usurpations" by the British was a matter for Congress to decide.

Declaring war was just one question Congress would decide; another question was the scale or magnitude with which the United States wished to wage war. This is an interesting facet to examine because it reveals the fact that Congress believed it had a role in defining the course and conduct of the war. This could encompass the extent of use of armed merchant vessels and privateers in the conflict. As most of Madison's message had centered on maritime issues, the option of waging war just on the sea came into consideration. This proved more appealing in the Senate than in the House, where war fever was higher, but some of Madison's cabinet, including the secretary of the Treasury, worried about the war's potentially high costs. Confining it to the ocean might be better. The economic and physical cost of a land war could be high. However, the prospect of a maritime conflict appealed to a rationale that had been part of American thinking since the revolution, and even before, thanks to its British heritage. Licensing and arming existing ships, either as privateers or simple armed merchant ships, could be faster and cheaper than depending on the US Navy. After all, private interests paid for these types of ships, not the government. Attacking British merchant ships could be more damaging than any attempt to fight the Royal Navy. Members of Congress probably did not have access to the types of information their modern successors do about the physical strength of their opponent, but they did know as straight fact that British naval power could not be matched. If they knew the actual numbers, they were not encouraging. The US Navy had twenty ships (eight frigates and twelve sloops), and seventeen of them could be sent to sea. The Royal Navy's strength was 584 ships, of which 124 were frigates and 102 were the larger ships of the line.[24]

Another reason for restricting the war to sea was the problem of French treatment of American merchant ships, which continued in spite of Napoleon's announced termination of the Continental Decrees affecting US shipping. Of course, his invasion of Russia had also changed the dynamic of that system. One appeal of this maritime option was that it might draw Federalist support, as Federalist merchants could choose which adversary their armed merchant ships and privateers could fight; France would be the preferable target. Yet, if Congress were to include France in the declaration,

American ships would lose any chance of using French ports. Ultimately, Congress did not limit the war to maritime measures or include France; the grievances were too identified with Britain, and the demand or aspiration for territory was too strong in much of the West and South. On June 18, the president secured a declaration of war against Great Britain, which included authority "to issue to private armed vessels of the United States commissions or letters of marque and general reprisal."[25]

The words in the declaration attested to the distinction that had evolved over time in practice and law between commissions for "private armed vessels," which would be privateers, and "letters of marque and general reprisal," the authority needed to arm a merchant vessel. Whether everyone really appreciated the distinction and what it could lead to is unclear; there are instances where use of the term *letters of marque* might include privateering, or vice versa. The confusion is increased by the fact that the commissions carried by "private armed vessels" were known as letters of marque and reprisal. A good example is from April 1812, when Representative Nathaniel Macon of Georgia, among others, urged Congress to authorize letters of marque rather than declare war. The move would only be a preparatory step for war in order to allow more time to mobilize troops. It is doubtful Macon was thinking just of arming merchant ships; that would have been a very cautious path, more so than privateers, as the latter's sole purpose was to attack shipping while the armed merchant ship was both a cargo vessel and an armed one. In principle, it had more choice (see below) facing it. Obviously, Congress did not pursue this path and chose to withhold use of either option until it included them within the declaration of war.[26]

In their purest form, privateers in the War of 1812 were literally, as described, "private armed vessels," which meant they were warships that paralleled their counterparts in the US Navy. These types of ships and crews went out with one single purpose: to attack enemy commerce and to earn the captain, crew, owner, and investors as much money as possible. The cargo "consisted solely of powder, shot, and other appurtenances of battle." Interestingly, contemporary terminology spoke of privateers being on a "cruise" while armed merchant vessels were on a "voyage."[27] Today's use of the word *cruise* to describe leisure journeys almost makes it impossible to appreciate why people would use two such words to make a distinction. Yet, one way to understand this quickly can be illustrated with wages. If you were a member of a crew on a voyage, you drew a wage, for the vessel was still a cargo ship carrying goods. Prize money came only if the ship had taken a prize. If you were on a cruise on a private armed ship, you received no wage, but, if luck came your way multiple times, you might enjoy sizable amounts of prize money, far more than would be expected from service on a vessel carrying cotton, grain, and so on.[28]

Almost all merchant ships were armed because of the need to protect themselves from pirates, but if the owner or owners wanted to convert it to an actual armed privateer to attack enemy commerce and nothing more, the preparations were not modest. Costs could run as high as $25,000 to $40,000.[29] It might be necessary to change the sails and rigging, reinforce decks to carry the weight of guns, rebuild the stanchions and railings of the ship to diminish the risk of flying pieces of wood after being hit by gunfire, and, of course, modifying the interior space of the ship to take a larger crew. We have seen the need for larger crews to be a consistent requirement for privateers in order to overtake the targeted prize and to sail it afterward. Purchase of cannon would obviously add more to the cost. This was plainly a business investment that could offer good returns on a single cruise if the ship took good prizes.[30]

The armed merchantman, the "letter of marque" vessel, sailed under different circumstances and expectations. As the ship remained a merchant vessel, it might not have required as much overhaul. The size of the crew was customarily smaller than a privateer's. On these voyages, such ships went from port to port, carrying their cargo and delivering goods and passengers as needed. The letter of marque served more as a convenient protection if the ship came upon another vessel that seemed a relatively risk-free and potentially lucrative target. Taking on a high-risk vessel was seldom a path taken by privateers, who wanted to make money rather than risk destruction or serious damage and loss of crew. Possessing the letter protected the captain and crew from charges of piracy. As wartime posed dangers to the flow of commerce, taking a prize could compensate for losses in traditional commerce. However, it was the decision of the owner, and particularly the captain, to act more like a privateer or to continue with the peaceful movement of goods.[31]

The US government now controlled the entire mechanism and process for privateering and letters of marque and reprisal. The Department of State was the issuing authority, and the actual paperwork was handled by the customs collectors in the various port cities. The process the owner or owners had to go through was very similar to that experienced by earlier generations in the American colonies or in Britain—provision of information about the characteristics of the ship, the identity of senior officers, and the posting of a bond. On receiving the letter or commission, the captain possessed a set of instructions very similar to those seen during the American Revolution: the right to exercise "the rights of war, with all the justice and humanity which characterizes the nation of which you are members." Privateers and holders of letters were required "to pay the strictest regard to the rights of neutral powers, and the usages of civilized nations" and "to give them as little molestation or interruption as will consist with the right of ascertaining their neutral character."[32] Initially the Treasury Department treated prize goods as regular imports, which meant the loss of about 40 percent of the value of the prize goods. The United States depended on privateering as part of its approach to the war, and privateers depended on the ability to make a good profit for themselves, owners, investors, and crews. Within five months of the declaration of war, merchants in Baltimore, the leading port of origin for privateers, had sent a delegation down the road to Washington, DC, to urge Congress to end this requirement for prize goods, which Congress did. Now all the prize good money went to the parties involved with the privateers—most importantly, perhaps, the crew, who had no other source of money if they had returned from a "cruise" on a privateer.[33]

Other aspects of federal control over privateers are interesting to consider because of what the government tried to reward and what it found difficult to address. After declaring war, Congress offered privateers a reward previously restricted to US warships—namely, a bounty of $20 for each crewman found on an armed enemy ship of equal or greater size. Congress would extend this bounty, and later increase it, for other prisoners brought in by privateers. The likelihood of privateers attacking a British armed ship of similar size was not high, so one could question the incentive. Its purpose, though, was to encourage both US Navy ships and privateers to take prisoners and sink the enemy ship rather than place crew on it to bring it into port as a prize. In an environment worried about available manpower for the navy, this was a real concern.[34] Privateers, of course, might commit crimes, and, if so, US practice and policy placed them under the jurisdiction of federal criminal law. With a war on its hands after June 1812, Congress realized this arrangement might not work well onboard actual ships; thus, it decided to place privateers under the criminal code and courts martial process of the US Navy. The privateer captain nonetheless retained authority over issues of discipline, including the commencement of a court martial. The actual trial had to wait until the privateer encountered a US warship or entered a US port, at which point US naval officers would actually conduct the proceeding. Given the small size of the US Navy, this proved difficult, and the challenge of finding an effective formula for legal accountability remained throughout the duration of the war.[35]

The single port that put the most privateers to sea was Baltimore. Well before the War of 1812 the port had built a reputation as one of the leading locations for shipment of a variety of goods and items—tobacco, coffee, flour, iron, sugar, salt, barrels, deerskins, and so on—and it was one of the American centers of shipbuilding, as shown from its contributions during the revolution. Baltimore merchants had suffered at the hands of both the British and French. In fact, the total number of Baltimore-owned ships seized by French vessels during the 1790s and early 1800s actually exceeded that taken by the British. The problem was that the British seizures involved a higher number of larger merchant ships involved in the trade with Europe, while the French had concentrated on ships in the West Indies. Thus, British actions hit profits more deeply. Yet, even in spite of noticeable losses, Baltimore merchants continued to trade aggressively; it was not just a proud tradition but the realities of livelihood in the local economy, the shipbuilders, the merchants, the laborers, and the farmers who depended on continuation of commerce.[36]

We saw Baltimore's role in privateering during the American Revolution, and that aspect of its maritime business had continued whenever circumstances invited it. Before the United States obstructed his activities, Edmond Genet and supporters of the French republic had commissioned about fifty privateers under the French flag from Baltimore alone, which investors, shipbuilders, outfitters, and seamen volunteering to serve on them welcomed. After 1798, when the Quasi-War officially commenced, Baltimore's fortunes obviously changed to the US side. Baltimore owners received seventy-four commissions from 1798 to 1800, about one-fifth of the total number issued by the United States during this undeclared war with France.[37] The city had a community of entrepreneurs who knew all aspects of shipbuilding, outfitting, commerce, and privateering. By 1810 its population, including nearby environs, was around 50,000. The workforce was there to support all of this, and so, too, were prospective sailors.[38]

In her study of American privateering during the War of 1812, Faye Kert estimates that easily 100,000 Americans participated in some aspect of privateering, running from owner to ship's crew.[39] Baltimore was just one of the centers of competence, one could say, in this particular type of business. Jerome Garitee, the historian who has most closely studied the Baltimore experience, estimates that of the 1,100 or so commissions issued by the US government during the war, Baltimore parties applied for 175 of them. Most received their commissions from customs officials right in Baltimore, but others did so from other Maryland port towns. The numbers may be a little misleading. Corporations formed to support a privateer sometimes for just one cruise operation and disbanded after the ship returned, only to be reformed separately for the next venture. The total number of shareholders in these privateering ventures amounted to around two hundred people. About half of them were one-time investors, while the rest were involved in multiple ventures. The one-time investors were usually small entrepreneurs, but there were instances of a sail maker, a tailor, or even laborers who bought into the business, many acquiring one-twentieth of it or less out of the hope of making some money. Garitee found that there were about fifty investors in the group whose identities are known who invested in four or more private armed ships. These investors came from some of the largest merchant houses in the city.[40]

During the American Revolution, the design and construction of vessels from Baltimore had already acquired a favorable reputation among those in privateering. The Baltimore clipper would become synonymous with the city's history and maritime tradition, but it should not be confused with the large Baltimore clippers that became such a visible, and even romantic, part of trade on the high seas before the American Civil War. The term clipper was simply a reference to the fact the ship could move at a fast speed or clip. The privateering clippers were possibly descendants of a type of sloop that had originated in Jamaica or Bermuda, but others argue for sources of heritage running from Scandinavia to the Mediterranean. The design was a response to conditions and necessity. A significant amount of American commerce, whether during the colonial or national periods, was coastal trade. For this, one needed neither large vessels nor large crews. The possible threat of impressment of service onto a British vessel during both periods of history added a need for a ship that could still be sailed if part of its crew had been taken by the Royal Navy. Thus, these ships needed to have speed, and to have that one had to be able to create a great deal of sail quickly. The Baltimore designers and builders made some adjustments that enabled the rigging to be more like a schooner than just a sloop. A clipper ship's crew could use these changes to their advantage—either in pursuit of a target or to escape the threat of a foreign warship or privateer. Many of them also had long oars that ran out of bulwarks found between the gun ports. If the wind died, or the vessel needed to try to move stealthily in certain conditions, these could be invaluable. These were not ships built for fighting; their guns could not match a frigate's or, worse, a ship of the line. US Navy officers did not regard them as optimal for their demands. Also, given their sail capacity, an inexperienced captain could capsize the vessel or have it swamped. Yet, even the Royal Navy recognized the merit of clipper ships for the purposes they were built. In 1813 Admiral Sir John Borlase Warren, who commanded the British vessels blockading Chesapeake Bay, informed the admiralty that he had purchased three ships "of the Baltimore built and most approved models" to handle his commands dispatch traffic. Speed was their virtue.[41]

Finding crew varied in difficulty and circumstance. The US Navy actually faced greater challenges than privateers, as it had to compete with the army, which offered a type of enlistment bounty or bonus, as well as privateers. A cruise might be just for two or three months, a far shorter commitment than required in the navy, which usually required at least a year. Navy sailors were not as well paid as crew on merchant vessels, and the navy began to offer its own bonuses to try to compensate for this disparity, but with additional money required for the period of service. Navy sailors and officers could get prize money if such opportunities appeared. Those serving on true privateers depended on the hope that they would take numerous prizes and earn far more than any salaried seaman could.[42] The size of the crew varied with the nature of the ship—privateer or a merchantman carrying a letter of marque. Crews of 100 to 140 were not uncommon for privateers, whereas merchant ships needed only about forty at most. Captains often did their own recruiting, and, if not, they relied on recruiting agents, who obviously received compensation for each recruit. The circumstances surrounding recruitment are not difficult to imagine. A few glasses of liquor, a little advance money, and a lot of promises could entice some of the men easily—timeless techniques to get men, and probably a few women, to commit to come aboard or to shoulder a gun. Garitee's research from Baltimore suggests at least 80 percent of them were under twenty-eight years of age. Most came from the port and surrounding area, but the entire crew represented origins throughout North America, the West Indies, Europe, and beyond. Ships were integrated, so blacks were among the recruited crew. The large number of crew for privateers allowed the luxury, in a way, of recruiting those who did not have nautical skills—perhaps as many as one-third—who could serve as cooks, stewards, clerks, surgeons, and even marines. Of course, the end of the privateer's cruise meant they could all leave, and the owners and captain would have to recruit another crew for a subsequent round.[43]

Any ship's crew obviously wanted to know what the division of prize money would be. The formula varied between letter of marque merchantmen and privateers. For those on a merchantman the prospective division was often between one-half to one-third of the money going to the officers and crew, and the rest going to the owners. No formatted formula existed for this type of business. Garitee found that on the *Decatur* the captain received sixteen shares, first lieutenant nine shares, the second mate seven shares, petty officers had three shares each, the cook, steward, and qualified seamen got two shares each, and the rest received one each. Each crewman had a prize ticket with his name on it and the designated segment of the prize to be received. Congress had legislated a formula for prize money in 1800, but no evidence exists to show that merchants or privateers used it. Only the navy held to this schedule. For privateers the division of prize money followed a division of more categories among the crew; after all, this was the only source of income the crew received from the cruise. The number of shares did not differ noticeably, but tasks and ranks were better enumerated. Generally, each of the crew was assured at least one share. As with armed merchantmen with letters of marque, the percentage of shares going to the owners varied.

Getting prize money on a voyage or cruise was not a certainty. Faye Kert has examined available records as closely as anyone, and she concludes that "fewer than half of all privateers captured any ships whatsoever, and almost two thirds of those prizes were either recaptured or lost before they ever reached port." In short, the lure of success was far stronger than the rate, but the latter was not so low to dissuade owners, investors, and crews from trying such ventures. Two hundred and fifty-four vessels with letters of marque (this tabulation seems to include both privateers and armed merchantmen) brought in about 900 prizes. Keep in mind again that at most, half of the armed vessels were responsible for this number. Interestingly for privateers licensed by the British or Canadians, the ratio, in its most simplified itera-tion, was more impressive—twenty-three privateers brought in 212 prizes for adjudication. The impressive number of prizes is offset, though, by the fact these were usually smaller ships that gained less money than many taken by the Americans. Yet, even if the odds were not great, success could mean a great deal to all concerned. Consider the case of the *David Porter*, a Boston privateer that captured the *Ann Dorothy* in 1814, which earned nearly $60,000 after expenses were deducted. Half of that went to the investors, the rest to the officers and crew. Each share was worth $300. For an average seaman who probably just received a single share, that was more than two years of wages in the navy or on a merchant ship. Returns like that could convince any number of people that the privateering venture was worth the risk. If one goes by name recognition as a measure of success, that award should probably go to Samuel Cunard of Liverpool, Nova Scotia, who took his prize money, invested it in cargo and mail packet ships, and became the founder of one of the world's most famous shipping lines. Kert has tried to determine the total amount of prize money received by the American side. Law required that 2 percent of the prize money go into the Seamen's Hospital Fund. From that figure, she calculated a total of $10,676,793.50. Of course, she would not claim this is a final and certain amount. The total also illustrates how successful the captors of the *Ann Dorothy* were, because obviously a lot of other prizes were smaller in total, but variables such as the division between investors and the ship's crew as well as the number of the latter did not mean that a small prize was always less lucrative.[44]

Evaluating the impact of privateering and letters of marque on the course and outcome of the War of 1812 is not easy, as archives have not offered historians exact and comprehensive numbers. Again Kert has provided the most recent, and arguably the best, estimate based on her review of a number of primary and secondary sources. At least 1,172 letters of marque were issued, but remember that these were for single voyages, and some of the ships would have been on repeat voyages. Also, the letters covered both true privateers and armed merchantmen. She concludes there were probably around 600 vessels with letters of marque, which is slightly higher than earlier counts. The Canadian provinces of Nova Scotia and New Brunswick appear to have licensed forty to forty-five vessels to support the British.[45] The period between the declaration of war by the United States in June and the end of the war arguably witnessed the peak period for American privateers. The count for the number of prizes seized by American privateers during this time runs as high as 450 to about 300.[46] Kert estimates that about one-third of the total count for American privateers and armed merchantmen received their commission during this time. That figure amounts to 227 vessels, of which 138 failed to capture any prize at all and 28 took only one. Yet, as explained earlier, the lure of success and profit was high enough to tempt owners and others to seek letters of marque—admittedly at reduced numbers—throughout the remainder of the war.[47]

The obstacle the Americans increasingly had to surmount was the blockade the British established around their coastline. For example, in 1813 only five American vessels succeeded in clearing Boston harbor. In just one month after news of the Treaty of Ghent had arrived in that port city in March 1815, 144 ships left Boston harbor, well over 100 of them bound for foreign ports. The United States probably lost over $8 million in customs revenue, the British seized over 1,400 American vessels, and there were about 21,000 America maritime prisoners of war.[48] The blockade not only had a negative effect on the pockets and profits of merchants, manufacturers, investors, and others, but also seriously affected American consumers. Interestingly, one problematic consequence affected both Americans and British alike, as American vessels well into 1813, with British acknowledgment, had continued to carry grain to feed the Duke of Wellington's army fighting Napoleon in the Iberian Peninsula.[49] As for the privateers, the blockade forced them to evade it and then sail to more distant waters, including the coasts of Europe and of Britain itself as well as along the coast of Africa. This additional distance required some adjustment in privateering tactics. Getting a prize vessel to port for adjudication became a lot more difficult, and, consequently, privateers had to destroy or burn their prizes, which obviously reduced profits. Probably the only unexpected benefit to the privateer was the obvious fact that there was no need to worry about the prize being recaptured—a fairly frequent outcome.[50]

However, if the likelihood for profit went down, thanks to the more distant voyages and cruises, the strategic benefit of privateering for the Americans may have increased. Even with a superior number of warships, the amount of American privateers created problems for the Royal Navy from the start. By the end of 1812 itself the governor of Barbados was complaining to London about the infestation of American privateers in Caribbean waters.

Noting the sizable imbalance that so favored the British, London's initial response was to tell him and others in the region that they already had on hand resources more than adequate to deal with the Americans. To add to their responsibilities, London instructed the commander of the Halifax and West Indies Stations, which indeed ran from Nova Scotia, along the US coastline, to the West Indies, to take on convoy escort duty—a practice the British had perfected in the previous century against pirates as well as privateers.[51] Even after the convoy system strengthened, merchants in the West Indies continued to complain about the depredations of privateers. Insurance rates increased by as much as three times on several transatlantic routes; adding to this burden was the fact that the West Indies merchants had depended on American suppliers for much of their grain as well as barrels used for shipping. Some officials in the Caribbean colonies took independent action to enable American imports to continue to arrive. Without the grain, military commanders feared they could not feed their troops and dependents.[52] Later in 1813–1814 the situation improved, but the combined effects of privateering remained until the war's end.

By 1814 the waters off of Great Britain were a major zone for American privateers. The Americans could take advantage of the fact that British vessels did not have to sail in convoy in these waters. Thus, attractive targets presented themselves with costly consequences, particularly for merchants in some cities who worried about their ability to sustain commercial shipping. Insurance providers, like the famous Lloyds, had to raise their rates, going as high as 30 percent on the sea lane from Halifax, Nova Scotia, to Liverpool. As had been the case in the West Indies, the admiralty responded that it had adequate strength to deal with the Americans, and it faulted merchants for not choosing to place their vessels into convoys. Lloyds also added its voice to the call to sail in convoy formation. Enough outcry resulted from the combined impact of all of these problems that Parliament established an investigative committee to review the conduct of war upon the sea. By late 1814, the British were even concerned about developments in the US Navy, noticeably the projected appearance in 1815 of American-made ships of the line. While these would not be large enough to threaten what the British called their ships of the line, ships under seventy-four guns were considered potentially endangered.[53]

American privateers and armed merchantmen may have seized as many as 2,500 British vessels during the war, although the actual number could be closer to 2,000. If so, this would have amounted to about 10 percent of the entire British merchant fleet, not enough to bring Britain anywhere close to its knees but definitely enough to cause concern and worry, particularly when the war against Napoleonic France continued during part of this American war.[54] Thus, American privateers had assuredly contributed to British interest in negotiating a peace with the United States, though, when put alongside its global concerns, their impact would not have been decisive. For the United States, the accomplishments of its small navy and its privateers became part of the national image and myth. Two hundred years later, US naval actions and privateering seem to be the sole aspects of the War of 1812 that catches American public imagination, whether in popular history or swashbuckling fiction. For the navy the war became part of its heritage, and it demonstrated the value of a standing and preferably larger US Navy. It is no surprise that a naval intellectual like Alfred Thayer Mahan would find the experience of the War of 1812 noteworthy and that a future president who read Mahan so closely, Theodore Roosevelt, would write a history of the naval war that is widely available. One would think privateering could have sailed alongside or in the wake of this navalism, but it did not. Interest in a navy and changing national and international standards were about to draw the history of traditional privateering to its end. War, if covered by law, was ever more a matter of the state, and the leaders of most rising states in the late nineteenth century would conclude large navies were the key instrument for exerting power.

A NARROWING WINDOW FOR PRIVATEERING AND THE SPHERE OF PRIVATE WAR

For the United States in the early nineteenth century, navalism was still over the horizon. As students of US foreign policy and commerce have noted, the United States adapted rather easily to British control of the world's sea lanes during the first half of the nineteenth century. The Americans entertained neither a strategy nor the effort to challenge the British Royal Navy, although they did support a navy large enough to represent and assert national interests when they thought it necessary—often in conjunction with the more sizable endeavors of their British counterparts, whether to fight piracy in the Caribbean, to restrict the slave trade, or to pressure for the opening of ports and commercial rights in China. Privateering and other means of state-sanctioned private violence played little to no role in this.

Yet, even if the United States abandoned the practice of privateering for all purposes by the middle of the century, it remained wedded to the notion that in times of actual war it could still be a supplement to the US Navy.[55] In other circumstances, private instruments of force were not the means respected states should use.

A small but interesting illustration of this attitude toward privateers could be found in a discussion over whether privateers and their families were entitled to the same benefits and reward that uniformed veterans of the War of 1812 were. George Coggeshall was a former privateer from that war who, over forty years after its end, wrote a book to remind his readers of the contributions made by privateers. Yet, the real purpose of the book was Coggeshall's lament about the unequal memory and treatment between US Navy officers and the captains of the privateers. "The former are cherished and supported by the whole nation; have fame and honor meted out for every meritorious act. If wounded, they receive pensions and are provided for in sickness and old age. Now look at the other side of the picture: What had the captains officers of privateers and letters-of-marque to expect from their country? Nothing; and from the enemy, nothing but hard knocks, prison-ships, and free lodgings in Dartmoor." Coggeshall's view of the deserving was admittedly limited—what of the regular crew and others who had received just a share or two, at most, for their endeavors? "How soon the services of these brave and gallant men are forgotten," he wrote. "While Congress has given thousands of broad acres to all those individuals who fought or were mustered into service in all our wars since 1790, as a reward for their services to their country, not one foot of land, or any other compensation has been given to privateersmen, and those who served in private armed vessels in the war of 1812, or to their widows and orphan children."[56] Coggeshall was making his plea at literally the same time the United States was involved in negotiations related to the Declaration of Paris in 1856 (discussed below) that would for all purposes end privateering. His words, though, even with their limited horizon for those deserving benefits, point to a timeless gap that has existed for those who have fought as employees of the state and those who bore arms for a private employer encouraged or officially sanctioned. Even in 2018 one could ask a similar question about state treatment of those and their kin who died or were injured while serving with private employers.[57]

Privateering was increasingly criticized, whether in the United States or in many other countries. One reason was that its odor seemed too similar to that of piracy. Privateering had always had its critics. To the owners, officers, and crews of captured ships, the distinction between being taken by a privateer or by a pirate must have seemed very fine. History had a long record of privateers who had crossed the line into piracy and back again. Residency around any major seaport offered examples of not only an adventurous life on the high seas but, in the eyes of some, a life filled with thievery, drunkenness, inexcusable behavior, and unmentionable sin. Pirates and their officially sanctioned counterparts provided some of the most colorful examples. William Rotch, a leading whaler in Nantucket, Massachusetts, at the time of the American Revolution, and a Quaker, strongly supported his faith's position that members should neither participate in privateering nor purchase prize goods from them. He deplored the suffering privateering had brought to innocent families in Nova Scotia who lacked adequate food thanks to American privateers.[58] Of course, not all members of the Society of Friends had been so adverse, as earlier discussion of the colonial period and American Revolution has shown.

Religious reformers, both during and after the War of 1812, took up the cause to ban privateering, even if many of their fellow citizens engaged in it while the national government openly encouraged it. Unitarian congregations in Massachusetts, New York, and Ohio were noticeably prominent in this campaign, which often organized itself around peace societies. The indiscriminate effect of privateering, which ran from the targeted ship to innocent people depending on the goods seized, was one strong objection. Another was the sanctioning by governments of violence for private gain, which was morally unacceptable. The reformers also worried, and not without cause, that some men could not turn away from the practices they had gained and perfected during their privateering and would transfer them to a life of crime. This behavior and its practices, claimed the Massachusetts Peace Society, "can hardly fail to engender . . . a rapacious and avaricious spirit, eager for riches, and little solicitous about the means by which they are acquired; negligent of others' rights, and ready to raise a specious pretext for invading them."[59] Thus, the fear was about not only the acquisition of undesirable traits but also the fact that such people could create circumstances that could bring about an actual war.

We have seen how arguments supporting the growth of commerce depended on the assertion that the movement of goods should be as unhindered as possible. This had been one of the core criticisms of mercantilism before and during the American Revolution. Evolving concepts about the rights of private property, of which commercial goods were an example, evolved alongside widening convictions that commerce could act as a peaceful bond among nations—especially if the conduct and rage of war could be confined just to those fighting it and not to the broader population. Of all his contemporaries, Benjamin Franklin may have been drawn the most strongly to such arguments. Franklin was a Quaker himself, but he was also a well-read and -traveled man of the eighteenth century who shared the beliefs of the Enlightenment and believed men and governments could limit war and build relations among states that rested on commerce. The premise that "free ships make free goods" had been central to this, especially if one agreed to a narrow definition of contraband that would leave so much else protected from seizure. This ideal had been placed in the Model Treaty that Franklin, Jefferson, Adams, and other American envoys tried to negotiate during and after the American Revolution. Franklin appears to have been responsible for the provision within to prohibit privateering—an aspiration that has to be considered alongside his solicitation of privateers and other independent agents during the revolution.[60] Certainly, Franklin's enthusiasm about halting privateering did not rub off completely on Jefferson and Adams.

Franklin may not have converted most of his fellow citizens to his view, given the Constitutional Convention's acceptance of letters of marque and reprisal, but his arguments had their followers, who grew in influence after the War of 1812. Also, one treaty at least, the Treaty of Amity and Commerce with Prussia (1785), did contain provisions that forbade both signers from issuing commissions to private armed vessels to attack and seize commerce. More frequently, the treaties the United States signed with foreign governments during the next several decades contained provisions promising adherence to the laws of war, which was assurance the United States would limit war in ways so as to not affect the population at large and much of the commerce. Such a stipulation did not prohibit privateering, but it set an expectation that the United States would not resort to it as willingly as it had throughout the War of 1812. Meanwhile the peace reformers of the early nineteenth century found ammunition in Franklin's arguments that so well-mirrored theirs. Franklin, too, had regarded privateering as a slippery political and moral slope that could spin out of control. The actions of a few privateers would invite more of the same, with a resulting arms race involving more ships, higher costs, and greater demand for additional action to compensate for the losses and mounting expenses that would lead to war. Unitarian congregations might not have shared Franklin's worry that even undertakers would be corrupted by this environment, thanks to the luxurious opportunities war provided them to adopt dissolute lifestyles, but they absolutely shared his moral disapproval of privateering and his fear that such sanctioned private actions were a preamble to actual war.[61]

By the 1820s more Americans entertained a belief, or hope, that their nation could move away from reliance on these measures that sacrificed peace and the aspiration for a more harmonious world to personal gain. Some believed it unfitting for the United States to depend on such tactics; a democracy should promote commerce to help shape an interdependent order for the world. A better world could be built. The nation's leading statesman during this time, John Quincy Adams, shared these convictions. Adams believed that eliminating "private war on the sea" would be a major step toward this peaceful world. Adams thought private property, whether on land or sea, enjoyed sacrosanct status that protected it from seizure; it should never be destroyed by states during their disagreements or conflicts, As James Monroe's secretary of state, Adams approached France, Russia, and Great Britain about the prospect of eliminating privateering and the practice of allowing warships to seize private merchant vessels. Since both the United States and Britain were having problems with privateers seizing ships in the Caribbean at the time, Adams thought this might be the opportune moment to move the British to accept his proposal. He portrayed the case for halting privateering in terms of the mounting sense of reform in parts of the Atlantic world, such as efforts to stop the slave trade, but ultimately his endeavors were to no avail. France had announced in 1823 that it would suspend its use of privateering if the British agreed to do so. But the time was not opportune, and London would not have been comfortable with that segment of Adam's argument for the sanctity of commerce against seizure.[62]

Adams's arguments reflected the hardening of American attitudes about the rights of private property in times of war. In his study of the laws of war in US history, John Fabian Witt has explained how the American position on private property on the high seas came to differ from that of most of Europe. The position of European writers—Vattel, Burlamaqui, and others—was that in times of war a belligerent had the right to seize enemy property.

This did not mean unrestricted looting and pillaging, which examples from hundreds of years of European conflicts showed could be counterproductive by undermining the discipline of one's own troops and hardening the resistance of the population they were invading. Franklin's approach, indeed the approach of the Model Treaty still favored by the Americans, sought to protect private property and its owners as much as possible. In an interesting case decided by the US Supreme Court during the War of 1812, *Brown v. United States*, which involved American claims to some British property in Rhode Island, Chief Justice John Marshall acknowledged the right of seizure of private property. Congress could authorize it, but, most importantly, a declaration of war provided by Congress would not be an authorization for it. This was not an argument shared by all on the court, particularly Justice Joseph Story, who argued that the laws of war had always recognized the right to seize private property. Marshall's opinion did not settle the question even at the national level, much less the international one, but it illustrated the different course the Americans were beginning to take.[63]

This argument over the place and rights of private property in war was part of a much larger development affecting thinking about war itself and the parties allowed to participate in it. While war can take many forms and embrace vastly different types of participants, its legal standing rests on the actions of states. This book explores one vein of the movement to place violence under state control. That aspiration has never been entirely successful, and states have found ways of exempting themselves from aspects of the legal code governing war if they are fighting or using force against nonstate actors. One would not even have to be a cynic to note that all of this concern about the rights of private property did not apply when US troops acted against Native Americans, their possessions, and their settlements. Major governments, however, were building on the legacies of the preceding century, which had witnessed attempts to harmonize standards, laws, practices, and institutions dealing with crime and war on the high seas. Placing states and war itself under law was going to be an evolving theme in the nineteenth century and beyond. The extent to which private property on the world's oceans was protected by international law from seizure would remain a contentious point between the United States and other powers—most notably, Great Britain, which regarded the American insistence on a wide exemption of private property, excluding contraband, as an argument aimed at challenging British sea power.[64]

Just how far or strong the rights of private property were in war at sea remained a matter of disagreement among major American legal thinkers at the time. A short examination of the views expressed by Joseph Story in his *Commentaries on the Constitution of the United States* (published in 1833) and by James Kent in his *Commentaries on American Law*, which appeared in four volumes between 1826 and 1830, illustrates where the difference existed. Both men had no disagreement on the place of international law in the conduct of war at the time; they shared the desire to see war by states held accountable to law. The disagreement, if one can call it that, was the range of actions states could take against private property during times of war and, in particular circumstances, peace. Story, as his opinion in *Brown v. United States* suggests, advocated the more traditional view on the subject. His observations on letters of marque and privateering were not extensive, but they testify to the tradition of thought that had governed most American discussion to this time.

Story looks at this subject in Chapter XXI of his *Commentaries*, in which he discusses "the Power to Declare War and Make Captures." The first instance where Story does so is important because he recognizes two levels of conflict—war declared by Congress, and conflict that may be conducted without a declaration but through other actions in Congress. Story explained it as such: "The power to declare war may be exercised by congress, not only by authorizing general hostilities, in which case the general laws of war apply to our situation; or by partial hostilities, in which case the laws of war, so far as they actually apply to our situation, are to be observed." Proponents of the argument that Congress should actually declare war in all cases would be apoplectic by this; those who take a more moderate position—that Congress need only authorize it—would be much more comfortable with Story's assertion. That, however, is not the point under discussion here. Interestingly, Story sees declared war as a condition where the law of war has stronger authority. "Partial hostilities" are more open-ended, and clearly the place of the law of war is more dependent on the nature of the operation as well as the position the actor or actors in it may take regarding the applicability of the law of war to the conflict. Modern governments still take advantage of this ambiguity in undeclared and other forms of limited or partial conflict. However, Story was writing at a time when much of the body of the law of war remained to be negotiated and written. It was not just convenient to make this argument; it was probably necessary at the time. Story helpfully provided examples of both declared war and "partial hostilities"—the War of 1812 and the "qualified war of 1798 with France," which Story reminds his readers "was regulated by divers [sic] acts of congress, and of course was confined to the limits prescribed by those acts." So much for the claim that war could become so convenient that presidents would act on their own.[65]

Story clearly had no difficulty with the power to issue such letters during times of war. He writes that "the power to declare war would of itself carry the incidental power to grant letters of marque and reprisal, and make rules concerning captures." Such measures can be part of the inventory of instruments of war, and Story obviously recognizes that this power includes the right of seizure of private property. He does not elaborate this, but he knew a body of law and custom existed from the colonial times and afterward, just in North America itself, which illustrated what was permissible by those legally holding these letters. He does add the observation that the absence of clarification during the Articles of Confederation made this language necessary in the Constitution.[66]

This right to seize property was not restricted, however, to periods of declared war. Here Story was relying on historical precedent as well as an argument for the exercise of such powers during times of peace. He observes that "the express power 'to grant letters of marque and reprisal' may not have been thought wholly unnecessary, because it is often a measure of peace, to prevent the necessity of a resort to war." By the early 1830s one could argue that this view was falling out of fashion, and clearly anyone who wanted to strengthen the rights of private property and the movement of commerce would oppose it. Condoning such actions in war was controversial; allowing them in times of peace, especially if used recurrently, could be abhorrent. Yet, Story adds that "individuals of a nation sometimes suffer from the depredations of foreign potentates; and yet it may not be deemed either expedient or necessary to redress such grievances by a general declaration of war." "Under such circumstances," Story adds, "the law of nations authorizes the sovereign of the injured individual to grant him this mode of redress." Certainly, neither Franklin nor his successors in the peace reform movement would have agreed with this opinion. Yet, "in this case," Story asserts, "the letters of marque and reprisal . . . contain an authority to seize the bodies or goods of the subjects of the offending state, wherever they may be found, until satisfaction is made for the injury." Here Story echoes the traditional argument about the rights of seizure during war. However, Story is not discussing declared war but rather a condition below or preceding it. He arguably covers his argument with the observation that "this power of reprisal seems indeed to be a dictate almost of nature itself, and is nearly related to, and plainly derived from that of making war. It is only an incomplete state of hostilities, and often ultimately leads to a formal denunciation of war, if the injury is unredressed, or extensive in its operations." This is a rather sweeping judgment that protects an historical practice in Story's eyes—a practice grounded in the circumstances of natural law and rights. Letters of marque and reprisal—the terminology Story uses had become redundant by this time—are instruments that often precede actual war itself and remain for use during the formal war that follows. Story rejects the argument that these practices can encourage and invite war, that they are stepping stones to war that should be eliminated by international agreement. Others, as we know, saw this very differently.[67]

James Kent was a prominent contemporary of Story. His own *Commentaries on American Law* reflected the life and work of a man who had held the state of New York's highest legal office, and Kent delved more into international law and the law of war than Story had. The result would have satisfied Adams more than Story. In peacetime, the right of movement of commerce was more absolute than that recognized by Story, who had seen a place for peacetime privateering. "No nation has a right," Kent writes, "in time of peace, to interfere with, or interrupt, any commerce which is lawful by the law of nations, and carried on between other independent powers, or between different members of the same state." The negotiation of commercial treaties was a fundamental characteristic and right of a state. "Every nation may enter into such commercial tries and grant such privileges, as they think proper; and no nation to whom the like privileges are not conceded has a right to take offence, provided those treaties do not affect their perfect rights." Kent stresses the United States has worked "to encourage, in its diplomatic intercourse with other nations, the most perfect freedom and equality in relation to the right and interests of *navigation* [emphasis is Kent's]."[68] There is not much space in Kent's view to allow for any form of state interference.

Kent does not dispute the right to seize enemy property during wartime. "The practice of nations is to appropriate it at once, without notice, if there be no special convention to the contrary." Citing the writing of Cornelius van Bynkershoek, a Dutch jurist of the early eighteenth century, Kent, however, adds there are circumstances where foreign parties have had "a reasonable time after the war breaks out to recover and dispose of their effects. . . . Such stipulations," Kent claims, "have now become an established *formula* [Kent's emphasis] in commercial treaties." The weight of Kent's argument rests on his understanding of Vattel. "Such treaties" are "an affirmance of common right, or the public law of Europe." "The sovereign who declares war," says Vattel, "can neither detain those subjects of the enemy who are in his dominions at the time of the declaration of war, nor their effects. They came into the country under the sanction of public faith. By permitting them to enter his territories, and continue there, the sovereign tacitly promised them protection and security for their return." The sovereign must "allow them a reasonable time to retire with their effects." In an addendum to the text that addresses a Spanish decree from February 1829, Kent (presumably, as he did update his own work) notes the rights Spain had extended to foreigners conducting commerce in the port of Cadiz; even as enemy aliens they "were to be allowed a proper time to withdraw, and their property was to be sacred from all sequestration or reprisal." The rights extended to private property owned by foreign nationals at war with a country were not limitless, but Kent was clearly advocating an internal restraint that allowed owners to act to protect their property. It is further worth noting that Kent views approvingly the example of the Spanish to protect such property from being a target for reprisal.[69]

Kent recognized a place for privateering, but he was not happy about the continued practice of it. "Privateering, under all the restrictions which have been adopted, is very liable to abuse. The object is, not fame or chivalric warfare, but plunder and profit. The discipline of the crews is not apt to be of the highest order, and privateers are often guilty of enormous excesses, and become the scourge of neutral commerce." Kent had written these words within just a few years of mounting attempts by the United States to act against privateers in the Caribbean. As will be seen very shortly, a number of these vessels had originated in US ports but then had taken foreign crews who certainly owed no allegiance to the United States. "Under the best regulations," comments Kent, "the business tends strongly to blunt the sense of private right, and to nourish a lawless and fierce spirit of rapacity." Kent praised the earlier attempts by Franklin to stop privateering, and he saw the treaty between Prussia and the United States as exemplary. But, alas, "the spirit and policy of maritime warfare" had not permitted "such generous provisions to prevail." Citing Bynkershoek again, he argues that privateers should be liable for the damages they inflict on the property of others. At the same time, though, he admits the current practices of both France and Britain make this impossible during times of war. With regret, he acknowledges that the practice of the United States is no better.[70] Although Kent was somewhat despondent about the state of existing law and practice regarding privateering, the overall trend was moving in the direction he wanted. Immediately after the War of 1812—which coincided, one should remember, with the end of the Napoleonic Wars in Europe— another wave of privateering broke out. It occurred along the coast of South America and into the Caribbean and Gulf of Mexico, where recently independent republics turned to it as a measure against their colonial ruler, Spain. This time, the United States had to ask itself whether it was in its interests to allow these ships and many of their crew to originate in US ports. What had seemed so worthwhile from 1812 through 1814 now seemed truly problematic.

The causes of the Spanish American revolutions were diverse, but a catalytic event was the French invasion of Spain in 1808 that created circumstances that made revolution easier to initiate. The revolutionaries and their new governments lacked the capability to muster and build military capabilities equivalent to that of Spain or Portugal. Thus, alongside the armies and navies they established, they resorted to some of the same measures their North American counterparts had pursued after 1775. Privateers could strike at Spanish and Portuguese commerce and weaken the position of the colonial powers. Neutral commerce would face the same precarious situation it had known before. Collectively these privateers were called the Patriot or Independent corsairs, but that name hardly aided ship captains, who had to distinguish as best as possible the myriad flags the privateers flew, depending on their affiliation. First to appear were privateers from Buenos Aires or other ports in Argentina, who after stopping almost all Spanish ships near Argentina spread their operations into the West Indies and along Spain's own coast. Soon after them, privateers from Cartagena in the future Colombia began to operate in the Caribbean and West Indies. Privateers from Venezuela and Mexico joined their counterparts, and they were later joined by those of the Banda Oriental, which became Uruguay. The Mexican privateers operated out of ports in Texas (Galveston and Matagorda), among other locations, and also even Amelia Island off of the coast of Spanish-controlled Florida until 1819, when the Adams-Onis Treaty transferred Florida to the United States.[71]

Finding willing privateers and crews was no problem for the revolutionary governments. Whether in the wake of earlier wars, the Napoleonic Wars alongside the War of 1812, or end of the Cold War after 1989–1991, thousands of veterans were on the market seeking work. Privateering offered an opportunity to use skills perfected in military and sea service, and the new governments were not particularly curious about asking where and how that service had been acquired. The historian Peter Earle found an especially colorful quote from The Times of London, which asserted, "This villainous heterogeneous mass of ocean highwaymen are the very ejectment of the four quarters of the globe." There is little reason to think that most of the privateer captains or crew held any strong passion for the cause of their commissioners. Employment and money were the major concerns. Some of the first originated from the privateering and piracy ranks in the formerly French West Indies, but others came from Europe, and a sizable number were from the United States as well. At least one hundred privateer vessels sailed from US ports to serve all the revolutionary causes. Buenos Aires recruited especially vigorously in the United States by sending agents to American ports with blank commissions that could be filled out on the spot.[72]

Citizens of the United States viewed these revolutions sympathetically. After all, their example seemed to confirm the course set forth by the American Revolution. Revolting against Spain looked very much like revolting against Great Britain. Expansionist ambition and the desire for Florida also encouraged an anti-Spanish stance that could be traced all the way back to the Madison administration before the War of 1812. The United States was committed to neutrality in relation to Spain, and the actions of privateers coming from US waters had forced it at times to apologize. As involvement of US-made ships and citizens had begun after the first acts of revolution in 1808, the Madison administration walked a nebulous line that sought to weaken Spain's hold on Florida through apparent involvement in incursions and revolt in both West and East Florida as well as tolerance of privateers like Jean and Pierre Lafitte, who operated momentarily under the flag of Cartagena.[73] Some US government officials dabbled in this latest round of privateering as investors, and prominent figures like Henry Clay delivered speeches that welcomed and encouraged the revolutions. Yet, the United States really did not want war with Spain, certainly not as war with Britain seemed more likely before 1812, nor afterward when US neutrality and the right to conduct commerce after the war were important and the United States hoped to resolve differences with Spain diplomatically. Revolutions in the Americas increased the chance for European intervention, which the United States wanted to avoid, and after James Monroe won the presidency in 1816 his secretary of state, John Quincy Adams, was insistent on the preservation of US neutrality. Adams, we already know, was a strong opponent of privateering for moral and political reasons, and he cast a very dim eye on its practice after he and Monroe took office in 1817.[74]

The port of Baltimore attracted both the aspirants for privateers and the strongest critics. The reputation of the ships built there immediately drew representatives from the revolutionary governments as well as large numbers of willing local investors and candidates for ship captain and crew. Baltimore and its shipbuilders had enjoyed a period of growth during the War of 1812 thanks partly to privateering. The end of the war accompanied a slowdown in Baltimore's economy, which some attributed to increased competition from European companies that charged advantageous rates for freight. Also, ports like Philadelphia, New York, and Boston enjoyed the advantage of shorter distance to much of Europe. Even before 1800, Baltimore had developed a lucrative trade with South American destinations, which some thought could expand in the wake of the recent revolutions there. What had seemed like an opportunity grew in investors' imaginations after the War of 1812. From 1816 to 1820 at least forty privateering vessels departed Baltimore to serve the various South American and Mexican revolutions.[75] These privateers sometimes obtained their commission in Baltimore from a representative from Buenos Aires or one of the other new governments; certainly, they would not have obtained them from US officials as Congress had provided no authority and the United States was neutral. These facts, though, did not prevent a number of captains from trying to return their prizes in a US port—obviously a tricky plan, as no legal authority existed to determine their worth. The reason for taking the risk was a combination of higher prices and a better market for the goods. One way to get around the legal hurdle was to obtain a transfer of title for the goods from a court representing the commissioning state, which, in effect, removed the latter's right to adjudicate the prize. Another way, and likely a more common one, was just to smuggle them into the United States. An innovative approach that proved popular was to declare that the ship had been "in distress" and that it had to enter a US port for the safety of ship and cargo. US merchants and investors could also send a merchant vessel to sea to meet the privateer and have the prize goods transferred to the former ship. Circumventing the law involved imagination and intellectual energy, which many easily possessed.[76]

Neutrality itself rested on two foundations. The first was Pinckney's Treaty in 1795 with Spain and existing international law and custom. The second was the Neutrality Law in 1794 that had "prohibited 'the arming or fitting out of any ship to be employed in the service of a foreign state to commit hostilities . . . upon a state with which the United States was at peace.'"[77] Adding a complication for the United States was the fact that Spain regarded all privateers carrying commissions from revolutionary governments as being pirates; the "governments" were not sovereign governments and thus lacked the standing and legitimate authority to do so—a position like that taken in earlier conflicts by many states.[78] It was in the interests of the United States not to allow its territory and citizenry therein to become host to privateering ventures commissioned by other governments. What a US national did while living abroad was a matter of personal risk in many ways; what transpired on US territory involving US citizens was a more serious matter. After 1816 the attacks by privateers on neutral shipping became more serious. Even semi-official vessels, such as packet ships carrying mail, were subject to attack. The distinctions between piracy and privateering were becoming increasingly unclear.[79] Such developments left the United States little choice but to enact measures prohibiting private actors from measures that undercut US neutrality by either privateering or piracy. Congress approved a Neutrality Act in 1817 that restated the language from the 1794 law. A year later a second Neutrality Act specifically prohibited citizens in the United States from serving on any privateer commissioned by a South American government.[80] In 1819, signature of the Adams-Onis Treaty included provisions in which the United States committed itself to protect commerce and to punish piracy. The treaty did not contain a definition of piracy, even though the Spanish had wanted the text to include as pirates those US nationals who had received commissions from foreign agents on US soil.[81]

Between 1819 and 1821 the fate of piracy and privateering in the Caribbean and in the Americas confronted more prohibitive actions. In early March 1819, in response to increased attacks on neutral commerce, Congress authorized the president to use a naval force to seize any privateers who were attacking US merchant ships, which were neutral vessels at the time.[82]

Subsequently, Commodore Oliver Hazard Perry took the *John Adams* into Caribbean and South American waters to try to protect US commerce. Perry received instructions to give private assurances to the new governments that the United States still supported them and would accept the status of privateers who had been properly commissioned by these governments, which excluded any commissions issued in the United States. A decision announced by a federal judge in Philadelphia in August 1819 illustrated the end to the looser practices of earlier days. The case involved a Baltimore-built and -outfitted privateer who brought a Spanish prize into Philadelphia harbor. "It is a disgrace," wrote Judge Richard Peters, "to the character of American citizens, thus to prostitute themselves in nefarious acts of robbery and plunder, under the mask of assisting the Spanish patriots of South America."[83] The message could not have been stated more clearly.

For privateers like the Lafittes, who had taken advantage of the disputed claims made by the United States and Spain over the possession of the port of Galveston, the stage for operations was narrowing. The Adams-Onis Treaty would end the US claim for the time being and undermine the shaky foundation that permitted an alleged admiralty court to operate there. The Lafittes and their ilk would have to find other sources for commissions, but these were disappearing as the governments in South America secured more control over their own territory. Simon Bolivar instructed the privateers to leave Colombian waters in 1821. Venezuela was the last of these new states to allow privateering, and its commissioned vessels found themselves being boarded by US naval ships to verify their papers were in order.[84] The war against piracy in the Caribbean and West Indies, which involved Britain, the United States, Spain, France, and others, in effect ended around 1830. This was so not only in that historical theater for piracy but also in the Mediterranean. Piracy continued in parts of East and Southeast Asia and in isolated incidents in other settings, but much of the world did not direct its attention to the word again until the last couple of decades of the twentieth century. Privateering, too, seemed as unlikely as piracy. If it remained at all, it clearly did so under specific conditions determined by states. However, the utility of it seemed questionable to all major states, including the United States, which had acted to place it under strict control. Yet, the Americans were not ready to surrender the instrument of privateering completely.

Elsewhere the United States was likewise acting to prevent private citizens from conduct and the use of force in ways that conflicted with national interests. The neutrality laws were proving to be a major instrument in this regard. Even if it is true, as observed in an earlier chapter, that no one has actually been prosecuted and sentenced for violation of these laws, their existence has provided an effective restraint. While privateering was falling under strict control, the United States still had to address another form of private warlike action that sometimes appeared alongside: filibustering. This word, mentioned in Chapter 2, is derived from the Dutch word for "freeboo-ter." Reaching a common definition for the term in US history is not easy. In her study of forms of private and nonstate violence, the political scientist Janice Thomson writes that "filibusters were individuals who launched military expeditions from US territory, usually against neighboring states, for a variety of reasons." She then surveys a series of actions undertaken by foreign nationals from US soil, US citizens, expeditions even instigated inadvertently by the actions of foreign governments, particularly Mexico, and then those that had the participation of "US Government Agents." The last category did not necessarily mean explicit government support, but, for certain, employees of the United States were involved.[85] The definition offered by the leading historian of filibustering, Robert May, does not ini-tially seem to differ that much from Thomson's: "American adventurers who raised or participated in private military forces that either invaded or planned to invade foreign countries with which the United States was formally at peace." The stress on "countries with which the United States was formally at peace" suggests the weight May's interpretation will rest on violations of US neutrality laws. May's use of the word "private" invites a narrower focus than Thomson's. He discounts cases where people acted "with either the explicit or implicit permissions of their governments."[86] May, thus, does not emphasize affairs like the US role in Florida in 1810, where a US officer and soldiers were involved; the latter were acting as volunteers, perhaps not unlike Russia's "little green men" in Ukraine. Senior US government offi-cials, especially Secretary of State Monroe, seemed to have known, but were able to offer something similar to plausible deniability.[87] Yet, this, as well as Thomson's use of William Eaton's role in the operation against Tripoli, seems to resemble something closer to modern covert operations, where a degree of actual government authority, even if only from the executive branch, was involved. Last, May concentrates on the period from the 1830s through the 1850s, as he see filibusters closely affiliated with the ethos of American expansionism and Manifest Destiny.

Filibusters were thus private actors, but in important ways they were not bedmates with those addressed in this book—mercenaries and, more so, privateers. Filibustering required private capital, investors, ships, outfitting, and some of the other attributes of the latter, but it was not regarded as an entrepreneurial activity. Certainly its initiators and participants hoped to make money, but filibustering lacked aspects of the formal monetary arrangements of mercenary activity, especially from the appearance of the *condottieri* and afterward, or privateers. Formulae for distributing gains did not appear as regularly, ownership of shares and the expected gains therefrom did not exist, and individuals did not turn to it as a business option when commerce slowed or as an investment to supplement their income. Creation of a government, seizure of territory, excitement, personal enhancement, and perhaps the hope of later annexation by the United States were the major drivers in filibustering. Most important, though, was the fact that filibustering, unlike mercenary activity or privateering, did not occur under the fabric of law. The presence of authority and some form of law had shaped privateering throughout its history in the Atlantic world; mercenary activity also had to be subject to contracts, terms of service, and other requirements. Although both had begun as private measures involving private individuals, they ultimately became privately owned and administered instruments of the state. Filibustering never enjoyed this status. It operated outside the law from the start, depending on where one wanted to have it commence, and it increasingly faced critical legal obstructions.

Janice Thomson wisely points to two factors that made the United States particularly vulnerable to the problems posed by filibustering. The presence of comparatively weak neighbors was an important consideration, and the number of weak neighbors increased after the revolutions elsewhere in the Americas. Filibustering expeditions were often not large of scale or well-equipped. Facing an effective army or navy would have been well beyond their abilities. As a feature of the United States during the first half of the nineteenth century, Thomson points out one cannot imagine a filibustering attempt in Europe at the same time. It would have promptly been crushed. That reality brings us to Thomson's second point—namely that filibustering in the United States resulted from the weak and decentralized characteristics of the US state at the time.[88] While the United States had shunned mercenaries from its start and established a framework for privateering in the Constitution, nothing initially existed to prevent filibustering, except arguably a provision in Article I, Section 8 of the Constitution that enabled Congress to punish "offences against the Law of Nations." More specificity would emerge in the Neutrality Act of 1818, which threatened up to three years in prison and fines as high as $3,000 for "persons who, within US jurisdiction, began or aided 'any military expedition or enterprise . . . against the territory or dominions of any foreign prince or state, or of any colony, district, or people with whom the United States are at peace.'"[89]

Putting laws on paper does not necessarily lead to results on the same scale. The history of US filibustering has recurrent examples of US officials, both civilian and military, who knew aspects of what was going on and did little to nothing to stop it and even abetted it. The support for expansionism permeated much of American society, whether in the street or behind a desk. However, there appears to be no explicit case where US officials actually initiated and supported such an expedition. All of the contradictions in American behavior can be found in the responses of President Andrew Jackson and American officials to the expedition led by former Mississippi governor John A. Quitman to aid the Texas rebellion in 1836. In December 1835 Jackson told Congress how he opposed filibustering, and he instructed his cabinet to tell their officials to act to stop the flow of volunteers into Texas. We know, of course, that this did not happen. Quitman rightly suspected that many officials probably supported his expansionist vision. Yet, even if officials had opposed the filibusters, the volunteers' numbers were so large that such efforts would have been hopeless. Robert May ultimately stresses in his history of filibustering that "dwelling on filibustering's federal travelers . . . is counterproductive." The correct question to ask is about the level of resources the government committed to efforts to stop it, and the answer is that the number of US marshals, soldiers, and attorneys was simply inadequate. If one counted on the navy, its vessels were deployed globally to try to protect American commerce. For US military officers the arrest of US citizens posed difficult questions related to possible charges of imposing martial law. Filibusters also found ways to try to circumvent neutrality laws by arguing their expeditions were not military or by outfitting them after they had left the United States.[90] The inadequacy of resources and the decentralized character of the American state were problems that remained until the approach of the Civil War.

Like their mercenary and privateering counterparts, filibustering attracted a variety of people. The end of the Mexican War would release a number of veterans looking for work. Their skills, combined with the camaraderie and other aspects of military life that some missed, helped provide volunteers for filibustering. Others came from less savory elements of society—adventurers, connoisseurs of violence, former criminals, and others who just hoped the experience would provide them a more rewarding life. By the 1850s the United States was experiencing the effect of both urbanization and a wave of immigration that created displaced individuals as well as people who simply needed a form of work. Even though filibustering lacked the more formal and structured arrangements found in entrepreneurial endeavors like privateering, recruiters did promise salaries and bounties or bonuses if the expedition was successful. Some army officers pursued or explored filibustering as an option that might prove more lucrative and rewarding than duty in the East or at a garrison on the frontier. Filibusters, as such, represented a diverse array of people, motives, and aspirations.[91]

Filibustering did capture the imagination of much of the American population. Perhaps the most noteworthy example was William Walker, a Tennessean who initially pursued a newspaper career in New Orleans and then San Francisco but found himself drawn to the dreams of expansionism, glory, and advancement. His first attempted expedition in 1853 was to try to conquer the Mexican state of Sonora, but the intervention of US authorities stripped him of much of his manpower and Walker had to settle for Baja California. He barely got into Sonora before being chased out by Mexican troops in 1854. Walker's next destination was Nicaragua, which he entered with his "Immortals" in 1855. Taking advantage of political divisions in Nicaragua's population, Walker was able to prevail and was sworn in as president in 1856. Ultimately, he was defeated by a coalition of Central American states, and he surrendered to a US naval officer who, as negotiated, evacuated him and his money to the United States. Walker returned to Nicaragua repeatedly while claiming he was still the country's president. In 1858 Walker openly challenged the US Navy for trying to thwart his activities and defied President James Buchanan's attempt to enforce the neutrality laws. US troops and federal marshals prevented Walker's men and ships from leaving the ports of New York and New Orleans the following year. In 1860 Walker turned his vision to Honduras and the British colony of the Bay Islands off of its coast. British and Honduran troops captured "the gray eyed man of destiny," as his supporters called him, and executed him by firing squad in September 1860.[92]

By the time of Walker's execution, the attention of the United States had turned to a presidential election and the divisive issues that would result in the Civil War. Walker's gray eyes perhaps had symbolized Manifest Destiny and the march of progress to some of his supporters. Southern expansionism and a desire to expand the slavery-dependent economy had played a prominent role in filibustering, but obviously not in all of it. The desire for Canada was obviously not driven by such ambitions. A heightened sense of nationalism, conviction about the right of expansion to natural boundaries, which, for example, the US-Canadian border was not, belief that bringing the political values and system of the United States to others would benefit them, and a racism that justified superiority over blacks, Native Americans, and Spanish-speaking peoples—all of these factors, and others like greed, ambition, and adventurism, fed the filibustering movement.[93] Certainly, the unwillingness of the US government to sponsor and promote it, combined with the determination of officials to resist and even detain those involved, helped to diminish its appeal and potential successes. As erratic and stretched as US resources were in dealing with filibustering, the United States would have suffered greatly in international standing if it had actively promoted, condoned, or shown itself indifferent to it. Control of national borders and the actions of citizens were two of the measures states use to judge the strength and legitimacy of their counterparts. Similar concerns and expectations had been evident in the American moves to place privateering under the control of Congress. The same had to apply to restless, ambitious dreamers like William Walker. Meanwhile, antebellum expansionism played a role in setting the stage for the Civil War, a war whose demands and outcome would produce a much stronger central state than had existed since its founding in Philadelphia.

THE UNITED STATES, THE INTERNATIONAL COMMUNITY, AND PRIVATEERING

While the United States was confronted with the surge in filibustering that followed the Mexican War, a war was emerging in the eastern reaches of the Mediterranean that would result in a direct challenge to American retention of privateering. France and Great Britain, confronted with an increasingly weak Ottoman Empire and an ambitious Russia, sought to protect their rights and position in the eastern Mediterranean and the Middle East. In 1853 the Crimean War began. To fight it successfully the British and French needed to remove any major differences that could hinder their conduct of the war. They announced they would suspend the practice of seizing enemy property, excluding contraband, found on neutral ships. The French interestingly also seized neutral property found on enemy vessels, and they announced they would end this as well. Both powers also agreed to suspend any privateering during the conflict. Their motives were not that hard to understand. The British were a major economic and industrial power dependent on exports throughout the world as well as imports of necessary raw materials—some of them carried by the vessels of neutral powers. Ordering the Royal Navy to search neutral ships could potentially damage important trade, and the practice would certainly divert naval vessels from participating in operations against the Russians. Furthermore, assurance that neutral ships could sail without this worry about seizure of neutral property would be a conciliatory gesture to maritime commercial powers like the United States. The offer not to license privateers added a level of security to the promise of respect for the rights of neutral shipping. In an era where maritime commerce was so important, reliance on privateers to attack merchant vessels seemed both dated and illogical.[94]

The Americans saw these developments as vindication of their struggle to get recognition of the doctrine of "free ships make free goods." Secretary of State William Marcy saw the potential of getting the doctrine established within international law. The date of March 28, 1854, when Paris and London made these announcements, seemed an apparent milestone in American foreign policy, even if calculations about the United States had not monopolized British and French thinking. Two years later in the Declaration of Paris the world's leading powers and others accepted this doctrine of neutral rights. The declaration also stated that blockades had to be "effective," which ended paper blockades that lacked any actual means of enforcement. Ships had to be present to enforce it. This was a document the United States could easily sign, but it did not. The reason was that the first provision of the declaration called for the abolition of privateering.[95]

The United States found itself confronted by a calculated British effort to challenge its maritime power and to "deprive" it "of a strategic weapon that endangered Britain's global trade empire." That weapon was not the US Navy; it was the nation's merchant fleet, to which the United States could turn for privateering if it believed necessary. It was the world's second-largest merchant fleet, and, if armed, it could pose a significant challenge to British dominance on the seas. Although privateering had largely become an unused instrument for most of the world's states, it was still a belligerent's right during times of war. In the immediate context of the Crimean War, the French and British had to worry about Russia turning to it. The military adviser to the tsar believed privateering was the only instrument Russia possessed to challenge British maritime supremacy. Unsure about what confronted them, British insurance companies began to raise rates for merchants. Not surprisingly, calls arose to explore an international agreement to ban privateering. Some British observers believed the volume of America's merchant traffic was so great that the United States would willingly surrender privateering for the sake of its prominent role in commerce. Several European governments, among them Sweden-Norway, Spain, the Kingdom of the Two Sicilies, and some ports in the Baltic announced their ports were closed to privateers. The king of Prussia proposed that all countries renounce privateering, and more governments followed with bans on privateers in their ports—Belgium, Austria, Portugal, Brazil, Argentina, Chile, and Hanover.[96]

The United States very much wanted an international agreement recognizing the rights of neutral shipping and trade, and it worked to that end. However, agreement to end privateering was unacceptable, as it would remove a major wartime instrument that was actually recognized within the Constitution. In his State of the Union address in 1854, President Franklin Pierce said that an end to privateering would place powers like the United States at a clear disadvantage opposite those that had large navies. A large foreign navy could damage US commerce much more than the US Navy could inflict on that of any major foreign state. Pierce also referred to traditional concerns the United States had had about large standing armies and navies—particularly their high cost to the government and the citizenry and the threat they posed to individual liberty and the preservation of democratic values and institutions. Nonetheless, Pierce offered what he and his cabinet regarded as a compromise by stating that the United States would be prepared to discuss an agreement banning privateering if the other major powers agreed to halt the seizure of private property (excluding contraband) by naval warships.[97]

A second objection some Americans harbored to the proposed ban was that issuance of letters of marque and reprisal was something specified in the Constitution. Could the United States sign a treaty that overruled a power set forth in the founding document? This question has recurred throughout US history, and it has sometimes been used by opponents of treaties as a reason not to sign or to have Senate consent and subsequent ratification. Yet, even in the 1850s, officials realized that it was possible for the United States to enter such a treaty. Yes, the United States could surrender such a power because an ultimate protection still remained. That protection was that Congress retained the Constitutional power to pass subsequent legislation reinstating the power, an action that would have precedence over any treaty provision.[98]

In a floor statement in the House of Representatives nearly two years later—in fact, after the 1856 Declaration of Paris took effect—Representative Timothy Davis (Massachusetts), a member of the new Republican Party, iterated some of the same concerns President Pierce had. Speaking in support of a bill to grant bounty land to officers and crews of privateers from previous wars, Davis reminded the House of the important role of the United States in world commerce and the size of its merchant fleet. The fleet employed 143,000 sailors and in the previous year had brought in at least $200,000,000 of imports. Yet, "for the protection of all these interests," the United States had "a naval establishment scarcely equal to that kept up by the most important maritime Power." Davis did not name that power; he did not need to. He added, "We are in a most unfavorable position to exhibit our utter disregard for the claims of the private armed service. . . . We cannot escape the fact, that we do rely, and must hereafter rely, upon it as the main prop of our national defense; the legitimate aid and support of our Navy; and a mode of assault and defense which, when guarded by proper restrictions, is deserving of the most careful and complete protection and support of the General Government." Davis urged his listeners to remember the dangers and high costs of a professional military. "It is our splendid array of citizen soldiery that enables us to avoid war," he observed. "Our militia system on the land and on the sea . . . gives us protection, and sustains us in position before the world. It is this system that helps us to rise above the baser passions, and, from an enlightened stand-point, view the demoralizing aspects of war." Davis echoed decades of tradition and thought about the risk of large standing militaries. Their very existence increased the cost, propensity, and likelihood of going to war. The "militia system on sea or land was grand enough not only to check the ambition of those threatening us but also to control the aggressor within us."[99]

The United States chose not to sign the Declaration of Paris in order to protect the right of privateering. Its allies in refusing to sign were Spain, Mexico, and Venezuela. Evidence points to US pressure on Venezuela, but, ironically, Spain and Mexico refused to sign out of concern about US ambition and belief that they might have to rely on privateers against it. The Americans realized they had been maneuvered by the British in particular into a disadvantageous position, but they believed national interest required protection of privateering. The clear winner in the declaration was Great Britain, who clearly knew what it had accomplished against the Americans. Perhaps less clear to the British at the time, but assuredly evident later, was the fact, as Jan Martin Lemnitzer, author of a recent study of the Declaration of Paris, has written, that the British had "turned the 'maritime balance of power' on its head" by transforming it from "a stand-off between Britain and the rest of the world into an international, even global regime, underwritten by British sea power." Britain's concession for this had been its recognition of the rights of neutrals in time of war. The British recognized that the rights of neutral shipping could be as important to them as others. Any state that tried to challenge this policy, whether by naval warships or privateers, would have to answer to the Royal Navy.[100] The United States was the only state that could feasibly so act. Possibly the British did not realize how unlikely it was the United States would ever turn to privateering again. The Americans almost assuredly did not grasp that either, but for all purposes the story of privateering by states had ended. The Civil War would demonstrate how strongly the United States would have to consider international law and practice in its actions.

In May 1863, in the midst of an ever-widening war now only at its halfway point, President Abraham Lincoln had the War Department issue General Orders No. 100, a legal code on the conduct of the war. The work was the product of a German immigrant, Francis Lieber, a veteran of the Battle of Waterloo who emigrated to the United States in 1827 and pursued a career as an educator, law professor at Columbia College in New York, and then self-volunteered adviser to Secretary of War Edwin Stanton, General-in-Chief of the Union Armies Henry W. Halleck, and, on occasion, even the president himself. Stanton and Halleck met with Lieber on Christmas Day 1862 to discuss preparation of what historians and lawyers now call the Lieber Code. There was a large array of questions to address. Could the Confederacy claim the legal rights of a nation-state? If so, the repercussions were immense both in its international status and legal rights as well as the treatment of captured Confederate soldiers, the status of irregulars and guerrillas, treatment of noncombatants, rights of property, and so on. The Lieber Code did not answer all of these questions with absolute authority, but it became a foundation for the modern-day law of armed conflict (also known as international humanitarian law).[101]

Lieber's definition of war has had repercussions ever since the first day people read it as part of a code issued by presidential authority. In plainest terms Lieber's legal definition of war confined its conduct to states. In Section I, Article 20 Lieber writes, "Public war is a state of armed hostility between sovereign nations or governments. It is a law and requisite of civilized existence that men live in political, continuous societies, forming organized units, called states or nations, whose constituents bear, enjoy, suffer, advance and retrograde together in peace and war."[102] The significance of this definition carries through to today. Even with a growing body "of rules regulating non-international armed conflict, the proliferation of non-state actors, or debates on the privatization of war, international law," the Finnish scholar Rotem Giladi writes, "continues to view war, paradigmatically, as interstate business. Other categories of belligerents or participants in political violence—militias, national liberation movements or private military companies, to name a few—are assessed, regulated [and] included or excluded based on their affiliation or similarity to State actors exercising a public function."[103] Whether retention of Lieber's perspective is correct is not central here. That point will be visited in the final chapter and Conclusion. Even though Lieber's guidance occurred in the middle of the Civil War, its insistence, perhaps one could claim its preference, reflected the unfolding of circumstances Lieber had weighed before and during the first part of the war. Letters of marque and privateering were not among the major questions, many of which had related to armed irregulars as well as the treatment of unarmed noncombatants in areas controlled by Union forces, but Lieber's conclusion about the state-centric character of war assuredly reflected the direction thinking had evolved in much of Europe and the Atlantic world.

In his discussion of the Lieber Code, Giladi also directs our attention to the second, longer sentence, in Article 20. Lieber's observation that it is "requisite of civilized existence that men live in political, continuous societies, forming organized units, called states or nations" is a reminder that this was not always so. War in those earlier times could have been in the hands of nonstate actors and others acting "independently of state-affiliation."[104] After a hundred years of state-centric conflict that would mark so much of the historical record after publication of the Lieber Code, the suggestive reference Lieber made to nonstate conflict might not have seemed so necessary, since war resting on the legal foundation Lieber provided required state authority. The particular aspects of the discussions surrounding privateering during the Civil War pointed in that very direction.

The very question of the relationship of a state to a national government was one of the festering thorns before and during the Civil War. Interestingly for states like South Carolina that wanted to challenge national authority, the matter of privateering posed the secessionists in that state the same question as to who should make decisions. Several days after its succession, South Carolina's convention considered providing the governor the power to issue letters of marque and reprisal but concluded it was best to delay and allow this power to be handled by the confederation of states that would follow. Georgia drew the same conclusion several weeks later.[105] As with many aspects of their constitution, the Confederates retained the agreements reached earlier in Philadelphia.

Yet, the Confederate arm of sea power was a very weak one, and if the Confederacy was going to have any instrument to try to challenge the Union on the ocean, necessity required it to consider privateering immediately. On considering Lincoln's mobilization of 75,000 men, the Confederacy's president, Jefferson C. Davis, concluded this was enough evidence to prove the South faced imminent invasion and subsequently announced on April 17, 1861, an invitation for "private armed vessels on the high seas" that would receive letters of marque and reprisal. Twelve days later Davis explained his action to the Confederate Congress that had convened in Montgomery, Alabama. Davis acknowledged he had acted without congressional consent, as he did not yet have a congress to rely on, but he wanted to set into motion applications so the new congress could hastily act. His statement expressed confidence that "you will concur with me in the opinion that in the absence of a fleet of public vessels it will be eminently expedient to supply their place by private armed vessels, so happily styled by the publicist of the United States 'the militia of the sea,' and so often and justly relied on them as an efficient and admirable instrument of defensive warfare." On May 6, 1861, the Confederate Congress provided that very authority.[106]

The act closely resembled the one the US Congress had legislated in 1812, but with obvious changes reflecting the passage of a half century. The new law affirmed the Declaration of Paris in 1856 in its commitment to "free ships make free goods" but added the obvious caveat that the Confederacy would exercise the right of privateering. Private vessels from the Union had thirty days to leave ports in the Confederacy—a very generous grace period considering the fact the Union had promptly seized private vessels from the Confederacy. Applications for commissions closely followed the procedures used during the American Revolution and the War of 1812. The Confederacy created admiralty courts to adjudicate prizes. The only segment of prize money that did not go to the investors, captain, and crew was 5 percent placed into a pension fund for casualties. Bounties of $20 to $25 were also provided for each person captured on a ship. Like their historical ancestors on both sides of the Atlantic, Confederate privateers had to keep a detailed journal of their operations and captures.[107]

The international community watched these events closely and cautiously. Whether the Confederacy was a rightful belligerent was a problematic question. The United States regarded these events as a state of rebellion and did not want to see the Confederacy receive any form of recognition that gave it standing as a state in the community of nations. Great Britain straddled the question in some ways. It treated the Confederacy as a belligerent state, which frustrated Union policy about Confederate privateering, but at the same time the British announced that their ports, and those throughout the empire, were closed to vessels from either belligerent that sought to bring in a prize for adjudication. Existing international law and custom did not require this decision, which other powers followed, but a desire to maintain neutrality in an uncertain situation and outcome as well as an acknowledgment of the Declaration of Paris's ban on privateering made this a politically safe choice for foreign governments. As the Confederacy hoped its privateers could wage a worldwide attack on Union commerce, the closure of neutral ports to prizes was a sizable blow. Privateers operating far from the ports of the American South counted on the opinion of taking prizes into such ports, and now that was closed. The North, it seemed, never fully appreciated the favor that the international community, at least in this case, had extended.[108]

This was one reason that Confederate privateering actually had a fairly short life and limited success. The other reasons were the size of the Union Navy and the comparative effectiveness of the blockade around the South.

The early months of the Civil War witnessed the apogee of Confederate privateering. Twenty-five privateers went to sea, most of them originating from Charleston and New Orleans, two cities with enough capital and investors to support privateers. These privateers took about forty prizes; the ultimate total for the Confederacy may have been around sixty prizes. By 1862 the Confederacy was beginning to consider other options, namely blockade running and the use of actual naval warships—several which the British built—that would become raiders on the high seas. Confederate naval raiders like the CSS *Alabama* and the CSS *Shenandoah* inflicted significant damage on Northern commercial shipping and whaling, but their story, as interesting as it is, is a form of public warfare best examined elsewhere.[109]

As the stronger military power and the state that claimed legitimacy in the international system, the United States seemingly with more determination than consistency sought to persuade the outside world that the Confederates were rebels and not representatives of a sovereign state. President Lincoln had little experience of the laws of war. On April 19, 1861, he announced a naval blockade against the South and also stated that Southern privateers would be treated as pirates or criminals rather than as privateers. In the eyes of a number of onlookers, foreign as well as some members of Lincoln's cabinet, such as Secretary of the Navy Gideon Welles, Lincoln's course of action seemed to reach for the best of both worlds for Northern convenience but found neither. Blockades were customarily acts taken by one state against another, and the president did not want to recognize the Confederacy as a state and extend to it as well the rights of a lawful belligerent. Yet, arguably, the blockade raised that very question. On the other hand, the president, while ordering the blockade, insisted Confederate privateers were mere pirates acting without any authority from a sovereign state.[110]

Blockades, for example, were measures of war, and there was some question as to whether the president could order a blockade without a declaration of war. No declaration of war existed, and if Lincoln had sought one he would have posed the danger of recognizing the Confederacy as a separate state. In spring 1861 Lincoln did not have the advantage of the Supreme Court majority ruling in the Prize Cases in 1863 that justified his actions constitutionally. Declarations of war cannot occur in civil wars. These types of wars are the result of a situation and facts on the ground; they are not the result of a government act. The best that can be done is more of an acknowledgment of the condition of war, rather than declaring or willfully making war.[111]

As to Lincoln's promised treatment of Confederate privateers, problems also emerged within a few months. The capture of the *Savannah* by the USS *Perry*, and more so the subsequent placement of its crew into New York prisons as common criminals rather than prisoners of war, led President Davis on July 6 to send Lincoln a blunt message that explained he had confined Union prisoners and would order similar treatment and the same fate that befell the crew of the *Savannah*. A central question in this entire controversy was whether privateers could enjoy the same rights, primarily treatment as prisoners of war, that was already in practice in relation to captured Confederate soldiers. In reality, the North was pursuing a "dualistic approach," in Stephen Neff's words—treating soldiers as prisoners of war, and privateers who thought they had the protection of law due to their commissions as pirates. The increased scale of violence, which was evident by the summer of 1861, compelled the North to conclude it would be best to begin to treat captured soldiers as prisoners of war, thereby assuring certain standards in accommodations, treatment, and even the prospect of exchange. It was thinking along these lines that led a judge in the Court of Common Pleas in New York City to urge in December 1861 that the captured privateers be given the same rights as soldiers. Union authorities ultimately decided to take this course of action.[112] By that time, the controversy surrounding Confederate privateers had begun to subside because the Confederacy was beginning to realize it needed to turn to other measures, discussed earlier.

The Union chose to control its war at sea through naval vessels, but it threatened to resort to letters of marque and reprisal as a measure to influence British policy. As could be expected, though, there were erratic moments as Lincoln and his cabinet put together the policy they pursued. Just days after the bombardment of Fort Sumter, a group of private citizens established the Union Defence Committee of the City of New York and solicited money that enabled the arming of a private steamship, the *Quaker City*, to venture out of New York harbor to protect it against privateers. Afterward the ship steamed to join Union vessels outside of Hampton Roads. The *Quaker City* had no commission to act as a privateer, but it saw action, seized at least three Confederate vessels, and by October 1861, operating with the same crew who had obtained ranks in the US Navy, began to operate as a naval ship. The members of the Union Defence Committee regarded their contribution with pride, argued it was proof of the value of privateering, and urged Lincoln to get rid of Secretary of the Navy Welles, who opposed privateering. After the Confederate ironclad

Virginia (often known as the *Merrimack*) attacked the Union fleet at Hampton Roads in early March 1862, the New Yorkers moved one of their most prominent citizens, Cornelius Vanderbilt, to arm a steamer, fittingly the *Vanderbilt*, and steam to aid the Union Navy. Vanderbilt released his namesake vessel to the US Navy in September 1862. He had never had a commission as a privateer, but Secretary of War Stanton had praised his patriotism and given him the authority to arm and use his ship.[113]

Similar sentiments and actions occurred in New England. The governor of Massachusetts, John A. Andrews, endorsed a motion by the Board of Trade of Boston to permit the arming of private vessels with crews of New Englanders "acting as a naval corps of volunteers." Some New England merchants did arm their ships, but by late 1861 these ships had also entered the service of the US Navy. Meanwhile, like their New York colleagues, prominent New England merchants, joined by Secretary of State William H. Seward and sometimes Secretary of the Treasury Salmon P. Chase, pressed for the release of commissions for privateers. Secretary of the Navy Welles opposed use of privateers because he believed such action would be tantamount to "recognition of the assumption of the insurgents that they are a distinct and independent nationality." Welles, who had worried about the inconsistency of Lincoln's position on a blockade and the status of Confederate privateers, did not want the president to pursue actions that might undermine the Union's standing even more.[114] Lincoln and Congress had indeed followed a cautious path on privateering. In August 1861 Congress approved legislation giving the president the power to authorize commanders of privateers to take Confederate vessels. However, the legislation was powerless, as Congress had not provided the actual authority to issues letters of marque and reprisal. The president could not give the order in the actual legislation if no ships were sailing as privateers.[115]

Seward even tried to move the British closer to the Union position that the South was engaged in insurrection by offering to have the United States accept the ban on privateering in the Declaration of Paris. The British found contradictions in Seward's offer with the Union's insistence on the blockade. The British were willing to accept Seward's offer regarding the declaration, but it would apply only in future conflicts and not the current one. Seward's counterargument was that US participation as a signatory should start immediately, since it would further undercut the Confederate claim that their privateers were acting with sovereign authority. The British reaction to this directly aimed at the contradiction in Union policy that denied Southern sovereignty but then surrounded the South with a blockade—an act taken by one state against another. That response left Seward little choice but to retreat from his proposal.[116]

Continued tensions with Great Britain in 1862 and 1863, especially over the construction of ships used by the Confederacy against Union commerce and warships, led Lincoln and Seward to continue to pose privateering as a choice the Union might have to take. The president told Seward in July 1862 to have Charles Francis Adams Jr., the American minister in London, convey this message to the British. In March 1863 Congress did authorize the president to issue letters of marque and reprisal. Seward immediately acted to establish the procedures, mechanisms, and forms for application. He did have Welles review his measures, which the latter conceded reflected the steps taken in 1812 but added that Seward might have assumed more authority than Congress provided. Lincoln and Seward knew of Welles's opposition to privateering and respectfully asked him to state his reasons in a memorandum to Seward. Welles's resistance had multiple concerns. He worried that privateering could create the competition for manpower and equipment that had occurred in previous wars. He feared that reliance on private vessels was going to invite more trouble than the endeavor was worth. "To clothe private armed vessels with governmental power and authority . . . will be likely to beget trouble, and the tendency must unavoidably be to abuse. Clothed with these powers reckless men will be likely to involve the Government in difficulty." Welles added, "It will be necessary to establish strict rules for the government of private armed vessels, so as to some extent they will be likely officered and manned by persons of rude notions and free habits."[117] Such concerns reflected the opposition, unease, and uncertainty that had surrounded reliance on private force for centuries. Would its participants act in ways that best served the interests and objectives of the government or state employing them?

What worried Welles most was the possible diffusion and erosion of power in the constitutional system and the national government. War, he clearly thought, was a matter of the state, and it should be commanded and conducted by representatives of the state. A pivotal reason for this was to assure accountability and adherence to law. "The powers of imposing penalties and inflicting punishments is the essence of legislative power, for it is the penalty of transgression that gives force to law." In a narrow sense, Welles was worried about a provision in the recent authorization that allowed the president to define the rules for the operation of privateers, including their punishment. These powers, he insisted, must be retained by Congress; otherwise, Congress could surrender its powers to other cabinet departments and offices as it saw fit. The consequences of this would not only be destructive in a constitutional sense but also, and Welles was implying this rather than explicitly stating it, could affect and diminish the conduct of war in ways that best complied with the Constitution, international law, and the objectives and interests of the Union. Senator Charles Sumner, a Radical Republican from Massachusetts, had spoken with Welles about his own opposition to issuance of letters of marque and reprisal, and he urged Welles to share his letter directly with the president. Welles did not like the idea of doing an end-run around his cabinet colleague, but he later learned that Lincoln had to press Seward repeatedly to see the memorandum Welles had written. Lincoln, after all, knew Welles had agreed to send it to Seward.[118] The Lincoln administration issued no letters of marque and reprisal. The matter of a private arm in the Union's conduct of the naval war had ended.

The Civil War arguably terminated for the United States the practice of purposely soliciting and using private actors and instruments in conflict. The development certainly paralleled the position adopted by much of the developed world by the closing decades of the nineteenth century. However, even if the United States had conformed its practices to the Declaration of Paris that ended privateering, its thinking did not completely abandon privateering until at least the 1880s. Questions about the resolve and conditionality of that position arguably remained into the early 1900s, and one scholar argues there are threads that can be traced into the years after World War II. No single factor ended privateering and this dimension of private war. It was a combination of technology, strategic thinking about states and war, and the growth of international law and its subset, the law of armed conflict.

The descent of the US Navy from 1865 to the late 1880s was almost astonishing, given the strengthening of the national government and a heightened sensitivity toward national ambition in the Western Hemisphere—the purchase of Alaska and American interest in the Caribbean and the Gulf of Mexico (a longing for Cuba and Santo Domingo, and an attempted purchase of the Virgin Islands from Denmark, which would have to wait almost fifty more years). Arguably, the United States was more concerned with internal consolidation and growth—Reconstruction, the settlement of the western interior, construction of transportation networks, and ongoing industrialization—than it was with the capabilities of projecting power beyond its borders. Both the army and navy diminished significantly, and the condition of naval ships became deplorable, even laughable, based on accounts of sinkings, horrible states of repair, and a failure to keep up with naval design and armament. Even before the Civil War the age of steam had begun to surpass the age of sail.

Possessing a navy that could not match that of European powers and even some South American states, the United States actually had to continue to entertain, at least in its imagination, the option of privateering. When Theodore S. Woolsey, a professor of international law at Yale, recommended that the United States join the Declaration of Paris, he had to concede the fact that privateering might be the only option left to the nation opposite a major naval power. In 1882 Congress considered the abolition of the practice of prize money for navy crews and officers, but the secretary of the navy had to caution against the action because it might leave the navy at a disadvantage for recruiting sailors against the promise of prize money for privateers. By the 1880s a series of naval cruisers were under construction with a purpose, among others, of waging war against foreign commerce.[119]

The plausibility of supplementing these ships with privateers, though, was becoming harder to accomplish. Converting a sail-powered merchant vessel in the eighteenth or early nineteenth century to a warship was not as costly an effort, comparatively speaking, as doing the same with a steam ship, armoring it, and outfitting it with more modern guns. The increased weight of modern naval guns required special construction. Both steam-powered naval cruisers and merchant ships could be built for fast speeds, so fast that some questioned whether privateers could either catch them or outrun them if it was a naval vessel. Still, traditional ideas die hard, and advocates of privateering remained in the navy through the 1890s. To be fair, the British continued to think their adversaries, including Russia and France, could still resort to privateers as well. However, the British, who had strong reason to preserve their naval supremacy, had to confront the reality that most steam-powered merchant ships ultimately could not be reconverted in ways that would enable them to outsail and outgun steam-powered naval cruisers. By 1899 the secretary of the navy even conceded that the cost of conversion of merchant vessels was so high that private investors would avoid investing in it. Furthermore, if the capability had been feasible, it is debatable that the US shipbuilding industry, which had undergone difficult times since the Civil War, could have met and sustained the requirements of this type of shipbuilding on the scale needed.[120]

It is ironic that one of those who believed in the feasibility of privateering was Alfred Thayer Mahan at the Naval War College, the very naval intellectual whose writing would provide the strongest thread of justification of the naval weapons race that was to ensue. Mahan had not credited privateering and commerce raiding as being very successful during the War of 1812, but he did continue to believe it was an option to be used. It would require other powers to disperse their navies to protect commerce. Furthermore, Mahan thought merchant raiding and blockades might prove to be more humane ways of war, as these would weaken the enemy economically—possibly a faster way to bring a war to termination than counting on military victories. Captain (later Rear Admiral) Charles H. Stockton, one of Mahan's contemporaries and an authority on international law, made the same argument. Even by the arrival of the twentieth century the Americans were still not at ease with British power, and Stockton emphasized that British dependency on imports for food made it more vulnerable than the United States, which was self-reliant for its food supply.[121]

These were not the arguments for which Mahan is most remembered and studied. The model of British naval power provided an understandable answer to officers, statesmen, politicians, and intellectuals who believed the United States needed to develop the capabilities to project power internationally and to protect its diverse and wide-ranging interests. Concern about economic and industrial growth, the need for exports for the US economy, the critical role of the sea for merchant traffic, the presence or growing interest of European powers in areas that also attracted American interest, or were even close by, such as the Caribbean—all of these and other factors, like Social Darwinism and the perception of the international environment as a testing ground for national prowess and destiny, fed the conviction that the United States needed a strong navy—a military instrument developed and built for the state, and commanded by the state for its own defense and advancement of international advantage. This type of navy needed capital ships and not just cruisers and lighter vessels to war against commerce. Some advocates of large naval expansion argued that war involving capital ships would be more humane than earlier forms that had integrated war against commerce as part of its operation—a view with which Mahan disagreed because of his conviction that blockades and commerce raiding might bring peace sooner. War in search of great sea battles could permit commerce to continue to flow largely without interruption—a retention of the important distinction between public war and private property. This was the vision the United States had consistently sought. Mahan essentially rejected this distinction between public and private. Private losses could have a significant bearing on the standing of the public and its ability to endure loss and avoid defeat.[122] However, those who envisioned and built large capital ship navies were not as concerned. Naval war was clearly a state matter, and it had to be conducted with instruments of the state. There was no designated and preferable place for the private actor requested and supported by the state.

The United States continued to press for the immunity of private property and commerce on the high seas, aside from contraband. President William McKinley disavowed privateering during the Spanish-American War, and his vice president and successor, Theodore Roosevelt, a fervent supporter of a larger navy, raised the status of private property in statements that helped initiate the Second Hague Peace Conference. The first conference had concentrated more on problems related to land warfare. The Russo-Japanese War delayed the opening of the second conference until June 1907. The final treaty that emerged had thirteen conventions in it; the United States accepted ten of them, opposed two, and offered acceptance with reservations for one more. One of two conventions the United States refused to sign dealt with "The Conversion of Merchant Ships into War-Ships." The negotiators had tried to extend the provisions of the Declaration of Paris in 1856 and strengthen them by stipulating that any merchant ship converted to a warship would have to be placed under the command and responsibility of the state it served. In some ways American opposition to this provision appeared arcane, as will be seen, because the United States really did not oppose the substance of the agreement. However, the United States still held out for a provision in the treaty protecting private property from seizure by warships from other nations. The delegates told their counterparts that they wanted this in spite of the fact the Constitution provided the authority to seize such property through letters of marque and reprisal. Ambassador Joseph H. Choate told the convention that by limiting naval war to naval warships it would make war at sea more humane. Wars should be confined to the public property of states and not include private property that was not contraband. Commerce was also more of a harmonizer among nations rather than an obstacle to peace. As to privateering itself, Choate agreed that it was obsolescent for all purposes—the costs of converting ships and building to the specifications needed for warships were just too high.[123]

The position of the United States on immunity of private property on the high seas would figure prominently in the sequence of events that transpired between the outbreak of World War I in 1914 and the declaration of war by the United States in April 1917. The United States was not able to convert the international community to a position that most members regarded as extreme and detrimental to their own national interests. Privateering and the use of private instruments of force in maritime war were at an end, even if the United States had not agreed to that portion of the Declaration of Paris. It still has not to the present day. Whether this matters at all is a subject for the next chapter. In his study of the arguments against privateering, Michael Crawford writes that, curiously, one might have to look all the way to 1955 to see the door finally close on privateering. Reviewing the US *Naval War Code* of 1900, Crawford found these terms to forces "recognized as armed forces of the state":

> The officers and men of the Navy, Naval Reserve, naval Militia, and their auxiliaries.
>
> The officers and men of all other armed vessels cruising under lawful authority.

The latter left a slight open door for privateering when it referred to "all other armed vessels cruising under lawful authority." That opening closed in 1955 when a US Navy publication, *The Law of Naval Warfare*, offered the following definition of *warships*: "vessels commissioned as a part of the naval forces of a State and authorized to display the appropriate flag or pennant as evidence thereof. Such vessels in addition must be commanded by a member of the military forces of a State and must be manned by a crew subject to military discipline."[124] The control of the state seems absolute, almost ironclad. Certainly, it does not exclude the placement of a private vessel into the service of the US Navy, but its reference to a "crew subject to military discipline" suggests US Navy sailors. Civilians are customarily not subject to military discipline and the Uniform Code of Military Justice. However, as always, one can find circumstances to probe into the exact meaning of all the above. These are questions that would recur more frequently within a few decades after that regulation appeared.

6 THE PRIVATIZATION OF WAR

He was one of the greatest fictional entrepreneurs in what was the greatest state-on-state war in history—World War II. First Lieutenant Milo Minderbender in Joseph Heller's *Catch-22* started small by selling eggs and goods to the US Army Air Force but ultimately went into the really big time. He traded and retraded throughout the Mediterranean, doing contracts with the Germans and even getting his planes to bomb a US airbase. Perhaps he was a man ahead of his times; certainly, in the eyes of some today he would serve as a harbinger of the stateless and soulless multinational company with no loyalty to nation or employees. Critics of private military and security firms would probably claim that Erick Prince, of the former Blackwater, would be his counterpart—a challenge that would certainly cause Prince, rightly or wrongly, to bristle and to claim, among other things, that he has shown concern and loyalty to his employees and country.

Milo Minderbender, however, seemed to be out of step with the prevalent mindset of World War II, and he might have proved too old to take advantage of developments forty or so years later. The Great Depression, World War II, and the rapid emergence of the Cold War created circumstances, requirements, and laws and institutions to develop stronger nation-states with expanded powers to defend themselves and to pursue policies that would prevent the return and ascent of conditions that caused the economic, social, and political turmoil of the previous thirty years. This welfare/warfare model and mission of the state took different forms thanks to history, ideology, and need. Those scarred most deeply by the war believed they had to enact laws and policies that would repress or heal the social and economic forces that had fed the surge of war. In some cases, like defeated Japan and Germany, they had little choice, as the victors wanted as little military capability inside their borders as possible. The Soviet Union, in physical control of eastern and part of central Europe, concluded it had to establish a large, more modern military to keep these occupied areas under control, prevent intervention there by the United States and its allies, and contend with the rise of US military might. Initially determined to downsize its military as it had after earlier wars, the United States believed it had to reverse itself to confront an increasingly strong Soviet Union, an emerging Communist China after 1949, and a perceived Sino-Soviet plan to overturn the West as demonstrated, it seemed, in the outbreak of war in Korea in late June 1950. In just one decade, 1950 to 1960, the United States created immense military might, thanks in part to the growth of a support-ing industrial sector rooted in World War II that had become so sizable and influential that President Dwight D. Eisenhower in his final address would express open concern about the undue, distorting influence of the "military-industrial complex."[1]

This same international community, however, had taken the greatest steps ever to harness war and place the use of violence under state and interna-tional control. The United Nations Charter, the Nuremberg Principles and Code, and the Articles of the Geneva Convention in 1949 created new laws and boundaries for the international community and states to follow related to the justification for war, its subsequent onset, and conduct and termi-nation. As discussed in Chapter 1, war, when it was legal, was to be an act reserved to states. Obviously, these agreements did not halt the emergence and actions of nonstate actors. Revolutions, wars of national liberation, insurgencies, ethnic and tribal wars, and other forms of low-scale or limited conflict continued as they always had. Absent, though, in this body of agree-ments, treaties, and law were provisions that sanctioned privateering and other state-sanctioned private groups on the high seas. Mercenaries were for all purposes unsupported as well, although these conflicts would attract volunteers and proxies who arguably resembled mercenaries. The culmina-tion of centuries of concentration of violence and war in the hands of states seemed as close as ever to establishment. That, however, was assuredly not the case. Private actors engaged in war, or so closely attached to its actions to be almost indiscernible, would grow in numbers and scale during the last three decades of the twentieth century. By the start of the new century, concepts and agents of actual private war became more visible—actors that might act outside of or without state control rather than be channeled through it as had the mercenaries and privateers of the previous centuries.

The reasons for this reversal are complex. Considerations that would move a recently independent country in Africa to turn to mercenaries contrast greatly opposite those shaping the decisions and actions of the United States or Great Britain. To appreciate the diversity of reasons that existed, or still do, it may be helpful to start with the broadest, even global, factors and work down to the reasons that affected specific countries. As we saw in earlier chapters, the spread of practices related to private armed force, privateering, and the laws that govern such actions followed the expansion of empires. In their introduction to a book on the history of private violence, Alejandro Colas and Bryan Mabee observe that "empires, far more than national territorial states, have been responsible for the transnational circulation of commodities, armies, manpower, and laws that have produced the forms of sea-borne and land-based violence explored in this volume."[2] The expansion of British state authority across the Atlantic as well as into the Indian Ocean, the Subcontinent, and Southeast Asia offers the most influential example. However, other European states acted likewise, as did some former colonies of the British themselves, particularly the United States. Imperial powers were the major beneficiaries of these forms of private violence, whether in the form of increased revenue, prize money, goods, and other profits made by these entrepreneurs. In instances, such as that of the young United States or Great Britain during the American Revolution, reliance on private violence saved states money that would have been spent constructing warships and paying sailors or soldiers.[3]

The dismantlement of these same empires that followed World War II also created some of the conditions that invited mercenaries by demand or default. Mercenaries have repeatedly been an instrument of the politically and economically weak state. Revenues for raising, training, and equipping armies are expensive and sometimes out of reach. So, too, is the pool of professionals required to train and command an army. If foreign governments, such as the United States, the United Kingdom, and the Soviet Union, did not offer the money and advisers for training—which they increasingly did in a global race to preempt and contain the influence of their Cold War rival—private companies could. The first modern private military company appears to have been WatchGuard International, established in 1965 by former members of Britain's Special Air Services (SAS). Working alongside the British government, but also sometimes on its own, this company and other British successors that followed were active initially in the Middle East but soon extended their operations to other parts of the world, including a number of former British colonies.[4] Africa was where these developments reached the highest visibility, either by newly independent governments that needed the help of outside training or by the appearance of for-hire adventurers who appeared in large numbers to fight these governments and UN forces for the sake of insurrections, tribal groups, and even private companies that wanted to protect their colonial advantages. This was the heyday of the types of gun-for-hire mercenaries personified by "Mad Mike" Hoare and the Les Affeux (The Frightfuls) hired by Union Miniere in the former Belgian Congo. These men were not like their cousins (arguably distant ones) working for WatchGuard, a company that sought a profit from its services, but freelancers with little interest in the principles of their employing side—perfect working material also for a Hollywood still skittish of war films so recent after Vietnam and over-the-hill actors looking for one last hurrah in a rented uniform. As the 1970s advanced, mercenaries in Africa acquired about as bad an international reputation as their Hessian predecessors had in the American colonies two hundred years earlier.[5] This resulted, as will be discussed later in the chapter, in an international effort to place mercenary activity under stricter control of international law.

These wars of "particularist identities," as Mary Kaldor describes them, were often waged against "cosmopolitanism," to borrow another of her categories for analysis. The cosmopolitans, of course, represented and served the more established and traditional positions and structure of the international system and states, including the latter's traditional posture on war. While conceding the fact that identity has been a recurrent issue in wars for a long time, Kaldor argues these new identity wars are about labels, based on some "nostalgic representation of the past" rather than the interests of a state or an ideological agenda the war hopes to fulfill and install.[6] Such conflicts, of course, were going to continue and even multiply in the wake of the end of the Cold War and the breakup of another empire of a sort, the Soviet Union, with immense reverberations worldwide, even if it had not held colonial control over these areas. Kaldor has questioned the legitimacy of applying the distinction of public and private to these types of wars, and her caution helps to avoid taking the dichotomy too far. Obviously the types of wars that concern Kaldor and so many other scholars, practitioners, combatants, and nearby civilians often have little to do with public and private, unless one makes the argument that a "public war" must be a declared one—a differentiation that seems very arbitrary, narrow, and unrealistic in the world of current conflict. Kaldor is not claiming that distinction, and neither am I.[7]

To refresh arguments made in Chapter 1, "Private war," writes Graham Parsons, "is war that is waged by persons who act with their own private authority.... Private warriors have no moral responsibility to seek approval from another person or entity prior to becoming warriors. They are moral representatives of themselves only." Some participants in private wars could question this claim about moral authority; God, after all, is a higher, more absolute authority than any state or legal code, and nonstate actors have invoked him. However, international law does not grant God stature as a foundation for existing law. Thus, "Public war . . . is war that is conducted under the legitimate authority of a political sovereign. It is war that utilizes the legitimate authority of a public body to employ violence." This does not mean the war must be declared; it does mean there has to be some form of authorization, consent, or order from a sovereign authority to initiate and conduct the war.[8] Kaldor and others could fairly question the state-centric nature of this definition, and that question will resurface in the Conclusion.

The erosion of and challenges to state authority and the international system that became apparent after the end of the Cold War have suggested to some that we are watching a "re-medievalization of the world." Sean Mc-Fate relied on this argument in his penetrating analysis of mercenaries and private military contractors in 2014, and I have made use, and will return again, to facets of this analysis. Writing in the late 1990s, by which time antecedents of this argument had appeared, Claire Cutler cautioned against it in one very important way that must never be forgotten. She points to "a crucial distinction between medieval and modern authority structures." "In the medieval period private authority operated by virtue of the absence of political authorities desirous or capable of disciplining international commerce, whereas in the modern period private authority operated with the full support of state authorities."[9] The conduct of private war in the early feudal period, briefly reviewed in Chapter 2, illustrates what Cutler means, and the remainder of the book until this chapter explores why and how forms of state authority evolved. Now we have entered a period where that authority is under challenge, and, in fact, parts of the very authority itself and the institutions implementing its wishes are being privatized and globalized, to paraphrase Cutler's own words.[10]

Authority often travels alongside accountability, and to diminish one is to undercut the other. The impact of globalization has been cited by almost every scholar on privatization and armed force as a leading factor, and it is important to examine the scope and consequences of its effects. The movements of people, currency, information, technology, and manufacturing have served as assaults, in the views of many, on the traditional place and authority of states and sovereignty. It is important, though, to treat globalization more cautiously than the diffusion of all the above as well as the alleged cause of degradation of state power and authority. In her book *Altered States*, Valerie Sperling offers a differentiated view of the impact of globalization. She starts with its impact on accountability, and she identifies levels of improved accountability as well as diminished. She reminds us of the two forms of accountability we commonly hold. The first is "answerability" in which "public officials are obliged to provide information about their actions, and to explain and justify publicly the decisions on which their actions are based." The other form is "enforcement," and here citizens expect that those in power who have failed to fulfill their official responsibilities should be sanctioned by law or removed through election. Another way of treating accountability is by using the terms *vertical* and *horizontal*. The former is the means by which an informed citizenry is able to decide whether an official should continue in his or office. Obviously, the existence and nourishment of a civil society is critical for "vertical" accountability. "Horizontal" depends on the ability of different institutions of government being able to check one another—the checks-and-balances system, for example, that the United States relies on in its Constitution.[11]

The creation of international and transnational organizations and multilateral bodies has been a cause as well as characteristic of globalization—the United Nations, the International Monetary Fund, the World Trade Organization (WTO), and more. By seeking to guide and control the actions of states in particular, these institutions have helped to "deterritorialize" the place and role of states. Holding states accountable implies an attempt to obtain answers and an authority to impose sanctions if necessary. Sperling adds that such organizations, such as human rights bodies, can make states respond to new or underrepresented parts of their population, another form of weakening of state authority. However, such developments create their own reaction, and they can become targets of those wanting greater accountability as well. This "democratic deficit" and a desire for greater democratic accountability has become a major feature and trend in the international environment in recent years, as witnessed by the Brexit vote to withdraw Great Britain from the European Union as well as the election of Donald Trump in 2016 as a candidate who favored American exceptionalism and the supremacy of bilateral agreements over multilateral and international arrangements.[12]

The problems resulting from a "democratic deficit" have attracted particular attention. Laura Dickinson has explained how multilateral bodies like the WTO and UN "are seen as even less amenable to public participation than are domestic delegations, where power is at least somewhat constrained by democratic processes." Brexit voters and other European critics of the EU would agree; so too would many American critics of the UN and various international treaties because of fears about loss of sovereignty. Dickinson acknowledges that both academics and policy professionals are divided on the problems and strengths of increased authority at the multilateral and international levels, but she remains concerned about the opportunities for public participation at these levels.[13] Obviously public participation depends as well on the interest and willingness of the public and its elected representatives, as well as other national officials, to insist on transparency and safeguards. In some ways this has been a recurrent issue in the history of the United States, especially Congress, toward the United Nations as well as security treaties like the North Atlantic Treaty Organization (NATO). While some scholars argue that US suspicions have rested more on isolationism, there is a more justifiable argument: that the assurances the United States has sought prevent it from being committed into war without the consent of its elected representatives.[14]

Globalization has also encouraged and fed forces and considerations that have brought states to relinquish some state function by default or design to the private sector. Across-the-border movements of money, technology, and knowledge often occur on a private level without prior authorization by the state, for example. In other instances, states have chosen to transfer state functions to the private sector because they think the latter can act more promptly and efficiently in the modern globalized environment. This has been a prominent consideration and conclusion many states have drawn about the current and future international security environment. For a host of reasons examined below, states have chosen to place more functions in private hands. Nothing on the horizon appears ready to staunch this trend, including a resurgence of nationalism and antiglobalization sentiment found throughout the world. There are too many other factors, as we will see, that drive against a restoration of state authority over violence and force as envisioned in the mid-twentieth century. As Sperling observes, this type of "privatization is . . . a form of deterritorialization, in that it moves decision making into a private realm, inaccessible to citizens." The "shrinking state," she warns, "may decline" as a target of public discontent and criticism because there are "no accessible institutions to which to protest. State accountability to a population can then slowly evaporate."[15] Whether that degree of concealment and distance from the public can occur in national security is a critical issue. Dickinson, for example, sees it as more of a divided or doubled delegation of authority in which "political debate might be skewed if private entities control large swaths of formerly bureaucratic sectors."[16] This does not sound as severe as the circumstances envisioned by Sperling, and Dickinson's worry focuses on bureaucratic settings like law enforcement and prison management. However, the distance and relationship of the public and state to war making may become greater than one wishes. The seriousness of war and death arguably make the use of violence for defense or advancement of national interest the most important decision a state can take. For such isolated decisions to happen, many unfortunate developments would have to transpire, especially the development of a disengaged and uninterested population. The challenge will be to prevent that in light of the dispersion of power and the development of capabilities and options that make such a choice easier and more appealing.

The end of the Cold War between 1989 and 1991 signaled, contemporaries hoped, the end of a massive state-on state confrontation that had sometimes boiled over in limited wars and conflicts in locations like Korea, Vietnam, Angola, Nicaragua, and others. Immediately afterward, governments concluded they could downsize their militaries and decrease national spending or shift it to other priorities. Peter Singer estimates that 7 million military personnel worldwide left the ranks and needed work. The United States alone reduced the size of the US military from around 2.2 million to 1.4 million, where it has basically remained to the present day. The US Army, for example, reduced its divisions from eighteen to ten in number. Joining this glut of trained personnel from the closure of the Cold War was a smaller but highly trained cadre of personnel from the Republic of South Africa, which had downsized its army and security forces after the end of apartheid. Of course, a large majority of these people went into other careers, lines of work, or joined the traditional defense companies that had supported national defense needs for decades. The recent private security and military firms only received a portion of them.[17]

Not only was there a large pool of people looking for work, there was also an immense inventory of weapons now available at bargain-basement prices. This was especially so with weapons from the former Warsaw Pact, whether held by former Soviet troops or their former Eastern European allies. For example, newly united Germany did not want to operate with these weapons; neither did other NATO states, and former Warsaw Pact states were now entertaining the possibility of becoming NATO members themselves, a prospect that raised hope for arms manufacturers in the West. These weapons spread at cheap prices into the developed world, particularly Africa, the Middle East, and parts of Central and South America. In time, they would appear in greater number on the streets of the United States itself. I remember encountering the chance to purchase an AK-47 when I was on a trip to Dresden, Germany, in the mid-1990s, provided, I was told, by Russian soldiers who sold theirs before departing garrisons in the Dresden area. This was a booming and lethal market for small arms whose repercussions last to the present day.[18]

The reduction in the size of standing militaries rested in part on a hope for a "peace dividend" (the term used in the United States during the early years of the first administration of President Bill Clinton) and a strategic estimate that the short, successful use of state power in coalition form against Iraq in the first Gulf War set a precedent for a stronger UN authority that might be part of a "New World Order" (a term from the preceding administration of President George H. W. Bush). These estimates and projections proved very short-lived as the international community found itself engaged in an array of conflicts that presented strategic challenges that outmatched both intellectual and political understanding of them as well as the size of the reduced militaries now expected to try to control and end them. The types of conflict that became more visible and frequent in the wake of the Cold War's end illustrated the effects of the consequences of globalization that made privatizing force and violence a viable, maybe even necessary, option. Many of these were the "particularist" conflicts discussed by Mary Kaldor and others above. Some were civil wars within countries; others were irredentist conflicts, tribal conflicts across borders, religious wars and struggles between sects in one religion, or fighting that followed the collapse of state authority or the migration of people because of drought and famine. These conflicts and their myriad causes required redefinition of security. As causes of a security crisis could be both external and internal, new words entered the vocabulary, such as *intermestic*, which referred to national security and foreign policy issues that had interwoven foreign and domestic dimensions.[19] To retell the course of these conflicts in the Balkans, Somalia, Rwanda, and other locations during the 1990s is not my purpose. The international community of the United Nations and the major states resorted to a combination of humanitarian intervention and peacekeeping missions to try to contain and settle them, but some, especially Somalia and Rwanda, ended badly or at best (in the Balkans) belatedly. For the United States, whose military, particularly its army, was still struggling with the scars from Vietnam, there was great reluctance among many in uniform to become committed to such operations. A chaotic mission in Somalia in 1993 that ended with eighteen dead US soldiers, including the broadcast images of one body being dragged through the streets, spelled almost an end of willingness of much of the public, the military, and many in Congress to support the commitment of US troops in such missions in spite of the efforts of presidents to underemphasize their scale and potential danger and to circumvent congressional authority through presidential order.[20]

Many states in the heart of such violence and tragedy could not afford a trained and well-equipped military, and they sometimes lacked the effectiveness in governing institutions to maintain internal order, meet other domestic needs, or to control their borders. "Failed state" became a popular, if at times somewhat questionable, label for them. What happened in Africa was illustrative of the problem. The Soviet Union's disintegration ended one source of assistance in some African states. Without worry about a Soviet presence, the United States reduced its assistance as well. Later, President George W. Bush would seek to reverse this trend in aid to Africa, and China would also emerge as a very visible player in aid, infrastructure spending, and even peacekeeping. Yet, the weakness of some of these states, and the relative ineffectiveness of their armies, saddled sometimes with corruption and factionalism that undermined a sense of professionalism, set many on a difficult and turbulent course. Even during the 1990s France, which provided important aid to twenty-two states, reduced its presence in Africa, only to see it would have to increase it after 9/11 and the spread of extremism by Islamic factions and other groups.[21] Deciding what measures to use to address these needs and developments became problematic because of the general reluctance of American and European publics to commit themselves to such missions even before the wars in Iraq and Afghanistan, and certainly during and after them.

Reinforcing this aversion to intervention and fear about the open-ended, unclear end-states that many of these missions seemed to promise was a schizophrenic recognition that the international community should act in such matters but that it also needed to find means by which it could do so with less risk to member states and their professional militaries. *Postmodern militaries*, a term popularized by scholars of the military like Martin Shaw and Charles Moskos, depended on a smaller number of personnel, often volunteers, whose strength and capabilities were supplemented by the adoption of the latest technologies. The large conscription armies prevalent in the first two-thirds of the twentieth century were no longer acceptable to much of the public. The staggering number of dead from World War II, declining birth rates in much of the Western world, the erosion of the vision of glorious and honorable death in battle, and a subsequent public intolerance for high casualties created a need for alternatives sources and means in warfare. States needed substitutes for segments of public militaries. These considerations helped create support for what Australian scholar Thomas Waldman has labeled as "vicarious warfare," which he defines as "modes of warfare that place a premium on shielding the military from danger and applying force by proxy or, if directly by American forces, in the shadows." Those "modes" could be substitutes or proxies from other states or regions, such as the Montagnards in Vietnam and the mujahideen in Afghanistan in the 1980s; or adoption of weapons requiring fewer personnel to operate them thanks to greater accuracy or killing power; or hiring contractors to do a lot of support roles while letting the professional military concentrate on the hardcore aspects of military operations.[22] Just where "casualty aversion" was deepest in the United States was the subject of much discussion and analysis during the 1990s and first decade of the next century. Politicians in both branches—Congress and the presidency—claimed it was strongest in the public; others argued it was in the buildings at opposite ends of Pennsylvania Avenue.

THE PUSH FOR PRIVATIZATION

Warfare itself had undergone immense change and even transformation, in the opinion of some, thanks to the introduction and dependency on advanced electronics, communications, software development, advanced materials, and other cutting-edge technologies. There was much talk about the revolution in military affairs (RMA)—the literal transformation of war that might occur thanks to electronics and communications resulting in concepts like information dominance, battlefield dominance, and so on— visions and aspirations that collided with the realities of the conflicts in Iraq and Afghanistan, where such dominance proved elusive. However, that is not the important point for this book. The critical consideration was that the military had to depend greatly on the commercial sector for everything from components to operating and weapons systems reliant on software from nonmilitary and commercial providers. The popular understanding of the commercial-defense relationship had been that most of the technological benefits flowed from the defense side to the commercial and, thus, to the citizenry at large. Indeed, that had been true in many instances running from the powdered orange drink Tang to advancements in computers and applications like global positioning systems (GPS). However, that trend was reversing by the closing decades of the twentieth century.[23] In 1994 I joined the faculty of the Industrial College of the Armed Forces, a college (since renamed) that is part of the National Defense University, which reports to the chair of the Joint Chiefs of Staff. The educational and research mission of the school is in part to assess and teach the characteristics and trends of the economic, commercial, and social segments of both the US and international system that affect US national security and defense capabilities.[24] For eleven years (1994–2005), before being ushered into department and college administration, I directed or codirected a seminar field study on the electronics industry (both US and international). To be told repeatedly by industry association and corporate executives that the US defense market accounted for about 5 percent of the total market for US firms in semiconductors was eye-opening. Several major US manufacturers told our study group that they would not manufacture components to meet military specifications; the market was too small and the capital costs too high in relation to the domestic and international markets they needed to serve. They would happily sell components made for the commercial or private sector for military use.

Reliance on the private sector was nothing new for US defense, as the dependence on private manufacturers during World War II for aircraft, vehicles, tanks, weapons, and so on suggested. However, that had occurred on a scale of defense and economic mobilization and conversion that was unimaginable by the 1990s and beyond, thanks to new technologies, foreign competition, and changing weaponry, among other things.[25] The US Air Force had been at the cutting edge of this movement toward privatization because it was more dependent on new technology as well as private industry for aircraft. Unlike its sister services, the army and navy, it did not have a system of arsenals and shipyards to support it. Paul Koistinen, a historian who has studied the US defense economy and national security policy, has described how the actions of the air force and the expansion of all the services brought about the privatization of the munitions industry as well as the gradual diminishment of arsenal and shipyards in manufacturing.[26] However, the situation in the 1990s had gone far beyond this. The Defense Department and Congress acted on measures to push for commercial-off-the-shelf (COTS) procurement. The military services, the Department of Defense (DOD) itself, and study groups like those mentioned above examined companies and interviewed executives to learn "best commercial practices." Faced with an environment that many thought would be highly dependent on information technologies as both a means of delivering information and the weapon itself, figures like Vice Admiral Arthur Cebrowski, USN, who became head of the Office of Force Transformation (2001–2005), even questioned whether the United States needed a traditional defense-industry sector. Reliance on the commercial, or private, sector might be enough to meet national security requirements.[27] A process of privatization that had picked up speed during the 1950s was operating on a far grander scale by the start of the present century.

This was an environment ripe for privatization—not only of the industry and manufacturing of weapons, systems, and components, but, equally, the movement of missions, tasks, and people from the government to the private sector. Globalization seemed to be challenging different aspects of state authority; newly independent states lacked the resources to develop effective professional militaries; new forms of war and conflict presented questions about the role and effectiveness of traditional militaries; millions of trained veterans were available for work outside of governments; populations, especially in modern postindustrial states, disliked the imposition of large conscription militaries and the types of mass war that had existed in the past; states and even international bodies needed more flexibility and diversity in the instruments they could use; and political leaders feared public backlash against the deployment of professional militaries into uncertainly defined and terminated peacekeeping and humanitarian missions. Worst of all, the international environment following the end of the Cold War and then the attacks of 9/11 appeared to be generating more of these types of conflicts. Traditional modes of response seemed neither effective nor desirable. Thus, there were many circumstances in which private actors could act alongside with specific arguments to justify resorting to them. The most important argument, though, particularly for the United States and the United Kingdom—the two leading countries in developing and providing such services—rested not only in requirements in the security environment but in a reexamination of the division of tasks assumed by government and by the private sector.

The pattern of privatization that was emerging was well-enough in motion that President Dwight D. Eisenhower cautioned the nation about it in his farewell address in January 1961. Noting how the United States had created "a permanent armaments industry of vast proportions," Eisenhower reflected on its necessity but warned, "We must guard against the acquisition of unwarranted influence, whether sought or unsought, by the military-industrial complex" as well as the danger that "public policy could itself become the captive of a scientific technological elite."[28] Eisenhower was not specifically warning against the privatization of military functions in war, although the remainder of the speech shows he was fully aware of future developments that might emerge from this complex that so troubled him. Contractors to serve as drivers or sutlers, or in the repair and construction of various items, had been a part of US history from the start. The ratio, in fact, had been one contractor to six soldiers during the American Revolution, one to five during the Civil War, one to twenty-four during World War I, and one to seven during World War II.[29] Thus, Eisenhower was not unfamiliar with the practice, especially as a support service for the US military. He inherently and wisely suspected, however, that whatever forms the expansion of interest by the military-industrial complex developed, it could compromise or distort national decision making.

Experts differ on the timing and circumstances of the move toward privatization by the Department of Defense and military services. Part of the reason is the question of whether covert military groups, proxies, and other types of special units should be grouped together with privatization. In her study of the outsourcing of national security, Laura Dickinson does place such Vietnam-era activities like the Civilian Irregular Defense Group, the tribal Montagnards, the Phoenix Program, and other activities related to or administered by the Central Intelligence Agency into the arena of outsourced policy and military activity. She even suggests the troops provided by the Philippines, South Korea, and Thailand could be a form of "quasi-contractor." In all fairness, one must consider that Dickinson is not concerned with privatization as such, if one defines it in terms of commercial, for-profit activities (as done in this book) with the broader question of outsourcing. Indeed, other governments, tribal groups, and various covert operations could be the agents for this type of outsourcing. She acknowledges that the types of activities involving contractors in Vietnam differed greatly from those in Afghanistan and Iraq. For certain, the ratio between contractors to military personnel was quite different—Vietnam was one to five and Iraq (2008) was at one to one. Nevertheless, Dickinson regards these Vietnam-era measures as precedent setting for the move toward ever greater privatization, reduction of effective accountability toward both the government and public it serves, and loss of a nurturing, interactive relationship between government actions and public values as espoused in "human dignity, public participation, and transparency."[30]

A similar argument is found in Paul Verkuil's *Outsourcing Sovereignty*, where he identifies the Iran-Contra affair as a decisive point in the move to privatizing national security policy. After Congress had prohibited the use of federal funds to support the Contras in Nicaragua, who were trying to topple the government of Daniel Ortega, members of the National Security Council staff in the White House fell back on a scheme to fund them through payments from Saudi Arabia, private donors, and money gained from the sale of weapons to Iran, an action also prohibited by Congress. Without question, this arrangement was a maneuver to circumvent the procedures set forth in the Constitution that the US government could not expend money not appropriated by Congress. Iran-Contra was a serious violation of the Constitution, and, yes, it was a form of privatization. The Contras were nonstate actors, and there had been examples before of the US government supporting such groups both overtly and covertly. Iran-Contra took this a step farther by relying on soliciting money from a foreign government as well as private donors and using profits from illegal arms sales. This was not US funding covered in some way to prevent tracing it back to its official origins. Arguably, Iran-Contra was more a symptom of an emerging pattern of trying to bypass congressional review and approval rather than a channel to enable private parties to assume government functions for profit. The arms sellers certainly hoped to make a profit, but unlike their distant predecessors, the privateers, or current private military firms and security firms that would follow in greater numbers, they operated without a contract or legal arrangement between the US government and the private party.[31]

When the United States abandoned conscription in favor of an all-volunteer force, it unknowingly took steps that assured privatization. Whether an all-volunteer force could be expected to perform all the duties of its conscription predecessors was unclear. To motivate people to enlist, conditions had to improve, including the transfer of some duties that were widely regarded as unappealing and even demoralizing. The military did not know much about how to advertise for itself, so it turned to advertising agencies to create the campaigns to get people to enlist.[32] "Be All You Can Be," a recruiting slogan for the US Army, would not have resonated very well to a soldier staring down toilet bowls while on latrine duty. Companies developed or changed their scope to assume the contracts offered to perform such duties and others, too. Such changes, and reliance on them by the military services, were almost common-sense in light of the circumstances and needs of an all-volunteer force. Old-timers, of course, lamented the better living conditions and barracks and the absence of character and discipline-building tasks that they believed created a tougher force.

During the 1970s and 1980s an ideological argument intensified on both sides of the Atlantic, particularly in some of the English-speaking countries, that revolved around the proper relationships among the state, economy, industry, and citizen. These were the latest editions of older arguments that Elke Krahmann, as discussed in Chapter 1, depicts between the advocates of republicanism and liberalism. The former stresses the community, increasingly the state, as the best means to guarantee the security of the citizenry; the latter formula stresses the power of the individual and the importance of protecting individual rights against an encroaching state.[33] This division is not the only way of understanding this philosophical and political disagreement, but it helps here because of Krahmann's focus on force. After over three decades of crisis containing a major depression, a world war, and the origins of the Cold War, critics of state power feared that it had grown so large that it threatened individual liberty as well as the ability to use the economy and its resources for the sake of commercial growth and freedom. A significant portion of the intellectual heritage shaping this argument originated from across the Atlantic, whether it was John Maynard Keynes's arguments for government activism and intervention or the free-market arguments raised by Friedrich Hayek and others—including the more extreme iteration made by Ayn Rand. All of these people had seen firsthand the political and physical destruction that followed the economic disorder of the interwar years, but they disagreed on what to do about it. Economists and political thinkers in the United States were greatly influenced by their arguments and took sides at universities and various public and political fora.[34] In the United States, a leading proponent of the neoliberal view was Milton Friedman from the University of Chicago, whose book *Capitalism and Freedom* (1962) provided a sizable amount of the intellectual muscle for the arguments that were to follow.[35]

Neoliberalism is important to this question because of how it contributes "to the transformation of the fundamental coercive properties of the state."[36] The election of Margaret Thatcher and the Conservative Party in 1979 in the United Kingdom could be seen as the political starting line for the installation of neoliberalism into actual government policy. Ronald Reagan's victory in the US presidential election in 1980 put a neoliberal advocate into the White House. Aaron Ettinger observes there were two stages in the neoliberal movement once it had hold of political offices. The first occurred in the 1980s and was "a rolling back of state-initiated market constraints." Such reforms "were active sets of state-initiated programs associated with attacks on organized labour, planning agencies, and bureaucracies cuts, downsizing, and privatization." Some of these reforms collided with broader realities that caused a momentary halt and an adjustment to what Ettinger describes as a new form of neoliberalism that "incorporate[d] technocratic, strategic, and market-oriented state interventions into the free market." This version of neoliberalism did not try so much to dismantle the state as operate it "with a deliberate series of state interventions and regulations." This included "networked forms of governance, multilateral economic surveillance, technocratic management, public-private partnerships, and market-complementing forms of regulation."[37] In many ways the changes made in the defense sector in the United States, the UK, and to some degree beyond reflected a combination of downsizing and privatization from the first phase with the forms of "technocratic management, public-private partnerships, and market-complementing forms of regulations" found in the second part.

A more aggressive evaluation of neoliberalism and national security is offered in the work of Anna Leander, from the University of Copenhagen's Business School. She describes it as the abandonment of "the conventional idea that states should be governing markets and make them socially useful" and replacing that "with the idea that markets should be relied upon to govern states." State bureaucracies in the view of the neoliberals were "self-serving" and potentially corrupt. Markets were the better governor and decider for what should occur. Leander reminds us very persuasively that this message carried beyond the shores of the United Kingdom and United States, due unquestionably to the efforts of these two parties, and became the aspiration of newly independent countries in Asia and Eastern Europe. This assertion of market power would check that of government and the state and offer its own ambiguity that promoted creative activity among entrepreneurs.[38] Without going into an extensive critique of Leander's entire argument, her insightful reminder of the effort to promote neoliberalism globally seems a distortion of what occurred, and still does, in the United States. First of all, Congress controls and engages in decisions related to military structures and force level in ways that hardly respond to market forces or efficiencies. What some commentators call the Iron Triangle in Washington, DC—the key links among Congress, the DOD, and the defense manufacturers—is almost the antithesis of free-market thinking, even though the following pages briefly discuss an attempt to make that so. If that indeed happened and took effect, it failed dismally.

Particularly after the end of the Cold War and the subsequent downsizing of major militaries, an increase in "operational tempo," the number and demand of new and competing operations, was the last thing any national leader and his or her military wanted, but that was the reality. There were many skill sets the military did not have or did not have in adequate amounts—the training, operation, and repair of new technologies and integrated systems. With the multiple needs the services faced as well as the variables for skill sets, it was implausible to consider having a trained force in uniform large enough to meet these requirements. It would be too large and arguably too expensive. Better to turn to the private sector, which could meet personnel needs for whatever the specific requirements of this surge were. Working in contract relationships, these people could be retained and released as necessary, not unlike mercenaries and privateers from centuries earlier who had offered specific skills, weapons, technologies, and numbers to supplement and complement existing forces. Critics of high defense spending who believe that large militaries and defense structures take away people and money that could better be used for national economic growth could also find reason to think that reliance on the private sector might avoid some of this sacrifice.[39]

With the expansion of the defense industrial sector as well as the civilian workforce supporting the Department of Defense and the military services, the DOD had to confront the fact that there were many jobs that could be performed by workers in the private sector. For example, later in 2001, the US government found 849,389 positions government-wide that met that description. As such, these jobs were not "inherently governmental."[40] Starting in the 1970s, the Office of Management and Budget in the Office of the President released A-76, a form that set forth the procedures that departments and agencies had to follow. This process, arcane to the outside world, helped set the stage toward a shift to outsourcing throughout the government, and not just the Defense Department and the Departments of the Army, Navy, and Air Force. This is not to say that its proponents regarded the process as the equivalent of outsourcing or privatization. After all, the award of the project or task could go to a government office as well as a private competitor. Arguably, though, it created a climate that made it easier to consider these next steps. In 1997, for example, the Office of the Undersecretary of Defense for Acquisition, Technology, and Logistics issued a report that found that between 1978 and 1994 the A-76 process saved on the average about 30 percent for each project in competition. That only amounted to an annual saving of about $1.5 billion annually—small change, cynics would say, in terms of overall defense spending. The complicated twists and turns of A-76 are beyond our concern here. Not surprisingly, government workers' unions disliked the policy, even though the overall government sector did not fare badly, and, at times, there was concern about the number of private actors willing to wade through the paperwork to enter the competition. Nonetheless, the process had become part of the culture because there was a demonstrable record of savings.[41]

The recurrent cycle of peacekeeping, humanitarian, stabilization, and other missions facing the military invited consideration of measures that could meet the ups and downs of personnel needs, especially in support functions. In December 1985 the chief of staff of the US Army signed an order establishing the Logistics Civil Augmentation Program (LOGCAP). The language in the key paragraph explaining the purpose of LOGCAP is worth quoting in full:

> The Army continually seeks to increase its combat potential within peacetime resource allocations. To achieve the maximum combat potential, maximum support from as many sources as possible is necessary. This requires pursuit of support from external resources. Host nation support (HNS) is one method of support through Government to Government agreements. LOGCAP is aimed at providing another support alternative by capitalizing on the civilian sector in CONUS and overseas locations.[42]

The critical words are in the last sentence, which stresses the importance of relying on contractors both in the continental United States (CONUS) and abroad. Put more straightforward, the army's explanation made clear that it regarded contractors (and admittedly the host nation where operations would be occurring) as a supplement and complement to a force whose size was restricted ultimately by Congress. The army could not count on the statutory size of the force being increased. Contractors were an obvious, necessary alternative.

The new regulation emphasized that its application applied particularly in settings where there would be support through multilateral or bilateral treaties. For example, if NATO defined the operation as an alliance matter, member states and their militaries could be counted on for providing various forms of support. Prior to the paragraph explaining the purpose of LOGCAP, a provision had stressed the need to establish contracts "quickly as needs are identified in wartime situations." The rather soft definition of "wartime conditions" offered in the regulation that stressed the term was a generic one "to denote a range of conditions from heightened international tensions or states of military readiness through periods of armed conflict up to and including a congressionally declared state of war" can seem frustrating, but it reflects contemporary thinking about the range of operations the military thought existed below the highly unlikely event of a declared war. In short, the bulk of these operations would resemble ones the military had recently experienced—especially in Lebanon and Grenada, which had occurred through presidential order without congressional authorization (although the Lebanon mission belatedly received authorization through use of the War Powers Resolution in 1983).[43] Declared war, as implied in the regulation, would inject an entirely different set of expectations and measurements, including a greater likelihood of increased force size and structure that would probably require military resumption of duties awarded to contractors.

Interestingly, the regulation adds the observation a little later that contractor performance is something that cannot be included as a "basis" in military planning. Toward the end, one finds recognition of the fact that contractors could become involved in "wartime planning" and assist the "wartime staffs" of the major commanders. The next sentence limits this role, however, to "selected combat support and combat service activities." They were not to assume duties that would make them combatants under law.[44]

This stipulation about remaining noncombatants was going to become a matter of controversy as the size and range of these types of military operations expanded. So, too, would a specification added just after the previous one—namely that "contractors will not be used to perform inherently governmental functions." The question of the status as combatants or noncombatants will be addressed later in this chapter, but it is worth considering how the army defined "inherently governmental" in this regulation. Readers should always remember that these regulations are written and reviewed by judge advocates general (JAGs, or military lawyers) before they are signed. The definition posed in a glossary to the regulation may again be worth quoting in full because of its important implications and possible ambiguities.

["Inherently governmental" is] a function which is so intimately related to the public interest as to mandate performance by Government employees. These functions include those activities which require either the exercise of discretion in applying Government authority or the use of value judgments in making decisions for the Government. Government functions normally fall into two categories: the act of governing, and monetary transactions and entitlements. The act of governing includes criminal investigations, judicial functions, management and direction of Armed Services, conduct of foreign relations, selection of program priorities, direction of Federal employees, and direction of intelligence and counterintelligence operations. Monetary transactions and entitlements include revenue disbursements, and control of treasury accounts.[45]

Max Weber would have regarded the management of violence in the state's service as an "inherently governmental function," even though the legal terminology had probably not been defined. When we return briefly to this matter later, we will see that the language in the above is not the final word. Lawyers and scholars do disagree. Certainly the historical record, as treated in this book, concluded that war and state violence are matters important enough "to the public interest as to mandate performance by Government employees"—thus the historical demise of privateering and most forms of mercenaries. It would be difficult to challenge the assertion that exercise of these powers does not "require" an "exercise of discretion" "or the use of value judgments." The "management and direction of Armed Services" means not only command but, arguably, decisions related to the conduct of war—strategy, tactics, rules of engagement, and so on. The addition of language regarding "intelligence and counterintelligence operations" is also worth considering, especially in light of both the contemporary discussion and implementation of the Iran-Contra affair and the subsequent reliance on contractors we have seen occurring in operations of the Central Intelligence Agency and other entities in Iraq, Afghanistan, and elsewhere. Bear in mind, however, that the above was the work of military attorneys and not those working in other government agencies or in the confines of the National Security Council during the mid-1980s.

The creators of LOGCAP knew that they were supporting a new environment that posed some risk. "The use of military contractors versus US military personnel," write the authors, "involved a higher degree of risk." At this stage it was difficult to predict their effectiveness. The management of this risk and decisions about it rested in the hands of the major army commander (MACOM, to use the terminology). He or she would have to assess the risk, decide on what functions were best suited for this, and determine what the best mix of contractor and military personnel was. Building in some "redundancy and multiplicity of sources of support" could help to prevent detrimental consequences and effects. For the contracting officers that were writing, judging, and awarding the requirements, there was need for attention to detail at all stages.[46] To be fair, the army anticipated there might be problems, and in instances there assuredly were.

The first use of LOGCAP by the army in a military operation was in the Balkans. By the 1990s the air force and navy followed with their own augmentation programs. The architecture of these military/private-sector relationships and operations had been set into place and motion. "Contract warfare," as Sean McFate labels it, was now more possible. Yet, many companies were really not in the business of providing surrogate militaries for actual combat. Categorizing these companies is not always easy, and scholars have offered different approaches. Peter Singer presents three of them: military support firms, military consultant firms, and military provider firms. The first specialize in various types of assistance and services that are nonlethal—essentially the types of support largely envisioned in the LOGCAP program. The second, military consultant firms, move into areas related to actual training and advisory functions, and these are the functions that the initial memorandum on LOGCAP cautions may have to occur based on the commander's assessment and needs. Here governmental and nongovernmental functions begin to blur more. The final category, military provider firms, depending on the national laws under which it must operate, may enter into actual combat functions and closely related command-and-execution responsibilities.[47] McFate, a US Army veteran who also worked for a private military firm before pursuing his academic and analytical career, uses a similar three-way division but with different terms that add a little more clarity: combat service support/general contractors, combat service/security support companies, and combat arms/private military companies.[48] The category "security support companies" is particularly problematic in McFate's view because these companies can become engaged in lethal actions but are usually unequipped for combat, since they often focus on evaluating intelligence, communications, interpreting, interrogation, and even the conduct of intelligence or spy operations.[49] Deborah Avant uses four categories, and importantly draws a distinction between "armed operational support" and "unarmed operational support on the battlefield."[50] David Shearer offers a fourth category below military or "logistical support," as he designates it, which he labels as "security services, which are involved in the protection of commercial property and personnel."[51] This description in itself illustrates the increased ambiguity that practitioners faced as they tried to define what was a matter of personal security, sometimes seen as more of a police function, and the traditional military roles identified with war and combat. This challenge reflects the characteristic of conflicts that merged matters of war and crime, among other things. Perhaps the key conclusion to make from all of the variations in typology is not to struggle among them and try to choose or compose the best one, but to acknowledge that each offers refinement and factors that have to be considered.

LOGCAP has undergone revisions since its inception over thirty years ago. Its first awards, and indeed most of its award for contracts, have gone to companies in the military or logistical support functions. Knight, Brown, and Root, for example, operated food, laundry, water, and fuel duties for US forces in Bosnia, thereby putting more military personnel into the field rather than behind stacks of potatoes or dirty underwear. In instances, military engineers helped the contractors in various construction projects. In East Timor, where a peacekeeping and humanitarian intervention was underway beginning in 1999, the US company DynCorp provided helicopters piloted by Russians and Bulgarians to support a UN effort in which the United States itself had no direct ground role. This was a way that the United States could be involved, support the operation, but avoid committing military personnel, which might have raised notification and authorization issues with a Congress skittish with concurrent US military operations in the Balkans. In the first Gulf War of 1990–1991, which one should remember involved a larger US Army still unaffected by the cuts that would soon follow, contractors predominantly served in support functions, but little doubt existed about the importance of their support for the overall war effort, which turned out to be very short-lived. The United States used a mix of US and foreign contractors to support its military as well as some related functions for coalition members.[52]

The lure of privatization continued during the Clinton administration, which, if anything, seemed more determined to pursue this as part of an effort to enable a reduction in the size of the military as well as a desired "peace dividend." Shrinking government had become a bipartisan crusade. For example, in March 1996 the Department of Defense released the report "Improving the Combat Edge through Outsourcing." After specifying the post–Cold War challenges facing the department, the authors claimed that "DoD can meet these challenges today and free up the additional resources required for modernization in the future by managing its internal operations and particularly its support activities more efficiently." The strategic environment of 1996 lacked a rival like the Soviet Union. The conviction was the United States had to be able to "to fight and win two nearly simultaneous regional conflicts."

"The conflicts," the document noted, "are often described as 'come as you are' wars, meaning that there will be little lead time for mobilization or surge of production capability. They will require rapid transportation, tailored and flexible maintenance support and greater reliance on private sector suppliers." A few sentences later the report added that "best business practices, tempered by risk and threat assessments, must be used to determine where outsourcing, privatization and competition can improve the performance of these activities." Since operational and support activities for the Defense Department and the services amounted to $93 billion of the budget for fiscal year 1996 (which ended on September 30, 1996), the department hoped it could "maximize effectiveness and save money by capabilities."[53]

In autumn 1997 Secretary of Defense William Cohen launched a Defense Reform Initiative to take advantage of the options posed by outsourcing as well as implementation of the much-vaunted "best business practices." With the reduction of the US Army from eighteen to ten divisions already underway, the army and other services tried to diminish the cuts in the military force by increasing cuts in the civilian workforce supporting the Defense Department and services. Thus, in 1998 the department reduced its acquisition staff by 38 percent. The implementation of this was not as drastic as it sounded, as the department tried to do it by attrition. Nevertheless, in the part of the Defense Department that handled contracting and procurement, the size of the workforce was going down while the volume of work was almost assuredly going up. I will add that one additional savior the department thought would rescue it was information technology and better computers—the lasting dream of organizations that hope to do more with less.[54]

The administration of George W. Bush continued this push for outsourcing and downsizing. Secretary of Defense Donald Rumsfeld was a critic of large government and regarded the DOD as a behemoth where resources needed to be shifted "from bureaucracy to the battlefield, from tail to tooth." On September 10, 2001, Rumsfeld told an assembled audience of Pentagon officials that the challenge was "to eliminate or shift to private suppliers any but the core activities of defense."[55] Of course, the environment was going to change quickly within the following twenty-four hours.

Given the surprise nature of the 9/11 attack, some disarray and adjustment was inevitable. Requirements for Iraq after the invasion on March 20, 2003 (Iraqi time), should have been more anticipated, but, inevitably, the nature of military operations creates some uncertainty. Civilian officials and US military officers handling the contracts were entering Iraq and Afghanistan prepared to act in accordance with the Federal Acquisition Regulations. Military commanders often wanted responses and needs filled very quickly, but the system was designed to be deliberate, often allowing contractors a few months to prepare their proposal and the officials a few months more to make the decision and award the contract. That did not work as easily in a setting with real military operations.[56] End runs around procedures, inside deals, and other violations did occur, enough to raise serious questions about accountability and even the purpose and legal status of the contractors in both theaters. The role of American contractors, specifically CACI International Corporation and Titan International, in the Abu Ghraib prison scandal due to abusive interrogations and apparent violations of US and international law raised serious questions. While most contractors were striving to do their best to respect law and regulations, even when they sometimes were not clear, recurrent cases in the coming years increased official concern in Washington, unease in the military services, and international criticism. There were cases involving physical assault on Afghan and Iraqi nationals, assault on other contractors, child pornography, and prostitution, among other things. Nowhere was this in any "best business practice." Closer, perhaps, to the application of that were billing irregularities and shortcuts around required procedures. In 2005 the chief contracting officer for the US Army Corps of Engineers, Bunnatine Greenhouse, charged in a congressional hearing that the Corps of Engineers had violated federal law and regulations in its award of a contract to Kellogg, Brown, and Root, now a subsidiary of Halliburton. Greenhouse had done so under the ostensible protection of the Federal Whistleblowers Protection Act, but the Army Corps demoted her anyway. The press, however, did not lose interest in the story.[57]

It did not take long for questions to begin to arise about the wisdom of privatization and the almost fawning enthusiasm that some had held for best business practices. In 2006 Congress received the latest iteration of the *Quadrennial Defense Review*, a reporting requirement Congress had established in 1996 to provide it with an evaluation every four years of the strategic environment, threats, and projected needs and courses of action. The *Review* expressed concern that the military was "hampered by inefficient business practices"—a less enthusiastic view of what could be gleaned from the private sector. The discussions of ensuing years showed a more restrained view of privatization but at the same time did not spurn or turn away from it.[58] Arguably, the Pentagon and the services had little option but to do so. Perhaps, as well, broader political considerations were also entering the arguments behind intervention and how to conduct it in the current strategic and political environment.

The *Review* from 2010 illustrated even greater misgiving. The legacy of the Nisour Square Incident in September 2007, reviewed in the Introduction, was still very much in play three years later and beyond. The Department of Defense realized it would have to assume more vigorous management over both the review and awarding of contracts as well as the behavior of the contractors. This did not mean halting outsourcing; in fact, the *Review* emphasized how the department had to do more to integrate public and private relationships. However, there was a stated desire to reduce the amount of the workforce in support services that came from the private sector. The announced reduction from 2010 to 2015 was supposed to be from 39 to 25 percent, which the department believed would enable a better balance of functions between the private and public sectors and a more effective use of tax dollars.[59]

Of course, one of the most appealing arguments for using private resources, whether for military support or actual combat, is that it is supposed to be a money saver. The answer is not that simple. Developing countries that lack a military, or have a weak one with little domestic base behind it, could possibly find it more economical to hire an outside force rather than build and equip one. Yet, a definitive answer is elusive because the expense of building a national army may be unknown or quite variable, the length of the conflict could cancel any gain elsewhere, and a foreign or contractor force may offer little for shoring national identity. The argument for postindustrial countries like the United States would initially seem more clear cut. The government does not have to pay as much for recruitment, training, equipping, and the like. The contractor can be committed for a set period of time and then released. Medical, retirement, and other expenses can fall on the shoulders of the employing company and not taxpayers. Some of these arguments resemble those from hundreds of years ago: that private forces could supplement national income or spare government expenditure, thanks to the backing of investors, be they from London or Baltimore, or modern-day stockholders. Once deployed, even when in a behind-the-lines support role or in advisory and training functions, companies have to provide their own security. Sometimes this has been the case even when the company's employees are involved in roles approaching actual combat or are involved in it.[60]

One factor that clearly affects cost is whether a contractor, if actually involved in military operations, can conduct an assignment more effectively than the state's military. The question can draw a completely different result for a state that has a weak military at the start versus one that has a modern military, or is capable of funding and supporting one, but has chosen not to in favor of outsourcing segments of its national security. Critics of Blackwater in Iraq, for example, have argued that the action of its employees contributed to a more complex, volatile situation on the ground, with portions of the population strongly alienated. If so, the consequence may be more military operations and a lengthier deployment.[61] A partial answer comes from research by Ulrich Petersohn, who found that the employment of a contractor force may add to the intensity and severity of the conflict.[62] This may or may not extend its length. Thus, there is no authoritative answer as to whether outsourcing national security functions saves money or adds expense. Many variables have to be considered in each situation to gauge this accurately. The fairest answer is probably provided by Robert Mandel, who, after considering the findings of the Government Accountability Office (GAO), uses the term "situational."[63]

THE PROBLEM OF ACCOUNTABILITY

Cost saving and efficiency were arguably the major justifications for the turn to the private sector that developed during the Cold War and accelerated afterward. The primary benefit, however, may have been the use and exploitation of an instrument in conflict that eludes the set of controls and laws that emerged on both the state and international levels during the past two centuries and earlier. Prior to then, rulers, heads of government, and states had been comfortable relying on private actors in warfare. There had been examples, such as during the Elizabethan period, where resort to private actors, especially privateers, had been a convenient way of concealing state support and allowing plausible denial. However, even alongside the most scheming ploys of Elizabeth I there had been a desire to save money, use private funds, and create additional sources of revenue from prizes. The concealing of state identity became more difficult, although probably never impossible if one was clever enough, as time progressed. By the 1990s the United States and others appeared to have rediscovered the convenience of private means that Elizabeth had so willingly used. Not only might these means be cheaper and more efficient, they also might circumvent some of the troublesome areas of congressional review and authorization and permit greater flexibility in what the United States, or other states, could do.

The central question takes us right back to that posed in Chapter 1: Are war and violence on behalf of the state official or "state" responsibilities and functions? The general answer that the international system and law had found was "yes," but if the state desired, there were circumstances where it could turn to the private arm. The marque-and-reprisal clause in the Constitution was an example of that, even though it fell into disuse as it seemed navies had taken on the functions of privateers. In the abstract, though, one could argue that states could still outsource national security, or at least parts of it, if it had laws, procedures, and an effective authority in place to sanction and control it. Whether states should do so is another question, an extremely important one, and a good caution against taking a strictly legalistic approach to the entire matter. It is on this latter point that just war theory, with its emphasis on legitimate authority and sanction, also enters consideration. Through the means of decision there is supposed to be a path or way for citizens and soldiers alike to identify and hold accountable those who have decided to use force. After all, war and violence are supposed to be done in the name and service of the people composing the state, if they are acts covered by international law that likewise satisfy the standards of just war thinking. In democracies and forms of representative government a strong argument insists that war and violence should represent the public's law and attest to what it cherishes, such as respect for law, the dignity and rights of human life, and adherence to international law and common standards of conduct. War and violence are the most serious actions a state, a people, or a group can take; in all of these one should see public engagement and approval. Measures to prevent corruption or other ill-gotten gains should exist. Even if a state, a multilateral body, or alliance believes it has effective laws, procedures, and review in place, can these prevent a breakdown of the relationship between the private agent and the state or society at large?[64]

The potential problems of accountability showed themselves quite early in the 1990s. The Clinton administration concluded it was necessary to send US troops to Colombia to train and assist the Colombian army in fighting the drug cartels. The poor human rights record of some in the Colombian military as well as the concern that the United States could find itself dragged into a conflict carrying elements of crime fighting as well as actual counterinsurgency led Congress to limit what US personnel could or could not do. They could not operate with Colombian military units with poor human rights records, and Congress stipulated they could not engage in counterinsurgency operations but only in antidrug measures. Involvement in the former could bring the United States into what some believed was more of a civil war. To those in the field—Colombian or US—the distinction between counterdrug and counterinsurgency measures could be difficult to discern. The challenges in Colombia continued into the following Bush administration. DynCorp did not believe it had to operate under the rules stipulated for US soldiers; therefore, in 2001 it flew helicopter gunships and other helicopters to bring in Colombian forces against the Revolutionary Armed Forces of Colombia (FARC).[65] Intentional or not, this option proved an effective way of circumventing restrictions in US law.

An arguably more troubling example occurred after Croatia declared its independence from disintegrating Yugoslavia in 1991. Croatia faced serious challenges from the Serbs, and its army badly needed training and equipping. At this stage in the Balkan conflict the United States was not prepared to send US ground troops; there was still a hope the Europeans, with the aid of airstrikes, could work out what some in Washington regarded as a European affair. In 1994 Croatia turned to Military Professional Resources Inc. (MPRI) for a contract to provide this training and other support functions, which MPRI did, after it had obtained the required approval of the Department of State. As explained, the major purpose of this contractual arrangement was to aid Croatia in improving its military so it could join in NATO's Partnership for Peace Program. MPRI, like a number of private military firms and corporations, employed retired officers at the ranks of admiral, general and below. In August 1995 the Croatian military entered the Krajina area, controlled by the Serbs, and successfully pushed most of them out, contributing to the appearance of about 120,000 refugees and charges of ethnic cleansing. The success of the operation was proof to some skeptics that MPRI had to have been involved to enable this to happen. MPRI has denied this, and after the negotiation and signature of the Dayton Peace Accords in November/December 1995 MPRI's business in the Balkans expanded, as did that of other US and foreign contractors. In fact, reports exist that the United States used the prospect of a contract for the Serbs with MPRI as an inducement to sign the accords, thereby offering the Serbs what had already benefited the Croats.[66]

Both of the above were contracts between a foreign government and a US contractor, an obviously different arrangement than that between a US military service, the Department of Defense, or other departments and agencies. US law treats a contract with a foreign country or customer as an arms export, a process set forth in the Arms Export Control Act of 1976. That law authorizes the president "to control the import and the export of defense articles and defense services and to provide foreign policy guidance to persons of the United States involved in the export and import of such articles and services." The licensing of exports is coordinated and issued through the Office of Defense Trade Controls in the Department of State, which has to decide whether the International Traffic in Arms Regulations (ITAR) affects the items or services being exported. A United States Munitions List details the arms and services available.[67] The fact the primary licensing authority is in the Department of State, rather than the DOD (or even the Department of Commerce), has been an issue of contention at different times but attests to the conviction that such sales are not just defense or commercial transactions but agreements that have major foreign policy repercussions.

Even though the laws and regulations do enable and require congressional review above certain thresholds, the overall process is not one that easily enables close congressional attention. To do so, Congress has to have the desire, plus an adequate number of knowledgeable staff, to follow these sales closely, and that is not always the case. Any export with a value of over $50 million requires a report to Congress. Congress can block the sale through a joint resolution, which the president can veto and Congress can attempt to override. Fifty million dollars may or may not be a lot of money depending on the service or items being provided. If there is concern about congressional reaction, the parties seeking to sell can divide the package into segments to keep its value below the threshold.[68]

There is nothing, then, that specifically mandates that the licensing offices or those in Congress reviewing the sales have to ask whether the specific tasks or project should be in the hands of private actors. This is not to suggest the question never arises, but, technically, it is not in the purview of the Office of Defense Trade Controls, or the counterpart offices in the Departments of Defense and Commerce, and other departments that are more focused on technology transfer and security. Its answer has potential foreign policy, political, and operational repercussions in the field, and these should be considered. These repercussions may reveal themselves quickly after the contractor has acted on the state and local level. T. X. Hammes, whose scholarship rests on extensive military service, warns that outsourcing functions that are part of military operations "can seriously undercut the legitimacy of both the host nation and US Government." Local nationals tend to expect the state to have a monopoly over such violence, and, if not, that reflects badly on it. When contracting firms decide to hire local nationals, this can have immense consequences. Those individuals receiving money can find their stature opposite the government or competing groups enhanced, as has occurred in Afghanistan. In other cases, locals resent the presence of nationals from other countries who have been given jobs by contractors they hoped would be future employers. US officials and commanders of provincial reconstruction teams in Afghanistan tried to prevent this by attempting to understand the future impact on the local economy, which may prove difficult. In Afghanistan US commanders learned from Afghan officials that the wages offered by contractors were so attractive that it was becoming hard for the Afghan government to meet its own recruiting needs and to maintain adequate numbers in uniform. Here was a problem that governments two hundred years earlier and before would have recognized! Even though then president Hamid Karzai faced a series of charges of corruption against him and his family and was a problematic figure, it was hardly surprising that in 2010 he tried to order all contractors out of Afghanistan within four months. Hammes cautions that US and International Security Assistance Force (ISAF) reliance on contractors could undermine one of the key tenets of US counterinsurgency doctrine that was then in place and guiding US policy—namely, the importance of establishing the legitimacy of the host nation's government.[69] Of course, the order did not work, and, given the dependence of the United States on its ISAF partners, and even of segments of Afghanistan itself, it could not have succeeded.

A recurrent question that the US government could never settle with necessary clarity and finality was the meaning of an "inherent government function." As the number of contracts and contractors expanded, along with tasks that came ever closer to actual combat operations, the issue stubbornly remained. The Federal Activities Inventory Reform Act of 1998 stated that "inherently governmental" meant something "so intimately related to the public interest as to mandate performance by government personnel."[70] This nobly sounding language certainly provided thoughtful commentary, but it was hardly a step beyond the army regulation discussed earlier. An aggressive advocate of private means could pose the question as to why they did not or could not serve "public interest" as well as public or government agencies. This might be especially so when the government or state had taken enough measures to insure that the private agent would so act. In 2006 the Department of Defense took a major step on this matter when it issued an instruction titled "Guidance for Determining Workforce Mix." Reflecting some of the experiences and encounters that military units had had with contractors (discussed below), the department made clear that "inherently governmental" included "combat operations, interrogations to the extent that they entail substantial discretion, and activities that require 'military-unique knowledge and skills,' such as the administration of US military correctional facilities, the provision of military advice and training, and the direction and control of intelligence operations." Security itself became inherently governmental "if it involves unpredictable international or uncontrolled, high threat situations where success depends on how operations are handled and there is a potential of binding the United States to a course of action when alternative courses of actions exist." To try to distinguish from operations that might not be inherently governmental, the key difference was the absence of the need for "substantial discretion," which could "include the security of buildings in secure compounds in hostile environments and security for 'other than uniquely military functions.'" Contractors were to be used with caution "in contingency operations where major combat operations are ongoing or imminent." Only the senior "combatant commander" for the region of operations could override this guidance.[71]

This tightening of the language affecting US policy was helpful in a legal and administrative sense, but it did not stem the movement toward dependence on more contractors. Others argued that US law on its own was not enough, and that the United States needed to bring itself more closely to the body of international law controlling mercenaries and other private actors. To appreciate that, however, requires a brief examination of the increased use of contractors and the types of incidents that posed growing political and legal questions. A US Army that had 700,000 in uniform at the end of the first Gulf War in 1991 had only two-thirds of that number in 2004. However, it faced a far more complex situation than it had in 1991—conflicts in Iraq and Afghanistan, a continuing operation in the Balkans, instability in parts of Africa and the Middle East, and the recurrent North Korea problem.[72]

Faced with an expanding commitment in Iraq, as well as a need not to diminish the mission in Afghanistan too greatly, the reality was that the United States was still not going to increase substantially the size of its military. Nor was it about to call up the National Guard and Reserves—at least not in an election year (2004) when such actions could stir controversy among a public still hoping for a short war in Iraq. The increased numbers had to come from the private sector and not just an expanded military commitment.[73]

The increases were rapid, even though numbers are not as exact before the last half of 2007, when the Department of Defense started collecting data more aggressively.[74] The figure of $5 billion the United States spent on contractors (DOD and others) in Iraq in 2003 tripled, to $15 billion in 2005. So, too, did the number of armed contractors, rising from 10,000 to 30,000 in 2005. Some nongovernment sources, such as the Private Security Association of Iraq (a trade association), estimated the figure of armed contractors at 48,000; keep in mind, though, the absence of a uniform definition of a contractor. The Departments of Defense and State were the largest employers by far, but several other cabinet departments and a number of agencies also hired contractors.[75] For some companies, the value of increased business was staggering. Blackwater, which figured prominently in US activities at the time, had $25,395,556 of contracts in 2003; by 2005 that rose at least fifteenfold, to $352,871,817. Not all of this was in Iraq or Afghanistan. Certainly a prominent amount of that boost had come from the decision of Coalition Provisional Authority Ambassador Paul Bremer in Iraq to extend Blackwater a no-bid contract to provide security to US officials. The following year the Department of State awarded the company a contract for worldwide services as needed.[76]

In 2007 President Bush supported an increase in the number of US military personnel to prevent a further deterioration of the situation in

Iraq. This, alongside the increase of personnel in Afghanistan by President Barack Obama after his 2008 election to improve the chance of winning the war he believed should have been the priority, fueled a faster increase in the number of contractors as well as the ratio between contractors and military personnel that saw the former outmatch the latter. One factor that reinforced this was the release in 2008 of *Army Field Manual 3-07*, which dealt with stability operations. This emphasized a "whole of government approach," which meant that US strategy and policy in both countries had to rest on a coordinated and better-integrated application of resources and instruments not only by the military but from all departments and agencies involved with national security and foreign policy. Building institutions became a major facet of this approach, and, here, as well as other arenas of activity, contractors had to figure prominently, whether they were supporting this activity, protecting its participants, or becoming more involved in actual military operations.[77] The "Surge," as the increase in size and operations in Iraq became known, peaked in numbers in April 2008 with 160,000 military personnel and 163,900 contractors—essentially a 50-50 breakdown. T. X. Hammes has observed how unlikely it would have been for the United States to have these numbers in Iraq if they had all been in the military. It is impossible to imagine Congress supporting such an increase at the time. There were three times as many contractors in Iraq working for the United States as there were British troops in that country, the commitment of a major ally.[78] The figures cited in the first paragraph of the introduction to this book illustrate the trends that followed. US strategy and operations, as well as those of its partners and allies, depended on contractors in all roles. If they had not been there, it is simply hard to imagine that the United States could have sustained its presence as long as it has and, possibly, as long as it will.

One portion of the contractor community especially concerned the United States and others: the number of people working for private security contractors or firms (PSCs or PSFs—I will use PSC). These were the contractors most likely to be armed. It is no surprise that incidents like that at Nisour Square heightened this concern. We are not talking about a proportionately high amount; usually the percentage of armed security contractors to total numbers in Iraq and Afghanistan was 5–10 percent; the numbers varied throughout each year.[79] Their roles, numbers in relation to armed troops, and national origins, among other factors, created questions about their effectiveness and impact on US and coalition strategies and accomplishment of objectives. Writing for staff and members of Congress, Moshe Schwartz with the Congressional Research Service (CRS) attempted to clarify this situation in a report in 2010. "Armed services" included security for sites and buildings, convoys, individuals traveling, and full-time protection for select people. Not all PSCs, Schwartz added, were heavily involved in such activities; some obtained more than half of their money from various unarmed activities like analyzing intelligence, training, or the operation of command, control, and communications centers. In late 2009–early 2010 Schwartz estimates there were about fifty PSCs in Iraq, with over 30,000 employees. In Afghanistan, the number of companies he identified came to fifty-two, with around 25,000 employees. Circumstances in Afghanistan operated under restraints and conditions set by then President Karzai due to his own suspicion of contractors. As a rule companies could not employ more than 500 people, and a majority of the PSCs did not work for the US government. Karzai still hoped to remove all of them from his country.[80]

By the time this report appeared, the United States had begun to reduce the number of troops it had in Iraq. Yet, as troop levels and even the overall number of contractors declined, the number, and, thus, the percentage of armed contractors in the total figure increased. In Afghanistan, as one entered 2010, all the numbers were increasing—US troops, contractors, and the number and percentage of armed contractors. The nationality of the contractors was an obvious point of concern. How strongly did they support US or coalition objectives or, more narrowly, the interests and objectives of their own government? The US approach had been to encourage hiring of Iraqi nationals because such actions could save money, as salaries were lower and jobs could reduce poverty and build economic opportunity and possibly support for the Iraqi government. Actually, the percentages of Iraqi nationals working for PSCs had declined from 25 percent of the workforce in late 2007 to 18 percent in late 2009. In Afghanistan, however, it was a very different story. In September 2009, 94 percent of the PSC employees there were armed, and of that armed group 90 percent were Afghan nationals. Literally in less than a year the number of armed security contractors there had increased by 236 percent, thanks to the increased number of military operations and the temporary increase of forward operating bases.[81]

The report illustrated how the Department of Defense, as well as the Congressional Research Service itself, had come to include and count armed contractors as part of the overall armed force that was at the beckon of the United States. As always, there will be disagreements over numbers because the DOD draws a distinction between offensive and defensive involvement in combat that defines what armed contractors can or cannot do. Its position is that PSC employees cannot be in offensive operations—only defensive ones. That difference can become a problem in itself. International law, as we will see, does not make this distinction, and its adherents regard PSCs as being bigger actors in US operations. As stability operations were part of the guiding doctrine for what the United States was doing in both Iraq and Afghanistan at the time, its view or treatment of who should be counted in a stabilizing force clearly influenced the counting as well—in this case probably expanding the number of those in combat operations. The figures used by both military sources and the CRS estimated that 13–18 percent of the armed forces in Iraq were armed contractors; the figure for Afghanistan was higher, at 22–30 percent.[82] These are significant percentages. One can imagine the political and budgetary difficulty of replacing all of these con-tractors (US, Iraqi, Afghan, and many other nationalities) with US troops. Neither the White House under President Obama for certain nor the Con-gress most likely would have been willing to seek or authorize the actual increase of personnel. The latter certainly would have explored and probably added conditions to the deployment, its duration, and possible conditions of outcome. There was no feasible way US policy or operations would have been sustainable, regardless of opinion on the wisdom of folly of doing so.

The silent, steady increase in contractor casualties was something the United States and the rest of the world did not watch. Sadly, they may not have felt the need or obligation to do so. You will not find contractor casu-alties listed by the Department of Defense as part of the overall force used for support or combat operations. One must go to a website with the US Department of Labor to see the number, and the figures it provides are based on insurance claims filed. At the end of 2016 there were 3,408 companies reporting from all theaters (including the Philippines, Somalia, Yemen, and Syria, as well as Iraq and Afghanistan). The total number of dead since September 11, 2001, came to 3,804. There were 118,556 wounded. Reports of contractor dead and wounded are very hard to find in newspapers, and it would be interesting to see how both the American public and Congress would respond if these numbers were added to the official casualties from all locations.[83] US military and Defense Department civilian casualties are much more up to date (generally within twenty-four hours). As of June 15, 2017, the total for all theaters with operations amounted to 6,930. Even half a year earlier, contractor fatalities were well over half of those for troops and Defense Department civilians. What is more unbalanced and disturbing, if one looks at this in terms of human cost and accountability, is the number of those wounded. There may be some discrepancy here as the DOD lists those wounded in action while the numbers for contractors describes them as "wounded," which may include those injured in noncombat situations. Since individuals in support functions, which are not part of combat, can also become victims of improvised explosive devices, terrorist attacks, and other incidents, the measurements can be evaluated from both directions. The Department of Defense states as of June 15, 2017, that 52,560 individuals had been wounded.[84] This is slightly under half of the figure for those wounded in the count for contractors, which may encompass noncombat circumstances. The figures are not reassuring for those in either setting, but for contractors they attest to sizable numbers that elude public attention.

T. X. Hammes was disturbed by the figures he found in 2010. As 2009 ended, nearly 1,800 contractors had been killed and 40,000 wounded in both Iraq and Afghanistan alone. In the first half of 2010, while writing, Hammes found that the number of contractor deaths in the two countries had exceeded those for the US military.[85] In 2014 Colonel Scott L. Efflandt, US Army, examined the problems affecting military professionalism and contractors and concluded that armed security contractors were "1.5 to 4.8 times more likely to be killed in Iraq or Afghanistan than US uniformed personnel."[86] Again, try to imagine the impact of these figures if they were all US military personnel (and a smaller number of Defense Department civilians) rather than contractors employed by companies. Public outcry would assuredly have been greater, even though many of the contractors employed by US companies were foreign nationals. Approval of troop increases to replace them would have been out of the question. US operations in Afghanistan are now in their seventeenth year; operations in Iraq are in the fifteenth, with a brief hiatus of sorts after 2011. Continuation of the US role in these conflicts depends on contractors, which parallels with a need to contain the amount of domestic political controversy that can arise if official US troop levels ascend too highly again.

The other side of this matter obviously suggests the reality that contractors are becoming more involved in combat or near-combat operations. The extent to which the Department of Defense, the US military, and their foreign counterparts in Iraq and Afghanistan expected this to happen is debatable, but little doubt exists that all knew it could happen. When stabilization operations became a greater justification for coalition and US actions, the presence of support workers and staff, as observed earlier, also made them easier targets. Acquiring accurate data on contractor involvement in hostilities is a consistent complaint among scholars and others trying to understand the situation. The scenario most inviting to contractor gunfire was the escort of motorcades and vehicles. Provision of documents by the Department of State (not the DOD, significantly) to the journalist Jonathan Cook in 2008 showed that between 2005 and 2007, 65 percent of the cases in Iraq where a contractor fired a weapon involved escort duty. However, the same data indicated that shots occurred on just 2 percent of all the escort missions these contractors had. Undoubtedly, other department and agencies in Iraq had experienced incidents, and even the ones reported by the Department of State had been voluntary reports. The figures had to be larger.[87] For example, ArmorGroup was a company that escorted nonmilitary convoys in Iraq. A publicly traded corporation, it had 9,000 employees at the time, of which 1,200 were in Iraq. In 2005–2007 it could escort as many as twenty-five convoys daily. ArmorGroup quickly and painfully learned that the insurgents in Iraq understandably made no distinction between military and nonmilitary convoys or between soldiers and contractor personnel. In Iraq in 2005, one out of every eighteen convoys came under attack (a figure for all carriers); by 2007 that number had dropped to one out of seven. The big trucks that often appeared were almost a modern counterpart, it seemed, to the landing ship tanks (LSTs of World War II) that had been dubbed "large, slow targets." In 2006 ArmorGroup escorted 1,184 convoys and found itself attacked 450 times. In short, any employee could count on an attack about every 2.6 times. By the end of 2006 the company's death count was surpassed by only three coalition partners in Iraq: the United States, Great Britain, and Italy. Company employees responded quickly with small arms fire when attacked.[88]

After the Bush administration and Ambassador Bremer with the Coalition Provisional Authority (CPA) decided in May 2003 to ban about 85,000 Baath Party members in Iraq from serving in a new Iraqi government and to dissolve Iraq's military, Interior Ministry, and presidential security forces, a complex, extremely difficult situation confronted the militaries and officials of the coalition forces in Operation Iraqi Freedom. Now hundreds of thousands of very disgruntled Iraqis were ready to support the insurgents. Even Bremer himself became a contracting officer, as the CPA arranged and offered contract agreements.[89] Under Bremer, Iraq was an occupied country until June 2004 and did not enjoy sovereignty. Perhaps unknowingly, given the consequences, the ambassador added to the problem of violence by contractors when he issued CPA General Order No. 17 in June 2003. It stated, "Coalition contractors and their sub-contractors, as well as their employees, not normally resident in Iraq, shall not be subject to Iraqi laws or regulations in matters relating to the terms and conditions of their contracts in relation to the Coalition Forces or the CPA." In short, these contractors were "immune from Iraqi Legal Process."[90]

There was an important loophole in this order that arguably enabled all contractors to act more aggressively, if needed, as well. The existing edition of the *Army Field Manual* then in force stated that contractors would not be "subject to Army regulations or the Uniform Code of Military Justice" with the exception of a declared war. Writing later for the US Army War College, Thomas Mockaitis commented that contractors "could easily interpret CPA Order No 17 as carte blanche." There was no way Operation Iraqi Freedom would be a declared war in spite of the clamor of a handful of critics in and outside of Congress to make it such.[91] Thus, contractors did not have to worry about the *Army Field Manual* or the Uniform Code of Military Justice. Obviously, contactors could be held accountable under US laws, but this was going to prove difficult and require Congress to legislate measures that arguably remain inadequate and ambiguous to this present day. In 2006 the Department of Defense announced an "interim rule" in the *Federal Register* to defense acquisition regulations that specifically authorized contractors operating with the US military "to use deadly force when necessary to execute their security mission to protect/assets/persons, consistent with the mission statement contained in their contract." The "combatant commander" was responsible for ensuring "that private security contract mission statements do not authorize the performance of any inherently Governmental military functions, such as preemptive attacks, or any other types of attacks."[92] Efforts to halt or overrule this regulation did not succeed, including one attempt to use the Anti-Pinkerton Act of 1893, which forbid the US government of the District of Columbia from hiring anyone from that detective agency or others like it, as it would prohibit this type of open-ended allowance for contractors. None of these succeeded.[93]

Thus, a climate of impunity seemed to exist, although most contractors acted cautiously and responsibly. The exceptions, though, became problematic. There were companies that acquired the reputation of having very trigger-happy employees. The House Committee on Oversight and Government Reform conducted hearings in 2007 that investigated the role and behavior of contractors in Iraq and Afghanistan. From January 1, 2005, through September 12, 2007, Blackwater employees under contract to the Department of State were in 195 incidents where they fired weapons. In 84 percent of the incidents, they were the first to fire.[94] Of course, one could work with different starting points for these numbers. Some incidents may have reflected a visible or arguable imminent threat of attack, which led to the first gunfire. For the benefit of doubt, some incidents assuredly can be treated as spontaneous gunfire with no purpose. The two other companies doing similar work for the Department of State—DynCorp and Triple Canopy—had a series of incidents that, combined, did not match Blackwater's number. Admittedly, this numerical difference could reflect the number of missions as well as the type, so caution is wise. Interestingly, incidents involving Blackwater produced more property damage than the combined number for the other two competitors. Most occurred from moving vehicles, which made it difficult to verify casualties and damage.[95] Nonetheless, the willingness to initiate firing may reflect differences in corporate culture and training as well.

Complaints from US and coalition commanders and soldiers did occur. One of the most quoted was made by Brigadier General Karl Horst, USA, deputy commander of the Third Infantry Division in Iraq in 2005, who strongly objected to the reckless acts of some contractors. "They shoot people, and someone else has to deal with the aftermath." Speaking of another company's employees, Zapata, Horst observed that they sometimes relied on the practice of "clearing by fire," which was an almost scythe-like approach that could include US soldiers as targets as well. Officers in the US Army and Marines that I had in seminars from 2003 until 2015 retold incidents off-the-record that they had witnessed or knew of through others or participation in subsequent investigations. No one intimated that this situation was the normal one, but the complications and dangers created for commanders and personnel in the field, Iraqi and Afghan civilians, and civilian personnel from other agencies, departments, and contractors could make the entire climate in a town, village, or area more difficult.[96] A bad incident could be a genuine setback for coalition objectives.

Steve Fainaru of the *Washington Post* did a series of stories in 2007 and 2008 on the contracting done by the US Army Corps of Engineers in Iraq. The Army Corps of Engineers was involved in many reconstruction projects in Iraq, and it issued contracts to two British companies, Aegis Defence Services and Erinys Iraq, to provide security for those working on the projects. The US general in Iraq in charge of all contracting even depended on Aegis for his own security. Aegis had been the subject of some controversy because of a video from around 2005–2006 that ostensibly showed Aegis employees shooting at Iraqi civilian vehicles while Elvis Presley's "Mystery Train" played in the background. Aegis's reputation in the eyes of its critics did not benefit from the fact that its founder was a former British army officer, Tim Spicer, who had acquired a reputation earlier as an old-style mercenary operating in Africa and Oceania. He definitely had a Hollywood flair surrounding his past. Yet, dependence on these companies, in the opinion of the civilian head of logistics in Iraq for the Army Corps of Engineers, was no matter of choice. Jack Holly, a retired marine colonel, had to deal daily with the protection of various projects and transportation supporting them. He permitted a representative of a trade association, the Private Security Company Association of Iraq, to be in his planning meetings. The association and its members were in Iraq, Holly observed, because of "the U.S. government's failure to recognize the problem." He expressed the situation directly. Most employees were not "here because of apple pie, mother, and the American flag. . . . There was supply and there was demand, and the supply and demand created a price." Continuing to reflect, he observed, "When you see the number of people I've had killed, the American public should recognize that every one of those people represents an American soldier or marine or sailor who didn't have to go in harm's way." Speaking of military personnel, he added, "I don't want a mother to know that her son was in a convoy coming up from Kuwait and he got killed guarding Frappuccino that was going to the fuckin' U.S. embassy. To me, soldiers and marines have a mission to do certain things, and on other things you can out-source risk." The risk could be very high, as Holly knew, since one of his convoys in 2005 escorted by a British firm, Hart Security, had lost thirteen of twenty people in just one attack.[97]

If thirteen troops from the United States or any other coalition partner had been killed in a single attack on a convoy, one can rest assured it would have been a lead news story for that day. However, these contractors died in a state close to anonymity and in a legally ambiguous climate that reinforced their situation as second-class citizens in various ways before both national and international law. Although my focus is on the United States, the fate of these thirteen people likely rested on domestic laws in their own countries—Great Britain, Iraq, or wherever—as well as international law. Turning to the United States, the relative indifference to contractors in the press, public, and Congress has played a serious part in eroding constitutional and even ethical boundaries for how the US government uses force and interacts with its citizens in the area of civil-military relations. It can easily do the same in any system of government that espouses public participation in decision making and the importance of accountability. Reflecting on this charge in his study of civil-military relations in the United States since World War II, William Taylor writes, "private security contractors have served to sever the vital connection between citizenship and military service. Civilian policy makers now have the expedient ability to avoid either clearly articulating the justification for additional service members or paring down international commitments to correlate top existing force levels." There is a "clear disconnect between military service and citizenship that the usage of private military contractors encourages." Furthermore, as shown in these pages, military commanders, both from necessity and learned habit, have now become comfortable in using contractors.[98] When teaching in professional military education I learned a term called "asset protection." Protection of assets, human and technological, is an obvious responsibility of a commander and national leaders. However, the term sometimes had a more negative meaning in discussion—namely a circumstance where protection of assets arguably becomes the primary objective. A particular aircraft or vessel is so expensive that it requires discretion on how and when to use it. Personnel in an all-volunteer system, in effect, acquire some of the same features because of their status, cost in training, and fear of public disapproval with high casualty rates. If one can find other assets, perhaps more disposable and usable, then it is tempting to turn to them, even if, ironically as contractors, they may be more expensively paid. The company, however, is paying the salary.

Arguably, the most egregious incident illustrating this form of "vicarious warfare" or "asset protection" and the political, legal, and moral questions that result does not involve the United States but Russia. On February 7, 2018, a force of around 500 pro-Syrian troops, including Russian mercenaries, attacked a position near Deir-al Zour in Syria controlled by around forty to fifty US personnel (Special Operations, Special Forces, and marines) as well as militia units alongside them. Several months later details remained rather murky, but the combination of ground-fire and rocket strikes, as well as air strikes, may have killed 200–300 of the attackers, including a number of the Russian mercenaries; estimates run as high as 100. Russia has military units in Syria, but Russian spokespeople said the people making the attack were not theirs. There were no US casualties.[99]

Russian use of mercenaries is not new. Evidence of their presence in Bosnia and in Transnistria surfaced in the 1990s, and they clearly played a role as the "little green men" in Ukraine after 2014. Technically, mercenaries are still illegal under Russian law, but a number of modifications of law have enabled their role in a variety of ways. For example, a change of law in 2008 permitted foreign security operations for some of the large Russian oil and energy companies. In 2011 revised laws permitted establishment of reserves for the armed services and foreign intelligence services. A 2013 law allowed private military corporations to have their own weapons and "to provide other military services." This was about the same time the first Russian private military companies appeared in Syria. President Vladimir Putin has plainly stated the value of contractor or mercenary-like activities as a means of "implementing national interests without . . . direct involvement." Putin and other Russian officials know Russian military losses in Afghanistan from nearly forty years ago and more recently in Chechnya still dwell on the public's mind. Also, Russia, like most other states, finds that private means can supplement and complement existing capabilities and perhaps avoid some additional expenditure.[100]

The origins and identity of the Russian private military companies and units in Syria present an interesting story on how informally such institutions develop and conduct themselves in Russia and beyond. Understanding the exact history of the employing company in Syria relies on studying linkages in Putin's inner circle and some trust in dotted lines. The apparent employer in Syria is known as Wagner, the Wagner Group, or Wagner Private Military Company. Its founder most likely is Yevgeniy Prigozhin, a man indicted by Special Counsel Robert S. Mueller for alleged actions interfering in the 2016 US presidential election. Certainly Prigozhin has a colorful past—nine years in prison for prostitution and robbery and a reputation as a restaurateur, a caterer, and recognition, so to speak, as "Putin's Chef." His multidimensional talents brought or enabled him to create the Wagner operation, which played a role in Ukraine and in Syria. Estimates suggest it has about 3,000 employees in Syria, roughly a thousand fewer than the number of Russian military personnel there in 2017. Its commander is a retired lieutenant colonel from the Russian military intelligence service (GRU) named Dmitry Utkin, who prefers to go by the name of Wagner (sometimes spelled Vagner) in honor of his favorite German composer and in memory of the Nazi ideology that reportedly fascinates him so much that witnesses claim he wears a helmet with horns and has a swastika tattooed on his shoulder. Utkin and others have targeted former Russian soldiers as recruits with sizable sums of money—far, far more than they would earn if they had stayed in uniform.[101]

The nebulous circumstances surrounding the legal status and fate of those employed by Wagner in Syria is an extreme case of what can befall men and women employed by many companies in conflict or war zones. The actual names of those killed do not appear in any official death notice or tally. As to those in Syria, in late February 2018 the British Broadcasting Corporation's (BBC) Russian Service interviewed Nina Atyusheva, whose son died in Syria in September 2017 as a company employee. A person brought her son's coffin and an insurance payment of around $90,000 to Atyusheva, but it was the lack of any official acknowledgment of her son's service and death that so distressed her. A death certificate stated he had died from a gunshot wound in the stomach area; a Russian consular official in Syria explained he died in a fire. Atyusheva asked the BBC reporters a question that any parent, whether in Russia, Iraq, the United States or elsewhere, could pose about the characteristics, purpose, and accountability for a son's death: "I want to ask this question: in what way are the children sent by the armed forces different from those like mine, who went as a volunteer."[102] The fact that US soldiers are volunteers is not the point here. It is rather the two-track system for treating sacrifice, injury, and death that demands our focus.

Although he was writing about the United States, Paul Koistinen in the last volume of his multivolume study of political economy and warfare observes that "the use of private firms today constitutes a much graver problem than in earlier centuries. They have acted to 'hollow out' the government's capacity to conduct national security functions in an increasingly turbulent world." What Koistinen does not ask, but assuredly understands, is, What if it is the government itself that chooses to allow these capacities or functions to be hollowed out? Other scholars mentioned in these pages—Deborah Avant, Laura Dickinson, Allison Stanger, and Elke Krahmann, among others—have expressed these same worries. A counterargument made by contractors, military leaders, and some writers would add that reliance on contractors has arguably enabled governments and international bodies to address the problems of this "increasingly turbulent world" because of their specific skills, faster availability, and flexibility in numbers as needed. It is harder, though to challenge Koistinen's conclusion that "privatization has enormously complicated civil-military relations and the ability of the executive to effectively monitor and control military activities and operations."[103] The conclusion obviously applies outside the United States as well.

It is hard not to see greater design in the American move, and that of others, to privatized instruments in war, rather than just the exploitation of special skills, flexibility, and other attributes that make them particularly useful in the conflicts of recent decades. Rebecca Thorpe reflects on this in the conclusion of her book on politics and military spending in the United States when she notes how the nation has found ways to finance and conduct conflicts in ways that do not lose public approval as quickly as in Vietnam or even later. The military became all voluntary; there was no national service obligation, and reliance on contractors kept the force size lower. Republicans and Democrats alike resorted to deficit spending and borrowing to finance these operations rather than raising taxes or shifting major domestic spending. New technologies invited the prospect and hope that conflicts could be fought more cleanly with fewer casualties (particularly to one's own country). I had tried to argue the same in a book chapter titled "Keeping War Usable: A Place for Imperfect War," and in subsequent parts of that work. Thorpe, however, states it much more eloquently and concisely when she writes, "The ability to obviate or reduce public sacrifices in wartime undermines the system of checks and balances that the Constitution's framers envisioned. Rather than imposing the sacrifices on political majorities with electoral power over governing officials, policymakers can promote initiatives that reduce the immediate costs of war for most Americans." "The broad extension of defense benefits and the shifting of war costs," she writes, "make it easier for elected officials to perpetuate military spending and exercise force abroad without fear of electoral reprisal."[104]

Even though Congress became more attentive and involved in the review and assessment of private contractors in Iraq, Afghanistan, and beyond after 2007, the inescapable fact remains that Congress does not choose and award the contractor. While it has tried other measures, such as placing a ceiling on the number of contractors, companies have worked around that by hiring local nationals, a pattern we saw earlier in this chapter.[105] Privateers under the American model had not received contracts from Congress either, and there were clearly loose and dubious arrangements that existed. Yet, the authorization for the letters of marque and reprisal had come from Congress. The president could not commence this on his own, nor the War Department (as it was then known) and US Navy; the actual authority had to come from Congress. Nothing that clear exists for modern contractors, aside from the fact that the United States has a long history of turning to private contractors for different functions and that the path to using contractors as they are today in many ways was just a continuation or evolution of old practices and policies. Why not outsource another function as well? This would seem a logical step. Congress does not often exercise the power to review what the contracting officers and their agencies, departments, and military services are doing. That power is more elaborate with military contracts than in some other settings, and evidence points to the expectation that contractors will do a fair amount of self-policing. This "market accountability" does work to some degree. Companies do not want to become known as poor performers, trouble makers, or as covers for illegal or corrupt actions. Governments and military services have no obligation to return to them for business. In instances where the company committed or was involved in noticeable human rights abuses, this monitoring has worked. Otherwise, the record of congressional oversight and regulation seems more problematic.[106]

Most of Congress's power and abilities over contracting rest in its budgetary and appropriating powers, although other committees, such as those with foreign affairs or government operations portfolios, can certainly examine these issues as well. A long-standing debate exists over whether Congress actually authorizes actions when it appropriates money. This is not the place to attempt to resolve it, but the fact that debate and uncertainty exist attests to the problem. Congress has organized much of its work around authorizing and appropriating committees; the first are supposed to review policy and authorize the various steps to be taken, and the latter decide on the amount of money actually appropriated to support the policy and its accomplishment. In reality, the process does not work that cleanly, and in recent years authorizing committees have sometimes failed to fulfill their obligations, thereby by default allowing the appropriators in the House and Senate to enter more into actual policy deliberation in addition to funding decisions. However, presidential requests for a declaration of war or an authorization to use force are not part of the budget process; they are separate. If there is no congressional authorization, the most prominent source of authority to use force comes from presidential orders under the authority of the commander in chief. Some analysts question the constitutionality of such action without congressional approval. Appropriating money for the military is not a specific authorization to use force. It is an action that funds a standing military in peace and war. The authorization comes either from a separate congressional authorization or by order of the president as commander in chief of US military forces.

When private contractors become part of this picture, the president's power is enhanced while Congress's decreases. The Constitution requires Congress to review military policy and spending every two years and to appropriate for a period no longer than two years. If segments of the military have been outsourced, Congress has lost some of its power to determine the numbers in the military, how to shape the military to best meet national security needs, and when to authorize the president to use it. "By possessing power over the conscription of American civilians and by regulating the standards of reserve activations," writes Jon Michaels, "Congress can potentially limit the size of a conflict and its relative duration. Without the prospects of an unlimited, fresh supply of troops as replacements and reinforcements, the president may feel constrained in initiative and continuing unilateral engagements." Michaels even reminds us of the easily overlooked fact that "Congress can limit the politicization of the military by legislating hierarchical promotional guidelines and by organizing units around civilian and military leaders whose positions require Senate confirmation pursuant to the Appointments Clause."[107] This seems arcane and trivial in light of the desire to retain "inherently governmental" functions in the Department of Defense and military services, but when one begins to shed tasks that were once so-regarded, the implications for the duration of a conflict and the limits of congressional and public control over it become more visible. It is hard to disagree with Michael's observation that if "there were some external, elastic source of troops, who could complement and supplement the US Armed Forces, provide needed reinforcements, and help the president avoid having to activate reservists and/or reinstituting a military draft, the costs of not acting conservatively and judiciously are lowered."[108] Admittedly, the presence of Reserve and National Guard units in Iraq and Afghanistan challenge this claim. Yet, again remember the increased dependence of these missions on contractors.

Of course, Congress can terminate funding for US military operations, as it did in 1973 to suspend US military operations in Southeast Asia. Yet, ways exist to circumvent that, as the Iran-Contra affair demonstrated in the intelligence community. Congress did not terminate money for military operations in Bosnia, but it did set a ceiling of twenty thousand troops, which the United States, in effect, circumvented by adding two thousand contractors.[109] Some Muslim countries, in fact, became a source for payments for these contractors. In Iraq, imbursement for the costs of contractors arranged by the CPA reportedly came from money obtained by the sale of Iraqi oil. Contractors clearly depended on a number of US government agencies and departments, and not just the Department of Defense, usually the most closely monitored by Congress and understandably so, since it disburses by far the largest amount of money.[110] This dispersion of contracts rests partly on budget rules that enable one government department to turn to "another to award or administer a contract." A prominent example of this were interrogators and interpreters employed by Titan working for the army at Abu Ghraib prison in Iraq who had been hired not by the US Army but by the National Business Center in the Department of the Interior. The army paid the National Business Center a fee for doing so, but the latter had no cause to manage the contract and, almost assuredly, it lacked the expertise to monitor or investigate what was occurring.[111] Congressional hearings on such practices and abuses usually occur after the fact—in so-called fire-alarm hearings, as Deborah Avant and Lee Sigelman call them, which occur after the problems have emerged and ripened. Yes, both are correct in noting that Congress seems to prefer to work this way, partly out of a desire not to tie the executive branch's hands too tightly.[112]

To operate in a setting for combat operations without clear authorization of one's government is to exist in a region where one's rights and status are not well-defined. That may benefit the enabling government through saving or diversion of costs as well as avoidance of public controversy, but it does little for the legal standing of those men and women working in these positions; furthermore, their exposure says less for the ethical measures used by many in the policy community. Turning to companies that offer larger salaries is not enough to compensate for this. The circumstances that have brought the United States and others to depend more on private actors results from and reflects a gradual surrender of congressional responsibility and authority in times of conflict and war. Over three decades ago when I worked on war powers matters as a staff member with the House Committee on Foreign Affairs, a popular wisecrack was that Congress likes to be in on the takeoff but it does not want to be around if there is a crash landing. In the arena of war powers, at least, it seems fewer and fewer want to be around for the takeoff, and even investigating the crash landing, if it happens, may be something they wish to avoid. Calls made by a handful of members of Congress and others for a more vigorous exercise of these responsibilities now almost resemble the clamor for higher rates of personal saving or calls for better deportment in American cinemas—perhaps old-fashioned and no longer reflective of the realities around us.

THE MERCENARY QUESTION AND WHAT TO DO

In those zones of law defining the place and rights of contractors on the international stage, Congress and the international community have shown activity on some fronts but less on others. As I've noted elsewhere, whether one approves or disapproves of the actions of contractors, they operate in a legally ambiguous environment in many ways. Perhaps the easiest place to begin with is whether they are mercenaries like their historical predecessors. In the broadest understanding of the term and how mercenaries were used, especially after states formed, one could answer that contractors are indeed mercenaries. Governments historically turned to mercenaries for special skills, equipment, and flexibility. They signed agreements or contracts with the *condottieri* or others who recruited, organized, and led them. Thus, the mercenary provided services for a set length of time or particular campaign or operation. Once completed, their services were no longer needed. The supply of mercenaries in the past (and of contractors today) often resulted from environments filled with change—the end of a cycle of war or confrontation that released armed men without jobs, overpopulation, or famine (definite factors in underdeveloped areas, where becoming a mercenary or joining a nonstate insurgency are among one's few options).

However, the differences that exist are equally important and arguably urge a redefinition of the term *mercenary* if one is going to apply it in 2018. In the feudal period the distinction between a mercenary and what we would call a soldier today was unclear. Lords turned to them because they might lack enough vassals. Many were freelancers. Mercenary groups did not operate as companies, as did privateers increasingly, which brings the latter closer in ways to today's contractor. There were no owners, anxiously awaiting investors, or other corporate arrangements, as privateers increasingly had and modern contractors know. Unlike their contractor descendants, mercenaries were not paid salaries; instead, they received a share of the loot and prize—a practice prohibited by international law and in modern contracts. By the late Middle Ages mercenaries increasingly were not nationals of the monarch or government that hired them. This is sometimes the case of those employed by a contracting company; its employees may originate from other countries rather than the country where the company is incorporated or the government is quartered that awarded the contract. However, unlike mercenaries until the seventeenth century, who did not place much value on "customer loyalty," the modern-day private military or security firm will argue that it desires and depends on such loyalty. It wants to be a long-term provider to its customer rather than an erratic provider that shifts sides. Modern business practice strongly reinforces this behavior because it promises longer profits and a diversity of contracts in the future. Also, the presence of many retired officers in the leadership of these companies ties them by political values and knowledge to their former service and its members. The dynamics as well as the corporate structure make this a very different arrangement than that of the classical mercenary. The hired private mercenary largely disappeared in Western war in the nineteenth century.

In Chapter 2 and earlier in this chapter, reference was made to the emergence of mercenaries in Africa and in other former colonial locations as they moved toward their independence. When these mercenaries appeared, there was little in international law since the beginning of the twentieth century that clarified their status. The Hague Convention in 1907 prohibited states from recruiting mercenaries in neutral territory; this included the neutral state itself as well as states beyond its borders. Interestingly, though, mercenaries could travel through neutral territory to offer their services to a warring state.[113] The Geneva Convention of 1949, which sought to define combatant and noncombatant status, did not elaborate on the mercenary question. It appeared that belligerent states could hire them, and some scholars have concluded that this tacit acknowledgment provided mercenaries combatant status on the battlefield. At the minimum, Common Article 3, which is in all four articles of the Geneva Conventions, provided a minimal base of protection for all noncombatants in actual hostilities, including the right of humane treatment and not to be tortured.[114]

The increased use of mercenaries moved the United Nations General Assembly to measures to try to prohibit or discourage hiring and using mercenaries. In 1965 and 1968, the General Assembly approved resolutions that asserted no state had the right to intervene in the internal affairs of other states and that the use of mercenaries against "national liberation and independence movements" was illegal and that mercenaries themselves were "outlaws." Yet, these resolutions, which were not binding, also traversed an ambivalent, almost contradictory path, such as in 1970 when the General Assembly backed away from the language of a few years earlier and urged states "to refrain from organizing or encouraging the organization of irregular forces or armed bands, including mercenaries, for incursion into the territory of another State." By 1973 the General Assembly returned to treating mercenaries as a criminal problem. The Security Council, whose actions carried more standing in international law, did approve resolutions demanding the withdrawal of mercenaries from the Republic of Guinea and condemning Portugal for permitting mercenaries to operate within its colonies.[115] It would take the United Nations until 1977 to try to resolve the status of mercenaries. Simultaneous to some of the UN's actions were those of African states themselves. Newly independent Angola established a commission in 1976 resulting from the use of mercenaries in its own recent war, which resulted in a recommendation to make the use of mercenaries an international crime. A year later, the Organization of African Unity (OAU) approved a Mercenary Convention that condemned the use of mercenaries to fight against "self-determination, stability, or the territorial integrity of another [OAU] state." These states could use mercenaries for other purposes, perhaps an acknowledgment that some states had to rely on them due to the lack of resources and people to create an effective military.[116]

Negotiations in Geneva, Switzerland, for the Diplomatic Conference on Humanitarian Law from 1974 to 1977 finally presented a protocol that would be added to the 1949 Geneva Conventions. Commonly called Protocol I, this addition had been backed by many African nations that wanted a stronger definition of *mercenary* to prevent their use. Some critics saw this as part of an anti-Western ploy, especially since Protocol I also promised better treatment of people involved in national liberation movements and other forms of rebellion or insurgency. Nevertheless, Protocol I provides the definition of mercenaries most widely accepted in much of the international community—although not all of it, since the United States has never added its signature from concern that the protocol gives combatant status to terrorists. This objection is derived from the extension of prisoner-of-war status to members of irregular forces and national liberation movements.[117] As a popular quip claims, one man's terrorist can be another man's freedom fighter.

Even though the text of the specific language in Protocol I appears in Chapter 2, I believe it is helpful to repeat it here, so its significance can be better appreciated. A mercenary is a person who

is specifically recruited locally or abroad in order to fight in an armed conflict;

Does, in fact, take a direct part in the hostilities;

Is motivated to take part in the hostilities essentially by the desire for private gain and, in fact, is promised, by or on behalf of a party to the conflict, material compensation substantially in excess of that promised or paid to combatants of similar ranks and functions in the armed forces of that party;

Is neither a national of a Party to the conflict nor a resident of territory controlled by a Party to the conflict;

Is not a member of the armed forces of a party to the conflict; and

Has not been sent by a State which is not a party to the conflict on official duty as a member of its armed forces.[118]

In 1989 the UN General Assembly tried to refine Protocol I with what is popularly known as the UN Mercenary Convention (the full name being the International Convention Against the Recruitment, Use, Financing and Training of Mercenaries). The convention reiterated Protocol I but made a couple of changes. The words "direct part" in paragraph (b) were modified to include participating "directly in hostilities or in a concerted act of violence." Obviously the latter raised questions about the meaning and boundaries of "concerted acts." The convention also said its language would cover not only "international armed conflicts," that is, conflicts between states or groups from two or more states, but also to conflicts within national borders, such as insurgencies or rebellion. As of the end of 2016 only thirty-five nations had ratified the convention; several major sources of private military corporations are noticeably absent—the United States, Great Britain, France, and Russia among them.[119]

The above is a restrictive definition that private military firms have been able to take advantage of to claim they are not mercenaries. Perhaps the biggest disadvantage to Protocol I is the fact that to be confronted with the charge of being a mercenary, the defendant, and thus the accuser as well, has to be able to meet the six criteria in cumulative fashion. Finding someone who would meet all six of the above criteria would be very challenging. Perhaps, as Lindsey Cameron has written, "a South African employee of a PMC guarding Paul L. Bremer, earning 1500 USD [dollars] per day and firing at resistance fighters who attack Bremer could conceivably meet all of the criteria of the definition." Yet, this is a lot of "ifs." The detaining party would have to prove all six standards. For contractors who are Americans, Iraqis, Afghans, and other nationals coming from countries who are parties to a conflict, there is no danger of being accused of being a mercenary because of the stipulation in the fourth paragraph.[120] Military support firms, which account for most employed contractors, do not easily fall into these criteria, unless one wants to try to press for a broad interpretation of "concerted acts." Even then, it would be hard to meet the other five standards. Another aspect that protects many modern contractors is that the common interpretation of international law specifies that the person has been recruited for a specific conflict or engagement. The corporate nature of private military firms or contractors is that they employ many of their people over lengths of time that surpass the duration of a conflict; these are employees sent to do a job and, afterward, be reassigned to another location and task that has nothing to do with the preceding.[121]

The plain fact is that being a mercenary is still not an actual crime under the law of armed conflict or in international humanitarian law. The UN General Assembly Resolutions above do not carry legal force, and the United Nations lacks an enforcement mechanism. It is possible that the International Criminal Court (ICC) could become a setting for trials based on charges of mercenarism, but, if so, the existing body of international law will need to be stronger.[122] Furthermore, some members of the ICC, and most definitely the United States, which is not a member of the court, would oppose efforts to strengthen the worldwide capacity of the ICC in this arena. Those wanting stronger laws against mercenaries have urged national governments to strengthen their laws to prevent it. The record of the United States is testimony to the difficulty—some might say hesitation and unwillingness—to take such measures very far.

A definite obstacle to placing mercenaries directly into combat is the fact that they do not enjoy the status and legal rights of a combatant on the battlefield. Under the Geneva Convention combatants have the right to prisoner-of-war status. This does not include mercenaries, although the language in Convention III offers some flexibility for support personnel. Article 4 states that prisoners of war can be "members of the armed forces of a Party in the conflict as well as members of militias and volunteer corps forming part of such armed forces." Combatant status even carries over to members of the latter groups who are part of "organized resistance movements belonging to a Party to the conflict. However, to be a combatant these individuals must "fulfill the following conditions":

> that of being commanded by a person responsible for his subordinates;
> that of having a fixed distinctive sign recognizable at a distance;
> that of carrying arms openly;
> that of conducting their operations in accordance with the laws and customs of war.[123]

Of course, most contractors do not carry weapons openly. Nevertheless, companies have sought to protect their employees by sometimes outfitting them in uniforms that closely resemble those of the United States, Great Britain, or other countries. Even while this doubtless reflects a hope that such appearance may create an impression of being a combatant, the negative side is assuredly that it makes it easier for insurgents or whoever to fire on contractors as regular combatants. A subsequent paragraph in Article 3 of Convention III offers some coverage by noting, "persons who accompany the armed forces without actually being members thereof, such as civilian members of military aircraft crews, war correspondents, supply contractors, members of labor units of services responsible for the welfare of the armed forces, provided that they have received authorization from the armed forces which they accompany," can be combatants.[124] Some scholars have argued that the preceding situation offers "de facto integration" into the armed forces of a state, a stance that the International Court of Justice has seemingly supported. The key consideration is being subject to military command.[125]

This entire question can pull one more deeply into interpretations of law and terminology than is necessary here. Remember the struggles over terminology that emerged in both Iraq and Afghanistan between lawful and unlawful (legal and illegal) combatants. The position that the United States and other coalition partners could treat unlawful combatants more harshly than lawful ones opened a genuine Pandora's box of legal, political, and image problems. As the status of contractors is murky at best—and almost beyond question in actual combat operations, where they seem to be in the unlawful category—it was not easy to find an accommodating answer. The United States draws a distinction between "defensive" and "offensive" operations. The distinction goes back to that problematic description, "inherently governmental." Defensive acts done as part of security may not be so treated if they do not involve "unpredictable international or uncontrolled high threat situations."[126] Stated another way, a lawful combatant is a person who has acted "in a public capacity," a stipulation that placed actions against state authority.[127] International law does not distinguish between offensive and defensive operations, so contractors publicly carrying arms and engaged in conflict are unlawful combatants. Like other unlawful combatants, contractors, if captured, have the protection of Common Article 3 found in all four of the Geneva Conventions of 1949, but that does not provide a lot of comfort if one is taken prisoner by either lawful or unlawful actors on the battlefield.

The rather tenuous claim to be a combatant rests on responsiveness to military authority (see above), but that depends on how obvious and effective that authority is. For US contractors, there never seems to be enough certainty about this matter, especially for those with contracts from other departments besides the DOD (including the military services). Could the Department of Defense and military commanders actually hold contractors accountable when they were acting under a contract from the Department of State, the Department of Justice, the Central Intelligence Agency, or whatever? Even if the Defense Department or, more importantly, a military commander held such authority, which they often did over their own contractors, could they bring a civilian into a military courtroom for judgment under the Uniform Code of Military Justice? These are very hard questions. The standing of civilians under military law was a troublesome question in the days of privateers or arguably in any setting where other US courts and civil law functioned simultaneously.

The territorial nature of criminal law creates challenges to enforce it overseas, so it is important to establish laws that permit recognized forms of the extraterritorial application of US law. There are five channels of US law that are on hand. The Uniform Code of Military Justice (UCMJ) covers criminal acts by members of the US Armed Forces whether home or abroad, although in the United States, depending on the crime and position of the military, the service member may be tried in a state or local court. Even in foreign countries, this can occur with the concurrence of the US command. The Military Extraterritorial Jurisdiction Act (MEJA) of 2000 "applies to certain felonies committed by those employed by or accompanying the Armed Forces abroad." The USA PATRIOT Act made changes in the US legal code to apply to crimes Americans committed on federal installations facilities and quarters or residences while abroad. Amendment in 2006 of the Mann Act, which relates to human trafficking, extended its jurisdiction to both government employees and contractors alongside US operations overseas.[128] A fifth law, the War Crimes Act of 1996, originally intended to enable the United States to prosecute those who tortured US personnel, underwent changes in 2006, noticeably after the Abu Ghraib scandal, that provided the authority to prosecute and punish US service people and civilians abroad when they violated Common Article 3 in the Geneva Conventions. So far, no contractor has faced prosecution under this law.[129]

The MEJA became a problem as soon as operations began in Afghanistan, Iraq, and beyond. The language about civilians was unclear. Application to Defense Department civilians was obvious, but it was initially an open question in relation to contractors. The push to place them under the MEJA resulted from the fact that Status of Forces Agreements that the United States signed with countries customarily exempted US nationals from prosecution under the law of the host nation. The orders Ambassador Bremer issued in 2003–2004 fell within this practice. Consequently, contractors working under the Department of Defense came under the jurisdiction of the act. However, those employed by other US offices did not, such as the interrogators from Abu Ghraib; nor did MEJA have jurisdiction over Americans who worked for private security and military firms serving other governments. The fact, too, that MEJA applied only to crimes punishable by more than a year excluded a lot of misdemeanors and outright shenanigans that could upset local populations and create resentment for the US and coalition personnel in the area. The Abu Ghraib scandal in early 2004 motivated members of Congress as well as DOD staff to close the loophole that excluded contractors employed by other departments. Henceforth all US citizens, as well as foreign nationals employed by US companies, could be prosecuted under MEJA if their misdeed occurred while working in support of the Department of Defense mission.[130] A related problem for MEJA was the willingness and ease of prosecution—either of which seemed overly abundant in the opinion of some observers. The Department of Justice carried responsibility for prosecution, but difficulty in obtaining adequate information from foreign settings could impair the process. In 2005 the Department of Defense issued a regulation to try to strengthen its cooperation with the Justice Department in investigations and compiling evidence. Between 2000 and 2008 only about a dozen cases were prosecuted under MEJA. Efforts by Congress to strengthen it in the wake of the Nisour Square incident in 2007 were unsuccessful, partly because the Bush administration feared that a stronger law would invite a host of lawsuits aimed at impairing US operations in Iraq. MEJA basically had little effect on accountability and a correction of abuses that were occurring.[131]

Having had limited success with MEJA, the next step was to try to widen the application of the Uniform Code of Military Justice. Legislated by Congress in 1950, the code's Article 2 (10) provided some foundation for military jurisdiction over civilian personnel when it stipulates, "In times of war persons serving with or accompanying the armed forces in the field are subject to court-martial and military law." What exactly "in times of war" meant was pivotal. A series of court rulings, the most significant being a decision by the United States Court of Military Appeals in 1970 (United States v. Averette), stated that the jurisdiction over civilians applied only in circumstances of declared war. Of course, Congress has not declared a war since World War II, and any declaration in the future is very unlikely. If this interpretation remained, prosecution of any civilian under the UCMJ seemed impossible.[132] With the revelations about contractor misconduct and possible violations of national and international law, some change in the language and criteria permitting jurisdiction over civilians was necessary. In 2006 Senator Lindsey Graham (R-SC and a former judge advocate in the US Air Force) introduced language to the National Defense Authorization Act of 2007 to replace "in time of war" with "in time of declared war or contingency operations" involving people "serving with or accompanying an armed force in the field." Graham's amendment was both more specific (declared war) and more flexible, because the term "contingency operations" arguably included the types of deployments occurring in Iraq, Afghanistan, and elsewhere since 2001.[133]

As well intended as this change was, it raised a new question and reopened an older one. The new question was whether Senator Graham's amendment allowed for prosecution of non–Defense Department contractors. Graham hoped the change would prevent future incidents like Abu Ghraib, which had involved non-DOD contractors. Therefore, some scholars argue the amendment does enable jurisdiction over all contractors and maybe even over other civilians (government and private) accompanying the armed forces. Others disagree. A memorandum from Secretary of Defense Robert Gates in March 2008 appeared to confine the new language just to those working with the Defense Department.[134] The older, reopened question is whether a trial of a civilian in a military court would go unchallenged on constitutional grounds. Doing so might require reclassifying the civilian as a member of the US military. That, in itself, poses legal questions, partly based on due process, which might be better handled by legislation in Congress than through a military command or court decision. Courts generally have not been supportive of actions that arbitrarily change the status of a civilian based on the absence of civilian court or factors reflecting convenience or even necessity.[135] Seventeen years after the attacks on September 11, 2001, the United States, as well as advocates of international humanitarian law and/or the law of armed conflict, have done little to settle the questions surrounding the legal status and use of private instruments of force. Privateers in the Atlantic in the early 1800s arguably enjoyed a clearer definition of their duties and rights than private military and security firms do in the second decade of the twenty-first century.

The simplest way to resolve the ambiguity and problematic role of contractors would be to "renationalize" their responsibilities and duties. Put back into military uniform the functions that have been "outsourced" during the past decades. That would arguably strengthen, even re-create, bonds that once existed between public values, state policy, and accountability on one side with those serving to accomplish and maintain state objectives on the other. That, however, is not going to happen. Although I have concentrated on the United States in this book, one can ask how many states and societies are willing to create and support militaries so large to accommodate all of these functions. This would require the expense of moving hundreds of thousands of men and women into military service. A modern *levee en masse*, tantamount to mass mobilization, would impose immense cost on governments and their publics and divert people from jobs and services in the domestic economy that are critical for national prosperity and well-being. The diversion of tax revenue and government spending into defense would take money away from national programs concerned more with health, education, public welfare, and advancement. Add to that the fact that the citizenry of many postindustrial societies, where birth rates have dropped, are not prepared to sacrifice sons and daughters as willingly. The range of special technical and information skills now required by the military services and other offices of government makes it harder and harder to retain such know-how permanently in uniform. Besides, many of these are skills easily developed and retained in a civilian setting, where they can be tapped as needed. This merger of civilian and military is characteristic of "postmodern" militaries.[136] I have had conversations with military professionals who have advocated a fundamental change in military recruitment—hire by skill, and offer set packages of salary and rank rather than requiring all to serve a set period for enlistment. This market approach to recruiting could solve some of the challenges facing the military, but the complex array of missions it faces as well as the diverse capabilities required will require reliance on private providers. The day of the mass military, except for a unique circumstance demanding it and, even more so, allowing the time to create and train it, is in effect over in military culture and operations.

A theme underlying every page of this book has been a belief that violence on behalf of a society and its people should be public. Killing is the most serious act a leader, a ruler, or a state can take against another, be it a member of one's own citizenry or a body of members or citizens of another group or state. Such acts should be public because they require deliberation, acts of discretion, and procedures to hold accountable those who have decided to commence them or are responsible for implementing them. Nonpublic wars either are private or are conducted in ways by governments that try to divert attention and accountability. The history I have tried to depict and summarize here has dealt with how evolving and existing states, largely in the Atlantic world, tried to place management over private violence. Ultimately by the late nineteenth century they had largely succeeded. Private actors disappeared because states chose to assume their roles or simply tried to outlaw them, as had been the case with privateers. This focus on the Atlantic world is admittedly limited, but rulers and states attempted to take similar measures elsewhere. Nowhere, should one conclude, did states completely succeed in taking over the management of violence. Nonstate groups and actors were always there, and recurrent periods emerged when they proliferated, such as in the decolonizing world following World War II, or the conflicts emerging in the wake of the end of the Cold War. What is important to recall, though, from the first couple of chapters as well as earlier parts of this one, is that it is states that largely shape and negotiate international law, and they understandably sought to guide the conduct of war along lines that required accountability and protected those serving them. Nonstate actors were often a form of outsiders who enjoyed certain rights, as expressed in Common Article 3 of the Geneva Conventions, but could not in effect receive the rights of those serving respective states.

The United States, in a very curious way, was something of an anomaly in this world, even while it played an instrumental role, especially during and after World War II, in the composition, negotiation, and advocacy of international law in peace and war. The oddity was not in its dislike of private force. Mercenaries acquired an odious reputation in American thinking due to the legacies of the American Revolution. During the nineteenth century, private actors who tried to enlist their own armies for adventure and expansion elsewhere usually received the cold shoulder, even if some sentiment might have existed in private circles, and ultimately under international pressure the United States used neutrality laws to restrict the filibusterers. I have not described volunteer groups, like those serving in China before the United States declared war on Japan on December 8, 1941, proxy groups like the Contras in Nicaragua receiving US assistance during the 1980s, or various covert activities, which some scholars of private force have included. I have not done so because I wanted to concentrate on the activities that existed more for monetary gain or were, in fact, actual business concerns. The anomaly in US policy and law is that it never prohibited the latter. In fact, its Constitution contained a provision sanctioning the practice of turning to private actors with letters of marque and reprisal if Congress authorized it. Whether such commissions had to be part of an actual declared war was unclear. Even as most of the international community in 1856 moved to outlaw privateering for a variety of reasons, dislike of the private aspect being less of a concern than a desire to prevent other countries with smaller navies resorting to it to supplement their navies, the United States defended the practice for that very reason (plus the fact it was in the Constitution). There the provision has remained, but, ironically, if it may not be the exact formula for handling the challenges of private force in the early twenty-first century, it is a reminder that it can be done if a government so chooses.

There are several factors beyond those in the preceding paragraphs that press for reliance on private force in the present and future, even while it offers repercussions that scholars, lawyers, and others rightly caution against. For poorer countries the option of relying on a private force may be politically and economically more feasible than recruiting and maintaining a standing military. This has been a recurrent question faced by some states in Africa. Some skills important to modern militaries, such as intelligence acquisition and analysis, may be beyond the resources of these countries. Relying on contractors for these as well as in other areas, such as training or logistics, is arguably a wiser option in such circumstances.[137] Peacekeeping is a mission that could be well served by use of private contractors. In his study of mercenaries, Sean McFate turned to data maintained by the Center for International Development and Conflict with the University of Maryland that illustrated how the number of interstate conflicts has dropped significantly since the end of World War II while intrastate or internal conflicts had tripled. These "neomedieval" conflicts, as McFate labels them, are exactly the types of conflicts in which many states have become reluctant to involve themselves.[138] One only need to remember the "lessons learned" by the United States after Somalia in 1993 as well as the recurrent debates over the size, duration, and objectives of US involvement in Iraq, Afghanistan, Libya, Syria, and Somalia again, to see the point. British reluctance to involve itself in the struggle in Syria in 2013 was another example. This type of political stammering by governments reluctant to commit their own troops and to engage in the arguments and expenditure of political capital to build domestic support has convinced some that reliance on private actors might be the better way to proceed. This would be especially so, if the United Nations, as well as nongovernmental organizations (NGOs), turned to private military firms to create such a force and to fund it. The availability of such a force would bypass some of the time-consuming measures needed to get contributions of troops from member states and also avoid debates in national legislatures over authorization and control of the deployment. Advocates of this approach pointed to the horrors of the massacres in Rwanda in 1994 as a situation where member-state reluctance was so central. The UN actually did consider turning to Executive Outcomes in 1996 when another refugee crisis in Rwanda developed. Peter Singer, Michael O'Hanlon, and others have argued that such a course might have saved thousands of lives.[139] Twenty years later the question remains about peacekeeping and humanitarian missions, which have almost become persona non grata in discussions about military roles in the United States and some other countries. If member states are unable or unwilling to commit troops to such missions, of if they do so but require so many conditions as to how they can conduct any operation, are there reasons for the United Nations to explore other options? The answer is yes.

Just considering the United States presents an illustration how this could work to the benefit of all concerned parties. The United States has had an ambivalent, even confusing, relationship with the United Nations on the role and command of US forces in UN missions. Historically, Congress has opposed any attempt to claim that a UN Security Council authorization to use force is the equivalent to a congressional authorization. Congress must provide the latter, although in reality it sometimes has failed to do so. The other consideration very much in play is that any operation using US troops must rely on money appropriated by Congress. In the first Gulf War a mechanism for bypassing this came close to being put in place. In what amounted to "tin cup diplomacy," the United States solicited donations from foreign governments to compensate for US military operations. When the Senate majority leader, Senator Robert Byrd (D-WV), protested that this was bypassing congressional authority over appropriations, a procedure was put into place to have the money placed in an account in the Department of the Treasury from whence Congress would vote to release the money.[140] In turn, imagine an option where the United States had a law similar to the marque-and-reprisal clause in the Constitution that offered private companies to conduct operations, as defined by the president and Congress, but operations, as had been the situation with privateers, funded through the mechanisms of private enterprise. On one hand, such a course would pose new options by which the United States could respond, and the question of congressional authorization would still be in play. Undeniably, however, other questions would arise about the ethics and imagery of explicit war for profit, the channels of command and accountability, and the lingering question that never disappeared about private actors—would they fight as strongly, willingly, and as loyally? What missions would this leave for the professional military and its own identity and purpose? An entire range of questions at the national and international levels would have to be answered as best as possible before the United States would resort to such measures. The prospect of such a debate in the future is not as remote as it would have sounded even thirty years ago.

One reason the likelihood of these debates grows is the globalization and spread of the private military and security industry. Though the United States and Great Britain are the leading providers of these companies, the companies themselves have offices and operations throughout the world. As shown earlier, they employ people from many countries. The location of a headquarters on US or British soil does not carry a requirement to employ predominantly one's own nationals. Like other multi- or transnational firms, the hiring of local employees builds better knowledge of that market, its needs, preferences, customs, laws, and so on. Also, like many of their counterparts in more commercial lines of business, these firms adjust with changes in the global market as well as domestic markets. This encourages them to diversity in the types of services and skills they provide. When demand for a specific service or skill diminishes or disappears in one setting, a company has to begin to explore other markets where it can apply its services, particularly, as is the case with most private military and security firms, with the needs of a government that wants to rely on them rather than developing or applying its own means. This rather borderless nature of globalized business conflicts in many ways with traditional notions of security and conflict that are tied to states and boundaries. The challenge of trying to regulate what a US company can offer through the legal framework of arms exports, for example, is already difficult and becoming more so as technologies and markets change. Consider, too, the fact that other countries do not want to leave the private security and military business in the hands of US and British suppliers. This worry about dependence is similar to that in areas of commercial technology or in categories of weaponry. The Chinese are figuring more prominently in the international marketplace, as are the French and other states. Another problem then emerges that mirrors that in the proliferation of any sensitive technology. Once multiple sources of supply become available, it becomes far more problematic in finding ways of stopping them or of reaching agreements among the suppliers to restrict its distribution and provision.[141]

There is little evidence to suggest that state control over violence and war is going to increase. This is not to suggest by any means the disappearance of states, but it is to point out that states have found reliance on private instruments of force and violence to be useful again. The pinnacle of state power that developed in the last half of the nineteenth century and carried over into most of the past century has begun to decrease. Indeed, in the segments of the historical record examined in this book, that situation was an anomaly. The question we face is whether private means of force can be kept under effective control at both the national and international levels. If not, we return to a type of free-for-all force that one finds in certain settings in history, particularly in late medieval and early Renaissance Italy. No one should want this. Machiavelli witnessed firsthand the costs of this system, if one wants to call it that, and warned his readers and later generations against it. The option should be a "mediated market for force," to borrow Sean McFate's characterization, where use of private force is negotiated and some mechanism of review and control is maintained.[142] At least three paths exist: self-regulation by the industry itself, stronger forms of national control, and a revision of international law that affects the status of private actors.

Like any industrial sector, companies in the private military and security contractor business have sought to organize themselves into trade associations to establish a stronger, more united voice; enable mutual understanding among member companies and other members, including governments in instances; serve as a forum for discussions and programs of common interest to members of the association; and establish codes of conduct for all members that enhance the reputation of the industry and discourage abuses. The most noteworthy of them is the International Stability Operations Association, founded in 2001 and known until 2010 as the International Peace Operations Association. The development of policies by government committed to stability operations, and the importance of private firms in implementing them, invited a renaming to include this more diverse range of missions. Its code of conduct is a means of getting members to pledge to adhere to the guidelines and standards within, which address many of the broader objectives of international humanitarian law. Although the association possesses no legal powers, its governing body can remove a company from membership if it believes it has grounds to do so. Other forms of sanctions also exist. Obviously, member companies also punish their own employees for violating company standards of policies.[143]

By 2006 the government of Switzerland along with the International Committee of the Red Cross had commenced negotiation with representatives from a number of governments, including the United States, Great Britain, Australia, China, France, South Africa, Iraq, and Afghanistan, to develop an international standard for companies in the private military and security sectors. The negotiations ended in September 2008 with agreement on what is commonly known as the Montreux Document. The formal part of the document runs for nearly twenty pages. It is not legally binding and does not undermine the commitment of any signing government to existing international agreements. Nevertheless, it creates a set of good practices for states in three categories: contracting (those hiring contractors), territorial (states where the contractors operate), and home (the state where the headquarters of the contracting company is located). While intended to address the circumstances primarily in Afghanistan and Iraq, the negotiators of the Montreux Document understood its significance could be carried on in both location and time.[144] Analyzing it several weeks later for the Center for Strategic and International Studies in Washington (a well-known think tank), Anthony H. Cordesman informed his readers that the document addressed "many of the concerns expressed by senior Afghans like President Karzai" in 2010 and earlier. The international dimensions of the comment also helped the United States avoid the accusation that it could "somehow dictate . . . terms and ignore the needs of host countries." An extra benefit was that the document enjoyed "broad enough European backing to set potential standards for a coordinated approach in Afghanistan."[145]

Simultaneous to this, the Swiss government through the Geneva Center for the Democratic Control of Armed Forces invited academics, private security and military company representatives, and government officials to negotiate an international code of conduct (ICOC) for private security service providers. It entered into effect in November 2010, and by September 2013, 708 companies had committed themselves to this code of conduct. To avoid confusion, this is not the equivalent of membership, which currently consists of 102 companies, governments, and nongovernment organizations. This sizable commitment, even if the document is again voluntary and without legal enforcement mechanisms, has been testimony to the importance that much of the industry places on its credibility and image. The ICOC particularly emphasizes the importance of adherence to international human rights law (separate from the law of armed conflict or international humanitarian law). With nearly a decade of operation in Afghanistan and Iraq alone approaching in 2010, the participants knew all too well the variety of complex environments and operations that faced them. To add muscle to the code, it outlines a process by which companies through use of the ICOC standards and establishing internal reporting procedures could obtain a certification of the fact they were adhering to the code's principles. The International Code of Conduct Association maintains a very active website that provides ongoing information about changes in laws as well as information and forms for application.[146]

Of course, no one will place total confidence into self-monitoring and reporting mechanisms and associations. There is a little too much of the "foxes minding the chicken coop," as Sarah Percy observes.[147] Yet the level of activity that has occurred since 2001—and I have not discussed every national or specialty association that also exists—attests to the fact that the industry sees itself as having a growing future and requiring a need to create standards before governments perhaps do so more emphatically with laws. In reality, the latter action by national governments is necessary, since companies may need to operate under a wide range of national laws before they enter the international market for private military and security services. No international association or code of conduct can completely accommodate that scale of diversity.[148] Several years ago, Renee de Nevers in a very important article rightly questioned the ability of the industry to regulate itself that well. His assertion that the companies in this sector have felt "little incentive to develop strong trade associations" might be challenged in light of developments since 2010, although, again, the benefit gained by becoming associated with an association or code, which enhances a company as well as an overall industry's image, has to be considered against questions about the effectiveness of those same endeavors. Foxes can look very dignified and respectable. Similar doubt maybe exists in regard to de Nevers's assertion that there is simply not a very strong sense of "community of fate" among these companies. Competition in the marketplace prevents some of that, and so can national laws, such as US antitrust laws, which restrict what companies can discuss in a trade association.[149] Yet, the efforts placed into establishing the associations and codes in recent years argue that there is some sense of common fate—that a few bad eggs can really spoil the stage for all and that they need to prevent unwanted controversy. The one area, though, where de Nevers's remarks are accurate, and especially with the United States, is the need for more government action at the national level.[150]

The United States has not seen much significant progress since the efforts discussed earlier in this chapter. Nor has much progress been made in some other key countries. Great Britain, if anything, has taken the arguments of neoliberalism even farther than the United States and has privatized significant portions of its land forces responsibilities—indeed, to the level where some military and public officials worry about the growing ignorance about the military and its place in national defense among the public at large. Germany's case is somewhat different because of its commitment to maintain a citizen's army that will discourage the practices and tendencies that led to World War II. Conscription remained in place until 2011, and the constitutional basis for it is still there in case it is needed again. In the republican/liberal (including neoliberal) dichotomy Elke Krahmann uses, Germany stands as an example of a state that has retained much of its republican outlook. Privatization has occurred, but in a more selective fashion. Furthermore, in 2005 the German Bundestag passed legislation that established stronger parliamentary control over foreign deployments of the Bundeswehr, making it, in the opinion of some, a parliamentary military force. It would be harder, although not impossible, for German contractors to find themselves in combat roles.[151] The decision Germany made in 2016 to expand the Bundeswehr has stirred ongoing discussions about the place of conscription, so the arguments about a citizen's military and privatization continue.

The focus of US activity has been more at the administrative and contract management levels rather than tackling the broader question of whether private armed force is a path of the future that requires a better constitutional framework for its use. Congress in 2008 established a commission on wartime contracting in Iraq and Afghanistan to try to develop a balanced assessment of the issue. It had two years to present its report. The results were not surprising. The commission found that government agencies treated "contracting as an administrative afterthought." This was troubling in light of the fact that the culture of so many agencies had "not yet recognized that success in contingency missions depends in large part on their decisions to use contractors at the right time, in the right place, in the right numbers, and for the right purposes." The report noted that both the DOD and State

Department found that they were over-reliant on contractors; in too many cases they were the "default option." Even before the commission had begun its work, the Pentagon had established an army contracting command and acted to hire more contracting officers—a reversal of the trend from recent years. All of these steps assuredly helped in dealing with problems of irregularities, poor performance, mismanagement, and corruption.[152]

The fact that states and the international system established institutions and processes to try to place violence in conflict and war under state and international control should serve as a strong, almost shrill warning not to let it be reversed. The reasons that rulers and governments assumed authority over such violence and war were intermingled with the emergence and growth of states themselves as well as a long-term absence in the international system of any institutionalized multilateral means of trying to negotiate or arbitrate settlements to avoid conflict. The critical word there is "institutionalized," because in modern history there were peace conferences, even prolonged "concerts" or "congresses" of powers, that tried to preserve stability, order, and peace in certain regions. The evolution and transformation of war into the mass-mobilized, total conflicts of the first half of the twentieth century compelled heavy state control and direction, but these changes also motivated a strengthening of the international system and institutions. Arguments over the proper roles taken by states never end, and we in the United States appear to be in a mood to question many of the assumptions that guided governments and societies after World War II. Perhaps the practices of the first half of the twentieth century could return, along with the demand for larger national militaries that would retake the responsibilities now given to the private sector. However, as observed earlier, few publics appear desirous of returning to that or willing to accept the sacrifices required to do so. The convenience of relying on private force will remain in front of us and continue to be much debated.

If private means of force are to be used for state ends, the most important step to take is for governments to establish constitutional or legal frameworks that enable and control this—frameworks that have benefited from public attention and debate rather than quiet evolution, default, and incremental surrender of government responsibilities. The authors of the Constitution were correct when they decided to place the marque-and-reprisal clause into war-related powers controlled by Congress. The reason is that any decision to resort to this option required congressional, and thus, in a governmental sense, public acceptance. The signature of a contract with the Department of Defense, a civilian cabinet department in the United States, or other government departments is not the magnitude of public consent that is needed. It is not that that consent is actually absent; public officials are there to judge, award, and review it. However, it is below the public's field of vision. There is no heavier duty that a US citizen can be asked to assume than to lay his or her life on the line. We have allowed for congressional authorization or consent from the beginning for members of the military sent into conflict, and it is now critically important that we establish such authority for those asked to provide national security services in private contract with a part of the US government. It is critical to keep conflict and war at the public level, even if its participants may partly come from the private, commercial world. That is the fundamental conclusion one draws from several centuries of history.

Simply turning to the marque-and-reprisal clause and saying we will restore the issuance of these licenses for private parties are not adequate answers. Much of the historical practice originated from an environment and period that recognized the right of private war for compensation. That, so far, has not been a major consideration. As governments did from the late Middle Ages onward, mercenaries and privateers in their respective ways were instruments used to supplement a military, provide special skills and technologies, and even, for poorer countries, to become the major military instrument on hand. Correctly sometimes, and horribly incorrectly in others, governments regarded them as cost-savers. Many of these motives exist today, along with different demographics and values assigned to human life. Congress and parliaments need to legislate laws that permit this form of private/public arrangement, explain its range of permissibility, and then authorize its use and mission. It should not happen and prevail by default or neglect. A separate office within each major department or agency is a better method of handling this than placing it alongside many other decisions that contracting officials must decide. Every agreement and contract signed between a company and an agency or department carries within it an aspect of accountability and public approval. However, the public's stake is not going to be as high for the arrangement of a cooperative research-and-development agreement or the sale of a software technology or piece of diagnostic medical equipment. For the potential loss of human life, that degree of public knowledge and stake must be there.

At the same time, change must occur at the level of international law and institutions, as ultimately the single most important development has to be here and not within national laws. Several scholars have argued for the UN's creation of a special office to strengthen oversight and maybe even to set up offices to monitor, register, and approve those firms meeting UN requirements. In a sense, one could build on the efforts undertaken just several years ago to establish the International Code of Conduct Association. This UN office would not offer in itself an authorization to use private actors. That would presumably be implied in a Security Council authorization to use force and the respective measures undertaken by participating member states. However, this would enable companies to carry, in effect, a seal of approval as a UN-approved provider.[153]

As important as the creation of such an office or organization could be, it really does not get to the fundamental question that follows. If the United Nations were to establish such an office that assisted states in arrangements with private contractors, should it not, alongside other governments and the International Committee of the Red Cross, also reexamine the Geneva Conventions' treatment of mercenaries, and by implication, contractors as noncombatants? If it were not to do so, it could almost be charged with a form of hypocrisy by permitting state use of noncombatants for state purposes. This would likely entail the challenging matter of reopening negotiations surrounding the 1999 Geneva Protocol, its definition of *mercenary*, and the status of other nonstate actors.[154] Most contractors go to great lengths to avoid association with the types of mercenaries that recall images more of Wallenstein or those in Africa forty years ago. The world does not need or desire their restoration and return, and, therefore, any amendment of existing laws and agreements should recognize that. Yet, the dualistic arrangement contractors find themselves in—combatant or noncombatant—borders on moral disgrace. The convenience, if one wishes to call it such, of enabling states to rely on private actors while treating them as largely nondescript noncombatants should be ended, if this is the path the United Nations and states of the international community wish to pursue. Life should not carry two prices—full value or discount.[155]

A recurrent fear is that the private option tempts governments to use force more frequently, arbitrarily, and secretly. Its appeal is the relative absence of accountability and visibility alongside a higher acceptability because of the nature of the worker, the contractor involved or killed. Such a death is a tragedy, but in the present environment it more easily becomes a statistic—if one can in fact find it. The inclusion of contractors as combatants could actually create a better restraint against their use. It allows for more equivalent status on the battlefield, even if there may not and perhaps should not be full equivalence between a contract employee and a publicly employed servant of the state. The injury and death of combatants can become single numbers more easily rather than two detached sets. If publics and their governments saw these figures in total, would their responses be different than they have been since the expansion of contractor-supported warfare in recent decades? It is hard not to think otherwise. Milo Minderbender in *Catch-22* probably would not care, but we should.

Private contractors in conflict and war deserve better protection by states and international law and bodies than they currently have. They are serving in missions that states have designated for them. The conflict may not be "public war" as the originators of that terminology used it nearly three centuries back, but it is not completely private war either. It is a form of state-sponsored conflict that tries to limit its visibility for purposes of national security objectives, political acceptance and support, and cost. It is in a way the "imperfect war" that writers in the eighteenth century explored. This is the environment in which most private military and security firms and their clientele governments are working. However, what happens if actual private war returns, which is indeed happening in one arena in particular: cyber. This is the final question, and one that returns us to the first chapters in this book.

CONCLUSION: THE RETURN OF PRIVATE WAR

The US presidential election of 2016 encountered an unprecedented effort by an outside power—Russia—to influence an American campaign and outcome. To some in the intelligence and law enforcement communities, this was no surprise. If not a surprise, though, the extent and skill to which the Russians appeared to have used cyber technologies and programs to seek such influence was alarming. The warnings and tell-tale signs had taken a disturbing appearance by September 2016, when the Federal Bureau of Investigation informed the Democratic National Committee (DNC) that it had evidence Russian hackers had penetrated one of the committee's computers. Neither the FBI nor DNC displayed serious concern at first, but when sensitive internal Democratic Party documents began to appear on WikiLeaks earlier that summer, concern rose quickly. Some of the documents reinforced an unflattering portrait of Hillary Clinton and senior DNC officials working to block the campaign of Senator Bernie Sanders (I-VT) to win the party nomination. In September 2016 President Barack Obama spoke personally with Russian president Vladimir Putin to stop the hacking.[1] Whether Putin did is unclear, and it will probably never be proved that Russian interference was the decisive factor in the election's outcome.

The evidence pointing to Russian interference continued to increase from late 2016 through summer 2018, even if some individuals, including President Donald J. Trump, disputed its role in shaping his victory. On December 9, 2016, the Central Intelligence Agency briefed congressional members that it had "high confidence" the hacks had occurred to assist Trump's candidacy. At the end of that month a joint action report from the FBI and Department of Homeland Security asserted Russia was responsible for hacking the DNC. Then, on January 16, 2017, the director of national intelligence, James Clapper, released unclassified and classified versions of a report prepared by the FBI, CIA, and National Security Agency titled *Assessing Russian Activi-*

ties and Intentions in Recent U.S. Elections: The Analytic Process and Cyber Incident Attribution, which claimed the Russians had sought to weaken "public faith in the U.S. democratic process."[2] Information pointing to Russian activity continued to accumulate. In March 2017 the Department of Justice charged two Russian hackers and two Russian intelligence agents with stealing 500 million Yahoo accounts for a variety of purposes, some of which were linked to the US election as well as gaining money and personal information. Four months later the General Services Administration, which handles much purchasing for the US government, removed Kaspersky Lab from its list of approved vendors. Kaspersky, a former KGB cryptographer and software engineer, had become a billionaire through his business in cybersecurity programs. Not surprisingly, the Department of Homeland Security ordered that all Kaspersky programs be removed from government computers. Interest in Kaspersky did not stop here, however. In October 2015 its US subsidiary had paid retired Lieutenant General Michael Flynn, US Army, to speak at a meeting in Washington. Flynn became President Trump's first national security adviser, but he also came under investigation by Special Counsel Robert Mueller and resigned in February 2017, in part because of ties he had not fully reported with Russian officials during the period of the presidential campaign. More stories emerged throughout 2017, including the revelation by Facebook that the Russians had purchased advertising space on it to run ads on domestic issues that were sensitive in the US election. Other developments, such as the indictment of Paul Manafort, Trump's campaign manager until August 2016, only added energy to the speculation about Russia's role because of meetings Manafort had had with the Russian ambassador to the United States and others.[3]

One of the most difficult aspects of the Russian endeavors was determining the exact roles of the Russian government and the hackers. Which was which and who was who are difficult questions to answer. In his study of the relationships between governments and private actors in the cyber world, Tim Maurer deems Russia as probably the most prominent example of "proxy relationships based on sanctioning." By sanctioning, "a state consciously but indirectly benefits from a malicious activity targeting a third party, an activity which the state could stop but chooses not to." Maurer offers two other forms of proxy relationships: "delegation . . . where the beneficiary has significant, at least overall or effective, control over the proxy," and "orchestration . . . where the state supports the state without necessarily providing specific instructions." By sanctioning, the state is more of an enabler. Not every expert would necessarily agree with Maurer; an argument might exist for more delegation in Russian actions rather than sanctioning, but it probably requires greater detail for proof. Maurer notes how some see Russian law enforcement as lax and marginal, but, if anything, he believes it to be the opposite in this situation. The Russian authorities know what is going on, even if some of it is illegal, but choose to do nothing as long as the hackers target others outside Russia's boundaries.[4]

Certainly the continuous remarks of President Putin that the hacking was something outside of his control lend credence to Maurer's argument. For example, in late summer 2016 Putin intriguingly described leaks from the Democratic National Committee in the United States, which were widely attributed to the hacks, as a "public good." Presumably, Putin meant for the American public, but the evidence that has emerged points to Putin's dislike of Hillary Clinton, his worry, even fear, about US intentions toward Russia, and his desire to try to shape an international environment more to Russia's advantage. If Putin meant the "public good" for Russia, even if it was just through a desire to push the United States away from its secular, materialistic, and sexually degenerate ways, then his explanation shows how such actions, in his mind, could serve state objectives. However, Putin added that "on a state level" Russia was not the perpetrator.[5] Nearly nine months later, Putin fueled the speculation about the hackers' role in an interview with NBC journalist Megyn Kelly by claiming that "the attacks could have been executed by anyone, even proud Russian patriots committing crimes against the Kremlin's adversary without his personal knowledge." This was almost a form of a nondenial, to use that term of art. He acknowledged the hacking likely originated in Russia, but he fell back on the claim that controlling what private Russians do was beyond his control. Admittedly, in the cyber world it is not so easy to dismiss that claim. Still, for a head of state who reportedly asserts strong surveillance and enforcement on segments of the population, the assertion was hard to accept at face value. It sounded too much like contorted answers in 2014–2015 about the role of Russian soldiers in Ukraine—described first as "local self-defense forces" but acknowledged about a year later as Russian volunteers, some of whom were mercenaries. US and European intelligence services found enough evidence and "cybertrails" to point to probable involvement by GRU (the foreign intelligence agency of the General Staff of the Russian Armed Forces).

Interestingly, private-sector sources in the United States, such as the cyber security company Crowdstrike, had come to this conclusion even before the US intelligence community, in January 2017. Crowdstrike and other sources reported that GRU had outsourced some or all of its efforts. One company, Esage Lab, was already on the sanction list of Russian companies established by the Department of State because of its research and development work for GRU. Other evidence pointed to reliance on criminal gangs in Russia and elsewhere—perhaps arranged by a quid pro quo that offered exemption from criminal prosecution if these individuals cooperated. Voluntary or not, their "patriotism" came under wide suspicion in the United States.[6]

None of this was a new ploy. Russia had relied on a large group of young hackers, "Nashi," in its cyber attack on Estonia in 2007, an event that heightened international awareness of the dangers to national security posed by cyber means. The excuses about the appeal and role of "patriotic" Russian hackers were similar to some of the explanations Elizabeth I of England had offered regarding the acts of privateers against Spain—it was fairly easy to cover one's tracks and claim these were the actions of overzealous or uncontrolled individuals. Whether Putin could have been as involved in these events as much as Elizabeth sometimes was is unclear. If so, this would have been more than just sanctioning such actions.[7]

Nor was a desire to use information, including distorted and fabricated versions of it, for government and state purposes hardly unique to Russia. Perhaps the historical conclusions made by some Russians about information's role and impact are more exceptional in their sweep and magnitude, particularly in the way they believe information helped bring about the downfall of the Soviet Union. The Soviets primarily had viewed information as a way of organizing and mobilizing the population rather than informing them. Western media and culture, Soviet leaders thought, challenged and undermined this approach to information through decades of assault and influence that helped create tension and dissatisfaction in parts of Russian society. However, this attitude did not dissipate with the collapse of the Soviet Union. It continued as the Russians in the mid-1990s explored unsuccessfully the idea of an information security treaty with the United States. Security in this instance did not just mean concentration on the mechanics and programs or security of the means of communication but implied a broader meaning of protecting or insulating against information that could fragment society. Putin clearly shares those concerns, as speculation continues about his conviction that the United States and Secretary of State Clinton wanted to undercut his election campaign in 2012. If information is a means that can be applied for internal purposes, and one that the West had used with such effect against the USSR, it was not a major leap to envision its use as an instrument against danger and adversaries from the outside.[8]

As analysts tried to comprehend the reasons and methods the Russians had used to influence the 2016 presidential election, they focused more on how Putin understands information and the extent to which he and others were relying on earlier lines of thought. One important thread of inquiry went all the way back to the 1960s, when Vladimir Lefebvre, a mathematical psychologist at the Military Institute of Electronics in Moscow, developed what became known as reflexive control theory. The theory stresses the development and use of means to send another party information that will influence him or her to make voluntarily a decision that has been predetermined by the initiator. The Soviets tried to apply this theory during the latter part of the Cold War, and the Russians have continued to use it. One of the most knowledgeable authorities on the Russian use of reflexive control theory is Timothy Thomas, recently retired from the US Army's Foreign Military Studies Office at Ft. Leavenworth. Thomas stresses the "holistic" approach the Russians take to information in both technical and psychological terms; they might act to compromise another country's cyberstructure as well as well as to undermine faith in the media. For example, Boris Rodionov, writing in 2004 in a journal published by the General Staff of the Russian Federation Armed Forces, argued that such information "will make it possible to influence the outcome of presidential elections, to form public opinion, and to exert pressure on processes capable of ensuring bloodless and effective control of states from the outside." Admittedly, such sweeping statements resemble some of the smoke-and-haze thinking made about "information dominance" on the battlefield in the United States during the 1990s. However, the broader point is a recurrent and fairly old one: How does one use information to one's advantage? How do you "weaponize" it, to use one term, or how to do you wage "doxfare" (the release of documents to influence decisions and actions)?[9]

In the Putin era, the United States did not directly witness the role of cyber in operations by the Russians until 2007 and 2008 with the respective attacks on Estonia (cyber only) and Georgia. It should have been no surprise, for by that time Russia was explicitly *articulating* a concept of "information warfare that regarded cyber as one dimension of it." This type of warfare seeks "disruption of the key enemy military, industrial and administrative facilities and systems, as well as bring[ing] information-psychological pressure to bear on the adversary's political-military leadership, troops and population." Customarily, Russian strategic thinkers had seen these as measures tied to an actual military or kinetic operation, but within the past decade opinions changed in order to see the application of information warfare in broader terms. Some experts pointed to Russia's reliance on "cyber mercenaries," such as Nashi and other groups. The capabilities of these groups were undeniable, and, so too, in the eyes of some analysts was the fact that Russia (for that matter, any state) lacked the means of effectively controlling them. The military probably needed them for their skills and their abilities to conduct some cyber campaigns. The resemblance of this relationship to that of traditional mercenaries with special skills was not so different.[10]

Since 2009, strategic writers in the United States and many European countries have been trying to wrap their intellectual arms around this Russian approach in order to decide whether it deserves a new name to spark their own thinking, even if in some ways the Russian emphasis on all instruments in warfare restated earlier approaches. The new label proposed, among those who thought it required a name, was "hybrid warfare." The purpose in these pages is not to investigate and judge this line of thought, but to highlight the part of the discussion that stresses the ability of Russia (or any state turning to this type of warfare) to turn to nonmilitary and nonstate actors. Rarely does the word *mercenary* or *privateer* arise in much of this discussion, but as types of nonstate actors they are part of the landscape. Frank G. Hoffmann, now with the National Defense University, highlighted the importance of "convergence" in this warfare: "the convergence of military force and the interagency community, of states and nonstate actors, and combatants and noncombatants." It was a "blurring of lines between modes of war." By no means did Hoffmann want to argue this type of war was unprecedented; even the blurring of forces "into the same force" or their application "in the same battlespace" was the distinctive, but not entirely new, feature. "In such conflicts," Hoffmann warned, "future adversaries (states, state-sponsored groups, or self-funded actors) will exploit access to modern military capabilities."[11] This analysis has generated an ongoing discussion—much of which has examined justifiably the underlying value of such a framework and argument, and less of which has gone to the level of specific types of nonstate actors. Some charge that "hybrid war" is merely the latest label found for a long, historical quest for a strategy that tries to accomplish victory more easily with new technology. Others accuse its usage of distorting the ability to evaluate Russian objectives. Some place more credence behind it, particularly in light of the emphasis that key senior Russian officers have given to it.[12] The critical point in these pages is that the proposed integration of nonstate and state means is not new, although this reliance on private military firms or mercenaries, if that be the case, reawakens a tradition that had largely disappeared from most warfare among the major powers during the past two centuries. Information, disinformation, misinformation, deception, or whatever, are not new measures in conflict by any means. However, the unprecedented reliance on new technologies for their dispersion as well as for penetration of the same is. As commentators thought of "hybrid warfare," though, one question they needed to pose was whether it was that unique to the Russians. The Russians might have excelled in some areas, such as the penetration of a nation's political channels and institutions, to distort and even disrupt them. However, in other areas the United States was arguably the leader, particularly in the dependence on private contractors. Hybrid warfare, if it is the right term, was for everyone.

The convergence of state and nonstate, of public and private, in hybrid warfare is a characteristic that draws little disagreement among those arguing over the accuracy and applicability of the term. For those who work in cyber or study and report it, the blurring of these worlds is a given. We have seen it in the aforementioned work of Tim Maurer. Shane Harris, a journalist who has covered cyber issues for years, writes, "Waging war in cyberspace is becoming a private affair. A burgeoning industry of cyber arms merchants and private security forces is selling its goods and services both to the government and to corporations that will no longer endure relentless espionage or the risk of cyber attack. The armies of nations will inevitably meet one another on the cyber battlefield. But the armies of corporations will meet there, too."[13]

Harris's characterization may sound futuristic, maybe even fantastical, but it actually reflects reality in the cyber world. As a network or system, the cyber world is heavily private. Estimates place 85–90 percent of the critical information infrastructure in the United States in private hands.[14] This plainly means sensitive national security information has to travel on privately owned networks. What is additionally interesting is that similar information from other countries may travel on these networks as well. Shane Harris estimates that "99 percent of the electricity and 90 percent of the voice communications services the military uses come from privately owned cables, routers, and other infrastructure."[15] Neither the US government nor the military owns or governs this infrastructure. The US government does not control internet protocol and addresses in the United States, though there has been some discussion of legislation to try to do this. Some countries have tried to block internet search engines and certain websites and even create search engines within their borders; China has tried all of the above with varying levels of success. A public debate continues in the United States over whether the government can establish a "kill switch" to shut the internet down for national security and emergency reasons. Even if the Department of Defense, the military services, the Department of Homeland Security, the National Security Agency, and other agencies have acted to strengthen internet or cyber security for the nation as well as their own departments and services, most security still remains in private hands. In fact, some of the best techniques or programs for security as well as means of hacking or attack originate with and become available from private sources.

Analysts and practitioners often speak of the *cyber domain*—the very term suggests a setting, like a territory, that can be governed. However, cyber itself knows no physical boundaries; the myriad ones and zeroes that cross its networked system are oblivious to national jurisdiction. Those persons, corporations, governments, and other entities programming and sending those coded numbers for whatever purpose—correspondence, banking, air traffic control, distance learning, and so on—are required to follow national laws, a factor that makes tracing and prosecuting troublemakers or aggressors on the internet so difficult at the international level. In reality, the cyber domain resembles the nebulous, ambiguous world largely ungoverned by law that pirates took advantage of on the high seas. Thus, hackers may be today's Blackbeards, depending on their objectives. We know, however, that bringing order and rule to the world's oceans was not easy and required an extensive period of time. It is not surprising that scholars have drawn analogies with the evolution of the law of the sea to explain the present situation and possible future of the cyber domain.[16]

The maritime world witnessed a form of private conflict—letters of marque and reprisal and privateering—that evolved in some ways from being largely private warfare between grieved parties to a private instrument available for rulers and states to supplement or act as a substitute for their navies. Some of the blurring of "hybrid warfare" occurred—privateers becoming pirates, or vice versa, or even naval officers and crew leaving their service to become privateers, or the reverse. The relationship between public and private is different, though, in the judgment of some scholars, from the forms of privatization that occurred with privateers or the private military and security corporations of today. In the past few years this analogy has attracted attention. Karen E. Eichensehr, who teaches at the UCLA School of Law, has recently described the similarities and differences in part of her continuous work. She accurately describes privatization as a model where "the government formally signs up a private company as an agent to carry out functions that the government itself previously performed and then supervises the private party's performance of the actions."[17] As I showed in Chapter 6, sometimes supervision has been less than desired. However, what concerns Eichensehr is the development of what she intentionally labels as "the public-private system." The word "system" is critical to her analysis because "rather than a public-private partnership," which is more the dynamic in an outsourcing contract, "the private sector and government do not always act as partners. Sometimes they are antagonists, and sometimes their relationship is ambiguous at best."[18] Informality is a recurrent trait in these arrangements. "In some circumstances," she writes, "private companies have stepped in independently to remedy cyber security problems out of frustration with the government's failure to act." There are instances where "private companies act as a force multiplier, cooperating with the government to undertake cyber security operations." Yet, she adds there are situations where "the government seems to have informally encouraged and even assisted private parties in doing things that the government does not want to do itself, but which it nevertheless finds useful." Much of this sounds like contracting, but Eichensehr cautions it is not. "The public-private cybersecurity system differs from traditional contracting out because the private actors—not the government—decide at the outset what functions they should perform, and the private actors operate outside of the contractual frameworks that governments have used to constrain private contractors in other circumstances."[19] These are more open-ended relationships than traditional contracts. They resemble more a relationship of convenience and necessity, and they invite questions as to who would be in the actual driver's seat.

An illustration of how this relationship works concerns the development of "zero day" methods of attack. This is a method or program of attack that benefits from unknown flaws in another system. In short, the targeted party has no forewarning and has "zero days" to prepare. In the United States the National Security Agency, among others, is interested in developing and possessing these capabilities. Development of "zero day" programs takes one into a murky part of the internet, for the people who create these are essentially hackers, although they would probably prefer a name like "security researchers" for business purposes. Many suppliers are outside of the government, and they offer their products and services to governments or to larger defense contractors who often act as a middleman between the government and developer.[20] Offices like the NSA try to stockpile these capabilities rather than purchasing them one at a time. Prices can vary, depending on the sophistication of the program to the type and capabilities of the target. According to Shane Harris, the Stuxnet program the United States and Israel codeveloped to attack centrifuges in Iran's nuclear program contained at least four "zero day" capabilities. The purchaser is not always certain that the provider is just selling it to a single customer. Some companies, like Vupen, a French provider, do sell to multiple customers; furthermore, there are no guarantees to prohibit diversion of the program to another party. Of course, these companies and many others will have to take steps to try to find the flaws in their own programs where a "zero day" attack could wreak havoc. Yet, even a large company like Google cannot hire all the people needed to do this type of work, so it, in turn, has to rely on hired hackers to try to protect itself.[21]

Shane Harris has described how some of these operations or companies have turned themselves into what he calls "boutique cyber mercenaries." He focuses on Endgame, a company that has sold packages as expensive as $2.5 million (with an apparent promise of twenty-five zero day attacks in one year for the customer). Endgame, based in the United States, has scoured networks and computers in Russia, the Middle East, China, and elsewhere to identify targets for existing or prospective customers. It stresses an "active defense" approach that Harris finds particularly troubling, as he observes "this kind of defense doesn't entail just erecting firewalls or installing antivirus software. It can also mean launching a preemptive or retaliatory strike." Harris adds that domestic law prohibits Endgame from doing so; the attack would be a governmental matter. Since 2013 some evidence suggests Endgame had begun to diversity its field of customers beyond US government agencies to some major corporations and banks. The founder of Endgame, Chris Rouland, has advocated allowing corporations, individuals, or groups to attack other parties. He claims the mounting costs of losses due to cyber hacking compel this as well as the relative difficulty of getting the government to do anything in the right time and at the right level of response.[22] Fighting back could entail measures at various levels, but the obvious question is when it would be tantamount to an attack that under the law of armed conflict could be justification for a comparable response, either unarmed or armed, depending on the scale of damage and possible loss of life.

The answer depends on how much or little relationship one believes cyber war, cyber conflicts, and cyber attacks have with international law and the law of armed conflict. Consider, for example, the fact that the law of armed conflict covers the actions of states and assumes that states or some other actor and procedure will be able to determine who the aggressor is. That is not a given in the cyber world; in fact, it is the difficulty in identifying responsibility that makes it harder to think the boundaries and procedures of existing law can be easily transferred into the cyber domain. Yet, some do argue this, while others believe such an approach is hopeless. Another view claims that a new form of international treaty for a new and different domain might be the solution, such as the role played by the Outer Space Treaty of 1967 and the Moon Treaty of 1979 (the Agreement Covering the Activities of States on the Moon and Other Celestial Bodies) for outer space. Stronger domestic laws dealing with cyber and its actors are an additional option some advocate. For example, the US Congress passed in 1984 and amended with a new name in 1986 the Computer Fraud and Abuse Act. The law is obviously important for what falls under US jurisdiction, but its origins come from over thirty years ago, in the era of clunky mainframes and the early days of software code and programming—ancient history in the cyber domain.[23]

Setting aside the pros and cons about the applicability of international law, any answers about placing a cyber attack within its definitions and boundaries have to address two definitions: Article 2 (4) of the United Nations Charter, which stipulates that states must "refrain from the threat or use of force against the territorial integrity or political independence of any state," and Article 51, which permits self-defense in case of "armed attack."[24]

Of course, what is "use of force" in a cyber setting? The laws reflect the consequences of physical attacks. Even the 1,100-plus pages of the *Department of Defense Law of War Manual*, released in June 2015 after a very long procedure of bureaucratic midwifery and updated a year later, has to acknowledge the continuous change in cyber technology but nevertheless points out that there are circumstances where the existing law of war would still apply. The primary means to determine a "use of force" is to look at the effects—a factor that various officials stressed even before the publication of the *Law of War Manual*.[25] It states that "if cyber operations cause effects that, if caused by traditional physical means, would be regarded as a use of force under *jus ad bellum*, then such cyber operations would likely also be regarded as a use of force." These could include the meltdown of a nuclear power plant, the opening of a dam above a populated area, and the impairment of air traffic control that could causes crashes. Crippling a military logistics system to the point where it could not support operations could also be a use of force.[26] If the nature and impact of the cyber operation "amount to an armed attack or the imminent threat thereof," then the United States could invoke Article 51 as a right of self-defense.[27] The reservation of the right to respond to an imminent attack is something on which the international community does not completely agree, as the United States has expressed this right in ways that cause some to argue it would act in both a preemptive and preventive fashion. Nevertheless, the United States holds the right "to take necessary and proportionate action in self-defense." The emphasis on proportionality, which is important in both law as well as just war theory, does not mandate a response in kind, which means the response does not have to be cyber. It could be an airstrike or a special operations mission. The response must meet the standards of proportionality and necessity, however it is done. There is also a legal and ethical expectation that any response will apply rules of discrimination or distinction to prevent disproportionate loss of life, especially among noncombatants.[28]

All of this sounds laudable and fairly clean on paper, but reality brings true difficulty to much of it. As noted earlier, attribution can be extremely difficult in the cyber world. The destructive program may have been routed through several countries, even including networks and routers in one's own country. Retaliation demands identification, and without it efforts can be misdirected and potentially harmful to innocent parties. The blurred distinction between public and private adds more complexity in determining the correct targets. Adding more uncertainty is assessing the intent of the attack. Knowing the originator helps; a group of mischievous or even malevolent hackers suggests reduced likelihood it is an armed attack but does not absolutely rule it out, given the capabilities of nonstate actors. Espionage is not an armed attack; in fact, international law does not prohibit it. Of course, cyber operations do not always remain contained within the target. This happened with the Stuxnet attack on Iran's nuclear program, where one of the programs in it ultimately made its way into computer programs outside of Iran. Thus, a very good case exists for placing strict procedures and control over how, when, and for what ends one relies on and uses cyber operations. A strong case exists for the supremacy of state authority in these decisions and, arguably, the actual execution as well. Certainly, the type of public/private system discussed above poses very troublesome implications, but is it realistic to expect that states, or even any international regime with limited resources, will effectively meet this challenge? The number of nonstate actors in the cyber world is so immense and diffuse that it is impossible to see any system or structure that could keep all of it within bounds.

The reference to *jus ad bellum* in the *Law of War Manual* is also a reminder of how closely international law builds on just war theory. However, what if the action taken does not rise to the level of war as commonly understood in that word's use—the question about war's meaning discussed briefly in Chapter 1? The rise of various types of limited or confined actions using special operations or forces, targeted killings, nonstate actors like a contractor, and cyber pose scenarios that fall short of war as most understand it and thus invite that very question. In 2006 in a revision of his classic *Just and Unjust Wars* from 1977, Michael Walzer argued for the application of a framework for *jus ad vim*—measures that fall short of war. At this point, one should not forget that law and just war theory can diverge in that such limited actions may technically be acts of war in terms of law but not in the eyes of much of the public or even governments. Matters of scale can make this question frustrating in law and just war theory. Walzer and others who have advocated *jus ad vim* realize that such low-scale measures are easier and more tempting for governments to use because they are so limited and often below the concern or scrutiny of the public, the media, and much of the international community. In these circumstances the temptation to bypass standards of just war such as sanction and authority, clarity of intention, proportionality, and discrimination is real, which gives even more reason to consider such factors in a jus ad vim operation. In fact, proponents of jus ad vim would insist that such measures should only be a last resort and not be done in a fashion that creates a high probability of escalation to war. If war is a likely result, then one must think in terms of jus ad bellum.[29]

Cyber presents especially difficult hurdles to the application of jus ad vim. While one can certainly make compelling arguments to require application of its standards, it will be very difficult to prove that the initiator purposely violated or dismissed them. If one cannot identify the first party, judgment about intent becomes difficult, although perhaps not impossible. Seeking accountability and identifying the person or persons who made the decision are going to be very challenging. Just war theory and the law of armed conflict are both dependent on notions of war that rely on physical objects controlled and used by people. It is this physicality, or kinetic nature, that contrasts with the means in the cyber realm, even though these nonphysical means may produce consequences that match the destructiveness of a physical means, such as a bomb. None of this discussion means one should dismiss just war theory in cyber. Quite to the contrary, there is true urgency in trying to get parties to respect and follow it. Finding and evaluating all the evidence is simply going to be harder.

Governments are responsible for what happen within their boundaries, and a series of laws do address that, including those against fraud, identity theft, and outright stealing of money. As mentioned earlier, the jurisdiction of many of these laws governs the actions of US citizens within the United States as well as measures they might try outside of its borders. In fact, laws criminalize actions US citizens would take in violation of agreements the United States has entered that deal with international communications, such as interfering with satellites or radio communications. A fair amount of international communications law developed under the auspices of the International Telecommunications Union, of which the United States is a member. Some international agreements, such as the aforementioned Outer Space and Moon Treaties, prevent the weaponization of space, although militarization, if one wants to push the word's meaning, has occurred abundantly in the form of monitoring and communications satellites. These types of arms control agreements, along with the Antarctic Treaty that bans all military activities, are seen as ways of perhaps limiting what can happen in the cyber domain.[30] Governments can use their adherence to these agreements to prohibit certain actions by both state and nonstate actors in these realms. Whether these types of international agreements can work in cyber is unclear, but that is a path many desire to explore.

The current position of the US government on cyber operations reflects the stance the United States has developed toward actions by either government offices or private actors against foreign parties. They are all under the jurisdiction of the US government, whether through congressional authorization, presidential order, or enforcement of existing laws and treaties that prohibit such actions by private citizens. The preponderant view has been that cyber is a domain that favors presidential power and action, arguably because speed and stealth may be instrumental for executive branch advantage. The matter of which branch of government is best for controlling cyber is a question US officials have wrestled with for more than twenty years. In 1997 President Bill Clinton received a report from the Commission on Critical Infrastructure Protection. The governing legislation was the War Powers Resolution of 1973, passed by Congress in the closing period of the Vietnam War to try to prevent the repeat of an incremental descent into a large war, even though Congress had provided the initial authorization to use military force in 1964 in the Gulf of Tonkin Resolution. Looking at the 1973 resolution with its definitions, emphasis on reporting requirements, and enactment of procedures that provided for congressional override of a presidential order to deploy force through the authority of the commander-in-chief clause, the commission concluded that the War Powers Resolution was so connected to the world of kinetic force and movement of troops that it was largely inapplicable. The acknowledgment by Congress in the resolution that presidents had the authority to send US forces into "hostilities" during an emergency without any congressional approval posed more questions than it answered. There was no definition of "hostilities." Admittedly, in 1973 the probability of a cyber attack was something contemplated only in science fiction rather than the corridors of Congress. Nevertheless, a real hole was there for the executive branch to exploit.[31]

That is largely what presidents have done since then. Perhaps the most forceful statement of presidential authority was made by President Barack Obama in Presidential Policy Directive 20 in October 2012. The text of the document became available through items illegally released by Edward Snowden the following year. The document itself exists in a limbo-like world. Even though the full text is available on websites and has been discussed in media and professional journals, the US government's position is that it remains classified because it was illegally released. The Obama administration had pursued a course similar to what the authors of the commission report had projected fifteen years earlier. For example, in defining the prospect of US intervention in Libya in 2011, the White House had seized on the same doubts about the meaning of "hostilities" expressed earlier. Although the Obama White House had generally reported to Congress in ways it believed "consistent with the War Powers Resolution," it had argued that the resolution did not apply in the case of Libya—the scale of the operation was too limited, no US casualties had occurred to that point, and escalation to that scale was unlikely. Congress's major concern in the resolution had been protection of US forces, and what was occurring in Libya, or that might occur, was not at that level.[32] Later in 2011 the Department of Defense had presented a report to Congress on cyber operations in which it argued that cyber operations "might not include the introduction of armed forces personnel into the area of hostilities," which appeared to be an intentional avoidance of a factor that could trigger the resolution. However, in all fairness, the report added that the operations could be a part of a much larger operation that could require reporting to Congress.[33] This important qualification highlights two characteristics that are problematic for Congress. Cyber operations can indeed be part of a preparatory set of actions preceding the actual physical movement of personnel and physical weapons. The duration of such measures could be just prior to their movement or weeks before. When would be the proper time for reporting them to Congress without the risk, some would argue, of compromising the mission? The report infers right before or just at the beginning of the "physical" part of the operation. Second, the launching, command, and actual execution of the mission may be performed by personnel residing in the United States. Some would argue this is not an "introduction" of personnel.[34] From the vantage point of any congressional desire to preserve a role in the authorization and use of force, these are very troublesome exemptions to claim. In fact, a whole range of questions have arisen in relation to these operations, as well as the command and control of unmanned aerial vehicles (UAVs, or drones) from the territorial United States. Are these people combatants? Arguably yes. Do their actions on US soil make their locations, and others supporting them, valid targets for attack? Answering all of these is another book in itself. The point is that existing laws are too far behind the technologies and capabilities at the beckon of the president, the military, and others supporting the military (including contractors). Waiting for "boots on the ground" before expecting a report would be one more step by Congress to put itself out of business on the war powers front.

It should be no surprise that Presidential Policy Directive (PPD)-20 makes no explicit reference to Congress and the War Powers Resolution, though it does stress that the United States "shall conduct all Cyber operations consistent with the US Constitution and other applicable laws and policies of the United States, including Presidential orders and directives." Similar assurance occurs in relation to obligations the United States had under international law and the law of armed conflict. The reference given to "Presidential orders and directives" signals a determination to hold to powers that may be derived either from statute or a president's determination to fulfill the expectations of the commander-in-chief clause and to protect the Constitution and the welfare of the public. It is a strong statement. PPD-20 contains an especially important discussion of presidential authority related to "cyber operations with significant consequences." The latter includes loss of life, "significant responsive actions against the United States," "significant" property damage, "serious adverse US foreign policy consequences," and "serious impact on the United States." The conduct of cyber operations with these probable consequences requires "specific presidential approval." However, there is an important exception to this under conditions of actual emergency. In these circumstances the secretary of defense, or another cabinet or agency official with authority from the president, can "conduct . . . Emergency Cyber Operations necessary to mitigate an imminent threat or ongoing attack using DCEO [Defensive Cyber Effects Operations] if circumstances at the time do not permit obtaining prior Presidential approval." Stipulations following this do point out these measures should be nonlethal and be of a nature unlikely to result in "significant consequences." They, too, have to comply with the Constitution, existing laws, and president directives and orders.[35]

In the area of defensive cyber operations the directive acknowledges the importance of government partnership with the private sector to take advantage of the range of capabilities. It does add, however, that the US Government will "retain DCEO, including anticipatory action against imminent threats, as governed by the provisions in this directive, as an option to protect . . . infrastructure."[36] The challenge, however, is that the types of programs the US government acquires from private companies or "boutique mercenaries" sometimes contain their own retaliatory programs. Reflecting on this relationship in light of President Eisenhower's famous warning about the military-industrial complex, Shane Harris has observed Eisenhower would not have been able to predict "that corporations would compete with government in the conduct of hostilities." Yet, in spite of the assurances stated in PPD-20, that capability does rest in private hands, and it is difficult to assure that it is not used. So-called hack backs, in which a company uses an offensive capability to strike back at an adversary, have occurred, even though these would arguably be outside the authority of PPD-20.[37] Do companies and private actors have the right of self-defense? The practice of letters of marque and reprisal, particularly during the earlier periods of their use, allowed that very easily, even though (as seen in Chapter 2) it did not take long for rulers to try to place this right of redress for damages and grievances in frameworks to contain their effect on just the injured parties and not on broader relationships. The question that arises here is whether it is desirable or practical to permit such actions again. They are occurring. However, they do unfold in a setting where, arguably, the stakes are much higher, thanks to the magnitude of weapons that state and nonstate actors have and the speed with which they can unleash them.[38]

The guidelines set forth in PPD-20 have been modified by the Trump administration to allow for greater military discretion in the use of cyber operations below the understanding of "use of force" in international law, which emphasizes death, physical destruction, and economic consequences. Trump reportedly decreased the role of interagency discussion and approval of such operations, and he elevated the status of US Cyber Command, established in 2010, to be equal to other combatant commands, such as Pacific Command (PACOM) and European Command (EUCOM). The National Security Presidential Memorandum, signed in September 2018, "authorized offensive cyber operations" below the "use of force." A new National Cyber Strategy, also released in September, iterated Trump's intention to strengthen US abilities to conduct cyber operations.[39] The president's national security advisor, John Bolton, has stated the United States is undertaking offensive operations, but he has not elaborated on what they are or who is implementing them. Presumably, they are under the authority of Cyber Command, but whether the executors are military personnel or contractors is unclear. Perhaps in anticipation of such developments, as well as the elevation of the status of US Cyber Command, the chair and ranking minority member of the House Armed Services Committee proposed legislation in June 2017 that requires the Department of Defense to notify congressional committees dealing with defense "within 48 hours of the conduct of 'any sensitive military cyber operation.'" The forty-eight-hour timeline fits into the framework of the War Powers Resolution. The proposal includes both defensive and offensive cyber operations that are "intended to cause effects outside a geographic location where United States armed forces are involved in hostilities." The language that survived in the final version of the legislation does not define offensive operations that clearly, reflecting in part a traditional congressional reluctance to tie the president's hands too tightly. Most likely, its intent mirrors the definitions in PPD-20, but those standards may now be looser and allow more presidential discretion, so Congress has more work in front of it. An additional problem, not surprisingly, is the limitation of the bill's authority to the Defense Department; after all, it is an amendment to the DOD authorization bill. Other departments are out of its purview, and the legislation requiring congressional notification would still not include intelligence operations, which are reported under a separate procedure to the intelligence committees.[40]

Thus, the United States, along with the rest of the international community, faces a fundamental question as to whether one can restrict or prohibit the role of private actors in conflict and war. If so, how can it be done? The really central question comes back to whether such state control remains possible. Proposals have emerged along different paths of argument, and most concede the virtually impossible and questionable task of placing it all under state or international authority. Consider the widening array of areas that have become part of the national security debate—environment, health, food, energy, cyber—just to mention several. Professional military schools now address all in their curricula, and defense ministries often have sections and/or specialists responsible for assessing how changes in these areas can alter the more traditional aspects of security and military activity.[41] Clearly, many of these fall outside the boundaries of traditional military activity, though some argue modern militaries should be more able to address them while others argue this dilutes the traditional role and function of the military. Wherever one stands, it can almost be certain that there is recognition of the fact that the military or government must turn to private entities for skills and support. Governments should rightly question whether they are the correct seat of responsibility and accept the reality that in instances they must rely on the private sector. Where to draw that line is the question facing us, as it faced earlier generations within the traditional range of tasks associated with armed force. Development and possession of weapons of mass destruction, for example, are arguably a domain where most people would agree states or some future international body retain control. However, since cyber as well as various chemical and biological weapons can pose weapons of mass destruction–like consequences, the degree of control will always be compromised, even if severe punishment is threatened. Larger weapon systems—aircraft, naval warships, missiles— also beg for the same type of state control, but there is a private marketplace for the purchase of some of these types of systems. Small firearms are another story; they are much more open to private purchase and distribution, legal or not. In addition, the need for such weapons by contractors serving in more traditional support and services, or those hired to protect them, places many in private hands.

Finding the appropriate level of state control is another challenge. There are levels of control that ascend from the local to the national, regional, and international levels. For such a tiered approach to be effective it would probably have to descend from the international level downward; otherwise, the laws, regulations, and practices would be so varied that control of force as well as the means behind it would approximate a morass. It is hard to conceive of this, especially at the level of small arms. One can only imagine the reaction of the National Rifle Association in the United States to efforts by Congress and any president to bring the policies concerning the sale and ownership of firearms in the United States into conformity with an international treaty. Acceptance and adherence to a "subsidiarity principle" that places local and state powers over use of force would collide directly with deeply entrenched views of sovereignty that are strong in parts of the United States.[42] Thus, as optimal as these efforts might be, it is hard to imagine there is much likelihood for their implementation. Such frameworks, along with the requirement to rely on private providers for many skills in the security arena, make it unlikely to envision stronger state control over force. Max Weber's assessment of a century ago now faces hurdles unforeseen when states were consolidating power to conduct mass-mobilized, total wars.

In the previous chapter I supported in general a proposal advocated by Peter Singer for a United Nations office that would certify willing private security and military contractors that meet a set of internationally negotiated standards. Singer's early iteration of this idea preceded some of the efforts coordinated by private companies with academics and representatives from key governments.[43] This may still be the best course, as it can take advantage of a growing appreciation among both the public (government) and private sectors that the status of private actors in conflict and war is a growing question. Such a realization comes from the obvious fact that significant numbers of private actors and their means have already entered into the realm of conflict or act in such close proximity that their status is not clearly defined. "Boutique mercenaries," which act differently than the traditional contractual arrangement with private firms, add to a dispersion of capabilities and people that falls outside of the reach of most of the ongoing efforts at self-policing and professional codes.

My recommendation, at least, for the United States has been to revisit the purpose and general constitutional and political framework behind letters of marque and reprisal. As I wrote earlier, the objective is not to restore letters of marque and reprisal per se, but to recognize the precedent of an option that enabled use of private means to serve state ends. There is an arguable similarity between the practice and purpose of letters of marque and reprisal in conflict at seas and the requirements of today. Importantly, this extends beyond the supplemental skills that private actors can provide or the fact their role may help obfuscate, or even conceal, the role of a state's government. In fact, the objective in the US Constitution was to prevent that by making the agreement a public matter. The establishment of offices to review and issue agreements with companies, in light of congressional authorization to create such offices, could handle much of the form of contracting seen in Iraq and Afghanistan, where the importance of skills and flexibility in personnel have proved so important.

However, another aspect of privateering does not apply as easily in settings like the conflicts in these two countries. Recurrently, much of the history of marque and reprisal, especially after the appearance of modern states, was to have at one's beckon a form of force that fell short of war—a set of measures, in this case attacks on commerce rather than warships, that might persuade another government to steer away from war and try to negotiate differences. Compensation had been the primary reason, but we have seen cases, such as in the debates preceding the US declaration of war in 1812, where advocates of privateering hoped it would demonstrate to the British the seriousness of US concerns by inflicting noticeable losses. Cyber presents us with a more complex environment. Yes, states may use its means to warn states, to indicate that severer, more physical measures, could follow if there is no adjustment of policy or a willingness to negotiate. Like maritime conflict, cyber can target nonmilitary targets, aim for limited damage, and avoid loss of life. These limited ranges are part of its attraction, but it can also aim for much more destructive results.[44] A true danger in the cyber domain is that private actors will retaliate on their own with no prior knowledge by the home government or any form of consent or authorization. This is occurring repeatedly in many settings, and governments often lack the means of knowing it until afterward at best or of determining the origins. What if such attacks were to reach the level of effect where death and significant physical damage occurred, but the attacker's identity and goal remained ill-defined? It could be a purposeful attack by a state or nonstate actor; it could also be a program created and released by a cyber sorcerer's apprentice who watches his or her scheme run out of control.

Setting and enforcing boundaries for action in physical warfare was hard enough and sometimes impossible, particularly when reliance on mercenaries or privateers was part of the practice. Captain Kidd and the ministries in London had had different opinions on where the laws and boundaries of conduct were, much to the captain's regret. However, London could monitor Kidd's actions in the Atlantic and Indian Oceans. That capability is not as certain in cyber. Companies, groups, and private actors will want compensation or redress for damages they have suffered in the cyber domain. Compensation by court, arbitration, or negotiation may be far too slow and unsatisfactory. Thus, it is no surprise to find arguments recently made that urge the US government to establish an office under congressional authority to issue licenses to companies and other actors who want the authority to see compensation and redress through cyber means. Those using the licenses, similar to a letter of marque, would have to report their actions for review. Those failing to do so would face the risk of losing their license, if caught, and additional criminal prosecution if necessary.[45] Such an arrangement may not work well unless the penalties are costly and the resources devoted to monitoring and enforcement are ample. Means would have to exist in which domestic and foreign parties targeted would have recourse to submit evidence to this office, or another deemed appropriate, for investigation of charges. After all, any process dependent on self-reporting is going to be undercut by those who choose not to out of confidence that they cannot be traced and identified. The proposal merely illustrates the immense hurdles that would have to be surmounted. Cyber is a largely commercial and private world in which most of the means of intrusion, hacking, attack, and destruction are in private hands. No one should expect a reversal of this fact.

The prospect of private war is now back with us to a degree not seen arguably since the Middle Ages. Partly because of cyber we now are in a world where private parties not only can commit traditional criminal acts like theft or fraud in new ways; we now know there are those who possess the capabilities of committing acts that are seen as aggression and components of war in ways that are much harder to track than attacks by small arms, improvised explosive devices, and even chemical, biological, or nuclear means. In that regard alone, we are witnessing a return of a medieval-like order, at least when the question comes down to access to a major means in conflict that the state does not control, probably cannot control on its own, and must rely on its developers and owners to use for state (or obviously nonstate) purposes, if possible. So, in this particular circumstance, the cyber mercenaries and private military and security firms may well resemble vassals from centuries back. However, that analogy can only carry one so far. Vassalage carried two-way understandings between lord or ruler and those serving and living in the realm. Many private firms stress their loyalty to the state in which they are located, but how far that extends to foreign nationals working for the company remains a question. The cyber mercenaries may or may not feel such loyalties or obligations. Indeed, there is a corner of the cyber community that regards states as an impediment to the movement of free information and the community that could result, they believe, from that.

Cyber has played a significant part in the erosion of state authority, along with many other factors, some of which have been in the historical landscape for a long time, such as the causes of migration or the reasons behind financial collapse, so I will not venture the prediction that states will eventually disappear due to cyber or any other factor. States, international bodies, and others realize that placing cyber under state and international authority is a critical step in preventing it from becoming an instrument in cyber-level conflicts that can escalate into genuine, kinetic warfare. As was the case with other means used in private warfare or by private parties, states struggled to place these and, more so, the decisions leading to conflict and war under state and international control. The same is so with cyber, although it will be much harder than any of its predecessors used in war. Not to do so, though, will leave us open to a chaotic order not as susceptible to common order and international harmony as some visionaries of the internet have argued.

Private war has always had monetary concerns at its center. Even those who volunteered hoped they would receive payment in some form of coin or property. The appeal of doing so as an actual soldier for the ruler or state seemed sound and attractive to those who preferred some certainty about payment over the division of booty. The lure of rich personal gain, whether for a mercenary or a privateer and his crew, could crash against the reality of no booty, prizes, or division of spoils. Rulers and states eventually came to rely on these providers as supplemental or complementary to what they had under their command in the state's ranks. The hope of money remained for the mercenary or the privateer, but by the 1700s both were coming more and more under state control, which means use in ways that served state objectives. Both the evolution of international law and standards for state behavior, along with the appearance and practice of total wars relying on almost all aspects of the state, spelled the end to any significant roles for private actors.

We have seen how different models of state structure, economic policy, and power in the international system have altered attitudes toward the benefits or detractions of private actors in conflict and war. The mercantilistic and imperial systems of Europe, especially that of Great Britain, called for stricter state control over commerce and the use of any supplementary private means during times of war, whether mercenaries or privateers. Ultimately, the Royal Navy took on roles that had once been left to privateers, and that development reflected London's desire for stronger control over the actions of all on the high seas. The Americans, partly out of their doubt about concentrated power and a standing military, as well as a desire to be a commerce trading nation, regarded privateers as a way of not having to build a large navy and a worthwhile instrument to wage commercial war against any major adversary. The American dream of being mainly a commercial power, however, collided with the realities of maritime power, in particular by several of the world's states, and their rejection of much of the American view about unhindered commerce on the seas for neutral powers in times of war and peace. The recognition that the United States needed a navy capable of asserting US interests worldwide essentially placed the last nail in the legend of American privateering.

The monetary hopes of privateers and mercenaries are now found amid the employees of contractors and cyber boutique mercenaries as well. There is nothing new here. Nor is there much new in the desire of governments to resort to these means because they have capabilities, technologies, skills, and so on that are better done there than in the government or military. One can increase or decrease their numbers as needed, which is arguably not as easy to do in modern militaries, especially if it is an all-volunteer force that has enlisted with understandings of service for a set duration.

The troubling difference from the past is the desire to use private means as a way of preventing controversy about the conflict on the home front. The outcry that would result from using a fully conscript force in the United States would be immense and politically damaging to anyone advocating it, unless there was a genuine national emergency. Outsourcing various duties and tasks customarily tied to the military has been a way of enabling those volunteers in uniform to concentrate on more combat-related skills. Terms like "inherently governmental" or "combat operations" seemingly provide adequate assurances that not all functions can be, or ever would be, outsourced to the private sector. For that to occur in the United States would require legislation from Congress, which is highly unlikely and arguably unconstitutional. If anyone were ever to advocate this, he or she would be proposing measures that would strip Congress of much of its remaining war power as well as its power over biannual appropriations for the military, as contractors could presumably be paid out of earnings from the company rather than government funding. This is not likely.

What is likely is an ongoing seepage of tasks and missions to the private sector that place more distance between the employee in the field and the Department of Defense or other agency or department making use of that person. Calls for increased defense spending will generally continue to receive congressional support, but maybe not at the scale the current president or future ones wish. The cost of sophisticated weapons, technology, and the training to operate them will continue to mount, and with that the urge for better efficiency and cost-saving where possible may likely push toward more and more outsourcing. The numbers of those contractors arguably in combat operations or up against the boundaries of them will probably increase. Unless the US government, and other governments in their respective settings, creates and strongly supports laws and offices to administer and review these practices, the lines of accountability will fray more each year. The level of public engagement in these decisions and deployment will lessen. Deaths will continue to mount in partly concealed and poorly visible ways, and wars will be fought by two categories—those in uniform for public service, and those hoping to get better pay but without recognition. It is a public/private way of doing conflict and war that may be convenient for current political ends. It is also an unfit way for a democracy, or any government that claims to regard and treat all its citizens equally, to fight a war.

NOTES

INTRODUCTION

1. Most of the numbers cited come from Heidi M. Peters, Moshe Schwartz, and Lawrence Kapp, *Department of Defense Contractor and Troop Levels in Iraq and Afghanistan: 2007–2015*, CRS Report R44116 (Washington, DC: Library of Congress, Congressional Research Service, December 1, 2015), 3, 5. The number for US military personnel in Iraq in 2006 is from Amy Belasco, *Troop Levels in the Afghan and Iraq Wars, FY 2001–2012: Cost and Other Potential Issues*, CRS Report 40862 (Washington, DC: Library of Congress: Congressional Research Service, July 2, 2009), 9. The figure for US contractors in 2006 is from Renae Merle, "Census Counts 100,000 Contractors in Iraq," *Washington Post* (December 5, 2006), http://www.washingtonpost.com/wp-dyn/content/article/2006/12/04/AR2006120401311.html. The numbers in Afghanistan had not changed significantly by the end of 2016—9,800 US military personnel and 25,197 contractors employed by DOD. The numbers in Iraq by January 2017 had risen from 5,262 military personnel and 3,592 DOD employed contractors. See the update to the same report above released on April 28, 2017, 5, 9.

2. The lexicon for these companies is populated by names that offer, or try to offer, important shades of distinction—*private military firms, private military contractors, private defense*

contractors, and *private security firms* being the most widely used. Their differences and similarities are discussed in Chapter 6, which examines the recent and current situation. One common purpose of all the labels, however, is to claim that the employees are not mercenaries—a very problematic word both politically and legally.

3. Noah Kirsch, "The Return of Erik Prince," *Forbes*, April 30, 2018, 107–110.

4. Erik Prince, *Civilian Warriors: The Inside Story of Blackwater and the Unsung Heroes of the War on Terror* (New York: Portfolio/Penguin, 2013), 211–216.

5. Ibid., 209–211 and 216–220. Prince states the number of dead as eleven. See also Matt Apuzzo, "Guards Guilty in '07 Killings in Iraq Square," *New York Times*, October 23, 2014, A1.

6. An observation the author heard repeatedly in a nonattribution setting by officers in his seminars at the National Defense University from 2006 to 2015.

7. Apuzzo, "Guards Guilty in '07 Killings." Spencer S. Hsu, "Murder Conviction in Blackwater Case Thrown Out, Other Sentences Overturned," *Washington Post* News Service, reprinted in *Chicago Tribune*, August 4, 2017, http://www.chicagotribune.com/news/nationworld/ct-blackwater-conviction-20170804-story.html. For the legal ambiguity facing both the Blackwater employees and the Iraqi witnesses, see David E. Price, "Private Contractors,

Public Consequences: The Need for an Effective Criminal Justice Framework," in Christopher Kinsey and Malcolm Hugh Paterson, eds., *Contractors and War: The Transformation of U.S. Expeditionary Operations* (Stanford, CA: Stanford University Press, 2012), 218; and Cindy Jung, "Lawless and Unpunished: Private Defense Contractors Spiraling out of Control," *Harvard International Review* (Spring 2016), 7–10. Finally, see "Recent Cases: Eighth Amendment— Mandatory Minimum Sentences—D.C. Circuit Holds It Cruel and Unusual to Impose Mandatory Thirty-Year Sentence on Military Contractors for Gun Charge," *Harvard Law Review*, 131 (2018), 1465–1472. For the 2018 trial and retrial see Sarah Grant, "Trial Preview: Third Attempt to Convict Blackwater Guard for 2007 Massacre of Iraqi Civilians," *Lawfare*, November 2, 2018; and Eileen Sullivan, "Blackwater Security Contractor Found Guilty, Again, in Deadly 2007 Iraq Shooting," *New York Times*, December 19, 2018.

8. Prince, *Civilian Warriors*, 133–138.

9. Andrew deGrandpre, "Blackwater's Founder Wants Trump to Outsource the Afghanistan War. Why That's so Risky," *Washington Post*, August 10, 2017, https://www.washingtonpost.com/news/checkpoint/wp/2017/08/10/blackwaters-founder-wants-trump-to-outsource-the-afghanistan-war-why-thats-so-risky/?utm_term=.33d204bdc495. See also Kirsch, "The Return of Erik Prince," 107–111; Josh Rogin, "Inside Erik Prince's Secret Proposal to Outsource the War in Afghanistan," *Washington Post*, August 9, 2017; and David A. Graham, "Are Mercenaries Really

a Cheaper Way of War?" *The Atlantic Online*, August 9, 2017. For the August 2018 proposal see Jared Keller, "Don't Let Erik Prince Anywhere Near the War in Afghanistan," *Task and Purpose*, August 20, 2018; and Tax Axelrod, "Report: Trump Considering Plan to Privatize Afghan War," *The Hill*, August 17, 2018.

10. A book that raises these questions, albeit in relation to more traditional types of conflict, is Mary L. Dudziak, *War Time: An Idea, Its History, Its Consequences* (New York: Oxford University Press, 2012). However, the impact of the Copenhagen School, represented by the work of Ole Waever, Barry Buzan, and others, in developing the concept of securitization is important here. Immensely oversimplified, *securitization* examines how a nontraditional issue can be reframed in ways to make it a security matter. A brief introduction to securitization is Ralf Emmers, "Securitization," in Alan Collins, ed., *Contemporary Security Studies*, 2nd ed. (Oxford: Oxford University Press, 2013), 136–150.

11. Max Weber, "Politics as a Vocation," in H. H. Gerth and C. Wright Mills, eds., *From Max Weber: Essays in Sociology* (Oxford: Oxford University Press, 1946, reprinted 1958), 78.

12. The term *national security* seems to have emerged in the 1930s and 1940s. See Mark Neocleous, "From Social to National Security: On the Fabrication of Economic Order," *Security Dialogue*, 37, 3 (2006), 363–384.

13. I joined this debate in articles and a book, Kenneth B. Moss, *Undeclared War and the Future of U.S. Foreign Policy* (Washington, DC, and

Baltimore: Wilson Center Press and Johns Hopkins University Press, 2008).

14. For example, see Jay Wexler, *The Odd Clauses: Understanding the Constitution through Ten of Its Most Curious Provisions* (Boston: Beacon Press, 2011), 119–137. Note that Wexler's book was published in 2011, when one could claim circumstances had developed that might breathe life back into this language.

CHAPTER 1. DEFINING THE SPHERES OF WAR

1. Philip Bobbitt, *Terror and Consent: The Wars for the Twenty-First Century* (New York: Alfred A. Knopf, 2008), 125.

2. Quincy Wright, *A Study of War*, abridged by Louise Leonard Wright (Chicago: University of Chicago Press, 1942; rev. 1964), 7.

3. Discussions of Just War theory will recur briefly in later stages in this book. A good introduction to the theory that reviews it historically as well as in terms of modern usage is Alex J. Bellamy, *Just Wars: From Cicero to Iraq* (Cambridge: Polity Press, 2006). The reference to proportionality in prehistorical or ancient warfare does not imply that its practitioners were always so moderate in their actions. See Lawrence H. Keeley, *War before Civilization: The Myth of the Peaceful Savage* (Oxford: Oxford University Press, 1996) as a reminder of the magnitude of brutality.

4. Gary D. Solis, *The Law of Armed Conflict: International Humanitarian Law in War* (Cambridge: Cambridge University Press, 2010), 21.

5. Mary Kaldor, *New and Old Wars: Organized Violence in a Global Era*, 2nd ed. (Stanford, CA: Stanford University Press, 2007), 2.

6. Jack S. Levy and William R. Thompson, *The Arc of War: Origins, Escalation, and Transformation* (Chicago: University of Chicago Press, 2011), 3.

7. Ibid., 6.

8. See Lawrence M. Friedman, *A History of American Law* (New York: Simon and Schuster, 1973), 166–178.

9. Carl von Clausewitz, *On War*, edited and translated by Michael Howard and Peter Paret (Princeton, NJ: Princeton University Press, 1976), 75.

10. Ibid., 7.

11. Ibid., 610.

12. Lawrence Freedman, "Defining War," in Julian Lindley-French and Yves Boyer, eds., *The Oxford Handbook of War* (Oxford: Oxford University Press, 2012), 20.

13. Ingrid Detter De Lupis, *The Law of War* (Cambridge: Cambridge University Press, 1987), 15, 19.

14. Hannah Tonkin, *State Control over Private Military and Security Companies in Armed Conflict* (Cambridge: Cambridge University Press, 2011), 18–19.

15. The similarities and differences between mercenaries and private military firms as well as the employees of the latter and professional soldiers are examined in Chapter 6.

16. Sean McFate, *The Modern Mercenary: Private Armies and What They Mean for World Order* (Oxford: Oxford University Press, 2014), xiv, 6.

17. David William Bates, *States of War: Enlightenment Origins of the Political* (New York: Columbia University Press, 2012), 35; Justine Fornhaber-Baker, "Seigneurial War and Royal Power in

Later Medieval Southern France," *Past & Present*, 208 (August 2010): 37–76, especially 37–38.

18. Wright, *A Study of War*, 191.

19. Maurice Keen, "Introduction: Warfare and the Middle Ages," in Maurice Keen, ed., *Medieval Warfare: A History* (Oxford: Oxford University Press, 1999), 1–2.

20. Paul Christopher, *The Ethics of War and Peace: An Introduction to Legal and Moral Issues*, 2nd ed. (Upper Saddle River, NJ: Prentice Hall, 2003), 29–42.

21. Frederic J. Baumgartner, *Declaring War in Early Modern Europe* (New York: Palgrave Macmillan, 2011), 21–22.

22. See Bellamy, *Just Wars*, 37–40.

23. James Q. Whitman, *The Verdict of Battle: The Law of Victory and the Making of Modern War* (Cambridge, MA: Harvard University Press, 2012), 17.

24. Baumgartner, *Declaring War in Early Modern Europe*, 22–23.

25. Albert E. Hindmarsh, "Self-Help in Time of Peace," *American Journal of International Law*, 26, 2 (April 1932): 316–318. Also see Fornhaber-Baker, "Seigneurial War and Royal Power," 41.

26. Andre Corvisier, *Armies and Societies in Europe, 1494–1789*, translated by Abigail T. Siddal (Bloomington: Indiana University Press, 1979), 41; Bruce D. Porter, *War and the Rise of the State: The Military Foundation of Modern Politics* (New York: Free Press, 1994), 25. The point about restrictions on who could duel comes from Wright, *A Study of War*, 175–176. For more on knights, chivalry, and commoners, see Maurice Keen, *Chivalry* (New Haven, CT: Yale University Press, 1984;

rev. 2005), 1–2, 220, 224–230; and James Turner Johnson, *Just War Tradition and the Restraint of War: A Moral and Historical Inquiry* (Princeton, NJ: Princeton University Press, 1981), 134–187.

27. Corvisier, *Armies and Societies in Europe*, 41; Norman Housley, "European Warfare, c.1200–1320," in Keen, ed., *Medieval Warfare*, 123.

28. Baumgartner, *Declaring War in Early Modern Europe*, 26.

29. Wright, *A Study of War*, 176.

30. Whitman, *The Verdict of Battle*, 53, 104, 111.

31. Rodney Bruce Hall and Thomas J. Biersteker, "The Emergence of Private Authority in the International System," in Hall and Biersteker, eds., *The Emergence of Private Authority in Global Governance* (Cambridge: Cambridge University Press, 2002), 5.

32. Claire Cutler, "Private International Regimes and Interfirm Cooperation," in Hall and Biersteker, eds., *The Emergence of Private Authority in Global Governance*, 32.

33. Laura A. Dickinson, *Outsourcing War and Peace: Preserving Public Values in a World of Privatized Foreign Affairs* (New Haven, CT: Yale University Press, 2011), 8.

34. Karen Lund Petersen, "Risk, Responsibility and Roles Redefined: Is Counterterrorism a Corporate Responsibility?" *Cambridge Review of International Affairs*, 21, 3 (September 2008): 408.

35. Patricia Owens, "Distinctions, Distinctions: 'Public' and 'Private' Force?" *International Affairs*, 84, 5 (2008): 980.

36. The information on Grotius is taken from Philip Bobbitt, *The Shield of*

Achilles: War, Peace, and the Course of History (New York: Alfred A. Knopf, 2002), 509–510; and Stephen R. Bown, 1494: How a Family Feud in Medieval Spain Divided the World in Half (New York: St. Martin's Press, 2011), 244–248. Also see Dona A. Hathaway and Scott J. Shapiro, The Internationalists: How a Radical Plan to Outlaw War Remade the World (New York: Simon and Schuster, 2017), 3–5, 13.

37. Martine Julia van Ittersum, "Introduction," in Hugo Grotius, Commentary on the Law of Prize and Booty, edited by Martine Julia van Ittersum (Indianapolis: Liberty Fund, 2006), xvi–xvii.

38. Ibid., xviii–xix. The emphasis on natural law in Grotius is also assessed in Lauren Benton, A Search for Sovereignty: Law and Geography in European Empires, 1400–1900 (Cambridge: Cambridge University Press, 2010), 132–133.

39. Grotius, Commentary, 50.

40. Thomas Hobbes, Leviathan, edited by Edwin Curley (Indianapolis: Hackett Publishing, 1994), 76, 78.

41. Bobbitt, The Shield of Achilles, 513–514.

42. Grotius, Commentary, 95.

43. Ibid., 104, 128, 195.

44. Janice E. Thomson, "State Practices, International Norms, and the Decline of Mercenarism," International Studies Quarterly, 34, 1 (March 1990): 43.

45. Ibid., 43.

46. Richard Tuck, "Introduction," in Hugo Grotius, The Rights of War and Peace, Book I, edited by Richard Tuck (Indianapolis: Liberty Fund, 2005), xxvii–xxx.

47. Adam Smith, An Inquiry into the Nature and Causes of the Wealth of Nations, edited by Edwin Canaan (New York: Modern Library, 1994), 430, 444, and 764. The quote is from the last page.

48. The author speaks from experience.

49. Smith, The Wealth of Nations, 764–765.

50. Ibid., 763.

51. Keep in mind the fact that there are regions where state development is not occurring along Western models. Due to its relationship with international law, discussion of the sanction and control of war has a heavy Western bias, for better and for worse.

52. Niccolo Machiavelli, The Prince, in The Essential Writings of Machiavelli, edited and translated by Peter Constantine (New York: Modern Library: 2007), 47.

53. Charles Tilly, Coercion, Capital, and European States, AD 990–1992 (Oxford: Blackwell Publishers, 1990; 1992), 15, 30.

54. Porter, War and the Rise of the State, 58.

55. Machiavelli, The Prince, 38.

56. Bates, States of War, 42.

57. Martin van Creveld, The Rise and Decline of the State (Cambridge: Cambridge University Press, 1999), 174.

58. Bobbitt, The Shield of Achilles, 86–87.

59. Hendrik Spruyt, The Sovereign State and Its Competitors: An Analysis of Systems Change (Princeton, NJ: Princeton University Press, 1994), 82–83. Of course, particular German states did do so, such as Prussia.

60. Ibid., 85–108.

61. Bates, States of War, 44–46.

62. Van Creveld, *The Rise and Decline of the State*, 176.

63. Ibid., 176–177.

64. Hobbes, *Leviathan*, 76, 86.

65. Van Creveld, *The Rise and Decline of the State*, 179.

66. Ibid., 179–180.

67. This distinction continues to be made by some "realists" who argue that one cannot apply models of law and governance from domestic systems to the international system.

68. Hobbes, *Leviathan*, 114.

69. Ibid., 114.

70. Elke Krahmann, *States, Citizens and the Privatization of Security* (Cambridge: Cambridge University Press, 2010), 24.

71. Ibid., 24–25.

72. John Locke, "The Second Treatise of Government: An Essay Concerning the True Original, Extent and End of Civil Government," in *The Selected Political Writings of John Locke*, edited by Paul E. Sigmund (New York: W. W. Norton, 2005), 83; Kenneth B. Moss, *Undeclared War and the Future of U.S. Foreign Policy* (Washington, DC, and Baltimore: Woodrow Wilson Center Press and Johns Hopkins University Press, 2008), 29.

73. Jean-Jacques Rousseau, *The Social Contract*, translated by Maurice Cranston (London: Penguin Books, 1968), 55–56.

74. Ibid., 56.

75. This discussion draws from Krahmann, *States, Citizens, and the Privatization of Security*, 25–27.

76. Ibid., 12, 36–39.

77. Ibid., 13, 9–4.

78. Rousseau, *The Social Contract*, 56.

79. This discussion draws partly from Brien Hallett, *The Lost Art of Declaring War* (Urbana: University of Illinois Press, 1998), 65–73.

80. Baumgartner, *Declaring War in Early Modern Europe*, 95–96.

81. Ibid., 100–101.

82. Ibid., 108–109.

83. Ibid., 120–121.

84. Ibid., 122–123.

85. Ibid., 126-127.

86. Moss, *Undeclared War*, 21–22. See also J. J. Burlamaqui, *The Principles of Political Law*, 5th ed., translated by Thomas Nugent (Boston: University Press, W. Hilliard, 1807), 1, 2, 5. Available at http://constitution.org/burla/burla_.htm.

87. Baumgartner, *Declaring War in Early Modern Europe*, 134–135.

CHAPTER 2. PRIVATE WAR: WHO ARE THE PARTICIPANTS?

1. Ulrich Schneckener, "Fragile Statehood, Armed Non-State Actors and Security Governance," in Alan Bryden and Maria Caparini, eds., *Private Actors and Security Governance*, Geneva Centre for the Democratic Control of Armed Forces (Münster: LIT Verlag, 2007), 25.

2. Ibid.

3. Ibid.

4. Ibid., 25–26. The label "little green men" became a popular, sardonic term for Russian personnel wearing no insignia who were engaged in the fighting in Ukraine. Their weaponry and tactics belied likely origin in the Russian army, but no one specifically confirmed that. Their "uncertain" origin inspired the reference to Martians or aliens. See Owen Matthews, "Putin's (Secret)

Army," *Newsweek*, January 26, 2018, 27–35.

5. Schneckener, "Fragile State-hood," 26.

6. Ibid. Also see John MacKinlay, "Defining Warlords," *International Peacekeeping*, 7, 1 (2000): 48.

7. Schneckener, "Fragile State-hood," 26–27; Ingrid Detter De Lupis, *The Law of War* (Cambridge: Cambridge University Press, 1987), 23, 21.

8. Phil Williams, "Transnational Organized Crime," in Paul Williams, ed., *Security Studies: An Introduction*, 2nd ed. (London: Routledge, 2013), 503–519. Quote is on page 507.

9. Schneckener, "Fragile State-hood," 27–28.

10. Frances Stonor Saunders, *The Devil's Broker: Seeking Gold, God, and Glory in Fourteenth-Century Italy* (New York: Fourth Estate, Harper Collins, 2004), 65–66.

11. Andre Corvisier, "Mercenaries," in Andre Corvisier, ed., *A Dictionary of Military History*, translated by Chris Turner (Oxford: Basil Blackwell, 1994), 501; William Urban, *Medieval Merce-naries: The Business of War* (London: Greenhill Books, 2006), 59.

12. Corvisier, "Mercenaries," 501–502.

13. See Sean McFate, *The Modern Mercenary: Private Armies and What They Mean for World Order* (Oxford: Oxford University Press, 2014), 36–37.

14. Adam Roberts and Richard Guelff, *Documents on the Laws of War*, 3rd ed. (Oxford: Oxford University Press, 2004), 447; also see concluding notes related to Geneva Protocols I and II, 493–512.

15. Kenneth B. Moss, *Undeclared War and the Future of U.S. Foreign Policy* (Washington, DC, and Baltimore: Wilson Center Press and Johns Hopkins University Press, 2008), 188–189.

16. See the discussion in Chapter 6 for an examination of the common terms in these contracts.

17. Corvisier, "Mercenaries," 502–503; Urban, *Medieval Mercenaries*, 21–22.

18. Urban, *Medieval Mercenaries*, 23–26.

19. I borrow the words *complement* and *supplement* from Andre Corvisier. See Corvisier, "Mercenaries," 502.

20. Norman Housley, "European Warfare, c. 1200–1320," in Maurice Keen, ed., *Medieval Warfare: A History* (Oxford: Oxford University Press, 1999), 123; Urban, *Medieval Mercenaries*, 38; McFate, *The Modern Mercenary*, 28.

21. Housley, "European Warfare," 125.

22. William H. McNeill, *The Pursuit of Power: Technology, Armed Force, and Society since A.D. 1000* (Chicago: University of Chicago Press, 1982), 65–72.

23. Thomas Ertman, *Birth of the Leviathan: Building States and Regimes in Medieval and Early Modern Europe* (Cambridge: Cambridge University Press, 1997), 62–65; Housley, "Medieval Warfare," 126.

24. McNeill, *The Pursuit of Power*, 67–68; Michael Mallett, "Mercenaries," in Keen. ed., *Medieval Warfare*, 213; John Gillingham, "An Age of Expansion, c. 1020–1204," in Keen, ed., *Medieval Warfare*, 72; Urban, *Medieval Mercenar-ies*, 141–142.

25. See Sean McGlynn, *By Sword and Fire: Cruelty and Atrocity in Medieval War-fare* (London: Phoenix, 2008), 197–244,

for a sobering depiction of medieval warfare.

26. McNeill, *The Pursuit of Power*, 70; Mallett, "Mercenaries," 211–213; Michael Howard, *War in European History* (Oxford: Oxford University Press, 1976), 24–29.

27. Alex J. Bellamy, *Just Wars: From Cicero to Iraq* (Cambridge: Polity Press, 2006), 37–40.

28. Mallett, "Mercenaries," 213.

29. Jurgen Brauer and Hubert Van Tuyll, *Castles, Battles, and Bombs: How Economics Explains Military History* (Chicago: University of Chicago Press, 2008), 85–89.

30. Ertman, *Birth of the Leviathan*, 63–65.

31. Howard, *War in European History*, 17; Andre Corvisier, *Armies and Societies in Europe: 1494–1789* (Bloomington: Indiana University Press, 1979, 42; Brauer and Van Tuyll, *Castles, Battles, and Bombs*, 101.

32. Urban, *Medieval Mercenaries*, 75–76; Brauer and Van Tuyll, *Castles, Battles, and Bombs*, 80.

33. Mallett, "Mercenaries," 216–217.

34. McNeill, *The Pursuit of Power*, 74.

35. Mallett, "Mercenaries, 217–226; Brauer and Van Tuyll, *Castles, Battles, and Bombs*, 81–83.

36. Brauer and Van Tuyll, *Castles, Battles, and Bombs*, 83–84.

37. Ibid., 89–92; McNeill, *The Pursuit of Power*, 74–75.

38. Brauer and Van Tuyll, *Castles, Battles, and Bombs*, 94.

39. Ibid., 93.

40. Howard, *War in European History*, 26–27.

41. Brauer and Van Tuyll, *Castles, Battles, and Bombs*, 96–99.

42. See discussion in Chapter 1.

43. Ertman, *Birth of the Leviathan*, 66.

44. McFate, *The Modern Mercenary*, 31.

45. Mallett, "Mercenaries," 228; Urban, *Medieval Mercenaries*, 269.

46. Philip Bobbitt, *The Shield of Achilles: War, Peace, and the Course of History* (New York: Alfred A. Knopf, 2002), 81.

47. Brauer and Van Tuyll, *Castles, Battles, and Bombs*, 106–110; McNeill, *The Pursuit of Power*, 78.

48. Howard, *War in European History*, 27–28.

49. Brauer and Van Tuyll, *Castles, Battles, and Bombs*, 113.

50. Ibid., 111–114.

51. Bruce D. Porter, *War and the Rise of the State: The Military Foundations of Modern Politics* (New York: Free Press, 1994), 66–67.

52. Ibid., 65–66.

53. Lauro Martines, *Furies: War in Europe, 1450–1700* (London: Bloomsbury Press, 2013), 44.

54. Porter, *War and the Rise of the State*, 66–67.

55. This discussion draws from Charles Tilly, *Coercion, Capital, and European States: AD 990–1992* (Oxford: Blackwell, 1990), 84–87.

56. McNeill, *The Pursuit of Power*, 114.

57. Geoffrey Parker, *The Military Revolution: Military Innovation and the Rise of the West, 1500–1800* (Cambridge: Cambridge University Press, 1988), 64.

58. McNeill, *The Pursuit of Power*, 121. William Urban even estimates Wallenstein had as many as 150,000 men under arms fighting in several armies on different fronts. See Urban, *Bayonets for Hire: Mercenaries at War*,

1550–1789 (London: Greenhill Books, 2007), 104.

59. Parker, The Military Revolution, 65–67.

60. Herfried Munkler, The New Wars (Cambridge: Polity, 2005), 42.

61. See the accounts of the sack of Magdeburg in Urban, Bayonets for Hire, 107; and Martines, Furies, 73–80. The quotation of the Jesuit priest, Gaspard Wiltheim, is found in Munkler, The New Wars, 43–44.

62. Munkler, The New Wars, 45–47.

63. Urban, Bayonets for Hire, 114–115.

64. The discussion draws upon Tilly, Coercion, Capital, and European States, 166–167.

65. Bobbitt, The Shield of Achilles, 120. The broader discussion is from pages 120–130.

66. Porter, War and the Rise of the State, 108; Urban, Bayonets for Hire, 282–283; Corvisier, Armies and Societies in Europe, 51–60; Janice E. Thomson, Mercenaries, Pirates, and Sovereigns: State-Building and Extraterritorial Violence in Early Modern Europe (Princeton, NJ: Princeton University Press, 1994), 28–29.

67. Urban, Bayonets for Hire, 282–283; Bobbitt, The Shield of Achilles, 130–132; Porter, War and the Rise of the State, 108–109; John Brewer, The Sinews of Power: War, Money and the English State, 1688–1788 (New York: Alfred A. Knopf, 1989), xvii.

68. McNeill, The Pursuit of Power, 103, 102.

69. Ibid., 105.

70. Henry A. Ormerod, Piracy in the Ancient World (Baltimore: Johns Hopkins University Press, 1924; reprinted 1997).

71. Thomson, Mercenaries, Pirates, and Sovereigns, 22. Thomas is quoting William Edward Hall, A Treatise on International Law, 8th ed., edited by A. Pearce Higgins (Oxford: Clarendon Press, 1924), 314.

72. William McFee, The Law of the Sea (Philadelphia: J. B. Lippincott, 1950), 87–88.

73. Rodolphe Durand and Jean Philippe Vergne, The Pirate Organization: Lessons from the Fringes of Capitalism (Boston: Harvard Business Review Press, 2013), 14–15.

74. See Daniel Heller-Roazen, The Enemy of All: Piracy and the Law of Nations (New York: Zone Books, 2009), 16. Heller-Roazen uses Marcus Tullius Cicero, On Duties, edited and translated by M. T. Griffin and E. M. Atkins (Cambridge: Cambridge University Press, 1991), 141.

75. David Armstrong, Theo Farrell, and Helene Lambert, International Law and International Relations, 2nd ed. (Cambridge: Cambridge University Press, 2012), 43.

76. Thomsen, Mercenaries, Pirates, and Sovereigns, 108.

77. Ibid, 108–109; Durand and Vergne, The Pirate Organization, 54–55.

78. Heller-Roazen, The Enemy of All, 11.

79. Ibid., 11.

80. Ralph T. Ward, Pirates in History (Baltimore: York Press, 1974), 2–22.

81. Ibid., 59–60.

82. Ibid., 102.

83. N. A. M. Rodger, The Safeguard of the Sea: A Naval History of Britain, 660–1649 (New York: W. W. Norton, 1997), xxv, 126–127.

84. Ibid., 127.

85. Peter Earle, *The Pirate Wars* (New York: St. Martin's Press, 2003), 18–19.

86. Rodger, *The Safeguard of the Sea*, 91–92.

87. Ibid., 27; Ward, *Pirates in History*, 104–105.

88. Rodger, *The Safeguard of the Sea*, 128–129.

89. Ward, *Pirates in History*, 102.

90. N. A. M. Rodger, "The Law and Language of Private Naval Warfare," *Mariner's Mirror*, 100, 1 (2014), notes 8 and 13.

91. Ibid., note 8.

92. Grover Clark, "The English Practice with Regard to Reprisals," *American Journal of International Law*, 27, 4 (October 1933): 701–702. It is important to avoid confusing the usage of reprisal here with its understanding in the context of more recent forms of war, which involve intentional retaliatory measures taken against the population by the military.

93. Ibid., 695–697.

94. Frederic L. Cheyette, "The Sovereign and the Pirates, 1332," *Speculum*, 45, 1 (January 1970): 48.

95. Christopher Beck, "Common Good and Private Justice: Letters of Marque and the *Utilitas Publica* in Fourteenth-Century Marseilles," *Journal of Medieval History*, 41, 1 (2015): 88–89, 102.

96. Lauren Benton, *A Search for Sovereignty: Law and Geography in European Empires, 1400–1900* (Cambridge: Cambridge University Press, 2010), 10.

97. Stephen R. Bown, *1494: How a Family Feud in Medieval Spain Divided the World in Half* (New York: St. Martin's Press, 2011), 2–3.

98. Ibid., 3–5.

99. Benton, *A Search for Sovereignty*, 22–23.

100. As quoted in Bown, *1494*, 205.

101. Ibid., 204–205.

102. Mark G. Hanna, "Well-Behaved Pirates Seldom Make History: A Reevaluation of the Golden Age of Piracy," in Peter C. Mandall and Carole Shammas, eds., *Governing the Sea in the Early Modern Era: Essays in Honor of Robert C. Ritchie* (San Marino, CA: Huntington Library, 2015), 137–139. Also see Mark G. Hanna, *Pirate Nests and the Rise of the British Empire, 1570–1740* (Chapel Hill: University of North Carolina Press, 2015), 106–107.

103. Halvard Leira and Benjamin de Carvalho, "Privateers of the North Sea: At World's End—French Privateers in Norwegian Waters," in Alejandro Colas and Bryan Mabee, eds., *Mercenaries, Pirates, Bandits, and Empires: Private Violence in Historical Context* (New York: Columbia University Press, 2010), 60.

104. The commission is quoted in Gardner Weld Allen, *Massachusetts Privateers of the Revolution*, Vol. 77, Massachusetts Historical Society Collections (Cambridge: Massachusetts Historical Society, 1927), 5.

105. Rodger, *The Safeguard of the Sea*, 149; Hanna, *Pirate Nests and the Rise of the British Empire*, 35.

106. Michael Kempe, "'Even in the Remotest Corners of the World': Globalized Piracy and International Law, 1500–1900," *Journal of Global History*, 5 (2010): 359, 358.

107. Ibid., 359; Heller-Roazen, *The Enemy of All*, 86.

108. Hanna, "Well-Behaved Pirates," 137.

109. Douglas C. Peifer, "Maritime Commerce Warfare: The Coercive Response of the Weak?" *Naval War College Review*, 66, 2 (Spring 2013): 84–85; J. Meyer and P. Masson, "Commerce-Raiding," in Corvisier, *A Dictionary of Military History*, 171–172.

110. Peifer, "Maritime Commerce Warfare," 85.

111. Leira and Carvalho, "Privateers of the North Sea," 57.

112. McNeill, *The Pursuit of Power*, 103–104.

113. Rodger, *The Safeguard of the Sea*, 176–177.

114. Steve Murdoch, *The Terror of the Seas: Scottish Maritime Warfare, 1513–1713* (Leiden: Koninklijke Brill, 2010), 6, 9.

115. Ibid., 25. 27.

116. Rodger, *The Safeguard of the Sea*, 182–189.

117. Ibid., 198–199; Jon Latimer, *Buccaneers of the Caribbean: How Piracy Forged an Empire* (Cambridge, MA: Harvard University Press, 2009), 13.

118. Rodger, *The Safeguard of the Sea*, 199; David Loades, *England's Maritime Empire: Seapower, Commerce, and Policy, 1490–1690* (Harlow: UK: Pearson Educated, 2000), 122.

119. Ibid.

120. Ibid., 127. See also David Childs, *Pirate Nation: Elizabeth I and Her Royal Sea Rovers* (Barnsley, UK: Seaforth Publishing, 2014), 7, 47.

121. Loades, *England's Maritime Empire*, 128.

122. Rodger, *The Safeguard of the Sea*, 201–202. See also Susan Ronald, *The Pirate Queen: Queen Elizabeth I, Her Pirate Adventurers and the Dawn of Empire* (New York: Harper Perennial, 2007), 112–125.

123. Ibid., 140–45.

124. McFee, *The Law of the Sea*, 106–108; Ronald, *The Pirate Queen*, 144–146.

125. Ronald, *The Pirate Queen*, 146–147.

126. This discussion draws from several sources. See in particular Kenneth R. Andrews, *Elizabethan Privateering during the Spanish War, 1585–1603* (Cambridge: Cambridge University Press, 1964), 3–5; Earle, *The Pirate Wars*, 25, and McFee, *The Law of the Sea*, 110.

127. Ronald, *The Pirate Queen*, 148–153.

128. Ibid., 198–205, 214–237. See also Kris E. Lane, *Pillaging the Empire: Piracy in the Americas, 1500–1750* (Armonk, NY: M. E. Sharpe, 1998), 43–49.

129. Andrews, *Elizabethan Privateering*, 3, 59, 10, 22. Quotation is from page 20. See also Ronald, *The Pirate Queen*, 279–290; and Lane, *Pillaging Empire*, 51–55.

130. Ronald, *The Pirate Queen*, 291.

CHAPTER 3. PRIVATE AND PUBLIC WAR IN THE ATLANTIC WORLD AND BEYOND

1. L. M. Hill, "The Admiralty Circuit of 1591: Some Comments on the Relations between Central Government and Local Interests," *Historical Journal*, 14, 1 (March 1971): 7.

2. Ibid., 7; John Brewer, *The Sinews of Power: War, Money and the English State, 1688–1783* (New York: Alfred A. Knopf, 1989), 64.

3. Elizabeth Mancke, "Chartered Enterprises and the Evolution of the British Atlantic World," in Elizabeth Mancke and Carole Shammas, eds.,

The Creation of the British World (Baltimore: Johns Hopkins University Press, 2005), 239–240.

4. Brewer, The Sinews of Power, 137. The preference of James I for "Great Britain" is mentioned by N. A. M. Rodger, The Safeguard of the Sea: A Naval History of Britain, 660–1649 (New York: W. W. Norton, 1997), 347.

5. Patrick K. O'Brien, "Inseparable Connections: Trade, Economy, Fiscal State, and the Expansion of Empire, 1688–1815," in P. J. Marshall, ed., The Eighteenth Century, Vol. 2 of The Oxford History of the British Empire (Oxford: Oxford University Press, 1998), 63–64.

6. Bruce D. Porter, War and the Rise of the State: The Military Foundations of Modern Politics (New York: Free Press, 1994), 73–78.

7. William H. McNeill, The Pursuit of Power: Technology, Armed Force, and Society since A.D. 1000 (Chicago: University of Chicago Press, 1982), 178.

8. Robert C. Ritchie, "Government Measures against Piracy and Privateering in the Atlantic Area, 1750–1850," in David J. Starkey, E. S. van Eyck van Heslinga, and J. A. Moor, eds., Pirates and Privateers: New Perspectives on the War on Trade in the Eighteenth and Nineteenth Centuries (Exeter, UK: University of Exeter Press, 1997), 10.

9. Ibid., 10.

10. Angus Calder, Revolutionary Empire: The Rise of the English-Speaking Empires from the Fifteenth Century to the 1780s (New York: R. E. P. Dutton, 1981), 118; Ronald Findley and Kevin H. O'Rourke, Power and Plenty: Trade, War, and the World Economy in the Second Millennium (Princeton, NJ: Princeton University Press, 2007), 238–240.

11. Ibid., 175–179.

12. P. J. Marshall, "Introduction," in Marshall, The Eighteenth Century, 4–7.

13. Findley and O'Rourke, Power and Plenty, 228.

14. Ibid., 228; Calder, Revolutionary Empire, 118–119.

15. Findley and O'Rourke, Power and Plenty, 227.

16. The discussion draws in particular from the work of Lauren Benton. See her A Search for Sovereignty: Law and Geography in European Empire, 1400–1900 (Cambridge: Cambridge University Press, 2010) and "Legal Spaces of Empire: Piracy and the Origins of Ocean Regionalism," Comparative Studies in Society and History, 47, 4 (2005), particularly pages 716–717 for the point on competing jurisdictions.

17. Benton, A Search for Sovereignty, 32–34.

18. Benton, "Legal Spaces of Empire," 702–703.

19. Benton, A Search for Sovereignty, 122–136.

20. See Chapter 1 for a discussion of this.

21. Benton, A Search for Sovereignty, 137–142. For another comparative view of the Atlantic and Asian worlds in British thinking see Philip J. Stern, "British Asia and British Atlantic: Comparisons and Connections," William and Mary Quarterly, 68, 4 (October 2006), 693–712.

22. Douglas R. Burgess Jr., "A Crisis of Charter and Right: Piracy and Colonial Resistance in Seventeenth-Century Rhode Island," Journal of Social History, 45, 3 (2012), 606–607.

23. Peter Earle, The Pirate Wars (New York: St. Martin's Press, 2003), 26–52.

24. Ibid., 64.

25. John A. C. Conybeare and Todd Sandler, "State-Sponsored Violence as a Tragedy of the Commons: England's Privateering Wars with France and Spain, 1625–1630," Public Choice, 77, 4 (1993): 881–882.

26. Ibid., 882–883; Rodger, The Safeguard of the Sea, 356–363.

27. Ibid., 379–382; Charles Wye Kendall, Private Men-of-War (New York: Robert M. McBride, 1932), 65.

28. Rodger, The Safeguard of the Sea, 411–424.

29. Carla Gardina Pestana, The English Atlantic in the Age of Revolution, 1640–1661 (Cambridge, MA: Harvard University Press, 2004), 2.

30. Ibid., 157.

31. Earle, The Pirate Wars, 77.

32. N. A. M. Rodger, The Command of the Ocean: A Naval History of Britain, 1649–1845 (New York: W.W. Norton, 2004), 7.

33. Calder, Revolutionary Empire, 267–268.

34. Burgess, "A Crisis of Charter and Right," 606.

35. Helen J. Crump, Colonial Admiralty Jurisdiction in the Seventeenth Century (London: Longmans, Greden, 1931), 104.

36. Earle, The Pirate Wars, 89–92.

37. Ibid., 92–94; Douglas R. Burgess Jr., The Politics of Piracy: Crime and Disobedience in Colonial America (Lebanon, NH: ForeEdge, University Press of New England, 2014), 26–29; Kris E. Lane, Pillaging the Empire: Piracy in the Americas, 1500–1750 (Armonk, NY: M. E. Sharpe, 1998), 104–107.

38. The charge of dismissal or neglect is echoed in Matthew Norton, "Temporality, Isolation, and Violence in the Early Modern English Maritime World," Eighteenth-Century Studies, 48, 1 (2014): 50.

39. Burgess, The Politics of Piracy, 29; Earle, The Pirate Wars, 92.

40. Burgess, The Politics of Piracy, 29.

41. This summary draws from Lane, Pillaging the Empire, 107–125; Burgess, The Politics of Piracy, 30–32; and Earle, The Pirate Wars, 94–96.

42. Burgess, The Politics of Piracy, 32.

43. Earle, The Pirate Wars, 97–98.

44. Halvard Leira and Benjamin de Carvalho, "Privateers of the North Sea: At World's End—French Privateers in Norwegian Waters,' in Alejandro Colas and Bryan Mabee, eds., Mercenaries, Pirates, Bandits, and Empires: Private Violence in Historical Context (New York: Columbia University Press, 2010), 61.

45. Ibid., 62. The point is made by H. M. Scott in his "Review Article: The Second 'Hundred Years War,' 1689–1815," Historical Journal, 35, 2 (1992), 454.

46. Leira and de Carvalho, "Privateers of the North Sea." 62–63.

47. Ibid., 64–65.

48. Ibid., 66–82.

49. Burgess, The Politics of Piracy, 143–145.

50. Ibid., 146–150.

51. Ibid., 146–147, 150–152.

52. John Franklin Jameson, Privateering and Piracy in the Colonial World: Illustrative Documents (New York: Macmillan, 1923), xi–xii.

53. Calder, Revolutionary Empire, 403.

54. Norton, "Temporality, Isolation, and Violence, 51.

55. Burgess, The Politics of Piracy, 51–52.

56. Calder, Revolutionary Empire, 402.

57. Kendall, Private Men-of-War, 153.

58. The description draws upon Marcus Rediker, Between the Devil and the Deep Blue Sea: Merchant Seamen, Pirates and the Anglo-American Maritime World, 1700–1750 (Cambridge: Cambridge University Press, 1987, 1993), 32–33, 107, 264; and Marcus Rediker, Villains of All Nations: Atlantic Pirates in the Golden Age (Boston: Beacon Press, 2004), 43–45. Also see Denver Brunsman, The Evil Necessity: British Naval Impressment in the Eighteenth Century Atlantic World Charlottesville: University of Virginia Press, 2013), 58–59, 68.

59. Kendall, Private Men of War, 153; Brunsman, The Evil Necessity, 58–59, 68.

60. Burgess, "A Crisis of Charter and Right," 614; Burgess, The Politics of Piracy, 193–194.

61. Burgess, "A Crisis of Charter and Right," 616–618.

62. Rodger, The Command of the Ocean, 156–157.

63. Tim Beattie, The British Privateering Voyages of the Early Eighteenth Century (Suffolk, UK: Boydell Press, 2015), 5–6 for both newspaper quotes.

64. Rodger, The Command of the Ocean, 158–159.

65. Earle, The Pirate Wars, 111–114.

66. I. K. Steele, Politics of Colonial Policy: The Board of Trade in Colonial Administration, 1696–1720 (Oxford: Clarendon Press, 1968), 45.

67. Ibid., 45.

68. Robert C. Ritchie, Captain Kidd and the War against the Pirates (Cambridge, MA: Harvard University Press, 1986), 27–40.

69. Ibid., 41–54; Tom Wareham, "More Than Just Kidd's Play," History Today (January 2013), 11–13.

70. Benton, A Search for Sovereignty, 116.

71. Ritchie, Captain Kidd, 62–68.

72. Ibid., 80–134; Benton, A Search for Sovereignty, 117.

73. Earle, The Pirate Wars, 146.

74. Ibid., 146–147.

75. Ritchie, Captain Kidd, 160–184 and 154 for the anti-piracy law.

76. Ibid., 203–227.

77. Steele, Politics of Colonial Policy, 57.

78. Earle, The Pirate Wars, 155.

79. Shinsuke Satsuma, "Politicians, Merchants, and Colonial Maritime War: The Political and Economic Background of the American Act of 1708," Parliamentary History, 32, 2 (2013): 321–322; J. S. Bromley, Corsairs and Navies, 1660–1760 (London: Hambledon Press, 1987), 114.

80. Colin Woodard, The Republic of Pirates: Being the True and Surprising Story of the Caribbean Pirates and the Man Who Brought Them Down (Orlando, FL: Harcourt, Harvest Books, 2007), 64.

81. Ibid., 64–65.

82. Ibid., 65–67.

83. Beattie, British Privateering Voyages, 46, 48.

84. Woodard, The Republic of Pirates, 65–84.

85. Ibid., 86; Earle, The Pirate Wars, 160–161.

86. Blackbeard's possible Stuart leanings are discussed in Woodard, The Republic of Pirates, 214. See also Earle, The Pirate Wars, 193–194.

87. Ibid., 189–91; Benton, "Legal Spaces of Empire," 720.

88. Benton, "Legal Spaces of Empire," 720.

89. Alejandro Colas and Bryan Mabee, "The Flow and Ebb of Private Seaborne Violence in Global Politics: Lessons from the Atlantic World, 1689–1815," in Colas and Mabee, Mercenaries, Pirates, Bandits, and Empires, 96–103.

90. Daniel A. Baugh, British Naval Administration in the Age of Walpole (Princeton, NJ: Princeton University Press, 1965), 112.

91. Ibid., 113.

92. Ibid., 113–114; Earle, The Pirate Wars, 194–195.

93. Richard Pares, War and Trade in the West Indies, 1739–1763 (London: Frank Cass, 1936), 46–48.

94. Baugh, British Naval Administration in the Age of Walpole, 114–115.

95. Roger Morriss, The Foundations of British Maritime Ascendancy: Resources, Logistics and the State, 1755–1815 (Cambridge: Cambridge University Press, 2011), 8; Brewer, The Sinews of Power.

96. John B. Owen, The Eighteenth Century, 1714–1815 (New York: W. W. Norton, 1974), 48–50; Calder, Revolutionary Empire, 549–552; Pares, War and Trade, 49.

97. Proceedings of the Council of Maryland, 1743/4, vol. 28, 326 and 311, https://archive.org/details/archivesof maryla28brow.

98. Pares, War and Trade, 49.

99. Henning Hillmann and Christina Gathmann, "Overseas Trade and the Decline of Privateering," Journal of Economic History, 71, 3 (September 2011), 731; Findlay and O'Rourke, Power and Plenty, 256.

100. Hillmann and Gathmann, "Overseas Trade and the Decline of Privateering," 732.

101. Ibid., 730–761.

102. Joyce Appleby, The Relentless Revolution: A History of Capitalism (New York: W. W. Norton, 2010), 46–47.

103. P. W. Klein, "The Origins of Trading Companies," in Leonard Blusse and Femme Gaastra, eds., Companies and Trade (Dordrecht, Netherlands: Leiden University Press, 1981), 23–24; Janice E. Thomson, Mercenaries, Pirates, and Sovereigns: State-Building and Extraterritorial Violence in Early Modern Europe (Princeton, NJ: Princeton University Press, 1994), 61.

104. James D. Tracy, "Introduction," in James D. Tracy, ed., The Rise of Merchant Empires: Long-Distance Trade in the Early Modern World, 1350–1750 (Cambridge: Cambridge University Press, 1990), 9.

105. Burke, quoted in Philip J. Stern, The Company State: Corporate Sovereignty and the Early Modern Foundations of the British Empire in India (Oxford: Oxford University Press, 2011), 3. The Burke quote can be found in Edmund Burke, The Work of the Right Honourable Edmund Burke, 7: Speeches on the Impeachment of Warren Hastings (London: Bell and Daldy, 1870), 23.

106. Andrew Phillips and J. C. Sharman, International Order in Diversity: War, Trade, and Rule in the Indian Ocean (Cambridge: Cambridge University Press, 2015), 11–12.

107. K. N. Chaudhuri, The Trading World of Asia and the East India Company, 1660–1760 (Cambridge: Cambridge University Press, 1978), 454–455.

108. Appleby, The Relentless Revolution, 46–47.

109. The Portuguese are discussed in Thomson, *Mercenaries, Pirates, and Sovereigns*, 33–34; in Philips and Sharman, *International Order in Diversity*, 76–79; and in George D. Winius, "Two Lusitanian Variations on a Dutch Theme: Portuguese Companies in Times of Crises, 1628–1662," in Blusse and Gaastra, *Companies and Trade*, 123–134.

110. Thomson, *Mercenaries, Pirates, and Sovereigns*, 63–64; Michael Howard, *War in European History* (Oxford: Oxford University Press, 1976), 52; Holden Furber, *Rival Empires of Trade in the Orient, 1600–1800* (Minneapolis: University of Minnesota, 1976), 105, 149.

111. P. C. Emmer, "The West India Company, 1621–1791," in Blusse and Gaastra, *Companies and Trade*, 76, 89; Patrick O'Brien, "Mercantilism and Imperialism in the Rise and Decline of the Dutch and British Economies," *De Economist*, 148, 4 (2000): 471, 483.

112. Appleby, *The Relentless Revolution*, 43–44.

113. Timothy Brook, *Vermeer's Hat: The Seventeenth Century and the Dawn of the Global World* (New York: Bloomsbury Press, 2008), 15–17.

114. Thomson, *Mercenaries, Pirates, and Sovereigns*, 35–36. For Grotius, see the discussion in Chapter 1.

115. Ibid., 36–38.

116. Ibid., 59–64.

117. Ibid., 34.

118. Furber, *Rival Empires of Trade in the Orient*, 40–41.

119. Phillips and Sharman, *International Order in Diversity*, 11–12, 103, 114–116; K. N. Chaudhuri, "The English East India Company's Shipping (c1660–1760)," in Jaap R. Burijhn and Femme S. Gaastra, eds., *Ships, Sailors and Spices: East India Companies and Their Shipping in the 16th, 17th and 18th Centuries* (Amsterdam: NEHA, 1993), 65; Stern, *The Company State*, 3, 6, 12.

120. Stern, *The Company State*, 50–51, discusses the treatment of "interlopers." See the overview of Captain Kidd in this chapter. See also Brian Gardner, *The East India Company* (New York: Dorset Press, 1971), 48–49.

121. Stern, *The Company State*, 77–82; quote is on page 77. Gardner, *The East India Company*, 42–44; quote is on page 44.

122. Adam Smith, *An Inquiry into the Nature and Causes of the Wealth of Nations*, Edwin Cannan, ed. (New York: Modern Library, 1994), 688–690. See also Nicholas Phillipson, *Adam Smith: An Enlightened Life* (New Haven, CT: Yale University Press, 2010), 265–266.

123. Roger Beaumont, *Sword of the Raj: The British Army in India, 1747–1947* (Indianapolis: Bobbs-Merrill, 1977), 31; Thomson, *Mercenaries, Pirates, and Sovereigns*, 38.

124. Stern, *The Company State*, 142–163; Gardner, *The East India Company*, 49.

125. Stern, *The Company State*, 185–196.

126. Furber, *Rival Empires of Trade in the Orient*, 105.

127. Gardner, *The East India Company*, 54–55; Thomson, *Mercenaries, Pirates, and Sovereigns*, 64.

128. Gardner, *The East India Company*, 55–56; G. J. Bryant, "British Logistics and the Conduct of the Carnatic Wars (1746–1783)," *War in History*, 11, 3 (2004): 282.

129. The general overview comes

from Gardner, *The East India Company*, 59–65. The quotations are from Furber, *Rival Empires of Trade in the Orient*, 156.

130. Gardner, *The East India Company*, 65–66; Bryant, "British Logistics and the Carnatic Wars," 286–287.

131. Owen, *The Eighteenth Century*, 189; Anthony Webster, *The Twilight of the East India Company: The Evolution of Anglo-Asia Commerce and Politics, 1790–1860*, Worlds of the East India Company, 3 (Woodbridge, Suffolk, UK: Boydell Press, 2009), 21.

132. Furber, *Rival Empires of Trade in the Orient*, 170.

133. Lucy S. Sutherland, *The East India Company in Eighteenth Century Politics* (Oxford: Oxford University Press, 1952), 77–79, 94.

134. Arthur Young quoted in H. V. Bowen, *The Business of Empire: The East India Company and Imperial Britain, 1756–1833* (Cambridge: Cambridge University Press, 2006), 14.

135. Owen, *The Eighteenth Century*, 189–190; and H. V. Bowen, "British India, 1765–1813: The Metropolitan Context," in Marshall, *The Eighteenth Century*, 536–540.

136. Ibid., 530; Gardner, *The East India Company*, 137–149.

137. Gardner, *The East India Company*, 122–123; Bowen, "British India, 1765–1813," 542–545.

138. Bowen, *The Business of Empire*, 43–44; George III quoted by Raymond Callahan, *The East India Company and Army Reform, 1783–1798* (Cambridge, MA: Harvard University Press, 1972), 45.

139. G. J. Bryant, "Asymmetric Warfare: The British Experience in Eighteenth Century Warfare," *Journal of Military History*, 68 (April 2004): 452–453.

140. Douglas M. Peers, "Gunpowder Empires and the Garrison State: Modernity, Hybridity, and the Political Economy of Colonial India, circa 1750–1860," *Comparative Studies of South Asia, Africa, and the Middle East*, 17, 2 (2007): 248–249.

141. Lawrence James, *Raj: The Making and Unmaking of British India* (New York: St. Martin's Press, 1997), 121.

142. Callahan, *The East India Company and Army Reform*, 49.

143. Bowen, *The Business of Empire*, 48–49.

144. Ibid., 73–73, 205–206.

145. Gardner, *The East India Company*, 171.

146. Ibid., 288–291.

CHAPTER 4. DEFINING THE BALANCE IN A REVOLUTION AND THE CONSTITUTION

1. See the discussion in the previous chapter as well as later in this chapter for more on this.

2. See later in this chapter for an examination of the placement of these words into the Constitution. The genesis of this book comes partly from a few pages of an earlier book I wrote, *Undeclared War and the Future of U.S. Foreign Policy* (Washington, DC, and Baltimore: Woodrow Wilson Center Press and Johns Hopkins University Press, 2008), 11–45, especially pages 30–34. In that book I leaned somewhat sympathetically, but not absolutely, to the arguments made for expanded definitions of marque and reprisal in the modern day. I scarcely considered

the question of "public" and "private" war and its implications, whether in the past, the present, or the future, which I have tried to do in this book.

3. Douglas Edward Leach, *Arms for Empire: A Military History of the British Colonies in North America, 1607–1763* (New York: Macmillan, 1973), 11–12.

4. The four categories and general descriptions come from John K. Mahon, *History of the Militia and the National Guard* (New York: Macmillan, 1973), 31–32.

5. Ibid., 31.

6. Ibid., 32.

7. Leach, *Arms for Empire*, 275–283.

8. Joseph Seymour, *The Pennsylvania Associators, 1747–1777* (Yardley, PA: Westholme Publishing, 2012), xii, xx, 40–41.

9. Matthew Underwood, "'Jealousies of a Standing Army': The Use of Mercenaries in the American Revolution and Its Implications for Congress's Role in Regulating Private Military Firms," *Northwestern University Law Review*, 106, 1 (2012): 324–325; Charles Patrick Neimeyer, *America Goes to War: A Social History of the Continental Army* (New York: New York University Press, 1996), 91–99.

10. John Grenier, *The First Way of War: American War Making on the Frontier* (Cambridge: Cambridge University Press, 2005), 41–43; Neimeyer, *America Goes to War*, 99–100. Also see Colin G. Calloway, *The American Revolution in Indian Country: Crisis and Diversity in Native American Communities* (New York: Cambridge University Press, 1995), 48–49.

11. Grenier, *The First Way of War*, 41–43, 61–65.

12. Leach, *Arms for Empire*, 132–133.

13. Grenier, *The First Way of War*, 41; Reginald C. Stuart, *War and American Thought: From the Revolution to the Monroe Doctrine* (Kent, OH: Kent State University Press, 1982), 14–15.

14. Carl E. Swanson, "American Privateering and Imperial Warfare, 1739–1748," *William and Mary Quarterly*, 42, 3 (July 1985): 357–382.

15. Herbert A. Johnson, "American Constitutionalism and the War for Independence," *Early American Studies*, 14, 1 (Winter 2016): 155.

16. A point made by Andre Corvisier in his essay "Mercenaries," in Andre Corvisier, ed., *A Dictionary of Military History* (Oxford: Blackwell Publishers, 1994), 501–503. The Declaration of Independence no doubt strengthened the judgment against mercenaries, which the French Revolution, Corvisier notes, strongly reinforced.

17. This discussion draws upon Underwood, "Jealousies of a Standing Army," 329–330.

18. Piers Mackesy, *The War for America, 1775–1783* (Lincoln: University of Nebraska Press, 1964, 1992), 39–40.

19. Ibid., 61–62. The figure of 32,000 is drawn from John Brewer, *The Sinews of Power: War, Money and the English State, 1688–1783* (New York: Alfred A. Knopf, 1989), 41. Also see Neimeyer, *America Goes to War*, 53–63.

20. Jeremy Black, *War for America: The Fight for Independence, 1775–1783* (Phoenix Mill, UK: Alan Sutton Publishing, 1991), 50.

21. Jackson Turner Main, *The Sovereign States, 1775–1783* (New York: Franklin Watts, 1973), 224; Sam Willis, *The Struggle for Sea Power: A Naval*

History of the American Revolution (New York: W. W. Norton, 2015), 81.

22. Willis, The Struggle for Sea Power, 82.

23. Louis Arthur Norton, Captains Contentious: The Dysfunctional Sons of the Brine (Columbia: University of South Carolina Press, 2009), 31.

24. Reuben Elmore Stivers, Privateers and Volunteers: The Men and Women of Our Reserve Naval Forces, 1766 to 1866 (Annapolis, MD: Naval Institute Press, 1975), 19–20.

25. Nathan Miller, Sea of Glory: A Naval History of the American Revolution (Charleston, SC: Nautical and Aviation Publishing, 1974), 35.

26. Norton, Captains Contentious, 13; James M. Volo, Blue Water Patriots: The American Revolution Afloat (Westport, CT: Praeger Publishers, 2007), 6.

27. Volo, Blue Water Patriots, 6; Willis, The Struggle for Sea Power, 85–87; John E. Selby, The Revolution in Virginia, 1775–1783 (Williamsburg, VA: Colonial Williamsburg Foundation, 1988), 76; Gene Williamson, Guns on the Chesapeake: The Winning of America's Independence (Bowie, MD: Heritage Books, 1998), 112–113, 177–178.

28. Main, The Sovereign States, 226–227.

29. Willis, The Struggle for Sea Power, 82–83; Robert H. Patton, Patriot Pirates: The Privateer War for Freedom and Fortune in the American Revolution (New York: Pantheon Books, 2008), 30–31.

30. Miller, Sea of Glory, 255. The description of the Massachusetts law and the quotes from it and by John Adams come from C. Kevin Marshall, "Putting Privateers in Their Place: The Applicability of the Marque and Reprisal Clause to Undeclared Wars," University of Chicago Law Review, 64 (Summer 1997), 960–961.

31. Miller, Sea of Glory, 255; Marshall, "Putting Privateers in Their Place," 961; Willis, The Struggle for Sea Power, 93–94.

32. Marshall, "Putting Privateers in Their Place," 961–962; Miller, Sea of Glory, 256. Also see Journals of the Continental Congress, 1774–1789, April 3, 1776, 25–254, http://memory.loc.gov/; and the letter written by John Hancock "to Hon Assembly of New Hampshire. To the Honorable the Assembly of Massachusetts Bay, Assembly of Rhode Island, Assembly of Connecticut. Convention of Virginia," April 12, 1776, Letter of Delegates to Congress, Vol. 3: January 1, 1776–May 15, 1776, https://memory.loc.gov/.

33. Marshall, "Putting Privateers in Their Place," 961–963.

34. Volo, Blue Water Patriots, 45–46; Miller, Sea of Glory, 257–258; Patton, Patriot Pirates, 125–126; Marshall, "Putting Privateers in Their Place," 968–970.

35. Patton, Patriot Pirates, 33–34; Miller, Sea of Glory, 256.

36. Patton, Patriot Pirates, 144–148; Volo, Blue Water Patriots, 45. Also see Richard Buel Jr., In Irons: Britain's Naval Supremacy and the American Revolutionary Economy (New Haven, CT: Yale University Press, 1998), 56–57.

37. Miller, Sea of Glory, 262, 126.

38. Stivers, Privateers and Volunteers, 36–42.

39. Marshall, "Putting Privateers in Their Place," 964–965.

40. The first letter is as quoted in Patton, Patriot Pirates, 47; see also

Robert Morris to William Bingham, December 4, 1776, in *Letters of Delegates to Congress: Vol. 5, August 16, 1776– December 31, 1776,* 573–575, https://memory.loc.gov/.

41. Marshall, "Putting Privateers in Their Place," 967–968.

42. Volo, *Blue Water Patriots,* 46.

43. Stivers, *Privateers and Volunteers,* 26.

44. Volo, *Blue Water Patriots,* 46–47. The figure for Connecticut is from Main, *The Sovereign States,* 247.

45. Volo, *Blue Water Patriots,* 46–47; Miller, *Sea of Glory,* 260–261.

46. Miller, *Sea of Glory,* 260–261.

47. John Adams to General Horatio Gates, March 23, 1776, in Charles Francis Adams, ed., *The Works of John Adams,* vol. I (Boston: Little, Brown, 1856), 206–207 (electronic edition).

48. Ibid., 207.

49. Letter from John Adams to Abigail Adams, April 12, 1776, *Adams Family Papers: An Electronic Archive,* Massachusetts Historical Society, http://www.masshist.org/digitaladams/.

50. Adams to Gates, March 23, 1776 in Adams, *The Works of John Adams,* 207.

51. Eliga H. Gould, *Among the Powers of the Earth: The American Revolution and the Making of a New World Empire* (Cambridge, MA: Harvard University Press, 2012), 114.

52. Geoffrey Best, *War and Law since 1945* (Oxford: Oxford University Press, 1994), 26–35; Harold E. Seleskey, "Colonial America," in Michael Howard, George J. Andreopoulos, and Mark R. Shulman, eds., *The Laws of War: Constraints on Warfare in the Western World* (New Haven, CT: Yale University Press, 1994), 59–85.

53. Gould, *Among the Powers of the Earth,* 18–21.

54. The discussion draws upon Gould, *Among the Powers of the Earth,* 33–40. Also see George William Van Cleve, *We Have Not a Government: The Articles of Confederation and the Road to the Constitution* (Chicago: University of Chicago Press, 2017).

55. Draft of Articles of Confederation, July 12, 1776, attached to the Draft Constitution by the Committee of Detail, 6 August 1787, *The Documentary History of the Ratification of the Constitution, Digital Edition,* ed. John P. Kaminski, Gaspare J. Saladino, Richard Leffler, Charles H. Schoenleber, and Margaret A. Hogan (Charlottesville: University of Virginia Press, 2009).

56. Ibid.; Garrett Epps, *American Epic: Reading the U.S. Constitution* (Oxford: Oxford University Press, 2013), 106–107.

57. Draft of Articles of Confederation, July 12, 1776; Stuart, *War and American Thought,* 27.

58. Draft of Articles of Confederation, July 12, 1776.

59. Act of Confederation of the United States of America, November 15, 1775, *The Documentary History of the Ratification of the Constitution, Digital Edition.*

60. Cathy D. Matson and Peter S. Onuf, *A Union of Interests: Political and Economic Thought in Revolutionary America* (Lawrence: University Press of Kansas, 1990), 31–35.

61. Act of Confederation of the United States of America, November 15, 1776.

62. Franklin, Lee, and Adams to

Sartine, September 17, 1778, *The Revolutionary Diplomatic Correspondence of the United States*, Vol. 2, http://memory.loc.gov.

63. Ibid; the argument that the Declaration of Independence is also a declaration of war is drawn from Brien Hallett, *The Lost Art of Declaring War* (Urbana: University of Illinois Press, 1998), 48, 52–56.

64. J. Adams to the President of Congress, January 18, 1781, *The Revolutionary Diplomatic Correspondence of the United States*, Vol. 4, electronic edition.

65. J. Adams to the President of Congress, August 8, 1781, ibid.

66. "Committee Report on Carrying the Confederation into Effect and on Additional Powers Needed by Congress, August 22, 1781," in *The Documentary History of the Ratification of the Constitution, Digital Edition*.

67. Douglas J. Sylvester, "International Law as Sword or Shield? Early American Foreign Policy and the Law of Nations," *Journal of International Law and Politics*, 32 (1999): 13–21. For Talbot and the *Betsey* see Theodore M. Cooperstein, "Letters of Marque and Reprisal: The Constitutional Law of Privateering," *Journal of Maritime Law and Commerce*, 40, 2 (April 2009): 226–231.

68. Joel H. Samuels, "How Piracy Has Shaped the Relationship between American Law and International Law," *American University Law Review*, 59, 5 (June 2010): 1235–1243. Pinckney as quoted in this article.

69. Extract of a letter from a merchant in London to his friend in America, dated October 3, 1787, *New York Journal*, December 6, 1787, *The Documentary History of the Ratification of the Constitution, Digital Edition*.

70. New York Assembly, Remarks on an Act for Regulating Elections, February 6, 1787, *Founders Online*, National Archives, last modified July 12, 2016, http://founders.archives.gov/documents/Hamilton/01-04-02-0017.

71. Emer de Vattel, *The Law of Nations* (Indianapolis: Liberty Fund, 2008), 83.

72. Anthony J. Bellia Jr. and Bradford R. Clark, "The Law of Nations as Constitutional Law," *Virginia Law Review*, 98, 4 (June 2012): 754.

73. Michael J. Klarman, *The Framers' Coup: The Making of the United States Constitution* (New York: Oxford University Press, 2016), 11–16.

74. Bellia and Clark, "The Law of Nations as Constitutional Law," 735–736 and 746–747; Frederick W. Marks III, *Independence on Trial: Foreign Affairs and the Making of the Constitution* (Baton Rouge: Louisiana State University Press, 1973), 142.

75. John Jay, *The Federalist No. 3* introduction by Garry Wills (New York: Bantam, 1982), 13.

76. Gilbert L. Lycan, *Alexander Hamilton and American Foreign Policy: A Design for Greatness* (Norman: University of Oklahoma Press, 1970), 21–22.

77. Bellia and Clark, "The Law of Nations as Constitutional Law," 759; James Madison, *Vices of the Political System of the United States*, April 1787, *Founders Online*, National Archives, https://founders.archives.gov/documents/Madison/01-09-02-0187.

78. *The Documentary History of the Ratification of the Constitution, Digital*

Edition, originally for Ratification by the States, Volume X: Virginia, No. 3.

79. James Madison, *Federalist No. 41*, introduction by Garry Wills, 244.

80. Stuart, *War and American Thought*, 60.

81. Ibid., 61.

82. Draft Constitution by the Committee of Detail, August 6, 1787, *The Documentary History of the Ratification of the Constitution, Digital Edition*.

83. Stuart, *War and American Thought*, 62, 89.

84. I draw on my own discussion of Burlamaqui in *Undeclared War and the Future of U.S. Foreign Policy*, but Burlamaqui is easily found online. See J. J. Burlamaqui, *The Principles of Political Law*, 5th ed. (Boston: University Press, W. Hilliard, 1807), electronic edition, http://constitution.org/burla/burla_.htm, 1, 2, 5.

85. Ibid.

86. Alexander Hamilton, *Federalist No. 25*, introduction by Garry Wills, 146.

87. In an article in 2008 Kathryn L. Einspanier argues that some of the framers knew these writers quite well. See her article "Burlamaqui, the Constitution, and the Imperfect War on Terror," *Georgetown Law Journal*, 96 (March 2008): 991, 1005–1006.

88. James Madison, *Notes of Debates in the Federal Convention* (New York: W. W. Norton, 1966), 475–476. The discussion draws upon David Gray Adler, "The Constitution and Presidential Warmaking," in David Gray Adler and Larry N. George, eds., *The Constitution and the Conduct of American Foreign Policy* (Lawrence: University Press of Kansas, 1996), 185; and Francis D. Wormuth

and Edwin B. Firmage, *To Chain the Dog of War: The War Power of Congress in History and Law*, 2nd ed. (Urbana: University of Illinois Press, 1989), 18. The question as to whether Congress has actual powers in the management and conduct of war remains unanswered in spite of the commander-in-chief clause in the Constitution (Article 2, Section 2) that many use to argue Congress should not have or exercise such powers. Yet, of course, it does by defining the size and configuration of force structure in legislation, providing funding, conducting hearings on the execution of a conflict, and passing legislation that may set deadlines for the conduct of military operations.

89. William Blackstone, *Commentaries on the Laws of England: A Facsimile of the First Edition of 1765–1769*, vol. I (Chicago: University of Chicago Press, 1979), 150. An electronic copy of this edition can also be found online.

90. The point about reprisals as a form of limited war is discussed in Michael D. Ramsey, *The Constitution's Text in Foreign Affairs* (Cambridge, MA: Harvard University Press, 2007), 221–222. Also see Jules Lobel, "Covert War and Congressional Authority: Hidden War and Forgotten Power," *University of Pennsylvania Law Review*, 134 (June 1986): 1060–1061.

91. *The Documentary History of the Ratification of the Constitution, Digital Edition*.

92. John Hart Ely, *War and Responsibility: Constitutional Lessons of Vietnam and Its Aftermath* (Princeton, NJ: Princeton University Press, 1993), 67, 74. An informative discussion of the pros and cons in this argument

about the meaning of the marque and reprisal clause is found in Jay Wexler, *The Odd Clauses: Understanding the Constitution through Ten of Its Most Curious Provisions* (Boston: Beacon Press, 2011), 119–137.

93. Louis Fisher, *Presidential War Power*, 2nd ed. (Lawrence: University Press of Kansas, 2004), 7.

94. Ibid.

95. Lobel, "Covert War and Congressional Authority," 1045–1046, 1058.

96. Ibid., 1051.

97. Marshall, "Putting Privateers in Their Place," 980–981.

98. John Yoo, *The Powers of War and Peace: The Constitution and Foreign Affairs after 9/11* (Chicago: University of Chicago Press, 2005), 147–148.

99. Ramsey, *Constitution's Text in Foreign Affairs*, 221–231.

100. Wormuth and Firmage, *To Chain the Dog of War*, 37.

101. Wexler, *The Odd Clauses*, 133.

102. George C. Daughan, *If By Sea: The Forging of the American Navy—from the Revolution to the War of 1812* (New York: Basic Books, 2008), 250–253.

103. Stuart, *War and American Thought*, 50–53.

104. Robert W. Tucker and David C. Hendrickson, *Empire of Liberty: The Statecraft of Thomas Jefferson* (New York: Oxford University Press, 1984), 40–41.

105. Daughan, *If By Sea*, 266.

106. Stanley Elkins and Eric McKitrick, *The Age of Federalism: The Early American Republic, 1788–1800* (New York: Oxford University Press, 1993), 337–340.

107. Ibid., 330–335.

108. Ibid., 335–336; Daughan, *If By Sea*, 272–273.

109. A good discussion and review of the events surrounding Genet's mission can be found in Elkins and McKitrick, *The Age of Federalism*, 330–373.

110. Ibid., Jefferson's meetings with Genet and the quotations come from pp. 345–346. Genet's life in the United States is on pages 372–373.

111. Alexander Hamilton to Richard Harison, June 13–15, 1793, Founders Online, National Archives, last modified December 28, 2016, http://founders.archives.gov/documents/Hamilton/01-14-02-0373.

112. Daughan, *If By Sea*, 276–277.

113. Elkins and McKitrick, *The Age of Federalism*, 378–406, offers a good overview of the lead-up to the negotiations of Jay's Treaty.

114. Daughan, *If By Sea*, 279–281, 293–294; John Adams to Abigail Adams, March 15, 1794, *Adams Family Papers: An Electronic Archive*, Massachusetts Historical Society, http://www.masshist.org/digitaladams/.

115. Daughan, *If By Sea*, 289–291.

116. Ibid., 296–298, 304.

117. Ibid., 304.

118. Ibid., 304–307.

119. Elkins and McKitrick give a very comprehensive overview of the events and personalities in *The Age of Federalism*, 549–579.

120. Ibid., 583.

121. Lycan, *Alexander Hamilton and American Foreign Policy*, 216–222, 251.

122. Ibid., 274–275, 313; Elkins and McKitrick, *The Age of Federalism*, 583–584; Alexander DeConde, *The Quasi-War: The Politics and Diplomacy of the Undeclared War with France, 1797–1801* (New York: Charles Scribner's Sons, 1966), 64–65. Also see Bellia and

Clark, "The Law of Nations as Constitutional Law," 774–776.

123. Elkins and McKitrick, *The Age of Federalism*, 584–585.

124. For an international context see Bruce D. Porter, *War and the Rise of the State: The Military Foundations of Modern Politics* (New York: Free Press, 1994), 252–255.

125. Daughan, *If By Sea*, 312–315.

126. Ibid., 314–315. The definitive study of this private/public divide in naval construction is Frederick C. Leiner, *Millions for Defense: The Subscription Warships of 1798* (Annapolis, MD: Naval Institute Press, 2000).

127. See Elkins and McKitrick, *The Age of Federalism*, 614, for historical context and part of the story. The remaining source, including the quotation of President Adams, comes from Michael V. Seitzinger, *Conducting Foreign Relations without Authority: The Logan Act*, CRS Report for Congress, RL 33265, January 20, 2010 (Washington, DC: Congressional Research Service, Library of Congress, 2010 version and updated as needed), 1–2.

128. Ibid., 2.

129. Gregory E. Fehlings, "America's First Limited War," *Naval War College Review*, Newport Papers (Summer 2000), 12–13, http://www.nwc.navy.mil/press/Review/2000/summer/art4-Suo.htm.

130. Daughan, *If By Sea*, 334–340.

131. DeConde, *The Quasi-War*, 103–107, 328.

132. Fehlings, "America's First Limited War," 14; J. Gregory Sidak, "The Quasi War Cases—and Their Relevance to Whether 'Letters of Marque and Reprisal' Constrain Presidential War Powers," *Harvard Journal of Law and Public Policy*, 28, 2 (2004): 484; William R. Casto, *The Supreme Court of the Early Republic: The Chief Justiceships of John Jay and Oliver Ellsworth* (Columbia: University of South Carolina Press, 1995), 121.

133. Fehlings, "America's First Limited War," 14–15; Sidak, "The Quasi War Cases," 484–485; also see the text of *Bas v. Tingy* 4 Dall. 37 (1800), http://press-pubs.uchicago.edu/founders/.

CHAPTER 5. THE RETURN AND RETREAT OF PRIVATE FORCE FOR PROFIT

1. The literature of the national security state is so immense that any effort to list it in an endnote would be unfairly arbitrary. Having worked in and around it for over three decades, I would say that my own outlook and conclusions were shaped by an endless interplay between daily responsibilities and a boundless literature that explained, justified, or attacked the assumptions, arguments, institutions, and practices of the national security state. However, the work that most captured my attention in noting the disparity between the early acceptance of private force and the more recent rejection or discomfort with it is in Nicholas Parillo, "The De-Privatization of American Warfare: How the U.S. Government Used, Regulated, and Ultimately Abandoned Privateering in the Nineteenth Century," *Yale Journal of Law and the Humanities*, 19, 1 (Winter 2007): 1–95.

2. David C. Hendrickson, *Peace Pact: The Lost World of the American Founding* (Lawrence: University Press of Kansas, 2003), 163–170.

3. Paul A. Gilje, *Free Trade and Sailor's Rights in the War of 1812* (Cambridge: Cambridge University Press, 2013), 14–28.

4. Peter S. Onuf, *Jefferson's Empire: The Language of American Nationhood* (Charlottesville: University Press of Virginia, 2000), 67–71.

5. Gilje, *Free Trade and Sailor's Rights*, 28–29.

6. Donald R. Hickey, *The War of 1812: A Forgotten Conflict* (Urbana: University of Illinois Press, 1989), 10–13.

7. Ibid., 13–16.

8. Reginald C. Stuart, *War and American Thought: From the Revolution to the Monroe Doctrine* (Kent, OH: Kent State University Press, 1982), 99.

9. Hickey, *The War of 1812*, 7–9. Hickey quotes the term "militia of the sea," although it may not have come into popular use until later in the nineteenth century; see Reuben Elmore Stivers, *Privateers and Volunteers: The Men and Women of Our Reserve Naval Forces, 1766 to 1866* (Annapolis, MD: Naval Institute Press, 1975), 105. Certainly others had expressed such sentiments; see John Adams's remarks in the previous chapter.

10. Thomas Jefferson, Fourth Annual Message to Congress, November 8, 1804, http://avalon.law.yale.edu/19th_century/jeffmes4.asp.

11. The article Jefferson wrote is reproduced in George Coggeshall, *History of the American Privateers and Letters-of-Marque during Our War with England in the Years 1812, 13 and 14* (New York: C. T. Evans, 1856), xliv. It is also interestingly provided in its entirety on the website of Feral Jundi, which is devoted to contemporary operations of private military contractors. See http://feraljundi.com/2392/letter-of-marque-thomas-jefferson-on-privateering-July-4-1812.

12. The points about convertibility and cost are drawn from Kevin D. McCranie, *Utmost Gallantry: The U.S. and Royal Navies at Sea in the War of 1812* (Annapolis, MD: Naval Institute Press, 2011), 17.

13. Roger H. Brown, *The Republic in Peril: 1812* (New York: W. W. Norton, 1964), 17–22; Hickey, *The War of 1812*, 16–22.

14. The role of international legal considerations is discussed in Stuart, *War and American Thought*, 109–113.

15. The characterization is from Garry Wills's biography, *James Madison* (New York: Henry Holt, Times Books, 2002), 63. I cannot say I have found anything to suggest otherwise.

16. Stuart in *War and American Thought*, 113–114, argues for Madison's consideration of limited war; Hickey in *The War of 1812*, 20–22, represents the more prevalent view of Madison.

17. Hickey, *The War of 1812*, 21–23; Brown, *The Republic in Peril*, 22–25; Gilje, *Free Trade and Sailors Rights*, 165.

18. J. C. A. Stagg, *Mr. Madison's War: Politics, Diplomacy, and Warfare in the Early American Republic, 1783–1830* (Princeton, NJ: Princeton University Press, 1983), 79–80.

19. Ibid., 91–110; Hickey, *The War of 1812*, 29–43.

20. See Adam Jortner, *The Gods of Prophetstown: The Battle of Tippecanoe and the Holy War for the American Frontier* (New York: Oxford University Press, 2012), 155–224.

21. Deborah Rosen, Border Law: The First Seminole War and American Nationhood (Cambridge, MA: Harvard University Press, 2015).

22. The entire text of Madison's message to Congress is in Russell D. Buhite, ed., Calls to Arms: Presidential Speeches, Messages, and Declarations of War (Wilmington, DE: Scholarly Resources, 2003), 25–31.

23. Ibid.

24. Hickey, The War of 1812, 44–45. The figures on naval strength come from Jon Latimer, 1812: War with America (Cambridge, MA: Belknap Press of Harvard University Press, 2007), 84–85.

25. Declaration of War, June 18, 1812, http://www.historyguy.com/war _of_1812_declaration_of_war.htm; Hickey, The War of 1812, 45–47; Brown, The Republic in Peril, 108–130.

26. Brown, The Republic in Peril, 110.

27. John Philips Cranwell and William Bowers Crane, Men of Marque: A History of Private Armed Vessels out of Baltimore during the War of 1812 (New York: W. W. Norton, 1940), 22.

28. Ibid.

29. Ibid., 163–164, 343; Faye M. Kert, Privateering: Patriots and Profits in the War of 1812 (Baltimore: Johns Hopkins University Press, 2015), 72; Jerome R. Garitee, The Republic's Private Navy: The American Privateering Business as Practiced by Baltimore during the War of 1812 (Middletown, CT: Wesleyan University Press, 1977), 37–38.

30. Kert, Privateering: Patriots and Profits, 71.

31. Cranwell and Crane, Men of Marque, 22–23.

32. Ibid., 18 and 45–46. The full text

of a commission is provided in the latter pages.

33. Ibid., 18.

34. Parrillo, "The De-Privatization of American Warfare," 25.

35. Ibid., 33–34.

36. Garitee, The Republic's Private Navy, 20–27.

37. Ibid., 26–28.

38. Ibid., 26–31.

39. Kert, Privateering: Patriots and Profits, 38.

40. Garitee, The Republic's Private Navy, 32–46.

41. Crandall and Crane, Men of Marque, 37–39.

42. Hickey, The War of 1812, 91–92.

43. Stephen Budiansky provides a vivid description of some of the recruiting conditions and practices in Perilous Fight: America's Intrepid War with the British on the High Seas, 1812–1815 (New York: Alfred A. Knopf, 2010), 290–291. Many of the details come from Garitee, The Republic's Private Navy, 91–92, 127–134.

44. Kert, Privateering: Patriots and Profits, 8, 36, 79, 87.

45. Ibid., 8.

46. Hickey, The War of 1812, 96; Budiansky, Perilous Fight, 288.

47. Kert, Privateering: Patriots and Profits, 78–79.

48. Ibid., 36–37, 85.

49. Latimer, 1812: War with America, 100–101.

50. Kert, Privateering: Patriots and Profits, 79.

51. Latimer, 1812: War with America, 99–102.

52. Troy Brickham, The Weight of Vengeance: The United States, the British Empire, and the War of 1812 (Oxford:

Oxford University Press, 2012), 152–155.

53. Hickey, *The War of 1812*, 217–219; McCranie, *Utmost Gallantry*, 248–249.

54. Budiansky, *Perilous Fight*, 288, uses this figure while Kert, *Privateering: Patriots and Profits*, 86, notes the range between 1,500 to 2,500 vessels and leans closer to nearly 2,000.

55. Kenneth J. Hagan, *This People's Navy: The Making of American Sea Power* (New York: Free Press, 1991), 20.

56. Coggeshall, *History of the American Privateers and Letters-of-Marque*, xlviii–l.

57. Admittedly, modern contractors often provide forms or insurance and other benefits, but standards are not uniform, and treatment of foreign nationals versus citizens of the employer's own country can vary. The broader question of who is remembered and who is forgotten painfully remains.

58. Michael J. Crawford, "Taking the Moral High Ground: The United States, Privateering, and Immunity of Private Property at Sea," *International Journal of Naval History*, 12, 1 (January 2015): 2–3, http://www.ijnhonline.org/2015/01/.

59. As quoted in ibid., 3.

60. Ibid., 5–6; John Fabian Witt, *Lincoln's Code: The Laws of War in American History* (New York; Free Press, 2012), 44–45.

61. This discussion draws from Witt, *Lincoln's Code*, 44–47.

62. Crawford, "Taking the Moral High Ground," 8–9; Gilje, *Free Trade and Sailors' Rights*, 298–300.

63. Witt, *Lincoln's Code*, 70–71.

64. Crawford, "Taking the Moral High Ground," 7–8.

65. Joseph Story, *Commentaries on the Constitution of the United States*, Chapter 21, "The Power to Declare War and Make Captures," 3–4, http://www.constitution.org/js/js_005.htm.

66. Ibid, 4.

67. Ibid., 4–5.

68. James Kent, *Commentaries on American Law*, Part I, Lecture II, "Of the Rights and Duties of Nations in a State of Peace" (New York: O. Halstead, 1826), 15–16, http://www.constitution.org/jk/jk.ooo.htm. Kent's *Commentaries* have undergone numerous revisions; this link reflects the fifteenth edition, done by Jon Roland 1997–2002. Using it requires caution to prevent citation of language added for later editions.

69. Ibid., Part I, Lecture III, "Of the Declaration, and Other Early Measures of War," 6–7; Witt, *Lincoln's Code*, 71.

70. Ibid., Part I, Lecture V, "Of the Rights of Belligerents," 8–10.

71. Peter Earle, *The Pirate Wars* (New York: St. Martin's, 2003), 212–214; Caitlin Fitz, *Our Sister Republics: The United States in an Age of American Revolutions* (New York: Liveright Publishing, 2016), 110, 170–172.

72. Fitz, *Our Sister Republics*, 170–172; Earle, *The Pirate Wars*, 214–215; David Head, "New Nations, New Connections: Spanish American Privateering from the United States and the Development of Atlantic Relations," *Early American Studies*, 11, 1 (Winter 2013): 163.

73. Earle, *The Pirate Wars*, 214–215; Joseph Gibbs, *Dead Men Tell No Tales: The Lives and Legends of the Pirate Charles Gibbs* (Columbia: University of South Carolina Press, 2007), 36–37; William C. Davis, *The Pirates Lafitte: The*

Treacherous World of the Corsairs of the Gulf (Orlando, FL: Harcourt, 2005), 69–70.

74. Gibbs, *Dead Men Tell No Tales*, 37; Patrick R. Browning, "The Gran Para: The Delicate Dance of South American Privateering from Baltimore," paper written in fulfillment of the Doctor of Jurisprudence, Francis King Carey School of Law (2015), 8.

75. Browning, "The Gran Para," 6–7.

76. Head, "New Nations: New Connections," 168–170.

77. Sean T. Perrone, "John Stoughton and the *Divina Pastora* Prize Case, 1816–1819," *Journal of the Early Republic*, 28 (Summer 2008): 217–218; Browning, "The Gran Para," 9.

78. Gibbs, *Dead Men Tell No Tales*, 38.

79. Earle, *The Pirate Wars*, 216–217, 234.

80. Browning, "The Gran Para," 9.

81. Davis, *The Pirates Lafitte*, 402–403.

82. Earle, *The Pirate Wars*, 234.

83. Davis, *The Pirates Lafitte*, 402–406.

84. Ibid., 419, 448–449.

85. Janice E. Thomson, *Mercenaries, Pirates, and Sovereigns: State Building and Extraterritorial Violence in Early Modern Europe* (Princeton, NJ: Princeton University Press, 1994), 118–142.

86. Robert E. May, *Manifest Destiny's Underworld: Filibustering in Antebellum America* (Chapel Hill, NC: University of North Carolina Press, 2002), xi, xv.

87. See Thomson's account in *Mercenaries, Pirates, and Sovereigns*, 135–137. May's account is about a page; see also May, *Manifest Destiny's Underworld*, 5–6.

88. Thomson, *Mercenaries, Pirates, and Sovereigns*, 118–119.

89. May, *Manifest Destiny's Underworld*, 7.

90. Ibid., 7–9, 143 (quotation), 143–156.

91. Ibid., 81–31.

92. Ibid., 40–51.

93. Ibid., 111–116.

94. Crawford, "Taking the High Moral Ground," 10–11; Jan Martin Lemnitzer, "'That Moral League of Nations against the United States': The Origins of the 1856 Declaration of Paris," *International History Review*, 35, 5 (2013): 1069; Robert C. Ritchie, "Government Measures against Piracy and Privateering in the Atlantic Area, 1750–1850," in David J. Starkey, E. S. van Eyck van Heslinga, and J. A. Moor, eds., *Pirates and Privateers: New Perspectives on the War on Trade in the Eighteenth and Nineteenth Centuries* (Exeter, UK: University of Exeter Press, 1997), 23.

95. Lemnitzer, "That Moral League of Nations against the United States," 1069; Witt, *Lincoln's Code*, 133–134.

96. Lemnitzer, "That Moral League of Nations against the United States," 1069, 1070–1071, 1073–1074; Crawford, "Taking the Moral High Ground," 11.

97. Ibid., 11, electronic edition; Lemnitzer, "That Moral League of Nations against the United States," 1077.

98. Crawford, "Taking the Moral High Ground," 12.

99. Remarks of the Honorable Timothy Davis, "The Privateer System," July 23, 1856, *Addenda to the Congressional Record, Congressional Record*, 34th Congress, 1st Session, U.S. House of Representatives.

100. Lemnitzer, "That Moral League of Nations against the United States," 1081–1082 (quotation on last page); Witt, *Lincoln's Code*, 135.

101. See Witt, *Lincoln's Code*, 1–4, 173–196, 229–246.

102. *The Lieber Code: Instructions for the Government of Armies of the United States in the Field*, General Orders No.100, promulgated on April 24, 1863, by Abraham Lincoln, http://www.msn.com/?ocid=U218DHP&pc=EUPP_U218.

103. Rotem Giladi, "Francis Lieber on Public War," *Goettingen Journal of International Law*, 4, 2 (2012): 450.

104. Ibid.

105. William Morrison Robinson Jr., *The Confederate Privateers* (Columbia: University of South Carolina Press, 1990; originally published by Yale University Press in 1928), 7–8.

106. Ibid., 13–17. Robinson reproduces the text of Davis's letter on 15–16.

107. Ibid., 18–24.

108. Ibid., 25–30.

109. Lindsey S. Butler, *Pirates, Privateers, and Rebel Raiders of the Carolina Coast* (Chapel Hill: University of North Carolina Press, 2000), 18–22; Stivers, *Privateers and Volunteers*, 229–230.

110. Witt, *Lincoln's Code*, 141–149.

111. Stephen C. Neff, *Justice in Blue and Gray: A Legal History of the Civil War* (Cambridge, MA: Harvard University Press, 2010), 32–34.

112. Ibid., 22–23; Robinson, *The Confederate Privateers*, 133–140; Burrus M. Carnahan, *Lincoln on Trial: Southern Civilians and the Law of War* (Lexington: University Press of Kentucky, 2010), 16–18; Stivers, *Privateers and Volunteers*, 188–189.

113. Robinson, *The Confederate Privateers*, 307–311.

114. Ibid., 311–313. The text of Welles's letter is on 312. Also see Stivers, *Privateers and Volunteers*, 190.

115. Stivers, *Privateers and Volunteers*, 191.

116. Witt, *Lincoln's Code*, 160–161; Crawford, "Taking the Moral High Ground," 12.

117. Stivers, *Privateers and Volunteers*, 192–193 and 419–420. The entire text of Welles's letter, dated March 31, 1863, is found in Stivers on 418–422.

118. Ibid., 192–196.

119. Parillo, "The De-Privatization of American Warfare," 73–76.

120. Ibid., 77–79, 82–84.

121. Crawford, "Taking the Moral High Ground," 12–14.

122. Parillo, "The De-Privatization of American Warfare," 85–90.

123. Ibid., 87; Crawford, "Taking the Moral High Ground," 14–17.

124. Ibid., 20–21.

CHAPTER 6. THE PRIVATIZATION OF WAR

1. See, for example, Bartholomew H. Sparrow, *From the Outside In: World War II and the American State* (Princeton, NJ: Princeton University Press, 1996); and James T. Sparrow, *Warfare State: World War II Americans and the Age of Big Government* (New York: Oxford University Press, 2011).

2. Alejandro Colas and Bryan Mabee, "Introduction: Private Violence in Historical Context," in Colas and Mabee, eds., *Mercenaries, Pirates, Bandits and Empires: Private Violence in Historical Context* (New York: Columbia University Press, 2010), 4.

3. Colas and Mabee make this same point on page 4 as well, even though

they do not use the United States or Great Britain as examples.

4. Sean McFate, *The Modern Mercenary: Private Armies and What They Mean for World Order* (Oxford and New York: Oxford University Press, 2014), 36–37.

5. This draws largely on ibid., 37, but also see David Shearer, *Private Armies and Military Intervention*, Adelphi Paper 316, International Institute for Strategic Studies (Oxford: Oxford University Press, 1998), 15.

6. Mary Kaldor, *New and Old Wars: Organized Violence in a Global Era*, 2nd ed. (Stanford, CA: Stanford University Press, 1990–2001), 6–7.

7. Ibid., 2.

8. Graham Parsons, "Public War and the Moral Equality of Combatants," *Journal of Military Ethics*, 11, 4 (2012), 299–300.

9. Claire Cutler, "Artifice, Ideology and Paradox: The Public/Private Distinction in International Law," *Review of International Political Economy*, 4, 2 (Summer 1997), 275.

10. Ibid., 275.

11. Valerie Sperling, *Altered States: The Globalization of Accountability* (Cambridge: Cambridge University Press, 2009), 8–10.

12. Ibid., 12–13.

13. Laura A. Dickinson, "Public Participation/Private Contract," *Social Justice*, 34, 3–4 (2007–2008), 150.

14. Kenneth B. Moss, *Undeclared War and the Future of U.S. Foreign Policy* (Washington, DC, and Baltimore: Woodrow Wilson Center Press and Johns Hopkins University Press, 2008), 76–77; Louis Fisher, *Presidential War Power*, 2nd ed. (Lawrence: University Press of Kansas, 2004), 88–94.

15. Sperling, *Altered States*, 15–17.

16. Dickinson, "Public Participation/Private Contract," 150–151.

17. P. W. Singer, *Corporate Warriors: The Rise of the Privatized Military Industry* (Ithaca, NY: Cornell University Press, 2003), 53; McFate, *The Modern Mercenary*, 43; Mark Erbel, "The Underlying Causes of Military Outsourcing in the USA and UK: Bridging the Persistent Gaps between Ends, Ways, and Means since the Beginning of the Cold War," *Defence Studies*, 17, 2 (2017): 138.

18. Singer, *Corporate Warriors*, 53–54; William D. Hartung, "The International Arms Trade," in Paul D. Williams, ed., *Security Studies: An Introduction*, 2nd ed. (New York: Routledge, 2013), 444–445.

19. Some of this discussion draws from Deborah D. Avant, *The Market for Force: The Consequences of Privatizing Security* (Cambridge: Cambridge University Press, 2005), 33–34. Also see Singer, *Corporate Warriors*, 50–51.

20. See my discussion in *Undeclared War and the Future of U.S. Foreign Policy*, 97–102, 138–142. Also see Sheena Chestnut Greitens and Theo Farrell, "Humanitarian Intervention and Peace Operations," in John Baylis, James J. Wirtz, and Colin S. Gray, eds., *Strategy in the Contemporary World*, 4th ed. (New York: Oxford University Press, 2013), 286–302.

21. Singer, *Corporate Warriors*, 55–60; Shearer, *Private Armies and Military Intervention*, 27–29. Also see for this endnote as well as the discussion addressed in several of the previous notes Mary K. Feeney, "Public Wars and Private Armies: Militaries, Mercenaries, and Public Values,"

paper presented at the Copenhagen International Public Value Workshop, University of Copenhagen, Denmark, May 28–31, 2008, 6–9, https://www.re searchgate.net/publication/267822422.

22. See Martin Shaw, *Post-Military Society: Militarism, Demilitarization and War at the End of the Twentieth Century* (Philadelphia: Temple University Press, 1991), 184–189; and Charles C. Moskos, John Allen Williams, and David R. Segal, "Armed Forces after the Cold War," in Moskos, Williams, and Segal, eds., *The Postmodern Military: Armed Forces after the Cold War* (New York: Oxford University Press, 2000), 2. Also see Thomas Waldman, "Vicarious Warfare: The Counterproductive Consequences of Modern American Military Practice," *Contemporary Security Policy*, 39, 2 (2018): 181–182; Robert Mandel, *Security, Strategy, and the Quest for Bloodless War* (Boulder, CO: Lynne Rienner Publishers, 2004), 48; and J. Marshall Beier, "Discriminating Tastes: 'Smart' Bombs, Non-Combatants, and Notions of Legitimacy in Warfare," *Security Dialogue*, 34 (December 2003): 413. A sample of the public opinion from the first decade after 2000 is discussed in Scott Bittle and Jonathan Rochkind with Amber Ott, "Confidence in U.S. Foreign Policy Index: Anxious Public Pulling Back from Use of Force," *Public Agenda*, 4 (Spring 2007): 10, www .publicagenda.org. Also see McFate's discussion on "humanizing war" in *The Modern Mercenary*, 44–45.

23. See the discussion in Jacques S. Gansler, *Democracy's Arsenal: Creating a Twenty-First-Century Defense Industry* (Cambridge: MIT Press, 2011), 254–258.

24. Since 2012–2013 the school has been known as the Dwight D. Eisenhower School for National Resource and Security Strategy, or to prevent one of the largest business cards around, the Eisenhower School.

25. See Paul A. C. Koistinen, *Arsenal of World War II: The Political Economy of American Warfare, 1940–1945* (Lawrence: University Press of Kansas, 2004); and *State of War: The Political Economy of American Warfare, 1945–2011* (Lawrence: University Press of Kansas, 2012), 4–7.

26. Koistinen, *State of War*, 74–80.

27. Peter Dombrowski and Eugene Gholz, *Buying Military Transformation: Technological Innovation and the Defense Industry* (New York: Columbia University Press, 2006), 29–31. Also see Erbel, "The Underlying Causes of Military Outsourcing in the USA and UK," 143.

28. "Military-Industrial Complex Speech, Dwight D. Eisenhower, 1961," http://avalon.law.yale.edu/20th_cen tury/eisenhower001.asp.

29. "Presence of Contractor Personnel during U.S. Military Operations," table 2, in Congressional Budget Office, *Contractor's Support of U.S. Operations in Iraq* (Washington, DC: Congress of the United States, August 2008), 13.

30. Laura A. Dickinson, *Outsourcing War and Peace: Preserving Public Values in a World of Privatized Foreign Affairs* (New Haven, CT: Yale University Press, 2011), 24–30; "quasi-contractor" is on 28. Also see pages 8–9 for discussion of public values. The ratio figures for Vietnam and Iraq are from Congressional Budget Office, *Contractors' Support of U.S. Operations in Iraq*, 13.

31. Paul R. Verkuil, *Outsourcing*

Sovereignty: Why Privatization of Government Functions Threatens Democracy and What We Can Do about It (Cambridge: Cambridge University Press, 2007), 9–13.

32. William A. Taylor, *Military Service and American Democracy: From World War II to the Iraq and Afghanistan Wars* (Lawrence: University Press of Kansas, 2016), 110–125.

33. See Chapter 1, 29–30; also Elke Krahmann, *States, Citizens and the Privatization of Security* (Cambridge: Cambridge University Press, 2010), 12–13.

34. See Mark A. Smith, *The Right Talk: How Conservatives Transformed the Great Society into the Economic Society* (Princeton, NJ: Princeton University Press, 2007); and Nicholas Wapshott, *Keynes Hayek: The Clash That Defined Modern Economics* (New York: W. W. Norton, 2011). A general history of neoliberalism is Daniel Stedman Jones, *Masters of the Universe: Hayek, Friedman, and the Birth of Neoliberal Politics* (Princeton, NJ: Princeton University Press, 2012). Also see the brief discussion in McFate, *The Modern Mercenary*, 41–43.

35. Krahmann, *Citizens and the Privatization of Security*, 34.

36. Aaron Ettinger, "Neoliberalism and the Rise of the Private Military Industry," *International Journal*, 66, 3 (Summer 2011): 750.

37. Ibid., 750.

38. Anna Leander, "The Impunity of Private Authority: Understanding PSC Accountability," paper presented at the International Studies Association Conference, February 28–March 3, 2007, 11–12. http://openarchive.cbs. dk/bitstream/handle/10398/6985/lean der_isa07_woc-wp89.pdf?sequence=1.

39. The summary is largely from Singer, *Corporate Warriors*, 60–64; and McFate, *The Modern Mercenary*, 45–48. The worry about economic dislocation caused by high defense spending had been one of Eisenhower's concerns as well.

40. Gansler, *Democracy's Arsenal*, 300. A brief discussion of "inherently governmental" occurs later in this chapter.

41. Ibid., 298–306.

42. Summary of Change, Army Regulations (AR) 700-137, Logistics Civil Augmentation Program, Headquarters, Department of the Army, Washington, DC, December 16, 1985. http://www.aschq.army.mil/support ingdocs/AR700_137.pdf.

43. Ibid., 6; the page numbers cited in this document are those as they would be numbered based on the entire document and not the numbering given by the army, which includes three or four pages of blank or regulatory clarification. Also see Moss, *Undeclared War and the Future of U.S. Foreign Policy*, 92–94, 132–136.

44. See AR 700-137, Section 2-4, Risk, 7, and chapter 3, Procedures, 8.

45. Ibid., Glossary, 10.

46. Ibid., Sections 2-4, Risk, and 3-2, Contract Considerations, 7. Also see Ettinger, "Neoliberalism and the Rise of the Private Military Industry."

47. Singer, *Corporate Warriors*, 91–100.

48. McFate, *The Modern Mercenary*, 16–17.

49. Ibid., 15.

50. Avant, *The Market for Force*, 16–17.

51. Shearer, *Private Armies and Military Intervention*, 25.

52. Deborah C. Kidwell, *Public War, Private Fight? The United States and Private Military Companies*, Global War on Terrorism Occasional Papers 12 (Fort Leavenworth, KS: Combat Studies Institute Press, 2005), 18–19.

53. Department of Defense, "Improving the Combat Edge through Outsourcing," *Defense Issues*, 11, 30 (March 1996). Pagination for this report varies depending which DOD website is used. See http://www.dod.mil/pubs/foi/Reading_Room/Selected_Acquisition_Reports/Improving%20the%20Combat%20Edge%20Through%20Outsourcing.pdf.

54. Dickinson, *Outsourcing War and Peace*, 30–33.

55. Martha Minow, "Outsourcing Power: How Privatizing Military Efforts Challenges Accountability, Professionalism, and Democracy," *Boston College Law Review*, 46 (September 2005): 1002; Ettinger, "Neoliberalism and the Rise of the Private Military Industry," 755. The speech is Donald H. Rumsfeld, Secretary of Defense, DOD Acquisition and Logistics Excellence Week Kickoff—Bureaucracy to Battlefield, September 10, 2001, http://www.pentagon.gov/speeches/2001/20010910-secdef.html.

56. Gansler, *Democracy's Arsenal*, 116–117.

57. Dickinson, *Outsourcing War and Peace*, 40–41, 65–68, 111–113. I had Ms. Greenhouse in my seminar for an entire year at the National Defense University in 1995–1996. Also see Ettinger, "Neoliberalism and the Rise of the Private Military Industry," 757–758.

58. Ettinger, "Neoliberalism and the Rise of the Private Military Industry," 756–757. Also see *Quadrennial Defense Review Report* (Washington, DC: Department of Defense, 2006), 63.

59. Ettinger, "Neoliberalism and the Rise of the Private Military Industry," 757–759.

60. See, for example, the point Elke Krahmann makes about the appeal of contractors to members of the International Security Assistance Force in Afghanistan, in Elke Krahmann, "NATO Contracting in Afghanistan: The Problem of Principal-Agent Networks, *International Affairs*, 92, 6 (2016): 1408.

61. The point is implied in Gerald Waite, "Outsourcing a War: What You Get for Your Mercenary Dollar," *International Journal on World Peace*, 31, 4 (December 2014): 82.

62. Ulrich Petersohn, "Private Military and Security Companies (PMSCs), Military Effectiveness, and Conflict Severity in Weak States, 1990–2007," *Journal of Conflict Resolution*, 61, 5 (2017): 1046–1072.

63. Robert Mandel, "Overview of American Government Expeditionary Operations Utilizing Private Contractors," in Christopher Kinsey and Malcolm Hugh Patterson, eds., *Contractors and War: The Transformation of U.S. Expeditionary Operations* (Stanford, CA: Stanford University Press, 2012), 17–18.

64. The last half of this paragraph again draws from the standards and concerns posed by Laura Dickinson in her *Outsourcing War and Peace*, 8–10.

65. Moss, *Undeclared War and the Future of U.S. Foreign Policy*, 192–193; Sperling, *Altered States*, 182–183.

66. This draws from different

accounts in Avant, *The Market for Force*, 99–109; Shearer, *Private Armies and Military Intervention*, 56–60; and Sperling, *Altered States*, 178–181. The offer of MPRI to the Serbs is discussed in Jon D. Michaels, "Beyond Accountability: The Constitutional, Democratic, and Strategic Problems with Privatizing War," *Washington University Law Quarterly*, 82 (Fall 2004): 1027.

67. Moss, *Undeclared War and the Future of U.S. Foreign Policy*, 194. Also see Carlos Ortiz, "Regulating Private Military Companies: States and the Expanding Business of Commercial Security Provision," in Libby Assassi, Duncan Wigan, and Kees van der Pihl, eds., *Global Regulation: Managing Crisis after the Imperial Turn* (Houndmills, Basingstoke, UK: Palgrave MacMillan, 2004), 212–214. See the Arms Export Control Act, U.S. Code Title 22, chapter 3, at http://wwwlawcornell.edu/us-code/22/usc_sup_01_22_10_39.html.

68. See citations in previous endnote. Also see Sarah Percy, *Regulating the Private Security Industry*, Adelphi Paper 384, International Institute for Strategic Studies (London: Routledge, 2006), 26.

69. T. X. Hammes, "Private Contractors in Conflict Zones: The Good, the Bad, and the Strategic Impact," Strategic Forum No. 160, Institute for National Strategic Studies (Washington, DC: National Defense University, November 2010): 6–10,

70. Marion E. "Spike" Bowman, "Privatizing while Transforming," *Defense Horizons*, 57, Center for Technology and National Security Policy (Washington, DC: National Defense University, July 2007), 6; Hannah Tonkin, *State Control over Private Military and Security Companies in Armed Conflict* (Cambridge: Cambridge University Press, 2011), 108–109.

71. Tonkin, *State Control over Private Military and Security Companies in Armed Conflict*, 110; Department of Defense, Instruction, Number 1100.22; September 7, 2006, http://www.dodea.edu/Offices/CSPO/upload/Guidance-for-Determining-Workforce-Mix.pdf.

72. Bowman, "Privatizing while Transforming," 2.

73. Thomas R. Mockaitis, *Soldiers of Misfortune* (Carlisle, PA: Strategic Studies Institute, U.S. Army War College Press, 2014), 9.

74. Moshe Schwartz, *The Department of Defense's Use of Private Security Contractors in Iraq and Afghanistan: Background, Analysis, and Options for Congress*, R40835 (Washington, DC: Library of Congress, Congressional Research Service, January 19, 2010), 5.

75. Mockaitis, *Soldiers of Misfortune*, 10–11.

76. "Additional Information about Blackwater USA," memorandum prepared by the Majority Staff of House Committee on Oversight and Government Reform for members of that committee, October 1, 2007, 3–4, http://psm.du.edu/media/documents/congressional_comm/house_oversight_gov_reform/us_house_oversight_report_blackwater.pdf.

77. William J. Flavin, "The Elephant in the Room," in Kinsey and Patterson, eds., *Contractors and War*, 86.

78. Hammes, "Private Contractors in Conflict Zones," 2–3.

79. Schwartz, *The Department of Defense's Use of Private Security Contractors*, 7.

80. Ibid., 2–3.

81. Ibid., 6–12.

82. Ibid., 12–15.

83. "Contractor Casualty Statistics," *Feral Jundi*, http://feraljundi.com/contractor-casualty-statistics/. Also see "Defense Base Act Case Summary by Employer," https://www.dol.gov/owcp/dlhwc/dbaallemployer.htm#content; Hammes, "Private Contractors in Conflict Zones," 3.

84. "U.S. Casualty Status," https://www.defense.gov/casualty.pdf.

85. Hammes, "Private Contractors in Conflict Zones," 3.

86. Scott L. Efflandt, "Military Professionalism and Private Military Contractors," U.S. *Army War College Quarterly Parameters* (formerly known as *Parameters*), 44, 2 (Summer 2014): 54. Efflandt draws his analysis from Schwartz; see note 74 above.

87. Mockaitis, *Soldiers of Misfortune*, 13.

88. Steve Fainaru, *Big Boy Rules: American Mercenaries Fighting in Iraq* (Philadelphia: DaCapo Press, 2008), 129–131.

89. Ann Hagedorn, *The Invisible Soldiers: How America Outsourced Our Security* (New York: Simon and Schuster, 2014), 40–42.

90. See Coalition Provisional Authority Order Number 17, Status of the Coalition, Foreign Liaison Missions, Their Personnel and Contractors, June 26, 2003, http://www.usace.army.mil/Portals/2/docs/COALITION_PRO VISIONAL.pdf. Also see Mockaitis, *Soldiers of Misfortune*, 16.

91. Mockaitis, *Soldiers of Misfortune*, 16–17.

92. https://www.federalregister.gov/documents/2006/06/16/E6-9499/defense-federal-acquisition-regulation-supplement-contractor-personnel-authorized-to-accompany-us. Also see Fainaru, *Big Boy Rules*, 69–70.

93. The text of the act can be found in 5 U.S. Code 3108; http://uscode.house.gov/view.xhtml?req=granuleid:USC-prelim-title5-section3108&num=0&edition=prelim. Also see endnotes in Fainaru, *Big Boy Rules*, 225, for quotations on page 70 of the book.

94. "Additional Information about Blackwater USA," October 1, 2007, 6–7. See note 76.

95. Ibid., 7.

96. Mockaitis, *Soldiers of Misfortune*, 15–16.

97. Fainaru, *Big Boy Rules*, 125–128.

98. Taylor, *Military Service and American Democracy*, 178.

99. Thomas Gibbons-Neff, "How a 4-Hour Battle between Russian Mercenaries and U.S. Commandos Unfolded in Syria," *New York Times*, May 24, 2018.

100. Levi Maxey, "A Wolf in Mercenary Clothing? Russian Contractors as Gray Zone Tool," *Cipher Brief*, November 26, 2017; "Private Military Companies in Russia: Carrying out Criminal Orders of the Kremlin," *InformNapalm*, http://informnapalm.rocks/private-military-companies-in-russia-carrying-out-criminal-orders-of-the-kremlin (*InformNapalm* is a website initiated by Ukrainian and Georgian journalists in the wake of the 2014 intervention in Ukraine); Sergei Khazov-Cassia and Robert Coalson, "Russian

Mercenaries: Vagner Commanders Describe Life inside 'The Meat Grinder,'" *Radio Free Europe/Radio Liberty*, March 14, 2018; and Owen Matthews, "Putin's (Secret) Army," *Newsweek*, January 26, 2018, 28.

101. Matthews, "Putin's (Secret) Army," 31; Adam Taylor, "The Shadowy Russian Mercenary Firm behind an Attack on U.S. Troops in Syria," *Washington Post*, February 23, 2018; Khazov-Cassia and Coalson, "Russian Mercenaries: Vagner Commanders Describe Life inside 'The Meat Grinder'"; "Private Military Companies in Russia," *InformNapalm*.

102. Nina Nazarova and Ilya Barabanov, "The Russian Guns for Hire Dying in Syria," *BBC Russian Service*, Archangelsk, February 20, 2018.

103. Koistinen, *State of War*, 42.

104. Rebecca U. Thorpe. *The American Warfare State: The Domestic Politics of Military Spending* (Chicago: University of Chicago Press, 2014), 184; Moss, *Undeclared War and the Future of U.S. Foreign Policy*, 112–148 and 187–198 in particular.

105. Avant, *The Market for Force*, 128.

106. Christopher Spearin, "Accountable to Whom? An Assessment of International Private Security Companies in South America," *Civil Wars*, 6, 1 (2003): 9.

107. Michaels, "Beyond Accountability," 1054–1057.

108. Ibid., 1063.

109. Sperling, *Altered States*, 185.

110. Michaels, "Beyond Accountability," 1074–1075.

111. Percy, *Regulating the Private Security Industry*, 27; Moss, *Undeclared War and the Future of U.S. Foreign Policy*, 196.

112. Deborah Avant and Lee Sigelman, "What Does Private Security in Iraq Mean for Democracy at Home?," paper prepared for presentation at McGill University and the University of Chicago, January 2008, 19.

113. Ellen L. Frye, "Private Military Firms in the New World Order: How Redefining 'Mercenary' Can Tame the 'Dogs of War,'" *Fordham Law Review*, 73, 6 (2005): 2624–2625; Adam Ebrahim, "Going to War with the Army You Can Afford: The United States, International Law, and the Private Military Industry," *Boston University International Law Journal*, 28, 181 (2010): 202.

114. Frye, "Private Military Firms in the New World Order," 2625; Ebrahim, "Going to War with the Army You Can Afford," 202–203.

115. Resolution 2131, "The Declaration on the Inadmissibility of Intervention in the Domestic Affairs of States and the Protection of their Independence and Sovereignty," was in 1965. Resolution 2465, "Declaration on the Granting of Independence to Colonial Countries and Peoples," was in 1968. Both are discussed in some detail in Frye, "Private Military Firms in the New World Order," 2626–2627; and Ebrahim, Going to War with the Army You Can Afford," 203–204.

116. Frye, "Private Military Firms in the New World Order,"2630.

117. Ibid.. Also see Michael Scheimer, "Separating Private Military Companies from Illegal Mercenaries in International Law: Proposing an International Convention for Legitimate Military and Security Support the [sic] Reflects Customary International Law," *American University International*

Law Review, 24, 3 (2009): 616–617; and note 11 in Ryan Good and Derek Jinks, "International Law, U.S. War Powers, and the Global War on Terrorism," Harvard Law Review, 118 (2005): 2655, which is discussed and cited in Moss, Undeclared War and the Future of U.S. Foreign Policy, endnote 19, 267–268. See also Ebrahim, "Going to War with the Army You Can Afford," 206–207.

118. Adam Roberts and Richard Guelff, Documents on the Laws of War, 3rd ed. (Oxford: Oxford University Press, 2004), 447; also see concluding notes related to Geneva Protocols I and II, 493–512.

119. Ebrahim, "Going to War with the Army You Can Afford," 208–210. Also see United Nations Treaty Collection, https://treaties.un.org/Pages /ViewDetails.aspx?src=IND&mtdsg _no=XVIII-6&chapter=18&lang=en.

120. Lindsey Cameron, "International Humanitarian Law and the Regulation of Private Military Companies," paper presented in Basel, Switzerland, in a conference on "Non-State Actors as Standard Setters: The Erosion of the Public-Private Divide," February 8–9, 2007, printed in Governance, Basel Institute on Governance, 3.

121. Frye, "Private Military Firms in the New World Order," 2638–2639.

122. Ibid., 2631–2632.

123. See Geneva Convention III, Geneva Convention Relative to the Treatment of Prisoners of War, of August 12, 1949, in The Geneva Conventions of August 12, 1949 (Geneva: International Committee of the Red Cross, June 1948), 76–77.

124. Ibid., 77.

125. Tonkin, State Control over Private Military and Security Companies in Armed Conflict, 86.

126. Ibid., 110.

127. Cameron, "International Humanitarian Law and the Regulation of Private Military Companies," 3. Also see Kenneth Watkin, "Warriors without Rights: Combatants, Unprivileged Belligerents, and the Struggle over Legitimacy," HPCR Occasional Papers (Cambridge: Program on Humanitarian Policy and Conflict Research, Harvard University, Winter 2005): 25.

128. Charles Doyle, Civilian Extraterritorial Jurisdiction Act: Federal Contractor Criminal Liability Overseas, R42358 (Washington, DC: Library of Congress, Congressional Research Service, January 28, 2013), 1–2. See also Eugene R. Fidell, Military Justice: A Very Short Introduction (Oxford: Oxford University Press, 2016), 4.

129. Jennifer K. Elsea, Moshe Schwartz, and Kennon H. Nakamura, Private Security Contractors in Iraq: Background, Legal Status, and Other Issues, CS Report RL32419 (Washington, DC: Library of Congress, Congressional Research Service, September 29, 2008), 22; Mockaitis, Soldiers of Misfortune, 27.

130. Elsea, Schwartz, and Nakamura, Private Security Contractors in Iraq, 23–24; Percy, Regulating the Private Security Industry, 28–29; Hagedorn, The Invisible Soldiers, 113; Marc Lindemann, "Civilian Contractors under Military Law," Parameters (Autumn 2007): 87.

131. Lindemann, "Civilian Contractors under Military Law," 87; Hagedorn, The Invisible Soldiers, 113–119; Elsea, Schwartz, and Nakamura, Private Security Contractors in Iraq, 24–25;

Percy, *Regulating the Private Security Industry*, 29.

132. Geoffrey S. Corn, "Contractors and the Law," in Kinsey and Patterson, eds. *Contractors in War*, 167–168; Elsea, Schwartz, and Nakamura, *Private Security Contractors in Iraq*, 26–27.

133. Ebrahim, "Going to War with the Army You Can Afford," 196; Grif Witte, "New Law Could Subject Civilians to Military Trial," *Washington Post*, January 15, 2007, A1, 11; Lindemann, "Civilian Contractors under Military Law," 88.

134. Lindemann, "Civilian Contractors under Military Law," 89; Mockaitis, *Soldiers of Misfortune*, 29.

135. Ebrahim, "Going to War with the Army You Can Afford," 196–197; Elsea, Schwartz, and Nakamura, *Private Security Contractors in Iraq*, 29.

136. The point about birth rate and conflict is explored in Edward Luttwak, "A Post-Heroic Military Policy," *Foreign Affairs*, 75, 4 (July 1996): 33–44; and James J. Sheehan, *Where Have All the Soldiers Gone? The Transformation of Modern Europe* (Boston: Houghton Mifflin Co., 2008). The postmodern military is discussed earlier in this book and in Martin Shaw, *Post-Military Society: Militarism, Demilitarization and War at the End of the Twentieth Century* (Philadelphia: Temple University Press, 1991).

137. Singer, *Corporate Warriors*, 182–183.

138. McFate, *The Modern Mercenary*, 92–93.

139. Singer, *Corporate Warriors*, 184–186; Michael O'Hanlon, *Saving Lives with Force: Military Criteria for Humanitarian Intervention* (Washington, DC:

Brookings Institution, 1997), 8; Todd S. Milliard, "Overcoming Post-Colonial Myopia: A Call to Recognize and Regulate Private Military Companies," *Military Law*, 176 (June 2003): 16–19.

140. No resolution to use force occurred for Korea in 1950 or in the Balkans in 1999. The Clinton administration argued that the scale of operations in the latter did not meet the equivalent of war. See Moss, *Undeclared War and the Future of U.S. Foreign Policy*, 77–109.

141. This paragraph draws several points from McFate, *The Modern Mercenary*, 149–155. The points about proliferation and controls are more my own but dependent, admittedly, on work in technology distribution and export controls earlier in my career as well as the literature I had to read.

142. McFate, *The Modern Mercenary*, 98–99.

143. See the ISOA website at http://stability-operations.org/. Also see Elsea, Schwartz, and Nakamura, *Private Security Contractors in Iraq*, 39.

144. The Montreux Document is found at https://www.icrc.org/eng/assets/files/other/icrc_002_0996.pdf.

145. Anthony H. Cordesman, "Private Security Forces in Afghanistan and Iraq: The Potential Impact of the Montreux Document," Washington, DC: Center for Strategic and International Studies, November 17, 2010. https://www.csis.org/analysis/private-security-forces-afghanistan-and-iraq-potential-impact-montreux-document.

146. See https://icoca.ch/en. A history of the ICOC can be found on its website. The paper is by Ann-Marie

Buzatu, *Towards an International Code of Conduct for Private Security Providers: A View from a Multistakeholder Process*, SSR Paper 12 (Geneva: Geneva Center for the Democratic Control of Armed Forces, 2015).

147. Percy, *Regulating the Private Security Industry*, 59.

148. Ibid., 59–60.

149. Renee de Nevers, "(Self) Regulating War? Voluntary Regulation and the Private Security Industry," *Security Studies*, 18, 3 (2009): 482. My observation on the impact of antitrust laws comes from personal experience as a company representative for Siemens (1990–1994) in multiple meetings with the National Association of Manufacturers and various associations in the electronics and semiconductor fields.

150. De Nevers, "(Self) Regulating War?," 482.

151. Krahmann, *States, Citizens and the Privatization of Security*, 84–118 and 156–193; Alan Cowell, "The Draft Ends in Germany, but Questions of Identity Endure," *New York Times*, June 30, 2011, http://www.nytimes.com/2011/07/01/world/europe/01germany.html. The status of the 2005 law is discussed in Ekkehard Brose, *When Germany Sends Troops Abroad: The Case for a Limited Reform of the Parliamentary Participation Act*, SWP Research Paper 9 (Berlin: Stiftung Wissenschaft und Politik, German Institute for International and Security Affairs, September 2013).

152. Commission on Wartime Contracting in Iraq and Afghanistan, *At What Risk? Correcting Over-Reliance on Contractors in Contingency Military Operations*, Second Interim Report to Congress, February 24, 2011, 21 and 14; Mockaitis, *Soldiers of Misfortune*, 23–14; Jacques S. Gansler and William Lucyshyn, "Contractors Supporting Military Operations: Many Challenges Remain," in Kinsey and Patterson, eds., *Contractors and War*, 283–284.

153. See Frye, "Private Military Firms in the New World Order," 2650–2653; and Peter W. Singer, "War, Profits, and the Vacuum of Law: Privatized Military Firms and International Law," 42, *Columbia Journal of Transnational Law* (2004).

154. See, for example, the points on mercenaries raised by Frye, "Private Military Firms in the New World Order," 2656–2659.

155. A number of writers have made an argument asking for reconsideration of contractors as combatants. See, for example, Milliard, "Overcoming Post-Colonial Myopia," 77–79; Moss, *Undeclared War and the Future of U.S. Foreign Policy*, 197–198; and Charles J. Dunlap Jr., "Technology: Recomplicating Moral Life for the Nation's Defenders," *Parameters*, 29 (Autumn 1999): 7.

CONCLUSION. THE RETURN OF PRIVATE WAR

1. William Banks, "State Responsibility and Attribution of Cyber Intrusions after Tallinn 2.0," *Texas Law Review*, 95 (2017): 1487–1488; Catherine A. Theohary and Cory Welt, "Russia and the US Presidential Election," CRS Insight IN 10635 (Washington, DC: Library of Congress, Congressional Research Service, January 17, 2017), 1–2. A recent account of this still unfolding story is in David E. Sanger, *The Perfect Weapon: War, Sabotage, and Fear in*

the Cyber Age (New York: Crown, 2018), 152–239.

2. Director of National Intelligence, "Assessing Russian Activities and Intentions in Recent U.S. Elections: The Analytic Process and Cyber Incident Attribution," January 6, 2017, ii, https://www.dni.gov/files/documents /ICA_2017_01.pdf; Banks, "State Responsibility and Attribution of Cyber Intrusions," 1490–1491.

3. Eric Blinderman and Myra Din, "Hidden by Sovereign Shadows: Improving the Domestic Framework for Deterring State-Sponsored Cybercrime," *Vanderbilt Journal of Transnational Law*, 50 (2017): 898–900; Minority Staff Report, "Old Tactics, New Tools: A Review of Russia's Soft Cyber Influence Operations," prepared for Democratic Members of the Subcommittee on Oversight Committee on Science, Space and Technology (Washington, DC: November 2017), 13–14; Mason Shuya, "Russian Cyber Aggression and the New Cold War," *Journal of Strategic Security*, 11, 1 (Spring 2018): 6–7.

4. Tim Maurer, *Cyber Mercenaries: The State, Hackers and Power* (Cambridge: Cambridge University Press, 2018), 20–21 and 94–95.

5. Justin Key Canfil, "Honing Cyber Attribution: A Framework for Assessing Foreign State Complicity," *Journal of International Affairs*, 70, 1 (Winter 2016): 218. Canfil uses a report by Jake Reudnitsky, John Mickelthwait, and Michael Riley, "Putin Says DNC Hack Was a Public Good, but Russia Didn't Do It," *Bloomberg News*, September 2, 1016.

6. Patrick Tucker, "Vladimir Putin and the Little Green Men of the Internet," *Defense One*, June 5, 2017, http:www.defenseone.com/technol ogy2017/06/vladimir-putin-and-little -green men. The comments on Putin's worldview are drawn from two books. Foremost is Timothy Snyder, *The Road to Unfreedom: Russia, Europe, America* (New York: Tim Duggan Books, 2018). The subtitle is a little misleading; Russia and what its leaders hope to do with the United States and Europe are the focus. The second book is Charles Clover, *Black Wind, White Snow: The Rise of Russia's New Nationalism* (New Haven, CT: Yale University Press, 2016), 1–20 and 249–332.

7. P. W. Singer and Allan Friedman, *Cybersecurity and Cyberwar: What Everyone Needs to Know* (New York: Oxford University Press, 2014), 110–112.

8. Maurer, *Cybermercenaries*, 58–61; Snyder, *The Road to Unfreedom*, 48–55.

9. Minority Staff Report, "Old Tactics, New Tools," 6–9. Timothy Thomas is quoted on 7 and Rodionov on 9. Also Ido Kilovaty, "Doxfare: Politically Motivated Leaks and the Future of the Norm on Non-Intervention in the Era of Weaponized Information," *Harvard National Security Review*, 9 (2018): 146–179.

10. Nikolas K. Gvosdev, "The Bear Goes Digital: Russia and Its Cyber Capabilities," in Derek S. Reveron, ed., *Cyberspace and National Security: Threats, Opportunities, and Power in a Virtual World* (Washington, DC: Georgetown University Press, 2012), 175–178 and 180–182. Gvosdev's quotation is of Roland Heickero, *Emerging Cyber Threats and Russian Views on Information Warfare and Information Operations*

(Stockholm: FOI, Swedish Defence Research Agency, 2010), 17. Maurer in *Cybermercenaries* sees Russia's use of Nashi, a youth movement, as a form of sanctioning, 97.

11. Frank G. Hoffmann, "Hybrid Warfare and Challenges," *Joint Force Quarterly*, 52 (1st quarter, 2009): 34–39.

12. See, for example, Michael Kofman and Matthew Rojansky, "A Closer Look at Russia's 'Hybrid War,'" *Kennan Cable*, 7 (Washington, DC: Woodrow Wilson International Center for Scholars, April 2015), 1–8; Eve Hunter with Piret Pernik, "The Challenges of Hybrid Warfare," ICDS Analysis (Tallinn, Estonia; International Centre for Defence and Security, April 2015), 3–7; Berttina Renz and Hanna Smith, *Russia and Hybrid Warfare: Going beyond the Label*, Papers Aleksanteri (Helsinki: Aleksanteri Institute, University of Helsinki, 2016); Charles K. Bartles, "Getting Gerasimov Right," *Military Review* (January–February 2016): 30–38.

13. Shane Harris, *@War: The Rise of the Military-Internet Complex* (New York: Houghton Mifflin Harcourt, 2014), xxii.

14. Kristen E. Eichensehr, "Public-Private Cybersecurity," *Texas Law Review*, 95 (2017): 494–495; Scott J. Shackelford, *Managing Cyber Attacks in International Law: Business and Relations* (Cambridge: Cambridge University Press, 2014), 79–80.

15. Harris, *@War*, 57.

16. See Jeremy Rabkin and Ariel Rabkin, "Navigating Conflicts in Cyberspace: Legal Lessons from the History of War at Sea," *Chicago Journal of International Law*, 14, 1 (Summer 2013): 197–258; Duncan Hollis, "An e-SOS for Cyberspace," *Harvard Journal of International Law*, 52, 373 (2011): 412–414.

17. Eichensehr, "Public-Private Cybersecurity," 471. Besides the works cited above by Maurer as well as Rabkin and Rabkin, see Florian Egloff, "Cybersecurity and the Age of Privateering," in George Perkovich and Ariel E. Levite, eds., *Understanding Cyber Conflict: Fourteen Analogies* (Washington, DC: Georgetown University Press, 2017), 231–247; and Natalie Vanatta, "Who Will Defend the Nation in the Digital Domain?" in Adam R. Bryant, Robert F. Mills, and Juan Lopez Jr., eds., *Proceedings of the 12th International Conference on Cyber Warfare and Security* (Sonning Common, UK: Academic Conferences and Publishing International, 2017), 367–373.

18. Eichensehr, "Public-Private Cybersecurity," 478.

19. Ibid., 471–472.

20. Harris, *@War*, 93–94.

21. Ibid., 95–102.

22. Ibid., 103–108.

23. Shackelford, *Managing Cyber Attacks in International Law*, 264–265; Blinderman and Din, "Hidden by Sovereign Shadows," 906–908.

24. As quoted by Kenneth B. Moss in "Challenges to International Regulation of Cyber Technology at War," DIIS Policy Brief (Copenhagen: Danish Institute for International Studies, May 2014), 2.

25. See, for example, the remarks made in 2012 by Harold Koh, then legal adviser to the Department of State, USCYBERCOM [US Cyber Command] Inter-Agency Legal Conference, Fort Meade, Maryland, September 18, 2012,

copy in possession of author but available online. Also see James E. McGhee, "Liberating Cyber Offense," *Strategic Studies Quarterly* (Winter 2016): 51–52.

26. *Department of Defense Law of War Manual*, June 2015, Updated May 2016, 987–989, https://www.documentcloud.org/documents/2997317-DoD-Law-of-War.

27. Ibid., 991.

28. Ibid., 991, 995–997.

29. Michael Walzer, *Just and Unjust Wars*, 4th ed. (New York: Basic Books, 2006), xv–xvi; Daniel Brunstetter and Megan Braun, "From Jus ad Bellum to Jus ad Vim: Recalibrating Our Understanding of the Moral Use of Force," *Ethics and International Affairs*, 27, 1 (2013): 87–106.

30. Shackelford, *Managing Cyber Attacks in International Law*, 274–277.

31. Discussed in Kenneth B. Moss, *Undeclared War and the Future of U.S. Foreign Policy* (Washington, DC, and Baltimore: Wilson Center Press and Johns Hopkins University Press, 2008), 89–90 and 98–101.

32. Jason Healey and A. J. Wilson, "Cyber Conflict and the War Powers Resolution: Congressional Oversight of Hostilities in the Fifth Domain," *Georgetown Journal of International Affairs* (March 2013): 61–62. Also see Harold Hongju Koh, "Testimony on Libya and War Powers before the Senate Foreign Relations Committee," http://www.foreign.senate.gov/imo/media/doc/Koh_Testimony.pdf, and "United States Activities in Libya," http://www.foreignpolicy.com/files/fp.

33. Healey and Wilson, "Cyber Conflict and the War Powers Resolution," 63–64; Department of Defense,

Department of Defense Cyberspace Policy Report: A Report to Congress Pursuant to the National Defense Authorization Act for Fiscal Year 2011, Section 934, November 2011, 9.

34. Healey and Wilson, "Cyber Conflict and the War Powers Resolution," 64–66.

35. Presidential Policy Directive, PPD-20, https://fas.org/irp/offdocs/ppd/ppd-20.pdf.

36. Ibid. For discussions of PPD-20 see Nicholas Ryan Turza, "Counterattacking the Comment Crew: The Constitutionality of Presidential Policy Directive as a Defense to Counter Attacks," *North Carolina Journal of Law and Technology*, 15 (2014): 134–169; Matthew Rinear, "Armed with a Keyboard: Presidential Directive 20, Cyber Warfare, and the International Laws Of War," *Capital University Law Review*, 43 (2015): 679–720; and Herbert Lin and Amy Zegart, "Introduction to the Special Issue on Strategic Dimensions of Offensive Cyber Operations," *Journal of Cybersecurity*, 3, 1 (2017): 1–5.

37. Harris, *@War*, 220, 117–120.

38. The points here are predominantly mine, but Harris does refer to them as well; see *@War*, 224.

39. Franz-Stefan Gady, "Trump and Offensive Cyber Warfare," *Diplomat*, January 16, 2017, http://thediplomat.com/2017/01/trump-and-offensive-cyber-warfare/; Patrick Barry, "The Trump Administration Just Threw Out America's Rules for Cyberweapons," *Foreign Policy*, August 21, 2018; Erica D. Borghard and Shawn W. Lonergan, "What Do the Trump Administration's Changes to PPD-20 Mean for U.S. Offensive Cyber Operations?," Council on

Foreign Relations, September 10, 2018, https://www.cfr.org/blog/what-do-trump-administrations-changes-ppd-20-mean-us-offensive-cyber-operations; Ellen Nakashima, "White House Authorizes 'Offensive Cyber Operations' to Deter Foreign Adversaries," *Washington Post*, September 20, 2018. Also see Executive Office of the President, *National Security Strategy of the United States*, September 2018.

40. Herb Lin, "A Notification Requirement for Using Cyber Weapons or for Unauthorized Disclosure of a Cyber Weapon," *Lawfare*, June 10, 2017. *Lawfare* is an online blog free to subscribers. Also see Joseph Marks, "Lawmakers to Pentagon: Tell Us When You Use Cyber Weapons," *Defense One*, June 8, 2017. *Defense One* is an online newsletter also available at no charge to subscribers. Robert Chesney, "The NDAA FY18's Cyber Provisions: What Emerged from Conference?" *Lawfare*, November 14, 2017.

41. I draw on my own experience at the National Defense University, but in scholarship one can find discussion of the same in studies of the private/public balance and national security. See, for example, Alyson Bailes, "The Private Sector and the Monopoly of Force," in Alyson Bailes, Ulrich Schneckener, and Herbert Wulf, *Revisiting the State Monopoly on the Legitimate Use of Force*, Policy Paper No. 24 (Geneva: Geneva Centre for the Democratic Control of Armed Force, 2006), 2–9.

42. Herbert Wulf, "The Future of the Public Monopoly of Force," ibid., 19–26. For the availability of weapons, especially small arms, see William D. Hartung, "The International Arms Trade," in Paul D. Williams, ed., *Security Studies: An Introduction*, 2nd ed. (London: Routledge, 2013), 441–156.

43. See discussion in Chapter 6.

44. This discussion refers to points made in Rabkin and Rabkin, "Navigating Conflicts in Cyberspace," especially 215, 224–234.

45. Christopher M. Kessinger, "Hitting the Cyber Marque: Issuing a Cyber Letter of Marque to Combat Digital Threats," *Army Lawyer*, DA PAM 27-50-483 (August 2013): 22.

BIBLIOGRAPHY

PRIMARY SOURCES

CORRESPONDENCE

Adams, John. *The Works of John Adams*, Vol. 1. Edited by Charles Francis Adams. Boston: Little, Brown, 1856.

Adams Family Papers: An Electronic Archive. Massachusetts Historical Society. http://www.masshist.org/digitaladams/.

Letters of Delegates to Congress, Vol. 3: January 1, 1776–May 15, 1776. Electronic edition, https://memory.loc.gov/.

Letters of Delegates to Congress, Vol. 5: August 16, 1776–December 31, 1776, 573–575. Electronic edition, https://memory.loc.gov/.

The Revolutionary Diplomatic Correspondence of the United States, Vol. 2. Electronic edition, https://memory.loc.gov/.

DOCUMENTS, SPEECHES, AND REPORTS

Arms Export Control Act, U.S. Code Title 22, chapter 3. http://wwwlawcornell.edu/uscode/22/usc_sup_01_22_10_39.html.

Bas v. Tingy 4 Dall. 37 (1800). http://press-pubs.uchicago.edu/founders/.

Belasco, Amy. *Troop Levels in the Afghan and Iraq Wars, FY 2001–2012: Cost and Other Potential Issues.* CRS Report 40862. Washington, DC: Library of Congress, Congressional Research Service, July 2, 2009.

Buhite, Russell D., ed. *Calls to Arms: Presidential Speeches, Messages, and Declarations of War.* Wilmington, DE: Scholarly Resources, 2003.

Coalition Provisional Authority Order Number 17. Status of the Coalition, Foreign Liaison Missions, Their Personnel and Contractors. June 26, 2003. http://www.usace.army.mil/Portals/2/docs/COALITION_PROVISIONAL.pdf.

Commission on Wartime Contracting in Iraq and Afghanistan. *At What Risk? Correcting Over-Reliance on Contractors in Contingency Military Operations.* Second Interim Report to Congress. February 24, 2011.

Congressional Budget Office. *Contractor's Support of U.S. Operations in Iraq.* Washington, DC: Congress of the United States. August 2008.

"Contractor Casualty Statistics." *Feral Jundi.* http://feraljundi.com/contractor-casualty-statistics/.

Declaration of War. June 18, 1812. http://www.historyguy.com/war_of_1812_declaration_of_war.htm.

"Defense Base Act Case Summary by Employer." https://www.dol.gov/owcp/dlhwc/dbaallemployer.htm#content.

"Defense Federal Acquisition Regulation Supplement." *Federal Register.* https://www

.federalregister.gov/documents/2006/06/16/E6-9499/defense-federal-acquisi
tion-regulation-supplement-contractor-personnel-authorized-to-accompany-us.

Department of Defense. *Department of Defense Cyberspace Policy Report: A Report to Congress Pursuant to the National Defense Authorization Act for Fiscal Year 2011, Section 934.* November 2011.

Department of Defense. *Department of Defense Law of War Manual.* June 2015, updated May 2016. https://www.documentcloud.org/documents/2997317-DoD-Law-of-War.

Department of Defense. "Improving the Combat Edge through Outsourcing." *Defense Issues,* 11, 30 (March 1996). Pagination for this report varies depending on which DOD website is used. See http://www.dod.mil/pubs/foi/Reading_Room /Selected_Acquisition_Reports/Improving%20the%20Combat%20Edge%20 Through%20Outsourcing.pdf.

Department of Defense. *Instruction,* Number 1100.22. September 7, 2006. http:// www.dodea.edu/Offices/CSPO/upload/Guidance-for-Determining-Workforce -Mix.pdf.

Department of Defense. *Quadrennial Defense Review Report.* Washington, DC: Department of Defense, 2006.

Director of National Intelligence. Background to "Assessing Russian Activities and Intentions in Recent U.S. Elections: The Analytic Process and Cyber Incident Attribution." January 6, 2017, https://www.dni.gov/files/documents/ICA_2017_01 .pdf.

The Documentary History of the Ratification of the Constitution, Digital Edition. Edited by John P. Kaminski, Gaspare J. Saladino, Richard Leffler, Charles H. Schoenleber, and Margaret A. Hogan. Charlottesville: University of Virginia Press, 2009.

Doyle, Charles. *Civilian Extraterritorial Jurisdiction Act: Federal Contractor Criminal Liability Overseas.* CRS Report R42358. Washington, DC: Library of Congress, Congressional Research Service, January 28, 2013.

Elsea, Jennifer K., Moshe Schwartz, and Kennon H. Nakamura. *Private Security Contractors in Iraq: Background, Legal Status, and Other Issues.* CRS Report RL32419. Washington, DC: Library of Congress, Congressional Research Service, September 29, 2008.

Executive Office of the President. *National Security Strategy of the United States.* September 2018.

5 U.S. Code 3108. http://uscode.house.gov/view.xhtml?req=granuleid:USC-prelim -title5-section3108&num=0&edition=prelim.

Founders Online. National Archives. Last modified July 12, 2016. http://founders .archives.gov/documents/Hamilton/01-04-02-0017.

Headquarters, Department of the Army. Summary of Change, Army Regulations (AR) 700-137, Logistics Civil Augmentation Program, Headquarters. Washington, DC. December 16, 1985. http://www.aschq.army.mil/supportingdocs /AR700_137.pdf.

House Committee on Oversight and Government Reform Majority Staff. "Additional

Information about Blackwater USA." Memorandum for members of that committee, October 1, 2007. http://psm.du.edu/media/documents/congressional_comm/house_oversight_gov_reform/us_house_oversight_report_blackwater.pdf.

International Committee of the Red Cross. Geneva Convention III, Geneva Convention Relative to the Treatment of Prisoners of War, of August 12, 1949. In *The Geneva Conventions of August 12, 1949*. Geneva, Switzerland: International Committee of the Red Cross, June 1948.

International Stability Operations Association. http://stability-operations.org/.

Jay, John, Alexander Hamilton, and James Madison. *The Federalist Papers*. Various editions.

Jefferson, Thomas. Fourth Annual Message to Congress. November 8, 1804, http://avalon.law.yale.edu/19th_century/jeffmes4.asp.

Journals of the Continental Congress, 1774–1789. http://memory.loc.gov/cgi-bin/query/r?ammem/hlaw:@field(DOCID+@lit(jc00041)).

Koh, Harold. "Testimony on Libya and War Powers before the Senate Foreign Relations Committee." http://www.foreign.senate.gov/imo/media/doc/Koh_Testimony.pdf; and "United States Activities in Libya," http://www.foreignpolicy.com/files/fp.

———. USCYBERCOM [US Cyber Command] Inter-Agency Legal Conference. Fort Meade, Maryland. September 18, 2012. Paper in possession of author but available online.

The Lieber Code: Instructions for the Government of Armies of the United States in the Field. General Orders No. 100. Promulgated on April 24, 1863, by Abraham Lincoln. http://www.msn.com/?ocid=U218DHP&pc=EUPP_U218.

"Military-Industrial Complex Speech, Dwight D. Eisenhower, 1961." http://avalon.law.yale.edu/20th_century/eisenhower001.asp.

Minority Staff Report. "Old Tactics, New Tools: A Review of Russia's Soft Cyber Influence Operations." Prepared for Democratic Members of the Subcommittee on Oversight Committee on Science, Space, and Technology. Washington, DC: November 2017.

Montreux Document. https://www.icrc.org/eng/assets/files/other/icrc_002_0996.pdf.

Peters, Heidi M., Moshe Schwartz, and Lawrence Kapp. *Department of Defense Contractors and Troop Levels in Iraq and Afghanistan: 2007–2015*. CRS Report R44116. Washington, DC: Library of Congress, Congressional Research Service, December 1, 2105.

Presidential Policy Directive, PPD-20. https://fas.org/irp/offdocs/ppd/ppd-20.pdf.

Proceedings of the Council of Maryland, 1743/4. Vol. 28, pp. 326 and 311. https://archive.org/details/archivesofmaryla28brow.

Remarks of the Honorable Timothy Davis. "The Privateer System." July 23, 1856. *Addenda to the Congressional Record, Congressional Record*, 34th Congress, 1st Session, US House of Representatives.

Roberts, Adam, and Richard Guelff. *Documents on the Laws of War*, 3rd ed. Oxford: Oxford University Press, 2004.

Rumsfeld, Donald H., Secretary of Defense. DOD Acquisition and Logistics Excellence Week Kickoff—Bureaucracy to Battlefield. September 10, 2001. http://www .pentagon.gov/speeches/2001s20010910-secdef.html.

Schwartz, Moshe. *The Department of Defense's Use of Private Security Contractors in Iraq and Afghanistan: Background, Analysis, and Options for Congress*. CRS Report R40835. Washington, DC: Library of Congress, Congressional Research Service, January 19, 2010.

Seitzinger, Michael V. *Conducting Foreign Relations without Authority: The Logan Act*. CRS Report for Congress, RL 33265. Washington, DC: Library of Congress, Congressional Research Service, January 20, 2010.

Theohary, Catherine A., and Cory Welt. "Russia and the US Presidential Election." CRS Insight IN 10635. Washington, DC: Library of Congress, Congressional Research Service, January 17, 2017.

United Nations Treaty Collection. https://treaties.un.org/Pages/ViewDetails .aspx?src=IND&mtdsg_no=XVIII-6&chapter=18&lang=en.

BOOKS

Blackstone, William. *Commentaries on the Laws of England: A Facsimile of the First Edition of 1765–1769*, Vol. I. Chicago: University of Chicago Press, 1979.

Burke, Edmund. *The Work of the Right Honourable Edmund Burke*, Vol. 7: *Speeches on the Impeachment of Warren Hastings*. London: Bell and Daldy, 1870.

Burlamaqui, J. J. *The Principles of Natural and Politic Law*, 5th ed., trans. Thomas Nugent. Boston: University Press, W. Hilliard, 1807. http://constitution.org /burla/burla_.htm.

Cicero, Marcus Tullius. *On Duties*, ed. and trans. M. T. Griffin and E. M. Atkins. Cambridge: Cambridge University Press, 1991.

Clausewitz, Carl von. *On War*, ed. and trans. Michael Howard and Peter Paret. Princeton, NJ: Princeton University Press, 1976.

Hobbes, Thomas. *Leviathan*, ed. Edwin Curley. Indianapolis: Hackett Publishing, 1994.

Kent, James. *Commentaries on American Law*. New York: O. Halstead, 1826, 15–16. http://www.constitution.org/jk/jk.ooo.htm.

Locke, John. "The Second Treatise of Government: An Essay Concerning the True Original, Extent and End of Civil Government." In *The Selected Political Writings of John Locke*, ed. Paul E. Sigmund, 17–125. New York: W. W. Norton, 2005.

Machiavelli, Niccolo. *The Prince*. In *The Essential Writings of Machiavelli*, ed. and trans. Peter Constantine, 3–100. New York: Modern Library, 2007.

Madison, James. *Notes of Debates in the Federal Convention*. Introduction by Adrienne Koch. New York: W. W. Norton, 1966, reprinted 1987.

Rousseau, Jean-Jacques. *The Social Contract*, trans. Maurice Cranston. London: Penguin Books, 1968.

Smith, Adam. *An Inquiry into the Nature and Causes of the Wealth of Nations*, ed. Thomas Canaan. New York: Modern Library, 1994.

Story, Joseph. *Commentaries on the Constitution of the United States.* http://www.constitution.org/js/js_005.htm.

Vattel, Emer de. *The Law of Nations*, ed. and with an introduction by Bela Kapossy and Richard Whatmore. Indianapolis: Liberty Fund, 2008.

SECONDARY SOURCES

Adler, David Gray. "The Constitution and Presidential Warmaking." In *The Constitution and the Conduct of American Foreign Policy*, ed. David Gray Adler and Larry N. George, 183–226. Lawrence: University Press of Kansas, 1996.

Allen, Gardner Weld. *Massachusetts Privateers of the Revolution*, Vol. 77. Massachusetts Historical Society Collections. Cambridge: Massachusetts Historical Society, 1927.

Andrews, Kenneth R. *Elizabethan Privateering during the Spanish War, 1585–1603.* Cambridge: Cambridge University Press, 1964.

Appleby, Joyce. *The Relentless Revolution: A History of Capitalism.* New York: W. W. Norton, 2010.

Apuzzo, Matt. "Guards Guilty in '07 Killings in Iraq Square." *New York Times*, October 23, 2014.

Armstrong, David, Theo Farrell, and Helene Lambert. *International Law and International Relations*, 2nd ed. Cambridge: Cambridge University Press, 2012.

Avant, Deborah D. *The Market for Force: The Consequences of Privatizing Security.* Cambridge: Cambridge University Press, 2005.

Avant, Deborah, and Lee Sigelman. "What Does Private Security in Iraq Mean for Democracy at Home?" Paper prepared for presentation at McGill University and the University of Chicago, January 2008.

Axelrod, Tax. "Report: Trump Considering Plan to Privatize Afghan War." *The Hill*, August 17, 2018.

Bailes, Alyson. "The Private Sector and the Monopoly of Force." In *Revisiting the State Monopoly on the Legitimate Use of Force.* Policy Paper No. 24, ed. Alyson Bailes, Ulrich Schneckener, and Herbert Wulf, 2–9. Geneva: Geneva Centre for the Democratic Control of Armed Force, 2006.

Banks, William. "State Responsibility and Attribution of Cyber Intrusions after Tallinn 2.0." *Texas Law Review*, 95 (2017): 1487–1513.

Barry, Patrick. "The Trump Administration Just Threw Out America's Rules for Cyberweapons." *Foreign Policy*, August 21, 2018.

Bartles, Charles K. "Getting Gerasimov Right." *Military Review* (January–February 2016): 30–38.

Bates, David William. *States of War: Enlightenment Origins of the Political.* New York: Columbia University Press, 2012.

Baugh, Daniel A. *British Naval Administration in the Age of Walpole.* Princeton, NJ: Princeton University Press, 1965.

Baumgartner, Frederic J. *Declaring War in Early Modern Europe*. New York: Palgrave Macmillan, 2011.

Beattie, Tim. *The British Privateering Voyages of the Early Eighteenth Century*. Suffolk, UK: Boydell Press, 2015.

Beaumont, Roger. *Sword of the Raj: The British Army in India, 1747–1947*. Indianapolis: Bobbs-Merrill, 1977.

Beck, Christopher. "Common Good and Private Justice: Letters of Marque and the *Utilitas Publica* in Fourteenth-Century Marseilles." *Journal of Medieval History*, 41, 1 (2015): 88–106.

Beier, J. Marshall. "Discriminating Tastes: 'Smart' Bombs, Non-Combatants, and Notions of Legitimacy in Warfare." *Security Dialogue*, 34 (December 2003): 411–425.

Bellamy, Alex J. *Just Wars: From Cicero to Iraq*. Cambridge: Polity Press, 2006.

Bellia Jr., Anthony J., and Bradford R. Clark. "The Law of Nations as Constitutional Law." *Virginia Law Review*, 98, 4 (June 2012): 729–838.

Benton, Lauren. "Legal Spaces of Empire: Piracy and the Origins of Ocean Regionalism." *Comparative Studies in Society and History*, 47, 4 (2005): 700–724.

———. *A Search for Sovereignty: Law and Geography in European Empires, 1400–1900*. Cambridge: Cambridge University Press, 2010.

Best, Geoffrey. *War and Law since 1945*. Oxford: Oxford University Press, 1994.

Bittle, Scott, and Jonathan Rochkind, with Amber Ott. "Confidence in US Foreign Policy Index: Anxious Public Pulling Back from Use of Force." *Public Agenda*, 4 (Spring 2007): 1–34. www.publicagenda.org.

Black, Jeremy. *War for America: The Fight for Independence, 1775–1783*. Phoenix Mill, UK: Alan Sutton Publishing, 1991, reprinted 2001.

Blinderman, Eric, and Myra Din. "Hidden by Sovereign Shadows: Improving the Domestic Framework for Deterring State-Sponsored Cybercrime." *Vanderbilt Journal of Transnational Law*, 50 (2017): 889–931.

Bobbitt, Philip. *The Shield of Achilles: War, Peace, and the Course of History*. New York: Alfred A. Knopf, 2002.

———. *Terror and Consent: The Wars for the Twenty-First Century*. New York: Alfred A. Knopf, 2008.

Borghard, Erica D., and Shawn W. Lonergan. "What Do the Trump Administration's Changes to PPD-20 Mean for U.S. Offensive Cyber Operations?" Council on Foreign Relations, September 10, 2018, https://www.cfr.org/blog/what-do-trump-administrations-changes-ppd-20-mean-us-offensive-cyber-operations.

Bowen, H. V. "British India, 1765–1813: The Metropolitan Context." In *The Eighteenth Century*. Vol 2: *The Oxford History of the British Empire*, ed. P. J. Marshall, 487–507. Oxford: Oxford University Press, 1998.

———. *The Business of Empire: The East India Company and Imperial Britain, 1756–1833*. Cambridge: Cambridge University Press, 2006.

Bowman, Marion E. "Spike." "Privatizing while Transforming." *Defense Horizons*, 57.

Center for Technology and National Security Policy. Washington, DC: National Defense University, July 2007.

Bown, Stephen R. *1494: How a Family Feud in Medieval Spain Divided the World in Half*. New York: St. Martin's Press, 2011.

Brauer, Jurgen, and Hubert Van Tuyll. *Castles, Battles, and Bombs: How Economics Explains Military History*. Chicago: University of Chicago Press, 2008.

Brewer, John. *The Sinews of Power: War, Money, and the English State, 1688–1788*. New York: Alfred A. Knopf, 1989.

Brickham, Troy. *The Weight of Vengeance: The United States, the British Empire, and the War of 1812*. Oxford: Oxford University Press, 2012.

Bromley, J. S. *Corsairs and Navies, 1660–1760*. London: Hambledon Press, 1987.

Brook, Timothy. *Vermeer's Hat: The Seventeenth Century and the Dawn of the Global World*. New York: Bloomsbury Press, 2008.

Brose, Ekkehard. *When Germany Sends Troops Abroad: The Case for a Limited Reform of the Parliamentary Participation Act*. SWP Research Paper 9. Berlin: Stiftung Wissenschaft und Politik, the German Institute for International and Security Affairs, September 2013.

Brown, Roger H. *The Republic in Peril: 1812*. New York: W. W. Norton, 1964, reprinted 1971.

Browning, Patrick R. "The Gran Para: The Delicate Dance of South American Privateering from Baltimore." Paper written in fulfillment of the Doctor of Jurisprudence, Francis King Carey School of Law (2015), https://digitalcommons.law.umaryland.edu/mlh_pubs/56/.

Brunsman, Denver. *The Evil Necessity: British Naval Impressment in the Eighteenth-Century Atlantic World*. Charlottesville: University of Virginia Press, 2013.

Brunstetter, Daniel, and Megan Braun. "From Jus ad Bellum to Jus ad Vim: Recalibrating Our Understanding of the Moral Use of Force." *Ethics and International Affairs*, 27, 1 (2013): 87–106.

Bryant, G. J. "Asymmetric Warfare: The British Experience in Eighteenth-Century Warfare." *Journal of Military History*, 68 (April 2004): 431–469.

———. "British Logistics and the Conduct of the Carnatic Wars (1746–1783)." *War in History*, 11, 3 (2004): 278–306.

Budiansky, Stephen. *Perilous Fight: America's Intrepid War with the British on the High Seas, 1812–1815*. New York: Alfred A. Knopf, 2010.

Buel Jr., Richard. *In Irons: Britain's Naval Supremacy and the American Revolutionary Economy*. New Haven, CT: Yale University Press, 1998.

Burgess Jr., Douglas R. "A Crisis of Charter and Right: Piracy and Colonial Resistance in Seventeenth-Century Rhode Island." *Journal of Social History*, 45, 3 (2012): 605–622.

———. *The Politics of Piracy: Crime and Disobedience in Colonial America*. Lebanon, NH: ForeEdge, University Press of New England, 2014.

Butler, Lindsey S. *Pirates, Privateers, and Rebel Raiders of the Carolina Coast*. Chapel Hill: University of North Carolina Press, 2000.

Buzatu, Ann-Marie. *Towards an International Code of Conduct for Private Security Providers: A View from a Multistakeholder Process.* SSR Paper 12. Geneva: Geneva Center for the Democratic Control of Armed Forces, 2015.

Calder, Angus. *Revolutionary Empire: The Rise of the English-Speaking Empires from the Fifteenth Century to the 1780s.* New York: R. E. P. Dutton, 1981.

Callahan, Raymond. *The East India Company and Army Reform, 1783–1798.* Cambridge, MA: Harvard University Press, 1972.

Calloway, Colin G. *The American Revolution in Indian Country: Crisis and Diversity in Native American Communities.* New York: Cambridge University Press, 1995.

Cameron, Lindsey. "International Humanitarian Law and the Regulation of Private Military Companies." Paper presented in Basel, Switzerland, at the conference "Non-State Actors as Standard Setters: The Erosion of the Public-Private Divide," February 8–9, 2007. Printed in *Governance*, Basel Institute on Governance.

Canfil, Justin Key. "Honing Cyber Attribution: A Framework for Assessing Foreign State Complicity." *Journal of International Affairs*, 70, 1 (Winter 2016): 217–226.

Carnahan, Burrus M. *Lincoln on Trial: Southern Civilians and the Law of War.* Lexington: University Press of Kentucky, 2010.

Casto, William R. *The Supreme Court of the Early Republic: The Chief Justiceships of John Jay and Oliver Ellsworth.* Columbia: University of South Carolina Press, 1995.

Chaudhuri, K. N. "The English East India Company's Shipping (c1660–1760)." In *Ships, Sailors, and Spices: East India Companies and Their Shipping in the 16th, 17th and 18th Centuries,* ed. Jaap R. Burijhn and Femme S. Gaastra, 49–74. Amsterdam: NEHA, 1993.

———. *The Trading World of Asia and the East India Company, 1660–1760.* Cambridge: Cambridge University Press, 1978.

Chesney, Robert. "The NDAA FY18's Cyber Provisions: What Emerged from Conference?" *Lawfare*, November 14, 2017.

Cheyette, Frederic L. "The Sovereign and the Pirates, 1332." *Speculum*, 45, 1 (January 1970): 40–68.

Childs, David. *Pirate Nation: Elizabeth I and Her Royal Sea Rovers.* Barnsley, UK: Seaforth Publishing, 2014.

Christopher, Paul. *The Ethics of War and Peace: An Introduction to Legal and Moral Issues.* 2nd ed. Upper Saddle River, NJ: Prentice Hall, 2003.

Clark, Grover. "The English Practice with Regard to Reprisals." *American Journal of International Law*, 27, 4 (October 1933): 694–723.

Clover, Charles. *Black Wind, White Snow: The Rise of Russia's New Nationalism.* New Haven, CT: Yale University Press, 2016.

Coggeshall, George. *History of the American Privateers and Letters-of-Marque during Our War with England in the Years 1812, 13 and 14.* New York: C. T. Evans, 1856.

Colas, Alejandro, and Bryan Mabee. "The Flow and Ebb of Private Seaborne Violence in Global Politics: Lessons from the Atlantic World, 1689–1815." In *Mercenaries, Pirates, Bandits, and Empires: Private Violence in Historical Context,* ed. Alejandro Colas and Bryan Mabee, 83–106. New York: Columbia University Press, 2010.

———. "Introduction: Private Violence in Historical Context." In *Mercenaries, Pirates, Bandits, and Empires: Private Violence in Historical Context*, ed. Alejandro Colas and Bryan Mabee, 1–14. New York: Columbia University Press, 2010.

Conybeare, John A. C., and Todd Sandler. "State-Sponsored Violence as a Tragedy of the Commons: England's Privateering Wars with France and Spain, 1625–1630." *Public Choice*, 77, 4 (1993): 879–897.

Cooperstein, Theodore M. "Letters of Marque and Reprisal: The Constitutional Law of Privateering," *Journal of Maritime Law and Commerce*, 40, 2 (April 2009): 1–50.

Cordesman, Anthony H. "Private Security Forces in Afghanistan and Iraq: The Potential Impact of the Montreux Document. " Washington, DC: Center for Strategic and International Studies, November 17, 2010.

Corn, Geoffrey S. "Contractors and the Law." In *Contractors in War: The Transformation of United States' Expeditionary Operations*, ed. Christopher Kinsey and Malcolm Hugh Patterson, 152–183. Stanford, CA: Stanford University Press, 2012.

Corvisier, Andre. *Armies and Societies in Europe, 1494–1789*. Trans. Abigail T. Siddal. Bloomington: Indiana University Press, 1979.

———. "Mercenaries." In *A Dictionary of Military History*, ed. Andre Corvisier, trans. Chris Turner, ed. and expanded by John Childs, 501–504. Oxford: Basil Blackwell, 1994.

Cowell, Alan. "The Draft Ends in Germany, but Questions of Identity Endure." *New York Times*, June 30, 2011.

Cranwell, John Philips, and William Bowers Crane. *Men of Marque: A History of Private Armed Vessels out of Baltimore during the War of 1812*. New York: W. W. Norton, 1940.

Crawford, Michael J. "Taking the Moral High Ground: The United States, Privateering, and Immunity of Private Property at Sea." *International Journal of Naval History*, 12, 1 (January 2015), (electronic edition without pagination), http://www.ijnhonline.org/2015/01/.

Creveld, Martin van. *The Rise and Decline of the State*. Cambridge: Cambridge University Press, 1999.

Crump, Helen J. *Colonial Admiralty Jurisdiction in the Seventeenth Century*. London: Longmans, Greden, 1931.

Cutler, Claire. "Artifice, Ideology and Paradox: The Public/Private Distinction in International Law." *Review of International Political Economy*, 4, 2 (Summer 1997): 261–285.

———. "Private International Regimes and Interfirm Cooperation." In *The Emergence of Private Authority in Global Governance*, ed. Rodney Bruce Hall and Thomas J. Biersteker, 23–42. Cambridge: Cambridge University Press, 2005.

Daughan, George C. *If By Sea: The Forging of the American Navy—from the Revolution to the War of 1812*. New York: Basic Books, 2008.

Davis, William C. *The Pirates Lafitte: The Treacherous World of the Corsairs of the Gulf*. Orlando, FL: Harcourt, 2005.

DeConde, Alexander. *The Quasi-War: The Politics and Diplomacy of the Undeclared War with France, 1797–1801*. New York: Charles Scribner's Sons, 1966.

deGrandpre, Andrew. "Blackwater's Founder Wants Trump to Outsource the Afghanistan War. Why That's so Risky." *Washington Post*, August 10, 2017. https://www.washingtonpost.com/news/checkpoint/wp/2017/08/10/blackwaters-founder-wants-trump-to-outsource-the-afghanistan-war-why-thats-so-risky/?utm_term=.33d2o4bdc495.

De Lupis, Ingrid Detter. *The Law of War*. Cambridge: Cambridge University Press, 1987.

Dickinson, Laura A. *Outsourcing War and Peace: Preserving Public Values in a World of Privatized Foreign Affairs*. New Haven, CT: Yale University Press, 2011.

———. "Public Participation/Private Contract." *Social Justice*, 34, 3–4 (2007–2008): 148–172.

Dombrowski, Peter, and Eugene Gholz. *Buying Military Transformation: Technological Innovation and the Defense Industry*. New York: Columbia University Press, 2006.

Dudziak, Mary L. *War Time: An Idea, Its History, Its Consequences*. New York: Oxford University Press, 2012.

Dunlap Jr., Charles J. "Technology: Recomplicating Moral Life for the Nation's Defenders." *Parameters*, 29 (Autumn 1999): 24–53.

Durand, Rodolphe, and Jean Philippe Vergne. *The Pirate Organization: Lessons from the Fringes of Capitalism*. Boston: Harvard Business Review Press, 2013.

Earle, Peter. *The Pirate Wars*. New York: St. Martin's Press, 2003.

Ebrahim, Adam. "Going to War with the Army You Can Afford: The United States, International Law, and the Private Military Industry." *Boston University International Law Journal*, 28, 181 (2010): 181–218.

Efflandt, Scott L. "Military Professionalism and Private Military Contractors," *U.S. Army War College Quarterly Parameters* (formerly known as *Parameters*), 44, 2 (Summer 2014): 49–60.

Egloff, Florian. "Cybersecurity and the Age of Privateering." In *Understanding Cyber Conflict: Fourteen Analogies*, ed. George Perkovich and Ariel E. Levite, 231–247. Washington, DC: Georgetown University Press, 2017.

Eichensehr, Kristen E. "Public-Private Cybersecurity." *Texas Law Review*, 95 (2017): 467–538.

Einspanier, Kathryn L. "Burlamaqui, the Constitution, and the Imperfect War on Terror." *Georgetown Law Journal*, 96 (March 2008): 985–1026.

Elkins, Stanley, and Eric McKitrick. *The Age of Federalism: The Early American Republic, 1788–1800*. New York: Oxford University Press, 1993.

Ely, John Hart. *War and Responsibility: Constitutional Lessons of Vietnam and Its Aftermath*. Princeton, NJ: Princeton University Press, 1993.

Emmer, P. C. "The West India Company, 1621–1791." In *Companies and Trade*, ed. L. Blusse and F. Gaastra, 71–96. Leiden, Netherlands: Leiden University Press, 1981.

Emmers, Ralf. "Securitization." In *Contemporary Security Studies*, 2nd ed., ed. Alan Collins, 136–150. Oxford: Oxford University Press, 2013.

Epps, Garrett. *American Epic: Reading the U.S. Constitution*. Oxford: Oxford University Press, 2013.

Erbel, Mark. "The Underlying Causes of Military Outsourcing in the USA and UK: Bridging the Persistent Gaps between Ends, Ways, and Means since the Beginning of the Cold War." *Defence Studies*, 17, 2 (2017): 135–155.

Ertman, Thomas. *Birth of the Leviathan: Building States and Regimes in Medieval and Early Modern Europe.* Cambridge: Cambridge University Press, 1997.

Ettinger, Aaron. "Neoliberalism and the Rise of the Private Military Industry." *International Journal*, 66, 3 (Summer 2011): 743–764.

Fainaru, Steve. *Big Boy Rules: American Mercenaries Fighting in Iraq.* Philadelphia: DaCapo Press, 2008.

Feeney, Mary K. "Public Wars and Private Armies: Militaries, Mercenaries, and Public Values." Paper presented at the Copenhagen International Public Value Workshop, University of Copenhagen, Denmark, May 28–31, 2008.

Fehlings, Gregory E. "America's First Limited War." *Naval War College Review.* Newport Papers. (Summer 2000): 101–139.

Fidell, Eugene R. *Military Justice: A Very Short Introduction.* Oxford: Oxford University Press, 2016.

Findley, Ronald, and Kevin H. O'Rourke. *Power and Plenty: Trade, War, and the World Economy in the Second Millennium.* Princeton, NJ: Princeton University Press, 2007.

Fisher, Louis. *Presidential War Power*, 2nd ed. Lawrence: University Press of Kansas, 2004.

Fitz, Caitlin. *Our Sister Republics: The United States in an Age of American Revolutions.* New York: Liveright Publishing, 2016.

Flavin, William J. "The Elephant in the Room." In *Contractors and War: The Transformation of United States' Expeditionary Operations*, ed. Christopher Kinsey and Malcolm Hugh Patterson, 85–111. Stanford, CA: Stanford University Press, 2012.

Fornhaber-Baker, Justine. "Seigneurial War and Royal Power in Later Medieval Southern France." *Past & Present*, 208 (August 2010): 37–76.

Freedman, Lawrence. "Defining War." In *The Oxford Handbook of War*, ed. Julian Lindley-French and Yves Boyer, 17–29. Oxford: Oxford University Press, 2012.

Friedman, Lawrence M. *A History of American Law.* New York: Simon and Schuster, 1973.

Frye, Ellen L. "Private Military Firms in the New World Order: How Redefining 'Mercenary' Can Tame the 'Dogs of War.'" *Fordham Law Review*, 73, 6 (2005): 2607–2664.

Furber, Holden. *Rival Empires of Trade in the Orient, 1600–1800.* Minneapolis: University of Minnesota, 1976.

Gady, Franz-Stefan. "Trump and Offensive Cyber Warfare," *Diplomat*, January 16, 2017, http://thediplomat.com/2017/01/trump-and-offensive-cyber-warfare/.

Gansler, Jacques S. *Democracy's Arsenal: Creating a Twenty-First-Century Defense Industry.* Cambridge, MA: MIT Press, 2011.

Gansler, Jacques S., and William Lucyshyn. "Contractors Supporting Military Operations: Many Challenges Remain." In *Contractors and War: The Transformation of*

United States' Expeditionary Operations, ed. Christopher Kinsey and Malcolm Hugh Patterson, 278–296. Stanford, CA: Stanford University Press, 2012.

Gardner, Brian. The East India Company. New York: Dorset Press, 1971.

Garitee, Jerome R. The Republic's Private Navy: The American Privateering Business as Practiced by Baltimore during the War of 1812. American Maritime Library, Vol. VIII. Middletown, CT: Wesleyan University Press, 1977.

Gibbons-Neff, Thomas. "How a 4-Hour Battle between Russian Mercenaries and U.S. Commandos Unfolded in Syria." New York Times, May 24, 2018.

Gibbs, Joseph. Dead Men Tell No Tales: The Lives and Legends of The Pirate Charles Gibbs. Columbia: University of South Carolina Press, 2007.

Giladi, Rotem. "Francis Lieber on Public War." Goettingen Journal of International Law, 4, 2 (2012): 447–477.

Gilje, Paul A. Free Trade and Sailor's Rights in the War of 1812. Cambridge: Cambridge University Press, 2013.

Gillingham, John. "An Age of Expansion, c. 1020–1204." In Medieval Warfare: A History, ed. Maurice Keen, 59–88. Oxford: Oxford University Press, 1999.

Good, Ryan, and Derek Jinks. "International Law, U.S. War Powers, and the Global War on Terrorism." Harvard Law Review, 118 (2005): 2653–2662.

Gould, Eliga H. Among the Powers of the Earth: The American Revolution and the Making of a New World Empire. Cambridge, MA: Harvard University Press, 2012.

Graham, David A. "Are Mercenaries Really a Cheaper Way of War?" The Atlantic Online, August 9, 2017.

Grant, Sarah. "Trial Preview: Third Attempt to Convict Blackwater Guard for 2007 Massacre of Iraqi Civilians." Lawfare, November 2, 2018.

Greitens, Sheena Chestnut, and Theo Farrell. "Humanitarian Intervention and Peace Operations." In Strategy in the Contemporary World, 4th ed., ed. John Baylis, James J. Wirtz, and Colin S. Gray, 286–302. New York: Oxford University Press, 2013.

Grenier, John. The First Way of War: American War Making on the Frontier. Cambridge: Cambridge University Press, 2005.

Gvosdev, Nikolas K. "The Bear Goes Digital: Russia and Its Cyber Capabilities." In Cyberspace and National Security: Threats, Opportunities, and Power in a Virtual World, ed. Derek S. Reveron, 173–190. Washington, DC: Georgetown University Press, 2012.

Hagan, Kenneth J. This People's Navy: The Making of American Sea Power. New York: Free Press, 1991.

Hagedorn, Ann. The Invisible Soldiers: How America Outsourced Our Security. New York: Simon and Schuster, 2014.

Hall, Rodney Bruce, and Thomas J. Biersteker. "The Emergence of Private Authority in the International System." In The Emergence of Private Authority in Global Governance, ed. Rodney Bruce Hall and Thomas J. Biersteker, 3–22. Cambridge: Cambridge University Press, 2002.

Hall, William Edward. A Treatise on International Law, 8th ed., ed. A. Pearce Higgins. Oxford: Clarendon Press, 1924.

Hallett, Brien. *The Lost Art of Declaring War.* Urbana: University of Illinois Press, 1998.

Hammes, T. X. "Private Contractors in Conflict Zones: The Good, the Bad, and the Strategic Impact." *Strategic Forum No. 160,* Institute for National Strategic Studies. Washington, DC: National Defense University, November 2010.

Hanna, Mark G. *Pirate Nests and the Rise of the British Empire, 1570–1740.* Chapel Hill: University of North Carolina Press, 2015.

———. "Well-Behaved Pirates Seldom Make History: A Reevaluation of the Golden Age of Piracy." In *Governing the Sea in the Early Modern Era: Essays in Honor of Robert C. Ritchie,* ed. Peter C. Mandell and Carole Shammas, 129–168. San Marino, CA: Huntington Library, 2015.

Harris, Shane. *@War: The Rise of the Military-Internet Complex.* New York: Houghton Mifflin Harcourt, 2014.

Hartung, William D. "The International Arms Trade." In *Security Studies: An Introduction,* 2nd ed., ed. Paul Williams, 441–456. New York: Routledge, 2013.

Hathaway, Dona A., and Scott J. Shapiro. *The Internationalists: How a Radical Plan to Outlaw War Remade the World.* New York: Simon and Schuster, 2017.

Head, David. "New Nations, New Connections: Spanish American Privateering from the United States and the Development of Atlantic Relations." *Early American Studies,* 11, 1 (Winter 2013): 161–175.

Healey, Jason, and A. J. Wilson. "Cyber Conflict and the War Powers Resolution: Congressional Oversight of Hostilities in the Fifth Domain." *Georgetown Journal of International Affairs* (March 2013): 59–69.

Heickero, Roland. *Emerging Cyber Threats and Russian Views on Information Warfare and Information Operations.* Stockholm: FOI, Swedish Defence Research Agency, 2010.

Heller-Roazen, Daniel. *The Enemy of All: Piracy and the Law of Nations.* New York: Zone Books, 2009.

Hendrickson, David C. *Peace Pact: The Lost World of the American Founding.* Lawrence: University Press of Kansas, 2003.

Hickey, Donald R. *The War of 1812: A Forgotten Conflict.* Urbana: University of Illinois Press, 1989.

Hill, L. M. "The Admiralty Circuit of 1591: Some Comments on the Relations between Central Government and Local Interests." *Historical Journal,* 14, 1 (March 1971): 3–14.

Hillmann, Henning, and Christina Gathmann. "Overseas Trade and the Decline of Privateering." *Journal of Economic History,* 71, 3 (September 2011): 730–761.

Hindmarsh, Albert E. "Self-Help in Time of Peace." *American Journal of International Law,* 26, 2 (April 1932): 315–326.

Hoffmann, Frank G. "Hybrid Warfare and Challenges." *Joint Force Quarterly,* 52 (1st quarter, 2009): 34–39.

Hollis, Duncan. "An e-SOS for Cyberspace." *Harvard Journal of International Law,* 52, 373 (2011): 374–432.

Housley, Norman. "European Warfare, c. 1200–1320." In *Medieval Warfare: A History,* ed. Maurice Keen, 113–135. Oxford: Oxford University Press, 1999.

Howard, Michael. *War in European History*. Oxford: Oxford University Press, 1976.

Hsu, Spencer S. "Murder Conviction in Blackwater Case Thrown Out, Other Sentences Overturned." *Washington Post* News Service, reprinted in *Chicago Tribune*, August 4, 2017. http://www.chicagotribune.com/news/nationworld/ct-blackwater-conviction-20170804-story.html.

Hunter, Eve, with Piret Pernik. "The Challenges of Hybrid Warfare." ICDS Analysis. Tallinn, Estonia: International Centre for Defence and Security, April 2015.

Ittersum, Martine Julia van. "Introduction." In Hugo Grotius, *Commentary on the Law of Prize and Booty*, ed. Martine Julia van Ittersum, xiii–xxi. Indianapolis: Liberty Fund, 2006.

James, Lawrence. *Raj: The Making and Unmaking of British India*. New York: St. Martin's Press, 1997.

Jameson, John Franklin. *Privateering and Piracy in the Colonial World: Illustrative Documents*. New York: Macmillan, 1923.

Johnson, Herbert A. "American Constitutionalism and the War for Independence," *Early American Studies*, 14, 1 (Winter 2016): 140–173.

Johnson, James Turner. *Just War Tradition and the Restraint of War: A Moral and Historical Inquiry*. Princeton, NJ: Princeton University Press, 1981.

Jones, Daniel Stedman. *Masters of the Universe: Hayek, Friedman, and the Birth of Neoliberal Politics*. Princeton, NJ: Princeton University Press, 2012.

Jortner, Adam. *The Gods of Prophetstown: The Battle of Tippecanoe and the Holy War for the American Frontier*. New York: Oxford University Press, 2012.

Jung, Cindy. "Lawless and Unpunished: Private Defense Contractors Spiraling out of Control." *Harvard International Review* (Spring 2016): 7–10.

Kaldor, Mary. *New and Old Wars: Organized Violence in a Global Era*, 2nd ed. Stanford, CA: Stanford University Press, 2007.

Keeley, Lawrence H. *War before Civilization: The Myth of the Peaceful Savage*. Oxford: Oxford University Press, 1996.

Keen, Maurice. *Chivalry*. New Haven, CT: Yale University Press, 1984; rev. 2005.

———. "Introduction: Warfare and the Middle Ages." In *Medieval Warfare: A History*, ed. Maurice Keen, 1–9. Oxford: Oxford University Press, 1999.

Keller, Jared. "Don't Let Erik Prince Anywhere Near the War in Afghanistan." *Task and Purpose*, August 20, 2018.

Kempe, Michael. "'Even in the Remotest Corners of the World': Globalized Piracy and International Law, 1500–1900." *Journal of Global History*, 5 (2010): 353–372.

Kendall, Charles Wye. *Private Men-of-War*. New York: Robert M. McBride, 1932.

Kert, Faye M. *Privateering: Patriots and Profits in the War of 1812*. Baltimore: Johns Hopkins University Press, 2015.

Kessinger, Christopher M. "Hitting the Cyber Marque: Issuing a Cyber Letter of Marque to Combat Digital Threats." *Army Lawyer*, DA PAM 27-50-483 (August 2013): 4–23.

Khazov-Cassia, Sergei, and Robert Coalson. "Russian Mercenaries: Vagner

Commanders Describe Life inside the 'Meat Grinder.'" *Radio Free Europe/Radio Liberty*, March 14, 2018.

Kidwell, Deborah C. *Public War, Private Fight? The United States and Private Military Companies*. Global War on Terrorism Occasional Papers 12. Fort Leavenworth, KS: Combat Studies Institute Press, 2005.

Kilovaty, Ido. "Doxfare: Politically Motivated Leaks and the Future of the Norm on Non-Intervention in the Era of Weaponized Information." *Harvard National Security Review*, 9 (2018): 146–179.

Kirsch, Noah. "The Return of Erik Prince." *Forbes*, April 30, 2018, 107–110.

Klarman, Michael J. *The Framers' Coup: The Making of the United States Constitution*. New York: Oxford University Press, 2016.

Klein, P. W. "The Origins of Trading Companies." In *Companies and Trade*, ed. Leonard Blusse and Femme Faastra, 17–29. Dordrecht, Netherlands: Leiden University Press, 1981.

Kofman, Michael, and Matthew Rojansky. "A Closer Look at Russia's 'Hybrid War.'" *Kennan Cable*, 7. Washington, DC: Woodrow Wilson International Center for Scholars, April 2015.

Koistinen, Paul A. C. *Arsenal of World War II: The Political Economy of American Warfare, 1940–1945*. Lawrence: University Press of Kansas, 2004.

———. *State of War: The Political Economy of American Warfare, 1945–2011*. Lawrence: University Press of Kansas, 2012.

Krahmann, Elke. "NATO Contracting in Afghanistan: The Problem of Principal-Agent Networks." *International Affairs*, 92, 6 (2016): 1401–1426.

———. *States, Citizens and the Privatization of Security*. Cambridge: Cambridge University Press, 2010.

Lane, Kris E. *Pillaging the Empire: Piracy in the Americas, 1500–1750*. Armonk, NY: M. E. Sharpe, 1998.

Latimer, Jon. *Buccaneers of the Caribbean: How Piracy Forged an Empire*. Cambridge, MA: Harvard University Press, 2009.

———. *1812: War with America*. Cambridge, MA: Belknap Press of Harvard University Press, 2007.

Leach, Douglas Edward. *Arms for Empire: A Military History of the British Colonies in North America, 1607–1763*. New York: Macmillan, 1973.

Leander, Anna. "The Impunity of Private Authority: Understanding PSC Accountability." Paper presented at the International Studies Association Conference, February 28–March 3, 2007. http://openarchive.cbs.dk/bitstream/handle/10398/6985/leander_isa07_woc-wp89.pdf?sequence=1.

Leiner, Frederick C. *Millions for Defense: The Subscription Warships of 1798*. Annapolis, MD: Naval Institute Press, 2000.

Leira, Halvard, and Benjamin de Carvalho. "Privateers of the North Sea: At World's End—French Privateers in Norwegian Waters." In *Mercenaries, Pirates, Bandits, and Empires: Private Violence in Historical Context*, ed. Alejandro Colas and Bryan Mabee, 55–82. New York: Columbia University Press, 2010.

Lemnitzer, Jan Martin. "'That Moral League of Nations against the United States': The Origins of the 1856 Declaration of Paris." *International History Review*, 35, 5 (2013): 1068–1088.

Levy, Jack S., and William R. Thompson. *The Arc of War: Origins, Escalation, and Transformation*. Chicago: University of Chicago Press, 2011.

Lin, Herb. "A Notification Requirement for Using Cyber Weapons or for Unauthorized Disclosure of a Cyber Weapon." *Lawfare*, June 10, 2017.

Lin, Herbert, and Amy Zegart. "Introduction to the Special Issue on Strategic Dimensions of Offensive Cyber Operations." *Journal of Cybersecurity*, 3, 1 (2017): 1–5.

Lindemann, Marc. "Civilian Contractors under Military Law." *Parameters* (Autumn 2007): 83–94.

Loades, David. *England's Maritime Empire: Seapower, Commerce, and Policy, 1490–1690*. Harlow, UK: Pearson Educated Limited, 2000.

Lobel, Jules. "Covert War and Congressional Authority: Hidden War and Forgotten Power." *University of Pennsylvania Law Review*, 134 (June 1986): 1035–1110.

Luttwak, Edward. "A Post-Heroic Military Policy." *Foreign Affairs*, 75, 4 (July 1996): 33–44.

Lycan, Gilbert L. *Alexander Hamilton and American Foreign Policy: A Design for Greatness*. Norman: University of Oklahoma Press, 1970.

Mackesy, Piers. *The War for America, 1775–1783*. Lincoln: University of Nebraska Press, 1964, rev. 1992.

MacKinlay, John. "Defining Warlords." *International Peacekeeping*, 7, 1 (2000): 48–62.

Mahon, John K. *History of the Militia and the National Guard*. New York: Macmillan, 1973.

Main, Jackson Turner. *The Sovereign States, 1775–1783*. New York: Franklin Watts, 1973.

Mallett, Michael. "Mercenaries." In *Medieval Warfare: A History*, ed. Maurice Keen, 209–229. Oxford: Oxford University Press, 1999.

Mancke, Elizabeth. "Chartered Enterprises and the Evolution of the British Atlantic World." In *The Creation of the British World*, ed. Elizabeth Mancke and Carole Shammas, 237–262. Baltimore: Johns Hopkins University Press, 2005.

Mandel, Robert. "Overview of American Government Expeditionary Operations Utilizing Private Contractors." In *Contractors and War: The Transformation of United States' Expeditionary Operations*, ed. Christopher Kinsey and Malcolm Hugh Patterson, 13–35. Stanford, CA: Stanford University Press, 2012.

———. *Security, Strategy, and the Quest for Bloodless War*. Boulder, CO: Lynne Rienner Publishers, 2004.

Marks, Frederick W., III. *Independence on Trial: Foreign Affairs and the Making of the Constitution*. Baton Rouge: Louisiana State University Press, 1973.

Marks, Joseph. "Lawmakers to Pentagon: Tell Us When You Use Cyber Weapons." *Defense One*, June 8, 2017.

Marshall, C. Kevin. "Putting Privateers in Their Place: The Applicability of the Marque and Reprisal Clause to Undeclared Wars." *University of Chicago Law Review*, 64 (Summer 1997): 953–981.

Martines, Lauro. *Furies: War in Europe, 1450–1700.* London: Bloomsbury Press, 2013.

Matson, Cathy D., and Peter S. Onuf. *A Union of Interests: Political and Economic Thought in Revolutionary America.* Lawrence: University Press of Kansas, 1990.

Matthews, Owen. "Putin's (Secret) Army." *Newsweek,* January 26, 2018, 27–35.

Maurer, Tim. *Cyber Mercenaries: The State, Hackers and Power.* Cambridge: Cambridge University Press, 2018.

Maxey, Levi. "A Wolf in Mercenary Clothing? Russian Contractors as Gray Zone Tool." *Cipher Brief,* November 26, 2017.

May, Robert E. *Manifest Destiny's Underworld: Filibustering in Antebellum America.* Chapel Hill: University of North Carolina Press, 2002.

McCranie, Kevin D. *Utmost Gallantry: The U.S. and Royal Navies at Sea in the War of 1812.* Annapolis, MD: Naval Institute Press, 2011.

McFate, Sean. *The Modern Mercenary: Private Armies and What They Mean for World Order.* Oxford: Oxford University Press, 2014.

McFee, William. *The Law of the Sea.* Philadelphia: J. B. Lippincott, 1950.

McGhee, James E. "Liberating Cyber Offense." *Strategic Studies Quarterly* (Winter 2016): 46–63.

McGlynn, Sean. *By Sword and Fire: Cruelty and Atrocity in Medieval Warfare.* London: Phoenix, 2008.

McNeill, William H. *The Pursuit of Power: Technology, Armed Force, and Society since A.D. 1000.* Chicago: University of Chicago Press, 1982.

Merle, Renae. "Census Counts 100,000 Contractors in Iraq." *Washington Post,* December 5, 2006. http://www.washingtonpost.com/wp-dyn/content/article/2006/12/04/AR2006120401311.html.

Meyer, J., and P. Masson. "Commerce-Raiding." In *A Dictionary of Military History,* ed. Andre Corvisier, trans. Chris Turner, ed. and expanded by John Childs, 170–175. Oxford: Basil Blackwell, 1994.

Michaels, Jon D. "Beyond Accountability: The Constitutional, Democratic, and Strategic Problems with Privatizing War." *Washington University Law Quarterly,* 82 (Fall 2004): 1003–1127.

Miller, Nathan. *Sea of Glory: A Naval History of the American Revolution.* Charleston, SC: Nautical and Aviation Publishing, 1974.

Milliard, Todd S. "Overcoming Post-Colonial Myopia: A Call to Recognize and Regulate Private Military Companies." *Military Law,* 176 (June 2003): 1–95.

Minow, Martha. "Outsourcing Power: How Privatizing Military Efforts Challenges Accountability, Professionalism, and Democracy." *Boston College Law Review,* 46 (September 2005): 989–1026.

Mockaitis, Thomas R. *Soldiers of Misfortune.* Carlisle, PA: Strategic Studies Institute, U.S. Army War College Press, 2014.

Morriss, Roger. *The Foundations of British Maritime Ascendancy: Resources, Logistics and the State, 1755–1815.* Cambridge: Cambridge University Press, 2011.

Moskos, Charles C., John Allen Williams, and David R. Segal. "Armed Forces after the Cold War." In *The Postmodern Military: Armed Forces after the Cold War,* ed.

Charles C. Moskos, John Allen Williams, and David R. Segal, 1–13. New York: Oxford University Press, 2000.

Moss, Kenneth B. "Challenges to International Regulation of Cyber Technology at War." DIIS Policy Brief. Copenhagen: Danish Institute for International Studies, May 2014.

———. *Undeclared War and the Future of U.S. Foreign Policy*. Washington, DC, and Baltimore: Wilson Center Press and Johns Hopkins University Press, 2008.

Munkler, Herfried. *The New Wars*. Cambridge, UK: Polity, 2005.

Murdoch, Steve. *The Terror of the Seas: Scottish Maritime Warfare, 1513–1713*. Leiden, Netherlands: Koninklijke Brill, 2010.

Nakashima, Ellen. "White House Authorizes 'Offensive Cyber Operations' to Deter Foreign Adversaries." *Washington Post*, September 20, 2018.

Nazarova, Nina, and Ilya Barabanov. "The Russian Guns for Hire Dying in Syria." *BBC Russian Service, Archangelsk*, February 20, 2018.

Neff, Stephen C. *Justice in Blue and Gray: A Legal History of the Civil War*. Cambridge, MA: Harvard University Press, 2010.

Neimeyer, Charles Patrick. *America Goes to War: A Social History of the Continental Army*. New York: New York University Press, 1996.

Neocleous, Mark. "From Social to National Security: On the Fabrication of Economic Order." *Security Dialogue* 37, 3 (2006): 363–384.

Nevers, Renee de. "(Self) Regulating War? Voluntary Regulation and the Private Security Industry." *Security Studies*, 18, 3 (2009): 479–516.

Norton, Louis Arthur. *Captains Contentious: The Dysfunctional Sons of the Brine*. Columbia: University of South Carolina Press, 2009.

Norton, Matthew. "Temporality, Isolation, and Violence in the Early Modern English Maritime World." *Eighteenth-Century Studies*, 48, 1 (2014): 37–66.

O'Brien, Patrick K. "Inseparable Connections: Trade, Economy, Fiscal State, and the Expansion of Empire, 1688–1815." In *The Eighteenth Century*, Vol. 2 of *The Oxford History of the British Empire*, ed. P. J. Marshall, 53–77. Oxford: Oxford University Press, 1998.

———. "Mercantilism and Imperialism in the Rise and Decline of the Dutch and British Economies." *De Economist*, 148, 4 (2000): 469–501.

O'Hanlon, Michael. *Saving Lives with Force: Military Criteria for Humanitarian Intervention*. Washington, DC: Brookings Institution, 1997.

Onuf, Peter S. *Jefferson's Empire: The Language of American Nationhood*. Charlottesville: University Press of Virginia, 2000.

Ormerod, Henry A. *Piracy in the Ancient World*. Baltimore: Johns Hopkins University Press, 1924, reprinted 1997.

Ortiz, Carlos. "Regulating Private Military Companies: States and the Expanding Business of Commercial Security Provision." In *Global Regulation: Managing Crisis after the Imperial Turn*, ed. Libby Assassi, Duncan Wigan, and Kees van der Pihl, 205–219. Houndmills, Basingstoke, UK: Palgrave MacMillan, 2004.

Owen, John B. *The Eighteenth Century, 1714–1815*. New York: W. W. Norton, 1974.

Owens, Patricia. "Distinctions, Distinctions: 'Public' and 'Private' Force?" *International Affairs*, 84, 5 (2008): 977–990.

Pares, Richard. *War and Trade in the West Indies, 1739–1763*. London: Frank Cass, 1936, reprinted 1963.

Parillo, Nicholas. "The De-Privatization of American Warfare: How the U.S. Government Used, Regulated, and Ultimately Abandoned Privateering in the Nineteenth Century." *Yale Journal of Law and the Humanities*, 19, 1 (Winter 2007): 1–95.

Parker, Geoffrey. *The Military Revolution: Military Innovation and the Rise of the West, 1500–1800*. Cambridge: Cambridge University Press, 1988, revised 1996.

Parsons, Graham. "Public War and the Moral Equality of Combatants." *Journal of Military Ethics*, 11, 4 (2012): 299–317.

Patton, Robert H. *Patriot Pirates: The Privateer War for Freedom and Fortune in the American Revolution*. New York: Pantheon Books, 2008.

Peers, Douglas M. "Gunpowder Empires and the Garrison State: Modernity, Hybridity, and the Political Economy of Colonial India, circa 1750–1860." *Comparative Studies of South Asia, Africa, and the Middle East*, 17, (2007): 245–258.

Peifer, Douglas C. "Maritime Commerce Warfare: The Coercive Response of the Weak?" *Naval War College Review*, 66, 2 (Spring 2013): 1–27.

Percy, Sarah. *Regulating the Private Security Industry*. Adelphi Paper 384, International Institute for Strategic Studies. London: Routledge, 2006.

Perrone, Sean T. "John Stoughton and the *Divina Pastora* Prize Case, 1816–1819." *Journal of the Early Republic*, 28 (Summer 2008): 215–242.

Pestana, Carla Gardina. *The English Atlantic in the Age of Revolution, 1640–1661*. Cambridge, MA: Harvard University Press, 2004.

Petersen, Karen Lund. "Risk, Responsibility and Roles Redefined: Is Counterterrorism a Corporate Responsibility?" *Cambridge Review of International Affairs*, 21, 3 (September 2008): 403–420.

Petersohn, Ulrich. "Private Military and Security Companies (PMSCs), Military Effectiveness, and Conflict Severity in Weak States, 1990–2007." *Journal of Conflict Resolution*, 61, 5 (2017): 1046–1072.

Phillips, Andrew, and J. C. Sharman. *International Order in Diversity: War, Trade, and Rule in the Indian Ocean*. Cambridge: Cambridge University Press, 2015.

Phillipson, Nicholas. *Adam Smith: An Enlightened Life*. New Haven, CT: Yale University Press, 2010.

Porter, Bruce D. *War and the Rise of the State: The Military Foundation of Modern Politics*. New York: Free Press, 1994.

Price, David E. "Private Contractors, Public Consequences: The Need for an Effective Criminal Justice Framework." In *Contractors and War: The Transformation of United States' Expeditionary Operations*, ed. Christopher Kinsey and Malcolm Hugh Paterson, 205–230. Stanford, CA: Stanford University Press, 2012.

Prince, Erik. *Civilian Warriors: The Inside Story of Blackwater and the Unsung Heroes of the War on Terror*. New York: Portfolio/Penguin, 2013.

"Private Military Companies in Russia: Carrying out Criminal Orders of the Kremlin.

InformNapalm, undated, http://informnapalm.rocks/private-military-companies -in-russia-carrying-out-criminal-orders-of-the-kremlin.

Rabkin, Jeremy, and Ariel Rabkin. "Navigating Conflicts in Cyberspace: Legal Lessons from the History of War at Sea." *Chicago Journal of International Law*, 14, 1 (Summer 2013): 197–258.

Ramsey, Michael D. *The Constitution's Text in Foreign Affairs*. Cambridge, MA: Harvard University Press, 2007.

"Recent Cases: Eighth Amendment—Mandatory Minimum Sentences—D.C. Circuit Holds It Cruel and Unusual to Impose Mandatory Thirty-Year Sentence on Military Contractors for Gun Charge." *Harvard Law Review*, 131 (2018): 1465–1472. No author listed.

Rediker, Marcus. *Between the Devil and the Deep Blue Sea: Merchant Seamen, Pirates and the Anglo-American Maritime World, 1700–1750*. Cambridge: Cambridge University Press, 1987.

———. *Villains of All Nations: Atlantic Pirates in the Golden Age*. Boston: Beacon Press, 2004.

Renz, Berttina, and Hanna Smith. *Russia and Hybrid Warfare—Going beyond the Label*. Papers Aleksanteri. Helsinki: Aleksanteri Institute, University of Helsinki, 2016.

Reudnitsky, Jake, John Mickelthwait, and Michael Riley. "Putin Says DNC Hack Was a Public Good, but Russia Didn't Do It." *Bloomberg News*, September 2, 1016.

Rinear, Matthew. "Armed with a Keyboard: Presidential Directive 20, Cyber Warfare, and the International Laws of War." *Capital University Law Review*, 43 (2015): 679–720.

Ritchie, Robert C. *Captain Kidd and the War against the Pirates*. Cambridge, MA: Harvard University Press, 1986.

———. "Government Measures against Piracy and Privateering in the Atlantic Area, 1750–1850." In *Pirates and Privateers: New Perspectives on the War on Trade in the Eighteenth and Nineteenth Centuries*, ed. David J. Starkey, E. S. van Eyck van Heslinga, and J. A. Moor, 10–18. Exeter, UK: University of Exeter Press, 1997.

Robinson Jr., William Morrison. *The Confederate Privateers*. Columbia: University of South Carolina Press, 1990; originally published by Yale University Press in 1928.

Rodger, N. A. M. *The Command of the Ocean: A Naval History of Britain, 1649–1845*. New York: W. W. Norton, 2004.

———. "The Law and Language of Private Naval Warfare." *Mariner's Mirror*, 100, 1 (2014): 5–16.

———. *The Safeguard of the Sea: A Naval History of Britain, 660–1649*. New York: W. W. Norton, 1997.

Rogin, Josh. "Inside Erik Prince's Secret Proposal to Outsource the War in Afghanistan." *Washington Post*, August 9, 2017. https://www.washingtonpost.com/news /josh-rogin/wp/2017/08/09/inside-erik-princes-secret-proposal-to-outsource-the -warinafghanistan/?noredirect=on&utm_term=.64468aaddda3.

Ronald, Susan. *The Pirate Queen: Queen Elizabeth I, Her Pirate Adventurers and the Dawn of Empire*. New York: Harper Perennial, 2007.

Rosen, Deborah. *Border Law: The First Seminole War and American Nationhood.* Cambridge, MA: Harvard University Press, 2015.

Samuels, Joel H. "How Piracy Has Shaped the Relationship between American Law and International Law." *American University Law Review,* 59, 5 (June 2010): 1231–1265.

Sanger, David E. *The Perfect Weapon: War, Sabotage, and Fear in the Cyber Age.* New York: Crown, 2018.

Satsuma, Shinsuke. "Politicians, Merchants, and Colonial Maritime War: The Political and Economic Background of the American Act of 1708." *Parliamentary History,* 32, 2 (2013): 317–336.

Saunders, Frances Stonor. *The Devil's Broker: Seeking Gold, God, and Glory in Fourteenth-Century Italy.* New York: Fourth Estate, Harper Collins, 2004.

Scheimer, Michael. "Separating Private Military Companies from Illegal Mercenaries in International Law: Proposing an International Convention for Legitimate Military and Security Support the [sic] Reflects Customary International Law." *American University International Law Review,* 24, 3 (2009): 609–646.

Schneckener, Ulrich. "Fragile Statehood, Armed Non-State Actors and Security Governance." In *Private Actors and Security Governance,* ed. Alan Bryden and Maria Caparini, 23–40. Geneva Centre for the Democratic Control of Armed Forces. Münster, Germany: LIT Verlag, 2007.

Scott, H. M. "Review Article: 'The Second 'Hundred Years War,' 1689–1815." *Historical Journal,* 35, 2 (1992): 443–469.

Selby, John E. *The Revolution in Virginia, 1775–1783.* Williamsburg, VA: Colonial Williamsburg Foundation, 1988.

Seleskey, Harold E. "Colonial America." In *the Laws of War: Constraints on Warfare in the Western World,* ed. Michael Howard, George J. Andreopoulos, and Mark R. Shulman, 59–85. New Haven, CT: Yale University Press, 1994.

Seymour, Joseph. *The Pennsylvania Associators, 1747–1777.* Yardley, PA: Westholme Publishing, 2012.

Shackelford, Scott J. *Managing Cyber Attacks in International Law: Business and Relations.* Cambridge: Cambridge University Press, 2014.

Shaw, Martin. *Post-Military Society: Militarism, Demilitarization and War at the End of the Twentieth Century.* Philadelphia: Temple University Press, 1991.

Shearer. David. *Private Armies and Military Intervention.* Adelphi Paper 316. International Institute for Strategic Studies. Oxford: Oxford University Press, 1998.

Sheehan, James J. *Where Have All the Soldiers Gone? The Transformation of Modern Europe.* Boston: Houghton Mifflin, 2008.

Shuya, Mason. "Russian Cyber Aggression and the New Cold War." *Journal of Strategic Security,* 11, 1 (Spring 2018): 1–18.

Sidak, J. Gregory. "The Quasi War Cases—and Their Relevance to Whether 'Letters of Marque and Reprisal' Constrain Presidential War Powers." *Harvard Journal of Law and Public Policy,* 28, 2 (2004): 465–500.

Singer, P[eter]. W. *Corporate Warriors: The Rise of the Privatized Military Industry.* Ithaca, NY: Cornell University Press, 2003.

————. "War, Profits, and the Vacuum of Law: Privatized Military Firms and International Law," 42. *Columbia Journal of Transnational Law* (2004): 521–549.

Singer, P[eter]. W., and Allan Friedman. *Cybersecurity and Cyberwar: What Everyone Needs to Know.* New York: Oxford University Press, 2014.

Smith, Mark A. *The Right Talk: How Conservatives Transformed the Great Society into the Economic Society.* Princeton, NJ: Princeton University Press, 2007.

Snyder, Timothy. *The Road to Unfreedom: Russia, Europe, America.* New York: Tim Duggan Books, 2018.

Solis, Gary D. *The Law of Armed Conflict: International Humanitarian Law in War.* Cambridge: Cambridge University Press, 2010.

Sparrow, Bartholomew H. *From the Outside In: World War II and the American State.* Princeton, NJ: Princeton University Press, 1996.

Sparrow, James T. *Warfare State: World War II Americans and the Age of Big Government.* New York: Oxford University Press, 2011.

Spearin, Christopher. "Accountable to Whom? An Assessment of International Private Security Companies in South America." *Civil Wars*, 6, 1 (2003): 1–26.

Sperling, Valerie. *Altered States: The Globalization of Accountability.* Cambridge: Cambridge University Press, 2009.

Spruyt, Hendrik. *The Sovereign State and Its Competitors: An Analysis of Systems Change.* Princeton, NJ: Princeton University Press, 1994.

Stagg, J. C. A. *Mr. Madison's War: Politics, Diplomacy, and Warfare in the Early American Republic, 1783–1830.* Princeton, NJ: Princeton University Press, 1983.

Steele, I. K. *Politics of Colonial Policy: The Board of Trade in Colonial Administration, 1696–1720.* Oxford: Clarendon Press, 1968.

Stern, Philip J. "British Asia and British Atlantic: Comparisons and Connections." *William and Mary Quarterly*, 68, 4 (October 2006): 693–712.

————. *The Company State: Corporate Sovereignty and the Early Modern Foundations of the British Empire in India.* Oxford: Oxford University Press, 2011.

Stivers, Reuben Elmore. *Privateers and Volunteers: The Men and Women of Our Reserve Naval Forces, 1766 to 1866.* Annapolis, MD: Naval Institute Press, 1975.

Stuart, Reginald C. *War and American Thought: From the Revolution to the Monroe Doctrine.* Kent, OH: Kent State University Press, 1982.

Sullivan, Eileen. "Blackwater Security Contractor Found Guilty, Again, in Deadly 2007 Iraq Shooting." *New York Times*, December 19, 2018.

Sutherland, Lucy S. *The East India Company in Eighteenth-Century Politics.* Oxford: Oxford University Press, 1952.

Swanson. Carl E. "American Privateering and Imperial Warfare, 1739–1748," *William and Mary Quarterly*, 42, 3 (July 1985): 357–382.

Sylvester, Douglas J. "International Law as Sword or Shield? Early American Foreign Policy and the Law of Nations." *Journal of International Law and Politics*, 32 (1999): 1–87.

Taylor, Adam. "The Shadowy Russian Mercenary Firm behind an Attack on U.S. Troops in Syria." *Washington Post*, February 23, 2018.

Taylor, William A. *Military Service and American Democracy: From World War II to the Iraq and Afghanistan Wars.* Lawrence: University Press of Kansas, 2016.

Thomson, Janice E. *Mercenaries, Pirates, and Sovereigns: State-Building and Extraterritorial Violence in Early Modern Europe.* Princeton, NJ: Princeton University Press, 1994.

———. "State Practices, International Norms, and the Decline of Mercenarism." *International Studies Quarterly,* 34, 1 (March 1990): 23–47.

Thorpe, Rebecca U. *The American Warfare State: The Domestic Politics of Military Spending.* Chicago: University of Chicago Press, 2014.

Tilly, Charles. *Coercion, Capital, and European States, AD 990–1992.* Oxford: Blackwell Publishers, 1990, revised 1992.

Tonkin, Hannah. *State Control over Private Military and Security Companies in Armed Conflict.* Cambridge: Cambridge University Press, 2011.

Tracy, James D. "Introduction." In *The Rise of Merchant Empires: Long-Distance Trade in the Early Modern World, 1350–1750,* ed. James D. Tracy, 1–13. Cambridge: Cambridge University Press, 1990.

Tuck, Richard. "Introduction." In Hugo Grotius, *The Rights of War and Peace,* Book I, ed. Richard Tuck, ix–xxxiii. Indianapolis: Liberty Fund, 2005.

Tucker, Patrick. "Vladimir Putin and the Little Green Men of the Internet." *Defense One,* June 5, 2017. http:www.defenseone.com/technology2017/06/vladimir-putin-and-little-green-men.

Tucker, Robert W., and David C. Hendrickson. *Empire of Liberty: The Statecraft of Thomas Jefferson.* New York: Oxford University Press, 1984.

Turza, Nicholas Ryan. "Counterattacking the Comment Crew: The Constitutionality of Presidential Policy Directive as a Defense to Counter Attacks." *North Carolina Journal of Law and Technology,* 15 (2014): 134–169.

Underwood, Matthew. "'Jealousies of a Standing Army': The Use of Mercenaries in the American Revolution and Its Implications for Congress's Role in Regulating Private Military Firms." *Northwestern University Law Review,* 106, 1 (2012): 317–349.

Urban, William. *Bayonets for Hire: Mercenaries at War, 1550–1789.* London: Greenhill Books, 2007.

———. *Medieval Mercenaries: The Business of War.* London: Greenhill Books, 2006.

"U.S. Casualty Status." https://www.defense.gov/casualty.pdf.

Vanatta, Natalie. "Who Will Defend the Nation in the Digital Domain?" In *Proceedings of the 12th International Conference on Cyber Warfare and Security,* ed. Adam R. Bryant, Robert F. Mills, and Juan Lopez Jr., 367–373. Sonning Common, UK: Academic Conferences and Publishing International, 2017.

Van Cleve, George William. *We Have Not a Government: The Articles of Confederation and the Road to the Constitution.* Chicago: University of Chicago Press, 2017.

Verkuil, Paul R. *Outsourcing Sovereignty: Why Privatization of Government Functions Threatens Democracy and What We Can Do about It.* Cambridge: Cambridge University Press, 2007.

Volo, James M. *Blue Water Patriots: The American Revolution Afloat.* Westport, CT: Praeger Publishers, 2007.

Waite, Gerald. "Outsourcing a War: What You Get for Your Mercenary Dollar." *International Journal on World Peace*, 31, 4 (December 2014): 81–102.

Waldman, Thomas. "Vicarious Warfare: The Counterproductive Consequences of Modern American Military Practice." *Contemporary Security Policy*, 39, 2 (2018): 181–205.

Walzer, Michael. *Just and Unjust Wars*, 4th ed. New York: Basic Books, 2006.

Wapshott, Nicholas. *Keynes Hayek: The Clash That Defined Modern Economics*. New York: W. W. Norton, 2011.

Ward, Ralph T. *Pirates in History*. Baltimore: York Press, 1974.

Wareham, Tom. "More Than Just Kidd's Play." *History Today*, January 2013, 11–13.

Watkin, Kenneth. "Warriors without Rights: Combatants, Unprivileged Belligerents, and the Struggle over Legitimacy." *HPCR Occasional Papers*. Cambridge, MA: Program on Humanitarian Policy and Conflict Research, Harvard University, Winter 2005.

Weber, Max. "Politics as a Vocation." In *From Max Weber: Essays in Sociology*, ed. H. H. Gerth and C. Wright Mills, 77–128. Oxford: Oxford University Press, 1946, reprinted 1958.

Webster, Anthony. *The Twilight of the East India Company: The Evolution of Anglo-Asia Commerce and Politics, 1790–1860*. Vol. 3 of *Worlds of the East India Company*. Woodbridge, Suffolk, UK: Boydell Press, 2009.

Wexler, Jay. *The Odd Clauses: Understanding the Constitution through Ten of Its Most Curious Provisions*. Boston: Beacon Press, 2011.

Whitman, James Q. *The Verdict of Battle: The Law of Victory and the Making of Modern War*. Cambridge, MA: Harvard University Press, 2012.

Williams, Phil. "Transnational Organized Crime." In *Security Studies: An Introduction*, 2nd ed., ed. Paul Williams, 503–519. London: Routledge, 2013.

Williamson, Gene. *Guns on the Chesapeake: The Winning of America's Independence*. Bowie, MD: Heritage Books, 1998.

Willis, Sam. *The Struggle for Sea Power: A Naval History of the American Revolution*. New York: W. W. Norton, 2015.

Wills, Garry. *James Madison*. New York: Henry Holt, Times Books, 2002.

Winius, George D., "Two Lusitanian Variations on a Dutch Theme: Portuguese Companies in Times of Crises, 1628–1662." In *Companies and Trade*, ed. L. Blusse and F. Gaastra, 119–134. Leiden, Netherlands: Leiden University Press, 1981.

Witt, John Fabian. *Lincoln's Code: The Laws of War in American History*. New York: Free Press, 2012.

Witte, Grif. "New Law Could Subject Civilians to Military Trial." *Washington Post*, January 15, 2007.

Woodard, Colin. *The Republic of Pirates: Being the True and Surprising Story of the Caribbean Pirates and the Man Who Brought Them Down*. Orlando, FL: Harcourt, Harvest Books, 2007.

Wormuth, Francis D., and Edwin B. Firmage. *To Chain the Dog of War: The War Power of Congress in History and Law*, 2nd ed. Urbana: University of Illinois Press, 1989.

Wright, Quincy. *A Study of War*, abridged by Louise Leonard Wright. Chicago: University of Chicago Press, 1942; revised 1964.

Wulf, Herbert. "The Future of the Public Monopoly of Force." In *Revisiting the State Monopoly on the Legitimate Use of Force*. Policy Paper No. 24, ed. Alyson Bailes, Ulrich Schneckener, and Herbert Wulf, 2–9. Geneva: Geneva Centre for the Democratic Control of Armed Force, 2006.

Yoo, John. *The Powers of War and Peace: The Constitution and Foreign Affairs after 9/11*. Chicago: University of Chicago Press, 2005.

INDEX